CUTTING A NEW PATTERN

UNIFORMED WOMEN IN THE GREAT WAR

EDITED BY BARTON C. HACKER AND MARGARET VINING

A SMITHSONIAN CONTRIBUTION TO KNOWLEDGE

Smithsonian
Scholarly Press

WASHINGTON, DC
2020

Published by
SMITHSONIAN INSTITUTION SCHOLARLY PRESS
P.O. Box 37012, MRC 957
Washington, D.C. 20013-7012
https://scholarlypress.si.edu

Front cover: Women's Machine Gun Squad Police Reserves, New York City, 1918 (Library of Congress, Prints and Photographs Division). *Back cover (clockwise from top left):* Nurses, in Army Nurse Corps dresses as uniforms, and medical officers from Base Hospital No. 12, of Northwestern University Hospital, with Sir Thomas Lipton in London, 10 June 1917 (Library of Congress, Prints and Photographs Division). Two New Zealand women in soldiers' uniforms, ca. 1905–1926 (National Library/He Tohu). Mina Van Winkle, head of the Lecture Bureau of the U.S. Food Administration, in the "Hoover apron" (Library of Congress, Prints and Photographs Division).

Library of Congress Cataloging-in-Publication Data:
Names: Hacker, Barton C., 1935– editor. | Vining, Margaret, editor.
Title: Cutting a new pattern : uniformed women in the Great War / edited by Barton C. Hacker and Margaret Vining.
Description: Washington, D.C. : Smithsonian Scholarly Press, 2020. | Series: A Smithsonian Contribution to Knowledge | Includes bibliographical references and index.
Identifiers: LCCN 2019037059 | ISBN 9781944466350 (hardcover)
Subjects: LCSH: Armed Forces—Women—Uniforms—History—20th century. | Military uniforms—History—20th century. | World War, 1914–1918—Clothing and dress. | World War, 1914–1918—Women. | Uniforms—History—20th century.
Classification: LCC UC480 .C88 2020 | DDC 940.40082—dc23
LC record available at https://lccn.loc.gov/2019037059

ISBN-13: 978-1-944466-35-0 (print)

Printed in the United States of America

♾ The paper used in this publication meets the minimum requirements of the American National Standard for Permanence of Paper for Printed Library Materials Z39.48–1992.

Dedication

To Margaret Vining
with love, respect, and admiration.
She amounted to something.

CONTENTS

PREFACE

Remembering Margaret

Margaret Vining, who coedited and contributed to this book, died before it appeared in print, but her inspiration and hard work made it happen. I take advantage of this preface to sketch Margaret's background and career to help explain the book's genesis, purpose, limitations, and focus.

It all began with the land, the rich black soil of lowland North Carolina that the Simmons family had been farming for two centuries when, on 22 May 1933, the newborn Margaret uttered her first squalls. She was the second of three daughters born to George and Keturah Garner Simmons. Like the Simmonses, the Garners had deep roots in lowland North Carolina. In addition to their parents and grandparents, Margaret and her sisters grew up amid a swarm of aunts, uncles, cousins, and other less clearly defined relatives. But their closest neighbors were the tenant farmers and sharecroppers, all African American, who regularly helped out on the farm and whose children were the Simmons sisters' summer playmates. Though the Great Depression might worry Mom and Dad, the girls suffered little of the insecurity that afflicted so many other children of the era. The 600-acre Simmons farm in Jones County, near New Bern at the confluence of the Neuse and Trent Rivers, provided ample food, and tobacco brought in enough cash to buy whatever else they needed. Margaret learned to roller skate (she titled her sadly unfinished memoir "Roller-Skating on a Dirt Road"), to catch fish, to ride horses, to take care of the animals, to tend the kitchen garden, and to transplant tobacco. By the age of 10, she was driving the pickup truck and the tractor on the farm, a particular joy because she didn't have to share, as she did with everything else; neither of her sisters was the least bit interested. Bright and quick, Margaret took to schooling like a duck to water. She became a voracious reader and dreamed of faraway places.

Turning dreams into reality was no easy thing. Her parents assumed college was wasted on girls, who were only going to marry anyway. By the time Margaret graduated from high school in 1951, she was already displaying that streak of stubborn independence that always after remained her hallmark. Six years later, she had saved enough money working in a New Bern auto dealer's office to move 40 miles up the road to Greenville and enroll in East Carolina University. She plunged into American history and began her lifelong love affair with the piano, largely unrequited, I'm sorry to say. She continued to work, of course, now to save money to make the dream of faraway places real. At the end of her second college year, she had enough for a summer in Europe. Three friends pooled their money to hire a driver, who chauffeured them from northern Scotland to London. Then they were off to France and Italy. Despite the travels of later years, Margaret always treasured memories of that first trip abroad; she still talked about it in her final days.

The next year, everything changed. In her mid-20s, Margaret combined striking beauty with charm, poise, good taste, and a lively intellect. She was also an outstanding athlete. No wonder the beaus flocked about. But it was young Air Force Captain Bob Vining who won her hand. Margaret never lost her love for North Carolina, especially the coastal enclave of Emerald Isle, to which she frequently returned. But she had long since decided that her destiny lay elsewhere. Not the least of Bob Vining's charms was that he was not tied to North Carolina. They married in 1960, and Margaret's college career was left unfinished when they soon departed for Bob's next assignment at Hanscom Air Force Base in Massachusetts. All their three children were born in Concord. Always a quick learner, Margaret soon mastered the intricacies of being a military wife. She only learned to call herself a feminist later, but she acted like one from the outset, seeking every opportunity to improve the lot of military women and soldiers' wives. Perhaps the highlight of Margaret's military career came in 1971–1973, when Bob was assigned to U.S. European Command Headquarters in Stuttgart, Germany. At Margaret's urging, they lived "on the economy," in the nearby small town of Warmbronn. The Vining's European assignment was cut short by Bob's promotion to colonel and recall to the Pentagon. Just a few years later, he died at the tragically young age of 49. Once again, everything changed.

Bob's untimely death left Margaret with three teenagers to raise and educate. North Carolina Congressman Jim Martin, an old family friend, hired her as a legislative researcher for the American Bicentennial; she wrote a biweekly series of well-documented essays on revolutionary North Carolina, read on the radio and distributed to high schools during the bicentennial year. Margaret, who had never lost her thirst for learning, also enrolled in George Washington University, where she finally completed the B.A. that she had postponed almost two decades earlier; she went on to win an M.A. in the then still novel field of museum studies, with minors in material culture and women's history. That was in 1982. The next year was no less momentous: Margaret turned 50 and began her illustrious 35-year career at the National Museum of American History.

Despite her advanced degree, Margaret's museum career started at the bottom. She was initially assigned to an inventory management project that took her through the numismatics, photographic history, political history, and ceramics collections. This turned out to be a wonderful introduction to the museum and a decisive turning point in her career. Her final stop on the inventory project was armed forces history, where an aging curator chided her for asking about the absence of women's material in the collections. "They didn't do anything, Margaret," he said. "They were only whores and laundresses." Her internal response, as she later told me more than once: "They needed me!" Before that, Margaret had shown no particular interest in military history. Now, it became the central focus of her museum career. Promoted in 1986 to curatorial historian in the Division of Armed Forces History, Margaret set out to expand the collections aside from weapons, or, as she often put it, "everything that didn't shoot or cut." She focused especially on objects related to women—not only women who served in the armed forces but also those who served with the armed forces, like military wives and camp followers. Continuing her outspoken feminism, she also became and remained throughout her years at the museum a fierce advocate for the museum's women, from janitors to managers. She played no small part in the shift during her years at the museum from a support, curatorial, and administrative staff that was predominantly male to one that is now much more evenly balanced. That the museum finally installed its first female director in 2019 owed more than a little to Margaret's tireless efforts.

Even as she was collecting women's military material culture, Margaret had also begun assembling archival material related to women's military history; although America was the focus, a substantial part of the growing collection represented women associated with military institutions around the world from earliest times to the present. Ultimately, her efforts culminated in the establishment of the online Smithsonian Women's Military History Collection in 2016, perhaps her proudest achievement (https://www.si.edu/object/sova_nmah-af.0001). Although she had plenty of help along the way from colleagues, fellows, interns, and volunteers, Margaret deserves most of the credit for making the National Museum of American History (NMAH) the preeminent resource for the study of women's military history that it is today.

Margaret's first exhibit opened in 1990. *G.I.: The American Soldier Experience in World War II* was a joint project of NMAH and the U.S. Army Center of Military History that focused on the process of turning civilians, many of them callow teenagers, into trained and disciplined soldiers. She also enjoyed considerable success in expanding the presence of women in exhibitions, culminating recently in the NMAH-centered Smithsonian American Women's History Initiative (https://womenshistory.si.edu/). Curiously, Margaret never succeeded in winning museum support for a major exhibit on women's military history, although she was able to mount several small-scale exhibits over the years. The most recent closed in April 2019: *Uniformed Women in the Great War*.

Margaret's premiere collecting achievement was persuading the National Society of the Colonial Dames of America to donate its unique and unparalleled collection of women's uniforms from the Great War to the Smithsonian. In the spring of 1998, I joined the National Museum of American History as a curator of armed forces history with no more experience of museums than having visited one or another from time to time. Shortly after I arrived, my new colleague Margaret showed me the Colonial Dames collection. It radically reshaped my ideas about military history in general and the Great War in particular. The 60 or so uniforms in that extraordinary collection represented the participation of tens of thousands of American women in the war. I was astonished. Although I'd been studying, teaching, and writing about American military history for 40 years and published my first article in women's military history in the early 1980s, I never realized how many thousands of American women had volunteered to serve in the Great War. The real surprise was how relatively few of these uniforms represented the armed forces or the Red Cross, which had by 1914 in the United States, as in other countries, become a military nursing service in all but name. More than half of them belonged to civilian organizations.

Inspired by this remarkable collection, I joined Margaret in focusing on uniforms as key to understanding the transformation of women's roles in the early twentieth century. Blending our long-standing interest in women's military history with Margaret's pathbreaking work as a museum curator and her persistent efforts to integrate women's uniforms and other material artifacts into historical research and writing, we embarked on a nearly two-decade-long research project, the results of which we regularly shared with our professional colleagues and the public in the form of talks, lectures, and publications. *Cutting a New Pattern* is the capstone of our long journey, though fervently, we hope not the last word on the subject.

Believing that the experience of wearing the uniform was instrumental in this process, we investigated exactly how, and to what extent, the uniform made the woman and the ways that women's entry into uniformed occupations shifted their social, political, and economic roles in the world. The Great War transformed the place of women in society, as many scholars have argued. But we went a step further and asked how. We attribute, to a significant degree, that transformation to women's use of uniforms during the war. Recognizing from the outset that this phenomenon was transnational, we concluded that the book we wanted to write surpassed our resources. So we enlisted the aid of an international group of scholars to help make *Cutting a New Pattern* a reality. In it, 20 authors now explore the meaning and practice of women's uniformed service during the Great War in greater depth and breadth than ever before. Their combined answers, we believe, move the question to a whole new level.

None of this would have happened without Margaret's dedication and persistence. She often wondered aloud, only half-jokingly, if she would ever amount to anything. Obviously, she did.

Bart Hacker
April 2019

INTRODUCTION

The Meanings of Women in Uniform

BARTON C. HACKER AND
MARIAN MOSER JONES

Women in unprecedented numbers wore uniforms in the Great War. The United Kingdom and the United States led the way, but every belligerent and many neutral countries followed suit. For the first time, women became full-fledged members of the armed forces in some countries, but many other women donned uniforms in such civilian occupations as driver, police officer, and postal worker; in paramilitary units; and in a wide range of war relief and welfare organizations. Why did so many women serve in uniform during the Great War? What did uniforms mean to the women who wore them and the organizations that employed them? Exactly how, and to what extent, did the uniform make the woman, as it surely seems to have done? What was the long-term significance of women in uniform? This book offers some answers to these and related questions. Bringing together a wide range of national perspectives, *Cutting a New Pattern* sheds light on the depth and breadth of women's uniformed service during the Great War. Although much remains to be done, one thing is quite clear. Wearing uniforms transformed women's place in society. And that was not least among the many ways that the Great War altered the course of history.

STUDYING UNIFORMS

What prompted nonmilitary organizations to clothe their members in military-style uniforms? What made civilians willing, often eager, to don uniforms? These questions have no simple answers. When Artemis Yagou in 2011 introduced a special issue of the *Journal of Design History* on uniforms, she observed that "research into uniforms is not only exciting but also puzzling, as the subject develops into a maze of interdisciplinary components and interconnections expanding far beyond the field of dress."[1] Organizational dress in general, of which uniforms form an important subset, plays important roles in organizational dynamics.[2]

Part of the uniform's effect reflects its physical attributes, as the U.S. Forest Service's 75-year search for an appropriate uniform demonstrates. Frequent shifts in fabrics, colors, and styles have reflected, at least in part, changes in the agency's perception of its need to express authority or other postures.[3] Since the nineteenth century, political activists from suffragists to Blackshirts found uniforms to be effective means of amplifying their political messages.[4] Uniforms also helped further the ambitions of nation builders in the non-Western world.[5]

Like other occupational dress, uniforms distinguish members of the organization from outsiders, often with a rise in status. In this regard, even the business suit may take on aspects of uniformity.[6] Uniforms also foster internal homogeneity, which in the case of military uniforms is stratified by badges of rank, insignia, and other characteristics. For individuals, uniforms confer status and may well seem liberating to female and youthful wearers.[7] But uniforms are more sharply gendered than most other clothing.[8] Historically, they have been inextricably intertwined with gender, with military-style uniforms, in particular, being perceived as intensely masculine, even to the point of fetishism.[9] Nurses' uniforms, especially those of nurses who work in hospitals—which like the military (and prisons) are total institutions[10]—share many of the characteristics of military uniforms, though they are, of course, gendered female rather than male.[11] Interestingly enough, patients have been known to adopt uniforms to establish their place in hospital hierarchies.[12]

Uniforms mean many things to those who wear them and those who see them, to those who order them worn and those denied them. Whether military or civilian, uniforms are complex social entities, laden with social connotations and multiple purposes. Historians have not traditionally addressed these issues with respect to military or military-style uniforms, tending to prefer descriptive or narrative approaches to analytical.[13] That is no longer so true as it once was, as some historians have adopted new approaches from social scientists or cultural critics.[14] Over the past half century, these scholars have done much to unravel the complexities of what uniforms mean. The meanings of uniforms clearly carry different weights and interrelate in various ways according to specific time and place—and each is itself the product of a tangled set of interrelated functions and purposes.[15] All these analyses tend to converge on five primary aspects of uniforms, which may be labeled gender, control/class, utility/practicality, identity/status, and symbol. With that caveat, we will now proceed briefly to preview some of the ways these aspects of uniforms emerge in *Cutting a New Pattern* with respect to women who wore them in the Great War. Readers should keep in mind that these aspects are more nodes of meaning than exclusive categories. On that note, we will now briefly highlight some of the ways gender, control, utility, status, and symbol emerge in *Cutting a New Pattern.*

GENDER NORMS AND UNIFORMS

Tension between women's uniforms as expressions of traditional femininity (largely nurse style) and women's uniforms as transgressive of traditional gender constructs (largely military style) surfaces repeatedly in *Cutting a New Pattern*. The nunlike uniforms worn by Russian nurses and the essentially men's uniforms worn by Russian female combatants described by Laurie Stoff (ch. 10) most sharply illustrate the two poles of this dyadic opposition. Russian Sisters of Mercy, professional and quasi-trained nurses in the Russian army, generally adopted highly feminine, traditional uniforms. Such uniforms, like those worn by war nurses in most other nations, suppressed their wearers' sexuality and concealed their individual identity and, in the process, amplified their social value as depersonalized signifiers of idealized femininity. By contrast, Russian women were almost alone among Great War belligerents in their unhesitating adoption of a military identity without seeking to mute its socially threatening aspects; they shaved their heads and made no effort to feminize their uniforms. Perhaps this explains why women combatants in men's uniforms did not provoke the anxieties that women of noncombatant auxiliaries in modified masculine khaki uniforms aroused in Great Britain and its dominions. In essence, Russian women in the Battalion of Death renounced their feminine identities completely; if they did not, their commander, Maria Bochkareva, would dismiss them from the unit or "beat the domestic foolishness out of them."[16]

Maria Bucur (ch. 13) informs us that something very similar occurred in the Balkans on the basis of customs in Albania, Serbia, Montenegro, and Macedonia of "sworn virgins" that allowed some women to dress as men and enter military service. Unlike the cross-dressing women who deceptively passed as men to enter the militaries of France, Italy, Great Britain, and other countries, these Balkan women were understood by their society as actually renouncing their womanhood and becoming men for the duration of the war. This discussion offers an important caution to historians against viewing all biologically female persons who engaged in combat in male dress as cross-dressing women. In these instances, the uniform may have actually decoupled gender and biology.

And perhaps this is precisely why the khaki-clad legions of British and Anzac Amazons provoked the reactions they did: Such women neither renounced their identities as women nor held to traditional notions of femininity. Instead, through adopting the man's khaki service coats, and sometimes even breeches, to their female forms, they seemed to challenge the very notion of what it meant to be women. Women claiming the power to define their own gender identities and roles threatened (or promised) to usher in a new world. Tammy Proctor (ch. 4) recounts how British officials reacted to this threat by banning breast pockets for officers of the Women's Army Auxiliary Corps (WAAC) and requiring their boots or leggings to reach above the uniform skirt hemline (to make pants or leggings invisible). These regulations illustrate the double-edged concern of these officials that WAACs avoid aping masculine military dress while also taking care not to slide into improper displays of femininity.

Both British and American uniforms expressed this ambiguity: Long skirts and capes with starched white shirts drew a bright gendered line between female and male members of the armed forces. British and dominion nurses also wore the veil as a symbol of chastity. Christine Hallett and her colleagues (ch. 3) point out that these feminine touches preempted any possible controversy that the overtly military aspects of their uniforms might inspire. In any event, as several authors note, opinion about women in uniforms during the war did not remain static. Often viewed by the public with amusement, disdain, or even anger early in the war, women in uniform had achieved full acceptance by 1919, their contributions widely acknowledged and often praised.

French officialdom adamantly opposed allowing women to wear military-style uniforms, fearing it would fuel demands for suffrage, as indeed it did elsewhere. French journalists did not hesitate to comment on the gender threat posed by these British uniformed women and their American counterparts, commenting on the "striking masculine appearance" of American women ambulance drivers or describing British women in military auxiliaries as "virile" "amazons," "formed for struggle, violent action, adventures and peril," who emasculated their male counterparts and made them look like "tranquil Sanchos."[17] These biting remarks implied that such transgressions by French women would not be tolerated.

Similar attitudes prevailed in Italy, as Allison Scardino Belzer (ch. 9) informs us. She also calls attention to the stylized representations of women postal carriers, porters, and barbers in military-style uniforms that Umberto Brunelleschi drew during the war. These women, in their high heels and sleek utilitarian uniform dresses, appear both revolutionarily modern and blatantly feminine. There is no way they could be mistaken for men performing these occupations, and this was exactly the reassuring point that these images made to a worried male public. For France, Italy, and other belligerent countries concerned about replacing a population decimated by war and worried about the adverse social impact that millions of broken, disabled soldiers would have on future productivity (and fecundity), it hardly seems surprising that allowing women into uniforms might provoke fears that war had completely upended the social order and left women unwilling or unfit to return to their traditional, now critically needed, roles as mothers and homemakers.

Wearing a uniform had real consequences. Uniforms transformed the interrelated social, occupational, military/civilian, and gendered aspects of women's identities during the war. These new identities were formed in the volatile wartime confrontation between tradition and modernity: They involved women performing traditional roles (caring, nurturing, helping, facilitating) but in increasingly close and dangerous proximity to the exclusively masculine space of the war zone or women performing nontraditional roles (railroad porter, barber, postal worker, munitions worker) in civilian society. In both cases, unmistakably feminine uniforms allowed women to operate in formerly masculine spaces. They also allowed some women to change the ways they lived their gender and sexuality. This tension between women's uniforms and the reinforcement or transgression of gender norms was ubiquitous in the Great War.

UNIFORMS AS MARKERS OF CONTROL AND CLASS

Uniforms enabled organizations to control their members. As Christine Hallett and her colleagues (ch. 3) observe, Queen Alexandra's Imperial Military Nursing Service and Territorial

Force Nursing Service uniforms, with their starched collars and cuffs and their signature scarlet tippets, both signified their professional and distinctly military identities and physically disciplined the nurses to carry themselves with a military deportment. They distinguished these schooled professional nurses from the lesser trained Voluntary Aid Detachment nurses. American farmerettes asserted that a "uniform makes . . . for a sense of responsibility [and] affects their whole attitude towards the work—they must live up to it; they must do it credit."[18]

By the twentieth century, military uniforms had ceased to be major markers of social class for men. Though a discerning eye might distinguish the tailored outfit of a well-to-do colonel from the standard issue (and often ill-fitting) costume of a low-class private (even without the badges of rank), officers and men alike wore pretty much the same uniform.[19] For women it was a different story. Volunteering could be an expensive proposition, especially, as was often the case, when the volunteer must outfit herself.

This way women's uniforms related to their class identity constitutes an additional aspect of their transformative power. Laurie Stoff (ch. 10) notes that both the masculine Russian combat uniform and the feminine nurse's uniform acted alike as class levelers—an important function in highly stratified imperial Russian society. The particular power of the uniform to conceal an aristocratic identity is something that Ilse Bogaerts and Luke De Munck (ch. 8) also emphasize. The particularly colorful example of Belgian Countess Maria van den Steen de Jehay, director of the Elisabeth Hospital, wearing the "British" khaki uniform of her nurses, with its boots and felt hat, to a royal reception in 1915 illustrates the ways that uniforms served to communicate solidarity across classes of a society under siege. But other chapters show that women's uniforms did not always mask class: Occupational uniforms, whether military style or not, male or female, identified their wearers as workers and thus enhanced working-class identities among women as well as men, as particularly noted by Margaret Darrow (ch. 7) with relation to France, Allison Scardino Belzer (ch. 9) on Italy, and Claudia Reichl-Ham (ch. 11) on the Habsburg Empire.

In other circumstances, women's uniforms became markers of elite class privilege. Where few women could afford more than a single dress, observes Maria Bucur (ch. 13), the uniform of British medical volunteers in the Balkans identified them as wealthy foreigners. Barton Hacker (ch. 14) notes that the American YMCA was only one among several organizations that required volunteers to pay for their own uniforms, their travel expenses to and from the war zone, and sometimes their own automobiles; obviously, such volunteerism could be undertaken only by the affluent.

Affluence may also help explain, at least in part, the plethora of self-designed uniforms by wealthy volunteers, flouting convention and uniform regulations alike, which appear in several chapters. Affluence could also assert itself by inversion. The simple, nurse-like uniforms that titled and bourgeois British women adopted in Voluntary Aid Detachments came to stand for the upper-class identity, and consequent sacrifice, of many of their wearers. The inversion of class hierarchies that ensued when they served, as they often did, under lower-middle-class nurse matrons who had graduated from nurse training schools caused no end of friction. Women's uniforms during the Great War, in short, bore conflicting and contradictory relationship to social class, sometimes concealing it but other times sharpening class lines.

THE UTILITY OF UNIFORMS

The utility of uniforms is too easily overlooked. It can range from the simple pleasure of avoiding the middle-class woman's everyday task of deciding what to wear—a Young Women's Christian Association (YWCA) worker enjoyed a "mind . . . free from the cluttery competitive feeling of 'what to put on' each day"[20]—to the enormous advantage of being instantly recognizable as a member of an important organization. Uniforms might offer the practical suitability of fitting garb to the job at hand. "Khaki skirts, flannel blouses, and campaign hats may not be the most beautiful of garments," remarked one young American about her first experience with one, "but they are among the most comfortable and the easiest to work in—and with plenty of pockets."[21] Although never the central theme in any chapter, the utility of wearing a uniform appears again and again.

Uniforms were often constructed in ways that allowed women new freedom of movement so they could do their jobs well. Others emphasize how the simple uniform, made of wool or cotton and free of elaborate trimmings that had been a feature of women's clothes during the Victorian era, itself emancipated them. Ilse Bogaerts and Luc De Munck (ch. 8) comment on how the bra came to replace the corset during the war and how the new uniforms worn by Belgian women volunteers were often made of flexible fabrics such as jersey and tricot—replacements for cotton and wool, which were often in short supply. Women in black two-piece suits, the standard dress of most Belgian women volunteers, performed their critical work in a country too busy fighting for its existence to notice that they were not wearing corsets.

UNIFORMS AS SOURCES OF STATUS AND AGENCY

Uniforms allowed women greatly to widen the scope of their activities and the performance of their social and political roles—as well as change the way they performed gender. Agency could be reflected as mundanely as the varied ways they wore the uniforms, adapting them to the increasingly "unwomanly" conditions in which they worked, or as boldly as demanding the vote in return for wartime service. One Canadian nursing sister in 1915 on Lemnos in freezing weather described herself as looking "like a tough," wearing "dirty skirt, two sweaters, raincoat, old gloves and a sou-wester on, tied under my chin, mud on everything."[22] Russian Sisters of Mercy working near the front might abandon the veiled garb of tradition for more practical "pants, . . . leather jacket, high boots, and . . . Cossack hat."[23] In less extreme circumstances, women merely adapted the uniform for utilitarian, aesthetic, or sentimental reasons. Nurses throughout the war zone rolled up sleeves that were supposed to be cuffed for reasons of occupational hygiene, whereas many Voluntary Aid Detachment nurses, as Hallett and colleagues (ch. 3) note, sewed large red crosses onto the front of their tabards, over their hearts, to convey their humanitarian sympathy. For women, as for men, increasing proximity to the front lines coincided with increasing neglect of uniform regulations.

Uniforms served a broader function in enabling women to transform their identities by enlarging their scopes of action. This theme has many facets. Uniforms allowed at least some women in every belligerent nation to move from the domestic sphere into areas of the public sphere. This was relatively straightforward for nurses. Even in the deeply traditional Ottoman Empire, where any military participation for women was out of the question, fledgling Red Crescent nurse training programs allowed some women to move out of seclusion into the educational realm and the hospital setting, recounts Nicole van Os (ch. 12). The Ottoman nurses' uniform, with its head covering and loose white overcoat, desexualized the nurse in a manner similar to those worn by nurses in Western nations—while at the same time adhering to *tesettür*, the Muslim requirement for women to be properly covered when meeting unrelated men. It was especially important for the Muslim war nurse's identity to remain a clearly nonmilitary, quasi-private one: Amidst social objections to good Muslim women caring intimately for men outside their families, reports on nurses' activities characterized them as fulfilling the role of a mother or sister who could not tend the wounded soldier, thus in principle retaining their domestic identities.

Wearing nurse-style uniforms in the Great War, in short, merely continued a process going on since the early nineteenth century of making nurses respectable and, increasingly, professional. Military-style uniforms represented something newer and more radical. Wearing a military-style uniform, whether as a paid or volunteer worker, gave women new everyday freedoms and new public identities. Women's public persona could be explicitly military, as it was for Canadian military nurses (who held commissioned rank and truly became sister soldiers), Russian and Balkan female soldiers, and U.S. Navy yeoman (f). More commonly, it was quasi-military. Military nurses other than Canadian belong in this category. British, Anzac, and American nurses all served in liminal status, officer-like and wearing military-style uniforms (at least off duty), but without officer rank, pay, or respect; British, Anzac, German, and Habsburg women's auxiliaries, most Red Cross nurses, and American telephone operators belong in this category as well. Public identity could even be civilian, such as for female bus drivers, mail carriers, and munitions workers in Britain, France, Italy, Germany, Austria, and the United States; volunteers for the YMCA and other relief and welfare organizations who wore military-style uniforms fit in this category as well. Civilian workers, in particular, needed uniforms, as the woman in charge of the American Library Association's war effort insisted, "so that they may have standing with the military authorities and be given the respect and attention which an official connection with the military gives."[24]

In addition to literal freedom of movement, uniforms reflected and enabled a host of new freedoms associated with new public roles: financial independence gained through salaried employment or higher wages, new access to public spaces and commercial or military buildings formerly off limits to women, new recreations they were permitted as contributors to the war effort, the travel that military or volunteer organizations might pay for—expensive overseas travel in the case of Canadian, Australian, New Zealand, and American nurses—and the social and professional networks they formed.

THE SYMBOLISM OF UNIFORMS

These aspects of gender, class, control, utility, identity, and status mattered about as much to women as they did to men, but the symbolic impact of uniforms may have mattered a good deal more to women. As hinted in the previous discussion, nurse-style uniforms functioned in way quite distinct from military-style uniforms. In the simplest formulation, for women, the major symbolic significance of the nurse's uniform was instrumental, whereas that of the military uniform was transformational.

Nurses' uniforms functioned in similar ways everywhere, enshrouding their wearers in such sartorial symbols of chastity and purity as veils and white cloth, raising them above the earthly, sexual realm of ordinary woman. This quasi-religious symbolism provided nurses with access to the otherwise masculine territory of the war zone and was supposed to grant protection against men's sexual advances. Individual scholars have previously demonstrated that Russian, British, and other nurses' uniforms served this function, but the wide-ranging scholarship in *Cutting a New Pattern* reveals this theme as truly transnational.

In many nations, the war nurse or other uniformed woman became a potent and effective symbol for wartime propagandists. Edith Cavell was perhaps the most famous uniformed woman turned signifier. A British nurse serving with the Belgian Red Cross, she was charged with secretly helping Allied prisoners escape occupied Belgium, then executed by a German firing squad. Cavell expressly chose not to wear her nurse's uniform to her execution since she was being condemned to death for reasons other than her nursing service. But Allied propaganda images showed her splayed dead on the ground in a white nurse's uniform. These jarring and inaccurate images were intended to stoke hatred of the Germans—the polar opposite of Cavell's last wish: "I realize that patriotism is not enough. I would have no hatred or bitterness for anyone."[25]

Similarly, the 18 Canadian nurses who perished when a U-boat torpedoed the hospital ship *Llandovery Castle* resurfaced on a wartime recruitment poster as drowning damsels in distress, Cynthia Toman (ch. 5) informs us. Every nation used nurses in uniform for wartime propaganda campaigns, often reducing them to quasi-religious images of battlefield angels offering comfort and salvation to wounded and dying soldiers (and therefore making the front more palatable to prospective recruits).[26] Photographs of monarchs, such as Queen Marie of Romania, in nurses' garb also served powerful nationalistic purposes, as Maria Bucur (ch. 13) observes—even if these rulers had no formal training and spent little time in hospitals. For propaganda purposes, the true complexities of women's experiences in uniform had no place: Instead, they were reduced to icons designed to exhort the population to support the war effort and recruit more men to serve.

Women in military-style uniform also frequently appeared in recruiting posters, but wearing that style of uniform arguably had more far-reaching meaning. Women in uniform became symbols used by propagandists on both sides of the conflict, but uniforms, military style in particular, also symbolized women's expanded agency during the Great War. Wearing the uniform invoked the ancient association of military service with citizenship and asserted women's claim to full citizenship, which in the early twentieth-century context meant the right to vote. Women from every walk of life volunteered, but suffragists played an especially interesting role, especially as officers. With the outbreak of war, women's suffrage organizations in both Britain and America decided to suspend their agitation for the vote and instead actively support the war effort. Many thousands of women donned uniforms, not only as members of military auxiliaries but in purely civilian agencies working alongside the armed forces. And that included stepping into such uniformed civilian jobs as police officer or tram conductor. Their material contribution to the war effort undoubtedly contributed to the success of the suffrage strategy, but that success also owed more than a little to the symbolic impact of women's uniformed service during the war.[27] Women also secured a foothold in the military hierarchy that the experience of two world wars would make a permanent place.[28]

The relationship between suffrage and uniformed service could be complicated. Krisztina Robert (ch. 2) draws the straightest line between suffrage and women in uniform. She identifies such officers as Evelina Haverfield, a militant suffragette, who applied what she had learned about publicity during the prewar suffrage campaign to obtain favorable press coverage of women's military activities. In contrast, Tammy Proctor (ch. 4) points out that the Women's Volunteer Reserve also sought to gain favorable publicity by *distancing* themselves from the suffrage movement.

The symbolism of uniforms mattered even in countries where the suffrage movement was less powerful. Women's wartime service failed to gain the vote in either France or Italy. Margaret Darrow (ch. 7) argues that this symbolic claim to citizenship was the very reason that French authorities refused to allow women in uniform, much less to grant military status to the 150,000 women the army employed. Women in uniform challenged a pillar of anti-suffragism—only men deserved the vote because only men paid the blood tax of military service. In December 1917, when the French army made an exception and allowed uniforms for women automobile drivers, military authorities found it necessary to publicly warn French citizens that a woman driver's uniform was not "an improper disguise" but a military necessity.[29] They knew that women in uniform threatened the suffrage status quo.

Although Italian women never served in the armed forces, they did don military-style uniforms to enter the public sphere as letter carriers, train porters, tram operators, and the like, observes Allison Belzer (ch. 9). Although these women may have not been allowed to serve in the army, their uniforms signaled that women, too, had a patriotic role to play. Uniformed service did not win them the vote, but it did provide them a newfound public power that Belzer links to the postwar popularity of Fascism among Italian women. Not the least of the ideology's attractions was that it offered uniforms to women as well as men. Notably, it was Mussolini's regime that first advanced women's suffrage in Italy in 1925. Italian Fascism was far from the only movement that made political uniforms a vital part of its message.[30]

A strong prewar suffrage movement was the most reliable predictor of whether or not uniformed service would secure the right to vote. Where the prewar movement was weak or nonexistent, as in France and Italy, uniformed service led some women to larger public roles but not to enfranchisement. Austria, however, broke the pattern, as discussed by Claudia Reichl-Ham (ch. 11). Women in uniform embodied women's new public expression of patriotism and a step toward emancipation from their traditional roles. But stepping into public fell short of full political participation when the Habsburg Empire disintegrated. Although Austrian women won the vote in 1918, postwar backlash in a much-diminished state frustrated what historian Maureen Healy called "the political arrival of a new cadre of incipient citizens eager to serve the state."[31] Political and economic turmoil led to a deeply retrogressive postwar order that pushed women back into traditional roles and unskilled jobs. Uniformed service was clearly an important factor in advancing women's claims to citizenship, but the franchise alone was no guarantee of true liberation. *Cutting a New Pattern* demonstrates how uniforms in many different political contexts enabled many women to move into the public sphere and advance their claims to political and social citizenship—albeit in varied ways and with sometimes limited or ephemeral effect.

ROADS LESS TRAVELED

Common themes aside, *Cutting a New Pattern* illustrates that European women's experiences in the Great War varied significantly from country to country, a point strongly emphasized by Maria Bucur (ch. 13). She challenges the idea that women's uniformed service became a widespread aspect of European mass culture by reminding us that the vast majority of women in the Balkan states could barely afford rudimentary civilian clothes; how could they possibly purchase a tailor-made uniform specific to wartime volunteering? Nicole van Os (ch. 12) underscores this point. Ottoman society only most reluctantly allowed Muslim women to wear nurses' uniforms; anything more was inconceivable.

The khaki-clad legions of military women parading the streets of postwar London highlighted by Krisztina Robert (ch. 2) found few parallels elsewhere. Equally unique was their triumph over reactionaries concerned about gender norms undermined and men's military service trivialized. Similarly, the United States, with its weak federal state and tradition of well-funded and widespread women's voluntarism, offered a wider panoply of volunteer women's uniforms than perhaps any other country, as exemplified by the Smithsonian's extraordinarily diverse collection of American women's Great War uniforms described by Barton Hacker (ch. 14).

Among all the nurses who served in the Great War, Canadian nurses alone ranked as commissioned officers in the Canadian army, as Cynthia Toman (ch. 5) explains, with the same pay and benefits as their male counterparts. Distinct uniforms enhanced social power through both women's status as commissioned officers and their proximity to the front lines. Having lost 60 of their own in the war, Canadian nurses after the war gained lasting respect and substantial benefits, including privileged access in graduate nursing courses as well as administrative nursing positions. They also became the first Canadian women to vote in federal elections: Canada allowed male and female members of the military and veterans suffrage in 1917 but only extended the franchise to all white women in 1918 and withheld it from indigenous nonveterans and Asian women for many decades.

These examples and others undercut the all-too-common tendency of writers to make sweeping generalizations about women in the Great War without considering the vast intercultural and class differences among these women. Yet by defining the subject of women's uniformed service broadly, *Cutting a New Pattern* also draws linkages between national experiences that might not otherwise have seemed obvious. Because they were prohibited from serving in military uniforms, Italian and Ottoman Muslim women have largely been ignored in previous literature on women in uniform during the Great War. But Allison Scardino Belzer (ch. 9) and Nicole van Os (ch. 12) show how unjustified their absence is. The war began to open up uniformed, if nonmilitary, occupations to women in these countries, allowing some young, unmarried women to escape home confinement and venture into the public realm. The social stakes were high. Women in male jobs were a serious threat to religious and cultural norms in the deeply conservative societies of Italy and the Ottoman Empire, but Belzer and van Os also highlight the creative ways that these societies adapted to such changes.

HOW WE ORGANIZED THE DISCUSSION

We decided to organize *Cutting a New Pattern* as a series of country studies because it seemed the simplest and most direct way to locate potential collaborators. Organizing the book along national lines may privilege nationality above other defining categories of analysis. Allison Belzer has suggested that a volume in which chapters were organized by generation, by geography, or by occupation, rather than by nation, might produce additional and different insights. Transnational analyses interrogating women's experiences at the front and the way they altered the world that Germans called the "front community" (*Frontgemeinschaft*), for example, could map this historical terrain in new ways. These are tasks for future researchers.

We set the broad framework of uniformed women in the Great War, stressing the importance we attached to including nonmilitary as well as military women, but otherwise left the author(s) of each chapter free to follow their own course. Editing has largely been limited to matters of style and usage, but the end result nonetheless reflects a gratifying convergence of the meaning and significance of uniforms for women.

The order of chapters is roughly the Allies, then the Central powers, modified in part by date of entry into the war. Moving west to east with the Allies, we commissioned three chapters on British women in uniform (military [ch. 2], nurses [3], and civilians [4]) and, for convenience, two on English-speaking members of the Commonwealth (Canada [5] and Australia and New Zealand [6]). Chapters on France (7), Belgium (8), Italy (9), and Russia (10) follow. We then proceed with the Central powers: the Habsburg Empire (11) and the Ottoman Empire (12). The Balkans, with their mixed allegiances and varied dates of entry into the war, receive a chapter of their own (13). The United States declared war only in April 1917, so we put those three chapters last, one on civilian women active before U.S. entry (14), one on medical personnel active throughout (15), and one on civilian and military women active only after U.S. entry (16).

Readers may wonder about what may seem a top-heavy bias toward anglophone countries. That has a relatively simple explanation. Women in uniform were far more prevalent in Britain, its Commonwealth, and the United States, and the body of scholarship on their participation is far more extensive than in other countries. *Cutting a New Pattern* has been shaped by its sources. Belligerent governments commissioned artists, photographers, and writers to record what was happening because their output could provide useful propaganda. But government officials also shared the widespread sense that the Great War somehow represented a world-historical event, so they tended to retain these newfangled records rather than discarding them.[32] Any number of amateurs and freelancers multiplied the work of government-sponsored image makers and wordsmiths in the archives. The quantity of material, both published and archival, is much richer in Western Europe and America than farther east and south. The west–east gradient, most likely reflecting relative levels of wealth and education, is decidedly more marked for women than men. The number of women who could afford the considerable costs of outfitting themselves as volunteers was notably lower in Eastern than Western Europe.[33] Social class also shaped our sources. Readers should keep in mind that women in uniform came mostly from the middle and upper classes; they were far more likely than those of the lower classes to be well educated and literate. That disparity meant they were also far more likely than their less educated sisters to preserve (or have preserved) records of their service in memoirs, diaries, and correspondence, whether published or archived.

Readers will note several obvious, and not so obvious, omissions from *Cutting a New Pattern*. Most blatant is the absence of a chapter on German women in uniform. Unfortunately, the scholar who agreed to write the chapter for us was forced to withdraw too late in the process feasibly to replace her.[34] We also hoped to include chapters on some nonbelligerents, in which women also served in uniform; although we commissioned chapters on the Netherlands and Scandinavia, neither in the end materialized. Notable also is the absence of chapters on the British Empire and Commonwealth (other than Canada, Australia, and New Zealand) and the French Empire in toto. Both empires drew extensively on the populations of their Asian and African possessions, as well as China, during the war.[35] We know that both South Africa and India sent nurses to France, but we were unable to locate likely authors. Overall, such scholarship remains sparse, and almost none has focused on the experiences of women, much less their uniforms, if any. Writing of Vietnamese Great War experiences, however, Kimloan Hill, has observed that women in French Indochina offered the colonial governor their willingness to work in the health service or factories "by the side of our French sisters" and found evidence that Indochinese worker camps in France housed women as well as men.[36]

Cutting a New Pattern makes no claim to have the last word on the subject, but it does illuminate the complexity and variety in women's experiences with uniforms and service during the Great War. Across vast national differences, uniforms became instrumental in transforming women's lives. Did the uniform make the woman, or did the woman make the uniform? This volume attests resoundingly that the answer to both is yes, literally and figuratively. Women not only made, wore, and sometimes altered their uniforms themselves; they inhabited their uniformed identities in ways that made an indelible mark on gender and power relations in days to come. Of the many ways the Great War divided the past from the present, few were more important than the altered place of women in society, as many scholars have observed.[37] This book argues that uniforms worn by women both catalyzed and symbolized that transformation. The Great War laid an irregular but critical foundation for women's advancement during the twentieth century, with consequences that are with us still.

NOTES

1. Artemis Yagou, "Foreword: Uniforms in Design—Historical Perspective," *Journal of Design History* 24, no. 2 (May 2011): 101.

2. Anat Rafaeli and Michael G. Pratt, "Tailored Meanings: On the Meaning and Impact of Organizational Dress," *Academy of Management Journal* 18, no. 1 (Jan. 1993): 32–55; Michael G. Pratt and Anat Rafaeli, "Organizational Dress as a Symbol of Multi-layered Social Identities," *Academy of Management Journal* 40, no. 4 (1997): 862–898. See also James Laver, *Modesty in Dress: An Inquiry into the Fundamentals of Fashion* (Boston: Houghton Mifflin, 1969), 63–74; Ruth P. Rubenstein, *Dress Codes: Meanings and Messages in American Culture* (Boulder, Colo.: Westview Press, 1995), 65–82.

3. Frank J. Harmon, "What Should Foresters Wear? The Forest Service's Seventy-Five-Year Search for a Uniform," *Forest and Conservation History* 24, no. 4 (Oct. 1980): 188–199.

4. Barton C. Hacker, "Utility, Control, Status, Symbolism: Reflections on the Multiple Historical Meanings of Uniforms," in *Uniforms: Yesterday, Today, and Tomorrow*, ed. Phillippe Thilly (Brussels: Musée Royal de l'Armée et d'Histoire Militaire, 2007), 72–81; Wendy Parkins, ed., *Fashioning the Body Politic: Dress, Gender, Citizenship* (Oxford: Berg, 2002).

5. Nicolas Cambridge, "Cherry-Picking Sartorial Identities in Cherry-Blossom Land: Uniforms and Uniformity in Japan," *Journal of Design History* 24, no. 2 (May 2011): 171–186; Dilek Himam and Burkay Pasin, "Designing a National Uniform(ity): The Culture of Sümmerbank within the Context of the Turkish Nation-State Project," *Journal of Design History* 24, no. 2 (May 2011): 157–170; Li Li, "Uniformed Rebellion, Fabricated Identity: A Study of Social History of Red Guards in Military Uniforms during the Chinese Cultural Revolution and Beyond," *Fashion Theory* 14, no. 4 (2010): 439–469.

6. Carol S. Saunders and Bette A. Stead, "Women's Adoption of a Business Uniform: A Content Analysis of Magazine Advertisements," *Sex Roles* 15, nos. 3/4 (1986): 197–205; Magnus Mörck and Maria Tullberg, "The Business Suit and the Performance of Masculinity" (paper presented at the Interdisciplinary Conference of Fashion and Dress Culture, Copenhagen, 26–28 Oct. 2005), www.dkds.dk/forskning/fashiondressconference2005/papers

/Magnus_Morck_Maria_Tullaberg.pdf. See also Christopher Breward, *The Suit: Form, Function and Style* (London: Reaktion Books, 2016).

7. Nathan Joseph and Nicholas Alex, "The Uniform: A Sociological Perspective," *American Journal of Sociology* 77, no. 4 (Jan. 1972): 719–730; Rafaeli and Pratt, "Tailored Meanings."

8. Joanne B. Eicher and Mary Ellen Roach-Higgins, "Definition and Classification of Dress: Implications for Analysis of Gender Roles," in *Dress and Gender: Making and Meaning*, ed. Ruth Barnes and Joanne B. Eicher (Oxford: Berg, 1992), 8–28.

9. Jennifer Craik, "The Cultural Politics of the Uniform," *Fashion Theory* 7, no. 2 (April 2003): 127–147; Jennifer Craik, *Uniforms Exposed: From Conformity to Transgression* (Oxford: Berg, 2005), 21–50; Sharon Margaret Peoples, "Military Uniforms in the Eighteenth Century: Gender, Power and Politics" (Ph.D. diss., Australian National University, 2008); Sharon Peoples, "Embodying the Military: Uniforms," *Critical Studies in Men's Fashion* 1, no. 1 (Oct. 2013): 7–21; Dinesh Bhugra and Padmal De Silva, "Uniforms—Fact, Fashion, Fantasy and Fetish," *Sexual and Marital Therapy* 11, no. 4 (1996): 393–406.

10. The term was publicized, if not coined, by sociologist Erving Goffman. See his *Asylums: Essays on the Social Situation of Mental Patients and Other Inmates* (Garden City, N.Y.: Anchor Books, 1961). It refers to organizations like prisons and hospitals that sequester their members, at least in part, from the wider society for a significant period of time; uniforms are a characteristic of total institutions. See also Samuel E. Wallace, ed., *Total Institutions* (New Brunswick, N.J.: Transaction Publishers, 1970).

11. Specifically on nursing garb as uniform, see Jill Mellor Carey, "Nursing Uniforms and Fashion," Inter-Disciplinary Net. See also Susan Hardy and Anthony Corones, "The Nurse's Uniform as Ethopoietic [Character-Making] Fashion," *Fashion Theory* 21, no. 5 (July 2017): 523–552. For an interesting discussion of the challenge to the gender order presented by British women in uniform during the Great War, see Laura L. Doan, "Topsy-Turvydom: Gender Inversion, Sapphism, and the Great War," *GLQ: A Journal of Lesbian and Gay Studies* 12, no. 4 (2006): 517–542.

12. Helen Bright, "Religious Wear (Uniforms) in Psychiatry," *Open Journal of Psychiatry* 4 (2014): 104–112; Stephen Timmons and Linda East, "Uniforms, Status and Professional Boundaries in Hospital," *Sociology of Health and Illness* 33, no. 7 (2011): 1035–1049; Donald J. Marcuse, "The "Army" Incident: The Psychology of Uniforms and Their Abolition on an Adolescent Ward," *Psychiatry: Interpersonal and Biological Processes* 30, no. 4 (1967): 350–375. During the Great War, British army patients also wore special uniforms, the so-called convalescent blues; see Jeffrey Stephen Reznick, *Healing the Nation: Soldiers and the Culture of Caregiving in Britain during the Great War* (Manchester: Manchester University Press, 2004), 99–115.

13. Among the innumerable histories of military uniforms, the following seem to us the most reliable and useful: Paul Martin, *Der Bunte Bock* (Stuttgart: Franckh'sche Verlagshandlung W. Keller, 1963), translated as *European Military Uniforms: A Short History* (London: Spring Books, 1967); John Mollo, *Military Fashion: An Interpretive History of the Uniforms of the Great Armies from the 17th Century to the First World War* (New York: G. P. Putnam's Sons, 1972); Ingrid T. Schick, ed., *Battledress: The Uniforms of the World's Great Armies, 1700 to the Present* (London: Weidenfeld & Nicolson, 1978); Herbert Knötel Jr. and Herbert Sieg, eds., *Uniforms of the World: A Compendium of Army, Navy, and Air Force Uniforms, 1700–1937*, trans. Ronald G. Ball from the 1956 ed. (New York: Charles Scribner's Sons, 1980); Tim Newark, *Brassey's Book of Uniforms* (London: Brassey's, 1998).

14. In recent years, several works have taken the history of men's military uniforms in less descriptive and more analytical directions. See, for example, Daniel Roche, *La culture des apparences: Une histoire du vêtement (XVIIe–XVIIIe siècle)* (Paris: Bayard, 1989), trans. Jean Birrell as *The Culture of Clothing: Dress and Fashion in the "Ancien Régime"* (Cambridge: Cambridge University Press, 1996), 221–256; Alison Matthews David, "Decorated Men: Fashioning the French Soldier 1852–1914," *Fashion Theory* 7, no. 1 (Jan. 2003): 3–34; John P. Dunn, "Clothes to Kill for: Uniforms and Politics in Ottoman Armies," *Journal of the Middle East and Africa* 2, no. 1 (May 2011): 84–107. Laura Ugolini sets the Great War uniform in the context of menswear marketing and consumption; see "Consumers to Combatants? British Uniforms and Identities, 1914–18," *Fashion Theory* 14, no. 2 (April 2010):159–182; "War-Stained: British Combatants and Uniforms, 1914–18," *War and Society* 33, no. 3 (Jan. 2014): 155–171.

15. In addition to the works cited in notes 1 and 4, see Nathan Joseph, *Uniforms and Nonuniforms: Communication through Clothing* (New York: Greenwood Press, 1986); Thomas S. Abler, *Hinterland Warriors and Military Dress: European Empires and Exotic Uniforms* (Oxford: Berg, 1999), 11–21; Paul Fussell, *Uniforms: Why We Are What We Wear* (New York: Houghton Mifflin, 2003); Carrie Hertz, "The Uniform: As Material, as Symbol, as Negotiated Object," *Midwestern Folklore* 32, nos. 1–2 (2007): 43–56.

16. As cited in Stoff, ch. 10, n44.

17. As cited in Darrow, ch. 7, n33.

18. As cited in Vining and Hacker, ch. 16, n51.

19. Jane Tynan, "'Tailoring in the Trenches': The Making of First World War British Army Uniform," in *British Popular Culture and the First World War*, ed. Jessica Meyer (Leiden: Brill, 2008), 71–93; Jane Tynan, *British Army Uniform and the First World War: Men in Khaki* (Basingstoke, U.K.: Palgrave MacMillan, 2013).

20. As cited in Vining and Hacker, ch. 16, n23.

21. As cited in Hacker, ch. 14, n25.

22. As cited in Toman, ch. 5, n30.

23. As cited in Stoff, ch. 10, n29.

24. As cited in Vining and Hacker, ch. 16, n40.

25. Christine E. Hallett, *Edith Cavell and Her Legend* (London: Palgrave MacMillan, 2018), 28.

26. For a useful discussion of the presentation of women, especially nurses, in Great War propaganda, see Elizabeth Prelinger and Barton C. Hacker, "'The Spirit of Woman-Power': Representations of Women in World War I Posters," in *A Companion to Women's Military History*, ed. Barton C. Hacker and Margaret Vining (Leiden: Brill, 2012), 453–484.

27. Margaret Vining and Barton C. Hacker, "From Camp Follower to Lady in Uniform: Women, Social Class and Military Institutions before 1920," *Contemporary European History* 10, no. 3 (Nov. 2001): 353–373; Margaret Vining and Barton C. Hacker, "Suffragists in Uniform: Women Volunteers in the World War" (paper presented at "The Gentler Sex? Responses of the Women's Movement to the First World War 1914–1919," London, Sept. 2005).

28. Margaret Vining, "Women Join the Armed Forces: The Transformation of Women's Military Work in World War II and After (1939–1947)," in Hacker and Vining, *A Companion to Women's Military History*, 233–289.

29. As cited by Darrow, ch. 7, n19.

30. Hacker, "Utility, Control, Status, Symbolism," 73–74.

31. As cited in Reichl-Ham, ch. 11, n123.

32. In the United Kingdom, for example, official photographers collected thousands of images of women at work during the war, most of them in uniforms of one kind or another; see Susan Grayzel, "Introduction: A Change in Attitude: The Women's Work Collection of the Imperial War Museum." See also Agnes Conway and the Imperial War Museum, *The Women at Work Collection from the Imperial War Museum, Lambeth, London* (Brighton, U.K.: Harvester Microform, 1984–1986).

33. In the United States, an Army nurse's full kit for service abroad (which the Army did not pay for) cost about $180, roughly equivalent to $3,172 in today's dollars; see Julia C. Stimson, "The Army Nurse Corps," in *The Medical Department of the United States Army in the World War*, vol. 13, part 2, ed. M.W. Ireland (Washington, D.C.: Government Printing Office, 1922), 301.

34. Germany trailed only the British Commonwealth and the United States in its mobilization of women during the Great War. In lieu of a chapter on German women in uniform in this book, see Bianca Schönberger, "Mobilising 'Etappenhelferinnen' for Service with the Military: Gender Regimes in First World War Germany" (Ph.D. diss., University of Oxford, 2002); Karen Hagemann, "'German Women Help to Win!' German Women and the Military in the Age of World Wars," in Hacker and Vining, *Companion to Women's Military History*, 485–511; Helen Boak, "'Forgotten Female Soldiers in an Unknown Army': German Women Working behind the Lines, 1914–1918," *Women's History Review* 23, no. 4 (July 2014): 577–594; Matthew Stibbe, "Women's Mobilisation for War (Germany)," in *1914-1918-Online: International Encyclopedia of the First World War*, ed. Ute Daniel, Peter Gatrell, Oliver Janz, Heather Jones, Jennifer Keene, Alan Kramer, and Bill Nasson (Berlin: Freie Universität Berlin, 2014), https://doi.org/10.15463/ie1418.10025.

35. Barton C. Hacker, "White Man's War, Coloured Man's Labour: Working for the British Army on the Western Front," *Itinerario* 38, no. 3 (Dec. 2014): 27–44.

36. Kimloan Hill, "Sacrifices, Sex, Race: Vietnamese Experiences in the First World War," in *Race, Empire and First World War Writing*, ed. Santanu Das (New York: Cambridge University Press, 2011), 55.

37. Birgitta Bader-Zaar, "Controversy: War-Related Changes in Gender Relations: The Question of Women's Citizenship," in Daniel et al., *1914-1918-Online: International Encyclopedia of the First World War*, https://doi.org/10.15463/ie1418.10036.

ONE

BEFORE THE GREAT WAR

The Appearance of Women in Uniform, 1854–1914

BARTON C. HACKER AND MARGARET VINING

Interactions between women and military institutions changed dramatically during the course of the nineteenth century. Republicanism and mass mobilization, which accompanied late eighteenth century political revolutions in America and France, combined with the near-contemporary and equally revolutionary economic consequences of industrialization to begin a transformation of Western society that would profoundly alter relationships between states and their armed forces, the structure of military institutions, and women's military roles. The lower-class women who had for centuries followed the army and helped to support it with their labor gave way during the course of the nineteenth century to middle- and upper-class women who, by the first decade of the twentieth century, were becoming full-fledged members of the armed forces. And unlike their predecessors, they wore uniforms, first as nurses, then in a growing number of civilian organizations, and, finally, as members of the armed forces themselves.[1]

THE FIRST WOMEN IN UNIFORM

Women have played significant, if largely unacknowledged, military roles since antiquity but rarely in any kind of uniform before the mid-nineteenth century.[2] The absence of uniforms may account, at least in part, for the invisibility of camp followers and army wives and thus their almost complete absence from the historical record.[3] From the seventeenth until well into the nineteenth century, small numbers of women wore uniforms to pass as soldiers; that practice by its very nature was largely invisible.[4] Much more visible were the women who wore modified nonofficer regimental uniforms as *vivandières* or *cantinières* and their Central European counterparts, the *Marketenderin*. This practice emerged in the eighteenth century; curiously, it became most visible in the mid-nineteenth century, when the practice had largely run its course.[5] These women, like most other female camp followers, came from the lower classes. Such women had largely vanished from armies by the end of the nineteenth century; they were increasingly replaced by middle- and upper-class women who more commonly wore uniforms. The first signs of the new order came during the French Revolution. Western thought borrowed from antiquity, Aristotle's *Politics* in particular, the idea that bearing arms in defense of the state defined citizenship.[6] French attempts to mobilize the entire nation encouraged some women, not all of them French, to claim the citizen's right and obligation to wear uniforms and bear arms, though the high hopes of the 1790s, in fact, remained unrealized for many decades.[7] During the course of the nineteenth century, nursing became the path that first brought middle- and upper-class women into military service—and into uniform.[8]

Nursing had become a target for reformers who wanted to transform what was in the early nineteenth century a menial lower-class occupation into a respectable middle-class calling.[9] This was the explicit goal of Lutheran pastor Theodor Fliedner and his first wife, Friederike, when in 1833 they founded the Institution of Deaconesses, a Protestant nursing sisterhood inspired by the Catholic Sisters of Charity. When Friederike died, Fliedner remarried; his second wife, Caroline, was equally enthusiastic about the project. Established in Kaiserswerth, a small town on the Rhine downriver from Düsseldorf, the institution proved a great success, its ideas quickly spreading to the English-speaking world.[10] The revival of Anglican nursing sisterhoods in the 1840s likewise reflected the significance of religiosity in nursing.[11] As Anne Summers observed, mid-nineteenth century nursing was, in fact, much more about saving souls than bodies. Respectable nursing, even military nursing, retained a significant element of religious calling throughout the nineteenth century and well into the twentieth.[12] This was certainly true of Florence Nightingale, who learned about Kaiserswerth practices during a two-week visit in the summer of 1850 and learned even more when she returned the following summer for three months of study.[13]

At Kaiserswerth, Nightingale also learned about the importance of uniforms in elevating the social standing of nurses. Uniforms formed an integral part of the Kaiserswerth nursing system from the beginning, essential to project the respectability and competence that distinguished new, modern nurses from their disreputable predecessors.[14] Uniforms also continued to symbolize the religiosity of nursing. The graduate deaconess nurse wore an unadorned dark-blue foot-length cotton dress and dark-blue apron with a white snug-fitting cap tied under the chin, white collar, and scarf (Figure 1.1). Modeled on the clothing of a middle-class married townswoman of the lower Rhineland, the uniform was washable and rugged enough to meet nurses' needs but was believed to be neither too menial nor too refined.[15]

Figure 1.1.
Uniforms helped establish the respectability of nursing for single middle-class women. This composite drawing based on original sources in the Fliedner Archive, Kaiserswerth, Germany, by Irene Schuessler Poplin shows a deaconess-nurse uniform from the 1830s. From Poplin, Nursing History Review. *Barbara Bates Center for the Study of the History of Nursing, University of Pennsylvania School of Nursing.*

Nightingale took the lesson to heart, demanding that her nurses in the Crimea be uniformed. "The rule about wearing the regular dress [uniform] applies *particularly* to when they are *out of* Hospital," she insisted. "The necessity of distinguishing them *at once* from camp followers is particularly obvious when they are *not* engaged in Hospital work."[16] Uniforms, Nightingale's "regular dress," distinguished her lady volunteer and trained nurses from lower-class camp followers, some of whom still nursed during the Crimean War, though only in token numbers. Most mid-nineteenth century hospital attendants were male orderlies. In such an environment, uniforms became all the more necessary for female nurses if they were to enjoy even a modicum of respect. Though perhaps less significant to Nightingale, uniforms also asserted nurses' professional status, something appreciated by those who actually made their living as nurses but unwelcome to the untrained ladies who also volunteered; they believed the uniform made them look like domestic servants.[17] Lady volunteer Martha Nicol, for instance, fully understood the rationale for uniforms but doubted its validity and resented the religious implications; though she did not dislike the uniform's gray color, she was less enthusiastic about its material and texture, to say nothing of its leveling of social class.[18]

The habits of nursing sisters served much the same function as uniforms and may, in fact, have served, at least in part, as models for nurses' uniforms.[19] Long inspired by their training and professionalism, Nightingale made nursing sisters, Anglican as well as Catholic, the core of her hospital nursing staff at Scutari, the main British army hospital on the Turkish coast.[20] Nursing sisters were even more prominent in the Russian and French armies. In Russia as in England, the plight of sick and wounded soldiers inspired humanitarian action. The tsar's sister-in-law, the Grand Duchess Elena Pavlovna, founded the semireligious Order of the Exaltation of the Cross, which drew volunteer female nurses primarily from the aristocracy and upper bourgeoisie. Unlike their British and French counterparts, the Russian Sisters of Charity often worked under fire.[21]

French Sisters of Charity represented a much older tradition of nursing the poor. Abolished in the French Revolution but restored by Napoleon I, the Sisters of Charity had reestablished their control of nursing in civilian hospitals early in the nineteenth century.[22] In the Crimean War, they also revived their military nursing legacy, accompanying French forces as essential staff members of military hospitals.[23] Although religious and secular tensions persisted, uniforms for military nurses became increasingly prevalent in the decades before the Great War. Whether in military nursing corps, the Red Cross, or other nursing services, uniforms had become commonplace well before the Great War.[24] By 1914, the secular nurse's uniform had become more or less standardized. Its distinctive characteristics were a full apron over a white or dark ankle-length dress, with flat shoes and a head covering, usually with a badge designating the organization. Nurses in uniform, in short, represented nothing new, though their numbers during the war far exceeded anything known before. Nurse-style uniforms were also worn by many women in wartime relief and welfare organizations, especially those dealing with refugees.[25]

WOMEN AND MILITARY-STYLE UNIFORMS IN THE LATE NINETEENTH CENTURY

Unlike nurses in uniform, the late nineteenth-century appearance of women in military-style uniforms represented something new. Infatuation with uniforms and their associated paraphernalia has long been recognized as one of the markers of militarizing society.[26] The equation of military service with citizenship may have stimulated, at least in part, the rage for uniforms that swept the later nineteenth-century Western world and beyond, from the highest social levels to the least. Apparel of uniformity spread from the armed forces and veterans' societies to the higher civil service, to professionals in several fields, to members of numerous fraternal and social organizations, to factory workers, to youth groups, and even to school children. Pervasive nationalism and a growing martial climate characterized many such organizations. Uniforms for such public servants as police, firemen, postmen, and railroad employees all date from this same period.[27] Women as well as men found reasons to wear uniforms. Even a young Queen Victoria found a uniform appropriate to wear on occasion (Figure 1.2), as did other female members of the ruling classes throughout Europe.[28]

Charity also became militarized in the late nineteenth century. Red Cross nursing may represent the most widespread, and most predictable, instance,[29] but the most unexpected was the Salvation Army, which clothed religious revivalism in military trappings. Defining missionaries as soldiers, William Booth modeled the regulations for the army he cofounded with his wife, Catherine, on the British army's *Field Pocket-Book for the Auxiliary Forces*.[30] Members also wore military-style uniforms, men and women alike. Unlike the British army, the Salvation Army welcomed women into its ranks.[31] Modeled on male military officer's

Figure 1.2.
By the nineteenth century, military-style uniforms had become acceptable court dress. This drawing shows a young Queen Victoria in uniform reviewing her troops in 1856. British Museum, London.

uniforms, women's uniforms normally featured a Norfolk-style jacket with four front patch pockets, two at the bodice and two at the skirt, worn over a shirtwaist, often with a tie. Women's uniforms substituted an ankle-length skirt for the male trousers.[32] Although this style did spread to women in several other organizations, the sight of a woman in a military-style uniform remained quite unusual on the eve of the Great War. But that changed decisively during the war. Many observers noted the ubiquity of women in uniform, frequently with disapproval early in the war, but more often with admiration toward the end. Even factory workers and clerks might appear in uniform-like garb (Figure 1.3).

Military-style uniforms of the kind pioneered by the Salvation Army were worn not only by military women but by women in a wide variety of paramilitary organizations and an even wider range of relief and welfare organizations. Hundreds of thousands of women in military uniforms were what made the experience of the Great War transformational. This style subsequently became standard attire for women in other organizations before the Great War and spread even more widely during the war, though often with such variations as bloomers or another form of pants beneath a shorter skirt. Female motor drivers typically wore breeches rather than skirts. Fabrics and colors varied, but blue, gray, and khaki were favored. Low-heeled black or tan boots or shoes; some kind of headgear, most often a military-style broad-brimmed campaign hat with a badge; and insignia completed the ensemble.

Policewomen, letter carriers, and tram drivers, among others on the home front, typically wore military-style uniforms on the job, too, just as men in the same positions did; again, like other women wearing military-style uniforms, they usually substituted skirts for

Figure 1.3.
Women as well as men wore uniforms as members of the Salvation Army. This 1880 magazine illustration by an unidentified artist shows Salvation Army women in uniform as they conduct their first dockside service in New York City. Salvation Army Historical Center, Atlanta, GA.

breeches.[33] Even military nurses, especially after the establishment of formal military nursing services such as the U.S. Army Nurse Corps (1902) and Navy Nurse Corps (1908)[34] (Figure 1.4), the British Queen Alexandra's Imperial Military Nursing Service and its naval equivalent (1902), the Territorial Force Nursing Service (1907), the First Aid Nursing Yeomanry (1907), and Voluntary Aid Detachments,[35] adopted military-style uniforms for wear when they were not on the wards, as this volume attests (Figure 1.5).[36]

UNIFORMING GIRLS

By the early twentieth century, perhaps most surprising of all, some girls had also begun to wear uniforms. Uniforming youth began with charity schools several centuries earlier. School uniforms seem to have developed quite independently of military uniforms, initially,

Figure 1.4.
The original U.S. Navy Nurse Corps comprised a superintendent, a chief nurse, and 18 nurses, all of whom had served in the Spanish-American War. U.S. Naval Historical Center, Washington, DC.

Figure 1.5.
Members of the First Aid Nursing Yeomanry (FANY) in military-style uniforms on parade in about 1909. Initially opting for elegant military dress—red tunics, riding skirts, and showy peaked caps—by 1911, they had shifted to more practical khaki, tunics, and divided skirts over riding breeches. FANY Organization.

at least, as a means of marking orphans and other needy children as the recipients of charity.[37] The use of uniforms to restrict and control, to mark a lower-status member of the community, long persisted.[38] But in more recent times, uniforms have, for the most part, been restricted to private schools, their punitive origins forgotten as they became markers of high status.[39] Discipline, hierarchy, and order were central to the argument for school uniforms from the beginning and have remained so, though not, in more recent years, with lower-class connotations.

Uniforms became part of the increasing militarization of both public and private schools in the late nineteenth and twentieth centuries, affecting girls as well as boys.[40] Advocates of discipline and hierarchy in the schools promoted uniforms and military-style drill

Figure 1.6.
The early Boy Scout movement attracted girls as well, leading to the British establishment of the Girl Guides. This 1909 photo shows the First Kidderminster Girl Guides in uniform. Girl Guides Association, London.

to sustain school order as well as enhance military preparedness.[41] Such training would not only benefit the schools and the nation, they believed, but also stimulate the mental development of the pupils.[42] Military drill and officer training in the public schools was controversial then and has remained so.[43] At the opening of the twentieth century, militarized schools were joined by an array of voluntary youth movements, foremost among them the Boy Scouts inspired by R.S.S. Baden-Powell in Britain; they shared a distinctly military cast often expressed by uniforms.[44] Despite the clear intent embodied in its name, the Boy Scouts attracted large numbers of girls from the beginning. Baden-Powell responded by founding the Girl Guides, like the Boy Scouts uniformed but with even more direct ties to the military (Figure 1.6).[45]

The Girl Guides were conceived, at least in part, as a kind of cadet branch or feeder organization for the Voluntary Aid Detachments. They also became involved with the First Aid Nursing Yeomanry. During the Great War, the Girl Guides expanded greatly through its members' participation in a variety of war-related volunteer work, eventually surpassing the Boy Scouts in numbers. The Girl Guides were but the most prominent of contemporary girls' organizations that sprang up everywhere in the Western world; to a notable degree, military nursing or first aiding provided a model for their members.[46] The British example inspired worldwide emulation, its commitment to voluntarism and internationalism largely counterbalancing its militaristic tendencies, which were, in any event, chiefly organizational.[47] For individual scouts, girls and boys alike, the movement represented freedom and individuality far more than regimentation. The uniform was central to both the repressive and liberating meaning of the scout movement.[48]

On the eve of the Great War, women, mainly of the higher classes, had won the right to wear uniforms in a growing number of charitable and noncharitable organizations. Many women fully bought into the period's growing nationalism and militarism. They were more than ready to respond to their nations' next calls for mobilization and to stake their claims for full citizenship. Military thinking pervaded the suffrage movement no less than the Red Cross and the Salvation Army. Military style inspired the uniforms worn by civilian volunteers who served with relief and welfare organization in the Great War. The Red Cross and the Salvation Army pioneered this development in the nineteenth century, and both uniformed their female as well as male members. Many other organizations followed suit. Similar in color, material, and style to what soldiers wore, the uniforms of civilian volunteers allowed them to fit into the military organizations with which they worked, a matter of particular importance to the tens of thousands of women who volunteered. Civilian uniforms also included insignia and badges of rank, clear indicators of the hierarchical assumptions they shared with the military. Such uniforms, like their military counterparts, also distinguished their wearers from the civilian population at large. They visually represented their wearers' loyalty, patriotism, and acceptance of the obligations of citizenship.

NOTES

1. This chapter draws extensively on several of the authors' previous publications, especially Barton C. Hacker, "Reformers, Nurses, and Ladies in Uniform: Industrialization and the Changing Status of Military Women (1815–1914)," in *A Companion to Women's Military History*, ed. Barton C. Hacker and Margaret Vining (Leiden: Brill, 2012), 137–187; Barton C. Hacker and Margaret Vining, "Cutting a New Pattern: Uniforms and Women's Mobilization for War, 1854–1919," in "Textile History and the Military," supplement, *Textile History* 41, no. 1 (May 2010), 108–143; Margaret Vining and Barton C. Hacker, "From Camp Follower to Lady in Uniform: Women, Social Class and Military Institutions before 1920," *Contemporary European History* 10, no. 3 (Nov. 2001): 353–373.

2. Hacker and Vining, *Companion to Women's Military History*, 1–140. On the history of women in uniform generally, see Elizabeth Ewing, *Women in Uniform through the Centuries* (London: B.T. Batsford, 1975).

3. Barton C. Hacker. "Women and Military Institutions in Early Modern Europe: A Reconnaissance," *Signs: Journal of Women in Culture and Society* 6, no. 4 (Summer 1981): 643–671; Doreen M. Lehr, "Do Real Women Wear Uniforms? Invisibility and the Consequences for the U.S. Military Wife," *Minerva* 14, no. 3 (Dec. 1996): 29–44.

4. C.H. Firth, *Cromwell's Army: A History of the English Soldier during the Civil War, the Commonwealth and the Protectorate* (London: Methuen, 1902), 300–301, may have been the first modern historian to call attention to the phenomenon of women using men's uniforms to disguise themselves as soldiers. Rudolf M. Dekker and Lotte C. van de Pol, *The Tradition of Female Transvestism in Early Modern Europe*, trans. Judy Marcure and Lotte C. van de Pol (New York: St. Martin's Press, 1989), identified 83 women who donned male attire and pursued military careers during the seventeenth and eighteenth centuries. The phenomenon persisted well into the nineteenth century. Some 240 women are known to have served in the American Civil War disguised as soldiers, and there may well have been hundreds more; see DeAnne Blanton and Lauren M. Cook, *They Fought Like Demons: Women Soldiers in the American Civil War* (Baton Rouge: Louisiana State University Press, 2002). See also Richard H. Hall, *Women on the Civil War Battlefront* (Lawrence: University Press of Kansas, 2006); and, more generally, Julia Wheelwright, *Amazons and Military Maids: Women Who Dressed as Men in Pursuit of Life, Liberty and Happiness* (London: Pandora, 1989).

5. Thomas Cardoza, *Intrepid Women: Cantinières and Vivandières of the French Army* (Bloomington: Indiana University Press, 2010); Cricket Bauer, "Viva la Vivandières: A Short History of Women in Pseudo-military Costumes," *MI: Military Images* 21, no. 6 (May–June 2000): 20–24; Gil Mihaely, "L'effacement de la cantinière ou la virilisation de l'armée française au XIXe siècle," in "Pour une histoire culturelle de la guerre au XIXe siècle," *Revue d'histoire du XIXe siècle*, no. 30 (2005), https://doi.org/10.4000/rh19.1008. For citations to examples of such uniforms, see Hacker, "Women and Military Institutions," 666.

6. Barton C. Hacker, "Military Institutions and Social Order: Transformations of Western Thought Since the Enlightenment," *War and Society* 11, no. 2 (Oct. 1993): 1–23.

7. Vining and Hacker, "From Camp Follower to Lady in Uniform"; Dale L. Clifford, "Can the Uniform Make the Citizen? Paris, 1789–1791," *Eighteenth-Century Studies* 34, no. 3 (Spring 2001): 363–364; Claudia Opitz, "Der Bürger wird Soldat—und die Bürgerin . . . ? Die Revolution, der Krieg und die Stellung der Frau nach 1789," in *Sklavin oder Bürgerin? Französische Revolution und Neue Weiblichkeit 1760–1830*, ed. Viktoria Schmidt Linsenhoff (Frankfurt: Historisches Museum Frankfurt, 1989), 38–54; David Hopkin, "Female Soldiers and the Battle of the Sexes in France: The Mobilization of a Folk Motif," *History Workshop Journal* 56, no. 1 (Autumn 2003): 78–104; David Barry, *Women and Political Insurgency: France in the Mid-Nineteenth Century* (New York: St. Martin's Press, 1996), 9–10.

8. On the general relationship between war and modern nursing, see especially Quinccalea Brunk, "Nursing at War: Catalyst for Change," *Annual Review of Nursing Research* 15 (1997): 217–236; Gail Mitchell, Mary Ferguson-Paré, and Joy Richards, "Exploring an Alternative Metaphor for Nursing: Relinquishing Military Images and Language," *Nursing Leadership* 16, no. 1 (2003): 48–60.

9. Sarah (Sairy) Gamp, an utterly disreputable nurse-midwife in Charles Dickens, *The Life and Adventures of Martin Chuzzlewit* (London: Chapman & Hall, 1844), came to symbolize the shortcomings of early nineteenth-century nursing. Such works as Anne Summers, "The Mysterious Demise of Sarah Gamp: The Domiciliary Nurse and Her Detractors, c. 1830–1860," *Victorian Studies* 32, no. 3 (Spring 1989): 365–386; Katherine Williams, "From Sarah Gamp to Florence Nightingale: A Critical Study of Hospital Nursing Systems from 1840 to 1897," in *Rewriting Nursing History*, ed. Celia Davies (London: Croom Helm, 1980), 41–75, deemed Gamp a caricature. More recently, Carol Helmstadter, "A Third Look at Sarah Gamp," *Canadian Bulletin of Medical History* 30, no. 2 (2013): 141–159, has reviewed both the literature and the original sources, concluding that Dickens was more realist than caricaturist.

10. E.D. Ferguson, "The Evolution of the Trained Nurse [Part 1]," *American Journal of Nursing* 1, no. 8 (May 1901): 535–538; John H. Lowman, "The Evolution and the Development of the Nurse," *American Journal of Nursing* 8, no. 1 (Oct. 1907): 8–17; Lee Chambers-Schiller, "The Single Woman Reformer: Conflicts between Family and Vocation, 1830–1860," *Frontiers: A Journal of Women Studies* 3, no. 3 (Autumn 1978): 41–48; Catherine M. Prelinger, "The Nineteenth-Century Deaconessate in Germany: The Efficacy of a Family Model," in *German Women in the Eighteenth and Nineteenth Centuries: A Social and Literary History*, ed. Ruth-Ellen B. Joeres and Mary Jo Maynes (Bloomington: Indiana University Press, 1986), 215–229.

11. Martha Vicinus, *Independent Women: Work and Community for Single Women, 1850–1920* (Chicago: University of Chicago Press, 1985), 46–84; Carol Helmstadter, "From the Private to the Public Sphere: The First Generation of Lady Nurses in England," *Nursing History Review* 9 (2001): 127–140; Richard Huntsman, Mary Bruin, and Deborah Holttum, "'Twixt Candle and Lamp': The Contribution of Elizabeth Fry and the Institution of Nursing Sisters to Nursing Reform," *Medical History* 46, no. 3 (July 2002): 351–380. More generally, see Susan Mumm, *Stolen Daughters, Virgin Mothers: Anglican Sisterhoods in Victorian England* (London: Leicester University Press, 1999); Susan Mumm, *All Saints Sisters of the Poor: An Anglican Sisterhood in the Nineteenth Century* (Woodbridge, U.K.: Boydell Press, 2001).

12. Anne Summers, "The Costs and Benefits of Caring: Nursing Charities, c 1830–1860," in *Medicine and Charity before the Welfare State*, ed. Jonathan Barry and Colin Jones (London: Routledge, 1991), 133–148. On the persistence of religiosity beyond the mid-nineteenth century, see Sioban Nelson, "From Salvation to Civics: Service to the Sick in Nursing Discourse," *Social Science and Medicine* 53, no. 9 (Nov. 2001): 1217–1225. See also Barbra Mann Wall, "Science and Ritual: The Hospital as Medical and Sacred Space, 1865–1920," *Nursing History Review* 11 (Feb. 2003): 51–68.

13. JoAnn G. Widerquest, "Florence Nightingale's Calling," *Second Opinion* 17, no. 3 (Jan. 1992): 108–121; Florence Nightingale, diary, 1850, in Michael D. Calabria, *Florence Nightingale in Egypt and Greece: Her Diary and "Visions"* (Albany: State University of New York Press, 1997), 79–81; Calabria, *Florence Nightingale in Egypt and Greece*, 147; E.D. Ferguson, "The Evolution of the Trained Nurse [Part 2]," *American Journal of Nursing* 1, no. 9 (June 1901): 620–626; Lucy R. Seymer, "Florence Nightingale at Kaiserswerth," *American Journal of Nursing* 51, no. 7 (July 1951): 424–426.

14. For persisting concerns about respectability as justification for nurses' uniforms, see Jane Brooks and Anne Marie Rafferty, "Dress and Distinction in Nursing, 1860–1939: 'A Corporate (as Well as Corporeal) Armour of Probity and Purity,'" *Women's History Review* 16, no. 1 (2007): 41–57.

15. Irene Schuessler Poplin, "Nursing Uniforms: Romantic Idea, Functional Attire, or Instrument of Social Change?" *Nursing History Review* 2 (1994): 153–167.

16. Florence Nightingale, letter to Lady Canning, 9 Sept. 1855, in *"I Have Done My Duty": Florence Nightingale in the Crimean War, 1854–56*, ed. Sue M. Goldie (Iowa City: University of Iowa Press, 1987), 154 (emphasis in original).

17. Anne Summers, "Pride and Prejudice: Ladies and Nurses in the Crimean War," *History Workshop* 16 (1983): 32–56; Anne Summers, *Angels and Citizens: British Women as Military Nurses 1854–1914* (London: Routledge & Kegan Paul, 1988), 29–66; Carol Helmstadter, "Class, Gender and Professional Expertise: British Military Nursing in the Crimean War," in *One Hundred Years of Wartime Nursing Practices, 1854–1953*, ed. Jane Brooks and Christine E. Hallett (Manchester: Manchester University Press, 2015), 23–41; David Stanley, "Lights in the Shadows: Florence Nightingale and Others Who Made Their Mark," *Contemporary Nurse* 24, no. 1 (Feb. 2007): 45–51; Christopher J. Gill and Gillian C. Gill, "Nightingale in Scutari: Her Legacy Re-examined," *Clinical Infectious Diseases* 40 (15 June 2005): 1799–1805; Ewing, *Women in Uniform*, 39–42; Richard Huntsman, Mary Bruin, and Deborah Holttum, "Light before Dawn: Naval Nursing and Medical Care during the Crimean War," *Journal of the Royal Naval Medical Service* 88, no. 1 (2002): 5–27.

18. Martha Nicol, *Ismeer; or, Smyrna and Its British Hospital in 1855, by a Lady* (London: J. Madden, 1856), 9–10.

19. On the long history of habits as worn by nursing sisters (generically and largely interchangeably referred to as Sisters of Charity or Sisters of Mercy), whether Catholic or Protestant, see Elizabeth Kuhns, *The Habit: A History of the Clothing of Catholic Nuns* (New York: Image Books, 2003), 91–94, 109–111, 124–129. For a discussion of the uniform-like characteristics of the habit, see Sally Dwyer McNulty, *Common Threads: A Cultural History of Clothing in American Catholicism* (Chapel Hill: University of North Carolina Press, 2014), 6–10.

20. Fanny M. Taylor, *Eastern Hospitals and English Nurses: The Narrative of Twelve Months' Experience in the Hospitals of Koulali and Scutari, by a Lady Volunteer* (London: Hurst & Blackett, 1856), 1:316; Evelyn Bolster, *The Sisters of Mercy in the Crimean War* (Cork: Mercier Press, 1964); Sioban Nelson, *Say Little, Do Much: Nursing, Nuns, and Hospitals in the Nineteenth Century* (Philadelphia: University of Pennsylvania Press, 2001), 76–77. See also Anna Jameson, *Sisters of Charity, Catholic and Protestant, Abroad and at Home*, 2nd ed. (London: Longman, Green, Brown & Longmans, 1855).

21. John Shelton Curtiss, "Russian Sisters of Mercy in the Crimea, 1854–55," *Slavic Review* 25, no. 1 (Mar. 1966): 84–100; Evelyn R. Benson, "On the Other Side of the Battle: Russian Nurses in the Crimean War," *Image: Journal of Nursing Scholarship* 24, no. 1 (Spring 1992): 65–68; T.S. Sorokina, "Russian Nursing in the Crimean War," *Journal of the Royal College of Physicians of London* 29, no. 1 (Jan.–Feb. 1995): 57–63.

22. Dora B. Weiner, "The French Revolution, Napoleon, and the Nursing Profession," *Bulletin of the History of Medicine* 46, no. 3 (May–June 1972): 274–305; Colin Jones, "Sisters of Charity and the Ailing Poor," *Social History of Medicine* 2, no. 3 (Dec. 1989): 339–348; Edward R. Udovic, "What about the Poor? Nineteenth-Century Paris and the Revival of Vincentian Charity," *Vincentian Heritage Journal* 14, no. 1 (Spring 1993): 69–94.

23. María Ángeles Infante, "The Daughters of Charity in the History of Military Health Care and in the History of Nursing," *Anales* 123, no. 4 (July–Aug. 2015): 327–343; Thomas Chenery, dispatch from the Crimea about French medical arrangements and the performance of the Sisters of Charity, published in *The Times*, 13 Oct. 1854, as quoted in Phillip Knightley, *The First Casualty: The War Correspondent as Hero and Myth-Maker from the Crimea to Kosovo* (London: André Deutsch, 1975), 14; L. Baudens, *On Military and Camp Hospitals and the Health of Troops in the Field; Being the Results of a Commission to Inspect the Sanitary Arrangements of the French Army and Incidentally of Other Armies in the Crimean War*, trans. Franklin B. Hough (New York: Baillière, 1862); Thomas Longmore, *The Sanitary Contrasts of the British and French Armies during the Crimean War* (London: Charles Griffin, 1883); A.J. Barker, *The War against Russia 1854–1856* (New York: Holt, Rinehart & Winston, 1970), 221; Stella Bingham, *Ministering Angels* (Oradell, N.J.: Medical Economics, 1979), 42; Helen Rappaport, *No Place for Ladies: The Untold Story of Women in the Crimean War* (London: Aurum Press, 2007), 22–23.

24. Margaret H. Darrow, *French Women and the First World War: War Stories of the Home Front* (Oxford: Berg, 2000), 28–30; Summers, *Angels and Citizens*, 125–153; Ewing, *Women in Uniform*, 45–46; Julia C. Stimson and Julia O. Flikke, *Nurses in Action: The Story of the Army Nurse Corps* (Philadelphia: J.B. Lippincott, 1943), 115–119.

25. Several chapters (notably, 3, 5, 8, 14, and 15) in this volume address the development of nurses' uniforms in specific countries before and during the Great War. For a general history of nurses' uniforms from the mid-nineteenth century through the Great War, see Christina Bates, *A Cultural History of the Nurse's Uniform* (Gatineau, Que.: Canadian Museum of Civilization, 2012), chs. 1–3. On the symbolism of the nineteenth-century nurse's uniform, see also Sibel Öner Yalçın, Serap Torun, and Funda Gülay Kadıoğlu, "Nurse Uniforms' Evolution as Part of Medicine Cultural History—Tıbbın kültür tarihi çerçevesinde hemşire üniformasının evrimi," *Mersin Üniversitesi Tıp Fakültesi Lokman Hekim Tıp Tarihi ve Folklorik Tıp Dergisi* 4, no. 1 (2014): 6–15.

26. Alfred Vagts, *A History of Militarism: Civilian and Military*, rev. ed. (New York: Meridian Books, 1959). See also John R. Gillis, ed., *The Militarization of the Western World* (New Brunswick, N.J.: Rutgers University Press, 1989), especially ch. 1, Geoffrey Best, "The Militarization of European Society, 1870–1914."

27. Ewing, *Women in Uniform*, ch. 5; Sally A. Hastings, "The Empress' New Clothes and Japanese Women, 1868–1912," *Historian* 55, no. 4 (Summer 1993): 677–679; Rachel Chrastil, "Military Preparation in Peacetime: Training Societies, 1871–92," *Dix-Neuf: Journal of the Society of Dix-Neuviémistes*, no. 4 (Apr. 2005): 35–51; "Military Training in Public Schools," in *Issues of the Day; Being a Text-Book on the Political Situation, Past and Present*, 5th ed. (Chicago: Conrad H. Oliver, 1903), 432–434; Barton C. Hacker, "Control, Utility, Status, Symbolism: Reflections on the Multiple Historical Meanings of Uniforms," in *Uniforms: Yesterday, Today, and Tomorrow*, ed. Phillippe Thilly (Brussels: Musée Royal de l'Armée et d'Histoire Militaire, 2007), 72–81.

28. Ewing, *Women in Uniform*, 52–67; Philip Mansel, *Dressed to Rule: Royal and Court Costume from Louis XIV to Elizabeth II* (New Haven, Conn.: Yale University Press, 2005), 11–27.

29. John F. Hutchinson, *Champions of Charity: War and the Rise of the Red Cross* (Boulder, Colo.: Westview Press, 1996), 202; see also Dieter Riesenberger, "Zur Professionalisierung und Militarisierung der Schwestern Roten Kreuz vor dem Ersten Weltkrieg," *Militärgeschichtliche Mitteilungen* 53, no.1 (1994): 49–72.

30. Richard Collier, *The General Next to God: The Story of William Booth and the Salvation Army* (Glasgow: William Collins, 1965), 64; Margaret Troutt, *The General Was a Lady: The Story of Evangeline Booth* (Nashville, Tenn.: A.J. Holman, 1980), 34; Roy Hattersley, *Blood and Fire: William and Catherine Booth and Their Salvation Army* (New York: Doubleday, 1999), 235–239; Pamela J. Walker, *"Pulling the Devil's Kingdom Down": The Salvation Army in Victorian Britain* (Berkeley: University of California Press, 2001), 113–117; Norman H. Murdock, *Origins of the Salvation Army* (Knoxville: University of Tennessee Press, 1994), 100–105; Diane Winston, *Red-Hot and Righteous: The Urban Religion of the Salvation Army* (Cambridge, Mass.: Harvard University Press, 1999), 143–190.

31. Diane Winston, "Living in the Material World: The Changing Role of Salvation Army Women, 1880–1918," *Journal of Urban History* 28, no. 4 (May 2002): 466–487; Andrew Mark Eason, *Women in God's Army: Gender and Equality in the Early Salvation Army* (Waterloo, Ont.: Wilfrid Laurier University Press, 2003).

32. Jennifer Le Zotte, "'Be Odd': The Contradictory Use of Dress in the Gilded Age Salvation Army," *Winterthur Portfolio* 47, no. 4 (Winter 2013): 248–258.

33. For numerous examples, see Elizabeth Ewing, *Women in Uniform*.

34. Mary T. Sarnecky, *A History of the U.S. Army Nurse Corps* (Philadelphia: University of Pennsylvania Press, 1999), 29–79; Susan H. Godson, *Serving Proudly: A History of Women in the U.S. Navy* (Annapolis, Md.: Naval Institute Press, 2001), 32–55.

35. Eric Gruber von Arni and Gary Searle, *Sub Cruce Candida: A Celebration of One Hundred Years of Army Nursing, 1902–2002* (London: Queen Alexandra's Royal Army Nursing Corps Association, 2002), ch. 2; Kathleen M. Harland, "A Short History of Queen Alexandra's Royal Naval Nursing Service," *Journal of the Royal Naval Medical Service* 70, no. 2 (Summer 1984): 60–61; Summers, *Angels and Citizens*, ch. 9; Janet Lee, *War Girls: The First Aid Nursing Yeomanry in the First World War* (Manchester: Manchester University Press, 2005), ch. 1; Bingham, *Ministering Angels*, 121–126.

36. See especially chs. 3, 5, and 15 in this volume.

37. Alexander Davidson, *Blazers, Badges and Boaters: A Pictorial History of School Uniforms* (Horndean, U.K.: Scope Books, 1990), 11–20; see also P. Cunnington and C. Lucas, *Charity Costumes of Children, Scholars, Almsfolk, Pensioners* (New York: Barnes & Noble, 1978).

38. Janice Lee, "Administrative Treatment of Women Students at Missouri State University, 1868–1899," *Missouri Historical Review* 87, no. 4 (1993): 372–386; Lauretta F. Byars, "Lexington's Colored Orphan Industrial Home, 1892–1913," *Register of the Kentucky Historical Society* 89, no. 2 (Spring 1991): 147–178; Sarah Dwyer-McNulty, "Hems to Hairdos: Cultural Discourse and Philadelphia Catholic High Schools in the 1920s, a Case Study," *Journal of American Studies* (Cambridge) 37, no. 2 (Aug. 2003): 179–200.

39. Davidson, *Blazers, Badges and Boaters*, 69–74.

40. D. Kirk and B. Spiller, "Schooling for Docility: Drill, Gymnastics and the Problems of the Body in Victorian Public Schools," in *Child and Citizen: Genealogies of Schooling and Subjectivity*, ed. D. Meredyth and D. Tyler (Brisbane: ICPS, 1993); Alan Penn, *Targeting Schools: Drill, Militarism and Imperialism* (Abingdon, U.K.: Routledge, 1999); Alison Happel, "Ritualized Girling: School Uniforms and the Compulsory Performance of Gender," *Journal of Gender Studies* 22, no. 1 (Jan. 2013): 92–96.

41. "Military Training in Public Schools," 432–435; D.C. Bliss, "Military Training in the High School," *School Review* 25, no. 3 (Mar. 1917): 161–167; Frederick S. Camp, "Physical Education and Military Drill: What Should Be Our Policy? A Superintendent's Report," *School Review* 25, no. 8 (Oct. 1917): 537–545.

42. L.R. Gignilliat, *Arms and the Boy: Military Training in Schools and Colleges* (Indianapolis: Bobbs-Merrill, 1916), especially 94–100, 112–126.

43. Lesley Bartlett and Catherine Lutz, "Disciplining Social Difference: Some Cultural Politics of Military Training in Public High Schools," *Urban Review* 30, no. 2 (June 1998): 119–136; cf. Gene M. Lyons and John W. Masland, *Education and Military Leadership: A Study of the R.O.T.C.* (Princeton, N.J.: Princeton University Press, 1959), especially part 2, 27–97. For a British view, see C.B. Otley, "Militarism and Militarization in the Public Schools, 1900–1972," *British Journal of Sociology* 29, no. 3 (Sept. 1978): 321–339.

44. John Springhall, *Youth, Empire and Society: British Youth Movements, 1883–1940* (London: Croom Helm, 1977); Michael Rosenthal, *The Character Factory: Baden-Powell's Boy Scouts and the Imperatives of Empire* (New York: Pantheon Books, 1986).

45. Sarah Mills, "Scouting for Girls? Gender and the Scout Movement in Britain," *Gender, Place and Culture: A Journal of Feminist Geography* 18, no. 4 (2011): 537–556. See especially the section "'Please, Sir, We're the Girl Scouts': Girl Scouting and the Creation of the Girl Guides (1908–1916)."

46. Summers, *Angels and Citizens*, 279–282; Tammy M. Proctor, "Scouts, Guides, and the Fashioning of Empire, 1919–39," in *Fashioning the Body Politic: Dress, Gender, Citizenship*, ed. Wendy Perkins (New York: Berg, 2002), 125–144; Lucy Noakes, *Women in the British Army: War and the Gentle Sex, 1907–1948* (London: Routledge, 2006), 25–27.

47. Charles William Hackensmith, "Contributors to the Scouting Movement in North America," *Canadian Journal of History of Sport and Physical Education* 4, no. 1 (May 1973): 48–57; David I. MacLeod, "Act Your Age: Boyhood, Adolescence, and the Rise of the Boy Scouts of America," *Journal of Social History* 16, no. 2 (Winter1983): 3–20; Tammy M. Proctor, "'A Separate Path': Scouting and Guiding in Interwar South Africa," *Comparative Studies in Society and History* 42, no. 3 (July 2000): 605–631.

48. Tammy M. Proctor, "(Uni)forming Youth: Girl Guides and Boy Scouts in Britain, 1908–39," *History Workshop Journal*, no. 45 (Spring 1998): 103–134; Proctor, "Scouts, Guides, and the Fashioning of Empire." On the paradox of uniforms' contradictory meanings, see especially Nathan Joseph, *Uniforms and Nonuniforms: Communication through Clothing* (New York: Greenwood Press, 1986), part 2, 65–128.

TWO

FASHIONING AND PERFORMING MARTIAL FEMININITIES

Military Uniforms, Modernity, and Gender Identities in the British Women's Corps, 1914–1921

KRISZTINA ROBERT

The Victory March in London on 19 July 1919 marked a historic occasion. Primarily, the event celebrated the official end of the Great War with a spectacular military parade, honoring the armed forces of the imperial nation and its allies.[1] Additionally, the parade also marked a significant moment in British gender history. Marching among the troops were several female units representing the women's services, including the Women's Legion, the Women's Army Auxiliary Corps (WAAC), the Women's Royal Naval Service (WRNS), and the Women's Royal Air Force (WRAF). Their inclusion in the parade, along with nurses and male auxiliaries, was in itself historic. As one newspaper noted the day before, "it will be the first time that women have marched as victors in a national triumph."[2] The preparations of the services indicate that their leaders hoped to live up to this portrayal by using the event as a national and global platform for displaying their corps' martial female identities. This is obvious from the selection and training of their parade squads. Choosing the tallest, smartest-looking members from the mass of applicants, corps leaders organized special training for the squads to smarten them up.[3] The WRNS used their best drill instructor to train their company in Hyde Park, whereas the Women's Legion unit received expert drilling and marching lessons from the corporal major of the Royal Horse Guards regiment.[4] Preparations also included "a great deal of . . . brushing and pressing of uniforms."[5] In addition, WRAF headquarters had been debating whether their commandant should ride ahead of her parade squad, whereas officers of the WRNS walked the entire 7-mile route of the parade the day before as practice.[6] These efforts produced flawless performances of the corps' martial identities. Wearing their military uniforms and medals, the auxiliaries marched in perfect step and formation, swinging their arms in the distinct style of their male parent organizations and saluting both the cenotaph and the king as they marched past.[7] Through this behavior, they distinguished themselves from more civilian units, like the naval nurses, who waved their handkerchiefs to the crowds and "couldn't march at all," and the mercantile marine, who marched with their union banner in their Sunday best and doffed their flat caps instead of saluting.[8]

The martial display of the services was a success with the crowds who lined the parade route. Lady Londonderry, director of the Women's Legion, recalled the friendliness of people, "especially on the south side of the river," exchanging greetings and jokes with the women and offering them fruit to eat during the intervals when the march halted. In addition, she praised the chivalry of the troops, who gave women's detachments loud cheers as they were approaching the royal saluting base.[9] Katharine Furse, director of the WRNS, also remembered the kindness of onlookers. Feeling overcome by the roaring crowds, she and her staff managed to relax after a policeman praised their marching, a spectator reminded them to smile, and a group of admirals applauded as they passed by.[10] The recollections of a WAAC worker suggest that these responses were inspired partly by the women's military uniforms. Not included in the parade, C.F. Murdin decided to overstay her leave in London to see her friends in the procession and enjoy the festivities with them afterward. Throughout the day, her khaki uniform served as a pass, allowing her to cross restricted areas, securing her invitations to share vantage points, and earning her, and her friends, congratulations and free drinks from revelers. Contemplating the reasons for such support, she wrote, "I think our uniforms appealed to them."[11] These reactions conveyed endorsement of the services' martial femininity, which conflicted with previous opposition from sections of the public and the armed forces to the auxiliaries' military image.[12] Significantly, the recollections refer to specific groups, such as working-class communities in south London, admirals, and troops, who had objected to women's martial uniforms and parades before.[13] The shift in attitudes raises questions about the means, course, and agents of this transformation. If military parades are rituals that can develop, proclaim, and legitimate identities through symbolic means, what was the nature and significance of the martial femininities displayed by the female corps, what agencies and agendas produced them, and, crucially, what role did women's military uniforms and their spectacular presentations play in this process?[14]

TOWARD UNDERSTANDING WOMEN IN UNIFORM: A METHODOLOGICAL NOTE

Despite growing interest in women's wartime uniforms, existing scholarship has not considered these questions sufficiently. The reason stems partly from disciplinary specialization, which has restricted the conceptualization, sources, and methodologies of enquiries. Most studies have focused on the symbolic meanings of women's uniforms and their impact on definitions of femininity. Gender historians, who regard language as the main vehicle of producing meanings, have analyzed official and public debates about the corps' uniforms in government, press, and literary records.[15] Emphasizing opposition in these circles to women's martial appearance, they have concluded that this limited the corps' ability to create new female identities through dress.

Design scholars have prioritized fashion as the key discursive system in the construction of femininities.[16] Using visual representations, such as magazine images, they have argued that portrayals of the corps' uniforms as fashionable allowed members to signal modern female identities through martial dress. Studies stressed, however, that such identities remained problematic because of the essentially masculine nature of military clothing. Recently, costume historians have explored the material impact of uniforms on women's war experience.[17] Drawing on artifacts and recollections, they have shown that although women often took up war work inspired by the prestige of uniforms, poorly designed clothing issued by employers exacerbated harsh working conditions, forcing women to supplement and alter their dress.

These approaches have identified several agencies, the cultural resources they used, and the methods they deployed in the creation of wartime femininities. Existing studies, however, have defined these factors in limited terms. They have underestimated the agency of female corps leaders, members, and their uniforms, disregarding their role in producing and performing clothed martial identities and much of the culturally specific military symbolism utilized in the process. In addition, by emphasizing the role of military authorities, public critics, and popular representations, scholars have misread power relations between the main participants, along with their respective contributions to the gendering process.

Adopting an interdisciplinary conceptual framework clarifies the complexity of these issues and identifies the analytical tools for their discussion. First, I draw on Judith Butler's work on gender construction to illuminate the relative agency and role of the main participants in this process.[18] Butler has defined gender identities as fluid and constituted through repeated performances by the gendered subjects themselves. As dramatized acts, however, the effects of these productions are shaped by the contexts in which they are performed. This includes their environments, the material properties of which influence the meanings of the acts, and their audiences, who respond to the performances by critiquing or validating them, depending on their attitudes and the quality of the acts.

I also utilize material culture studies on dress to determine the role of uniforms in such performances.[19] Anthropologists in this field have stressed the performative agency of clothing in these practices.[20] They argued that instead of merely symbolizing identities by being displayed on human bodies, the material features of clothing actively shape performances by dictating and enabling certain physical actions while becoming animated themselves through these acts. Scholars have emphasized the inseparable connection between clothes, bodies, and their environments during such performances, especially in ritual contexts, arguing that they create joint spatial, material, and embodied discourses that should be analyzed together. Additionally, they have highlighted the links between the production and consumption of clothing in the enactment of identities, pointing out that wearers often alter outfits on the basis of audience responses to improve subsequent acts.

The discussion combines these approaches with the methods of cultural histories of materiality. These studies have explored artifacts as windows on past experiences otherwise inaccessible, especially of subjects who left no written records.[21] Historians have stressed the need to interpret discourses by locating them in their contemporary cultural, political, and socioeconomic contexts. Nevertheless, studies of object biographies have shown that in addition to changing, historically specific meanings, artifacts often carry older, historic connotations inherited from objects of the same kind dating from previous centuries.

This chapter explores the uniforms of the women's corps as the main means through which corps members, including the official services and their volunteer forerunners, constructed new martial femininities. To identify the cultural and material resources used by the corps, the discussion starts with a brief survey of the historical meanings and uses of civilian and military dress. The main section focuses on the material production and performative displays of the uniforms through which the corps developed a series of distinct, but overlapping, identities. I demonstrate variations of class, regionality, and military traditions through a material analysis of the designs and their presentations. Besides regulation patterns and their formal spectacles, I also examine subversive alterations of the uniforms and their routine displays through which corps members created their own military identities individually and in small groups. The discussion traces the development of martial femininities in four distinct periods of the war, characterized by different military, socioeconomic, and cultural conditions.

I also examine the interaction between the corps' uniformed practices and other agencies participating in the gendering process. Municipal and military authorities, members of the fashion industry, the press, the public, popular culture, and the armed forces contributed to definitions of martial female identities by endorsing particular designs and displays and criticizing others, thus shaping the nature of the constructs. I identify the social composition and agendas of all participants in a brief section before the main discussion to clarify their power relations and contributions to the process.

This chapter defines the historical significance of the corps' uniforms in facilitating women's entry into the armed forces as auxiliary troops by making femininity and soldiering compatible through the construction of martial female identities. By controlling their uniform designs, women were able to negotiate this process on their own terms. As a result, by the end of the war, the corps had obtained symbolic, if not formal, military status. I attribute this success to corps leaders' willingness to adapt their designs and displays to changing war conditions, including shifting discourses of modernity and national service through which the British war effort was defined.

THE CULTURE OF MARTIAL FEMININITY: DRESS CODES, UNIFORMS, AND GENDER IDENTITY

The strategy of the women's corps, to claim new martial roles by constructing higher-status female identities through uniforms, drew on a long tradition of using dress to mark and negotiate social status and gender boundaries.[22] The main material resource for the corps' new identities was provided by the uniforms of the British armed forces. Defined by their insignia, accoutrements, and spectacular displays, these included the dress of the regular army, the navy, and the air force, along with their prewar and wartime auxiliaries, such as the 1859 Volunteer Force and the Edwardian Territorial Force, Royal Naval Volunteer Reserve, and Boy Scouts.[23] Through their part in the conflicts of the prewar decades, their dress had come to represent a series of gendered attributes coveted by the female corps. Primarily, military uniforms symbolized an active, martial model of citizenship.[24] In an age when war was redefined as a national undertaking, the outfits of the Volunteers and Territorials indicated citizens' readiness to defend Britain from invasion, whereas army dress signified the expansion and protection of the empire.[25] Naval uniforms denoted both activities, accounting for their popularity.[26] The royal prerogative over the armed forces, whose troops wore "the King's uniform," reinforced these associations.[27]

Martial clothing also signaled inclusion in the male national community. Epitomizing level-headed self-control, stoic determination, and heroic sacrifice, it symbolized national identity and, collectively, the nation in arms.[28] The adoption of the standardized khaki service dress in 1902 underlined this meaning. Worn by all regular, territorial, and colonial army troops, it signified national and imperial unity. Related to these meanings were positive connotations of modernity. Besides Victorian associations of action, adventure, and supremacy, the khaki uniforms also signaled a new modernization of the forces, including utility, economy, and efficiency, driven by the problems of the Boer War.[29] Military parades were the main public representation of these attributes. As symbolic performances, they demonstrated martial skills, like drilling and marching, while displaying the qualities of discipline, stamina, and patriotism.[30] Additionally, parades also glamorized soldiers' bodies through the ostentatious display of close-fitting uniforms and swaggering deportment that emphasized erect postures, square shoulders, and forward-thrust chests associated with male sexuality.[31] Thus, when adopting martial dress and practices for their new identities, the corps had to feminize these signifiers to avoid associations of masculinity.

Military nurses' uniforms offered an ideal resource for softening the more masculine features of martial dress. Worn by members of the prewar army, navy, and territorial nursing unit and the Voluntary Aid Detachments (VADs), the costumes provided a female model of institutional dress that could be used as an alternative signifying system to martial uniforms.[32] These outfits were designed specially for women working in male-dominated public environments. They followed the pattern set by the habits of religious nursing orders and the liveries of female staff in early modern charity schools and hospitals. Consequently, nurses' costumes were the opposite of martial uniforms. Instead of glamorizing, they were intended to protect their wearers from sexual advances by shrouding their bodies in layers of loose, softly tailored or folded garments.[33] This was achieved by ankle-length, high-necked, and long-sleeved dresses with starched collars, cuffs, bibbed aprons, shoulder capes, and caps or veils in the soft hues of blue luster, gray, and white. These costumes conveyed respectability, physical and moral purity, obedience, and selfless sacrifice.[34] The presentation of the outfits matched their traditional design. Nurses were forbidden to alter the austere simplicity of their dress with any ornamentation, did not participate in public parades until World War I, and were trained to move quietly to avoid disturbing their patients.[35]

Simultaneously, however, the uniforms of the military nursing corps also demonstrated how to use discourses of modernity to attract female recruits. In order to stress nurses' military value and reference their links to the armed forces, reformers added martial symbols to the outfits, including scarlet, navy, and gray capes; regimental badges; rank insignia; and prestigious medals to win.[36] As a result, military nursing became highly fashionable, leading to a stampede of applicants during the Boer War and the creation of the voluntary First Aid Nursing Yeomanry and other similar organizations. These units, along with the VADs, extended their roles beyond nursing, for which they adopted additional khaki-and-navy uniforms, attracting criticism for being excitement-seeking "fashionable fads."[37]

THE PRODUCERS, PERFORMERS, AND AUDIENCES OF THE CORPS' UNIFORMED DISPLAYS

The women's corps' uniformed parades developed out of power struggles between the contributors involved in their production. These conflicts stemmed from the controversial nature of the martial femininities constructed by the displays. Since the identities facilitated women's military war participation, which disrupted existing gender norms, their construction generated heated internal, public, and official debates.[38] Whoever controlled the design and presentation of the uniforms could shape the identities that they developed and thus the terms of women's entry into the armed forces. Consequently, the various groups involved in the production of the uniforms and their displays competed with each other for their control.

Producers included corps leaders, along with the audiences of their displays, who became part of the production process by responding to the performances that shaped consecutive shows. Among these spectators turned producers were young women who, as potential recruits, sought exciting new openings for war work.[39] Also included were military authorities, who, as potential employers, were concerned about the disruption of their troops' discipline by female workers.[40] The British public, sections of which were anxious about the destabilization of the gender order by martial femininity, was an essential participant; its consent was necessary for obtaining recruits and official sanction for their military work.[41]

The producers of the uniformed displays also included skilled experts hired or co-opted by corps leaders to ensure that the costumes and their presentations were produced to high professional standards. Members of the garment trade were engaged as consultants and outfitters; military experts acted as drill instructors, and corps leaders courted popular artists and the press to generate favorable publicity about the uniformed spectacles. Inspired by their professional agendas, these groups also sought to shape the construction of martial femininities.[42] Influencing the design, display, and cultural impact of the uniforms depended on the ability of all participants to build alliances, to create effective performative representations of the costumes, and to alter dress designs and their presentations in line with the changing demands of the war effort and the shifting power relations that they generated.

The main responsibility for producing the uniformed displays was assumed by the female leadership of the corps movement.[43] Besides initiating the parades, they designed the dress patterns in consultation with fashion experts, organized their procurement in independent units, obtained sanction for them in the official services, altered the designs to accommodate public critics, and arranged drilling and marching instruction for their membership.[44] These actions were driven by a shared ambition to contribute to the war effort in a military capacity. To realize this objective, women's corps leaders had to form female military units and qualify them for auxiliary service with the armed forces. Therefore, they established a series of volunteer corps between 1914 and 1916 and organized the official services for the authorities in 1917 and 1918.[45] Uniforms and parades were central to this project. Putting troops in uniform and drilling them were recognized methods of instilling in them discipline and efficiency. Thus, by adopting martial dress and training for their units, corps leaders could demonstrate their readiness for military employment.[46]

These objectives and strategies were inspired by corps leaders' prewar activities. Many of them were veterans of the suffrage campaign who strove to prove women's fitness for the vote through military service. Militant suffragettes and hunting–shooting country women were hoping for physical action in the corps.[47] Other members of the leadership were eager to use their VAD or professional training for national service in more prestigious positions than unpaid nursing or charity work.[48] All these groups knew the importance of creating new identities through costumed displays when claiming novel roles and had experience in these practices. They also understood the value of organization and publicity and were adept at their techniques.[49] Finally, many came from military families and were acquainted with martial symbolism and traditions.[50] Because of their varied backgrounds, however, corps leaders envisaged different martial identities based on distinct types and degrees of militarism. The resulting rivalries split the movement into a range of volunteer and government-sponsored units, each with its own martial femininity, attracting different recruits.

After women's corps leaders, members of the female units exercised the greatest influence over the design and display of uniforms. Their agency stemmed from their multiple roles in the production of dress patterns and parades, starting with their part as the main target audience for the corps' uniformed spectacles. Seeking young, adventurous, and trained women for their units, corps leaders tailored the presentation of their outfits to the perceived tastes of potential recruits.[51] Once uniforms were issued, however, control over their design and display shifted considerably. Corps leaders' power over clothing patterns and conduct was limited to scheduled inspections and, from 1918, to checks carried out by female military police. Between these occasions, members could alter their outfit and wear it according to taste.[52] This was particularly easy during working hours since military managers were largely oblivious to the corps' uniform regulations.

Members had various reasons for modifying their dress. Like their leaders, many women imagined their war participation through particular uniform designs. A.B. Baker fantasized about going to the front in breeches, whereas Dorothy Young sent a sketch of the sailor dress she was hoping to wear when applying to the WRNS.[53] Popular portrayals of the uniforms as fashionable dress fueled such fantasies, inspiring women to transform the official design into their idealized models.[54] Correcting functional defects in the uniforms was another reason for alterations. Initially, WAAC uniforms came in limited sizes, requiring members to make their dresses fit either by joint efforts with friends or by taking their costumes to tailors.[55] Through such collective alterations, the auxiliaries also expressed smaller group identities based on shared rooms, huts, or offices.

Corps members' uniform adjustments could alter the official designs. Popular modifications often became so widespread that they were impossible to suppress. Therefore, to maintain their authority, corps leaders incorporated some of these changes into the regulation patterns.[56] The degree and frequency of such alterations increased with the expansion of the services, as the other ranks became more daring, realizing the power in their growing numbers.[57] They also represented their new designs through private studio portraits that they exchanged with each other as mementoes of friendship.[58]

As the employers of the corps, military authorities became key allies of corps leaders in the production of uniformed parades. Their support stemmed mainly from the worsening military manpower shortage. Having started the war seriously undermanned, the armed forces struggled to replace their losses throughout the conflict and relied increasingly on the labor of female auxiliaries to release male troops from support positions for combat.[59] Since army officers preferred to employ disciplined female units, they were generally supportive of women's corps leaders' dress, training, and publicity policies.[60] Expressions of their support included authorizing the corps' uniforms and facilitating their parades by providing training advice, lending bands, and inviting female units to participate in prestigious military spectacles.[61] This extended the corps' publicity opportunities and provided vital legitimacy for their martial identities.

Military authorities had little interest, however, in shaping women's uniform designs. Regarding women workers' clothing as a welfare matter, they delegated this task entirely to female corps leaders.[62] The only area where they retained control concerned the use of the armed forces' rank insignia, which they denied to the official services on the grounds that women lacked military status.[63] This denial was less a matter of gender discrimination than the legal and practical difficulties of extending military status to women.[64] Granting female auxiliaries military status would have necessitated applying the same disciplinary code to them that applied to soldiers, including the death penalty for desertion.[65] Neither public opinion nor women's corps leaders would have accepted this. Had women received the status of the troops without the same penal code, it would have been almost impossible to persuade servicemen to accept substitution by women without damaging their discipline and morale.[66] Nevertheless, by the end of the war, interservice rivalry and competition for female recruits prompted military authorities to share some of their prestigious symbols with the auxiliaries as an incentive to joining the services.

Another major influence in shaping the corps' uniformed displays came from popular portrayals. As part of their audience, journalists, artists, and the public were expected by corps leaders to reward their spectacles with positive reports and images.[67] Public approval was vital for a new and radical women's movement, facilitating recruitment, recognition, and employment. Conversely, public criticism could threaten the units' survival.[68] Good publicity depended on the perceived ability of the corps, conveyed through popular displays, to help meet the shifting demands of the war effort, which were represented through discourses of modernity. Therefore, corps publicists had to tailor representations of their uniformed identities to changing war conditions and their public portrayals.[69] In this task, they could rely on the press, which was generally supportive of the women's corps. Journalists appreciated the topical news stories and photo opportunities provided by the female units at a time of censorship and praised their uniformed parades as expressions of modern femininity.[70]

Public opinion was more divided. Garrison and naval towns, areas with strong volunteer traditions, and feminist and conservative political circles supported the corps.[71] Elsewhere, approval fluctuated with the military situation, which determined the value of the auxiliaries. A vocal minority, however, remained critical and could mobilize opposition through letters to the press or by spreading malicious rumors, especially when corps parades seemed at odds with war requirements.[72] These letters and allegations could generate more publicity, as newspapers and popular culture responded to such topical concerns with reports or visual portrayals. Corps leaders sought to neutralize criticism by challenging opponents in the press and by altering uniform patterns and representations.[73] Thus, public opinion shaped the definition of martial femininity through approval or condemnation of the parades, marking the lines and limits of gender transformation. On the basis of this interaction between corps leaders, members, the armed forces, military requirements, and popular representations, four main constructs of martial femininity emerged during the war.

THE PRODUCTION AND PERFORMANCE OF UNIFORMED MARTIAL FEMININITIES

The first construction of the corps' military identity was the female "volunteer." This model emerged in the initial months of the war out of the revival of Britain's amateur military tradition. Evoking the spirit of the Victorian Volunteer Force created for home defense, tens of thousands of men joined newly formed Volunteer Training Corps, mustering for evening drill and rifle practice.[74] The movement grew out of invasion fears generated by press reports about the German threat to the Channel ports. Government policies fueled concerns by refusing to publish defense plans to avoid causing panic while inviting territorial defense units to volunteer for fighting abroad.[75]

Unlike previous invasion fears, anxieties now assumed a new gendered dimension, which stemmed from official propaganda deployed to raise Kitchener's New Armies to reinforce the small regular forces on the continent. Appealing to masculine chivalry to boost enlistment rates, recruiters used exaggerated stories of gruesome atrocities committed by German troops against Allied women and children.[76] Such graphic images heightened invasion fears among women. Writing to the press, many of them urged following the men's example by forming a women's "Rifle and Revolver Corps" so that they could train to defend themselves in a potential invasion.[77] Inspired by this mood, suffrage and scouting activists established three paramilitary female corps appealing for recruits and funds. Their success varied according to the martial tradition they embraced.

The Women Signallers Territorial Corps and the Women's Defence Relief Corps adopted the Edwardian Territorial Force's centralized county organization to release men for enlistment by replacing them in signaling and civilian jobs.[78] In contrast, the Women's Volunteer Reserve assumed the more popular local company structure of the Victorian Volunteer Force, which it adapted to the demands of the time. As the War Office called all eligible men to enlist for foreign service, the reserve defined women as the new volunteers for home defense, claiming all combat support and civil defense duties for its units.[79]

The uniform policies of the Women's Volunteer Reserve indicate that founders of the corps used the Volunteer Force model strategically. Despite adopting the independent ethos of the early 1859 Volunteer Force to tap into the popular wartime mood, they modeled their uniform procurement on the late Victorian stage of the movement, when its centrally controlled clothing regulations imitated army procedures.[80] This system standardized uniforms by preventing deviations from the official pattern—a key consideration for female soldiers portrayed in satirical cartoons as a ragtag band of cranky Amazons.[81] Seeking a professional uniform look to convey efficiency and discipline, and thus inspire respect from military authorities, the Women's Volunteer Reserve adopted this policy. Through this strategy, they hoped to follow the example of their male predecessors in gaining official recognition and integration into the army.[82]

According to regulations, all uniforms and shoes had to be ordered and paid for through Women's Volunteer Reserve headquarters. Headquarters then gave written authorization to its official tailors to outfit members on the basis of sealed uniform patterns developed with corps leaders. Likewise, headquarters issued all insignia on payment of a deposit. To prevent unauthorized use, insignia had to be returned if members resigned.[83]

As the reserve expanded, corps leaders allowed provincial companies to replicate this process through local outfitters.[84] However, they also issued strict regulations about the correct way of wearing the outfits and introduced inspections by headquarters staff to uphold them.[85] Significantly, the reserve did not permit home production of its uniforms. Instead, it copied the policies of the Volunteer Force for helping poorer recruits buy their costumes by appealing for donations and allowing payment in installments.[86]

In contrast, the Women Signallers Territorial Corps and the Women's Defence Relief Corps followed the "semimilitary" uniform policies of the prewar Guide and Scout movements. Besides making uniforms optional and unregulated, the Women Signallers disregarded the advice of specialist outfitters, whereas the Women's Defence Relief Corps encouraged home production of its costumes. These policies produced a rather amateurish, motley, and "scallywag" appearance, which contrasted with the smart look presented by the Women's Volunteer Reserve on formal occasions.[87]

The uniform patterns of the Women's Volunteer Reserve symbolized the corps' active martial ambitions. Designed for strenuous outdoor activity, the outfits were a militarized version of the dress worn by elite women for colonial travel and country sports. This pattern reflected the background of corps leaders, like Evelina Haverfield, a militant suffragette and sportswoman, who had accompanied her army officer husband to the Boer war.[88] The tailor-made woolen costume, in frieze for privates and finer gabardine for officers, featured a full mid-calf-length skirt, buttoned at the front so it could be removed for riding when worn with breeches underneath.[89] Accessories included plain felt hats; flat, square-heeled shoes; spat puttees; and strong leather gloves. Recommended by outfitters for climbing, cycling, and motoring, these facilitated the Women's Volunteer Reserve's training in driving, signaling, dispatch riding, and camp cooking.[90] The martial nature of the uniforms was signified by their khaki color and military jackets. Imitating army privates' service dress, the reserve's other ranks wore loose-fitting, cloth-belted coats with two pleated breast pockets and cross flaps at the bottom, whereas officers adopted a fitted version of this with leather belts and patch pockets, similar to army officers' field service tunics. Shoulder straps, flannel shirts, ties, and collars fastened with gold safety pins worn by all ranks increased the costumes' similarity to army patterns.[91]

The Women's Volunteer Reserve's rank insignia also imitated the army. Besides the Austrian knots of the 1859 Volunteer Force adopted by provincial companies, the regulation badges worn by all officers were the army's old fleur-de-lis and Garter stars arranged in the

Figure 2.1.
Private and officer of the Women's Volunteer Reserve. Imperial War Museum (Q 30382).

same pattern as army officers' post-1880 crowns and Bath stars.[92] These features conveyed deliberate ambiguity about the Women's Volunteer Reserve's martial ambitions. Formerly, khaki service dress could denote home defense since both the Volunteer and Territorial Forces adopted them. But as the territorials were urged to volunteer for overseas while the new male volunteers were forbidden to wear khaki, this outfit now symbolized combatant duties.[93] The Women's Volunteer Reserve's rifle training and oft-stated objective to evacuate and defend civilians in a potential invasion reinforced this meaning.[94]

Seeking to boost their membership, founders of the Women's Volunteer Reserve marketed their uniformed identities through wartime discourses of modernity. This strategy drew on popular images of army recruiting, which depicted khaki uniforms as the new fashion for "real" men and portrayed soldiering as an exuberant experience of outdoor adventures.[95] Inspired by this, corps leaders promoted their uniforms as the patriotic fashion for modern women. They contrasted their outfits with last season's hobbles and picture hats, which they described as dowdy, incapacitating, and ridiculous, as well as with the latest "ultrafashionable" styles, which they branded exaggerated, ostentatious, and unpatriotic. Rejecting these extremes, corps leaders presented their costumes as simple, sensible, and practical, suitable for daytime work, evening drill class, and outdoor holidays.[96] They also argued that when combined with martial training, the uniforms expressed and stimulated fitness, endurance, and discipline, preparing women to meet the stern demands of the war. Isabel Margesson called "every woman who wishes to be smart . . . in her dress" to join the Women's Volunteer Reserve "as a patriotic act."[97]

Staging crosstown uniformed route marches accompanied by music was an even more effective way of advertising the Women's Volunteer Reserve's new identity. These performances brought to life the qualities of the female volunteer by combining the discourses of suffrage processions, fashion parades, and military pageants.[98] Besides conveying assertiveness, energy, and momentum through their rhythmic tramp and drumbeat, the marches also demonstrated the Women's Volunteer Reserve's efficient organization, training, and discipline. Thus, they could appeal to both potential recruits and employers.[99] Utilizing their suffrage campaigning experience, corps leaders used modern publicity methods to gain wider exposure for their displays. Adjutants of the reserve doubled as press officers, informing newspapers about upcoming parades and alerting photographers to march routes for the best pictures. These policies generated extensive illustrated press coverage, advertising the Women's Volunteer Reserve's uniformed identity nationwide and abroad.[100]

The Women's Volunteer Reserve's modern military image made the "Volunteer" the dominant brand of martial femininity. By mid-1915, the corps had over 30 companies with 8,000–10,000 women, representing a diverse membership.[101] Recruits included suffrage activists attracted by the Women's Volunteer Reserve's self-reliant ethos and claim to martial citizenship, whereas country sportswomen, "athletic" college students, and former Girl Guides were drawn by the prospect of outdoor adventure. Many of the latter were lower-middle-class teachers and clerks encouraged to join by the promise of free uniforms.[102] Portrayals of the corps' khaki parades through fashion discourses appealed to many recruits. In early 1915, khaki dress, "short" full skirts, and martial deportment, including an upright posture, the "military stride," and swinging arms, were highly fashionable among young women.[103]

The marches also secured the corps' first official military jobs. Impressed by the Women's Volunteer Reserve's parades, army officers invited units to join their recruiting processions, believing that the sight of women soldiers would shame "slackers" into enlisting. The uniforms further helped the corps obtain canteen, clerical, and transport work in munitions factories, recruiting offices, and military hospitals.[104]

In comparison, the Women's Volunteer Reserve's rivals lagged behind. During the same period, the Women's Defence Relief Corps formed 11 local units with approximately 2,500 members doing mainly farming work, whereas the Women Signallers Territorial Corps enrolled 200 women to train army recruits.[105] This was due partly to their dated, civilian, and comical appearance. Shapeless uniforms, slouching postures, and obscure equipment lent the signalers an old-fashioned and eccentric image. In contrast, the Swedish drill displays of the Women's Defence Relief Corps' "Helpers" lacked military relevance, similar to their cocked slouch hats, a symbol of make-believe soldiering when worn by noncombatants.[106]

From mid-1915, however, the popularity of the female volunteer was undermined by changing demands of the war effort and shifting discourses of modernity. As mounting casualties and falling enlistment had exposed dashing offensives and voluntary recruitment as outdated, there were increasing calls for modernizing the conduct of the war by centralizing armaments production and adopting conscription.[107] In this sobering climate, army uniforms were redefined as sacred emblems of sacrifice, rather than swanky fashion.[108] Thus, the Women's Volunteer Reserve's khaki parades were now out of tune with the public mood, especially as many members treated their uniforms as fashion items. Following the advice of magazines about well-dressed elegance, volunteers often flouted regulations by altering their outfits to express individual character. This alteration ranged from "dressing up" uniforms with high-heeled shoes, low-cut blouses, hat pins, and jewelry to masculinizing the costumes by adopting male attire and mannerisms.[109] Colonel W.M. Charlesworth, the Women's Volunteer Reserve's new commanding officer, led army recruiting marches riding astride, wearing breeches under her unbuttoned skirt, with tall boots, hunting stock, and a jacket buttoning from left to right. Members also sported breeches, wore their hair hidden under hats, and slapped their riding boots with whips or swagger sticks.[110]

These practices generated growing criticism of the Women's Volunteer Reserve. Letters to the press accused members of abusing "the King's uniform" by "playing at soldiers" and "aping" the men and demanded that authorities banned women's use of khaki.[111] Simultaneously, cartoons depicted the volunteers as frivolous flappers, posing in the affected style of fashion plates, with hands on hips, legs crossed over short skirts, smoking, and wearing service jackets with army badges and Sam Browne belts.[112] Such attacks damaged recruitment, causing deep divisions among staff officers about the image and work of the corps. In the end, several headquarters officers broke away from the reserve and established new female corps.[113] The most successful of these units was the Women's Legion, which legitimized the corps' military role by adapting its martial femininity to the shifting demands of the war effort.

From 1916, the Women's Legion's "army cook" and "driver" represented the corps' new identity. Designed by Lady Londonderry, director of the unit, it aimed to expand the legion's military employment and membership by reassuring army authorities and potential members about the propriety of women's martial work. Through this, Londonderry sought to obtain paid army jobs and extend recruitment for the legion's cookery and transport

Figure 2.2.
Colonel W. M. Charlesworth, Commanding Officer, Women's Volunteer Reserve. Author's personal collection.

Figure 2.3.
Euan Lyne, "Shades of Our Grandmothers!" Bystander, *18 August 1915. Illustrated London News Ltd/Mary Evans, 10237043.*

sections to working-class and trained middle-class women.[114] To achieve this, she developed a more feminine and work-focused identity emphasizing vocational training and skills. She also included class-based distinctions of militarism to accommodate working-class women's alleged hostility to the concept.

Londonderry conveyed these attributes through subtle changes to the uniforms of the Women's Volunteer Reserve. To indicate her corps' military nature, she retained the two-piece khaki suits but feminized them by adopting for all ranks the looser, softly tailored, cloth-belted jackets worn by rankers of the Women's Volunteer Reserve, instead of the officers' severe, fitted, leather-belted coats. Following the reserve's policy, she also used different fabrics and pockets to denote rank. These distinctions, however, now also signified members' perceived class-based attitudes to militarism. All workers received frieze jackets and flannel shirts, as opposed to officers' silk shirts and woolen coats. But working-class cooks' jackets featured civilian cross flaps, whereas middle-class drivers' jackets also had breast pockets, and officers' tunics sported both breast and army patch pockets.[115]

The other items of the Women's Legion's uniforms signified feminine work roles in the army. Instead of the Women's Volunteer Reserve's buttoned skirts and spat puttees facilitating outdoor adventure, members of the legion received khaki overalls, with Dutch caps for the cooks, to protect their shirts and full, mid-calf skirts when working in army kitchens and garages. A military overcoat and sensible brown shoes

Figure 2.4.
Member of the Women's Legion Military Cookery Section, ca. 1916. Author's personal collection.

completed the kit, which workers received free after a month's probation. The outfits were supplied by Selfridges and were paid for by the War Office.[116]

The Women's Legion's insignia emphasized the prestige of the corps by linking its martial femininity to Britain's imperial tradition. This was conveyed by the corps' cap badge, the main symbol of its identity. Depicting a classically robed female figure holding a laurel wreath, the emblem was identified as Victory, guardian goddess of imperial Rome.[117] But the missing wings of the figure and the sword in her other hand revealed that the image was a composite. These attributes referenced Athena, bringer of victory and protector of just warriors, and wartime Britannia, who exchanged her trident for a sword to rally troops and guard Britain, besides honoring and mourning heroes.[118] The badge also alluded to Britain's warrior queens, Elizabeth and Victoria, revered as the epitomes of the classical goddesses for assuming martial leadership and expanding the Empire.[119] Their presence was signified by Tudor roses framing Victory and by the figure's similarity to Boudicca's Edwardian statue associated with Victoria. Through these symbols, Londonderry legitimized martial femininity as a time-honored tradition facilitating the establishment of the Roman Empire and its modern successor, Britain. She also justified her members' roles in contributing to victory by providing troops with sustenance and speed.

Using classical and religious symbolism allowed Londonderry to seamlessly combine masculine-military and feminine qualities in her redefinition of martial femininity. Along with their soldierly virtues of resolution, strength, and courage, Athena and Britannia bequeathed their morality, compassion, and technical skills to the Legion's cooks and drivers.[120] In addition, Londonderry explained that the corps' name, represented by its initials at the top of the badge, was designed to instill in members the values of patriotic state service, discipline, and efficiency associated with the ancient Roman legions.[121] To add devotion to duty and God to her ideal of martial womanhood, she borrowed the Benedictines' motto, "Ora et Labora" (work and pray), inscribed at the base of the badge. Officers' collar badges used the same design, whereas rank insignia combined the laurel wreath, Tudor rose, and the corps' initials with fleur-de-lis and stars.[122]

Figure 2.5.
Women's Legion cap badge, ca. 1916. Imperial War Museum (INS 7778).

Seeking to update martial femininity, Londonderry promoted the legion's identity through emerging discourses on women's war participation. Public debates between mid-1915 and late 1916 called for women to take up factory, farm, and public service jobs to increase munition and food supplies and release men from civilian posts for conscription. Reformers also urged boosting the efficiency of the war effort by cutting waste, incompetence, and untrained labor.[123] These requirements were summarized by the popular slogan "Men must fight and Women must work" and images of the "woman war worker."[124] Press photographs portrayed this new social type by depicting female workers in overalls operating machinery in munitions factories and on farms or fixing cars in the Women's Volunteer Reserve's garage.[125] However, the somber mood about mounting casualties discouraged women's self-promoting public parades.

To avoid criticism, Londonderry adopted a cautious marketing strategy for the Women's Legion. Thus, the first units of its cookery and driving sections had no publicity until they proved successful since by replacing soldiers in Britain for foreign service, they represented a radical departure in women's military work.[126] Then, coinciding with their official recognition by the War Office, tightly managed press campaigns introduced women army cooks and drivers to the public. Articles portrayed legionaries as trained workers whose efficiency and utility exceeded those of the troops they replaced. Reports argued that women chauffeurs matched soldiers' stamina and technical skills but kept their cars cleaner, whereas female cooks served more appetizing and cost-saving meals than untrained soldiers. In addition, women were said to have double value by also releasing troops for the front.[127] Official photos reinforced this workmanlike and industrial modern-military image. Female cooks were depicted in their caps and overalls with sleeves rolled up, using high-tech catering equipment in army kitchens supervised by uniformed officials. Drivers were shown in their khaki outfits at the wheels of their vans or receiving orders from army officers at garage yards.[128]

The Women's Legion's new identity achieved its aim to facilitate the expansion of the corps' membership. Attracting applicants from a wider range of classes, it increased recruitment for the movement significantly. One appeal produced over 15,000 applications, and most new positions were filled from waiting lists.[129] At a time when munitions work and VAD nursing offered popular alternatives for women's war work, this appeal was due largely to

Figure 2.6.
"The Women's Legion and Army Waste," Illustrated Sporting and Dramatic News, *26 February 1916. Illustrated London News Ltd/Mary Evans, 10694198.*

the legion's softer martial femininity and work-focused modernity. Domestic servants joining the legion's cookery units chose lower wages with free khaki uniforms over better paid munitions work partly for the prestige of being the first women to officially serve with the army.[130] Proud to be women army cooks, they combined the symbols of this identity by pinning their outdoor cap badge on their overalls or work caps when on kitchen duty and even when posing for their private portrait photographs.[131] Likewise, thousands of middle-class women opted for the legion's motor squads as opposed to voluntary nursing posts or driving jobs in the volunteer corps.[132] They received not only free training and khaki uniforms but also the chance to drive for the Royal Army Service Corps and the Royal Flying Corps, which issued their prestigious cap badges to female staff.[133]

The Women's Legion's new image also improved public and official attitudes to women's army work, thus facilitating their mass military employment. This is indicated partly by the lack of popular criticism. In this respect, signaling distinct female identities and unambiguous vocational roles through the uniforms while avoiding spectacular displays, flaunting martial femininity, proved crucial. Equally importantly, the legion's new identity helped convince military authorities that female units could be attached to army formations without compromising soldiers' discipline.[134] Instead of a traditional female presence

Figure 2.7.
Women's Legion cooks, ca. 1916. National Army Museum (1995-01-21-60).

distracting troops from their duties, corps members were uniformed workers under strict discipline enforced by their own officials that included a ban on socializing with soldiers privately.[135] The resulting expansion of the legion's work contributed to the formation of the official female services in 1917 and 1918. These were created to ease the forces' manpower shortage by replacing troops with female auxiliaries in military support jobs across Britain and the Western Front.

ATTAINING SYMBOLIC MILITARY STATUS

The establishment of the official services—the WAAC, the WRNS, and the WRAF—transformed the construct of martial femininity. The new mass organizations extended the prevalence of military womanhood, turning a marginal local concept into a nationally recognized identity. This was due partly to the huge expansion of the membership. From some 10,000 volunteers, by 1919, the movement grew to over 100,000 auxiliaries whose visibility was increased by the services' enormous government-sponsored publicity.[136] By 1918, images of uniformed auxiliaries became ubiquitous, displayed in posters, parades, photographs, postcards, advertisements, and newsreels.[137] Official sanction also improved the status of military womanhood, though greater visibility increased the potential for public criticism.

The creation of the women's services altered the character of martial femininity as well. Formerly, with the exception of the Women's Legion cooks, it was an overwhelmingly middle-class identity, whose chief variety lay in different traditions of popular militarism adopted by the various volunteer corps. From 1917, the military nature of the identity became more diverse. Despite utilizing some popular traditions of volunteering, the services drew mainly on the regular militarism of their respective armed forces when crafting their image. These distinct military, naval, and aerial femininities became key recruiting tools and were used to develop esprit de corps among the membership.[138] Likewise, martial femininity became more varied and divided along class lines. This division stemmed partly from the influx of tens of thousands of working- and lower-middle-class women into the domestic, technical, and clerical units of the services, who eventually outnumbered middle-class officers and drivers.[139] On the basis of these occupational groups, distinct, class-based martial femininities developed that were reinforced by the adoption of formal distinctions between officers and other ranks. The services' new uniforms both produced and reflected these transformations. Their shifting patterns and displays reveal that the changes developed gradually between 1917 and 1919 through a process of trial and error.

In 1917, the WAAC's two-tiered uniform system signaled the shift toward the regular militarism of the armed forces. Previously, the single-tier model of the Women's Volunteer Reserve and the Women's Legion, which specified similar suits for all members and denoted rank by stylistic detail, symbolized the egalitarian ethos and horizontal structure of the 1859 Volunteer Force.[140] In contrast, the WAAC followed the more vertical hierarchy of the regular army. Designed to generate discipline, it was based on a strict division between officers and other ranks, reinforced by different uniform patterns, spatial segregation, and a ban on fraternization.[141] The WAAC was required to adopt this model by the War Office. Through this measure, military authorities sought to allay army officers' concerns about deploying female auxiliaries on the Western Front where the women initially worked. Commanding officers in France were unfamiliar with the Women's Legion's successful employment in Britain. Therefore, they doubted whether women had the necessary self-control to work with soldiers in harsh frontline conditions without engendering "the sex difficulty," undermining the troops' discipline.[142] The dual structure was also designed to prevent fraternization between female rankers and male officers and thus facilitate smooth working relations between soldiers and auxiliaries attached to army units for work.[143]

Chief controllers of the WAAC embraced this policy because it advanced their own political ambitions. Both Helen Gwynne-Vaughan and Mary Chalmers Watson hoped to facilitate the integration of the WAAC into the army and establish the corps on a permanent basis after the war.[144] The two-tiered uniform model furthered this goal by signaling that the WAAC would enforce discipline among its members by the time-honored method of the armed forces: a class-based hierarchy of different ranks.[145] The dual uniform system also had a practical impact on controlling WAAC members. Lacking their male colleagues' disciplinary powers, female officials relied partly on their higher-status clothing to bolster their authority over the other ranks.[146] Thus, uniform designs played a strategic role in overcoming army officers' opposition to women's auxiliary employment.

The hierarchical dress patterns defined the WAAC's martial femininity by distinct, class-specific qualities. Female officials' outfits were designed to identify them as "lady officers"—educated gentlewomen serving as military administrators.[147] Denied commissioned rank and even the title of "officer," chief controllers of the WAAC were determined to claim symbolically equal social and professional status with their male counterparts.[148] To achieve this goal, they militarized professional women's "coat and skirt" by combining it with key features of army officers' uniforms. The result was a tunic in "officer's khaki," sporting shoulder straps, patch "service" pockets, and bronze "general service" buttons worn over khaki shirts, ties, and collars fastened with gold safety pins.[149]

This design was not dictated by officials' duties, which included hostel administration, clerical work, and housekeeping. Instead, the costumes were meant to convey authority, control, and competence based on professional qualifications.[150] WAAC controllers also stressed their officials' status as ladies through the quality and procurement of their uniforms. The suits were individually made to measure, paid for by a £20.00 grant from the War Office, whereas hats and sealed patterns were supplied by exclusive firms, such as Woodrow of Piccadilly and Marshall and Snelgrove on Oxford Street.[151]

Efforts to style WAAC officials as "lady officers" were a partial success. Seeking a respectable look, chief controllers followed the assistants' advice at Marshall's to soften their costumes with feminine traits.[152] Thus, the tunics were made slightly double-breasted and loosely cut with long lapels, self-cloth belts, and no breast pockets to avoid accentuating the bust and were worn with crepe de Chine veils over tight-fitting caps. These attributes were meant to balance the "daringly short," calf-length skirts adopted for muddy front conditions and eliminate the more military aspects of the Women's Legion's uniforms to avoid tensions with army officers.[153] However, the feminine features overwhelmed the outfit's militarism. Gwynne-Vaughan redressed the balance by replacing the caps with the hats of the Women's Volunteer Reserve. She also insisted on wearing army insignia even after the WAAC's civilian status was confirmed, instead of crafting a new martial identity for her corps through distinctive badges. Eventually, the War Office adopted the Women's Legion's fleur-de-lis and roses as rank insignia that WAAC officials wore in the same pattern as army officers' crown and stars.[154]

Figure 2.8.
Officer and forewoman (noncommissioned officer) of the Women's Army Auxiliary Corps, 1917. Imperial War Museum (Q 30379).

In contrast, the other ranks' uniforms were designed to present members as sturdy auxiliary workers. The intention behind this image was to help overcome army officers' doubts about women's physical ability to work in harsh front conditions.[155] To achieve this, chief controllers defined auxiliaries as the female counterparts of private soldiers: young, strong, and primarily working class. This was indicated by the official term, "worker," which was adopted as the WAAC equivalent for "private."[156] Recruiting appeals revealed a similar stereotyping, calling for "strong, healthy and active women" and portraying members as sturdy and gritty Amazons, performing strenuous work.[157] This conceptualization determined the other ranks' uniforms. Analyzing the regulation patterns suggests that WAAC leaders designed the outfits with specifications similar to the criteria that shaped soldiers' service dress.

The defining characteristic of members' outfits was utility. Seeking a practical uniform, controllers adopted a coatdress as the basic garment, with an adjustable self-belt, washable collars, and two large pockets in the front for carrying identification documents.[158] A wartime invention, the coatdress was praised by fashion writers for its easy, "throw-on" simplicity and all-purpose usefulness as the uniform of the modern working girl.[159] These qualities appealed to WAAC leaders, who aimed for an outfit that was quick to get into and suitable for all occasions.[160] Like soldiers' dress, the uniforms were intended to be hard wearing. To complete their attire, the auxiliaries received thick, ribbed stockings, gaiters, and heavy shoes with cleats for drilling and marching, along with heavy army greatcoats to protect them from the cold.[161] In addition, the gabardine dresses and woolen stockings were designed for all seasons and meant to last a year before new kit was issued.[162] Finally, the patterns also conformed to the military principles of standardization and esprit de corps. All members received the same kit, regardless of their occupation, and their army connection was denoted by the khaki fabric of their dresses, shoulder straps, and titles.[163]

These uniform patterns were unpopular with the rank and file of the WAAC because of poor functionality, quality, and style. Designed with indoor workers in mind, the loose dresses were unsuitable for the outdoor physical duties of drivers handling cars and gardeners tending war graves.[164] The standardized dresses, initially in only three sizes, were also unsuited to a socially diverse membership. For lower-middle-class signalers and clerks, the ill-fitting, mass-produced clothes signified a demeaning loss of their class status, summarized by one clerk with the statement "an orphanage was better turned out."[165] Working-class cooks and mechanics were more appreciative of the free clothing. Like other members, however, they viewed the long, high-necked dresses, heavy shoes, and coats as frumpy and mannish.[166]

Consequently, most auxiliaries altered their regulation clothing. Drivers completely refashioned their outfits by having tunics and skirts made by tailors from extra coatdresses they obtained and by wearing warm hats, scarves, and gloves in their exposed cabs.[167] In contrast, gardeners discarded their dresses, adopting instead the tunics, breeches, and leggings of the Women's Land Army.[168] Other members modified the size and style of their dresses, which included shortening hemlines, narrowing waistlines, and substituting noncommissioned officers' cream collars for the regulation brown ones.[169] In addition, better-off auxiliaries embellished their costumes with silk or lisle stockings, high-heeled shoes, and fur collars on their greatcoats.[170] Unable to afford such luxuries, lower-paid members tucked their lacy handkerchiefs into their cuffs and created fashionable V-necks on their dresses by undoing the top buttons and turning in and fastening the edges with a brooch. Most women also personalized their hats and wore jewelry and makeup, against regulations.[171]

Unauthorized alterations contributed to the WAAC's weakly defined public image. The concept of female auxiliaries serving in the war zone was a radical novelty that should have been defined and marketed to the public in terms of corps members' uniformed identity. Initially, however, WAAC leaders omitted to do this. Inexperienced chief controllers overlooked the need for designing a distinctive cap badge for the corps, leading the War Office to adopt a nondescript emblem with the WAAC's initials surrounded by a laurel wreath.[172] Nor did WAAC propaganda create strong images of the corps' martial character. Disapproving of women's militarism, female directors of the National Service Department responsible for publicity failed to produce compelling posters or parades featuring the WAAC's uniform.[173] Thus, public opinion became confused about the corps' military character and role. Irregularity of dress among members reinforced this confusion, further diluting the WAAC's collective identity.

Its ill-defined public image generated by poor publicity damaged the reputation of the WAAC. Existing gender definitions recognized two types of women working in military environments: nurses and prostitutes.[174] WAAC members' fashionable uniform alterations associated them with the latter, linking the auxiliaries with negative wartime definitions of modern femininity. Government propaganda urged women's enrollment for war work by criticizing fashion and leisure as selfish indulgences that hindered the war effort.[175] Yet, instead of parades, WAAC publicists sought recruits by highlighting the auxiliaries' comfortable housing, plentiful food, and entertainments with their "soldier friends."[176] Such stories jarred with austerity conditions in Britain, generating hostility toward the WAAC. As public opinion sought scapegoats for the ongoing war and military setbacks, morality campaigners blamed high venereal disease rates in the army resulting from prostitution practiced allegedly in music halls.[177] Inadequate publicity linked these allegations to the WAAC. Lacking an authorized collective term, such as "WAACs," journalists named the auxiliaries after their uniforms "khaki girls," "chocolate soldiers," or "Brownies": the names of popular music hall entertainers.[178] Consequently, by late 1917, rumors were rife that the auxiliaries were army prostitutes, generating ribald jokes and illustrations that depicted the women soliciting in short dresses and sitting on soldiers' laps. These allegations hit WAAC recruitment hard.[179]

Figure 2.9.
"Just Waiting for a Couple of WAACs!" A&H "Now Smile" series, No. 480, Art and Humour Publishing Co., London. Author's personal collection.

The final model of the corps' martial femininity, "the servicewoman," successfully rebranded the construct between 1918 and 1919. This rebranding started with the militarization of the auxiliaries' uniformed identity by the armed forces. Following the example of the Royal Army Service Corps and the Royal Flying Corps,

Figure 2.10.
D. Tempest, "I've never been wounded, but I've had an awful W.A.A.C. on the knee!" Witty Comic Series, Bamforth & Co, Holmfirth, United Kingdom. Author's personal collection.

which shared their cap badges with female drivers, army formations in France, including the Signal Corps and the First Army, issued their brassards and colored patches to WAACs attached to their companies.[180] Initially, this was a practical measure to foster greater esprit de corps between auxiliaries and their army units. Later, it was also used as a gesture through which army officers expressed their appreciation for the women's good work and conduct.[181] Interservice rivalry extended this practice nationally. The worsening manpower shortage created competition between the armed forces for female labor, as the army expanded the WAAC while the navy and air force set up their own women's corps. Since terms and conditions were the same in the three units, the war ministries hoped to attract recruits by authorizing smarter uniforms and more prestigious insignia for them.[182]

Exploiting this situation, corps leaders claimed symbolic equality with the men by obtaining higher-status emblems for their units. When designing their officers' costumes, Katharine Furse and other WRNS directors copied their male colleagues' uniforms "in all essentials," adopting double-breasted reefer jackets in navy with eight gilt buttons and one breast and two slash pockets worn with matching skirts.[183] The rings on their cuffs also imitated naval officers' rank insignia, except for using blue rather than gold braid and a diamond shape instead of the curl.[184] WAAC controllers followed suit. Utilizing her good rapport with local army formations, Gwynne-Vaughan introduced saluting between male and female units in France, extending the practice to Britain later.[185] Her real triumph, however, came in autumn 1918. When ordered to take over the WRAF, she exploited the Air Council's desperation to turn around the failing corps and gained authorization for issuing female units with the uniforms and insignia of the RAF, including the prestigious "wings."[186]

Growing in confidence, corps leaders produced new, distinctly female, military identities for their units. These increased the services' respectability by smartening up their appearance and balancing masculine and feminine aspects of their uniforms, thus reducing irregularity of dress. Corps leaders achieved this by combining symbols of their respective armed forces with stylish, but affordable, markers of modern femininity. WRNS officers' tricorn hats and ratings' new blue-and-white sailor collars and caps glamorized their severe

Figure 2.11.
Officer of the Women's Royal Naval Service, 1918. Author's personal collection.

navy outfits by referencing Nelson's legacy.[187] Likewise, the WAAC brightened members' drab khaki outfits by authorizing unofficial cream collars and belted mackintoshes.[188] Such measures also aimed to raise morale, similar to WRAF policies that issued the RAF's new, attractive air force blue suits with a feminized version of soldiers' peaked service caps. The structured features of these caps prevented alterations, whereas their softer look offset the mannish RAF jackets.[189] Functional adjustments to uniforms stressed the auxiliaries' skilled work. Drivers and gardeners' modified suits were authorized, technical workers received tunics and trousers, and motorcyclists were issued with breeches and high boots.[190]

Finally, corps leaders boosted the martial female status of their units through royal patronage. WRNS directors obtained permission for using the royal title in their name and adopted a feminized version of the naval cap badge for their officers. Using royal blue rather than gold thread, the emblem combined the crown and anchor with the corps' initials.[191] This example eased the way for the other two services. The WRAF adopted the royal title and insignia of the RAF on its establishment, whereas chief controllers and the War Office used this strategy to give the defamed WAAC a clean bill of health. The new cap badge of the unit featured the queen's name with the corps' initials inside a laurel wreath surmounted by the crown, referencing the new commandant-in-chief of the service, which was renamed Queen Mary's Army Auxiliary Corps.[192] By emphasizing the auxiliaries' patriotism, royal patronage discouraged allegations of immorality against them.

A new publicity campaign highlighting the auxiliaries' uniforms completed the rebranding of the services' image. Its objective was to expand recruitment and urgently release troops for the front by selling martial femininity to young women as an exciting and positively modern identity. To achieve this, professional publicists at the Ministry of Labor promoted the corps through modern marketing techniques.[193] Adopting the style of commercial advertising, new colored posters depicted the auxiliaries as symbolic brand characters, representing military units that recruited members for auxiliary work. Recruiting marches were transformed into elaborate themed pageants, using advertising floats, bunting, and music to popularize the corps' female identities.[194]

Figure 2.12.
"The Girl behind the Man behind the Gun," recruiting poster for the Queen Mary's Army Auxiliary Corps (formerly WAAC), 1918. Imperial War Museum (PST 3570).

In these representations, the corps' uniforms became distinctive trademarks. Combined with their wearers' physical attributes, military environments, and activities, the outfits signified different types of martial femininity, providing recruits with alternatives to choose from. The WAAC's khaki dress denoted an active, outdoor army life in cheery company. This image was conveyed by the swinging skirt and ruddy cheeks of the WAAC girl, portrayed near her wooded campsite with comrades hiking and drilling in the background.[195] The WRNS uniform symbolized the dauntless spirit of Britain's seafaring traditions. Posing at the coast with white cliffs, a lighthouse, and a destroyer as a backdrop, Jenny Wren's earnest expression and wind-blown skirt implied her resolute support for Britain's naval defense.[196] The WRAF costume referenced the corps' modern technical expertise assisting Britain's flying aces, communicated by the sky-blue color linking the WRAF girl's stylish, professional suit with bobbed hair under her hat and the clear skies over an RAF airfield with flying and parked aircraft.[197] At joint pageants, uniformed auxiliaries enacted shared attributes of their martial identities. In the Silver Royal Wedding Anniversary and Edith Cavell's funeral, they demonstrated female patriotism and sacrifice, whereas in the 1918 Lord Mayor's Show, they performed skilled work roles in a mobile aircraft workshop and field kitchen.[198]

The successful rebranding of the corps' martial femininity was indicated by a growing desire among both the public and the auxiliaries to embrace symbols of this identity. Commercial companies started using images of uniformed auxiliaries to advertise a range of products, including luxury soap, waterproof shoes, and fountain pens.[199] Such positive images reinforced the impact of official publicity, boosting recruitment for the three services. Within a year, enrolment in the WAAC jumped from some 16,000 to over 40,000, whereas the WRAF rose from about 10,000 to more than 32,000 in eight months.[200] Considering the novelty of martial femininity, these numbers reveal increasing popularity of the corps among women.

The auxiliaries' recollections also indicate a growing identification with symbolic markers of their identity. Many WAACs who initially donned their ill-fitting uniforms reluctantly were proud to receive their new cap badge featuring the crown, viewing it as an elevation of their status.[201] Likewise, the new sky-blue suits inspired greater esprit de corps in the WRAF because they were "distinctive" and more attractive than the WAACs' khaki costumes.[202] Although many women disliked drilling, participation in public parades was highly popular. Such events, especially with royal visitors, figure prominently in corps members' memoirs.[203] Remembering the excitement of being selected for the Aldershot royal review, Lia Parfitt described weeks of drilling practice before the event. "None of us minded it though," she wrote, for "we wanted to show . . . that we were a smart outfit in the Aldershot Command."[204] The high point of the parade was marching past and saluting the royal party. Twenty-four years after the event, Parfitt recalled how members of her unit performed their martial identity to their new commandant-in-chief:

> Finally, the one command we have been waiting for is given by our U.A. "Company A—for'ard—MARCH!"—and we are marching in perfect rhythm; our skirts swinging in unison; the sun reflects a myriad of flashes from our badges, numerals and insignias; our gloved hands swinging straight up in front, practically level with our shoulders, in true British style of parade marching . . . our ranks perfectly straight and true. We are nearing the reviewing stand . . . here it is: Company—Eyes—RIGHT!" Every head in the ranks is turned as one . . . the Administrators and N.C.O.s snapping to a smart salute which we hold until everyone of our company has passed the reviewing stand. . . . We've been reviewed by the King and Queen. . . . —what a memorable day![205]

CONCLUSION

The construction of martial femininities enabled members of the women's corps to fill the armed forces' support jobs as auxiliary troops. Military uniforms became the primary means of achieving this goal. Because of their complex character, they could facilitate all aspects of collective identity formation. Signifying specific martial attributes and traditions, uniforms enabled corps leaders to develop a range of military identities and modify them according to the shifting demands of the war effort. Spectacular displays, another defining feature of martial dress, provided the corps with an ideal vehicle to proclaim and perform their soldierly qualities in public. Through parades, corps members could attract more recruits while convincing authorities about their fitness for auxiliary work. The spectacles also allowed the movement to generate additional representations of their identities and test popular reactions, helping to fine-tune their constructions.

Martial uniforms bestowed unique agency on corps members. The gendered and material character of the clothing allowed members to retain control over their designs, despite official, public, and media efforts to mold the patterns and meanings of the outfits. Additionally, the novelty of women's military uniforms gave corps members greater freedom to construct new identities than other women war workers. Through this agency, female volunteers and auxiliaries could actively shape the nature of their war participation and consciousness. Martial dress enabled them, both physically and culturally, to engage in new work and leisure activities and, through this, to perform nationally and internationally relevant public roles and join prestigious rituals acknowledging their contribution. By adopting martial uniforms, corps members also influenced cultural definitions of wartime Britain and women's long-term opportunities for public participation and employment.

NOTES

1. Film 439, Imperial War Museum, London (hereafter IWM).

2. "Full Details of Victory March; Women in the March," *Globe*, 17 July 1919, 6.

3. Sound 3137, IWM; Katharine Furse, *Hearts and Pomegranates: The Story of Forty-Five Years, 1875–1920* (London: Peter Davies, 1940), 386; Marchioness of Londonderry, *Retrospect* (London: Frederick Muller, 1938), 135–137.

4. Furse, *Hearts and Pomegranates*, 386; Londonderry, *Retrospect*, 135–136.

5. Furse, *Hearts and Pomegranates*, 386.

6. Alice Chauncey, *Women of the Royal Air Force* (London: WRAF Old Comrades Association, 1922), 48; Furse, *Hearts and Pomegranates*, 386; Sound 997, IWM.

7. Furse, *Hearts and Pomegranates*, 387; Londonderry, *Retrospect*, 136; "The Pageant of Victory," *Sheffield Daily Telegraph*, 21 July 1919, 7; Chauncey, *Women of the Royal Air Force*, 48; Photographs Q 28777, Q 28778, IWM; Film 439, IWM.

8. Sound 997, IWM; Furse, *Hearts and Pomegranates*, 387; "Celebrating Peace. March of the Troops," *Lancashire Evening Post*, 21 July 1919, 2; "The Pageant of Victory," *Sheffield Daily Telegraph*, 21 July 1919, 7.

9. Londonderry, *Retrospect*, 136.

10. Furse, *Hearts and Pomegranates*, 386–388.

11. C.F. Murdin, "The Day I Remember Best," *QMAAC Old Comrades' Association Gazette*, September 1929, 3–5.

12. Lucy Noakes, "'Playing at Being Soldiers'?: British Women and Military Uniform in the First World War," in *British Popular Culture and the First World War*, ed. Jessica Meyer (Leiden: Brill, 2008), 123–145.

13. Interview with Mary Andrews, daughter of Gladys Brotherton (née Spencer), a Women's Legion driver, 2 August 2005; Furse, *Hearts and Pomegranates*, 364; Sound 172, IWM.

14. David I. Kertzer, *Ritual, Politics, and Power* (New Haven, Conn.: Yale University Press, 1988), 41, 73–74, 155–156, 180; Maoz Azaryahu, "The Independence Military Parade: A Political History of a Patriotic Ritual," in *The Military and Militarism in Israeli Society*, ed. Edna Lomsky-Feder and Eyal Ben-Ari (Albany, N.Y.: SUNY Press, 1999), 89–116.

15. Susan Kingsley Kent, *Making Peace: The Reconstruction of Gender in Interwar Britain* (Princeton, N.J.: Princeton University Press, 1993); Sharon Ouditt, *Fighting Forces, Writing Women: Identity and Ideology in the First World War* (London: Routledge, 1994); Suzan R. Grayzel, "'The Outward and Visible Sign of Her Patriotism': Women, Uniforms, and National Service during the First World War," *Twentieth Century British History* 8, no. 2 (1997): 145–164; Noakes, "'Playing at Being Soldiers'?"; Janet S.K. Watson, *Fighting Different Wars: Experience, Memory, and the First World War in Britain* (Cambridge: Cambridge University Press, 2004).

16. Elizabeth Ewing, *Women in Uniform through the Centuries* (London: Batsford, 1975); Cheryl Buckley and Hilary Fawcett, *Fashioning the Feminine: Representation and Women's Fashion from the Fin de Siècle to the Present* (London: I.B. Tauris, 2002); Jennifer Craik, *Uniforms Exposed: From Conformity to Transgression* (Oxford: Berg, 2005).

17. Lucy Adlington, *Great War Fashion: Tales from the History Wardrobe* (Stroud: History Press, 2013); Nina Edwards, *Dressed for War: Uniform, Civilian Clothing and Trappings, 1914 to 1918* (London: I.B. Tauris, 2015).

18. Judith Butler, *Gender Trouble: Feminism and the Subversion of Identity* (New York: Routledge, 2006); Judith Butler, *Bodies That Matter: On the Discursive Limits of "Sex"* (New York: Routledge, 1993).

19. Lou Taylor, *The Study of Dress History* (Manchester: Manchester University Press, 2002).

20. Karen Tranberg Hansen, "The World in Dress: Anthropological Perspectives on Clothing, Fashion, and Culture," *Annual Review of Anthropology* 33, no. 1 (2004): 369–392; Susanne Küchler and Daniel Miller, eds., *Clothing as Material Culture* (Oxford: Berg, 2005); Carrie Hertz, "The Uniform: As Material, as Symbol, as Negotiated Object," *Midwestern Folklore* 32–33, nos. 1/2 (Spring/Fall 2006): 43–58.

21. Karen Harvey, *History and Material Culture: A Student's Guide to Approaching Alternative Sources* (New York: Routledge, 2009), 1–26; Catherine Richardson, ed., *Clothing Culture, 1350–1650* (London: Routledge, 2016).

22. Christopher Breward, *The Culture of Fashion: A New History of Fashionable Dress* (Manchester: Manchester University Press, 1995); Diana Crane, *Fashion and Its Social Agendas: Class, Gender, and Identity in Clothing* (Chicago: University of Chicago Press, 2000).

23. R. Money Barnes, *Military Uniforms of Britain and the Empire: 1742 to the Present Time* (London: Seeley, 1960); Amy Miller, *Dressed to Kill: British Naval Uniform, Masculinity and Contemporary Fashions, 1748–1857* (London: National Maritime Museum, 2007); Andrew Cormack and Peter Cormack, *British Air Forces 1914–1918 (2)* (Botley, U.K.: Osprey, 2001); Tammy M. Proctor, "Scouts, Guides, and the Fashioning of Empire, 1919–39," in *Fashioning the Body Politic: Dress, Gender, Citizenship*, ed. Wendy Parkins (Oxford: Berg, 2002), 125–144.

24. Stephen J. Heathorn, *For Home, Country, and Race: Constructing Gender, Class, and Englishness in the Elementary School, 1880–1914* (Toronto: University of Toronto Press, 2000), 48–55; Proctor, "Scouts, Guides, and the Fashioning of Empire."

25. Anne Summers, *Angels and Citizens: British Women as Military Nurses, 1854–1914*, 2nd ed. (Newbury, U.K.: Threshold Press, 2000), xvii–xix, 103–111; Spencer Wilkinson, *Citizen Soldiers: Essays towards the Improvement of the Volunteer Force*, 2nd ed. (London: Swan Sonnenschein, 1894).

26. Mary A. Conley, *From Jack Tar to Union Jack: Representing Naval Manhood in the British Empire, 1870–1918* (Manchester: Manchester University Press, 2017).

27. Scott Hughes Myerly, *British Military Spectacle: From the Napoleonic Wars through the Crimea* (Cambridge, Mass.: Harvard University Press, 1996), 30–40.

28. Myerly, *British Military Spectacle*, 10–11, 110–111, 139–168; Glenn R. Wilkinson, *Depictions and Images of War in Edwardian Newspapers, 1899–1914* (Houndmills, U.K.: Palgrave, 2003), 16–22, 29–36, 39–41; Roger T. Stearn, "Boer War Image-Maker: Richard Caton Woodville," in *The Boer War: Direction, Experience, and Image*, ed. John Gooch (London: Frank Cass), 213–223.

29. Jane Tynan, *British Army Uniform and the First World War: Men in Khaki* (Houndmills, U.K.: Palgrave, 2013), 3–13, 30–42, 116–123.

30. Myerly, *British Military Spectacle*, 139–169.

31. Myerly, *British Military Spectacle*, 16–20, 25–26, 57–59; E. John Solano, *Drill and Field Training* (London: Murray, 1915), 20–23.

32. Summers, *Angels and Citizens*.

33. Irene Schuessler Poplin, "Nursing Uniforms: Romantic Idea, Functional Attire, or Instrument of Social Change?" *Nursing History Review* 2 (1994): 153–167; Ewing, *Women in Uniform*, 37–51, 12–19, 22–27; Cecil Woodham Smith, *Florence Nightingale, 1820–1910* (New York: McGraw-Hill, 1951), 93.

34. Ewing, *Women in Uniform*, 41–46; Ouditt, *Fighting Forces*, 17–22.

35. Ewing, *Women in Uniform*, 41–45; Ouditt, *Fighting Forces*, 17–22; Summers, *Angels and Citizens*, 93–99.

36. Summers, *Angels and Citizens*, 147–152; Ewing, *Women in Uniform*, 42, 47–51.

37. Summers, *Angels and Citizens*, 162–172, 203–250; Ewing, *Women in Uniform*, 76–84; Katharine Furse, "War Work and Its Lessons," Furse Collection, 196/9/A1, Bristol University Library.

38. "Women Volunteers. Newcastle and London Disagree," *North Mail*, 29 June 1917; Sound 44, IWM; Noakes, "'Playing at Being Soldiers'?"; Minute 4, AG1 to F6, 8 February 1917, WO 32/5250, The National Archives, Kew (hereafter TNA); FM to AG, 24 May 1917, WO 32/5530, TNA.

39. Krisztina Robert, "Gender, Class, and Patriotism: Women's Paramilitary Units in First World War Britain," *International History Review* 19, no. 1 (1997): 52–65, 59, 61–62.

40. Field-marshal Douglas Haig's report, 11 March 1917, Army 3.4/7, Women at Work Collection (hereafter WWC), IWM.

41. Watson, *Fighting Different Wars*, 54–56; Krisztina Robert, "'All That Is Best of the Modern Woman'? Representations of Female Military Auxiliaries in British Popular Culture, 1914–1919," in Meyer, *British Popular Culture*, 97–122.

42. Tom H. Sawyers, "Women's Volunteer Reserve," *Tailor and Cutter*, 3 August 1916, 581; "Women's Volunteer Reserve," *Tunbridge Wells Advertiser*, 6 March 1915; Lia Parfitt, "I Was a WAAC," 14, 1998-01-87, National Army Museum, London (hereafter NAM); Robert, "'All That Is Best,'" 101.

43. For the corps movement, see Krisztina Robert, "Gendering Class, Patriotism, and Militarism: The Women's Corps Movement in Britain during and after World War I" (Ph.D. diss., University of Houston, 1998).

44. Sawyers, "Women's Volunteer Reserve," 3 August 1916, 581; Tom H. Sawyers, "Women's Volunteer Reserve," *Tailor and Cutter*, 2 November 1916, 856–859; "Rules for Recruits," Vol. 2/17, WWC, IWM; Furse, *Hearts*

and Pomegranates, 364–365; "Tunbridge Wells War Notes, Women's Volunteer Reserve," *Kent and Sussex Courier*, 12 March 1915, 5.

45. Krisztina Robert, "The Unsung Heroines of Radical Wartime Activism: Gender, Militarism, and Collective Action in the British Women's Corps," in *Labour, British Radicalism and the First World War*, ed. Lucy Bland and Richard Carr (Manchester: Manchester University Press, 2018), 145–165.

46. Solano, *Drill and Field Training*, 1–97.

47. Robert, "Gendering Class, Patriotism, and Militarism," 174–175, 186–187, 191–192; W.M. Charlesworth, "Women for the Army?" *Daily Graphic*, 27 July 1916.

48. Robert, "Gender, Class, and Patriotism," 59, 62–64.

49. Furse, "War Work and Its Lessons"; Furse, *Hearts and Pomegranates*, 291–292; Robert, "'All That Is Best,'" 101; Wendy Parkins, "'The Epidemic of Purple, White and Green': Fashion and the Suffrage Movement in Britain, 1908–11," in Parkins, *Fashioning the Body Politic*, 97–124.

50. These included Evelina Haverfield, Lady Londonderry, Katharine Furse, and Helen Gwynne-Vaughan. See also ADM 318/35, 93, 205, 211.

51. "Women Who Are in Khaki," *Daily Sketch*, 24 December 1916; "Woman and Her Motorcycle. What Military Women Are Wearing," *Motor Cycling*, 21 May 1918.

52. J.M. Cowper, *A Short History of Queen Mary's Army Auxiliary Corps* (Guildford: Women's Royal Army Corps Association, 1967), 55–56; Chauncey, *Women of the Royal Air Force*, 45.

53. A.B. Baker, "The Story of a W.A.A.C.," in *Everyman at War: Sixty Personal Narratives of the War*, ed. C.B. Purdom (New York: E.P. Dutton, 1930), 380–386; Dorothy Young to Furse ADM 318/51, TNA.

54. "A Happy W.A.A.C.," postcard no. 4929 (London: Raphael Tuck, 1918); Reginald Higgings, "WRAF-ish," *Sketch*, 22 January 1919, 105.

55. Parfitt, "I Was a WAAC"; Sound 42, IWM.

56. Helen Gwynne-Vaughan, *Service with the Army* (London: Hutchinson, 1942), 18–19; Cowper, *A Short History*, 49, 59.

57. Sound 44, IWM.

58. Krisztina Robert, "The Khaki Portrait" (paper presented at the International Conference on the First World War, Queen Mary's College, University of London, August 2014).

59. Keith Grieves, *The Politics of Manpower* (Manchester: Manchester University Press, 1988); Charles Messenger, *Call to Arms: The British Army, 1914–1918* (London: Weidenfeld & Nicolson, 2005), 243–264; "Memorandum on the Proceedings of Conference of April 10 1917," Army 3.7/15, WWC, IWM.

60. "Employment of Women," report by Lt. Gen. H.M. Lawson, 20, Army 3.3/2, WWC, IWM; Minute 4, Lt. Colonel J. Earl, AG1 to F6, 8 February 1917, WO 32/5250, TNA.

61. "Women's Volunteer Reserve. Parade to Glen Parva Barracks," *Leicester Mail*, 7 May 1915; Minutes 1, 3, and 21, "Proposals Regarding Uniform and Badges," 12 and 19 March and 12 April 1917, WO 32/5252, TNA; Furse, *Hearts and Pomegranates*, 365.

62. Minute 1 and "Uniform of Officials," memorandum by Mary Chalmers Watson and Helen Gwynne Vaughan, WO 32/5252, TNA; Furse, *Hearts and Pomegranates*, 364–365.

63. Minutes 3, 13, and 15, WO 32/5252, TNA; Furse, *Hearts and Pomegranates*, 364.

64. For arguments about gender discrimination, see Grayzel, "The Outward and Visible Sign of Her Patriotism"; Noakes, "'Playing at Being Soldiers.'"

65. See minutes in WO 32/5253, TNA.

66. The impact of women's military work on troop morale was an important consideration. See Haig's report, Army 3.4/7, WWC, IWM.

67. Robert, "'All That Is Best,'" 101.

68. Furse, *Hearts and Pomegranates*, 319–321; Londonderry, *Retrospect*, 111–115.

69. "Travelling Canteens. Work for the Women's Volunteer Reserve," *Birmingham Gazette*, 9 June 1915; "Playing Hockey with Convalescent Soldiers," *Daily Mirror*, 14 May 1918.

70. Robert, "'All That Is Best,'" 102.

71. Robert, "'All That Is Best,'" 101.

72. Robert, "'All That Is Best,'" 103. See also letters under "Playing at Soldiers," *Newcastle Chronicle*, 19 March and 1 April 1915; "The King's Uniform," *Morning Post*, 16, 19, 20, 21, 22, and 26 July 1915.

73. See letters by Minnie G. Davison and Minnie F. Reay, *Newcastle Chronicle*, 31 March 1915, and by Isabel Margesson, a Uniformed Woman, and Another Woman, "The King's Uniform," *Morning Post*, 19–20 July 1915.

74. J.M. Osbourne, "Defining Their Own Patriotism: British Volunteer Training Corps in the First World War," *Journal of Contemporary History* 23 (1988): 59–75.

75. Catriona Pennell, *A Kingdom United: Popular Responses to the Outbreak of the First World War in Britain and Ireland* (Oxford: Oxford University Press, 2012), 124–131; Peter Simkins, *Kitchener's Army: The Raising of the New Armies, 1914–1916* (Manchester: Manchester University Press, 1988), 41–46.

76. Kent, *Making Peace*, 22–26.

77. Gwynette Chapman, *Daily Herald*, 28 August 1914, 4; "Women and Home Defence," *Hull Daily Mail*, 8 September 1914, 5.

78. Women Signallers Territorial Corps, leaflet, vol. 7/58, WWC, IWM; Mrs. Dawson Scott, *The Official Handbook of the Women's Defence Relief Corps* (Southall, U.K., 1915), 10–22.

79. E. Haverfield, "Women's Volunteer Defence Force," *Evening Standard*, 4 September 1914, 11; "Women Soldiers," *Illustrated Chronicle*, 14 April 1915.

80. Ian F.W. Beckett, *Riflemen Form: A Study of the Rifle Volunteer Movement, 1859–1908* (Aldershot, U.K.: Ogilby, 1982).

81. See cartoon in *Lloyd's Weekly*, 3 March 1915, suppl. 38/27, WWC, IWM.

82. Women's Volunteer Reserve leaflets, vols. 2/15, 2/27, WWC, IWM; Lady Frances Balfour, "Of What Use?" *Evening Standard*, 15 July 1915; Women's Volunteer Reserve leaflet, vol. 2/25, WWC, IMW.

83. "Rules for Recruits" and "Constitution and Regulations," vol. 2/17–18, WWC, IWM.

84. Sawyers, "Women's Volunteer Reserve," 2 November 1916, 856.

85. "'Uniform,' Its Meaning and How It Should Be Worn," vol. 2/33, WWC, IWM.

86. The Walthamstow company, whose members sought to make their own, was expelled. See "Women's Volunteer Reserve in Essex," *East London Advertiser*, 17 April 1915; "Rules for Recruits," vol. 2/17, WWC, IWM; Beckett, *Riflemen Form*, 48–49, 80.

87. Women Signallers Territorial Corps, leaflet, vol. 7/58, WWC, IWM; Sawyers, "Women's Volunteer Reserve," 3 August 1916, 581; Dawson Scott, *The Official Handbook*, 10–12, 27–28, 30; "Bexhill Women's Help," *Bexhill-on-Sea Observer*, 4 September 1915, 9; Q30625, IWM.

88. Boyce Geddes, *Evelina: Outward Bound from Inverlochy* (Braunton, U.K.: Merlin, 1995), 13–63.

89. Sawyers, "Women's Volunteer Reserve," 2 November 1916, 858–859.

90. Women's Volunteer Reserve, leaflet, vol. 2/15, WWC, IWM.

91. Tom H. Sawyers, "Women's Volunteer Reserve Uniforms," *Tailor and Cutter*, 12 August 1916, 574; Sawyers, "Women's Volunteer Reserve," 3 August 1916, 581; 2 November 1916, 856–859.

92. Sawyers, "Women's Volunteer Reserve," 3 August 1916, 581; 2 November 1916, 856.

93. Osbourne, "Defining Their Own Patriotism," 65–66.

94. Women's Volunteer Reserve, leaflet, vol. 2/15, WWC, IWM; "Lady Volunteers!" *Hampstead Chronicle*, 21 December 1914.

95. Tynan, *British Army Uniform*, 35–43, 105–129; "Be in the Fashion and Wear Khaki," *Cheshire Observer*, 1 May 1915, 5; PST 5111, IWM; 1977-06-81-12, NAM.

96. Lady Jellicoe, "The Women's Army," *Daily Mail*, 10 February 1915; "Women's Volunteer Reserve. Local Corps to Be Formed," *Tunbridge Wells Advertiser*, 13 March 1915; "Fashions in War-Time," *Daily Chronicle*, 19 March 1915, suppl. 38/23, IWM.

97. "Fashions in War-Time."

98. Lisa Tickner, *The Spectacle of Women: Imagery and the Suffrage Campaign, 1907–14* (Chicago: University of Chicago Press, 1988); "Parade of Living Models," *Leeds Mercury*, 8 April 1909, 8; Myerly, *British Military Spectacle*.

99. *Daily Graphic*, 12 April 1915, suppl. 38/35, WWC, IWM; Balfour, "Of What Use?"

100. Robert, "The Unsung Heroines," 145–147.

101. "Branches," *Women's Volunteer Reserve Magazine*, January 1916, 20–21; February 1916, 41.

102. Robert, "Gendering Class, Patriotism, and Militarism," 155–160, 174–175, 183–197; "Women's Volunteer Reserve," *Ilford Recorder*, 16 April 1915.

103. "The New Full Skirts," *Chester Chronicle*, 27 March 1915, 2; "Women's Chat," *Sterling Observer*, 13 March 1915, 7; "Notes by the Wayside," *Milngavie Herald*, 12 February 1915, 4.

104. Krisztina Robert, "Constructions of 'Home,' 'Front,' and Women's Military Employment in First-World-War Britain: A Spatial Interpretation," *History and Theory* 52, no. 3 (October 2013): 319–343.

105. Dawson Scott, *The Official Handbook*, 7–9; "Women Signallers," *Daily Record*, 3 August 1915, 3.

106. Q 30625, Q 67400, Q 108031, Q 30623, IWM; "In England–Now!" *Bystander*, 10 March 1915, 12; "Woman's Ways," *Sketch*, 31 March 1915, 24; Tim Jeal, *Baden-Powell: Founder of the Boy Scouts* (New Haven, Conn.: Yale University Press, 2007), 397.

107. Simkins, *Kitchener's Army*, 104–161; Grieves, *The Politics of Manpower*, 11–18.

108. "The King's Uniform," *Morning Post*, 22 July 1915, 5.

109. "The Woman of To-morrow," *Fashions for All*, April 1914, 65–66; "'Uniform,' Its Meaning and How It Should Be Worn."

110. "Woman Colonel," *Daily Mail*, 26 April 1915, 8–9; "A Neat and Practical Uniform," *Newcastle Chronicle*, 15 July 1915; "The King's Uniform," *Morning Post*, 16 July 1915, 6.

111. "The King's Uniform," *Morning Post*, 16 July 1915, 6; 20 July 1915, 8.

112. Euan Lyne, "Shades of Our Grandmothers," *Bystander*, 18 August 1915.

113. Londonderry, *Retrospect*, 112–115.

114. "War Service Legion and Women's Legion Report, 1915–1918," 10–11, Army 1/11, WWC, IWM.

115. UNI 8962, IWM; photograph of Margaret Caswell, 1998-01-34-3, NAM; "A Patriotic Peeress," *Sketch*, 20 December 1916, 7; "Constitution of the Women's Legion," Adair-Roberts, Document 153, WWC, IWM.

116. Cowper, *A Short History*, 12; ACI No. 2034, 27 October 1916.

117. INS 7778, IWM; 1998-01-34-3, NAM.

118. Marina Warner, *Monuments and Maidens: The Allegory of the Female Form* (London: Vintage, 1996), 38–55, 104–176; PST 5109, IWM; J.M. Staniforth, "Fame and Shame," *Western Mail*, 19 July 1915, 3.

119. Antonia Fraser, *The Warrior Queens: Boadicea's Chariot* (London: Phoenix, 2002), 47–118, 226–251, 331–360.

120. Warner, *Monuments and Maidens*.

121. "War Service Legion," 11–13.

122. INS 7778, 7775, 7776, 7781, 7783, 7770, IWM.

123. Simkins, *Kitchener's Army*, 119–161.

124. Tickner, *The Spectacle of Women*, 229–233; "Some Types of Women War-Workers," *Western Mail*, 10 March 1916, 7.

125. "The Woman behind the Gun," *Graphic*, 19 February 1916, 253; news cuttings, suppl. 38/94, 38/168, 38/175, IWM.

126. Cowper, *A Short History*, 11.

127. "Women Army Cooks," *Derbyshire Courier*, 15 February 1916, 4; "The Motorists of the Legion," *Cheltenham Looker-On*, 16 September 1916, 8.

128. "To Avert Senseless Waste," *Sheffield Independent*, 15 February 1916, 8; "The Modern Amazons: Women in the Army," *Sunday Mirror*, 22 October 1916, 3.

129. "War Service Legion," 19–20; "Women's Legion. Rules for Superintendents," 1998-01-80, NAM.

130. "Women Camp Cooks," *Daily Mail*, 26 May 1916; "Women Who Are in Khaki," *Daily Sketch*, 24 December 1916; Annie Bartlett, "The Day I Remember Best," *QMAAC Old Comrades' Association Gazette*, December 1929, 5–6.

131. Photographs, 1994-07-226-8, 1995-01-21-60, NAM.

132. "War Service Legion," 11, 24–32.

133. Molly Coleclough, *Women's Legion, 1916–1920* (London: Spearman, 1940), 11–12; "Women Drivers for the Flying Corps," *Yorkshire Evening Post*, 14 September 1916, 4; "Wears R.F.C. Badge," *Daily Record*, 21 September 1916, 4.

134. Lawson, "Employment of Women," 20; Lord Derby, minute, 25 January 1917, Army 3.6/3, WWC, IWM.

135. "House Rules for Members of the Women's Legion" and "Rules for Superintendents," 1998-01-80, NAM.

136. Robert, "Gender, Class, and Patriotism," 53.

137. Robert, "'All That Is Best,'" 115–119.

138. PST 13167, 2766, 5898, IWM.

139. Robert, "Gender, Class, and Patriotism," 59–60; WRNS, 9/41, IWM.

140. Beckett, *Riflemen Form*, 111–112, 174–175.

141. Gary Sheffield, *Leadership in the Trenches: Officer-Man Relations, Morale and Discipline in the British Army in the Era of the First World War* (Houndmills, U.K.: Macmillan, 2000), 1–12.

142. Haig's report, Army 3.4/7, WWC, IWM; Gwynne-Vaughan, *Service*, 26.

143. Gwynne-Vaughan, *Service*, 15–16, 157–158.

144. Gwynne-Vaughan, *Service*, 15–18, 28–32; "Report of the Women's Reserve Committee," 23 December 1920, WO 163/26, TNA.

145. Sheffield, *Leadership in the Trenches.*

146. Gwynne-Vaughan, *Service*, 18–19; Leared, R.I., Document 13794, IWM.

147. O.B. Graham, 1998-01-59, NAM.

148. Molly Izzard, *A Heroine in Her Time: A Life of Dame Helen Gwynne-Vaughan* (London: Macmillan, 1969), 136–142; Chalmers Watson, "Comments on Leigh Wood's Report of Conference of 10 April," Army 3.7/14, WWC, IWM.

149. Memorandum by Chalmers Watson and Gwynne-Vaughan, WO 32/5252, TNA.

150. Robert, "Gendering Class, Patriotism, and Militarism," 159–163.

151. Minute 1 and memorandum by Gwynne-Vaughan and Chalmers Watson, WO 32/5252, TNA; UNI 469, IWM.

152. Izzard, *A Heroine*, 134–135.

153. Izzard, *A Heroine*, 134–135; memorandum by Gwynne-Vaughan and Chalmers Watson, WO 32/5252, TNA; Gwynne-Vaughan, *Service*, 17.

154. Gwynne-Vaughan, *Service*, 16–18; Minutes 13 and 17, WO 32/5252, TNA.

155. Douglas Haig to War Office secretary, 25 February 1917, WO 32/5093, TNA; Haig's report, Army 3.4/7, WWC, IWM.

156. Gwynne-Vaughan, *Service*, 16.

157. "The Women's Army Auxiliary Corps," *Nantwich Guardian*, 9 October 1917, 3; *Yorkshire Post*, 1 December 1917, 9; Jesse Pope, "The WAACs," *Sunday Mirror*, 25 November 1917, 4.

158. Gwynne-Vaughan, *Service*, 18; UNI 4446, 4447, 8135, IWM.

159. *Fashions for All*, January 1916, 3; October 1916, 6–7, 12; November 1916, 7; February 1917, 6.

160. Gwynne-Vaughan, *Service*, 18.

161. Parfitt, "I Was a WAAC."

162. Gwynne-Vaughan, *Service*, 18

163. UNI 8135, 4446, IWM; 1994-04-291, 1994-04-300, 1995-09-330, NAM.

164. Sound 579, 9731, IWM.

165. Sound 44, 3137, 42, IWM.

166. Sound 7444, 9731, IWM; Daisy A. Philp, 1998-01-92-1, NAM.

167. Sound 579, IWM.

168. Sound 9731, IWM.

169. Sound 42, IWM; Gwynne-Vaughan, *Service*, 19; UNI 4446, IWM.

170. Sound 42, IWM; Parfitt, "I Was a WAAC;" Leared, R.I., Document 13794, IWM.

171. Gwynne-Vaughan, *Service*, 47–48; Chauncey, *Women of the Royal Air Force*, 45; Sound 7444, IWM; Parfitt, "I Was a WAAC."

172. "Proposals Regarding Uniform and Badges," WO 32/5252, TNA.

173. Violet Markham, deputy director of the Women's Section, NSD, strongly criticized the Women's Volunteer Reserve's khaki parades. See "The King's Uniform," *Morning Post*, 22 July 1915, 5; PST 7816, IWM; Robert, "'All That Is Best,'" 112.

174. Robert, "Gendering Class, Patriotism, and Militarism," 306.

175. "Call to Service," *Western Morning News*, 13 November 1917, 5; "War-Time Extravagance," *Middlesex Chronicle*, 17 November 1917, 1.

176. Robert, "'All That Is Best,'" 112–115.

177. Trevor Wilson, *The Myriad Faces of War: Britain and the Great War* (Cambridge: Polity, 1986), 402–403, 507–516; Jan Rüger, "Entertainments," in *Capital Cities at War: Paris, London, Berlin, 1914–1919*, ed. Jay Winter and Jean-Louis Robert, vol. 2, *A Cultural History* (Cambridge: Cambridge University Press, 2007), 105–140.

178. "With the Khaki Girls in France," *Londonderry Sentinel*, 24 November 1917, 7; "The Brownies," *Eastbourne Gazette*, 8 November 1916; The Khaki Girls was a music hall dance group between 1900 and 1907, but the name also conjured up a popular song from the Boer War, "The Girl in the Khaki Dress." See John Mullen, *The Show Must Go On: Popular Song in Britain during the First World War* (Abingdon, U.K.: Ashgate, 2015), 80–81.

179. Robert, "'All That Is Best,'"112–115.

180. Sound, 579, 42, IWM; Gwynne-Vaughan, *Service*, 27, 34.

181. Cowper, *A Short History*, 34.

182. See Furse, *Hearts and Pomegranates*, 361.

183. Furse, *Hearts and Pomegranates,* 364; UNI 1007, 1011, National Maritime Museum (hereafter NMM).

184. Furse, *Hearts and Pomegranates*, 364–365; UNI 1005, NMM.

185. Gwynne-Vaughan, *Service*, 28–30.

186. Izzard, *A Heroine*, 195–199; Chauncey, *Women of the Royal Air Force*, 44–45; Cormack, *British Air Forces,*15–21, 29; Gwynne-Vaughan, *Service*, 67–68.

187. UNI 0996, 0994, 1008/1, NMM.

188. Cowper, *A Short History*, 49, 59; 1994-07-241-77, NAM; Gwynne-Vaughan, *Service*, 18–19.

189. Gertrude A. George, "The Orders for the Day," in *Eight Months with the Women's Royal Air Force* (London: Heath Granton, 1920); "Uniforms for the WRAF," *Aberdeen Evening Press*, 31 July 1918, 3.

190. Gwynne-Vaughan, *Service*, 18; 1995-01-24-1, NAM; Cormack, *British Air Forces*, 20; Q12291, Q12293, Q27255, IWM; Sound 7486, IWM.

191. Furse, *Hearts and Pomegranates*, 364; UNI 1661, 1018/2, NMM.

192. UNI 8611, IWM.

193. Robert, "'All That Is Best,'" 115–116; "Regulations for the QMAAC," p. 50, Army 3.13/46, WWC, IWM.

194. Robert, "'All That Is Best,'" 117; PST 13167, 2766, 5898, IWM; Myerly, *British Military Spectacle*, 8, 18; "W.R.A.F. Recruiting Rally," *Folkestone Herald*, 2 November 1918, 7.

195. PST 13167, IWM.

196. PST 2766, IWM.

197. PST 5898, IWM.

198. Cowper, *A Short History*, 56–57; "The Arrival of the Remains of Nurse Cavell at Dover," *Dover Express*, 16 May 1919, 5; "A Unique Lord Mayor's Show," *Graphic*, 16 November 1918, 548.

199. "Price's Court Bouquet" soap, *Illustrated London News*, 22 June 1918, 733; "Dri-ped" shoes, *Tatler*, 18 September 1918, 33; "Swan" fountain pen, *Tatler*, 28 August 1918, 2.

200. *Statistics of the Military Effort of the British Empire during the Great War, 1914 – 1920* (London: HMSO, 1922), 206; Chauncey, *Women of the Royal Air Force*, ix.

201. Olive Castle, Document 9190, IWM; Jenny Swann, Document 9373, IWM; Marjorie Mullins, 1998-01-83, NAM.

202. Sound 12178/4A, 8857, IWM.

203. Victoria Bramble, 1998-01-24, NAM; Marjorie Holme, 1998-01-70, NAM; Mullins, 1998-01-83, NAM; Castle, Document 9190, IWM.

204. Parfitt, "I Was a WAAC," 16.

205. Parfitt, "I Was a WAAC," 17.

THREE

PROFESSIONALISM, PATRIOTISM, AND PURITY OF PURPOSE

Symbolism and Identity in British and Other Allied Nurses' Uniforms

CHRISTINE E. HALLETT, ALISON SPIRES, AND KEIRON SPIRES

In the first decades of the twentieth century, the British nursing profession still held a precarious foothold in respectable society. Because of its association with the handling of bodies and waste products, nursing work was seen as potentially dangerous and polluting to those who performed it. This was particularly so for military nurses, not only because war hospitals were seen as hazardous and even brutalizing places but also because an older image of the war nurse as nothing more than a camp follower persisted in the popular imagination.[1] That image first began to change in the mid-nineteenth century, with the work of Florence Nightingale and other reformers doing much to promote a vision of the nurse as a genteel and devoted professional doing vital work out of religious and civic duty.[2]

The founding in 1902 of the British Queen Alexandra's Imperial Military Nursing Service (QAIMNS) marked a new departure.[3] The design of a uniform that would make a clear statement about both the professionalism and the moral probity of its members was an urgent project for its founders. Building upon blueprints created over a long latent period from 1861 to 1902, during which a small cadre of nurses had begun to claim a distinct identity, the QAIMNS uniform was designed to be both modest and practical. It featured a full-length skirt, neatly tailored bodice, and such hygiene-related accessories as collar, cuffs, and apron.[4] This chapter traces the design and development of the QAIMNS uniform during World War I, when the service enjoyed a rapid and significant increase in recognition and influence. It also compares and contrasts the uniforms of regular army nurses in British service with uniforms worn by four other categories of war nurses: (1) nurses of the official military nursing services in the self-governing British Dominions of Australia, New Zealand, and Canada; (2) volunteer British nurses with limited training who served only "for the duration"; (3) nurses of the U.S. Army Nurse Corps; and (4) those nurses in countries such as France, Belgium, Romania, and Russia, where lay professional nursing services had only begun to be developed and where religious orders of nurses, widely referred to as Sisters of Mercy, still had a prominent role in war nursing.

CREATING THE BRITISH AND DOMINION ARMY NURSE

During the nineteenth century, senior nurses in charge of professional schools of nursing in large cities throughout the developed world were creating an image of genteel femininity. By the first decades of the twentieth century, nurse leaders had, effectively, established more than a foothold within the male-dominated environment of the civilian hospital.[5] Professional nursing care was regarded as essential to patient well-being and survival.[6] However, although these highly professional women achieved a degree of acceptability in a civilian environment, they faced a tougher challenge in gaining recognition as part of the military medical services of industrial nations. War had always been seen as a masculine affair: Men waged war; women remained at home, providing both the justification for the fight—the protection of women and children—and the nurturing environment to which soldiers could return.[7] Breaking down these assumptions was to be a long-term project.

Although the modern-day Queen Alexandra's Royal Army Nursing Corps (QARANC) traces its heritage back to Nightingale's work in the Crimea, a formal British Army Nursing Service was slow to develop. Seven nurses were employed at the Royal Herbert Hospital in Woolwich in 1861, with Jane Shaw Stewart, a veteran of the Crimean War, at their head; a further six were recruited for the Royal Victoria Hospital, Netley, in 1863.[8] These women, who had civilian nursing status at the time of their appointment, can be viewed as pioneers of military nursing, female professionals intruding into an environment so exclusively male that their presence was, to many, an affront to the natural order of things.

The creation of the Army Nursing Service in 1881, as part of the so-called Childers Reforms, provided the first real formal recognition of female nursing in the British army. Further formal acknowledgement came with the publication of a new set of official regulations in 1883. Yet throughout the second half of the nineteenth century, the cadre of formally recognized professional military nurses remained small, the service fragmented. Approximately 60 women worked as nurses at 16 military hospitals by 1890, their numbers supplemented in 1897 with formation of Princess Christian's Army Nursing Reserve.[9] Their uniform, however, already marked them out as military nurses. Gray dresses and scarlet capes ("tippets") made a clear statement about their distinction from civilian nurses. Uniforms of civilian nurses varied in color according to which hospital they worked in; capes, if worn, were made from dark material, avoiding the militaristic overtones created by the army uniforms' gray and scarlet.[10] During the Second Anglo-Boer War (1899–1902), male medical orderlies exclusively staffed many forward field hospitals. Women had only just begun to gain access to such highly masculine environments. But mortality rates during that war, particularly from disease, were reported as scandalous in the British press, and the sense of crisis that was engendered provided women with a powerful argument for the need to bring the professionalism, caring skills, and clinical expertise of female nurses into military hospitals.[11] In 1902, shortly before the end of the war, the Queen Alexandra's Imperial Military Nursing Service was formed in Britain.[12]

The nursing professions of self-governing British dominions such as Australia, New Zealand, and Canada had been developing along broadly parallel lines. Historians have debated the relative influence of the Nightingale School of Nursing at St Thomas's Hospital, London (founded in 1860), and other significant British schools.[13] Whatever the actual chronology of the development of the British model of nursing, by the late 1860s, it was clearly influential throughout in the British dominions. Kirsty Harris has argued that "the spread of the Nightingale system in Australia from 1868 was ample evidence that the roots of Australian nursing were firmly British."[14] Although emerging slightly later, military nursing services in Australia and New Zealand mirrored the British experience. At the outbreak of World War I, each had a small Army Nursing Reserve, which expanded rapidly from August 1914 onward.[15] In Canada, the development of the army nursing service took a slightly different route, gaining more support from its army medical service colleagues. Here, by the outbreak of the war, nurses had officer-equivalent status, reflected in the more militaristic appearance of their uniforms, which were trimmed with epaulettes and brass buttons.[16]

By the time war began in 1914, nascent military nursing services in Britain and its self-governing dominions, particularly Canada, Australia, and New Zealand, were already using the design of nurses' uniforms as a means of projecting an image of a highly efficient cadre of professionals, who also had a distinctly military identity and who could be recognized by "their own" soldiers. By doing so, they were, perhaps inadvertently, identifying themselves as part of a movement among women who were demanding their right to do their national duty among their male compatriots, by participating in war service.[17] Recognizing that such claims might court controversy, nurses were careful to incorporate overtly feminine elements into their uniforms.

PRESERVING FEMININITY AND DECORUM

In 1998, Olwen Hufton identified the fate of the woman of the past as one in which she was regarded as "a reproductive object, a second-class citizen, someone without a history, whose growth was stunted to prevent her realizing her capacities."[18] As these disadvantages became apparent to female historians, many identified the need to "refocus the past" to bring women more clearly into a field of vision that had, previously, recorded only the contributions of men.[19] Nowhere, perhaps, has there been a greater need for this recalibration of our field of vision than in the medical history of World War I, a field in which the contribution of female nurses has, until recently, been almost entirely neglected.[20] Yet feminist historians have been remarkably reticent about paying attention to female nurses, viewing them, perhaps because of their apparent acceptance of a subjugated role, as difficult subjects for feminist study.

Bringing professional women into the exclusively male environment of the military hospital was a difficult project. By 1914, nurses had largely won the argument for their inclusion in the civilian hospital environment. They had done so on professional grounds; their work was increasingly seen as essential to patients' survival and recovery. Yet, as feminist writers from Simone de Beauvoir to Sheila Rowbotham have argued, modern industrial societies like Britain were so steeped in notions of patriarchal authority that women's identity was compromised by their cultural identification as "the second sex."[21] A female profession was, in itself, an anomaly, and any such profession was bound to have to both justify its place and avoid any ambiguity by clearly identifying its members as women.[22] Nurses' uniforms in both civilian and military practice denoted the femininity of their wearers. During the second decade of the twentieth century, it would have been unheard of for women to wear short skirts or breeches. Such a costume would have been seen as compromising the morality of its wearer. Hence, regular and reserve members of the QA wore long gray skirts. Notwithstanding a bodice attractively gathered at the waist, no one could be in any doubt of the modesty and probity of the wearer, as clearly displayed by Sister Kate Luard in Figure 3.1.[23]

Perhaps the most striking feature of British army nurses' uniforms was the veil worn by all fully qualified professional British and dominion military nurses. These military uniform veils contrasted sharply with civilian nurses' caps, which varied widely and often denoted the wearers' hospital. Wearing veils clearly distinguished military nurses from their civilian counterparts. Although a nurse might owe allegiance to one or other civilian training institution, taking the veil marked her, for the duration of the war, as a military nurse.[24] But the primary message of the nunlike veil, undoubtedly, was to identify its wearer as a woman of purity and chastity. It shielded her from unwanted male attention in the highly masculine environment of the military base and, later, in the forward areas known, significantly, as the "zone of the armies." It also reinforced the message to nurses themselves, as well as to those around them, that neither romantic entanglements nor sexual liaisons would be tolerated. Spending time unchaperoned outside the boundaries of the military hospital with a man (even with one's own brother) was absolutely forbidden, as was dancing, even in one's own mess.[25] The uniform's messages of discipline, purity, and decorum were a deliberate outward signifier of the behavior the nurse was expected to adhere to.

Preserving the right "look" entailed much hard work on the part of nurses, who were not issued a uniform; rather, they were given an allowance and had to find an approved tailor to make the uniform from stringent War Office specifications. Even though most nurses

Figure 3.1.
Sister Kate Luard in the uniform of the Queen Alexandra's Imperial Military Nursing Service (Reserve). Reproduced by kind courtesy of Caroline Stevens.

obtained their uniforms from Boyd Cooper Ltd. (then at 12 Bruton Street, London, W1), close inspection of the dresses reveals slight differences. Nurses had difficulty maintaining their uniforms once deployed overseas. The standard army supply chain did not provide for repairs of nurses' clothes or shoes; hence, they often had to purchase items locally or undertake repairs themselves. They also, at times, had to find local laundresses to wash their dresses and aprons.

The New Zealand Army Nursing Service met with particularly intractable male opposition during its formative years. Bureaucratic delays and a lack of enthusiasm from the hierarchy of the New Zealand Army Medical Corps meant that it was the spring of 1915 before the reserve's determined matron-in-chief, Hester Maclean, was able to formally inaugurate the Army Nursing Service around the small cadre of existing reserve nurses. And the chauvinism with which the service was confronted may have had an impact on the design of its uniform. The earliest version was, as Maclean herself commented, highly impractical; it was designed, it seemed, more to acknowledge and preserve femininity than to enable clinical practice. As Anna Rogers has described it, the uniform comprised "dark grey Pentone cloth ankle-length dresses and cloaks, with a touch of scarlet on [the] collars and cuffs, and plain grey bonnets."[26] The bonnets were later replaced by hats and the cloaks by long, buttoned coats. As the war progressed, the uniforms of professional military nurses were adapted to the realities of military service; skirts, in particular, were shortened. Not only did this heightening of hems prevent skirts from trailing in the mud and becoming dirty and unkempt (a totally unacceptable situation for military nurses), it was also a safety feature. On ambulance trains, in particular, it was a practical solution to activities such as "footboarding," the rather acrobatic technique required for exiting one carriage and crossing the gap to the next, to attend to patients in the next ward.[27]

UNIFORM: A SIGNIFIER OF PROFESSIONALISM AND MILITARISM

Figure 3.2.
Sister Volta Billing in the uniform of the Territorial Force Nursing Service. Reproduced by kind courtesy of Sue Light.

British QAIMNS and Territorial Force Nursing Service (TFNS) uniforms were designed to set their wearers apart from unqualified caregivers. Although QAIMNS nurses were not part of the army, not even of the Royal Army Medical Corps, the scarlet and gray colors, along with the stripes and badges they wore, conveyed the message that they had a genuine and significant role within the military and were an integral part of the war effort. The dresses were ankle length, with hidden fastenings down the front. The bodice was pleated at the front, and gathered in at the waist, with a long skirt. The bodice was lined with a white cotton fabric, and the collar had button holes for collar studs. The tippet, a short shoulder cape, was an important element of the uniform. It was designed to drop to a level just below the breast; its message was one of modesty and decorum, though its actual effect was to accentuate the wearer's feminine curves. The sepia coloration of many contemporary photographs masks the striking nature of the tippet's color. Regular QAIMNS nurses had entirely scarlet tippets, whereas reserve sisters had a broad scarlet stripe around the edge of an otherwise gray tippet.

Starched very stiff, detachable white collars and cuffs indicated the highly disciplined nature of the nurses' deportment and behavior. Cuffs had very little practical value; a nurse would actually remove them and roll up her sleeves when she entered a ward to attend her patients. Practical or not, they were a mandatory part of the uniform outside the wards, as one volunteer nurse learned to her chagrin. In her fictionalized autobiography, Irene Rathbone recounted a cuffless encounter with matron. Scurrying on an errand between wards, "she met Matron coming toward her—thin as a greyhound in her grey uniform, lynx-eyed and stony-faced." Attempting to pass with a murmured "good morning, Matron," she was brought up short: "Where are your cuffs, Nurse?" Rathbone continues the story:

> Joan looked at her bare arms and blushed. It was a strict rule that, except in the wards, cuffs should always be worn. In the hurry of her errand Joan had forgotten.
>
> "What ward do you belong to?" inquired Matron.
>
> "Ward 33."
>
> "Sister Ewart's? I am amazed that a nurse of hers—that any nurse—should appear in such a condition. I thought for a moment . . . that it was one of the housemaids."
>
> With which withering remark Matron went on her way.
>
> When Joan . . . returned to the ward, she told Sister Ewart what had happened. If she expected the slightest sympathy from that quarter . . . , she was disappointed. Sister's frosty little reprimand showed her that breaches of hospital etiquette . . . could not be lightly passed over.[28]

Long before they were admitted to military hospitals in an official capacity, civilian nurses organized themselves into hierarchies of command with rather militaristic etiquettes of behavior.[29] A probationer would, for example, stand in the presence of a staff nurse, who would stand in the presence of a sister. Exercising almost absolute authority over the nurses, hospital matrons were at the pinnacle of these nursing hierarchies, although they themselves were completely under the sway of the hospitals' boards of governors. Sleeve stripes often indicated a nurse's status, but uniform color might serve the same purpose. When Queen Alexandra's Military Nursing Service formed in 1902, it was natural for its founders to organize around hierarchies of command similar to those of civilian hospitals; fortunately, these sat comfortably alongside the military lines of command of the Royal Army Medical Corps, which mirrored British military hierarchies. From its foundation, the QAIMNS paid close attention to the uniforms of its senior staff. A portrait photograph of its second matron-in-chief, Caroline Keel, who held office from 1906 to 1910, reveals the careful use of materials (silk for formal wear; cotton for clinical wear; wool or silk for cloaks and tippets), a form of elaborate embellishment, known as frogging, which also

Figure 3.3.
Portrait of Dame Maud McCarthy, matron-in-chief to the British Expeditionary Force in France and Flanders, 1914–1919. Reproduced by kind permission of the Museum of Military Medicine, Mytchett, United Kingdom.

appeared on the military uniforms of the day, and a rather impractical bonnet topped by a large velvet bow.[30]

When the Territorial Force Nursing Service was created as part of the Haldane Reforms in 1908, it adopted the command structure of the QAIMNS, with a matron-in-chief, sisters, and staff nurses. Its first matron-in-chief was Sydney Browne, a veteran of the Boer War.[31] Browne had previously served as the first matron-in-chief to the QAIMNS, and her appointment to the newly created TFNS upon her retirement from the QAIMNS set the

Figure 3.4.
Image of Caroline Keel, matron-in-chief of the QAIMNS, 1906–1910, in her dress uniform. Reproduced by kind permission of the Museum of Military Medicine, Mytchett, United Kingdom.

pattern for the remainder of the twentieth century: It became commonplace for a retiring QAIMNS matron-in-chief to take over command of the TFNS. Careful attention was paid to the design of the TFNS uniform, and it was decided that it would be, essentially, the same as that worn by members of the QAIMNS. Its significance as a mark of recognition by the state was emphasized in a lecture given by Sydney Browne, in which she described the formation of the service:

> Every member receives a silver badge designed by Her Majesty Queen Alexandra, the President of the Service, and is entitled to wear the uniform of the TFNS which is a blue grey dress with a short cape faced with scarlet. It is a distinctive military dress and quite serviceable, and it is neat and appropriate for nurses, but it must not

be worn except at Territorial functions with the permission of the Matron-in-Chief. The wearing of the uniform ensures the recognition and respect which is always accorded to Army Sisters. Members are not obliged to provide uniform in time of peace as the allowance for uniform is not given until the Service is mobilized, but it is certainly an advantage to possess it, for the Territorial Force Nursing Service is a Government Service and its members are recognised by the Government, for example, in State functions such as the Coronation of the King and Queen, and the Thanksgiving Service for their Majesties' safe return from India, a certain proportion of the members who could attend officially in uniform are invited to be present. Members are also invited to be present at Reviews and Exhibitions, receptions and other entertainments.[32]

Because the uniforms of the QAIMNS, its reserve QAIMNS(R), and the TFNS were so similar, badges held particular significance in distinguishing between types of nurse. Indeed, as they worked together on active service within military hospitals of World War I, professional military nurses could sometimes be distinguished *only* by their badges: a QAIMNS service badge for regular QAs; a "Reserve" badge for the QA Reserve nurses, and the small silver badge in the form of a T, mentioned by Browne in her lecture, for Territorial Force nurses.[33] As the war continued, some nurses earned the right to wear medals alongside their badges: the Royal Red Cross (first or second class) for distinguished service and the Military Medal for acts of particular courage or gallantry.[34]

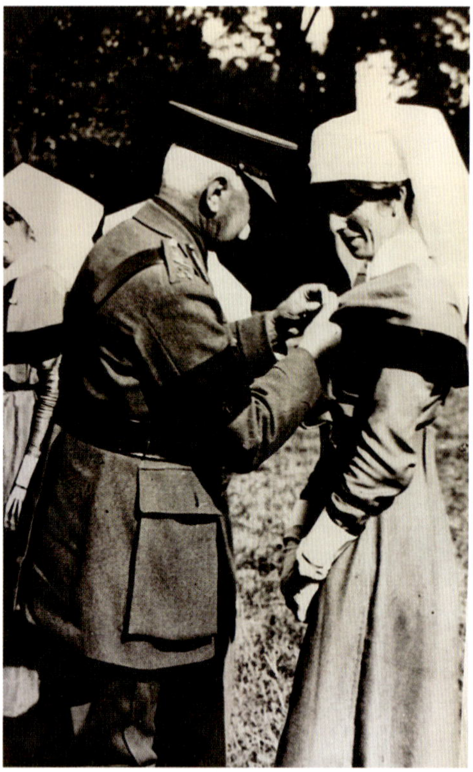

Figure 3.5.
Nursing sister of the QAIMNS(R) being awarded the Military Medal. Reproduced by kind permission of the Museum of Military Medicine, Mytchett, United Kingdom.

The supervisory roles of senior nurses were seen as important to the smooth running of the service, and uniform stripes and badges were used to orient both staff and patients to the level of seniority of any given nurse; staff nurses had no sleeve stripes, sisters had two, and matrons wore scarlet cuffs. Matrons-in-chief wore very distinctive uniforms, designed to indicate their status as part of both the nursing services and the war effort itself. Ethel Hope Becher, QAIMNS matron-in-chief during World War I, wore a rather old-fashioned looking uniform, a slightly updated version of the dress uniform worn by her predecessor, Caroline Keel.[35]

At the 1919 Victory Parade held in London, senior nurses marched together at the head of their regular nursing staffs.

Figure 3.6.
A portrait of Ethel Hope Becher, matron-in-chief of the QAIMNS during World War I, wearing her dress uniform. Reproduced by kind permission of the Museum of Military Medicine, Mytchett, United Kingdom.

Figure 3.7.
Nurses marching in the 1919 London Victory Parade. Reproduced by kind courtesy of Sue Light.

The intention was probably to convey the message that these women had not just been the nurturers who had cared for the wounded as they made their way back home to safety (important though this side of their role was). They were also a formidable military force in their own right and had made a significant contribution to the war effort.[36]

Following the war, regulations governing QAIMNS and TFNS uniforms continued to be stringent. Take, for example, the orders published by the QAIMNS in 1936, just prior to World War II:

> The Queen's badge for Queen Alexandra's Imperial Military Nursing Service, which is issued on confirmation of appointment, will always be worn by members when in uniform. It will be worn on the right breast on the red cape. . . . This badge is the property of the State and must be returned to the Matron-in-Chief when members leave the service. . . . Uniform will be purchased by the members themselves, an allowance towards this purpose being granted. The establishments authorized to supply the uniform are: Messrs. Boyd Cooper, 4 George Street, Hanover Square, W.1., and Messrs Harrods, Ltd., Knightsbridge S.W.1. . . . Members will provide themselves with the following uniform, which must be made exactly to specifications. . . . One dress, grey beige, three dresses, grey washing. Sisters to have two scarlet bands ½ inch wide above the cuffs. One coat and skirt, grey beige, collar

> edged with ½ inch scarlet facing. White silk shirt, grey tie. Eight aprons, collars, and cuffs as required. Overcoats and jackets, grey collar, edged ¾ inch and 5/8 inch scarlet respectively. Overalls, for use in acute wards and operating theatres, and when nursing women and children. . . . One cape, scarlet cloth. Six capes muslin with badge in red embroidered on one corner. One hat grey velour (winter), one hat grey felt (summer), both with regulation hat ribbon. One coat grey cloth, long, with special facings of rank. A special evening dress of approved pattern, with cap and without apron. Grey waterproofs may be worn when required.[37]

Clearly, although the uniform acquired a slightly more practical design during the interwar period, the precision and uniformity of its colors, materials, and dimensions continued to be carefully regimented. This was probably, in part, a reaction to professional military nurses' wartime experiences. Even on the front lines of war service, they had found themselves working alongside nurses of many nations, some of whom had very little professional training. The leaders of the QAIMNS and the TFNS viewed it as imperative that their members could be very clearly distinguished from volunteer assistants, including a particularly British type of volunteer nurse, the so-called Voluntary Aid Detachment (VAD).

PURITY, VIRTUE, AND THE BRITISH VAD

Working alongside professional nurses in military hospitals at home were semitrained volunteers, members of the Voluntary Aid Detachments universally known as VADs. The shortage of trained nurses at the outbreak of war was a dilemma for British nurse leaders. A significant group had been campaigning vigorously for full professional recognition since about 1887. Many of the more powerful nurse leaders wanted legislation entered into the statute books that would allow for the creation of a professional register into which a nurse's name could be entered only if she had received three-year training from a recognized nursing school.[38] The presence of VADs with six-month apprenticeship training and a few certificates in first aid and sick cookery was, therefore, something of an embarrassment to the nursing hierarchy; their resentment was shared by many of the rank and file, who would have preferred not to have had to accept the assistance of these volunteers.[39]

The British Voluntary Aid Detachments were founded in 1909.[40] Created to provide support for troops during wartime, particularly for the sick and wounded, they saw nursing as one of their most important functions, and their nurse members were seen as highly dedicated to the war effort.[41] Their volunteer nurses were uniformed in a way that was very different from their professional counterparts. They wore blue dresses—a color chosen to denote purity—with white aprons. Their head coverings resembled headscarves and were tied at the back to ensure that they did not look like the veils of the professionals. On their arms, they wore brassards to which were sewn the symbols of the Red Cross or the order of St. John of Jerusalem, both of which mobilized VAD units. To coordinate their efforts, the hierarchies of the two organizations came together to form a single Joint War Committee in

October 1914.[42] As the war progressed, many VADs chose to wear a red cross on the front of the tabard, directly over the heart, a powerful symbol of their humanitarian purpose. British VADs made a deep imprint on the psyche of the British and have been remembered as the self-sacrificing heroines of the war.[43]

SUBVERSION AND SABOTAGE OF THE NURSING IMAGE

VADs were not the only volunteer nurses to serve overseas. Some wealthy female volunteers established their own field hospitals in the early months of the war. Among them was American millionaire Mary Borden, who donated her hospital—"Mobile Surgical No. 1"—to the French Service de Santé des Armées. Borden was pursuing a career as an author, and she drew around herself a cadre of trained nurses from Britain, Australia, Canada, and the United States. Her hospital became a cauldron of literary creativity; three of its nurses, as well as Borden herself, published significant memoirs of their time there.[44]

The uniforms of British nurses and VADs symbolized, in part, their belonging to a particular, recognized nursing service. Borden's unique uniform, although bearing many similarities to that of a French Red Cross nurse, symbolized her independence. It was also designed to be glamorous, the veil flamboyant, the skirts rather short, and the white shoes higher heeled than was practical. Borden's uniform is, in many ways, a subversion of the

Figure 3.8.
Mobile Surgical No. 1. Mary Borden standing behind a seated patient toward the right of the photograph. Reproduced by kind courtesy of the Provincial Archives of Alberta, Edmonton, Canada.

devices used by others to depict purity, restraint, and discipline. It is unlikely that this was a deliberate act of rebellion. It is more likely that Borden, who appears always to have dressed elegantly, was unwilling to cast off that elegance for something more practical.[45] Because she was the "directrice" of her hospital and was funding its operating costs, her appearance was controlled only by her own recognition of the need for restraint.

Although her career was highly unusual, Mary Borden was not unique. Other women found their own way to the front lines, among them trained nurse Elsie Knocker and her assistant, Mairi Chisholm (see figure 8.1). The two had joined a volunteer unit funded and directed by the eccentric supporter of women's suffrage, Hector Munro.[46] After working for some time for Munro's unit at Furnes, Knocker and Chisholm decided to set up their own forward field ambulance on the Belgian front lines in the small village of Pervyse. They too wore veils, but like Borden, they chose to subvert the nurses' uniform, and they did so in ways that went way beyond Borden's glamorized image. Their "uniforms" were highly practical. They wore breeches and overcoats, and their veils were made from a rough material, suggesting that they were the female equivalent of soldiers in the trenches. They cared for wounded men in a Belgian front line aid post, underground in what they referred to as their "cellar-house," a shelter very like a military bunker. The message that these women were soldiering in their own way is emphasized by their highly practical but very masculine and militaristic leather boots. These two set out to create an impression, and they succeeded, becoming celebrities and gaining the award of the Military Medal, even though they belonged to no recognized professional unit.[47]

THE RELIGIOUS AND THE SECULAR: OTHER ALLIED NATIONS

The uniforms of British military nurses differed significantly from those of nurses on the European continent. Yet there were also points of similarity. One of the ways in which military nurses in most combatant nations carved a niche for themselves as part of their nation's war effort was to identify themselves as the symbolic "mothers of the nation."[48] The Madonna-like veil of the nursing services of many nations (including Britain) were, in part, designed to convey this image. This identification of maternal care with the protection of the sick and wounded was particularly powerful in such Catholic countries as France and Belgium.[49] Because there were very few secular schools of nursing in these countries, their nursing services were complex; hospital wards were staffed by nurses belonging to religious orders, a few professional nurses who had trained in secular schools, and lady volunteers drawn mainly from the upper classes. Both secular nurses and volunteers adopted a carefully tailored and slightly old-fashioned style of uniform that was almost entirely white, emphasizing the purity and authenticity of the nurse's purpose. Working alongside these lay nurses were the "religieuses" in the dark habits of nuns, complete with veils and wimples, presenting a severe image of discipline and self-sacrifice. The image of the French war nurse was a subject of great

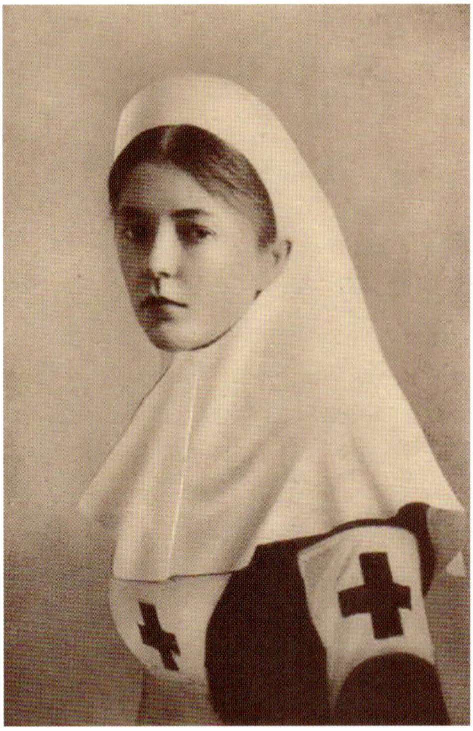

Figure 3.9.
Portrait of Mary Britnieva. Frontispiece to her memoir, One Woman's Story.

fascination for photographers and artists. The costume of the nun-nurse was often used in French propaganda images, very large numbers of which were sent home to soldiers' families as postcards. Many nurses, including British nurses serving in French field hospitals as part of the French Flag Nursing Corps, received postcards from their former patients that carried highly romanticized images of nurses caring for soldier-patients.[50]

Perhaps the most overtly religious nurses' uniform of the war, however, was that of the Russian Sister of Mercy. Here, the veil is pulled tight around the face, and the elimination of any sight of the nurse's hair conveys the message that she has renounced all worldly things and is devoting herself to the service of her patients. This uniform, too, could be slightly subverted. Anglo-Russian memoirist Mary Britnieva included a photograph of herself in the frontispiece of her memoir, *One Woman's Story,* a poignant tale of romance, loss, and service to country. In this image, her hair is clearly visible, the red crosses on her uniform are very prominent, and she seems to be at pains to convey the message that she is, effectively, a secular Red Cross nurse, albeit one powerfully motivated by a religious calling. Another memoirist, volunteer nurse Florence Farmborough, also included in her book several images of herself wearing the Russian uniform. Yet she also chose as the frontispiece of her *Nurse at the Russian Front* an image of herself wearing the highly practical and very masculine uniform issued to nurses serving with a so-called flying column.[51]

Women belonging to the royal families of European nations often donned military nurses' uniforms in order to denote their sense of devotion to their people. By adopting the nurse's uniform, such socially elite women could, in one sense, be seen as hijacking the nursing identity for propaganda purposes since they had no formal nurse's training. However, they were welcomed with gratitude and approval into the military hospital wards of their countries. Queen Elisabeth of the Belgians often made morale-boosting visits to Belgian military hospitals, spending time on the wards and, sometimes, actually working in dressing rooms and operating theaters, supporting the work of trained nurses and surgeons. Her highly individualistic "uniform," a white dress and a stylish white turban, was designed to be both practical and elegant.[52] Similarly, Queen Marie of Romania donned a Red Cross nurse's

Figure 3.10.
Portrait of Florence Farmborough. Frontispiece to her book, Nurse at the Russian Front.

uniform and toured the wards of Romanian military hospitals, distributing gifts and spending time talking to patients. Her image was consciously dramatic and strikingly clinical. "My white Red Cross dress had become a symbol," she wrote in her memoir.[53] Her uniform was probably designed to convey an impression of a queen who was not afraid to come into close contact with the wounded while, at the same time, protecting her from such vector-borne diseases as typhus. In this way, British-born Marie was able to telegraph her commitment to her Romanian subjects and dedication to their well-being.[54]

Soon after the United States entered the war in April 1917, it deployed base hospitals to Europe. A prestigious civilian hospital equipped and staffed each base hospital. Nurses were enlisted under the auspices of the American Red Cross and wore its distinctive uniform, a "blue serge dress with a heavy blue overcoat, a blue-brimmed velour hat, dark tan shoes and gloves."[55] The indoor uniform was an all-white dress (in part, to distinguish them from the British and dominion nurses) with a white apron, a cap (rather than a veil), and a prominently displayed red cross. This distinctive dress emphasized continuity with these nurses' earlier civilian work, making the point that these women were all highly trained professionals whose work was part of a preexisting tradition of humanitarian work. The neatness and elegance of its cut enabled nurses to lay claim to the "cool, detached, competent, and disciplined clinical performances" that formed the foundation of their claim to professional status.[56] It probably also served to protect nurses from the overt chauvinism that has been identified by Kimberly Jensen as a feature in some American base hospitals.[57] The continuity between civilian and military U.S. nurses' uniforms perhaps illustrates the confidence of members of the U.S. Army Nurse Corps, who saw no need to wear a veil if serving in a U.S. military hospital.

CONCLUSION: THE USES AND ABUSES OF NURSES' UNIFORMS

Nurses' World War I uniforms were deliberate signifiers of the aspirations and intentions of the groups they represented. As Julia Hallam has argued, "how nurses construct themselves . . . is an integral aspect of nursing's occupational identity."[58] Whether they wished to project a sense of professionalism, militarism, purity, or altruism, nurse leaders were aware of the symbolic power of the uniform and mobilized its potential in purposeful and often quite ingenious ways. Little wonder, then, that the image of the nurse was often used, and at times subverted, for propaganda purposes. Images of nurses in uniform figured prominently in war propaganda, from photographs of silent film actress June Caprice wearing a jaunty nurse's cap on posters encouraging American citizens to buy Liberty Bonds to graphic (if wildly inaccurate) images of Edith Cavell in military nurse's uniform lying dead on the ground, a German officer standing over her with a smoking revolver, intended to stoke hatred of the foe. Throughout the war, governments everywhere deployed posters depicting Red Cross nurses in uniform to persuade their citizens to support the war effort. For men, this support could mean volunteering for active service at risk of life. The fact that the nurse's uniform could be such an emotive and persuasive propaganda tool highlights its power as a signifier of nursing values. Such power had to be carefully controlled. Army Nursing Service leaders designed uniforms with skirts that were just the right length (becoming shorter only as raised hems became more acceptable); veils that were carefully bleached and folded; and pristine aprons, collars, and cuffs.

The uniform was performing a highly complex task. On the one hand, it was intended to indicate the femininity, even docility, of its wearer. Colors were carefully chosen: gray for professionals, blue for volunteers, and white for all nurses in Catholic countries. On the other hand, the uniform symbolized the newly won professionalism of its wearer. Trained military nurses, particularly those operating at very senior levels, wore prominent badges and lengths of braid, whereas the indoor (or ward) uniforms at all levels of the hierarchy included highly starched collars and cuffs and spotlessly white aprons. In Britain, only full members of the QAIMNS wore scarlet tippets. As well as indicating her femininity and professionalism, the uniform also signified the patriotism of its wearer, along with her status as a part of her nation's war effort. Its military features were inescapable: the severe cut, the mixture of scarlet and gray, the use of badges, stripes, and well-polished boots. Nurses' uniforms of World War I might differ from nation to nation, and those differences were, as we have shown, significant. However, all performed an impressively complex function; they protected and promoted nurses from home front to "zone of the armies" while, at the same time, creating a professional military nursing identity that was to endure for well over a century.

NOTES

1. For a discussion of these issues, see Margaret Vining and Barton C. Hacker, "From Camp Follower to Lady in Uniform: Women, Social Class and Military Institutions before 1920," *Contemporary European History* 10, no. 3 (Nov. 2001), 353–373; Christine E. Hallett, *Veiled Warriors: Allied Nurses of the First World War* (Oxford: Oxford University Press, 2014), 1–30.

2. There is an extensive literature on the work of Florence Nightingale. For an overview of her life and work, see Mark Bostridge, *Florence Nightingale: The Woman and Her Legend* (London: Viking, 2008). On her work in the Crimea, see Carol Helmstadter, "Class, Gender and Professional Expertise: British Military Nursing in the Crimean War," in *One Hundred Years of Wartime Nursing Practices, 1854–1953*, ed. Jane Brooks and Christine E. Hallett (Manchester: Manchester University Press, 2013), 23–41; Carol Helmstadter, "Navigating the Political Straits in the Crimean War," in *Notes on Nightingale: The Influence and Legacy of an Icon*, ed. Sioban Nelson and Anne Marie Rafferty (Ithaca, N.Y.: Cornell University Press, 2010), 28–54. On her later work in developing nurse education, see Roy Wake, *The Nightingale Training School, 1860–1996* (London: Haggerston Press, 1998), 1–93. See also Carol Helmstadter and Judith Godden, *Nursing before Nightingale, 1815–1899* (Farnham, U.K.: Ashgate, 2011).

3. On the history of the QAIMNS, see Juliet Piggott, *Queen Alexandra's Royal Army Nursing Corps* (London: Leo Cooper, 1975); Anne Summers, *Angels and Citizens: British Women as Military Nurses, 1854–1914*, rev. ed. (Newbury, U.K.: Threshold Press, 2000); Eric Taylor, *Wartime Nurse: One Hundred Years from the Crimea to Korea, 1854–1954* (London: Robert Hale, 2001). On the enlargement and development of the service at the beginning of World War I, see Hallett, *Veiled Warriors*, 16–26, 31–40, 47–60.

4. This uniform was building upon that of the earlier Army Nursing Service/Princess Christian's Army Nursing Service (Reserve) already in use in South Africa

5. Some of the earliest published claims to professional status came from British and American nurses who wrote histories of their profession. See, e.g., Sarah A. Southall Tooley, *The History of Nursing in the British Empire: Primary Source Edition* (London: S.H. Bousefield, 1906); M. Adelaide Nutting and Lavinia L. Dock, *A History of Nursing*, 4 vols. (New York: G.P. Putnam's Sons, 1907–1912).

6. Brian Abel Smith, *A History of the Nursing Profession* (London: Heinemann, 1960), 81–98; Celia Davies, *Rewriting Nursing History* (London: Croom Helm, 1980), 11–17; Susan McGann, *The Battle of the Nurses: A Study of Eight Women Who Influenced the Development of Professional Nursing, 1880–1930* (London: Scutari Press, 1992), 35–57; Sue Hawkins, *Nursing and Women's Labour in the Nineteenth Century: The Quest of Independence* (London: Routlege, 2010), 11–34; Helmstadter and Godden, *Nursing before Nightingale*, 169–189.

7. Gerard J. De Groot and Corinna Peniston-Bird, *A Soldier and a Woman: Sexual Integration in the Military* (London: Routledge, 2000); Lucy Noakes, *Women in the British Army: War and the Gentle Sex, 1907–1948* (London: Routledge, 2006); Trudi Tate, *Women, Men and the Great War* (Manchester: Manchester University Press, 1995); Susan Kingsley Kent, *Gender and Power in Britain, 1640–1990* (London: Routledge, 1999), 262–286.

8. Summers, *Angels and Citizens*, 72; Piggott, *Queen Alexandra's Royal Army Nursing Corps*.

9. Sue Light, "Army Nursing Service," Scarlet Finders, http://www.scarletfinders.co.uk/8.html (accessed 16 February 2018).

10. Sue Light, "The Fairest Force: 7. Uniform," http://www.fairestforce.co.uk/13.html (accessed 23 April 2018).

11. Keiron Spires, "Nurses in the Boer War (1899–1902): What Was It about the Collective Body of Nurses Caring for the Sick and Wounded during the Boer War That Shaped the Future of Military Nursing?" (Ph.D. diss., The South Bank University, London, 2013; Keiron Spires, Boer War Nurses Database; Charlotte Dale, "Traversing the Veldt with 'Tommy Atkins': The Clinical Challenges of Nursing Typhoid Patients during the Second

Anglo-Boer War (1899–1902)," in *One Hundred Years of Wartime Nursing Practices, 1854–1953*, ed. Jane Brooks and Christine E. Hallett (Manchester: Manchester University Press, 2013), 58–77.

12. Piggott, *Queen Alexandra's Royal Army Nursing Corps*, 37–40. For a firsthand account of nursing work during the Second Anglo-Boer War, see Eleanor C. Laurence, *A Nurse's Life in War and Peace* (London: Smith, Elder, 1912).

13. Monica Baly, "The Nightingale Nurses: The Myth and the Reality," *Nursing Times*, 3–9 August 1983, 40–42, reprinted in Christopher Maggs, ed., *Nursing History: The State of the Art* (London: Croom Helm, 1987); Helmstadter and Godden, *Nursing before Nightingale*.

14. Kirsty Harris, *More Than Bombs and Bandages: Australian Army Nurses at Work in World War I* (Newport, N.S.W., Australia: Big Sky, 2011), 16.

15. On the development of the Australian Army Nursing Services, see Jan Bassett, *Guns and Brooches: Australian Army Nursing from the Boer War to the Gulf War* (Melbourne: Oxford University Press, 1992), 1–31; Ruth Rae, *Scarlet Poppies: The Army Experience of Australian Nurses during World War One* (Burwood, N.S.W.: [Australian] College of Nursing, 2004); Ruth Rae, *Veiled Lives: Threading Australian Nursing History into the Fabric of the First World War* (Burwood, N.S.W.: [Australian] College of Nursing, 2009). On the New Zealand service, see Sherayl Kendall and David Corbett, *New Zealand Military Nursing: A History of the Royal New Zealand Nursing Corps, Boer War to Present Day* (Auckland: Authors, 1990); Jan Rodgers, "Potential for Professional Profit: The Making of the New Zealand Army Nursing Service, 1914–1915," *Nursing Praxis in New Zealand,* 11, no. 2 (July 1996): 4–12; Jill Clendon, "Potential for Professional Profit: The Making of the New Zealand Army Nursing Service, 1914–1915," *Nursing Praxis in New Zealand,* 12, no. 1 (March 1997): 24–28; Anna Rogers, *While You're Away: New Zealand Nurses at War, 1899–1948* (Auckland: Auckland University Press, 2003), 45–174. See also the contribution of Bruce Scates et al. to this volume (ch. 6).

16. Cynthia Toman, *Sister Soldiers of the Great War: The Nurses of the Canadian Army Medical Corps* (Vancouver: University of British Columbia Press, 2016). See also Toman's contribution to this volume (ch. 5).

17. On women's involvement in World War I, see Claire Tylee, *The Great War and Women's Consciousness: Images of Militarism and Womanhood in Women's Writings, 1914–64* (Basingstoke, U.K.: Macmillan, 1990); Angela K. Smith, *The Second Battlefield: Women, Modernism and the First World War* (Manchester: Manchester University Press, 2000). See also Toman's contribution to this volume (ch. 5).

18. Olwen Hufton, "Women, Gender and the *Fin de Siècle*," in *Companion to Historiography*, ed. Michael Bentley (London: Routledge, 1997), 929–940.

19. The quotation is taken from the title of Linda K. Kerber, *Women's America: Refocussing the Past*, 8th ed. (Oxford: Oxford University Press, 2015). On these issues, as they related to World War I, see also Joan W. Scott, "Rewriting History," in *Behind the Lines: Gender and the Two World Wars*, ed. Margaret Randolph Higonnet, Jane Jenson, Sonya Michel, and Margaret Collins Weitz (New Haven, Conn.: Yale University Press, 1987), 19–30; Margaret R. Higonnet and Patrice L.R. Higonnet, "The Double Helix," in Higonne et al., *Behind the Lines*, 31–47.

20. In histories of modern warfare written in the late twentieth century, the contributions of nurses were entirely absent. See, e.g., Roger Cooter, Steve Sturdy, and Mark Harrison, *War Medicine and Modernity* (Stroud, U.K.: Sutton, 1999). In more recent histories, such as Mark Harrison, *The Medical War: British Military Medicine in the First World War* (Oxford: Oxford University Press, 2010), they received a brief mention. The contributions of male nurses—or military orderlies—are also almost entirely absent.

21. Simone de Beauvoir, *The Second Sex,* trans. Constance Borde and Sheila Malovant-Chevallier (New York: Vintage Books, 2009); Sheila Rowbotham, *Hidden from History: 300 Years of Women's Oppression and the Fight Against It*, rev. ed. (London: Pluto Press, 1992). See also Joan Scott, *Gender and the Politics of History* (New York: Columbia University Press, 1988).

22. On the roles women played in the British military during World War I, see Lucy Noakes, "Eve in Khaki: Women Working with the British Military 1915–1918," in *Women and Work Culture: Britain c.1850–1950*, ed. Krista Cowman and Louise A. Jackson (Aldershot, U.K.: Ashgate, 2004), 213–228.

23. This image also appears on the cover of Christine E. Hallett, *Nurse Writers of the Great War* (Manchester: Manchester University Press, 2016). For other images, see Kate Luard, *Unknown Warriors: The Letters of Kate Luard, RRC and Bar, Nursing Sister in France 1914–1918*, ed. John and Caroline Stevens (Stroud, U.K.: History Press, 2014), 127–129.

24. Many portrait photographs of nurses gave particular emphasis to the veil, which appears to have been carefully arranged before the photograph was taken. See, e.g., the portrait of Matron Ball, QARANC/PE/1/336/

BALL, Museum of Military Medicine, Keogh Barracks, Mytchett, Surrey. On the anxieties that surrounded the adoption of military-style uniforms by British women, see Tammy M. Proctor (ch. 4).

25. Special permission was given for British nurses to hold dances in their own messes immediately after the Armistice of 11 November 1918 (Hallett, *Veiled Warriors*, 249).

26. Rogers, *While You're Away*, 39; Christine E. Hallett, *Nurses of Passchendaele: Caring for the Wounded of the Ypres Campaigns, 1914–1918* (Barnsley: Pen & Sword Books, 2017), 88–89. See also Scates et al. (ch. 5).

27. On "footboarding," see Hallett, *Veiled Warriors*, 175. Krisztina Robert (ch. 2) offers valuable insights into an anthropological analysis of uniform. In addition to its purely symbolic value, uniform could "actively shape performances by dictating and enabling certain physical actions."

28. Irene Rathbone, *We That Were Young, a Novel* (1932; repr., New York: Feminist Press, 1989), 221–222.

29. These norms of etiquette were described in the nursing textbooks of the time. See, e.g., Eva Luckes, *General Nursing*, 9th ed. (London: Kegan Paul, Trench, Trubner, 1884); Isla Stewart and Herbert E. Cuff, *Practical Nursing*, 4 vols. (Edinburgh: William Blackwood, 1899–1903).

30. Photograph of Caroline Helen Keer, matron-in-chief, QAIMNS, 1906–1910, QARANC/P6/1/344/Keer, Museum of Military Medicine, Keogh Barracks, Mytchett, Surrey.

31. Sydney Browne Papers, box 1, QARANC Collection, Museum of Military Medicine, Keogh Barracks, Mytchett, Surrey.

32. Sydney Browne, facts and figures about TFNS from 1908 onward, QARANC/PE/1/141/BROW, Museum of Military Medicine, Keogh Barracks, Mytchett, Surrey.

33. Light, "The Fairest Force."

34. See, e.g., a photograph of nurses being awarded the Military Medal, QARANC/CF/4/3/7/PHOT, Museum of Military Medicine, Keogh Barracks, Mytchett, Surrey.

35. Photograph of Ethel Hope Becher in outdoor uniform, QARANC/Pt/1/349/BECH, Museum of Military Medicine, Keogh Barracks, Mytchett, Surrey.

36. Krisztina Robert (ch. 2) makes similar comments about the involvement of other uniformed women in London's Victory Parade.

37. *Conditions of Service in Queen Alexandra's Imperial Military Nursing Service* (London: War Office, 1936), 13–16; Boyd Cooper, *Queen Alexandra's Imperial Military Nursing Service, Uniform Price List* (London: Boyd Cooper, Oct. 1933), 4; Uniform and orders, QARANC/PE/1/410/QAIMNS, Museum of Military Medicine, Keogh Barracks, Mytchett, Surrey.

38. On the campaign for nurse registration, see Eve R.D. Bendall and Elizabeth Raybould, *A History of the General Nursing Council for England and Wales, 1919–1969* (London: H.K. Lewis, 1969), 1–37; Winifred Hector, *The Work of Mrs Bedford Fenwick and the Rise of Professional Nursing* (London: Royal College of Nursing, 1973), 36–45.

39. Sharon Ouditt, *Fighting Forces, Writing Women: Identity and Ideology in the First World War* (London: Routledge, 1994); Christine E. Hallett, "'Emotional Nursing': Involvement, Engagement and Detachment in the Writings of First World War Nurses and VADs," in *First World War Nursing: New Perspectives*, ed. Alison S. Fell and Hallett (New York: Routledge, 2013), 87–102; Janet Watson, "'Wars in the Wards': The Social Construction of Medical Work in First World War Britain," *Journal of British Studies* 41, no. 4 (Oct. 2002): 484–510.

40. Thelka Bowser, *The Story of British V.A.D. Work in the Great War* (1917; facsimile repr., London: Imperial War Museum, 2003), 13–42.

41. A number of significant war memoirs offer insight into the experiences of VAD nurses. See, e.g., Olive Dent, *A VAD in France* (London: Grant Richards, 1917); Lesley Smith, *Four Years out of Life* (London: Philip Allan, 1931); Enid Bagnold, *A Diary without Dates* (1918; repr., London: Virago, 1978); Vera Brittain, *Testament of Youth: An Autobiographical Study of the Years 1900–1925* (1933; repr., London: Virago Press, 2004); Rathbone, *We That Were Young*. See also Ouditt, *Fighting Forces, Writing Women,* ch. 1.

42. See Bowser, *The Story of British V.A.D. Work*, 33–40.

43. Hallett, *Veiled Warriors*, 4–6.

44. Agnes Warner, *My Beloved Poilus* (St. John, N.B., Canada: Barnes, 1917); Ellen N. La Motte, *The Backwash of War: The Human Wreckage of the Battlefield as Witnessed by an American Hospital Nurse* (New York: G.P. Putnam's Sons, 1916); Maud Mortimer, *A Green Tent in Flanders* (New York: Doubleday, Page, 1918); Mary Borden, *The Forbidden Zone* (London: William Heinemann, 1929). On Mobile Surgical No. 1, see Hallett, *Nurses of Passchendaele*, 48–52, 57–60, 82–85.

45. On the life and work of Mary Borden, see Jane Conway, *Mary Borden: A Woman of Two Wars* (Chippenham, U.K.: Munday Books, 2010); Hallett, *Nurse Writers of the Great War*, 48–59.

46. G.E. Mitton, ed., *The Cellar-House of Pervyse: A Tale of Uncommon Things from the Journals and Letters of the Baroness de T'Serclaes and Mairi Chisholm* (London: A. & E. Black, 1916); Elsie Knocker, Baroness de T'Serclaes, *Flanders and Other Fields: Memoirs of the Baroness de T'Serclaes* (London: George G. Harrap, 1964); Diane Atkinson, *Elsie and Mairi Go to War: Two Extraordinary Women on the Western Front* (London: Preface, 2009).

47. Atkinson, *Elsie and Mairi Go to War*; Hallett, *Nurses of Passchendaele*, 17, 25, 31.

48. The significance of motherhood to the imperial projects of Western nations was emphasized by Anna Davin in her influential article "Imperialism and Motherhood," *History Workshop Journal* 5, no. 1 (March 1978): 9–66. On the emergence of a secular nursing tradition in France, see Katrin Schultheiss, *Bodies and Souls: Politics and the Professionalization of Nursing in France, 1880–1922* (Cambridge, Mass.: Harvard University Press, 2001). On the development of the nursing services in one significant military base hospital in Belgium during the war, see Luc De Munck and Luc Vanderweyer, *Het Hospital van de Koningen: Rode Kruis, L'Ocean en De Panne* (De Panne, Belgium: Gemeetebestuur de Panne en de auteurs, 2012). We are indebted to Luc de Munck for translations of material from this book. See also Ilse Bogaerts and Luc De Munck (ch. 8).

49. Margaret H. Darrow, "French Volunteer Nursing and the Myth of War Experience in the First World War," *American Historical Review* 101, no. 1 (Feb. 1996): 80–106; Margaret H. Darrow, "Making Sister Julie: The Origin of First World War French Nursing Heroines in Franco Prussian War Stories," in Fell and Hallett, *First World War Nursing*, 17–34. See also Darrow (ch. 7); Schultheiss, *Bodies and Souls*.

50. Hallett, *Veiled Warriors*, 1–16 (on the image of the nurse), 24–25 (on French military nursing services).

51. Mary Britnieva, *One Woman's Story* (London: Arthur Baker, 1934); Florence Farmborough, *Nurse at the Russian Front: A Diary 1914–18* (London: Book Club Associates, 1974). See also Laurie S. Stoff (ch. 10).

52. De Munck and Vanderweyer, *Het Hospital van de Koningen*.

53. Marie, Queen of Roumania, *Ordeal: The Story of My Life* (New York: Charles Scribner's Sons, 1935). On uniforms worn by nurses in the Balkans, see Maria Bucur (ch. 13).

54. On "queen-nurses" or "warrior-nurses," see Hallett, *Veiled Warriors*, 41–42, 204–206.

55. Mary T. Sarnecky, *A History of the U.S. Army Nurse Corps* (Philadelphia: University of Pennsylvania Press, 1999), 84.

56. Patricia D'Antonio, *American Nursing: A History of Knowledge, Authority and the Meaning of Work* (Baltimore: Johns Hopkins University Press, 2010), 44.

57. Kimberly Jensen, "A Base Hospital Is Not a Coney Island Dance Hall: Nurses, Citizenship, Hostile Work Environment, and Military Rank," *Frontiers: A Journal of Women Studies* 26, no. 2 (2005): 206–235, reprinted in *Mobilizing Minerva: American Women and the First World War* (Urbana: University of Illinois Press, 2008), 116–141. See also Marian Moser Jones (ch. 15).

58. Julia Hallam, *Nursing the Image: Media, Culture and Professional Identity* (London: Routledge, 2000), 8. On the role of uniform in the image of the nurse, see also Philip A. Kalisch and Beatrice J. Kalisch, *The Changing Image of the Nurse* (Menlo Park, Calif.: Addison-Wesley, 1987).

FOUR

CIVILIAN WOMEN AND UNIFORMS IN BRITAIN

TAMMY M. PROCTOR

On 12 June 1917, the *Nantwich Guardian*, the main newspaper for the small British market town of Nantwich in Cheshire, published an article on the new vogue for women in uniforms. On the basis of an article published earlier in *Pearson's Magazine*, the *Nantwich* piece focuses on the changes one could easily observe on the streets of any town in the United Kingdom. From trouser-wearing female window cleaners to uniformed women conductors on omnibuses to khaki-clad women reservists, uniforms for women seemed to be everywhere. As the article notes, "There is no getting away from it. Women have taken to uniform like ducks to water. Will they ever again bow their necks to the tyranny of frocks, frills, and furbelows?"[1] Indeed, by the last years of the war, a craze for uniforms and militarized clothing had seized the nation, and women more than any other group highlighted the shift in norms that appeared to be on the horizon. Countless media accounts describe the jarring nature of first seeing a woman in pants or of a fully uniformed female in a voluntary organization saluting soldiers in the streets. Yet this display of apparent militarization raised uncomfortable questions about women's role in war and its aftermath. Because the Great War not only militarized men, women, and children but also created an atmosphere in which the general public expected a display of patriotism and sacrifice, uniforms and other clothing proved an important way to exhibit citizenship. At the same time, patriotic clothing raised concern about the blurring of gender lines and the long-term impact of war on the home.[2]

THE AMBIVALENCE OF UNIFORMS

Typically, uniforms are designed for a purpose, but they also have a history that is both hidden and apparent. Krisztina Robert (ch. 2) examines in some detail the varied historiographical approaches to uniforms in British history, noting how women's agency has not received the scholarly attention that it should. Likewise, Christine Hallett, Alison Spires, and Keiron Spires (ch. 3) demonstrate how nurses in Britain and its empire sought to project a highly professional image with their uniforms, one that defined their status and role. Whereas those two chapters center on women in formal military corps and in nursing organizations, this chapter focuses on the ways in which civilian women sought to co-opt uniforms in wartime for their own purposes.

Clothing expresses multiple meanings for both wearers and viewers, simultaneously empowering an individual or group with a sense of identity and dividing people according to status. The ambiguity of clothing seems less obvious with a uniformed movement since members are presumably dressed alike, but the fact of uniformity meant that any deviations in style, color, or function were highlighted even more. For example, uniforms might reflect class distinctions in the quality of the fabric or the buttons. In addition, complicated undercoding goes on with uniforms, so that uninitiated outsiders might not recognize the subtle cues of difference, whereas the insiders note and experience every deviation, signaling placement in the hierarchy of the organization. A good example of the multiple meanings of uniforms is a military parade. From a distance all the soldiers might look as if they were identical, cogs in a machine, but up close, their regimental markers, the angles of their hats, their medals, and any accessories they added to their bodies express something individual about a soldier in this machine.

For civilians in the Great War, uniforms existed on a continuum that expressed everything from fully uniformed women in government-produced togs to females sporting modifications and adornments on ordinary clothes. Such alterations were designed to mimic or convey the idea of military attire or wartime status. Although citizenship was undoubtedly a key motivating factor for display of uniform, consumption and practicality played roles as well. Women worried about the attractiveness and utility of uniforms, and they accessorized or personalized uniforms where possible. This chapter examines civilian individuals and organizations that sought some form of uniform during the war. Women's uniforms, whether full official uniforms or other smaller material signs of wartime participation, demonstrated women's investment in war service, displayed their patriotic citizenship, and provided the opportunity to parade their public virtue. In so doing, uniformed females challenged the prerogative of uniforms for men.

BEFORE THE GREAT WAR

Prior to the Great War, people of all ages wore uniforms for a variety of reasons. Sports leagues, which had become popular by the Edwardian period, featured team colors, jerseys, and uniforms. Religious organizations such as the Salvation Army created uniforms for their personnel who engaged in public evangelism; so-called hallelujah girls had particularly striking dark-blue military-style uniforms.[3] Likewise, workplaces used specialized clothing to identify and protect laborers in particular occupations such as policing, mining, and transport. In addition, many political movements utilized armbands, sashes, and coordinated clothing to show belonging and solidarity. A good example of this strategy was the Women's Social and Political Union, whose members donned purple, white, and green for their public events promoting female suffrage.[4]

Also, by the early twentieth century, preparedness concerns among civilian and military officials had spawned a large number of social clubs, paramilitary organizations, and "training" forces designed to improve Britain's military readiness. Men could learn soldiering by joining the Territorial Force (1908) or the Officer Training Corps (1908), whereas women could train in nursing as part of the First Aid Nursing Yeomanry (1907) and the Voluntary Aid Detachment (1909).[5] Even youth joined such uniformed movements as the Boys' Brigade, Girls' Brigade, Boy Scouts, and Girl Guides, sporting their signs of membership at meetings, in schools, in churches, and on parade.[6] Because manufacturers and shops in Britain already produced and sold uniforms and accessories, their move to a wartime footing was not as difficult as it might have been.

All of these prewar peaceful service movements had military undertones and militarized appearances. Even before 1914, commentators worried about uniformed women aping men. As Cynthia Enloe has argued, "every uniform has been designed" by someone, vesting the clothing with meaning.[7] Such design decisions reflect political reality, which is particularly true for the history of gender. Leaders of women's and girls' organizations fretted about how to keep uniforms both practical and "feminine," relying on skirts to provide the main feminizing element. Long debates over skirt lengths, footwear, headwear, and color of uniforms suggest much anxiety over maintaining gender distinctions in uniforms. For example, Girl Guide uniforms were dark blue because khaki was considered too military for girls. Guides also had to accept flowers as troop symbols and badges, rather than the animals boys used, in order to maintain the gender distinction between Boy Scouts and Girl Guides.[8]

Despite such concerns in the years before 1914, only with the war and its accompanying militarization of society did uniforms take on a different and more charged meaning. Things that might have seemed relatively innocuous before the war, such as the wearing of khaki or the color of a uniform, now mattered in new ways. War significantly increased anxieties about gender and uniform in many locations, as Bruce Scates et al. (ch. 6) argue as well. Women's adoption of masculine styles, adornments, or uniforms therefore heightened concerns that the Great War might undermine "proper" masculinity and femininity. This concern was particularly visible in government debates about units under army jurisdiction. For example, British officials banned breast pockets from the Women's Army Auxiliary Corps (WAAC) officers in the Great War and required that their boots or leggings reach above the hemlines of uniform skirts, which were mandated at 8 inches from the ground for those serving at home in England. Those same uniform skirts had to be 1.5 inches longer for foreign service, reflecting fears about what a female force in a staging zone for war might face.[9] Of particular concern to military and civilian leaders was the protection of women's virtue; uniforms served as one way to distinguish "proper" women from the "easy" women of the streets.

Debates about the appropriate clothing for men and women during wartime played out in local households, workplaces, and the media. One expression of this fear of gender-bending came in the form of a public dispute about whether women could wear khaki, which was associated with male soldiers. Critics of khaki-wearing women's service organizations chided females for trying to falsely claim a badge of heroism and blood sacrifice for themselves. One British newspaper emphasized this point in 1917: "Khaki is sacred to those for whom it forms a shroud . . . it should not be lightly donned."[10] Beyond the prewar notion that khaki was reserved for men, khaki fabric now served as a way of defining military service as a blood sacrifice. It was not to be defiled. To ensure that military uniforms and insignia did not fall into the wrong hands, the British government amended the Defence of the Realm Act (DRR41) several times between 1916 and 1918 in an attempt to prohibit the sale of uniforms, insignias, or medals (or anything that looked like a uniform) to "unauthorized" people.[11] Yet as Laura Ugolini has demonstrated, there was a thriving market in illicit uniform sales; she cites one instance of a 16-year-old girl acquiring a full officer's uniform in 1917.[12] Such examples of misuse of uniforms only heightened public anxiety about how widespread uniforms had become among those who did not number among His Majesty's services.

One other consideration in the transition from prewar to wartime clothing is significant, namely, the pressure to express patriotism and civic engagement with the war effort. For civilians, whether young or old, man or woman, demonstrating citizenship and service was vital in order to avoid charges of slacking, shirking, profiteering, or simply not caring about the deaths of young men.[13] In this context, uniforms or clothing with visible signs of war service helped display public virtue. A woman with a Red Cross armband driving an automobile faced praise rather than censure because of this tangible indication that her automobile was necessary for the war effort. Media accounts focused on men of military age who faced public shaming and verbal abuse in the streets of Britain.[14] Uniforms, in other words, drew important distinctions not only on the battlefields but on the home front.

WHY WOMEN CHOSE UNIFORMS

For women, uniforms signified a certain excitement and adventure even as they also provided an opportunity to do something noticeable for the national war effort. Women recorded their sense of belonging and of being part of a larger effort. Teenager Cicely Stewart-Smith joined the Girl Guides because it provided the chance for war service. In her diary, she noted that "the idea of doing proper war work was really thrilling. . . . Perhaps it was because the whole world was in uniform then."[15] A sense of pride in both wearing the uniform and in serving the nation permeated accounts by women from the Great War. Cicely Spencer, a member of the Women's Forage Corps of the Royal Army Service Corps, repeatedly refers to this pride in her unpublished memoir about the experience:

> Best of all I was given a badge to wear . . . just a circular disc not more than an inch in diameter, but the thrill it gave me when I fixed it on the lapel of my jacket comes back to me even now, after fifty-six years. In my imaginations it was as large as a plate; I have it still, a very dear treasure.[16]

For women, the experience of public service in uniform was both unique and significant to their sense of themselves as citizens in the nation. Most strove to be worthy of the clothing they were wearing.

Women in uniforms experienced a sense of authority, and some recorded feeling better protected in public. With females filling public roles in new ways, some women felt vulnerable in civilian clothing, whereas others simply worried about the dangers of war itself. In this atmosphere of heightened patriotism and fear of attack, women's uniforms gained a foothold by the last couple of years of the war. Protection became a concern for female civilians, especially after some particularly deadly zeppelin raids in 1916. Women ambulance drivers adopted steel helmets to protect themselves during air raids, and firms marketed gas protection to women on the home front, playing on their fears of poison gas.[17] Such small reminders of the costs of war for civilians had an impact as well on the perception of women's clothing in wartime.

Those who faced the most risk and who were also the most visible and celebrated groups of women in Great War Britain were the various nursing organizations and the women's auxiliaries, which were branches of the armed services.[18] Their uniformed presence in wartime Britain became a commonplace sight. These groups varied widely in function and acceptability, but each contributed to the larger debate about the public role for women in a wartime society. Nurses and members of formal auxiliary corps had an official presence that shielded them from some of the public debate, but civilian women in wartime garb proved to be a jarring and uncomfortable sight. These females included the Women's Land Army, Green Cross (Women's Volunteer Reserve), and the Girl Guides Association, but uniformed women workers also became ubiquitous by 1917. These civilian women raised real concerns about what might happen after the war and, especially, whether females would be content with a return to the home and to "normal" clothing.

It is important to note that not all uniforms took official form, and many women donned wartime clothing that was not standardized but was nonetheless recognizable as being associated with the conflict. British clothing shops such as Burberry began producing clothing for men in the trenches that later was adapted for use by women in the services and at the home front. The "weatherproof" Burberry, later known commonly as the trench coat, proved a lasting success after its introduction during the war. In a 1918 advertisement in the *Illustrated London News*, women were urged to try this comfortable and protective coat. Burberry also marketed caps for motoring and other clothing with military stylings.[19]

Yet full uniforms did not entirely capture the meaning of militarized clothing for females during the war. Some wore other signs of their commitment to loved ones who were fighting or to the war effort. This was particularly true of widows, who dressed in uniforms of mourning during the war. Despite shortages in fabric and thread, women wore signs of bereavement that ranged from black "widow's weeds" to armbands or silk flowers.[20] The swelling numbers of bereaved meant that the sight of widows and other close family members wearing improvised mourning clothing became commonplace. Adrian Gregory estimates that roughly 3 million British people lost a close relative in the war, which does not include the numbers of extended family or friends experiencing grief.[21] Although mourning clothing does not constitute a traditional "uniform" as such, the presence of bereaved relatives garbed in mourning had a significant impact on the politics of clothing in the public sphere during the war.

Women with family members overseas contributed to this spectacle of war display by wearing jewelry, lace, armbands, or insignia that associated them with their menfolk or with war service. Women fashioned special jewelry from objects associated with war such as trench art, shells, or trinkets sent from the fronts, and they incorporated military insignia into brooches, belts, and other adornments. The tradition of "sweetheart" jewelry showing a woman's connection to a particular soldier also featured in the communities of Britain.[22] In another instance, Girl Guides after May 1915 could earn War Service badges to display prominently on their uniforms when they had completed the tasks associated with the badge. These were highly sought after symbols of girls' participation in the war effort, and rather than being sewn onto uniform sleeves along with ordinary badges, these patches fastened to the front of the tunic above the breast pocket.[23]

UNIFORMS FOR WORKING-CLASS WOMEN

Wartime clothing for women was particularly ubiquitous in heavy industry, policing, and transport. Munitions workers wore heavy overalls, voluminous caps, and trousers as safety measures, but accounts from women employed in this field suggest both that they enjoyed the freedom of movement the clothing gave them and that they personalized their outfits to make them more "feminine." Because metal jewelry was a hazard on the work floor, women accessorized with posies or brightly colored shoelaces. One former worker at the munitions depot in Woolwich described the scene: "First the 'cap shop' girls strutted proudly with emerald green ribbons in their shoes, the 'new fuse' girls followed with yellow, and soon the whole Arsenal was in the fashion."[24] Munitions workers, fancy shoelaces or not, were among the most recognizable and acceptable symbols of female war workers in Britain during the war. Widely depicted in recruiting drives for female volunteers and workers, their clothing signified patriotic service. In fact, one of the most well-known propaganda posters of the war featured a woman donning her uniform for munitions work. This 1916 recruiting poster produced by the British government reinforced the idea that women performing

Figure 4.1.
This 1916 recruiting poster, produced by the British government, reinforces the idea that munitionettes retained their femininity when putting on uniforms. The action shot here also implies an immediate need for volunteers. Artist: Septimus Scott. © Imperial War Museum (Art.IWM PST 3283).

munitions work retained their femininity when putting on uniforms. The rose hue of the central figure speaks to civilian and feminine occupation, whereas the action shot implies a need for volunteers immediately. She appears to be rushing to the factory urgently.

Munitions workers captured the attention of the public as young women "doing their bit" for the duration of the war, and the danger of their work only heightened the need for extraordinary clothing to protect them. Munitions workers were not the only women to adopt masculine styles and uniforms for their wartime occupations. Tram and train conductresses, bank tellers, window cleaners, policewomen, miners, and dockworkers are only a fraction of the women who wore special uniforms during the war. The government tried to normalize this regiment of women for popular audiences through its public Women's War Work exhibitions held throughout the war in various parts of the country. These exhibitions featured women in a variety of roles supporting the war; through photographs, live demonstrations, and models, women's work was explained. For city and town dwellers, it was not necessary to visit an exhibition to see women in uniforms at work. As one newspaper noted in summer 1916, "London is to-day a city of uniforms . . . the woman in uniform is now one of the familiar features of metropolitan life."[25]

MIDDLE AND UPPER-CLASS WOMEN IN UNIFORM

Whereas female industrial workers inhabited working-class districts of cities, middle-class and elite women dressed for war in their more upscale neighborhoods as well. Many of these volunteers spent considerable money on stylish uniforms and accessories for their wartime duties. For example, the Women's Legion and the Women's Volunteer Reserve provided a particularly flashy appearance since, initially, members had to purchase their own khaki uniforms with markings that designated their various divisions, such as clerical or motor work. As these organizations expanded to include women cooks, drivers, and manual laborers, the uniform policy provided for allowances. Still, wealthy women, many driving their own automobiles, wore smart khaki outfits for their work in the Women's Volunteer Reserve, and they made a splash. The Women's Volunteer Reserve uniforms, designed by women, had breast pockets and a smart military-style belt.[26]

Leaders of the Women's Volunteer Reserve, however, remained alert to the public atmosphere and tried to influence debates about these dashing women in uniform. They consistently described their clothing as "serviceable" and practical in that the color did not show the dirt, and they emphasized that women would not become Amazons fighting next to men.[27] Additionally, these leaders emphasized that the Women's Volunteer Reserve did not wear cosmetics and that their hope was to foster "that esprit de corps which existed among men of a regiment." Women's Volunteer Reserve founder and former suffragette Evelina Haverfield even suggested that the Women's Volunteer Reserve was a sort of adult extension of Girl Guiding.[28] It was important for the Women's Volunteer Reserve to emphasize service and to separate their activities from any notion that they were "militant suffragettes in disguise."[29] This campaign to normalize the Women's Volunteer Reserve uniforms paid off with positive press for women's war service as the war continued.

Another organization associated with Haverfield, the Women's Reserve Ambulance (also known as the Green Cross) received a boost for its members with a defense of uniforms by the *Daily Mirror* in 1916: "The Green Cross girl is the 'handyman' . . . [and] is in uniform and is drilled and trained as a soldier. She has a woman's heart and a woman's sense of humour that carries her through all trials."[30] While defending the uniforms for this important work, the newspaper found it necessary to remind readers that the uniformed "girls" were still womanly throughout it all. Green Cross recruits faced a number of rules when donning their khaki uniforms, including restrictions on smoking, cosmetics, and jewelry. Green Cross members also had to carry ID cards, which they produced when requested. Green Cross rules made the women's role clear: "Members must never forget that the wearing of the Uniform entails a distinct responsibility and that their conduct must only be such as will reflect credit on the Corps . . . it is the woman who has learned to 'play up and play the game' who will prove a national asset."[31]

UNIFORMED WOMEN ON THE LAND

Uniformed women were not confined to cities and large towns in Britain during the war. In fact, rural areas experienced an invasion of uniformed women after the creation of the Women's Land Army (WLA) in 1917. Smaller corps that had been organized to collect and distribute forage or to work in forestry already existed, but the Women's Land Army eventually enrolled more than 113,000 women for agricultural work on farms across Britain. At first, the members of the Women's Land Army wore skirts 14 inches from the ground with coats and boots, but the practicalities of life on farms in Britain meant that women farm workers soon adopted multiple pieces of "male clothing"—trousers, breeches, puttees, and gaiters. As the photograph in Figure 4.2 demonstrates, such changes to the WLA uniforms

Figure 4.2.
The Women's Land Army wore uniforms that challenged feminine tropes. Their breeches and puttees, although practical, raised the hackles of many local communities. Imperial War Museum (Q 54607).

challenged feminine tropes of the time about respectable dress. In some ways, the WLA members looked like schoolboys, with their collared shirts and ties. More alarming for public opinion were their breeches and puttees, which although practical, raised the hackles of many local communities. Individual accounts from land army members provide a good case study of the meaning and challenges for women of wearing uniforms during the Great War.

The Women's Land Army placed young women into difficult agricultural work at farms and in forests throughout Britain. These women typically had little experience in the labor they were expected to perform. Recruiters explained that their role was vital—they would be feeding the nation as well as the soldiers and sailors defending Britain. As the Women's Land Army song reminded recruits,

> The men must take the swords,
> And we must take the ploughs,
> Our Front is where the wheat grows fair,
> Our Colours, orchard boughs.[32]

This notion, that women were soldiers fighting on a different front, the food front, attracted thousands of young females who wanted to do their part in the war. Uniforms helped reinforce their status as food soldiers, and the fact that members received free uniforms helped recruit a wide range of social classes to the work.

Because of the nature of the work and because of typical British weather (wet!), practical uniforms that protected women from the elements became a necessity for the WLA. Women wore trousers or breeches, many of which were ill fitting. One woman described the odd sensation of wearing pants: "They wasn't proper seams. They were raw inside. Of course you wore your underclothes, but it did [rub], in different places, under your knees, till you got used to it."[33] Even wearing trousers, keeping uniforms clean was a trial. Beatrice Bennett, a land army member, recorded in her diary the conditions she faced on her assigned farm. Not only was the work strenuous and the weather terrible, but she spent evenings trying to clean and dry her uniform to maintain the standards her unit expected:

> THURSDAY: got up to our knees in mud
> FRIDAY: In all your travels you never saw such a lane for mud, without any exaggeration it came above our knees. You cannot stick a pin on my nice velvet breeches for white mud an inch thick. . . . I have been down (washed boots and leggings) and now for bed.
> SATURDAY: mud
> SUNDAY (after a week of leave): Imagine us all day fighting to stand in mud a foot deep. I got one foot stuck and while trying to get that one out the other one got fixed. Our hats and macs were dripping . . . I had to go down to dinner in civvies.[34]

Beatrice's diary continues with descriptions of mud, dust, and constant attempts to clean or dry out her uniform and boots. As her account demonstrates, uniforms were not merely for looks; they did have to be serviceable and safe for the work that women were doing for the war effort. Yet even Women's Land Army members themselves recognized the impression they made in their masculinized attire: "It is strange to see the girls dancing, breeches and jerseys, [in] a log hut with a stove in the middle."[35]

Official literature exhorted women to behave themselves while in uniform. The *Women's Land Army Handbook* warned, "You are doing a man's work and so you are dressed rather like a man; but remember that just because you wear a smock and breeches you should take care to behave like an English girl who expects chivalry and respect from everyone she meets."[36] Women's Land Army members followed strict rules that forbade jewelry, cosmetics, and smoking, and they were reminded never to walk with their hands in their breeches' pockets. As with all uniformed women's groups during the war, members took seriously the idea that they represented something bigger than themselves, namely, work of national importance. The uniform symbolized that commitment.

THE LEGACY OF WOMEN'S UNIFORMS

In the immediate aftermath of the war, crowds celebrated anyone in uniform. Vera Brittain, who served in the Voluntary Aid Detachment, remembered the night of the Armistice and the mood that reigned:

> Outside the Admiralty a crazy group of convalescent Tommies were collecting specimens of different uniforms and bundling their wearers into flag-strewn taxis; with a shout they seized two of my companions and disappeared into the clamorous crowd, waving flags and shaking rattles. Wherever we went a burst of enthusiastic cheering greeted our Red Cross uniform, and complete strangers adorned with wound stripes rushed up and shook me warmly by the hand.[37]

This sheer enthusiasm for all who had contributed to victory and for the uniforms they wore soon gave way to a call for the uniforms to be put away and for women to return to the home.

War workers in munitions, transport, and armed forces all received communications similar to the one received by Women's Legion motor driver D. Reynolds, which released her from service "on account of 'being surplus to requirements.'"[38] Women who relied on their wartime wages or who just enjoyed their new freedoms faced a backlash. The media dubbed those who resisted going back to a prewar sensibility as selfish, hard, and unnatural women. As Laura Lee Downs argues in her work on women metalworkers, "The laudatory image of a woman 'doing her bit' in the war factory rapidly shape-shifted. In her place appeared a menacing apparition: The wage-hungry woman muscling aside the honest veteran."[39] Return to "normalcy" became the order of the day for women, who were expected to make homes for returning soldiers.

Putting the genie back in the bottle was not that easy. The wartime enthusiasm for uniforms and the association of uniformed movements with public service ensured that such entities continued. Boy Scouting and Girl Guiding expanded significantly during and after the war, reaching their membership heights in the early 1930s; for adult leaders and older members, the uniform was vital to their interwar identities. Veterans' associations also displayed their uniforms on commemorative occasions, and military accoutrements and souvenirs from the war enjoyed brisk sales. The rage for more masculine styles shaped women's fashions in the 1920s, both in terms of clothing styles and with a new interest in short haircuts. Uniforms never entirely disappeared from workplaces, schools, and clubs, although many resumed their prewar styles.

Perhaps the most important legacy of women's civilian uniforms in the Great War was in the normative function that uniforms assumed. By the time civilians began donning official and unofficial trappings again in 1939 for World War II, the sight of a woman or a child in uniform had lost its shock value. The Women's Land Army revived in 1939, as did women's auxiliaries for service in the army, navy, and air force. Women returned to factories and served as air raid wardens. In fact, many of the uniformed females of the Great War donned militarized clothing again to fight this new war. Cicely Spencer remembered her pride in wearing her new green uniform as a member of the Women's Voluntary Service from 1939 to 1945. As she recorded at the end of her memoir, echoing the sentiments of thousands of British women from the Great War, "uniform[s] always carried more authority than ordinary clothes. I was very proud of mine."[40]

NOTES

1. "Magazine Forum; the War from Many Points of View; the Influence of Uniforms," *Nantwich Guardian*, 12 June 1917, 4.

2. Susan R. Grayzel, "'The Outward and Visible Sign of Her Patriotism': Women, Uniforms, and National Service during the First World War," *Twentieth Century British History* 8, no. 2 (Jan. 1997): 146. Another interesting article exploring the act of uniforming women is Elizabeth Hillman, "Dressed to Kill? The Paradox of Women in Military Uniforms," in *Beyond Zero Tolerance: Discrimination in Military Culture*, ed. Mary Fainsod Katzenstein and Judith Reppy (New York: Rowman & Littlefield, 1999), 65–80.

3. Jennifer Le Zotte, "'Be Odd': The Contradictory Use of Dress in the Gilded Age Salvation Army," *Winterthur Portfolio* 47, no. 4 (Winter 2013): 245.

4. Wendy Parkins, "'The Epidemic of Purple, White, and Green': Fashion and the Suffragette Movement in Britain 1908–14," in *Fashioning the Body Politic: Dress, Gender, Citizenship*, ed. Wendy Parkins (Oxford: Berg, 2002), 101–107. See also Lisa Tickner, *The Spectacle of Women: Imagery of the Suffrage Campaign* (Chicago: University of Chicago Press, 1988).

5. Tammy M. Proctor, *Female Intelligence: Women and Espionage in the First World War* (New York: New York University Press, 2003), 20–21.

6. Tammy M. Proctor, "(Uni)forming Interwar Youth: Girl Guides and Boy Scouts in Britain, 1908–1939," *History Workshop Journal* 45 (Spring 1998): 117.

7. Cynthia Enloe, *Maneuvers: The International Politics of Militarizing Women's Lives* (Berkeley: University of California Press, 2000), 261.

8. Proctor, "(Uni)forming Interwar Youth," 124.

9. WAAC uniforms of officers, WO 32/5251, The National Archives, Kew. Yet women changed their uniforms to fit their own understanding of fashion and utility, as Krisztina Robert (ch. 2) explains.

10. Susan R. Grayzel, *Women's Identities at War: Gender, Motherhood, and Politics in Britain and France during the First World War* (Chapel Hill: University of North Carolina Press, 1999), 193–194. For more information on the public debate about women's uniforms, see Jenny Gould, "Women's Military Services in First World War Britain," in *Behind the Lines: Gender and the Two World Wars*, ed. Margaret Randolph Higonnet, Jane Jenson, Sonya Michel, and Margaret Collins Weitz (New Haven, Conn.: Yale University Press, 1987), 118–120.

11. Alexander Pulling, ed., *Defence of the Realm Manual*, 5th ed., rev. to 28 Feb. 1918 (London: HMSO, 1918), 146–147.

12. Laura Ugolini, "The Illicit Consumption of Military Uniforms in Britain, 1914–1918," *Journal of Design History* 24, no. 2 (May 2011): 125–126. Women after the war often tried to use uniforms to demonstrate status as veterans, in both real and fraudulent ways. See Alison Fell, *Women as Veterans in Britain and France after the First World War* (Cambridge: Cambridge University Press, 2018).

13. In an article on women's services in World War I, Krisztina Robert identified several motivations for paid and voluntary work during the war, including patriotism, desire for better pay or working conditions, and adventure. Krisztina Robert, "Gender, Class, and Patriotism: Women's Paramilitary Units in First World War Britain," *International History Review* 19, no. 1 (Feb. 1997): 52–65.

14. On the white feather campaign, see Nicoletta F. Gullace, "White Feathers and Wounded Men: Female Patriotism and the Memory of the Great War," *Journal of British Studies* 36, no. 2 (Apr. 1997): 178–206.

15. Cicely Stewart-Smith, "The Log of a Loafer in the Guides," unpublished handwritten diary, 1923–1925, Guiding UK Archives, London.

16. Cicely M. Spencer, "Wait for the Wagon," sec. I, 6, Papers of Mrs. C.M. Spencer, 11603, 01/40/1, Imperial War Museum, London.

17. "Green Cross Helmets," *Sunday Mirror*, 23 Dec. 1917, 12; Susan R. Grayzel, "Defence against the Indefensible: The Gas Mask, the State and British Culture during and after the First World War," *Twentieth Century British History* 25, no. 3 (Sept. 2014): 423.

18. Krisztina Robert (ch. 2); Christine Hallett et al. (ch. 3).

19. A.E.L., "Ladies News," *Illustrated London News*, 9 Nov. 1918, 20. See also Lucy Adlington, *Fashion: Women in World War One* (Stroud, U.K.: History Press, 2014), 7–8.

20. Nina Edwards, *Dressed for War: Uniform, Civilian Clothing and Trappings, 1914 to 1918* (London: I.B. Tauris, 2015), 161.

21. Adrian Gregory, *The Silence of Memory: Armistice Day, 1919–1946* (Oxford: Bloomsbury Academic, 1994), 19.

22. Edwards, *Dressed for War*, 98. See also Adlington, *Fashion*, 8.

23. Tammy M. Proctor, *Scouting for Girls: A Century of Girl Guides and Girl Scouts* (Santa Barbara, Calif.: Praeger, 2009), 27–28.

24. Quoted in Edwards, *Dressed for War*, 60–61; Angela Woollacott, *On Her Their Lives Depend: Munitions Workers in the Great War* (Berkeley: University of California Press, 1994), 211–212.

25. "In London Town; the Woman in Uniform," *Cheltenham Looker-On*, 19 Aug. 1916, 13–14.

26. Women's Volunteer Reserve, Photograph 9194, misc. 28, item 505, Imperial War Museum, London.

27. "Inauguration of a Dover Unit," *Dover Express*, 27 Aug. 1915, 5; "Women's Volunteer Reserve; Trained to Resist Armed Invaders," *Manchester Courier and Lancashire General Advertiser*, 17 Dec. 1914, 2. The Women's Legion uniform is also described as "serviceable" in articles such as one in the *Aberdeen Press and Journal*, 16 Aug. 1917, 2.

28. "Women's Volunteer Reserve: A Local Unit Formed," *Kent and Sussex Courier*, 26 Feb. 1915, 2. Haverfield founded three war service organizations for women (Women's Emergency Corps, Women's Volunteer Reserve, and Women's Reserve Ambulance) before traveling to Serbia to serve with the Scottish Women's Hospitals there. See Boyce Gaddes, *Evelina: Outward Bound from Inverlochy: A Biography of the Hon. Evelina Haverfield* (Braunton, U.K.: Merlin Books, 1995), 63–71.

29. Grayzel, "'The Outward and Visible Sign,'" 155–156.

30. "The 'Green Cross' Girl," *Daily Mirror*, 7 Aug. 1916, 2.

31. *The Green Cross Society (WRA) Rules and Regulations*, n.d., Papers of Miss E.A. Cother, 18912, 16/14/1, Imperial War Museum, London.

32. "Land Army Song," in *Women's Land Army Handbook* (London: Board of Agriculture, 1917); Papers of Mrs. G. Mazey, 11169, box P406, Imperial War Museum, London.

33. Quoted in Edwards, *Dressed for War*, 63.

34. Handwritten manuscript, "Land Army Hostel," 2–10, Papers of Miss Beatrice Bennett, 2762, 94/27/1, Imperial War Museum, London.

35. "Land Army Hostel," 14.

36. *Women's Land Army Handbook*, 5–6.

37. Vera Brittain, *Testament of Youth* (New York: Penguin, 1989), 462.

38. "Certificate of Separation from Service," 1920, Papers of the Women's Legion, 10709, misc. 28, item 503, Imperial War Museum, London.

39. Laura Lee Downs, *Manufacturing Inequality: Gender Division in the French and British Metalworking Industries, 1914–1939* (Ithaca, N.Y.: Cornell University Press, 1995), 190.

40. Spencer, "Wait for the Wagon," sec. II, 3.

FIVE

"IF IT MADE THE MAN, IT CERTAINLY MADE THE WOMAN"

Uniformity and Canadian Military Nurses

CYNTHIA TOMAN

The wearing of uniforms was standard practice for trained nurses in Canada by the 1900s. Uniforms distinguished them from both untrained and semitrained women who offered care to ill or injured persons, either for free or for pay. Indeed, uniforms formed part of a nurse's professional identity from early student days, when the uniform identified her visibly with a specific hospital training school. Schools of nursing inculcated Victorian and Edwardian ideas of femininity and gentility into uniform styles for their student nurses.[1] Relatively few historians, however, have studied nursing uniforms. Christina Bates, for one, points out,

> Uniforms are the public face of an institution, designed to communicate the functions and values of that institution. Within the organization, they also serve to create group identity and loyalty. . . . The nurse's uniform was more than the outward representation of the accepted behaviours and values a school and hospital imposed on their students. The uniform literally disciplined the student's body to create those behaviours and values. Each day, student nurses pinned, pulled, buttoned, fastened and put together their complex outfit. . . . Like all clothing, the uniform was not only a symbol, but also an active participant in the formation of personal or social *mentalités*.[2]

Carrie Hertz's analysis of uniforms in general points out that "In reality . . . their meanings can also be interpreted and manipulated by both wearers and viewers."[3] She cautions that "uniform scholarship tends to focus on the stated 'regulations' of uniform codes while assuming that individuals both follow these regulations precisely and lack personal motivations or interpretations beyond what is intended by the uniform designers or regulators."[4] Hertz calls for studies to explore the perspectives of the wearers, asserting that the wearers were not passive and "the function of uniforms is polyphonic."[5]

This chapter begins to address the gap in the scholarship on uniformed women by examining first-person perspectives of Canadian Army Medical Corps (CAMC) nursing sisters, who both shaped and were shaped by their military officer uniforms within the gendered colonial context of the Great War (1914–1918). Only three CAMC nursing sisters ever published memoirs. Dozens more kept diaries, partial diaries, and/or letters. Many more, however, saved photographs taken during the war. Significantly, if a nursing sister had only one photograph from this period of her life, it was usually of herself in uniform.

THE CANADIAN ARMY MEDICAL CORPS NURSING SERVICE

Prior to the Great War, the Canadian militia had contracted with small groups of civilian nurses for short-term needs, as during the North-West Rebellion (1885) and occasional summer training camps. Twelve civilian nurses had served overseas under contract with the British Expeditionary Force during the South African War (1899–1902). The first (and only) women to enlist in the Canadian army during the Great War were members of the fledgling CAMC nursing service. They enlisted as officers in a specially created, all-female rank known as "lieutenant/nursing sister." On the basis of responsibility and experience, they progressed through the ranks as captains (typically matrons in charge of a medical or surgical unit) and majors (the rank held by Matron-in-Chief Margaret Macdonald during the Great War). Although authority was limited to hospital units and troops under their care, their pay and perks were equal to men of the same rank—a very unusual achievement for women of their era.

This fledgling nursing service originated with two women selected from distinguished Canadian families in 1904—a significant decision that ultimately set the CAMC nursing service apart from other allied services. The first nursing sister commissioned was Georgina Fane Pope, daughter of William Pope (one of the "Fathers of Confederation" in 1867) and sister to Joseph Pope (a cabinet member in the Wilfrid Laurier government, 1896–1911).[6] Her social influence and political connections established the nursing service on a firm footing within the Canadian army as commissioned officers—the only female commissioned officers in any army until the 1940s.[7] Together with Margaret Clotilde Macdonald, a Canadian who had served under contract with the U.S. Army during the Spanish-American War (1898), Pope developed a military nursing course, which she and Macdonald subsequently offered to small groups of civilian nurses, thus forming a small military nursing reserve leading up to the war.[8]

Apart from this reserve, civilian nurses knew very little about military nursing or being part of the army. Pope had written about her experiences during the South African War for both the *Canadian Nurse* and the *American Journal of Nursing*. Her reports certainly piqued civilian nurses' interest and created a favorable, even exciting, portrayal of what military service involved.[9] When England declared war against Germany and the call came to mobilize a nursing service in August 1914, Anglo-Canadian nurses were eager to participate. Mabel Clint enthusiastically counted herself among those "ready to stand with King and Empire as champions of liberty and honour." She described the Canadian contingent as sons and daughters of the empire "returning home" and as "a loyal body of Empire citizens, eager to aid in defence of the old home."[10]

Indeed, the number of nurse applicants far exceeded the CAMC quota, as it continued to do throughout the war. Nurses competed for coveted overseas postings and often wrote about being part of "history in the making." They were not willing to be left behind by brothers and fathers going off to war. By the time the service demobilized and returned to a token force of five permanent members, a total of 2,845 nursing sisters had served in Canada, England, and Russia as well as on the Western Front and in the Mediterranean theater in Lemnos, Egypt, Malta, and Macedonia. Their fuller history is available elsewhere, complete with demographics, biographies, first-person experiences on both the European and Mediterranean fronts, the conditions under which they served in these postings, and their postwar lives.[11] These nursing sisters clearly identified themselves as "sister soldiers" engaged in a deadly battle against organisms, trauma, and pain with a mandate to "save the world" (or at least the British Empire) through the care of sick and injured soldiers who could be returned to the front lines as soon as possible. Their passport into this entirely masculine military world of war was their uniforms, which permitted them to go where other women were not allowed, ever closer to the front line and into the heart of the action.

CAMC nursing sisters were extremely proud of their uniforms with their associated officer rank and status. Highly recognizable and quite distinct from the uniforms of other allied nursing services, the blue work uniform earned them the nickname "bluebirds." Initially, according to Edith Hudson in referring to the dress uniform, "surprised citizens usually mistook [us] for women police, suffragettes or members of an orphan asylum."[12] The Montreal *Gazette* pronounced the CAMC uniform "a very pleasing combination of feminine grace and military usefulness."[13] Emma Griffis even declared herself "in love, so to speak, with the uniforms. I think the full dress uniform a thing of beauty & a joy forever."[14] As Katharine Wilson recalled, "Oh, I was certainly excited at the thought of wearing my new uniform (for if it made the man it certainly made the woman!)."[15] The uniform was held in such high esteem that in 1926, Matron-in-Chief Margaret Macdonald even suggested veteran nursing sisters purchase a new one for special occasions as well as for their "burial dress."[16] The CAMC uniform clearly identified them as officer soldiers, enabling them to capitalize on its socially constructed power and navigate the intricacies of rank that it bestowed and privileged them regarding postwar careers.

IDENTIFICATION AS SISTER SOLDIERS AND OFFICERS

Georgina Pope is credited as designer of the original nursing sister uniform, which continued in use, with slight variations, until the 1950s.[17] The uniform package actually comprised two sets of clothing, mandated for different occasions: the dress or "walking out" uniform and the "working" uniform. Official regulations specified that nurses were to wear full dress uniform "for state ceremonies and entertainments" but not "whilst actually engaged in ward duties."[18] The winter version was navy blue, with scarlet collar and cuffs and white piping. The summer version was a medium blue, two-piece uniform, comprising a double-breasted jacket with appropriate rank stars on each shoulder, brass buttons, a brown leather belt, and brass belt clasp. This dress uniform—worn with black stockings and shoes, as well as either a navy-blue felt hat with the CAMC badge on the front for winter or a white Panama hat with a navy band for summer—included a navy-blue great coat, a navy cape with scarlet lining, and a navy waterproof raincoat. Muslin veils, an often-admired feature of the CAMC uniform, could be worn with either dress or work uniforms depending on the occasion. Ella Mae Bongard served with the American Expeditionary Force and commented with envy in her diary, "We'd all love to wear [veils] too if we could."[19]

The working uniform was more practical and was intended for use on all other occasions. Edith Hudson itemized the parts of her working uniforms this way:

> 4 working dresses of light blue; 14 gilt buttons with A.M.S. letters on them; rank badges; 2 stars (as a lieutenant) on each shoulder; 12 full aprons with square bibs, crossed straps, and square pocket on each side; 8 collars (Eton style) and cuffs (Bishop pattern); 8 muslin veils, 1 yard square each with 1″ hem; tan leather belt with A.M.C. clasp; laced tan boots; tan stockings; tan coloured gloves; military hat and coat; sweater; and an umbrella.[20]

Maude Wilkinson recalled humorously that those umbrellas became problematic during military drill: "I recall one morning when it was raining and we all arrived with umbrellas, much to the embarrassment and annoyance of the sergeant. 'Put down the umbrellas, roll them, and use them as canes!' he barked."[21]

The CAMC mandated the uniform to be worn for all occasions with few exceptions. Edith Hudson's instructions on enlistment stated, "Uniform only to be taken no plain clothes are required."[22] Matron Elizabeth Russell, later during the war, inquired specifically if it was acceptable to wear mufti (civilian clothing) on their half days off duty. The assistant director of medical services replied, "I do not consider that it is proper for them to wear mufti even when they are off duty or when going to London or when playing golf or tennis. I consider that Nursing Sisters are Officers and consequently are not permitted to wear mufti."

Figure 5.1.
Major/Matron-in-Chief Margaret C. Macdonald in the formal dress uniform of the Canadian Army Medical Corps nursing service. Canadian War Museum, George Metcalf Archival Collection, 19660092-001.

Matron-in-Chief Macdonald apparently turned a blind eye to the practice on occasion, however, if a nursing sister was completely away from her unit on leave. But she never authorized mufti for any activity in France.[23]

Although *gender* was not a term they used in first-person accounts, the nursing sisters were definitely aware of being on the edge of highly gendered spaces. Reading between

Figure 5.2.
Lieutenant/Nursing Sister Gertrude Halpenny in the working uniform. Gertrude Halpenny fonds, Canadian War Museum, George Metcalf Archival Collection, 19620016-005.

the lines and against the grain, one catches glimpses of gendered differences and gender-bending roles in their diaries and letters. They also wrote about a need to feel feminine and how the war was affecting them over the five years of CAMC involvement. Although determined to look as military as possible, they were equally determined to reassure others that they were still women, countering public and familial anxieties that the war would "harden" their feminine sensibilities and make them unfit as future girlfriends, wives, and mothers. A big part of "looking good" included feeling good when in uniform. For example, after Emeline Robinson resigned from the British nursing service, she referred to her new Canadian uniforms as "some nifty outfit!" that made her feel "much admired."[24] Helen Fowlds proudly claimed that

> the English nurses are openly jealous of our uniform and every day we notice little changes they are making in order to look like us—and imitation in this case is certainly flattery. They all say "Your uniform is so becoming and ours makes us look like maids. . . . No English women can criticize Canadian feet—our girls are much better shod. They all wear heavy tan boots while the English affect strap slippers with French heels—and usually run over at the ankles.[25]

Mediterranean settings particularly challenged their ability to look or feel good. Lemnos and Salonika, where Canadian army nursing sisters cared for soldiers from the ill-fated Gallipoli campaign, had formidable reputations as the worst postings of the war, both for endemic diseases and living conditions. Upon arrival at Lemnos during August 1915, for example, Mabel Clint overheard a soldier say, "No place for Sisters."[26] Frances Upton, in true soldierly tradition, wrote, "I have heard that we are going to Lemnos, and also that whoever suggested sending white women there, should be shot. However, it's up to Canada."[27] Hunger and food preoccupation were recurrent themes in the Lemnos accounts as well as flies, malaria, and lack of water, which made dirt a constant challenge. Katharine Wilson painted this bleak picture at No. 3 Canadian Stationary Hospital:

> Entering a square marquee, the mess hut, we found a table utterly devoid of any sort of covering to hide the wooden surface. . . . Two orderlies were in charge. From large iron pots they served us steaming hot stew (McConachies). With this, we had pale gray bread, on which we spread Swiss margarine [*sic*] that looked like butter but tasted like lard . . . Matron [Jessie] Jaggard sat at the head of the table. . . . She simply asked us to remember the men in the trenches, and that we were all part of the army, all working for a victory that would come. . . . She finished with the quotation "Ours not to question why, ours but to do or die". Looking down at the pale gray bread and wax margarine, I wondered, "How soon?"[28]

Nursing sisters in the Mediterranean theater, where, try as they might, it was almost impossible to maintain idealized images of uniformed femininity, became increasingly concerned about physical looks and bodily changes. They often related stories to their families about looking unfeminine and less military as they improvised according to the conditions in which they were working. In November 1915, for example, May Bastedo described her changed appearance at Lemnos, where they lived in four-person tents, with coal oil stoves for heat, straw mats over earthen floors, and "perpetual rain."[29] There rubber boots were essential for the "dreadful" mud, worn with raincoats and hats in an attempt to stay dry. Then snow and freezing temperatures set in over the Mediterranean region, and Bastedo wrote home, "you wouldn't know me, I'm like a tough; dirty skirt, two sweaters, raincoat, old gloves and a sou-wester on, tied under my chin, mud on everything."[30] Many described tying hot water bottles to their chests and backs during long cold night shifts. Others caused curiosity about the increased requests for riding breeches from England—which they then used under the uniform skirts. By mid-December, things had not improved, and Bastedo complained, "I get tired of wearing rubber boots but the mud is so sticky it pulls your rubbers off. We don't wear the white caps and aprons but short skirts, rubber aprons and small caps. . . . I have a woolen one for bad days and a jolly warm coat the matron got for us."[31] Frances Upton, writing from "somewhere in Greece" in January 1917, suggested that her family try to "imagine us in tents with all our beds filled, up to our ankles in mud—wearing rubber boots to our knees—three sweater coats—woolen gloves—our issue ones—men's coats . . . anything but ladylike." She added later that those boots had not been off for three weeks, except to go to bed.[32]

Regardless of their circumstances, nursing sisters worked hard to maintain their uniforms in the best possible condition. Helen Fowlds recalled the effort expended to keep their uniforms looking new at Lemnos: "It cost a small fortune to have my uniforms dipped [redyed]. . . . They were all so faded. Some of the girls [arriving as reinforcements] are appearing in gorgeous new ones of heavy silk or linen."[33] Keeping veils clean and white was particularly difficult, given the extremely limited supply of water on Lemnos, where each person received only "one quart that was to serve for drinking and cleansing purposes, for twenty-four hours."[34] So Fowlds asked her mother to send new ones periodically: "How I have blessed you for those two veils which arrived in good condition today. My stock is very low. If you could send me about two or even three a month it would be heavenly especially while we're out here."[35]

Figure 5.3.
Lieutenant/Nursing Sister Helen Fowlds in a letter home, dated 3 June 1915, observed that "the English nurses are openly jealous of our uniform."
Helen Fowlds Marryat fonds, Trent University Archives, 69-001.

Matrons Jaggard and Mary Frances Munro died from dysentery and were buried on Lemnos with full military honors. Their coffins were draped by three significant symbols—a flag, their uniform veils, and their belts—reinforcing their identities as both uniformed nurses and soldiers who had made the ultimate sacrifice. Still other nursing sisters died during the bombing of hospital units at Étaples and Doullens (France) on 19 and 29–30 May 1918, respectively. Just as at Lemnos, the funerals for Agnes McPherson, Eden Pringle, and Dorothy Baldwin at Bagneux British Cemetery (near Doullens) featured their uniforms prominently displayed atop the coffins. The sinking of the hospital ship *Llandovery Castle* on 27 June 1918 resulted in the deaths of all 18 nursing sisters on board. A German submarine torpedoed the ship in spite of its highly visible Red Cross markings, then surfaced to strafe survivors who had made it into lifeboats.[36] This incident caused great outrage at home and became a propaganda tool for recruitment—an image of nurses drowning in the water with the ship going down behind them and the call to arms: "Remember the *Llandovery Castle*."

SOCIAL POWER AND THE ARMY UNIFORM

The CAMC uniform bestowed enhanced social power at home and overseas to the nursing sisters through their uniqueness as commissioned military women and their proximity to the front lines. Part of this social power arose from their heightened visibility as uniformed military women in public media. Other aspects of social power arose from the access to military men and political figures that their officers' uniform provided. CAMC nurses also enjoyed opportunities for travel in their off-duty time, during which their officers' pay enabled them to take full advantage of any bargains they found.

Historian Françoise Thébaud claims that of all the women engaged in various forms of war work, nurses drew the most praise for their wartime contributions.[37] Uniformed nurses received so much public attention both at home and overseas that the writer of a letter to the editor of one newspaper questioned if nurses' uniforms were the only ones of value.[38] Canadian newspapers covered both individual nurses and units as they left Canada, as families received news from them, as they received honors and medals, as they returned on leave, and even as they married and left the service. This public focus brought trained, semitrained, and untrained women into conflict with one another over "who" should be allowed to do nursing work. Women of Voluntary Aid Detachment units (VADs) were typically young, often from wealthy, upper-class families. They had a great deal of enthusiasm but relatively little training for the charitable work they performed as part of the war effort.

British class structure positioned VADs as superior and privileged in relation to trained nurses, who came primarily from working- and middle-class backgrounds and worked for pay, in contrast to VADs who volunteered for temporary patriotic war service.[39] The Great War inverted this relationship, however, by privileging trained nurses through the inherent power of their role and their access to soldiers.[40] Nora Saltonstall, an American VAD with a French mobile surgical hospital, searched for "a man's size job," which led her to pursue hospital work in spite of her parents' refusal to allow her to train as a nurse. The search inched irresistibly toward assisting nurses, although officially she was an ambulance driver. Saltonstall described herself as "kicking my heels and frothing at the mouth because I am so untrained and can help so little. . . . It mortifies me to think how much more the nurses work than I."[41]

Not only did the uniform with its associated rank enable Canadian army nurses to move ever closer to the front line action; it also disrupted the traditional social space of the officers' mess where male officers enjoyed private time away from the troops, meals, and camaraderie with fellow officers as well as other privileges. The introduction of nursing sisters as officers stirred up controversy regarding women's access to the mess and how to negotiate their place there. In 1914, for example, Col. George Nasmith observed that nursing sisters were doubly privileged as officers and women:

> There seemed to be about a thousand nurses aboard the Franconia—the real number was about a hundred but they multiplied by their ubiquity; they swarmed everywhere; sometimes they filled the lounge so that the poor Major or Colonel could not get in for his afternoon cup of tea. The daily lectures for officers, particularly on subjects like "artillery range finding," had an abnormal fascination for the nurses while subjects like "the Geneva Convention" and "Hygiene" which they might have found useful held little attraction for them. Such is the perversity of the nurse when given the rank of an officer and freed from all hospital restraint. At the concerts few officers could obtain seats and a few of us were mean enough to wish that it would get rough enough to put some of the nurses temporarily down and out. The nurses were in a doubly fortunate position in that they could demand the rights of both officers and women, according to which happened to be advantageous at the moment.[42]

This privileged access to masculine spaces came with mixed consequences. As Wilhelmina Mowat (and many others) pointed out, "We had been instructed as Officers to not mingle with the lower ranks."[43] While the uniform restricted their social relationships to other officers, it also provided opportunities for developing close relationships in settings where they lived and worked together continuously, especially in active theaters of war. While on Lemnos, for example, British naval officers invited the Canadian army nursing sisters for dinners and social times aboard ship whenever they were in harbor. Frances Upton wrote home about these outings that

> to be thrown among so many wonderful & manly men & yet receive the treatment that we girls receive at their hands is something marvelous. The respect, admiration and devotion which we constantly receive, is too lovely for words. Just four men, up to date, have asked me to take their name and each one of them finer than anything I've ever seen.[44]

Some of these close relationships led to marriages between nursing sisters and medical officers both during and after the war. Marriage to officers was not forbidden, and historian Susan Mann describes Matron-in-Chief Macdonald as having an intense interest in the romances and overseas marriages of her nurses, to the extent that she was accused of running a "matrimonial agency."[45] Emma Griffis married Dr. Harold McGill soon after enlisting and resigned her commission as required by regulations.[46] Laura Hanham Harper, however, paid her own way to England, where she married soon after arrival, and, lying about her marriage, enlisted with the CAMC there.[47]

The uniform and rank could prove problematic when it came to "mingling with the lower ranks." Regulations against fraternization with "other ranks" constrained nursing sisters (who were overwhelmingly single) to socializing within the mess—that is, with medical officers who were typically married. Ruth Hays married prior to the war, and husband Billy Hays was serving as a stretcher bearer in France while she was "stuck in England" where she had been posted. Her officer status and rank made it all but impossible for them to get together. She found the separation very difficult with all the budding romantic relationships around her. In her diary, she confessed guiltily,

> I tell you one thing I do like tho' and that is the Captain himself. I'm getting crazier about him every day. I can't get to sleep for thinking of him and to think he is every bit of forty-three years old, and has a wife and three of the best kids in London—not to mention myself having a husband in France, of course![48]

But when Ruth and Billy did finally cross paths briefly, the time together was even more unsettling. He had never seen her in uniform (or considered that she outranked him). In her diary, Ruth wondered, "What passed thro' his mind when he saw me in my veil, and blue and brass uniform. Being a Scotchman, he did not remark upon it at all, and probably I will never know, whether he fancies his 'Sister-Wife' or not."[49]

In other situations, the CAMC uniform provided political and social capital that gave access to privileged experiences. Dorothy Cotton, for example, capitalized on her perceived status when she was chosen for a unique posting to Petrograd as part of a "political entente" between the British and Russian governments.[50] England had responded to Russian requests for Allied support by opening the Anglo-Russian Hospital at Petrograd (1916–1917), staffed by 37 "nurses from the Dominions." Situated in the palace of Grand Duke Dmitri, it was complete with ballrooms, reception rooms, and state apartments converted into wards.[51] Nurses at the Anglo-Russian Hospital wore the uniform of Russian Red Cross sisters, "except for Miss Dorothy Cotton of the Canadian contingent. . . . She will still be under the Canadian contingent and will wear their uniform."[52] Whether or not this was a hard-fought battle, Cotton was very pleased with the decision and wrote, "My uniform is certainly very taking (!) and all the sisters here are terribly interested in it, and call me the 'Officer Prince.'"[53] From her privileged position as Canada's representative, she reveled in opportunities to mingle with the royal family of Tsar Nicholas II and other prominent people in Petrograd and to attend cultural events such as the Bolshoi Ballet. As she wrote to a Montreal friend,

> Being 'Canada,' I always come in for everything that is going on, and my brass buttons make an awful disturbance. By the way, my nickname is 'Sister Buttons.' Everyone here is so thrilled with the generous gift from the Canadian government [£10,000] to the Anglo-Russian Hospital. I pretend to think it is nothing, but all the time I am nearly bursting with pride.[54]

Opportunity for travel, tourism, and enhanced purchasing power were other manifestations of social power linked to the uniform, thanks partially to the accompanying officer's pay. When Katharine Wilson compared her pay of $4.10 per day to that of other nurses without officer rank, for example, she claimed that "we were called the 'Millionaire Colonials.'"[55] An anonymous nurse was particularly effusive, writing in the *Canadian Nurse*,

> Another feature of the communal life which suggests Utopia is the delightful manner in which Sisters are paid. Their money is paid directly into the bank and is drawn by cheque, giving one the glorious feeling of being cared for as 'the sparrows and clothed as are the lilies of the field' by a beneficent Providence . . . as Manna into our bank account.[56]

Additional privileges included preferential first-class travel arrangements, access to special leave centers, release from meal preparations, and even "home sisters" to take care of housekeeping and shopping needs. These perks were more typically associated with a work pattern reserved for men, and as Susan Mann points out, it must have seemed too good to be true: "All the women had to do was work."[57]

Historian Cecilia Morgan suggests that prewar travel to Europe was quite popular among Canadian travelers from upper-middle-class backgrounds who had the resources to travel.[58] Some nursing sisters would have had such opportunities, but most of them had not. So armed with officers' pay and leave entitlements, nursing sisters made the most of time off to explore as much of England, Scotland, Ireland, and France as possible. They were entitled to 14 days every 6 months if they could be spared. After all, the army had transported them across the Atlantic, and they had worked hard to earn time off duty. For many of them, these were trips of a lifetime that they recorded in detail in diaries and photographs.[59] As Ruth Hays wrote home, "You see when this war is over or if any of us should have to go home we would feel very badly to think we had not seen as much of this country as possible."[60] England offered seemingly endless opportunities to explore. Elsie Collis made sure to visit St. Paul's Cathedral, the Lister Institute, and Dover Castle, among other sites. Likewise, Emeline Robinson began a round of serious sightseeing on her arrival. On the fourth day of touring, she recorded, "Had a peek into 'Ye Old Curiosity Shop,' bo't cards. etc. Finally ended up in 'Ye Old Cheshire Inn'—I sat in Dr. Johnson's chair while we ate bread, butter and jam and drank tea out of a very old mug." On her fifth day, "Lady Trotter conducted us thru St Thomas Hospital [site of the original training school established by Florence Nightingale] where the Matron served special tea. —Rather antiquated. But beautifully clean."[61] While stuck in Alexandria, Egypt, with No. 5 Canadian General Hospital, Elsie Collis used her time to visit the Blue Mosque, zoological gardens, and the pyramids (traveling by electric car and then by camel). She took a trip down the Nile on a felucca. And when posted temporarily to a British hospital within sight of the pyramids, Collis described the "magic" of the pyramids on several moonlight expeditions within her diary.[62]

CAMC nursing sisters certainly made the most of their enhanced purchasing power. Their diaries and letters are full of the descriptions of items either already shipped home to family members for safekeeping or coming with them when they returned. Indeed, in reading Helen Fowlds's letters of 1915–1916, one would think that little nursing work was being done at all! Fowlds and her friends, especially Myra Goodeve, seemed to take every free opportunity in France, Egypt, Greece, and England to shop for clothes, especially feminine silk underwear, pajamas, and other goods, as well as to have shampoos and manicures: "Miss

Goodeve, Boultbee and I spent our afternoon in Boulogne, and certainly had a time. We had a bath at the [Crislot], bought a wonderful cake, and inspected most of the stores. The lingerie shops are a great temptation and I must lay in a stock while I am over here."[63] After a trip to Cairo, she wrote that she "got half a dozen prs. [pairs] of silk knickers made. . . . We found the silk best as it took up little space and was easily laundered. I also got a cheap pair of Chinese silk pajamas—I like them better than night-gowns."[64] Even Salonika had its attractions for Fowlds: "We are about 3 or 4 miles out of Salonika by the road but not more than 2 across country. . . . There are several good stores where one could get almost anything but prices are simply terrific. . . . We bought lamps and can get boots made etc."[65] By the end of the war, Fowlds had even spent her savings on furs and a stylish hat: "At last I have got my furs. I saved all winter and got a set of black fox when I was in London. They cost $125, and are quite good value. I am delighted to have them as furs always make you look clothed. I got a very pretty hat too, made from a model."[66]

Indeed, the CAMC uniform provided the nursing sisters with more than national identity; as military officer women, they enjoyed a number of material and social benefits. On the one hand, they capitalized on the uniform's associated opportunities and social power, whereas on the other hand, they found it necessary to negotiate their place and power.

NAVIGATING MILITARY HIERARCHY AND RANK

Both military men and other allied nursing services found the CAMC nursing sister uniform, with its visible display of officer status and rank, to be initially confusing as well as unsettling. Col. George Adami referred to Florence Nightingale in 1918 as "the despair of the official, making it impossible to incorporate her and the organization she controlled as an integral part of the Medical Service." He went on to explain that

> thus it was that in 1906 the Minister deliberately created the Army Nursing Sisters as an integral portion of the Army Medical Service, under the command of a matron who, in her turn, is responsible to the [director general medical services]. . . . the Canadian Nursing Sisters have thus military status, and are under direct military control. This explains their uniform and their "stars," which apparently have given offence to the illogical.[67]

Adami noted stiff opposition in some parts of the military to the granting of rank to nursing sisters (a clear sign of masculinity).[68] Col. Robert Rudolf, in a 1916 address, also suggested that their rank "mixed things up a bit at first" in relation to other nursing services: "The English nurses do not have as much freedom of action as do the Canadians, and would never be allowed the liberty of dancing or of having afternoon tea with the officers at the Sisters' Mess [a privilege limited to other officers]."[69]

Rank confused and inverted socially constructed relationships between English and Canadian nurses, who were referred to frequently as "colonials."[70] Colonial nurses were supposed "to show deference to the English ways of doing things"—not an altogether unreasonable expectation since Allied nurses needed to be able to work together especially during "big pushes."[71] Katharine Wilson recalled, however, that "we were not accepted very graciously" and one English matron declaring to her, "I'll never consider you *my* Nursing Sisters" (emphasis in the original).[72] Rank was a contentious issue with animosity on both sides, as Ruby Peterkin noted:

> In fact, I fear the Eng[lish] sisters do not love us. You see we have two stars and they hadn't, and altho they spend a great deal of time in assuring us that they "rank as officers" it is not as convincing as those two stars. We just calmly survey their uniform which is hideous—a gray chambray, apron like ours, and a little grey cloth cape edged with scarlet about two inches wide. The[n] we as calmly glance at our own, which believe me, looks pretty smart in these surroundings, and you can fairly see them turn green.[73]

But rank, although a very sore point, did not account for all the animosity between the English and Canadian nursing sisters. Variations in practice, organization, and ideology likely played a part as well.[74] Matron Eleanor Charleson, for example, included the "Canadianizing of an English hospital" as an item on her list of duties when setting up hospital wards in previously used facilities, although she didn't specify just what that involved.[75] In at least one recorded situation at Malta, jealousy over rank manifested itself in poor treatment of CAMC nurses. A medical officer described them as having had a "rotten time" with "hardly enough to eat," being made to "sleep in the same quarters as the servants," while enduring "nasty remarks about them wearing a uniform with lieutenant's stars and receiving lieutenant's pay."[76] It is doubtful, however, that CAMC nursing sisters were completely innocent parties to these controversies.

Authority was an inherent aspect of rank, although as a semiseparate rank within the Canadian medical corps structure, nursing sisters did not disrupt mainstream gendered military hierarchy. Medical officers automatically enlisted as captains and, accordingly, ranked over most nursing sisters, thus ensuring that no woman would have authority over a military man beyond the wards. The authority of matrons and nursing sisters was limited to other nursing sisters, assistants within the various hospital units and, most importantly, their patients. In a reversal of usual gender roles, nursing sisters outranked these "other ranks" (noncommissioned men who comprised the bulk of their patients).

Rank required careful negotiation related to orderlies who provided invaluable, although not unproblematic, assistance in the care of soldiers. They comprised the largest group of enlisted men working regularly with the nursing sisters, who were also responsible for their training. Orderlies did much of the cleaning of the wards and the equipment, as well as making beds and providing dependent patients with personal care such as bathing, shaving, dressing, and toileting. If the nurse and orderly did not get along or if the orderly went "missing" frequently from the ward, work did not go smoothly since he was the only helper the nurse usually had. When Alice Isaacson transferred to a new ward in 1917, for example, she found 20 suspected cases of typhoid fever awaiting laboratory tests, and the ward was "gloomy and dark" with "only two electric lights for the whole ward." But more importantly, the orderly was "very disagreeable."[77] The situation did not look promising. Alice Ross valued a particularly good orderly, noting how they "had 35 pts. last night so Cartwright & I didn't waste much time. Cartwright is off this morning for which I am extremely sorry, for he is A1. I hope Jack, who succeeds him will prove good as an orderly for no laggard is wanted on the Enteric Suspects in the mornings."[78] Although orderlies could be a great irritation to nursing sisters, they were usually appreciated and respected for their ability to extend the range of nurses' eyes, ears, hands, and legs. They greatly extended the number of patients for whom a nursing sister could be responsible.

POSTWAR PRIVILEGE

As CAMC medical units demobilized throughout 1919–1920, nursing sisters found themselves in a different situation from medical officers who had been appointed to specific positions with various regiments, sanitary stations, and field ambulances—units that continued to function after the war on a smaller scale. Physicians could combine these reduced military responsibilities with private practice. But very few military positions remained for nursing sisters after the Canadian Expeditionary Force ceased to exist. A newly created civilian organization, the Department of Soldiers Civil Reestablishment (DSCR), assumed responsibility for invalided soldiers returned to Canada.[79] Initially, 400–500 nursing sisters transferred to these rehabilitation hospitals, but as patients gradually recovered well enough for discharge, nursing positions tapered off as well.[80] Maude Wilkinson stayed with the DSCR for four years after demobilization, for example, acknowledging "that I was still occupied with the returned veterans and had not, professionally speaking, successfully re-entered civilian life."[81] She subsequently left the DSCR to become director of the Red Cross Outpost Hospital Service, Ontario Division—a position that took her all across northern Ontario and into many adventures over the next 13 years.

CAMC nursing sisters, like other soldiers, were entitled to a war service gratuity calculated on the number of days served overseas. The maximum gratuity equated to 183 days' pay and allowances and was graduated according to rank. This gratuity could be substantial for long service, ranging from $700 to $1,000 or more. Thus, Frances Upton pondered her postwar options strategically. She had served since January 1915 and decided that "it would be wiser to remain here [with the army], as long as there is need. . . . I think it would be wasting money to give it up now . . . for if I stay in the service until the finish, I'll receive six months' salary as Government Gratuity."[82] Similarly, Ruth Hays wrote her sister that she was "coming home with about $1000 in savings plus six months' pay to come."[83]

In general, civilian women were expected to give up paid employment after the war, in deference to returning soldiers and conforming with traditional roles in the home. Nursing sisters, however, had engaged in paid work before the war with expectations to continue working. Almost half of them (46.2%) were over 30 years old on enlistment and older yet on demobilization, beyond the usual marriage age of the time. Marriage did claim some of them, but far more nursing sisters lost potential or actual sweethearts and fiancés to the war. They returned to a society of excess single women due to both war and influenza that had decimated the population of men, including male relatives who would have traditionally supported unmarried female relatives.

The majority of CAMC nurses had worked in private-duty nursing previously. But private duty was the one area that almost all of them wished to avoid after the war. As Luella Denton wrote, "The big question is, am I going back to private nursing? I think sometimes not but again, I must do something."[84] Private duty lacked the stability and financial security of salaried positions that were increasingly available in newly emerging types of nursing work.

Some nursing sisters had been highly qualified operating room nurses, instructors, and supervisors before the war and built upon their war time experiences to take up the few hospital positions available to trained nurses. Many had developed further specialized skills in surgery, dietetics, anesthesia, and radiology by completion of special courses while overseas. They were able to transfer these skills, for example, to emerging roles within civilian hospital anesthesia and radiology departments. As Frances Upton reasoned, "I do not ever intend to do private nursing again, so will probably end up by taking a hospital position again, seeing that no nice man wants to keep me in idleness and pay me for it."[85]

To forestall nursing sisters flooding into the civilian workforce, professional leaders promoted new work opportunities such as the convalescent military hospitals, Red Cross nursing outposts just opening up in remote areas,[86] the Victorian Order of Nurses (a district nursing service),[87] "mental" hospitals in need of nurses as psychiatry began to expand as a specialty, and the new field of public health nursing that was just emerging in Canada.[88] Both CAMC and civilian nursing leaders agreed that nursing sisters who had served overseas should have priority for the top administrative positions in civilian nursing—a practice greatly resented by civilian nurses.[89] In addition, new educational opportunities were offered to military nurses first, privileging them over nurses who had not served.[90]

But the public health field benefited most from these returning veterans who were given preference for university courses as well as the public health and social work positions that required these credentials.[91] Marguerite Carr-Harris, for example, took mental hygiene and public health courses at the University of Toronto, after which the provincial health department hired her for its Ontario Rural Child Welfare Project, designed to demonstrate the value of public health to local communities. Edna Moore went to New York in public health for a period before joining the Ontario Department of Health, becoming its chief public health nurse in 1931, as well as director for the Division of Public Health Nursing in 1944. The School Hygiene Branch of the Department of Education appointed Jean Urquhart as health supervisor for the Normal School at Regina to teach teachers about health for students.[92] Catherine Isabella Stewart became the first supervisor of the Red Cross Nursing Service in Saskatchewan in 1920, a position she held for the next 24 years.[93]

Wearing the army uniform was initially a novelty, one that visibly denoted the unique position of CAMC nurses within the masculine military environment as commissioned soldiers with officer rank and status. They could go where other women could not go—ever closer to the front lines of war. Materially, nurses were pleased with the overall design, femininity, and quality of their uniforms as well as its symbolic identification as distinctly Canadian; they were not mere colonials coming to England's defense. The uniform came with embedded expectations and rights. It not only established nursing sisters' credibility and authority but conveyed expectations for proper deportment, both as officers and as women, especially with regard to public anxieties about women in the military. Putting on the uniform began a process of transforming civilian nurses into soldiers, enabling them to embody the culture and values of the military (such as healing soldiers only to send them back to the front lines again). Few nursing sisters anticipated the impact of having worn the uniform on their postwar careers. After all, the Great War was to have been over by Christmas (a hope repeated each year, as it turned out). These postwar privileges, along with the military nurses, quietly disappeared from public view for the most part until a second world war threatened in 1939.

For many CAMC nursing sisters, the uniform transformed their lives substantially from a relatively solitary life of private-duty nursing to increased opportunities for regular paid work. It exposed them to travel and cultural experiences that would have been previously unaffordable. Their wages as officers were not only higher than going rates in private duty, but the work was regular and predictable, plus many of them received a substantial war service gratuity at the end of the war. They had privileged access to university education in public health after the war, which paved the way for expanded roles and autonomy. They held enhanced public respect (especially in light of the 60 deaths among their cohort). Because they were soldiers, they were eligible to vote in the special 1917 Canadian federal election and thereby were enfranchised a full year before other women. They developed a lifelong bond with other nursing sisters based on shared war experiences, which led to the formation of a national organization with local chapters dedicated to looking after one another, especially when health or financial resources dwindled. It endured almost a century, closing down in 2004.

NOTES

1. Kathryn McPherson, "The Nightingale Influence and the Rise of the Modern Hospital," in *On All Frontiers: Four Centuries of Canadian Nursing*, ed. Christina Bates, Dianne Dodd, and Nicole Rousseau (Ottawa: University of Ottawa Press, 2005), 73–87; Kathryn McPherson, *Bedside Matters: The Transformation of Canadian Nursing, 1900–1990* (Toronto: Oxford University Press, 1996), 165–167; Christina Bates, *A Cultural History of the Nurse's Uniform* (Ottawa: Canadian Museum of Civilization, 2012), 21.

2. Bates, *A Cultural History*, 7.

3. Carrie Hertz, "The Uniform: As Material, as Symbol, as Negotiated Object," *Midwestern Folklore* 32, nos. 1–2 (2007): 43.

4. Hertz, "The Uniform," 45.

5. Hertz, "The Uniform," 53.

6. Katherine Dewar, *Called to Serve: Georgina Pope, Canadian Military Nursing Heroine* (Charlottetown, Prince Edward Island: Island Studies Press, 2018).

7. Cynthia Toman, *Sister Soldiers of the Great War: The Nurses of the Canadian Army Medical Corps* (Vancouver, B.C.: UBC Press, 2016), 15.

8. Toman, *Sister Soldiers of the Great War*, 13.

9. Georgina Pope, "Army Nursing," *Canadian Nurse* 10, no. 10 (Oct. 1914): 597–601; G.F. Pope, "Nursing in South Africa during the Boer War, 1899–1900," *American Journal of Nursing* 3, no. 1 (Oct. 1902): 10–14.

10. Mabel B. Clint, *Our Bit: Memories of War Service by a Canadian Nurse* (Montreal: Barwick, 1934): 3, 11.

11. Toman, *Sister Soldiers of the Great War*.

12. Edith Hudson, "'War Memoirs' of Miss Edith Hudson," RG 64-7-21, folder 21, McGill University Archives; P. Bonner, "Canadian War Nursing Service," 2432/1/2/30-664, McGill University Archives.

13. "McGill Hospital Staff is Chosen," *Gazette* (Montreal), 2 Feb. 1915, 4.

14. Emma Griffis McGill, diary, 29 Mar. 1917, Glenbow Museum, http://www.albertaonrecord.ca/iw-glen-159 (accessed 23 July 2013).

15. Katherine [*sic*] M. Wilson-Simmie, *Lights Out! A Canadian Nursing Sister's Tale* (Belleville, Ont.: Mika, 1981), 14. The phrase "clothes make the man" has been variously attributed to Shakespeare (from *Hamlet*) and Mark Twain, according to *The Oxford Dictionary of Phrase and Fable*, http://www.encyclopedia.com/humanities/dictionaries-thesauruses-pictures-and-press-releases/clothes-make-man (accessed 27 Mar. 2017).

16. Margaret Macdonald, "A Message to the Nursing Sisters," *Canadian Nurse* 22, no. 7 (July 1926): 367.

17. Susan Mann, *Margaret Macdonald: Imperial Daughter* (Montreal: McGill-Queen's Press, 2005), 61–62.

18. *Instructions for Members of Canadian Army Medical Corps Nursing Service (When Mobilized)* (London: Vacher & Sons, 1917), 7.

19. Eric Scott, ed., *Nobody Ever Wins a War: The World War I Diaries of Ella Mae Bongard, RN* (Ottawa: Janeric Enterprises, 1997), 31.

20. Edith Hudson, diary, 20 Sept. 1914, held privately by Allan Kerr, Edmonton, Alberta.

21. Maude Wilkinson, *Four Score and Ten: Memoirs of a Canadian Nurse* (Brampton, Ont.: Margaret M. Armstrong, 2003), 44.

22. Hudson, diary, 20 Sept. 1914.

23. "Nursing Overseas, WWI, Correspondence Regarding Dress Regulations, Code of Conduct," RG 9, III, B-1, vol. 3419, file N-6/7-47, folder 3, Library and Archives Canada (hereafter LAC).

24. Emeline Robinson, diary, 25 and 27 Oct. 1917, held privately by Deborah Brummell, Ottawa.

25. Helen Fowlds, letter, 3 June 1915, Helen Marryat fonds, 69-001/1/1, boxes 1–2, Trent University Archives (hereafter cited as Fowlds letters, autograph book, or diaries).

26. Clint, *Our Bit*, 50.

27. Fowlds, autograph book.

28. Wilson-Simmie, *Lights Out*, 61.

29. May Bastedo, letter, 26 Nov. 1915, "My trip abroad," May Bastedo fonds, 58A 1 2.1, Canadian War Museum.

30. Bastedo, letter, 29–30 Nov. 1915.

31. Bastedo, letter, 12 Dec. 1915.

32. Frances Upton, letters of 26 Jan. and 3 Feb. 1917, collection held privately by Jon Johnson, Calgary, Alberta.

33. Fowlds, letter, 17 Sept. 1916. Alice Ross also dyed her uniforms just before leaving Salonika, as noted in her diary entry for 26 Apr. 1917, diaries held privately by Pam and Tom Graham, Kingsville, Ont.

34. Wilson-Simmie, *Lights Out*, 61.

35. Fowlds, letter, 23 Sept. 1915.

36. These incidents occurred in spite of the prominent display of Red Cross symbols and colors intended to protect those providing humanitarian care for all victims of war. There were at least 60 deaths among CAMC nursing sisters, according to Dianne Dodd, "Canadian Military Nurse Deaths in the First World War," *Canadian Bulletin of Medical History* 34, no. 2 (Fall 2017): 327–363. See also J.G. Adami, "The Enemy Air Raids upon Canadian Hospitals, May 1918: A Report to the D.G.M.S. Canadian Contingencies," *Bulletin of the Canadian Army Medical Corps* 1, no. 5 (Aug. 1918): 64–69; J.G. Adami, "The Sinking of H.M.H.S. 'Llandovery Castle,'" *Bulletin of the Canadian Army Medical Corps* 1, no. 5 (Aug. 1918): 69–73.

37. Françoise Thébaud, "The Great War and the Triumph of Sexual Division," in *A History of Women in the West*, ed. Georges Duby and Michelle Perrot, vol. 5, *Toward a Cultural Identity in the Twentieth Century* (Cambridge, Mass.: Harvard University Press, 1994), 21–75.

38. Janet S.K. Watson, *Fighting Different Wars: Experience, Memory, and the First World War in Britain* (Cambridge: Cambridge University Press, 2004), 58.

39. Watson, *Fighting Different Wars*, 61. Watson differentiates VAD volunteers from trained nurses who were paid workers, suggesting that war work required less dramatic change in life circumstances than it did for middle and upper-class VADs.

40. Henriette Donner, "Under the Cross—Why V.A.D.s Performed the Filthiest Task in the Dirtiest War: Red Cross Women Volunteers, 1914–1918," *Journal of Social History* 30, no. 3 (Spring 1997): 687–704.

41. Judith S. Graham, ed., *"Out Here at the Front": The World War I letters of Nora Saltonstall* (Boston: Northeastern University Press, 2004), 158–159.

42. George C. Nasmith, *On the Fringe of the Great Fight* (Toronto: McClelland, Goodchild, & Stewart, 1917), 7–8.

43. Wilhelmina Mowat-Waugh, "'White Veils, Brass Buttons and Me': Memoirs of a Nursing Sister in World War I in the Canadian Army Medical Corps 1915–1920," Brandon General Hospital Archives, Brandon, Manitoba.

44. Upton, letters, n.d. The letter is sequenced between one dated 20 Dec. 1915 and one dated 17 Mar. 1916; both were written from Lemnos.

45. Mann, *Margaret Macdonald*, 132–136, 250n93. For recent research, see Toman, *Sister Soldiers of the Great War*, 50–51. Macdonald's records estimated the marriage rate at 10% to 15%, although Toman's analysis shows the rate closer to 3.7%.

46. Marjorie Barron Norris, *Sister Heroines: The Roseate Glow of Wartime Nursing, 1914–1918* (Calgary: Author, 2002), 99–127.

47. Laura Hanham Harper, audiotaped interview with Margaret M. Allemang at Toronto, Ont., in 1978, "Canadian Nursing Sisters of World War I," Canadian Nurses Association fonds, Accession 2001-0164, LAC.

48. Ruth Honour Johnson Hays, diary, 1 July 1917. Diary and photographs held privately by Margaret Chalus, Edmonton, Alberta.

49. Hays, diary, 14 Mar. 1918.

50. Dorothy M. Cotton, "A Word Picture of the Anglo-Russian Hospital, Petrograd," *Canadian Nurse* 22, no. 9 (Sept. 1926): 486; Cynthia Toman, "Eyewitness to Revolution: Canadian Military Nurses at Petrograd, 1915–17," in *One Hundred Years of Wartime Nursing Practices, 1854–1954*, ed. Jane Brooks and Christine E. Hallett (Manchester: Manchester University Press, 2015), 122–143.

51. Edith Hegan, Gertrude Squire, and Mabel Lindsay joined Cotton at Petrograd later. Toman, "Eyewitness to Revolution"; "War Diaries and Letters: Dorothy Cotton," R. C. Fetherstonhaugh fonds, vol. 8, Rare Books and Special Collections, McGill University Library.

52. "The Anglo-Russian Hospital," *British Journal of Nursing* (9 Oct. 1915): 294. The other three nursing sisters also continued to wear the CAMC uniform.

53. Cotton, letter to her mother, 24 Nov. 1915, Fetherstonhaugh fonds.

54. Cotton, letter to Bob [Robert Fetherstonhaugh] from Petrograd, 16 Dec. 1915, Fetherstonhaugh fonds.

55. Wilson-Simmie, *Lights Out*, 31. Pay varied depending on the posting and how much sick time, vacation, or leave of absence time a nurse took. Those who served overseas typically earned between $100 and $130 per month.

56. CAMC nursing sister, "Military Nursing," *Canadian Nurse* 13, no. 8 (Aug. 1917): 483–484.

57. Susan Mann, "Where Have All the Bluebirds Gone? On the trail of Canada's Military Nurses, 1914–1918," *Atlantis* 26, no. 1 (Fall/Winter 2001): 39.

58. Cecilia Morgan, *'A Happy Holiday': English Canadians and Transatlantic Tourism, 1870–1930* (Toronto: University of Toronto Press, 2008), 21–22.

59. Pocket-size cameras for general public use were relatively new. Many nursing sisters bought one and put it to good use documenting both travels and wartime experiences, including Alice Isaacson, Frances Upton, Helen Fowlds, Dorothy Cotton, Edith Hudson, Edna Moore, Elsie Collis, Clare Gass, and Florence Hunter.

60. Hays, letters, 23 Nov. 1917.

61. Robinson, diary, n.d., but the events took place on arrival in England, April 1916.

62. E.D. Collis, "A Nursing Sister of #5: Diary of E.D. Collis, June 1915–March 1919," in possession of the author.

63. Fowlds, letter, 9 Apr. 1915.

64. Fowlds, letter, 13 Feb. 1916; diary, 3 Feb. 1916.

65. Fowlds, letter, 11 Mar. 1916.

66. Fowlds, letter, 18 Apr. 1918.

67. J. George Adami, *War Story of the Canadian Army Medical Corps*, vol. 1, *The First Contingent to the Autumn of 1915* (Toronto: Canadian War Records Office, 1918), 33–34.

68. Adami, *War Story*, 34–35.

69. "Legislation Needed to Protect Nurses," *Globe* (Toronto), 25 May 1916, 8. Rudolf was with No. 11 Canadian General Hospital in France according to Brian Douglas Tennyson, *The Canadian Experience of the Great War: A Guide to Memoirs* (Lanham, Md.: Scarecrow Press, 2013), 346–347.

70. Cynthia Toman, "'A Loyal Body of Empire Citizens': Military Nurses and Identity at Lemnos and Salonika, 1915–1917," in *Place and Practice in Canadian Nursing History*, ed. Jayne Elliott, Meryn Stuart, and Cynthia Toman (Vancouver, B.C.: UBC Press, 2008), 9–10.

71. CAMC nursing sister, "Military Nursing," 482–490; Toman, "A Loyal Body of Empire Citizens."

72. Katharine Wilson-Simmie, audio-taped interview with Julia Harvey at Wiarton, Ont., 18 Oct. 1977, "Canadian Nursing Sisters of World War I," Canadian Nurses Association fonds, Accession 2001-0164, LAC.

73. Ruby Peterkin, letter, 20 June 1915, MG 30 E160, Ruby Gordon Peterkin fonds, "Letters and Photographs, 1915–1917," LAC.

74. Toman, *Sister Soldiers*, 192–193.

75. "Abstracts from War Diary: No. 1 CSH," Margaret Clotilde Macdonald fonds, MG 30 E45, folder XII, "War Diaries of Matrons," folder XIII, "Nursing Overseas: General Descriptions," LAC.

76. J.J. Mackenzie, *Number 4 Canadian Hospital: The Letters of Professor J. J. Mackenzie from the Salonika Front with a Memoir by His Wife, Kathleeen Cuffe Mackenzie* (Toronto: Macmillan, 1933), 50.

77. Alice Isaacson, diary, 24 Feb. 1917, Alice E. Isaacson fonds, R11203-0-1-E, "Diaries and Photographs, 1917–1919," LAC.

78. Ross, diary, 5 Sept. 1915.

79. Andrew Macphail, *The Medical Services: Official History of the Canadian Forces in the Great War, 1914–1919* (Ottawa: King's Printer, 1925), 310–313.

80. Bill Rawling, *Death Their Enemy: Canadian Medical Practitioners and War* (Ottawa: Author, 2001), 117–119.

81. Wilkinson, *Four Score and Ten*, 92.

82. Upton, letter, 5 Jan. 1919.

83. Hays, letter, 5 Jan. 1919.

84. Luella Denton, letter, 26 Jan. 1919, "A Canadian Nursing Sister," Letters of Luella Denton, the Lorna Towler Collection, PF131S1F112, Grey Roots Museum & Archives, Owen Sound, Ont., https://greyroots.com/story/canadian-nursing-sister (accessed 28 October 2019). See also "Canadian Army Medical Nursing Service Department," *Canadian Nurse* 17, no. 1 (Jan. 1921): 96.

85. Upton, letter, 16 Feby 1919.

86. Jayne Elliott, "A Negotiated Process: Outpost Nursing under the Red Cross in Ontario, 1922–1984," in *Caregiving on the Periphery: Nurses and Midwives in Nineteenth- and Twentieth-Century Canada*, ed. Myra Rutherdale (Montreal: McGill-Queen's University Press, 2010), 245–277.

87. Beverly Boutilier, "Helpers or Heroines? The National Council of Women, Nursing, and 'Woman's Work' in Late Victorian Canada," in *Caring and Curing: Historical Perspectives on Women and Healing in Canada*, ed. Dianne Dodd and Deborah Gorham (Ottawa: University of Ottawa Press, 1994), 31–40.

88. Meryn Stuart, "Ideology and Experience: Public Health Nursing and the Ontario Rural Child Welfare Project, 1920–1925," *Canadian Bulletin of Medical History* 6, no. 2 (Jan. 1989): 111–132.

89. M. Lesley Newell, "'Led by the Spirit of Humanity': Canadian Military Nursing, 1914–1929" (M.A. thesis, University of Ottawa, 1996).

90. Mélanie Morin-Pelletier, "Héritières de la Grande Guerre: Les infirmières militaires canadiennes durant l'entre-Deux-Guerres" (Ph.D. diss., University of Ottawa, 2010).

91. Morin-Pelletier, "Héritières de la Grande Guerre."

92. Marguerite E. Robinson, *The First Fifty Years* (n.p.: Saskatchewan Registered Nurses' Association, 1968), 102–104.

93. Robinson, *The First Fifty Years*, 103.

SIX

"SHE PREFERS KHAKI TO THE FEMININE MODE OF DRESS"

Australian and New Zealand Women in Uniform during the Great War

BRUCE SCATES, MARGARET HARRIS,
AND RAELENE FRANCES

In autumn of 1916, a small contingent of Australian Army nurses took their first leave in London. "We made the Strand Palace Hotel our headquarters," Sister Tilton wrote, and "ventured forth resplendent in the new regulation army uniform." It was, she continued, "a smart outfit." A "grey Norfolk coat and skirt, with stars on our brown shoulder straps," conferred pride in the wearer, identified her as an army nurse, and instilled a sense of belonging. Well-dressed shoppers smiled approvingly and solicitous police waved their way through busy streams of city traffic. But the visual codes of such a uniform, a sartorial marker that connoted status, hierarchy, and role, were not apparent to everyone. A few days later, May Tilton and her companions embarked on an excursion to Llandudno, a tourist resort in northern Wales. Awaiting the return bus from Conway castle, another stranded tourist approached them. Tilton's account of the incident tells us much about new unsettling roles women played in wartime and the ambiguous status of a woman in uniform:

> "What time does your bus leave, Madam?"
>
> "It is not my bus, Sir."

> "Well, whose is it? What is that uniform you are wearing? I thought you were bus drivers."
>
> I told him what it represented. He growled:
>
> "How was I to know? Every woman you see is wearing a newfangled uniform."
>
> And so they were. One seldom saw a woman wearing ordinary dress in England. There were girls in blue uniforms acting as luggage porters, pushing great trucks loaded with goods along railway platforms while others acted as ticket collectors. They drove buses, taxis, and lorries and worked in offices and factories and munitions works, hard and long. In every branch of work, girls and women did their bit. We were proud of our sex.[1]

Pride, on the one hand, was countered by discomfort at the "newfangled" ideas of dress and occupation on the other. Although Tilton admired the sight of "women at all kinds of work" and the dashing figure of "little girls" in all kinds of uniform, others found such scenes deeply disquieting.[2] The meanings embodied in a uniform, for wearer and beholder, were complex and contested. Uniform lifted women out of their traditional domestic role, subverted normative notions of feminine behavior, and encroached on areas long the domain of men. In Tilton's case, it would carry women to the very center of the war zone, securing a measure of autonomy, freedom, and personal empowerment largely unknown in peacetime.

All this was quite new. Although women had played "significant military roles" throughout history, active participation was limited almost entirely to lower-class women (the "camp follower")[3] and "the occasional elite female leader." By the early twentieth century, the onset of total war meant that military mobilization involved the whole of society and men and women alike. A new phrase was coined, "the home front," and as Tilton observed, women donned uniform to work in ways and occupations previously unimaginable. Uniformed women spoke of "mobilising" for the war effort and "joining the forces," likening their service to the military service of men.[4] But "total war" was fought differently by different societies. Unlike Britain, neither Australia nor New Zealand had large-scale industrial military manufacturing, largely closing off munitions as an avenue of semiofficial uniformed work.[5] Nor did women take men's place "in every branch of work." Women, uniformed and otherwise, moved into some occupations but not others.[6] The women Tilton observed worked in "men's" industries for many reasons, including financial and patriotic ones and the quest for suffrage.[7] As Barton Hacker observed of nursing, war work "validated [women's] claim to citizenship."[8] White women in Australia and New Zealand had gained the vote in the late nineteenth century; taking on war work asserted the rights and responsibilities of citizenship in other ways. Finally, neither Australia nor New Zealand (nor for that matter any of the Dominions) created military services for women. There was no Women's Army Auxiliary Corps, no Women's Royal Navy Service, Women's Royal Airforce, or First Aid Nursing Yeomanry, nor did more than a very few Australian or New Zealand women journey "home" to serve in such units.[9] Throughout the war, nursing—and the auxiliary work undertaken by Voluntary Aid Detachments—remained the only government-sponsored service women could legitimately undertake.

Figure 6.1.
A smart outfit. Nurses from the Australian Army Nursing Service marching during a procession, South Australia, ca. 1918. National Library of Australia (http://nla.gov.au/nla.obj-152282029/view). Photo by Samuel Middleton Ware.

This belies the truth that Australian and New Zealand women wore many kinds of uniforms and inhabited them as actors. Government uniforms were only a small fraction of this riotous total. Women donned the femininely coded uniforms as Girl Guides, Red Cross workers, Young Men's Christian Association workers, and other charity organizers; women organized their wardrobe around the dress codes required in male-run office spaces; women wore sporting kit as part of organized workplace athletic clubs; and they caused discomfort among military authorities wearing uniforms as part of their membership of paramilitary groups. Women also wore uniforms for petty crime, as gestures of intimacy, and as genuine attempts at impersonating men. There were even instances of women dressing as soldiers and marching aboard troopships destined for the front. Whereas male parties

Figure 6.2.
Complex negotiations. Two New Zealand women don soldiers' uniforms, ca. 1905–1926. On one level, this portrait confirms the militarization of civil society throughout the war years; on another, it may read as a gesture of intimacy, connecting women to menfolk serving overseas. National Library/He Tohu, from Maclay, Adam Henry Pearson, 1873–1955: Negatives (Ref: 1/2-185135-G).

and organizations coded uniforms to create and constrain ideal female behavior, the women inside those uniforms sought agency, identity, and social recognition, requiring complex negotiations in a time of social change. As one alarmed newspaper columnist observed, these disruptive women "seemed to prefer khaki . . . to the feminine mode of dress."[10]

Having said that, nursing was, and remains, the preeminent lens through which female participation in the First World War was understood.[11] In war museums in both Australia and New Zealand, the nursing uniform is the sole garment granted legitimacy as a symbol of female

Figure 6.3.
A symbol of female war service. Napier Waller's mural of an Australian Army nurse in the nation's war memorial. Note the masculine appearance of her uniform and the blocking of the female form. Hall of Memory, Australian War Memorial. Photo by Bruce Scates.

war service.[12] As such, the greater part of this chapter deals with Tilton's story and that of some 3,000 other Australian and New Zealand nurses who donned a uniform and served overseas. Our emphasis here is not just what others said of them (the view of the onlooker) but what they thought of themselves—their deeply subjective investment in wearing that uniform. In this, we have been aided by a rare and, to date, underutilized archive. In the immediate aftermath of war, hundreds of Australian nurses were interviewed about their war service. These wartime narratives, along with the raw testimony of nurses' diaries and letters, restore women's voices to a historiography that has overwhelmingly privileged men. In the second half of this chapter, we consider the role uniformed women played on the home front. There, no less than in the case of nursing, the uniforms women donned were not just garments but symbols, a vehicle through which to perform agency and assert identity. A uniform's use and abuse—the way dress embodied duty, gained advantage, and denoted relationships—are a rich and complex field of historical inquiry.

UNIFORMED WOMEN IN THE WAR ZONE

Tilton called her memoir *The Grey Battalion* (1933), and that title in itself is telling. As Jennifer Craik has argued, uniforms shape who we are and how we perform our identities.[13] In Tilton's case, her uniform was linked firmly to discipline and moral authority. It was also a dense site of symbolism and meaning, encoding the way she came to remember the war years. The act of putting on that uniform separated her from wider society, granting status, signifying her devotion to national service, and identifying her as an Australian army nurse. Donning a uniform, for Tilton and all her compatriots, was a complex act of enablement and constraint. It was also a simple requirement of active service. Despite the exceptions noted below, nurses were told they "must always wear uniform." "You can imagine the outcry here," May Aston wrote from Egypt, "some of the Sisters have such pretty frocks."[14]

Uniforms for nurses served to mark them to an outside gaze as professionals worthy of respect. A nurse was set apart physically and socially from other women occupied in war work, such as prostitutes, merchants, and civilian dependents.[15] Nurses held an unshakable right to uniforms in the eyes of society at large in a way that groups such as the paramilitary Khaki Girls did not. This being so, the nurses who wore those uniforms jealously guarded them from interlopers. As early as 1915, the secretary of the New Zealand Nurses' Association objected to untrained volunteers being granted their use. We have "the approbation of our colleagues the world over," Miss J.M. Jones informed the New Zealand government, "and we feel we have a right to safeguard our privileges." The minister in question responded almost immediately: Untrained volunteers would not be given accoutrements.[16] That was no small concession; the quasi-military features of New Zealand and Australian nursing uniforms (including identification disks, medals, and badges of rank) were what placed the wearer within a hierarchical military structure. The nurse "feels invested with authority when she is in uniform," one Australian nurse explained in her local newspaper, "and carries a weight of influence [denied] the everyday garb of the ordinary untrained woman."[17]

DRESSED FOR THE JOB: MILITARIZING FEMININITY

What form did that uniform take? The short answer is several. Ostensibly, uniforms signify order and homogeneity.[18] But there was a complex dress code associated with nursing within and beyond the Australian Army Nursing Service (AANS). The "smart" attire much admired by Tilton was parade (or "walking out") dress: a gray serge tailored tunic, "bodice fashioned with military buttons, high neck and long sleeves," lace up boots and jacket topped by a felt hat, "trimmed with our colours, brown and red." The last replaced ugly and impractical bonnets (with a chocolate bow and a long silk tail) issued to nurses at the beginning of the war years. That dreadful bonnet died "a natural death," one nurse noted thankfully in her diary, perhaps because "we disliked [it] so much."[19] The "absurdity of a bonnet" was confirmed by the heat of Egypt, as was the "danger of eyestrain." Australian sisters took to wearing khaki helmets (substantial "investments" at the cost of 18s. a piece), and "one felt ready to hunt elephants."[20] Clearly, not all features of a uniform evoked pride and admiration. One sister dismissed her entire kit as "rotten": impossible to wear, expensive to buy, and "badly cut at David Jones [a department store in Sydney]."[21] Another (among the first to wear "the cloak and *the* bonnet" in England) recalled the "astonishment" of London's citizens on a visit to the British museum: "I suppose they had never seen such freaks before," she remarked. "We should have been inside as specimens."[22] All agreed that the length of the heavy gray skirt posed a problem. In summer, it "swirled up the thick dust"; in winter, "mud clung and soaked through everything."[23] "I believe 6 inches below the knee [must be] the limit in the future," an exasperated nurse informed the authorities. "[The] South African was a delight," but theirs "nearly killed" them.[24]

For all the stress on standardization implicit in a uniform, regulation attire was constantly evolving. Olive Haynes counted 11 different patterns of coat and skirt in the first three years of service, and in the early days of the war each state contingent sent overseas wore a different uniform, sporting significant differences in "quality, colour and details."[25] The *Kyarra*, one of the first hospital ships to sail from Australia, carried 160 nurses and a "queer" array of improvised costume unimaginable a few years later. Elise Eglinton thought the hobble skirts, which a few of the New South Welshman and Tasmanians were wearing, not quite "the thing" for active service: "They could never run if occasion occurred."[26]

Such apparel mirrors a common trend in women's uniforms throughout the war years. As Vining and Hacker have noted, they "exhibited overt military features and suppressed gender distinctions," removing women from a traditional domestic context, proclaiming their status as nursing professionals, and legitimizing their incursion in the male space of wartime.[27] The uniforms donned by the New Zealand Army Nursing Service (NZANS) shared the same masculine features. Matron-in-Chief Hester McLean likened their "coats of grey and scarlet" to the sharp, formal attire of British nurses, "but with a silver badge of fern leaf and a red cross to represent New Zealand."[28] Both services' uniforms signaled fine but clear gradations of rank, permanent (chocolate stripes on the sleeve and, later, stars) and temporary. "I'm an orderly sister today," Elsie Eglinton wrote home from the hospital ship *Karoola*, "that is I wear a red ribbon on my sleeve and am responsible for the . . . ward."[29] Uniforms also acknowledged periods and places of service. In November 1917, Australian troops who served in the Dardanelles campaign were entitled to attach a small brass A to their color patch. In January 1918, that privilege was extended to nurses who served on transports and hospital ships off Gallipoli, admitting women to the masculine Fellowship of Anzac. And all Australian nurses sported standard army insignia, their "Red Cape fastened at the neck with rising sun brooch."[30]

Uniforms were "overtly" masculine and military—but never entirely so. For nurses, this was a point of particular delicacy. Our uniform "must accentuate neither beauty nor plainness," Matron Kellett told the official historian. "It should be soothing to the distressed digger yet not accentuate the suspicions of the gutter press and party politician." "Decent" but attractive, "light yet substantial," a uniform sent complicated messages, often confusing gendered codes of dressing. As our subsequent analysis will show, the *way* a uniform was worn could convey a range of meanings, including (to Matron Kellett's chagrin) a brazen assertion of female sexuality.[31] Craig Wilcox's recent reading of AANS dress uniform is more nuanced. Streamlined and military parade dress might be, but it still sent a mixed message about women adopting male codes of dress: "dourly feminine from the hips down and almost masculine from the waist up."[32] Not surprisingly, perhaps, a party of Australian sisters was mistaken for Girl Scouts in London, much to the amusement of the nurses.[33]

Although parade dress empowered and modernized women, presenting them as symbols of authority and legitimizing their "resplendent" entry into the public sphere, ward attire reasserted women's domestic virtues and imbued them with the nurturing, angelic qualities long associated with nursing. The ward (or working) uniform donned by nurses took a different form from parade dress and drew on quite divergent traditions. To tend to the wounded, Australian and New Zealand nurses donned a gray ankle-length dress with starched collars, a white apron, and stiff veil. The last were borrowed from nuns' habits and conveyed the same message of devotion and self-denial. Religious dress, like the term sister itself, was a "desexualisation strategy."[34] A nurse quickly acquired an intimate knowledge of male anatomy, but the clothing she wore carefully concealed the female form, evoked the saintly images of a convent, and defused the sexually charged dimension of women tending men's (naked) bodies. Appropriately, working dress was maintained by immense domestic labor. "The caps and collars are the worst fly in the ointment," one exasperated nurse complained, "we iron them, with my little flat iron heated on the spirit stove; on a rug spread on the floor of the tent."[35] The sweaty heat of Egypt or Salonica necessitated an endless regimen of laundering.

A "small scarlet cashmere shoulder cape" completed the uniform of the ward and continued to be worn despite its cumbersome impracticality.[36] Introduced to the British nursing service by Florence Nightingale and known since then as a tippet, the cape was by far the most distinctive mark of an Australian nursing sister's uniform. Its appropriation by Australian and New Zealand forces caused a great deal of comment and "roused the ire of the permanent Army nursing sisters." In Queen Alexandra's Imperial Military Nursing Service, "only matrons wore the entire red cape, those of less exalted rank had gray capes with a scarlet border." In the AANS and NZANS (both technically reserve forces), all were entitled to wear it. "I would rather be with Australians than Imperials," Tev Davies wrote from her posting in a British hospital, "the regulars look on us as usurpers because we wear the scarlet cape."[37] Some British matrons demanded their "removal," prompting yet another challenge to military hierarchy. "The red cape was given to us at the time of the Boer War," one observer responded, "and we have as much right to keep it as the regular English army sisters."[38] Clearly, women were well aware of the symbolism and privilege even newfound uniforms embodied; nursing veterans of the South African war proudly asserting their service "traditions."[39] Although uniforms codified hierarchies, in the complex theatre of dominion service in an imperial war, they could also serve to challenge them.

For all the uniform demanded of its wearers, it nonetheless enabled women to work alongside male doctors, although never quite as their equals. It is telling that offers by female doctors to serve abroad were politely, but firmly, declined.[40] Disruptions to the military hierarchy did occur. During desperate fighting in France, with too few doctors to cope with the incoming wounded, women were hurriedly trained to administer anesthesia. It was a skill that women exercised with some enthusiasm; in strict demarcations of medical practice, this role had long been the exclusive preserve of men. But that breach of the gender order was short-lived and concessionary. When the push was over, women returned to their older (and subordinate) role in the wards.[41]

BREACHING THE CODE: ADAPTATION AND DEPARTURE

The uniform code was situational. It changed over the course of the war and in different theaters of service. Occasionally, uniform codes were relaxed altogether, even by the British army. "This summer we've been allowed to wear white dresses," Laura Grubb announced with some relief to her mother. In the oppressive heat of Salonica, "the girls [were] so glad to get out of [heavy] grey." Grubb had brought her dress with her, but other nurses fashioned what white garments they could from sheets and aprons and "a good many of [them] have never attempted such a thing as sewing." In so distant an outpost, the authorities turned a blind eye, as they did to Grubb's own liberties with uniform. With her own regulation felt hat looking "very tired," she replaced it with "the only thing she could get," a "cheap looking thing," slightly chocolate in color. "I am waiting [to see it] condemned as non-military," she continued, "but [the head] is not overstrict providing we always wear our stars and no low-necked dresses, no tan boots or stockings and no fancy Peter Pan collars."[42]

Carrie Hertz has cautioned historians against placing too much stress on the stated regulations of uniform codes, noting individuals seldom follow these regulations precisely.[43] Indeed, the demands of active service often made it impossible for them to do so, and by the end of the war, Grubb's own uniform was certainly "more patch than garment."[44] On active service and far from supply lines, standards slipped very quickly. A posting to the island of Lemnos began badly from the outset. Arrayed in parade uniform, Australian nurses lined up in fours to be piped into camp. "I must say we made a hash of it," one later recalled. "We had forgotten whether the odd or even numbers moved [first] so to be on the safe side we all moved!!"[45] It was several kilometers over rocky terrain to the site of the makeshift hospital. The "rough ground" was "fearfully hard" on their boots, another nurse remembered, and ankle-length skirts slowed their uneven progress.[46] Worse was to come. As winter approached, almost every item of uniform they were issued proved "inappropriate and inadequate." Embarking for the island, each nurse took with her one gray outdoor cape, two red capes, one outdoor bonnet, six linen collars, six cuffs, two pairs of ward shoes, four gray aprons, eight white aprons, boots, galoshes, and sundry other items of underwear and uniform.[47] Virtually any serviceable cloth was torn up for bandages and washers in the first influx of casualties. Then there was the weather to contend with. "We are nearly frozen," Sister Donnell wrote, "even in our balaclavas, mufflers, cardigans, raincoats and wellingtons."[48] The authorities had no choice other than to breach any standard dress code and issue a motley array of clothing. Much of it was drawn from the Tommies' stores, including coats ("ugly things without any shape or fit"), puttees ("quite an art to put them on"), and men's trousers ("we will wear our dresses over").[49] The results made a travesty of any kind of uniform: "We are being supplied riding pants, tunics and gumboots," Tev Davies wrote home to her mother. "Golly! Won't we look tragic?"[50]

Wearing trousers was one extreme. Even more at variance with normative feminine characteristics was Louise Young's drastic adaptations. First, she cut off most of her hair, the only relief to be found from the burrs and lice of the island. Then, when her tent collapsed in pouring rain and gale force winds, Young gave up any attempt to stay dry and equipped herself accordingly. The other nurses, she recalled, put on gumboots, "tucked up" their dresses, and donned Macintosh capes. "I got into my bathing costume and sailed down to the mess-tent to see what was to be done. I shall not forget Matron's face in a hurry. All the girls roared, and the matron asked me what I had on." Matron knew all too well. Young's willful improvisation flouted any regard for uniform.[51]

Departures like these were not confined to the early stages of the war. In the blazing heat of an Egyptian summer, some women abandoned attempts to starch their drooping collars and dressed as "scantily" as they could.[52] Staff Nurse Fay McKellar found her uniform "most unsuitable" for India, high collars and heavy material proving "impossible to wear."[53] Exposed to the "piercing winds" of Salonica, Sister/Nurse Payne wore "goat skin coats or leather jerkins" as well as "gum boots, overcoats and SouthWesters."[54] "Wintering" near the Khyber Pass, Tev Davies draped a battered gray cape fashioned in Australia with a wad of native shawls.[55] But arguably, the freezing conditions of the Somme were the worst. One fronted for duty, Sister Taylor recalled, "dressed in crowds of warm clothing—great coat, thick stockings, gumboots and work[ed] in them most of the time."[56]

Climate and geography forced one range of concessions; the exigencies of war forced another. When a push was on or a base was under attack, nurses dressed quickly in whatever came to hand. In France, Sister Muriel Doherty recalled rushing to duty "just as we were in our macintoshes and gumboots."[57] Nursing cholera victims in "the East," most nurses dispensed with ward uniform altogether: "We dressed in rubber costumes," Sister Vickers Foote recalled, "with masks, overalls, and rubber boots" shielding them from patients' vomit.[58] And a uniform, soiled or damaged by war, came to be charged with special significance. "We are

Figure 6.4.
Straight from the trenches. A group of Australian sisters at Brandhoek Australian Casualty Clearing Station (CCS). Although the photograph is posed, it suggests the range of attire donned at the front line on active duty. The CCS was exposed to shelling, hence the helmets and gasmasks. May Tilton, The Grey Battalion *(Sydney: Angus & Robertson, 1933).*

a disgrace the way we are," Kittie Naughton confessed after months on the Salient, "our dresses are torn and dirty." But we are "straight from the trenches," she added, that torn uniform a badge of pride.[59]

Like any article of wardrobe, a uniform could also be subtly individualized. Longing to "feel decently clad again," Olive Saloway had a "smart" new outfit made up in Italy. "Serviceable grey" it might be but stylish pockets in the coat and box pleats in the skirt were "not quite uniform." "It may be a trifle too smart for Matron's sharp eye," she told her mother, "so I shall have to be cautious and look ugly."[60] Many decorated uniforms with symbols of the Empire they served. Although far from regulation dress—standing orders forbade jewelry of any sort[61]—Sister Dorothy White pinned a gilt and enamel patriotic badge to her tunic. It read "A UNITED EMPIRE WHAT WE HAVE WE'LL HOLD" and featured a kangaroo, a beaver, an elephant, and an ostrich, all led by a British bulldog.[62] Most opted for less elaborate assertions of national identity. From the isolation of India's North-West Frontier, Tev Davies was delighted to receive an "awfully nice badge" sent out by patriotic workers in Melbourne. It was a "disc shaped in red, white and blue enamel . . . gold lettering . . . [reading] 'Australian Army Nursing Service 1916.' In the centre is A.I.F. in coloured enamel, while on the back is engraved, 'Australia's Appreciation.' . . . I tell you Mum dear I am proud of being Australian and I always wear it."[63]

THE COLORS OF WAR: UNIFORMS ON THE FRONT LINE

Color, as that glistening badge suggests, was one of the strongest visual signifiers of a uniform. Despite the red capes and white aprons commonplace in the wards, Australia's nurses, as Tilton's memoir attests, were styled "the grey battalion," and "adopting the grey" became nurses' vernacular for enlisting.[64] McNaughton (who served with Tilton in the Dardanelles) described her cohort as "the grey clad forms of Australian womanhood."[65]

Gray could be oppressive, especially on the long voyage out from Australia. "I feel almost as tho' I'd been at sea all my life," Laura Grubb wrote to her mother, "we are so tired of seeing nothing but grey uniform morning to night."[66] Remembering the bright dress of a civilian, Christine Strom also tired of "the monotony and the greyness." "We are indeed sick of grey!" she declared. "Once I get out of the Army I shall never wear it again." "*Everything* is grey here," she continued, "thank goodness I brought a vivid rug."[67] With time, Grubb came to accept the colored constraints of army life, "almost forgetting" such a thing as summer blouses ever existed. "I am quite used to grey now," she wrote from Cairo, "and I can't imagine anything else."[68] Strom, on the other hand, raged against the discomfort and ugliness of uniform. "[In] our charming suits of grey serge," she wrote facetiously, "five of us sallied forth . . . gently simmering."[69]

Gray grew on some. To others, it was always welcome. Color encoded difference, and uniforms conveyed at a glance a strong sense of individual and collective identity.[70] The gray attire of Australian sisters was readily contrasted with the uniforms of other nursing contingents, "the glowing blue" of the Canadians, the "pink sisters" of Voluntary Aid Detachments, and "the snowy whiteness" of American units, clad in what one nurse called "overalls."[71] Gray became, in time, a signifier of national belonging amid the "khaki hoards [*sic*]" of what seemed an entire world in uniform.[72] Anne Donnell, who described her sense of nationality as "quite akin to religion," fancied she could recognize an Australian from afar; there was something in the way her kinsfolk moved that asserted a "broadminded and independent spirit." But it was the color of the uniform and the flash of a rising sun badge that always "confirmed" that.[73] And one other color code was paramount in Sister Donnell's mind: A civilian nurse looked nothing like a sister serving with the Australian army.

As the first contingent of Red Cross nurses readied themselves to sail abroad, a popular journal in Sydney announced their bold "New Uniform": "As these nurses are not permitted to wear anything approaching the military uniform in colour, the Red Cross Society has decided on a neat dark-blue uniform, consisting of a Norfolk coat and skirt, with a very slight piping of pale blue on collar and coat sleeve." A dark-blue overcoat, a blue felt hat, and an "indoor uniform [of] a pretty dark blue striped Zephyr" completed a "very neat and serviceable" outfit.[74] It also determined the nickname soon conferred on Australia's Red Cross nurses (a title no doubt borrowed from the Canadians), "the bluebirds."[75]

"Pretty" was not a word nurses often used to describe themselves. "Smart" implies a less ornamental set of values, suggestive as it is of readiness, self-control, and confidence. But although Red Cross nurses were proud of their civilian status, they too succumbed to the strident nationalism and militarism of the age. That, again, was expressed through their uniforms. Special badges identified the wearer not just as a nurse but also as a member of a national contingent sent to aid the Empire. As the war ground on, the Red Cross became less a humanitarian, philanthropic agency than an arm of a belligerent state.[76]

The bluebirds served in "self contained units." Although paid the same as military nurses and placed at the disposal of the military authorities, they were largely exempt from military discipline. That did not prevent Nellie Crommelin from seeing herself as "military in every sense of the word." She began her war service sewing the badges of allied nations around her ward dress. And she ended it on the Somme, witnessing line after line of Allied troops marching bravely toward enemy lines.[77] Crommelin's field hospital was just a few kilometers from the fighting. For five days, "the roar and thunder of the cannon" shook the windows and doors of the ward. The surrounding villages were evacuated, but Crommelin kept to her post. "Sharing the dangers," she explained, brought her "a little closer to our men, . . . to prove to them we can also play a little part." Women might seem "so useless, so helpless, against the awful strain of the present."[78] But a nurse's uniform, even the "pretty" outfit of a bluebird, proved otherwise. It legitimized her entry into the male world of wartime, thrust women into the very center of the conflict, transformed them from helpless bystanders left at home to active participants on the world stage. Crommelin concluded her account with an appeal to menfolk who chose to stay at home, not that she thought "men" the right word to describe them. What "*real men*" would "want to stay behind with the . . . children?"[79]

Figure 6.5.
The female version of Anzac. A recruiting poster by Norman Lindsay. Here, women are thrust into the male space of battle, shaming men into volunteering for service. Ironically, such potent imagery also empowered women, asserting their independence and agency. Bulletin (Sydney), 29 July 1915.

That same image of nurses standing steadfast by "their men" was mobilized tirelessly by recruiting agencies. In the most emotive imagery, women are depicted in the center of the war zone, defiant in their stance, emboldened by their uniform. Civilian onlookers (or shirkers, as they were often called) seem weak, passive, and effeminate. Uniforms thus subverted conventional gendered paradigms. Paradoxically, they also reinforced them. In measuring war effort, valor and sacrifice were paramount, and as Nicoletta Gullace has observed, "the discourse of citizenship and patriotism . . . as well as military obligation and service to the state, became an authoritative way to measure civic worth."[80] Nurses' association with the battlefield enhanced their status throughout the war. Dressed in those "torn and dirty dresses," they claimed to be "diggeresses": the female version of the Anzac.[81]

A uniform spoke of duty, service, and sacrifice "nudging its wearer towards greater effort, discipline and loyalty."[82] Notwithstanding the vocal exceptions noted above, a nurse's attire comprised honored, revered, and treasured items. Uniforms were also an entitlement to privilege, even pleasure, especially behind the lines. "Those of us who go about in uniform," Anne Donnell confided to her diary, "have a distinct courtesy shown to us which is lacking if wearing civilian clothes. So I say the wise wear uniform." The wise and the canny. Wearing her "bright and effective" uniform, Donnell paid half the fare of her civilian counterpart, gained admission to select clubs, and sat in "circle seats and first stalls reserved for us."[83]

The parade dress of Staff Nurse F.N. Gregson may have been "plain and shabby" after a long and grueling posting to Salonica. Even so, she noted, it retained "certain advantages": sisters "who swank it in mufti" paid 6d. or 1s. for the privilege.[84] A uniform (and the pay that went with it) enabled women a degree of freedom and mobility unequaled for most in peacetime. Uniformed women rode donkeys about the pyramids, sailed in feluccas down the Nile, motored through England's Lake District, and stormed the finest shops of European capitals. They also ate for a good deal less.[85] Nurses were given special rates for meals. An extra serving, even an extra meal, compensated for the "very scanty suppers" of "food famine" England.[86] And in many cases, a uniform conferred privileged access to what were seen as male spaces. Wealthy and connected, Elsie Cook's war was a near-continuous round of outings and engagements, often with the elite of British and French society. Of far more modest social origins, Kit McNaughton took immense pleasure in touring the gambling parlors of Monaco.[87]

Off duty, a uniform could confer power, privilege, and rank on women traditionally subordinate to men. On duty, many "entitlements" were far less secure. Women serving in the British nursing units had been granted honorary rank as officers as early as 1904; Canadian nurses enjoyed a comparable status to men. Australian sisters went to war with no rank at all. Drawn from civilian hospitals, most had little grasp of military hierarchy, why, as one bewildered nurse wondered, "some wore stripes, and others stars, and some stars with a crown": "I fancied a Sergeant [was] by far the most important person in the Army." Even untrained male orderlies were not under her command.[88] The situation changed in 1916. Australian sisters were granted officer status, and with that, a new uniform sporting "stars on the shoulders *a la Canadian.*"[89] But unlike Canadian nurses, neither the AANS nor the NZANS secured the pay and conditions that went with men's commissions. A nursing sister was paid 9s. a day; a staff nurse received 2s. less. Compare that with their equivalent rank in male services—a first lieutenant earned 17s. 6d. a day, not including field allowance. Even so, nurses were expected to buy much of their uniform and kit and, unlike male officers, were given no allowances for replacements.[90] It was a sore point with women whose years of professional training had already imposed considerable financial hardship. Tev Davies advised her mother not to give another penny to patriotic funds: "It is humbug from start

Figure 6.6.
Freedom and mobility. A group of Australian Army Nursing Sisters take in the pyramids. Wearing a uniform enabled a range of movement unknown in peace-time and conferred clear authority over the "natives." Australian War Memorial (AWM A05410).

to finish, look at how much it cost in Australia, then since coming to London we have had to buy Primus Stoves, Macintoshes, Gum Boots, Mess Kit and several odds and ends. . . . Strikes me someone is making a good thing out of this war."[91]

Australian nurses were divided over the compulsory conferring of commissions. Some senior ranks welcomed the move, including those tired of evasive orderlies and the less than respectful attitude of imperial authorities. So too did several nurses from privileged backgrounds, including Elsie Cook, whose own marriage to an officer was in flagrant breach of AIF (Australian Imperial Force) standing orders. For the daughter-in-law of a former prime minister, the introduction of badges of rank, "used to indicate seniority within the Australian army and provide a hierarchical structure where members may be superior, equal or subordinate in rank," reflected her own social standing.[92]

But many nurses felt otherwise. Although "pips" on their uniforms offered new opportunities for some, they also regulated and restricted social behavior, in particular relationships between nurses and other ranks. "Matron gave us the biggest thunderbolt we have ever had," an indignant Annie Donnell wrote in her diary. "Now that you Sisters have been given the rank of Officers and wear Stars [she told us] you are not to go out with NCOs or privates or even speak to them except on duty." The response of one astonished sister suggests the way nurses continued to resist the imposition of military discipline and a rather self-serving view of the etiquette of uniform: "Could we dress up in Mufti [then] and go out with them[?]" Another pressed matron for a telling point of clarification. "I have a little Brother fighting in France that I haven't seen for 6 years. Does it mean that if he gets his furlough and comes over here I mustn't speak to him?"

Donnell's own response was more expansive. It again suggests ambivalence toward military structure and a need to negotiate the contradictory roles women experienced in wartime. Women may have donned a uniform, but in doing so, they had not discarded older identities as siblings and sweethearts. "We never asked for stars—in fact we dislike them. We have never received a commission from the King. We left Australia as Nursing Sisters and so we wish to be. . . . Our boys have left home and country to give their lives—if need be—in a strange land. Could we slight them so?"[93]

Commissions offended the democratic sensibilities of many nurses, some of whom fervently believed "we should all be one rank."[94] Finally, such distinctions jarred with the aesthetics of nursing, a sense of feminine "smartness" many of these women clearly valued. With so much metal pinned to their shoulders, one nurse disappointedly remarked, "I feel like an ironmongers shop."[95]

OUT OF LINE: THE ASSERTION OF WOMEN'S AGENCY

Jan Bassett has argued that one of the main reasons for the nurse's opposition to badges of rank was "their whole hearted acceptance of the ideology of separate spheres for men and women."[96] Perhaps that argument is overstated. Nursing (as we have seen) involved constant renegotiation of the boundaries that divided male and female spheres. Stepping into uniform, sisters entered a nebulous terrain, clouding any clear distinctions of gender and sexuality. But stepping *out* of uniform was also an option for nurses, and that move in and out of mufti also suggests other ways women evaded and subverted military culture. "Thou shalt not covet Civilian clothes" was one of the 10 shipboard commandments Elsie Tranter set down in her diary, "nor liberties, nor drinks, . . . for thou art on active service." Encoded in the uniform was strict self-denial, in particular a repudiation of female agency and sexuality. "Thou shalt not adulterate thy nurse's life with joy," the commandments continued, "Thou shalt not steal kisses in the dark, cosy corners on the deck or in covered areas."[97] But for Elsie and many of her contemporaries, the lure of life away from uniform was often irresistible.

There is a kind of bifurcation in the diaries and letters written by New Zealand and Australian nurses, regardless of which service they were attached to. Time in the ward and near the front lines was regulated by the exigencies of military service—it was uniformed. But hours outside the army were not. Elsie and her colleagues dressed in all manner of attire when not actually on duty. Photographs suggest a kaleidoscope of costume, elegant or intimate, practical or homely. Nurses on the voyage out delighted in shipboard concerts, one of the rare opportunities to wear "evening dress." "The Bluebirds," Elsie Cook scribbled excitedly in her diary, "gave a fancy dress Dance to the Grey Sisters. Great scheming and excitement over planning costumes."[98] And in Colombo, nurses slipped out of uniform and skipped gleefully into town. Many years later, Linda Watson still recalled a dinner dance put on by the "Tea Plantation Men": "Those in uniform could not attend, [but] there were a few of us who had evening frocks and I was one. We knew the Matrons would not know us so we were quite safe. [We] had great fun, they gave us French champagne."[99]

Shedding a uniform (despite or perhaps because its wearing was mandated) was a chance to escape the constraints Tranter referred to and to openly express one's sexuality. Often, that led to an open defiance of military authority. "I remember one sister leaving the steamer in Melbourne," Sister A.K. Isambert wrote, "with a low neck dress and turn down collar, in spite the fact she had been spoken to."[100] Lesser rebellions were no less eloquent. Craving feminine embellishment, Tranter and her friends "adorned" themselves with sprigs of wattle: "It looks quite gay in our scarlet capes" she noted, indulging a levity seldom seen in wartime.[101] Kit McNaughton may well have worn her war-torn uniform with pride, but the elegant shops of Paris full of "the loveliest of clothes" quickly seduced her.[102] Sometime later, she was posted to a rest home outside Boulogne, and there she resolved to escape uniform altogether. Women at the home faced the intrusive supervision of Lady Gifford, a typical lady bountiful, "all dressed up like a matron" and "drilling us like children": Nurses were repeatedly "strafed" for not wearing capes or for donning articles of mufti. McNaughton's response was to remove her cape and cap, then argue "in a very dignified manner" that officers did not wear belts off parade. "I'm afraid the old girl thinks the Australians rather beyond her," she wrote defiantly in her diary.[103]

The episode is rife with meaning. It attests an Irish Australian's contempt for the pretensions of "this Royal household," upholds the legitimacy of her own uniform, as opposed to the "lovely shade of grey" that impostor Lady Gifford got about in, and, most important of all perhaps, proclaimed her right to dress in uniform on terms of her own choosing. Whatever reading one chooses, uniform became a vehicle through which women asserted their agency in wartime.[104] Clearly, as Hertz has observed, personal motivation and intention gave uniforms a purpose never intended by their designers or regulators.[105] Uniform could even be molded to suit the wearer's mood. Tev Davies arranged no fewer than three studio photos, most in regulation dress: "Send the solemn one in uniform to Ida," she instructed her mother, "the smiling one in uniform and one without uniform to Nurse Werdenhofer Austin Hosp."[106]

THE MALE GAZE: UNIFORMS AS OBJECTS OF DESIRE

Army dress might seem solemn, but a uniform could also be sexualized, either by wearer or beholder. Klaus Theweleit has argued that the virginal white of a nurse's clothing was "a terrain for female fantasies."[107] There is ample evidence for that in the letters, journals, and scrapbooks kept by Australian nurses. Forward patients write verse, pen sketches, and compose letters that present their uniformed caregivers as objects of desire. *The Night Sister: or Eve,*

Figure 6.7.
Conflicting caricatures of women at war. A hospitalized patient's view of his nurses. Her uniform spans the male gaze—in one case attractive, in the other repugnant. National Library of Australia (MS 3637).

a pen and ink drawing by David Sharpie, is fairly typical. Here, the male patient is tucked tightly in his bed—a denial of agency and movement. The nurse, by contrast, plays the role of temptress, one leg raised ready to climb into his cot, a hand reaching out to pull down his bedclothes. The veiled nurse wears the semblance of a uniform, but her ward shoes sport a stylish high heel, and her gown reveals a shapely figure. As Katie Holmes's study of nurses' sexuality points out, this depiction of a uniformed woman as sexually active mirrors a disruption to the traditional order of gender roles common in the ward: "Women (nurses) carried the authority (and healing power), men (patients) were dependent and emasculated."[108]

Fantasies, by their very nature, need little grounding in reality. The rules governing relationships between men and women were strict; most stayed well within the boundaries. Nurses addressed their charges as "boys" (their own desexualization strategy) and played the part of sisters and mothers, rather than potential, flirtatious lovers. "Mother" and "sister" were likely roles; nursing staff were usually a good deal older than the men they cared for, and the busy wards they worked in were seldom steeped in romance. Nor is it entirely true that men were weakened by women's care. As Kirsty Harris has noted, nurses returned injured men to health, in effect restoring their masculinity.[109] But clearly, as Tranter's reference to "stealing kisses in the dark"[110] attests, men were also the objects of female desire, and outside the wards, the war did offer opportunities for sexual liaisons. Several nurses married former patients, even though it cost them dismissal from the service and the loss of that fetching uniform.[111] Men, for their part, presented uniformed women in different ways, ranging across relationships both real and imagined. *Oranges and Lemons* conveyed conflicting caricatures of women at war—one uniformed figure is a blushing comely nurse; the other is a stern, bespectacled matron.

"MINISTERING ANGELS"? THE RED CROSS, THE "ARMY IN WHITE," AND EMOTIONAL LABOR

Military nursing was the major field in which Australian and New Zealand women served abroad but not the only one. In the first year of the war, the Australian Red Cross set up headquarters in London. One voluntary bureau dealing with the search for the missing and a second arranging comforts for the prison camps were undertaken in close association with the military. For that, women thought it fitting to wear a uniform.

Historians have dubbed such work "emotional labour."[112] Sifting through conflicting accounts of a man's death in the battle and helping a distant family visualize and accept his loss built a rare bond of trust and intimacy. Red Cross women played the part of fictive kin, representing families at a grave they would never see, softening the cruelest blow of wartime.[113] In the case of prisoners of war, women provided physical aid as much as emotional comfort. A staggering 20,000 letters were answered every month, and most parcels contained the food and medicine that emaciated prisoners badly needed. Incarcerated men described Red Cross women as ministering angels: "We do appreciate everything you do," one wrote, "we know it is a labour of love."[114]

But that is not how these women necessarily saw themselves. Mary Chomley was in charge of over 30 volunteers and organized them with "the precision of a watch maker." Posing proudly in her uniform, she cuts a masculine figure of power and control. Her tailored blazer sports an officer's pips, the brim of her hat is as wide as a digger's, and a tie befits her methodical work in the office. Women like Mary Chomley challenged Edwardian conventions of femininity; her uniform claimed an authority and a purpose seldom seen before wartime. And like the sisters considered above, a rising sun badge was pinned to her lapel.[115]

Figure 6.8.
A masculine figure of power and control. Mary Chomley poses for a studio portrait in uniform. Courtesy State Library of Victoria (H2013.231/54).

New Zealand volunteers dressed in a similar style. Ettie Rout's service abroad negotiated the complex and contradictory roles of women's war work. On the one hand, her New Zealand Volunteer Sisterhood seems unexceptional. Like many patriotic leagues, it arranged outings for men, organized social events, and distributed comforts from home. But in Cairo and Paris, Rout also confronted "the social evil." Australian and New Zealand troops frequented bars and brothels, and many contracted venereal diseases. In response, Rout put together a prophylactic kit, issued condoms, and organized "safe" (that is to say, inspected) brothels. A committed feminist, Rout recognized the ravages gonorrhea and syphilis would wreak at home but was too much of a realist (and too little of a prude) to counsel restraint alone. For such unconventional work, Rout donned

Figure 6.9.
Complex and contradictory roles. Two images of Ettie Rout in uniform socializing with soldiers. One suggests sisterly companionship, the other sexual license. Courtesy Australian War Memorial (H03653 and H03654).

the Volunteer's Service uniform, borrowing from attire sported by Red Cross, YMCA, and Australian and New Zealand armed forces. There was nothing angelic about Ettie Rout's dress code; it was striking, practical, and imbued with the symbols of military authority. And Rout at once asserted and repressed female sexuality. One image of her in uniform is safe, comfortable, and domestic, seated passively beside "her" men, enjoying an innocent game of cards. The next is little short of Bacchanalian: Rout feeding grapes to soldiers lounging around her, their uniforms suggestively loose. Such were the extremes of uniformed women in wartime.[116]

For Rout, Chomley, and, indeed, most of the women featured in this volume, military clothing denoted work. But cross-dressing (commonplace throughout the war) reminds us of a uniform's recreational use. In New Zealand, the National Library and Te Papa, the museum of New Zealand, hold between them five professional studio photograph plates from the period of the Great War showing young women in men's military uniforms. Four of these five were acquired as part of liquidated photography studio stock sets. The fifth photograph, held by the National Library, was probably taken by an amateur and donated to a local library. Yet another photograph is held at the State Library of Victoria, a postcard-sized picture from the Great War showing two women in men's Australian Army clothing.[117]

Most of these photographs were professionally staged, and of the nine women featured, only one can be fully identified—Kathleen Veronica O'Brien.[118] All (bar a "Miss Wright" dressed in a sailor suit) are dressed in army kit.[119] Uniforms include the key unit signifiers, hat, badges, and belts, and all the women wear pants. Swagger sticks appear in three of the six photographs, and one (New Zealand) woman stands ready to draw a sword. Although many of the uniforms fit surprisingly well, at least three of the women wear tunics far too large (most notably Miss Wright in her navy jacket).[120]

These pictures raise more questions than answers. The time and monetary expense required for a professional photograph suggests that these were intentionally staged, especially those depicting two women, thus requiring multiple uniforms. Only the amateur photograph is explicitly of women in "costume." Far less rigid in composition, it shows women smoking comically large cigarettes and wearing the uniforms outside. Not incidentally, this is the only photograph to have been donated by relatives rather than acquired through a company. The silence around the production and use of these photographs is probably attributable to their nature. In private, the meanings of these images could be established through negotiation with no fear of public censure or criticism. Only one of these photographs shows women in a semipublic setting. Taken in the early days of the war (and long before the release of casualty lists), it has an almost playful character. We cannot say for certain why such photographs were taken, perhaps as an innocent distraction while a male relative or friend waited for his appointment, perhaps as keepsakes for men going overseas. Sweethearts or children could visually demonstrate their closeness through the intimacy of wearing their menfolk's clothing.

Clearly, not all uniforms donned in wartime involved a challenge to the gender order. Australasia's "Army in White" is a case in point. Throughout the war years, no fewer than 10,000 clubs, leagues, and societies produced comforts for soldiers, raised war funds, cooked meals, mounted entertainments, and recycled materials useful to the war effort. Much of this effort was undertaken by women in crisp white uniforms, "the noble duty of volunteer work" very much in keeping with normative female roles. South Australia's Cheer-Up Clubs were said to attract "winsome clear eyed girls, full of the sweetness and freshness of life." Dressed in ankle-length gowns with white veils sweeping back their hair and white aprons always at the ready, they cooked for and fed as many as 3,000 men in a month and washed a daunting pile of dishes afterward. Their saintly uniform and unblemished character ensured that "even the roughest men paid them the most studied respect."[121]

Here, too, uniform played a number of familiar roles. The Army in White tended the sick as did nurses; they rallied, marched in processions on Anzac Day, and performed the most menial duties with "utmost obedience."[122] A common uniform expressed "a great and glorious sisterhood." Social distinctions were said to go "by the board" as "ladies of leisure found themselves side-by-side with [young women] employed in offices."[123] Many of these claims are exaggerated; even in the most zealously patriotic circles, ladies held executive positions, whereas Cheer-Up girls scrubbed the dishes. But a uniform expressed a common identity. It was celebrated, commodified, and sometimes actively subverted. "Christmas stunts" were marked—predictably—by a concert, ham, and plum pudding. Less expected was the reversal of roles, where dazzling white Cheer-Ups sat down to "a splendid repast ... waited upon by men in Khaki." Women, it seems, were not alone in cross dressing:

> A feature of the afternoon was the "best dressed lady" . . . pride of place was unhesitatingly given to Trooper Thomas, whose saxe-blue coat and skirt was a dream, and his flaunting of it a delicious nightmare. When handed the trophy, "her" face was suffused with maiden like blushes, and the last I saw was a band of Cheer Ups carrying their "sister" off to be covered with complexion powder.[124]

Figure 6.10.
A great and glorious sisterhood. Cheer-Up workers flanked by boy scouts in Adelaide. Lined with memorial notices to the "fallen" and occupied by physically and mentally damaged men, work in the Cheer-Up Hut could not have been that cheerful. Courtesy State Library of South Australia (PRG 280/1/42/94).

Figure 6.11.
Induction in a military culture. Girls dressed in Red Cross uniforms assemble in readiness for Anzac Day. These children were charged with laying wreaths on war memorials in public rituals that valorized military service. Archives of the Australian Red Cross, New South Wales Division, 1914–2014, Vol. 10, Mitchell Library, PXE 1692.

Here again, uniform alerts us to a paradox in how gender identities were expressed and constructed. Patriotic work might be seen as a simple extension of women's traditional roles. Closely aligned with the female spheres of household and child care, it connotes women's powerlessness and isolation in war. But the Army in White suggests a rather different reading. Invested with emotional energy, even the most mundane work seemed valued and creative. And no less than men in war, a uniformed collective fostered a sense of fellowship and common purpose. Women may have tended to the needs of men, but they also took to the public sphere. Cheer-Ups were not confined to organizing concerts; they rallied in the streets in favor of conscription and raised thousands of pounds in support of the war effort. From an early age, children were inducted into a military culture, dressed in uniform, marshaled in units, and issued with wreaths to commemorate Anzac Day. In all this, we see what John Hutchison called "the militarisation of charity."[125] Patriotic work gave women a chance "to share in the great struggle," wearing a uniform distinctly their own.[126]

CRAVING KHAKI: PARAMILITARY GROUPS, CIVIL SERVICE, AND SPORTS

Australia and New Zealand's home front was thousands of miles from the nearest theater of war. That made the need to serve, and thus connect with menfolk fighting overseas, all the more urgent. Again, a uniform, and preferably one colored khaki, made that imagined kinship possible. But unlike nurses serving abroad (and a small contingent of Voluntary Aid Detachment workers), women at home had no official sanction to wear such a uniform.[127] To the contrary, military-style uniforms symbolized a desire to step outside the normal gender roles, and the right of women to wear them was fiercely contested. The Australian Women's Service Corps (AWSC) was one such discomforting organization seeking recognition, although many others existed (including the Khaki Girls of Victoria and the Woman's Khaki Corps of Western Australia). Branches of the AWSC were established across Australia, and as many as 700 women enrolled by mid-1917 in New South Wales and Queensland alone.[128]

The Australian Women's Service Corps was not content with the charity work expected of most Australian women. Craving proximity to the war, they petitioned to be allowed military rear-echelon jobs in England, Australia, and France. A range of duties—cooking, clerking, and driving—would free manpower to fight at the front.[129] Wearing "rough uniforms" to mark out their willingness to serve and undertaking "physical culture classes" to prepare their bodies for the rigors of possible war work, the AWSC women held frequent meetings and repeatedly lobbied for official status as military auxiliaries.[130] The Sydney branch, commanded by the formidable Miss Eleanor Jacob, set about proving their resolve by clearing 5 imperial tons of tree roots from Frenchs Forest in New South Wales, in uniform.[131] "Home life is dull," one khaki-clad woman was heard to remark, "anyone can . . . knit socks. [We are] meant for something bigger."[132] Repeated applications for war work caused considerable discomfort in governmental circles, and the use of the masculine and privileged color, khaki, infuriated some veterans' groups. The Woman's Khaki Corps of Western Australia created enough ire among returned AIF men that they petitioned the state premier for the organization to be banned.[133] The Australian Defence Department consistently declined the AWSC women's attempts to gain meaningful war-related military employment.[134] "The Woman's Service Corps in Sydney . . . offers its services to the nation, and the offer is declined with thanks," wrote one frustrated commentator in the woman's section of the Melbourne edition of *Punch*. "Federal authorities say there are no positions available wherein the services of women can be utilised. . . . We cannot believe it."[135]

Men, for their part, could not believe any kind of uniform suited "the gentler sex" for active service. "It seems absurd to picture these gentle hearted women roughing it with the boys in muddy dugouts and trenches," a columnist in the *Soldier* wrote:

> I wondered what prompted the idea until Miss Jacob explained: 'When I went to "The Great Push" [propaganda film screened across the Empire] one thing struck me particularly: I noticed a man, and the back of his pants wanted a patch. I thought there is work waiting for the Women's Battalion.' So, . . . if you find a [queer] battalion coming in from the rear with needles thimbles and thread, you will remember I gave you earlier intimation.[136]

The satire was pointed. The proper role for women was the knitting of socks at home, not dramatic female gestures in the war zone. In Britain, "khaki fever" (as it came to be called) had to be channeled and regulated. In Australia and New Zealand, there was even less tolerance of dress, work, or behavior that breached binary codes of gender identity.[137]

In Britain, women wore uniforms in a host of civil occupations. In New Zealand, the superintendent of police quashed the idea of female police officers as a "folly." In Australia, the idea of female police officers did see limited implementation during the war years.[138] In July 1915, the first female police were recruited in New South Wales after years of agitation by organizations such as the National Council of Women. Four more states would also recruit women police by the end of 1917.[139] But none of these women wore uniforms. The idea of placing a masculine police uniform on a female body was denounced immediately in the Australian press. "Before long the visiting Sydneyite will see the spectacle of a lot of hard-faced, hardhearted hussies patrolling the streets of the Southern capital," wrote the *Sydney Stock and Station Journal*. "It would be funny if it were not so pathetic."[140] Other newspapers openly mocked the idea of a female uniformed police officer:

> We see her garbed in uniform
> A figure trim and neat
> Replica, of a bobby bold
> But minus bobby's feet . . .
> At night where will her duty lie?
> We long to know the street
> Where Jane with baton, cuffs, and all
> Will pace upon her beat.[141]

The introduction of uniforms for Australian female police officers began only in 1951, with the last state adopting them in 1978.[142]

Government-owned trains and tramways offered another potential avenue of uniformed work for Australian and New Zealand women, as did postal work. These uniforms were imbued with patriotic symbolism. The jobs they symbolized were deemed essential. In New Zealand, women actively agitated for the right to work as conductors, and many hoped to follow the example of their sex in Britain. "Owing to my misfortune in not being born a boy," one young woman argued to the Tramway Board, "the next best thing would be to offer my services as a tramcar driver or conductor, to take the place of one who wishes to go and fight for his country."[143] Three other women also offered their services on the same day. On a national level, the Woman's National Reserve determined to provide qualified female railway workers for service and duly provided instruction to women in motor mechanics.[144] But it was all to no avail. In this sphere, as many others, efforts to wear a uniform were stymied.

Uniforms for New Zealand and Australian private sector workers also remained surprisingly static during the war. Subtle uniforms in the form of dress codes already existed for domestic servants, waitresses, and shop assistants. De facto uniforms were also suggested for wartime office workers and clerks. "Women have not until lately flocked to business and professions in such numbers that their dress was in any way of importance," wrote one anonymous woman in a Sydney newspaper, but now "it is more than likely that women's dress will be standardised, either officially or by tacit consent."[145] Other women wrote of the difficulties of sustaining clothing on par with male office worker standards on the lower wages earned by females.[146] That said, formal uniforms, or even dress codes stronger than those found before the war, did not appear during the period 1914–1918 in New Zealand or Australia.

Sport offered yet another arena for women to wear uniform. Against a backdrop of class issues in general and the conscription debates in particular, large department stores in Perth sponsored workplace Australian rules football. These female-only games could draw large crowds: The *West Australian* reported ticket sales fetching over £60 for one match in 1917.[147] Matches often doubled as fund-raisers, recruitment drives, and conscription rallies.[148] Male sport was criticized for keeping men from service overseas; female sport was seen as supporting the war effort. But women took up the game (and donned the uniform) for other reasons as well. "Although the patriotic imperative was clearly a strong factor in the women's matches," Peter Burk notes, "games played between the unionized workroom women and the women of the shop floor at Foy and Gibson [also] gave vent to the traditional workplace jealousies . . . between the working-class factory employees and the lower middle-class shop employees."[149] No similar sporting teams were sponsored in New Zealand; the lack of large-scale industrial employment, coupled with the contrastingly smooth implementation of conscription, probably worked against similar sporting incursions across the Tasman.

WHAT SERVING IN UNIFORM MEANT TO WOMEN

This chapter began on the streets of London, with May Tilton "venturing forth resplendent" in her army nurse's uniform. It ends in that same city with Laura Grubb awaiting repatriation in 1919. "I hope you are not worrying about me being let loose in this alarming place," she wrote home to her mother within weeks of the war ending, "Everyone is wonderfully good to us because we are Australians and our boys have made a name to be proud of. I'm very glad I'm in an Australian uniform."[150]

For Sister Laura Grubb, wearing a uniform laid her own small claim to war service. It symbolized duty, patriotism, and self-sacrifice; it also signaled loyalty to nation and fidelity to empire. But women's place in war was still not the same as men's. A nurse was not quite the equal of an Anzac. Grubb believed her countrymen had won a name "to be proud of." Wearing their uniform allowed them to bask in their reflected glory. But that may be far too dismissive a reading. As we have demonstrated, donning a uniform in wartime opened up possibilities unimaginable in peacetime, enabling women in diverse and complex ways. Grubb had traveled the world, seized positions of influence and authority, witnessed first-hand the struggles of great armies and the shaping of history. Her uniform may have embodied its own constraints and located her within a male hierarchy, but it also let Grubb loose on the world stage, affirmed and empowered her. Most important of all, Grubb and the women she served with wore uniform in ways that best suited themselves. The uniform became a costume to play out a role they themselves determined.

The extent to which the experience of war changed women's status in Australia and New Zealand is a subject of ongoing debate for historians. Similar questions have been posed by all the contributors to this volume. What is beyond dispute is that what John Horne has called the "demoblisation" of war cultures was neither simple nor inevitable.[151] And neither nurse nor war worker nor any of the uniformed women examined in this chapter would return very easily to the restrictive roles of prewar society.

NOTES

The authors thank the editors and contributors for insightful comment on this article. This research was partly funded by an Australian Research Council Grant LP110100264 exploring the Anzac mythology, and we thank Jayne Regan for her valuable assistance.

1. May Tilton, *The Grey Battalion* (Sydney: Angus & Robertson, 1933), 139–146. See also Susan R. Grayzel, "'The Outward and Visible Sign of Her Patriotism': Women, Uniforms, and National Service during the First World War," *Twentieth Century British History* 8, no. 2 (Jan. 1997), 146.

2. Elsie Tranter, diary, 27 Feb. 1917, 3DRL 4081, Australian War Memorial, Canberra (hereafter AWM).

3. Lucy Noakes, *Women and the British Army: War and the Gentle Sex, 1907–1948* (London: Routledge, 2006), 20.

4. Margaret Vining and Barton C. Hacker, "From Camp Follower to Lady in Uniform: Women, Social Class and Military Institutions before 1920," *Contemporary European History* 10, no. 3 (Nov. 2001): 360; Elizabeth S. Rogerson, 41 1032, AWM.

5. For a pioneering British study, see Angela Woollacott, *On Her Their Lives Depend: Munitions Workers in the Great War* (Berkley: University of California Press, 1994). See also Susan R. Grayzel, *Women and the First World War* (London: Pearson Education, 2002); Gail Braybon, *Women Workers in the First World War* (London: Routledge. 1989); Deborah Thom, *Nice Girls and Rude Girls: Women Workers in World War 1* (New York: I.B. Tauris, 1998). A small number of Australian women did work in small arms factories in Victoria and New South Wales; see Bruce Scates and Raelene Frances, *Women and the Great War* (Cambridge: Cambridge University Press, 1997), ch. 3.

6. Raelene Frances, "Women's Mobilization for War (Australia)," in *1914-1918-Online: International Encyclopedia of the First World War*, ed. Ute Daniel, Peter Gatrell, Oliver Janz, Heather Jones, Jennifer Keene, Alan Kramer, and Bill Nasson (Berlin: Freie Universität Berlin, 18 Dec. 2014), https://doi.org/10.15463/ie1418.10516.

7. Susan R. Grayzel, *Women's Identity at War: Gender, Motherhood, and Politics in Britain and France during the First World War* (Chapel Hill: University of North Carolina Press, 1999).

8. Barton C. Hacker, "Reformers, Nurses, and Ladies in Uniform," in *A Companion to Women's Military History*, ed. Barton C. Hacker and Margaret Vining (Leiden: Brill, 2012), 137–138.

9. Selena Estelle Williams, "'Taking the Long Journey': Australian Women Who Served with Allied Countries and Paramilitary Organisations during World War One" (Ph.D. diss., Australian National University, 2015), "Introduction"; Janet Lee, *War Girls: The First Aid Nursing Yeomanry in the First World War* (Manchester: Manchester University Press, 2005).

10. "In the Harbour City," *Punch* (Melbourne), 11 May 1916, 11; for the case of soldier stowaway Maud Butler, see Bruce Scates and Raelene Frances, *Women and the Great War* (Cambridge: Cambridge University Press, 1997), 43–44.

11. The literature is extensive. Key texts include Marianne Barker, *Nightingales in the Mud: The Digger Sisters of the Great War 1914–1918* (Sydney: Allen & Unwin, 1989); Jan Bassett, *Guns and Brooches: Australian Army Nursing from the Boer War to the Gulf War* (Melbourne: Oxford University Press, 1992), 31–9; Scates and Frances, *Women and the Great War*, ch. 2; Anna Rogers, *While You're Away: New Zealand Nurses at War, 1899–1948* (Auckland: Auckland University Press, 2003); Ruth Rae, *Scarlet Poppies: The Army Experience of Australian Nurses during World War One* (Sydney: College of Nursing, 2004); Janet Butler, *Kitty's War: The Remarkable Wartime Experiences of Kit McNaughton* (Brisbane: University of Queensland Press, 2013); Melanie Oppenheimer, *Oceans of Love: Narelle—An Australian Nurse in World War I* (Sydney: ABC Books, 2006); Kirsty Harris, *More Than Bombs and Bandages: Australian Army Nurses at Work in World War 1* (Newport, N.S.W., Australia: Big Sky, 2011); Peter Rees, *Other Anzacs: Nurses at War, 1914–18* (Crows Nest, N.S.W., Australia: Allen & Unwin, 2008). For recent work, see Jaclyn Hopkins, "'Not

Like Ordinary Times': Aspects of Australian Nurses' Experiences during the Great War" (B.A. honors thesis, University of Wollongong, 2014).

12. For example, fewer than 10 women are represented in Peter Jackson's Great War Exhibition in Wellington.

13. Jennifer Craik, *Uniforms Exposed: From Conformity to Transgression* (Oxford: Berg, 2005).

14. May Ashton, letter, 13 Sept. 1915, PR 88/25, AWM.

15. Barton C. Hacker and Margaret Vining, "Cutting a New Pattern: Uniforms and Women's Mobilization for War, 1854–1919," *Textile History* 41, no. 1 (May 2010): 110.

16. "Voluntary Nursing Sisters," *Wellington Press,* 6 Aug. 1915, 5. Australian nurses resented any similarity between Voluntary Aid Detachment uniforms and their own; see Melanie Oppenheimer, *Red Cross VAs: A History of the VAD Movement in New South Wales* (Walcha, N.S.W., Australia: Ohio Productions, 1999), 21; Rupert Goodman, *Voluntary Aid Detachments in Peace and War* (Brisbane: Boolarong Publications, 1991).

17. "Woman and Uniform Dress," *Barrier Miner* (Broken Hill), 14 Aug. 1915, 7.

18. Craik, *Uniforms Exposed,* 5.

19. E.M. Paten, "Reminiscences of Nursing," 3DRL 4145, AWM; Anne Donnell, circular letter with diary, MSS 1022, 91, Mitchell Library, Sydney (hereafter ML).

20. Irene Bonnin, letter, 3 Oct. 1915, PRG621/19, State Library of South Australia, Adelaide; G. Douglas, 41 969, AWM, Butler Collection of nurse narratives.

21. Beatrice Glasson Club, 41 1033, AWM, Butler Collection of nurse narratives.

22. N.F.S. Smith, 41 966, AWM, Butler Collection of nurse narratives; Papers of Minnie Schrader, Hermann Schrader Collection, MS 9734, National Library of Australia, Canberra.

23. See reminiscences by Grace Wilson, *Women's Day and Home,* June 1953, clipping in 3DRL 7819, AWM.

24. Matron Kellett, 41 175, AWM, Butler Collection of nurse narratives.

25. Olive Haynes, letter, 11 Mar. 1917, in *We Are Here, Too: The Diaries and Letters of Sister Olive L.C. Haynes, November 1914 to February 1918,* ed. Margaret O. Young (Adelaide: Australian Down Syndrome Incorporated, 1991), 197 (all subsequent citations of Haynes are taken from this anthology); Report of Matron, H.H.A.H.S. Kanowna, 41 1072, AWM.

26. Elsie Eglinton, letter, 7 Nov. 1914, PR 86/068, AWM; note similar variation in gray bonnets and white caps, Evelyn Davies, letter, 2 May 1915, AANS, AIF, 3 DRL 3398B, AWM.

27. Vining and Hacker, "From Camp Follower to Lady in Uniform," 363.

28. Hester Maclean, *New Zealand Army Nurses* (Auckland: Whitcombe & Tombs, 1923), 89.

29. Elsie Eglinton Papers, letter, 25 Dec. 1915, PR 86/068, AWM.

30. Peter Dennis, Jeffrey Grey, Evan Morris, Robin Prior, and Jean Bou, *The Oxford Companion to Australian Military History* (Melbourne: Oxford University Press, 2008), 36–37; E.M. Paten, "Reminiscences of Nursing," 3DRL 4145, AWM.

31. Matron Kellett, 41 175, AWM, Butler Collection of nurse narratives.

32. Craig Wilcox, *Badge, Boot and Button: The Story of Australian Uniforms* (Canberra: National Library of Australia, 2107), 65.

33. Evelyn Davies, "Just a Little Book to Keep a Record of Our Doings," 3 DRL 3398B, AWM.

34. Katie Holmes, "Day Mothers and Night Sisters: World War 1 Nurses and Sexuality," in *Gender and War: Australians at War in the Twentieth Century,* ed. Joy Damousi and Marilyn Lake (Cambridge: Cambridge University Press, 1995), 43–59.

35. C.E. Strom, diary, 9 June 1918, 41 1068, AWM.

36. G. Douglas, 41 969, AWM, Butler Collection of nurse narratives.

37. Elsie Sheppard Cook, diary, 14 Aug. 1915, PR 82/135, AWM; Evelyn Davies, letter, 21 July 1917, 3 DRL 3398B, AWM.

38. "Australian Sisters in England," *Una,* 29 July 1916, 109; "A Protest from Our Nurses," *Leader* (Orange), 8 Dec. 1916, 3. We thank Kirsty Harris and Craig Wilcox, respectively, for these references.

39. E.J. Gould, 41 975, AWM, Butler Collection of nurse narratives.

40. Susan J. Neuhaus and Sharon Mascall-Dare, *Not for Glory: A Century of Service by Medical Women to the Australian Army and Its Allies* (Brisbane: Salisbury, 2014).

41. Scates and Frances, *Women and the Great War,* 26.

42. Laura Grubb, letter, 21 June 1918, PR 83/40, AWM.

43. Carrie Hertz, "The Uniform: As Material, as Symbol, as Negotiated Object," *Midwestern Folklore* 32, nos. 1–2 (2007): 43. We thank Cynthia Toman for drawing this source to our attention.

44. M. Brown, 41 947, AWM, Butler Collection of nurse narratives.

45. N.F.S. Smith, 41 1045, AWM, Butler Collection of nurse narratives.

46. Evelyn Davies, letter, 19 Nov. 1915, 3 DRL 3398B, AWM.

47. Bassett, *Guns and Brooches,* 48. See also Alice McConnell, *Lemnos–Gallipoli, 1915: Women in War* (Richmond, Australia: Artek Productions, 2015), chs. 3–5.

48. Anne Donnell, circular letter with diary, MSS 1022, 69, ML.

49. E. Henson, letter, 23 Nov. 1915, DRL 4063, AWM.

50. Evelyn Davies, letter, 12 Nov. 1915, 3 DRL 3398B, AWM.

51. Louise Young, published letter to her sister, *Sydney Morning Herald,* 2 Feb. 1916. We thank Alice McConnell for this reference.

52. Evelyn Davies, letter, 29 Feb. 1916, 3 DRL 3398B, AWM.

53. Fay Mackellar, 41 1001, AWM, Butler Collection of nurse narratives.

54. L.M. Payne, 41 1020, AWM.

55. Evelyn Davies, letters, 12 and 24 Nov. 1916, 3 DRL 3398B, AWM. Some departures from ward dress imperiled nurses. "In the malaria season we were supposed to wear veils, long gloves and putties," one nurse remembered from her time on Lemnos, "which made it quite impossible to carry out our duties." Discarding such protective garb to attend to "vomiting men" exposed them all to infection (L.T. Armstrong, 41 941, AWM, Butler Collection of nurse narratives).

56. B.A. Taylor, 41 1049, AWM.

57. E. Vickers Foote, 41 1054, AWM.

58. Muriel Doherty, 41 966, AWM.

59. Diary of Kit McNaughton, cited in Butler, *Kitty's War,* 189.

60. Olive Saloway, letter, 21 Feb. 1918, Saloway Papers, MS 6442, National Library of Australia, Canberra.

61. Orders cited by Rupert Goodman, *Our War Nurses: The History of the Royal Australian Army Nursing Corps* (Brisbane: Boolarong, 1988), 86.

62.Patriotic Badge, REL 28323, AWM. We thank Kirsty Harris for this reference.

63. Evelyn Davies, letter, 14 Dec. 1916, 3 DRL 3398B, AWM.

64. Laura Grubb, letter, 1 July 1918, PR 83/4, AWM.

65. Diary of Kit McNaughton, cited in Butler, *Kitty's War,* 94.

66. Laura Grubb, diary, 8 July 1917, PR 83/4, AWM.

67. C.E. Strom, 41 1068, AWM, Butler Collection of nurse narratives.

68. Laura Grubb, letter, 21 Aug. 1917, PR 83/4, AWM.

69. C.E. Strom, 41 1068, AWM, Butler Collection of nurse narratives.

70. Craik, *Uniforms Exposed*, 5–8

71. Elsie Tranter, diary, 1 July 1917, 3DRL 4081, AWM; Tilton, *The Grey Battalion,* 201.

72. Nurses were aware of the many different national components of that legion of khaki, and many took to collecting cap badges. Writing some years after the end of hostilities, Sister E.G. Dobson confessed she had "many souvenirs of that time—capbadges from almost every Canadian regiment-, but I could not remember the history of each badge, each scrap of war" (E.G. Dobson, 41 964, AWM, Butler Collection of nurse narratives).

73. Anne Donnell, circular letter with diary, MSS 1022, 47, ML. Uniform facilitated mutual recognition. Note Jean Bisset's experience as she approached an AIF soldier boarding a hospital ship off Gallipoli. "'I see you've got an Australian hat. Are you from Australia?' The man's face broke out in a smile, 'Yes, and I noticed your badge the minute I saw you.'" Jean Bisset, "Letter from Sister Bisset," *Una*, 29 Jan. 1916, 346.

74. Nellie Crommelin, undated press clipping, PROOO65, AWM.

75. Elsie Sheppard Cook, diary, 13 July 1916, PR/82, AWM; Melanie Oppenheimer, "Gifts for France: Australian Red Cross Nurses in France, 1916–1919," *Journal of Australian Studies* 17, no. 39 (Dec. 1993): 65–78.

76. Vining and Hacker, "From Camp Follower to Lady in Uniform," 357–358. For the wartime transformation of the Red Cross in Australia, see Melanie Oppenheimer, *The Power of Humanity: 100 Years of the Australian Red Cross* (Melbourne: HarperCollins, 2014).

77. Nellie Crommelin, letters, 4 Jan. and 3 and 14 Apr. 1915, PROOO65, AWM.

78. Crommelin, letters, 22 and 27 Mar. 1918, PROOO65, AWM.

79. Crommelin, letter, 14 Apr. 1918, PROOO65, AWM.

80. See, e.g., the work of Norman Lindsay, *Bulletin* (Sydney), 29 July 1915; Nicoletta F. Gullace, *The Blood of Our Sons* (New York: Palgrave Macmillan, 2002), 3, 150.

81. Elsie Tranter, diary, 25 Dec. 1916, 3DRL 4081, AWM; Joy Damousi, "'Marching to Different Drums': Women's Moblisations 1914–1939," in *Gender Relations in Australia: Domination and Negotiation*, ed. Kay Saunders and Raymond Evans (Sydney: Harcourt Brace Jovanovich, 1992), 357.

82. Wilcox, *Badge, Boot and Button*, 39.

83. Anne Donnell, circular letter with diary, MSS 1022, ML.

84. F.G. Gregson, 41 977, AWM, Butler Collection of nurse narratives.

85. Anne Donnell, circular letter with diary, MSS 1022, 30, ML.

86. L.M. Loxton, scrapbook entry for 6 Mar. [1917], 2DRL/1172, AWM.

87. Elsie Cook, diary, PR 82/135, AWM; Butler, *Kitty's War*, 101. McNaughton was obliged to remove her cape. The nurses' "grey Quaker like figures" were much stared at.

88. Narrative of a sister in the AANS, 41 1069, AWM.

89. Evelyn Davies, 23 Oct. 1916, 3 DRL 3398B, AWM.

90. E. Vickers Foote, 41 1054, AWM. British nurses had better uniform entitlements than Australian nurses. The former were provided with a uniform and allowed £10 a year for replacements. An initial grant of less than £21 for the AANS proved woefully inadequate; "Uniform, Pay and Allowances, Nurses, AIF"; "List of Articles to be Supplied by the Department to Nurses or Their Equivalent Cost"; Laura Grubb, letters and diaries, PR 83/40, AWM.

91. Evelyn Davies, letter, 15 July 1915, 3 DRL 3398B, AWM.

92. Elsie Cook, diary, PR 82/ 135, AWM; L.I. Terrett and S.C. Taubert, *Preserving Our Proud Heritage: The Customs and Traditions of the Australian Army* (Sydney: Big Sky, 2011), 55.

93. Anne Donnell, circular letter with diary, MSS 1022, 138–139, ML.

94. Muriel Knox Doherty, letter, 16 June 1918, papers, 3DRL 2518/1, AWM.

95. Mimie Proctor, letter, 1 Oct. 1916, as cited by Bassett, *Guns and Brooches*, 55.

96. Bassett, *Guns and Brooches*, 55.

97. Elsie Tranter, diary, 18 Jan. 1917, 3DRL 4081, AWM.

98. Elsie Cook, diary, PR 82/ 135, AWM.

99. Linda Watson, diary, 12 June 1917, PR01246, AWM.

100. A.K. Isambert, 41 982, AWM, Butler Collection of nurse narratives.

101. Elsie Tranter, diary, 18 Jan. 1917 and 26 Jan. 1918, 3DRL 4081, AWM.

102. Diary of Kit McNaughton, cited in Butler, *Kitty's War*, 117.

103. Butler, *Kitty's War*, 154.

104. Butler, *Kitty's War*, 154.

105. Hertz, "The Uniform," 45, 53.

106. Evelyn Davies, letter, 20 May 1915, 3 DRL 3398B, AWM.

107. Klaus Theweleit, *Male Fantasies*, vol. 1, *Women, Floods, Bodies, History*, trans. Chris Turner, Carter Erica, and Stephen Conway (Minneapolis: University of Minnesota Press, 1987), 126. We owe this reference to Katie Holmes.

108. Holmes, "Day Mothers, Night Sisters," 55, 57.

109. Harris, *More Than Bombs and Bandages*, ch. 6.

110. Elsie Tranter, diary, 18 Jan. 1917, 3DRL 4081, AWM.

111. Ruth Rae notes that around 100 nurses left the service to marry "and how many had sexual relations outsides the confines of marriage is impossible to estimate," *Scarlet Poppies*, 159.

112. Bruce Scates, "'The Unknown Sock Knitter': Voluntary Work, Emotional Labour, Bereavement and the Great War," *Labour History*, 81 (Nov. 2001): 29–50.

113. Jay Winter, *Sites of Memory, Sites of Mourning: The Great War in European Cultural History* (Cambridge: Cambridge University Press, 1995), ch. 2; Bruce Scates, *Return to Gallipoli: Walking the Battlefields of the Great War* (Cambridge: Cambridge University Press, 2006), ch. 1.

114. Nola Anderson, "Dear Miss Chomley," *Wartime*, no. 21 (2003): 45; Wat Finley to Mary Chomley, 15 July 1918, Papers of Miss M.E. Chomley, Australian Red Cross Society, POW section, 1DRL615 [749/19/20], folder 3, AWM.

115. Bruce Scates, Rebecca Wheatley, and Laura James, *World War One: A History in 100 Stories* (Melbourne: Penguin, 2015), 173–183. We thank Jo Kildea for alerting us to the files above.

116. Ettie Rout, *Two Years in Paris* (London: E. Hornibrook, 1923); Scates et al., *World War One*, 70–73.

117. Te Papa collection, "Departing Shots: Berry & Co Portraits of World War One Soldiers," http://collections.tepapa.govt.nz/Topic/648 (accessed 27 February 2017); "Half-Length Portrait of Two Young Women in Military Uniform," 1916, H99.218/51, State Library of Victoria.

118. Te Papa collection, "Departing Shots: Berry & Co Portraits of World War One Soldiers," http://collections.tepapa.govt.nz/Topic/648 (accessed 27 February 2017); Te Papa collection, "Portrait of Kathleen Veronica O'Brien, Wearing a Soldier's Uniform," 1914, B.046503.

119. Te Papa collection, "Miss Wright," ca. 1920, B.044230; Te Papa collection, "Woman Dressed as a Regimental Sergant-Major of the NZ Rifle Brigade [inscribed Johnson]," 1915–1919, B.044278.

120. "Two Women Wearing World War 1 Soldier's Uniforms," 1914, Strand Collection, ref. no. 1/2-125254-F, National Library of New Zealand; "Studio Portrait of Two Unidentified Young Women in World War 1 Soldier's Uniforms," n.d. [ca. 1914–1926], ref. no. 1/2-185135-G, National Library of New Zealand.

121. Frederick J. Mills, *Cheer Up: A Story of War Work* (Adelaide: Cheer-Up Society, 1917), 24.

122. Mills, *Cheer Up*, 192.

123. Mills, *Cheer Up*, 27.

124. Mills, *Cheer Up*, 32.

125. John Hutchison, *Champions of Charity: War and the Rise of the Red Cross* (Boulder, Colo.: Westview Press, 1996); Scates, "The Unknown Sock Knitter," 43–45; Joan Beaumont, "Whatever Happened to Patriotic Women, 1914–1918," *Australian Historical Studies* 31, no. 115 (Oct. 2000): 273–287.

126. H. E. Harbutt, "Vaucluse," *Red Cross Record* (Sydney) 2, no. 1, 12 Jan. 1916, 31.

127. "Letters from a V.A. Who Went with Detachment to Serve under B.R.C.S at Their Invitation," *Red Cross Record* (Sydney) 3, no. 2, 2 Feb. 1917, 34.

128. "Willing Women Workers," *Punch* (Melbourne), 11 Jan. 1917, 5.

129. "Australian Women's Service Corps," *Evening News* (Sydney), 8 June 1918, 4.

130. "Australian Women's Service Corps," *Queensland Times* (Ipswich), 2 Feb. 1918, 6.

131. "Woman War Workers," *West Australian* (Perth), 4 May 1917, 9.

132. "Women and the Firing Line," *Sydney Mail*, 7 Mar. 1917, 21.

133. "Condensed Correspondence," *West Australian* (Perth), 18 July 1917, 8.

134. "Women Offer Service," *Kalgoorlie Miner*, 28 July 1917, 6.

135. "Willing Women Workers," *Punch* (Melbourne), 11 Jan. 1917, 5.

136. Vera, "From One Nurse to Another," *Soldier* 1, no. 20, 10 Nov. 1916, 17.

137. The literature is extensive; see Angela Woollacott, "'Khaki Fever' and Its Control: Gender, Class, Age and Sexual Morality on the British Home Front during the First World War," *Journal of Contemporary History* 29, no. 2 (Apr. 1994): 325–347; Viviene Cree, "'Khaki Fever' during the First World War: A Historical Analysis of Social Works' Approach towards Young Women, Sex and Moral Danger," *British Journal of Social Work* 46, no. 7 (Oct. 2015): 1839–1854; Janet S.K. Watson, "Khaki Girls, VADs, and Tommy's Sisters: Gender and Class in First World War Britain," *International History Review* 19, no. 1 (Feb. 1997): 32–51; Lucy Noakes, "Eve in Khaki: Women Working with the British Military, 1915–1918," in *Women and Work Culture: Britain, 1850–1950*, ed. Krista Cowman and Louise A. Jackson (Aldershot, U.K.: Ashgate, 2005), 213–228.

138. "Policewomen," *Marlborough Express*, 18 Oct. 1916, 8; Raelene Frances and Bruce Scates, *Women at Work in Australia from the Gold Rushes to World War II* (Cambridge: Cambridge University Press, 1993), 120–121.

139. Tim Prenzler, *One Hundred Years of Women Police in Australia* (Samford Valley, Qld.: Australian Academic Press, 2015), 3. A table lists when other states allowed policewomen: South Australia in Dec. 1915, Victoria in July 1917, Western Australia in Sept. 1917, and Tasmania in Oct. 1917.

140. "Women in the Force," *Sydney Stock and Station Journal*, 4 Aug. 1914, 4.

141. "Current Comment," *Mail* (Adelaide), 28 Feb. 1914, 8.

142. Prenzler, *One Hundred Years of Women Police in Australia*, 82.

143. "Recruiting," *Otago Daily Times*, 3 Nov. 1915, 10.

144. [Untitled], *Sun* (Sydney), 9 Feb. 1917, 6.

145. "Woman's Dress," *Mercury* (Hobart), 22 Dec. 1917, 11.

146. "Woman Worker's Uniform Wanted," *Inverall Times*, 29 Nov. 1918, 3.

147. "Ladies Fancy Dress Match," *West Australian* (Perth), 1 Oct. 1917, 5.

148. Peter Burke, "A Social History of Workplace Australian Football" (Ph.D. diss., RMIT University, 2008), 157.

149. Burke, "Workplace Australian Football," 156.

150. Laura Grubb, letter, 28 Feb. 1919, PR 83/40, AWM.

151. John Horne, "Demobilizing the Mind: France and the Legacy of the Great War, 1919–1939," *French History and Civilization* 2 (2009): 101–119.

SEVEN

MADEMOISELLES IN UNIFORM

Women Employed by the French Army during the Great War

MARGARET H. DARROW

Files of the French army's Automobile Service contain publicity stills of a young woman in a tailored coat, skirt, and beret. In one photograph, her hand grasps the starter crank of a truck; in another, she pours petrol into its tank.[1] She is, supposedly, one of the 300 or so women employed by the French army as drivers during the Great War. But how many women drivers ever wore this uniform is unclear. The Ministry of War took a year to decide that the women drivers needed a uniform and several more months to design it, and in all probability, the war ended before many of these snappy suits were delivered to the women. Nonetheless the decision that some army-employed women should wear uniforms was significant; a uniform implied that the woman who wore it was part of the military, performing military duties. As many of the articles in this collection demonstrate, this was everywhere a controversial premise, but it carried particular risk in France. Unlike Britain and its dominions and the United States, in the nineteenth century, France had instituted universal male conscription. In French republican ideology developed since the French Revolution, military service justified political rights, in particular the right to vote, that were denied to French women. Uniformed women military drivers, although few in number, opened perspectives that, unsurprisingly, the French army was anxious to contain.

Figure 7.1.
A driver for the French army posing in her new uniform, January 1918. © Musée d'histoire contemporaine-BDIC, reproduction by Archipel.

WORKING FOR THE ARMY

For most of the nineteenth century, the French army had informally employed women, disparagingly called camp followers, to provide a variety of services to soldiers: food, laundry, nursing, and sex. The Ministry of War also officially authorized a few women as *cantinières*, sutlers, assigned to each regiment, to sell food, tobacco, and liquor. These women accompanied the regiment on maneuvers and to war. By mid-century, they had acquired picturesque costumes, usually a skirted version of the regiment's uniform and had become familiar figures in popular culture. However, as Barton Hacker and Margaret Vining (ch. 1) note, this was their swan song. Prussia's crushing victories over the Habsburg Empire in 1866 and over

France in 1871 led to major military reforms in both defeated countries that purged women from their armies. By the summer of 1914, only a few *cantinières* remained in the French army, all of them elderly, confined to the garrison and deprived of their uniforms.[2]

In the spring and summer of 1915, a shortage of manpower coupled with a push for efficiency led the Ministry of War to contemplate hiring women once again, although in an entirely new and modern role: Ministry circulars mentioned women only as appendages to typewriters! By late fall, however, General Gallieni, minister of war, was thinking more broadly of women's potential usefulness to the army. He ordered regional commanders to envision "the replacement of military personnel by women in all possible posts and employment."[3] By 1917, the army was employing some 150,000 women in a wide variety of jobs such as clerical workers, telephone and telegraph operators, laundresses, cooks, cleaners, warehouse workers, carpenters, and drivers, but always as civilians and never in uniform.

Unlike the Russian army, which, in 1917, enrolled women in combat battalions, and the British and American militaries, which created women's auxiliaries for noncombat duties, the French Ministry of War refused to militarize women, even as auxiliaries. The ministry firmly rebuffed requests for enlistment by women pilots.[4] At least one women's volunteer battalion, the Volunteer Corps of French and Belgian Women for the National Defense, was created in the spring of 1915. Its founder, Madame Arnaud, announced that the women volunteers would wear soldier-blue uniforms and *képis* and carry rifles, thus proclaiming their readiness for military duty in the war zone. After receiving no response from the Ministry of War, she modified the uniforms—khaki with wide-brimmed Boy Scout–like hats—so they no longer resembled French soldiers. So attired, the corps, some 100 strong, drilled in the Tuileries garden. Madame Arnaud also modified her plans for their use in the war zone, suggesting instead that the corps should be confined to rear area duties like guarding depots. The Ministry of War continued to refuse to meet with her, however, and the press gleefully reported that ministry guards chased a delegation from the corps from one ministry door to another before finally dispersing them.[5]

By contrast, the Women's Automobile Club (Club Féminin Automobile) did receive authorization to work with the army's medical corps, the Service de Santé. The Service de Santé had been caught woefully short of motorized vehicles and, in the first year of the war, turned desperately to private individuals to fill the void.[6] The club's main publicist, feminist Marguerite Durand, declared these women had suitably feminine rather than military aspirations: to aid wounded soldiers. The drivers would wear uniforms but "not to play soldier, to be decked out in flashy gold braid or to strut around. On the contrary, [a uniform] would avoid feminine whimsy and even elegance inappropriate in the circumstances." It would be "nothing more than a simple blue suit . . . that costs 80 francs, an oil-cloth hat at 5 francs 50 and the club's insignia: an automobile wheel in white circled in dark purple with the three letters CFA in ruby red. This costume attracts no attention." The women would appear to be uniformed only when they were gathered in a group, and that would be rare, she believed. By presenting such an inconspicuous appearance, club members wanted to appear professional and official but also hoped to allay the Ministry of War's evident anxiety about militarized women. Durand proposed that CFA drivers receive permission to carry out evacuations from the war zone, but they were restricted to ferrying army personnel from hospital to hospital in Paris.[7]

Both Arnaud and Durand struggled to design a woman's costume that would solve the conundrum Krisztina Robert (ch. 2) defines as "making femininity and soldiering compatible." Until late in 1917, the French Ministry of War would deny that any such reconciliation was possible. The women the French army hired would be, and would remain, emphatically civilians. And they would be hired as individuals rather than enrolled in an auxiliary organization, even a civilian one like the Habsburg Empire's Women's Auxiliary Labor Force in the Field discussed by Claudia Reichl-Ham (ch. 11). They would not live in barracks or eat in military mess; they would not drill like Arnaud's volunteers and certainly not parade like Britain's women's corps; of course, they would not wear uniforms, not even armbands or badges.

Also, the ministry imagined that future women employees would be dependent widows and daughters of soldiers killed in the war and thus deserving the army's paternal support. Early circulars from the Ministry of War about the employment of women focused on establishing a hierarchy of applicants based upon their male relatives' war service rather than the women's job qualifications. Within several months, Gallieni recognized the problem with this approach. He cautioned commanders against "a too narrow interpretation" of these directives. "These priorities do not exclude the essential condition of proven professional experience," he warned.[8]

Such concerns notwithstanding, Ministry of War officials did not sufficiently recognize that by hiring civilians, the army would be competing in the commercial labor market that, as the war dragged on, became increasingly tight. Officers tasked with hiring women discovered that the pay scale set down by the ministry was often inferior to what civilian employers offered. For example, the postal service paid experienced telephone operators up to 9 francs a day and included meals at a reduced price, whereas the army's top pay was only 7.50 francs without any meal privileges.[9] In industrial areas, the army had trouble retaining even unskilled workers because factories offered higher wages. In 1917, one general reported that recently, the entire housekeeping and laundry staff of a military hospital in his region threatened to "defect" to a recently opened munitions factory unless their wages were increased. Commanders of garrisons in rural areas had no trouble hiring manual workers but could not recruit skilled secretaries and typists. Besides low wages, they faced the issue of "the isolation and distance" of these work sites from women's homes. They complained that the ministry refused to pay commuting costs or compensate women for the cost of relocation and lodging. The commanders of the military regions of Tarbes, Le Mans, Orléans, and Tours all raised these issues with the Ministry of War. The officer in charge of recruiting women workers in the Besançon region reported the impossibility of filling some 70 posts unless the army would provide transportation.[10]

The general perception that army jobs were unstable and temporary, especially in comparison with clerical jobs in the civilian administration and commerce, further hindered recruitment. Women assumed that jobs in the military would not outlast the war. Minister of War Roques called women's belief that their employment was a temporary expedient a "misperception" and counseled officers to reassure women that they were trying to recruit that "quantities of positions may continue after the end of the war," albeit without offering any guarantees.[11] Moreover, many army installations moved from place to place. As one officer reported in November 1917, "experience shows that a large number of the women we hire refuse to follow the regiment in case of relocation," particularly when it moved to the war zone. An officer in the war zone noted that "after successive bombardment the number [of women employees] has diminished more and more and has now fallen to only 6 (four secretaries and two warehouse workers)" as the civilian population had been evacuated.[12]

Many commanders responded to the Ministry of War's pressure to hire women with a barrage of stereotypical objections; women were inherently frivolous, indiscreet, incompetent, unfamiliar with military procedures, and subject to "vapors" and periodic indisposition, in short, disruptive to efficient operation and army morale. Once the experiment was underway, some officers grudgingly and sometimes wholeheartedly recorded their appreciation of their female employees. But although the more vociferous anti-feminine complaints faded, the problems attributable to women's civilian status remained. As General Drude of Rouen complained, "women are not bound by any enlistment."[13]

Of all women employed by the French army, those whose civilian status posed the most problems were women drivers of the Automobile Service. Official instructions forbade civilians to eat in the soldiers' mess, to avail themselves of military postal and travel privileges, and even to ride in military vehicles. These restrictions caused problems for all commanders who employed women but particularly for the Automobile Service whose women drivers often operated in the war zone. Unlike the archive of interviews that has enriched Bruce Scates, Margaret Harris, and Raelene Frances's (ch. 6) study of Australian women in uniform, there are no accounts of the experiences of French women drivers for the Automobile Service. Historians have discovered no interviews, diaries, memoirs, or letters that would enable us to understand what the job meant to them. However, British novelist and playwright Enid Bagnold, who drove briefly for the French army, described her life in a novel, *The Happy Foreigner* (1920):

> The early start at dawn, the flying miles, the winter dusk, the long hours of travel by the faint light of the acetylene lamps. . . . On and on and on rolled the days, and though one might add them together and make seven, they never made Sunday. For there is no Sunday in the French Army, there is no bell at which tools are laid aside and not even the night is sacred.[14]

One officer employing women drivers responded to a questionnaire in terms that confirm Bagnold's depiction. The work of women drivers, he insisted,

> is impossible to limit; the maintenance of their vehicles, as well as the services they provide to the medical teams and following evacuations require their permanent availability and cause daily unforeseen demands. . . . Moreover they are exposed in all weather, often in danger at night in locations under bombardment.[15]

Officers who employed women drivers complained that the Ministry of War's rigid definition of their civilian status made their arduous work even more difficult. Civilian employees were forbidden to eat in the soldiers' mess, even in the war zone, where there were few amenities. Although women drivers were posted far from their homes and required by the nature of their work to move around, they were denied military postal and travel privileges. In particular, how was the Automobile Service to interpret the regulation that denied authorization to ride in military vehicles to all women except "nurses in uniform"?[16]

That "uniform" was underlined in this directive raised in high relief the most insistent and contentious demand made by the Automobile Service: that their women drivers be issued official military uniforms. The initial instructions for hiring women drivers did not consider what they were to wear. Since, unlike nurses, there was no standard costume for a "conductrice," women's driving outfits varied considerably from the severely practical, which raised complaints about their lack of femininity, to what their commanders considered to be the fantastic, like the young noblewoman who wore knee-high boots and a cape or the driver Bagnold described as wearing "a bit of old ermine round her neck, knickerbockers and yellow check stockings."[17]

But it was not so much that their dress could bring discredit upon the Automobile Service that worried their bosses but that it hindered their work. Military police repeatedly stopped women drivers as suspicious persons, stretching short trips into long ordeals. A regional inspector reported that one of his drivers "experienced a regrettable incident with an agent of the *special morals police* who misunderstood the real reason for her presence in Amiens." Like the Italian commentator quoted by Allison Belzer (ch. 9), he and other officers pointed to the British army as an excellent model to follow regarding female personnel. Insisting that the army provide food, lodging, and especially uniforms for his drivers in the war zone, he pointed out, "This is the way the British army operates in order to oversee particularly the good conduct of women; all those who are employed are housed in barracks and each of them wears the distinctive uniform of her employment." He and other Automobile Service officers believed that morale, discipline, and, most of all, efficiency required women drivers "to present the appearance of military units."[18]

With much trepidation, the Ministry of War finally agreed. In December 1917, the Automobile Service issued a press release to prepare the public for the sight of French women in military-like dress.

> In a little while our citizens will see women wearing the uniform of our soldiers. Some will think this is a masquerade and they may protest what they think is an

improper disguise. It is nothing of the sort. The women who wear this uniform are volunteers incorporated into the Automobile Service where they work as drivers. Regulations require them to wear military uniform.[19]

The Ministry of War obviously considered the decision to put women drivers into uniform to be an explosive one. Why? What caused so much anxiety about the prospect of French women in military uniform?

CONCERNS ABOUT WOMEN IN UNIFORM

In the early twentieth century, a French woman in uniform was a subject of music hall and cartoon humor. An article published in 1912 entitled "When Women Are Soldiers" mocked British "amazons," in particular the Women's Sick and Wounded Convoy Corps and the Girl Scouts. It concluded with a drawing of a music hall version of a woman soldier, hour-glass figure bursting out of a grenadier's tunic, eyes peeking saucily from under her cap, asking "What will our pretty and spirited Parisiennes think of this?"[20] The prospect of women soldiers continued to be represented in this way during the war in illustrated magazines, stage shows, and postcards.

Parisians met the reality behind this image as early as August 1914 when British paramilitary women arrived as nurses and ambulance drivers in the First Aid Nursing Yeomanry

Figure 7.2.
"When? The Woman Soldier." A wartime postcard imagines women in the army. The caption at the top left reports, "Her presence will make a stay in the trenches more agreeable." © Musée d'histoire contemporaine-BDIC, reproduction by Archipel.

and the Women's Sick and Wounded Convoy Corps.[21] By the time the British Women's Army Auxiliary Corps (WAAC) was formed in 1917, Parisians had become accustomed to the sight of English "misses" in military-style uniforms. In 1918, contingents of the U.S. Army Signal Corps women arrived as well. French women, too, were wearing uniforms, although not military ones: Red Cross nurses and Green Cross canteen workers, and as more and more French men were mobilized, women performed the work—and wore the uniforms—of letter carriers, tram drivers, metro gate keepers, and others.

The Parisian press, although often neglecting to discuss the important work that these women did, always detailed what they wore. The "factrice," that is, the female letter carrier, appeared in Paris in May of 1917. In her enveloping black raincoat with its armband emblazoned with PPT (Postes, Télégraphes, et Téléphones), oilcloth wide-brimmed hat, and rectangular letter box slung from her shoulder, she seemed an exotic figure.[22] The previous autumn, the gas company had begun to employ women meter readers, dressed in dark suits and Panama hats with GAZ in gold letters on the hat band.[23] The metro hired women as keepers of the gates that controlled entrance to the platforms. Originally decked out in light-colored sailcloth outfits with a lapel pin composed of the Allies' flags, practicality soon replaced this with a belted black smock and cap.[24] The outfits of women tram drivers and fare collectors received the most attention. The female fare collector, as early as the spring of 1915, wore "a black smock, a kind of little fatigue cap coquettishly tilted over her hair, a numbered badge embroidered in silver thread pinned to her shoulder, satchel slung like a bandolier."[25] It took the tram company longer to hire women as drivers; the company immediately ran into trouble over their uniforms. The women drivers rejected the round oilcloth hats they were supposed to wear, adopting the visored caps of the male drivers. Eventually, the tram company gave in and approved the drivers' caps for women as well as men.[26]

One article published in January 1916 imagined a man who had fallen asleep in September 1914 and had just awakened to take a stroll through Paris. In each venue, he was astonished at the "curious spectacle" of women in uniform doing men's jobs.[27] The salacious humor magazine *La vie parisienne* made a joke of the phenomenon, claiming that the uniforms had imbued these working women with "a clan spirit analogous to that of the Knights Templar, an irreducible pride and really the ferocity of amazons." The magazine's 20 January 1917 issue ran a double-page spread imagining women police, fire fighters, customs' officers, and others in sexy uniforms.[28]

The press reported the new phenomenon of women in uniform with astonishment, fascination, and mockery, but not all reactions were benign. If the uniformed women who sold tickets on the tram or delivered the mail drew little public criticism, this was not the case for uniformed women volunteers. Even Red Cross volunteers came in for criticism; they were accused of caring more for the prestige of a fancy uniform than for the self-sacrifice that nursing entailed.[29] Rather than signaling modesty and self-abnegation as befitted charitable women, uniforms were self-aggrandizing and made the women who wore them conspicuous.

Figure 7.3.
A tramway driver and a fare collector in uniform. © Musée d'histoire contemporaine-BDIC, reproduction by Archipel.

A second criticism was that women in uniform debased the honor of men in uniform, the soldiers. By wearing uniforms, women seemed to be enacting a claim to national service comparable to military service. Supporters gave credence to this accusation by praising women volunteers as an "army of charity," fighting on the "battlefield of good works," and calling volunteering "mobilization."[30] Even worse were the women who affected military-style costumes. When fashion magazines in the fall of 1914 predicted women's winter outfits would have a "touch of the martial" about them, critics reacted with outrage. For frivolous women to wear "the glorious beret of our Alpine troops" or felt copies of trench helmets was an intolerable insult to French soldiers' sacrifices. "It does no honor to our troops to ape what they have made glorious under enemy fire," sputtered a columnist.[31] Madame Arnaud seems to have changed the uniforms of her women's volunteer corps (discussed earlier in this chapter) in response to such sentiments.

As was the case in nearly every country discussed in this anthology, French women in military-style uniforms also provoked fears and accusations of gender transgression; not only were they aping soldiers, they were aping men! Many people were already made uneasy by the sight of women doing "men's jobs," such as driving automobiles.[32] Uniforms only exacerbated such fears, evident in descriptions in the French press of the British women's paramilitary units and, later, the WAACS. Drilling in their khaki uniforms, they were "virile" "amazons," "formed for struggle, violent action, adventures and peril," according to one commentator. Their beauty, if they had any, was "a male beauty"; beside them, the British "tommies" looked like "tranquil Sanchos."[33] No better was the "striking masculine appearance" of American women ambulance drivers reported by *Le Petit Journal* in 1915.[34] A woman reporter in the *Petit Parisien* tried to soften such disturbing images with the claim that the WAACs' uniforms were not really masculine, just simple and practical, even attractive on the typically boyish British figure.[35] Nonetheless, even this favorable reporting left few doubts that such an experiment would be too risky for French notions of femininity and masculinity.

THE MEANINGS OF UNIFORMS

The symbolic value of a uniform magnified such fears. Uniforms gave women legitimacy and authority outside the domestic sphere. As Christine Hallett et al. (ch. 3) point out, in Catholic countries like France, as well as in Orthodox Russia, the model for the nurse's uniform was the nun's habit that, for centuries, had allowed women to move about society on their own without male escort, endowed with some of the authority of the church.[36] All French nurses' uniforms copied nuns' habits. Red Cross nurses, for example, wore long white veils with a red cross on the headband and, as outerwear, an enveloping dark-blue cape with a red cross badge over the heart. Neither the veils nor that capes were practical work clothes; they were designed to remind both their patients and the public of nuns. Dr. Anna Hamilton noted, "Traveling, being out on the streets sometimes late at night due to their duties, this uniform is a protection for our nurses."[37] Uniforms signaled that their wearers were members of, and thus protected by, powerful institutions. Women who wore uniforms were authorized to go places and do things that other women could not without endangering their reputations and even their physical safety. It was this kind of legitimacy that army officers sought for their women drivers.

But with this protection, permission, and authority came other symbolism that many French women sought but which the French polity was loath to accord them. In her history of Catholic nuns, Jo Ann McNamara points out the paradox of the nun's habit, which, while binding a woman to obedience to the church, simultaneously liberated her from the ordinary patriarchal authority of father, husband, or brother that legally controlled all French women

Figure 7.4.
A French Red Cross nurse on the right in the impractical long cape. The nurse on the left has exchanged the cape for a coat. © Musée d'histoire contemporaine-BDIC, reproduction by Archipel.

until the mid-twentieth century. Tram conductresses, nurses, and military drivers, of course, had not taken vows of obedience and celibacy, but their duties to their employers could be imagined to take priority over their traditional family obligations. Red Cross nurses signed up for definite periods and could be posted away from home; similar rules and penalties bound the women employed as military drivers. In point of fact, both the Red Cross and the army let women out of their contracts when family emergencies occurred, but nonetheless, their uniforms did indicate emancipation from patriarchal authority.

UNIFORMS, SUFFRAGE, AND THE ARMY

Such emancipation had political implications; it was here that the army's practical need for women in uniform ran into its most serious obstacle. The decades before the Great War saw the emergence of a women's suffrage movement in France. Although not as large or militant as the British movement at this time, it had steadily gained adherents and forced opponents to abandon one argument after another.[38] Marie Curie had proven women as intellectually qualified as men; Marguerite Durand's daily newspaper, *La Fronde*, written, edited, and published by women, had proven women capable of understanding politics. A straw poll published in *Le Journal* in the spring of 1914 received over 500,000 replies from women who wanted to vote.[39]

By 1914, the one remaining argument against granting French women the vote was the "blood tax." When suffragist Hubertine Auclert was arrested for mounting a women's tax strike in 1880 on the principle of no taxation without representation, the judge informed her that although women did pay taxes in money, they were not liable for the far more important tax in blood; that is, they did not perform military service.[40] In the years following this decision and especially after the 1905 conscription reform made male military service truly universal, the claim that women were not full citizens because they did not do military service became the main pillar of anti-suffrage argument.[41]

When, at the outbreak of the war, women rallied to their nations' defense, feminists in France as in Italy, Russia. and elsewhere saw this pillar cracking. Women were doing important national service: nursing, making munitions, growing food, working for the government and in public services. The war effort could not succeed without them. Women in the army would finally push women's suffrage over the top. As Thérèse Casevitz-Rouff wrote in the feminist journal *La Française,* this would "remove the last argument of those who refuse women their political rights on the pretext that they don't have the same duties as men and are exempt from military service." Or as Gaston Rageot later put it, "The day when the colonel of a provincial regiment allowed typists and orderlies in skirts to come through the gate, he has killed the last prejudice that still resisted the new mentality."[42] While Casevitz-Rouff and other feminists exulted, social and political conservatives shuddered. Although the founders of the British women's paramilitary organizations were not militants of the Women's Social and Political Union, as Jane Misme had pointed out early in the war, conservatives were convinced that all British women in uniform were militant suffragettes and that it was their action that was forcing the British government to prepare the Representation of the People Act that would give some British women the vote.[43]

So much was riding on the army's decisions about its women employees. The women who drove for the Automobile Service, like all of the women employed by the French military, were civilians. From the first, the army had striven to keep their civilian status unequivocal by denying women the rights of soldiers, such as dining in the mess, postal and travel privileges, and, of course, uniforms. It was the officers of the Automobile Service who pushed these issues most insistently, querying and complaining about restrictions on women drivers that hindered their work. Although the Ministry of War continued to refuse women drivers the right to eat in the mess and reprimanded Automobile Service officers for granting women postal privileges, a month before the war ended the ministry did finally agree with regard to travel vouchers that "women drivers may be treated similarly to soldiers."[44]

The most serious blurring of the line between civilian and military status was the uniform. Given the shortage of qualified drivers and under mounting pressure from the Automobile Service over harassment of women drivers, the ministry did finally agree to provide uniforms. The uniform design that the ministry approved was not nearly as military or as masculine as that of British paramilitary and military auxiliary women. Tammy Proctor (ch. 4) points out skirts and color difference were the most common ways of setting militarized women apart from soldiers. The French Ministry of War used both to identify its women drivers. The drivers' uniforms would not be the same color as French army uniforms—the latter were blue gray, whereas the women's uniforms were navy—and they would have skirts regardless of skirts' impracticality, particularly for motorcycle riders. But nonetheless, they would be military uniforms. As the press release stated, "Regulations require them to wear military uniform." That it took the Ministry of War a year to reach this decision indicates the trepidation with which the army approached the issue. Furthermore, the army appears to have been in no hurry to implement the decision. Despite the publicity photos taken in January 1918 (see Figure 7.1), there is no record of the uniforms' actual delivery or any photographs of women drivers on duty wearing them.[45] The Ministry of War probably felt that if the last obstacle to French women's political rights was to go down, someone other than the army should be responsible.

THE ARMY'S UNEXPECTED POSTWAR EMPLOYMENT OF WOMEN

Unlike British, American, and German women, French women did not get the vote after the First World War; the blood tax still stood in the way. For this, the army's shilly-shallying over the drivers' uniforms bears only a minute fraction of the blame. Nonetheless, at stake in French women's desire to wear uniforms was their claim to citizenship, and at the end of the war, this remained ambiguous.

Ironically, French women's lack of full citizenship may have contributed to their continued employment by the army after the war. Only three days after the armistice, the Ministry of War ordered a halt to all hiring of women, and some commanders immediately began to fire women employees. A report from the controller-general's office in August 1919, after repeating all of the earlier criticisms of women employees as inherently undisciplined and incompetent, vehemently recommended replacing them with male conscripts as soon as possible to return the army to an entirely male enterprise. As historian Andrew Orr has recently pointed out, however, this never materialized.[46]

As demobilization went forward, the army needed its clerical staff that, during the war, had largely been feminized. Budgetary constraints, a labor shortage, and then the reduction of the length of military service conspired to preserve some women's employment in the army in the 1920s, although much reduced from its wartime height. When, in 1923, conscription was reduced to 18 months and then, in 1928, was reduced further to one year, women employees appeared experienced and competent in comparison to these raw recruits. Moreover, in the increasingly fraught political climate of the 1920s and 1930s, the fact that women could not vote and thus were assumed to be apolitical was an asset; women appeared to be more disciplined and professional than radicalized young conscripts. In the mid-1920s, the army was employing over 7,500 women, almost all as clerical workers.[47]

The employment of women by the French military, undertaken during the Great War, turned out to be a more permanent innovation than anyone had imagined in the fall of 1915. By contrast, the army's experiment with uniformed women was exceedingly limited and temporary, lasting for only a few months in 1918 and confined to a few hundred women drivers. The potential political implications of French women performing military service were too serious for the army to broach except in an extreme crisis and for the briefest possible time period. The several thousand women the French army continued to employ after the war remained, emphatically, civilians.

NOTES

1. The originals are in the Musée d'histoire contemporaine (BDIC), accessible online at https://argonnaute.parisnanterre.fr/ark:/14707/a0115154188298xCD5c (accessed 12 October 2019). They were not widely published in France, but one does appear in a British publication, the *Illustrated War News*, 16 January 1918, 35.

2. See Claudia Reichl-Ham (ch. 11) on the Habsburg army and Thomas Cardoza, *Intrepid Women: Cantinières and Vivandières of the French Army* (Bloomington: Indiana University Press, 2010), 210–214, on the French army.

3. The correspondence from the Ministry of War about female employment is contained in the archives of the Service Historique de l'Armée de Terre, Château de Vincennes (hereafter SHAT), 7N 159 main d'oeuvre féminine. This circular is dated 10 November 1915.

4. Dossier 629, Femmes dans l'aviation, Bibliothèque Marguerite Durand, Paris; articles in *Le Petit Journal,* 28 September 1917, and *Le Petit Parisien,* 30 September 1915.

5. "Un régiment de femmes est en formation à Paris," *Le Petit Parisien*, 19 April 1915; "Les femmes qui veulent servir la France," *Le Petit Journal,* 22 April 1915; "Une manifestation du Corps volontaire des femmes," *Le Petit Parisien*, 12 January 1916; Jean Lecoq, "Les amazones parisiennes," *Le Petit Journal*, 15 January 1916.

6. Jean Pierre Fournier, "Evolution du Service de santé militaire française pendant la guerre de 1914–1918" (master's thesis, Montpellier III, 1996), 52–60.

7. Dossier 367, Club Féminin Automobile, Bibliothèque Marguerite Durand, Paris; Thérèse Casevitz-Rouff, "Chez les automobilistes militaires," *La Française*, 30 October 1915.

8. SHAT 7N 159 main d'oeuvre féminine. His successor in the ministry, General Roques, reiterated this directive in December 1916.

9. SHAT 16N 2449 main d'oeuvre féminine.

10. SHAT 7N 495 main d'oeuvre féminine.

11. SHAT 7N 159 main d'oeuvre féminine circular 2-12-1916.

12. SHAT 7N 495 main d'oeuvre féminine.

13. SHAT 7N 495 main d'oeuvre féminine.

14. Enid Bagnold, *The Happy Foreigner* (New York: Century, 1920), 19, 23.

15. The records of the French army's employment of women drivers are contained in SHAT 16 N 2767 Direction Service Automobile (hereafter DSA) personnel féminin.

16. SHAT 16 N 2767, DSA personnel féminin.

17. SHAT 16N 2767 DSA personnel féminin, regarding the Marquise de Saint-Leger; Bagnold, *Happy Foreigner*, 144. The narrator of Bagnold's novel wears a khaki uniform, presumably from one of the British women's corps, and a long leather coat that she had purchased herself.

18. SHAT 16N 2767 DSA personnel féminin.

19. SHAT 16N 2767 DSA personnel féminin.

20. Maurice Dekoba, "Quand les femmes seront soldats . . . ," *Le Gaulois du Dimanche*, no. 164, 13–14 April 1912. A similar article, "Un bataillon de femmes soldats," *Lectures pour tous,* February 1909, discussed women soldiers in Serbia.

21. Elisabeth Shipton, *Female Tommies: The Frontline Women of the First World War* (Stroud, U.K.: History Press, 2014), 60–66.

22. "Les 'factrices' font leur apprentisage," *Le Petit Parisien*, 16 May 1917.

23. Gabriel Perreux, *La vie quotidienne des civils en France pendant la grande guerre* (Paris: Librairie Hachette, 1966), 58.

24. Perreux, *La vie quotidienne des civils*, 191; "Celles qui remplacent les mobilisés. Les employées de métro," *Le Petit Parisien*, 5 September 1916.

25. "Les hommes combattent, les femmes travaillent," *Lectures pour tous*, 15 January 1916, 604–612; "Brosseuses et receveuses de tramway," *Le Petit Parisien*, 15 August 1916; Jane Simone, "Journal d'une remplaçante," *Je sais tout*, 15 September 1916, 319–328.

26. Perreux, *La vie quotidienne des civils*, 190.

27. "Les hommes combattent, les femmes travaillent."

28. Francis de Miomandre, "Chez les amazones," *La vie parisienne*, 17 February 1917, 154–157; "Ce que la mobilisation féminine nous fera peut-être voir," *La vie parisienne*, 20 January 1917: 58–59.

29. See, e.g., Michel Corday, *The Paris Front: An Unpublished Diary: 1914–1918* (New York: E.P. Dutton, 1934): 12; Félix Lejars, *Un hôpital militaire à Paris pendant la guerre: Villemin, 1914–1919* (Paris: Masson, 1923), 145; Georges Docquois, preface to Geneviève Duhamelet, *Ces Dames de l'hôpital 336* (Paris: Albin Michel, 1917).

30. See, e.g., Berthe M. Bontaoux, *Les Françaises et la grande guerre* (Paris: Bloud & Gay, 1917), 74; Marie de la Hire, *La Femme française: son activité pendant la guerre* (Paris: Librairie Jules Tallandier, 1917), 9–10; Tony d'Ulmès, "La mobilisation féminine en France," *Revue hébdomadaire,* 7 August 1917, 73–83; Emilie Borel, *La Mobilisation féminine en France (1914–1919)* (Paris: Imprimerie "Union," 1919).

31. "La mode féminine en temps de guerre," *Le Petit Parisien,* 30 November 1914; "Les ridicules de la mode," *Le Petit Parisien,* 22 September 1916.

32. Chantal Antier, *Les Femmes dans la Grande Guerre* (Paris: Soteca, 14–18 Editions, 2011), 17–18.

33. Léon Abensour, *Les Vaillantes: Héroïnes, martyres et remplaçantes* (Paris: Librairie Chapelot, 1917): 140–142. The British press expressed the same fears. See Barton C. Hacker and Margaret Vining (ch. 1) and Jenny Gould, "Women's Military Service in First World War Britain," in *Behind the Lines: Gender and the Two World Wars*, ed. Margaret R. Higonnet, Jane Jenson, Sonya Michel, and Margaret Collins Weitz (New Haven, Conn.: Yale University Press, 1988): 114–125.

34. *Le Petit Journal*, 20 June 1915.

35. Andrée Viollis, "Avec le corps d'armée des femmes anglaises," *Le Petit Parisien,* 7 and 14 January 1918.

36. Jo Ann Kay McNamara, *Sisters in Arms: Catholic Nuns through Two Millennia* (Cambridge, Mass.: Harvard University Press, 1996): 623–624.

37. Anna Hamilton, "Service des gardes malades de la Maison de santé protestante de Bordeaux pendant la première année de guerre," *Revue philanthropique* 37, no. 228 (15 August 1916): 373.

38. See Karen Offen, *Debating the Woman Question in the French Third Republic, 1870–1920* (Cambridge: Cambridge University Press, 2017). See also Steven C. Hause and Anne R. Kenney, *Women's Suffrage and Social Politics in the French Third Republic* (Princeton, N.J.: Princeton University Press, 1984).

39. Christine Bard, *Les filles de Marianne: Histoire des féminismes, 1914–1940* (Paris: Fayard, 1995), 80.

40. Steven C. Hause, *Hubertine Auclert, the French Suffragette* (New Haven, Conn.: Yale University Press, 1987), 68–76.

41. Margaret H. Darrow, *French Women and the First World War*, (Oxford, UK: Berg, 2000), 30–36.

42. Thérèse Casevitz-Rouff, "Les femmes aux services de l'armée," *La Française,* 4 March 1916; Gaston Rageot, *La Française dans la guerre* (Paris: Attinger frères, 1918), 14.

43. Jane Misme, "Les femmes dans l'armée," *La Française*, 3 June 1915.

44. SHAT 7N 2767 DSA personnel féminin, October 1918. In fact, other records in this file show that DSA officers had been signing travel vouchers for their women drivers for months prior to this decision.

45. There are no records in either the army's photography library at Fort d'Ivry or in the larger and more general collections of war photographs at the Musée de l'Armée in the Invalide and the Bibliothèque Nationale.

46. Andrew Orr, "'Too Numerous to Be Controlled': Women, Professionalism and Anti-republicanism in the French Army, 1914–1928," *French Historical Studies* 19, no. 2 (April 2016): 287–313. See also Andrew Orr, *Women and the French Army during the World Wars, 1914–1940* (Bloomington: Indiana University Press, 2017).

47. Orr, "Too Numerous to Be Controlled," 301–311.

EIGHT

BELGIAN WOMEN IN THE GREAT WAR

Uniformed or Not?

ILSE BOGAERTS AND LUC DE MUNCK

The collection of the Royal Museum of the Armed Forces and Military History in Brussels, one of the military museum sites of the War Heritage Institute, does not include military uniforms for Belgian women from the Great War. Women were not allowed in the Belgian army until 1975. An exception is the uniform of a certain sutler dating from around 1910. Female sutlers, like their male counterparts, were petty merchants who had been following European armies and selling drinks, tobacco, and other small comforts to the troops at least since the seventeenth century. By the late nineteenth century, some armies had granted them semiofficial status and dressed them in a female version of the uniform of the regiment in which they were serving. The collection also contains uniforms of Belgian nurses who were active in field hospitals during the Great War. This chapter takes a closer look at women's uniforms shortly before, during, and even after the war. Did their uniforms give women a new status and a certain legitimacy in a period where they were assuming new professional and charity functions? Were their uniforms formalizing a new role for women, inspired by fashion, and contributing to their emancipation? To what extent did these uniforms contribute to the professional identity of women?

WOMEN IN RELIEF AND WELFARE

The enormous scale on which the Great War was fought accelerated women's military roles. The British were the first to establish a female auxiliary corps as part of the army structure: the Women's Army Auxiliary Corps. Women were involved in a number of different activities, including driving, administration, cooking, and communication.[1] They were given khaki uniforms that closely resembled those of their male colleagues. Compared to other allied military forces, the Belgian army would trail far behind when it came to integrating female soldiers into their armies. Women were admitted to the Belgian army Medical Service only after the Great War, in 1921; previously, they were all civilian volunteers.

If one saw a khaki-clad female emergency medical worker on a motorcycle early in the war, she was almost certainly a foreign volunteer, like Elsie Knocker (later Baroness de T'Serclaes) and Mairi Chisholm, two of the women whom the slightly eccentric Dr. Hector Munro, an outspoken suffragist, recruited for his Flying Ambulance Corps in Flanders[2] (see also Hallett et al., ch. 3). The well-known propaganda images of women in overalls, working in the factory so that the men could fight, is also not an accurate depiction of Belgian reality. Manufacturing had, of course, come to a halt, and the Germans who occupied most of the country controlled the economy. As a result, life was difficult during the Great War in both occupied and nonoccupied Belgium. The situation varied from region to region. The women on the Belgian front were mainly nurses who kept the hospitals up and running and cared for the sick and injured. There were also women—often prostitutes—who opened the

Figure 8.1.
Elsie Knocker and Mairi Chisholm, close friends and ardent motorcyclists, soon parted ways with Munro's Flying Ambulance Corps to set up their own operation very near the front lines in northern Belgium at Pervyse. Private collection, Patrick Vanleene, Ghent.

many cafés and cabarets where the soldiers could go to relax. They were not the regimental girls, or *filles de régiment*, who once accompanied the army, but rather single women who saw prostitution as the only way to survive. In occupied Belgium, women also suffered greatly. Famine and unemployment were widespread. Many of the relief and welfare organizations established in Belgium, mainly by elite women, since the outbreak of the war continued their work in the occupied territory.

Competing women's suffrage organizations united to found the Patriotic Union of Belgian Women (Union Patriotique des Femmes Belges) right at the start of the war. Their goal was to provide aid following the German invasion. In the first phase, they offered their services in caring for the injured and refugees, but they were soon displaced in that role by the Belgian Red Cross. Union women were then called on to help in the kitchens and laundries and to clean the premises. The emergency relief service became well known. Initially an organization largely drawn from the bourgeoisie and upper classes, the union became more inclusive as the war progressed and acted to provide work for seamstresses and women who had been robbed of their normal income.[3] Their way of working changed completely under German occupation. In this second phase, the union became a service for providing employment to women who knew their way around needle and thread. They would sew shirts and knit socks for the injured and the soldiers. The union was also an information center that offered work to service staff, as well as a center for referring women to other charity organizations that distributed milk, soup, or clothes.

Established in November 1914, the National Aid and Nutrition Committee (Comité National de Secours et d'Alimentation [CNSA]), with its many regional, provincial, and local departments, saved the Belgian population from famine.[4] This private organization provided the Belgian population with food that was purchased via the Commission for Relief in Belgium, the large-scale U.S. aid program, and, after 1917, via the Spanish-Dutch Committee (Comité Hispano-Néerlandais). Toward the end of the war, 125,000 volunteers were working for the CNSA. Most of them were women who, apart from food, also distributed clothing and shoes. Unemployed government officials were appointed to run CNSA's large public cafeterias. Other activities included bread and soup kitchens, baby milk distribution, housing services for homeless people, food packages for prisoners (Le Petit Paquet [The Little Package]), children's canteens (Les Petites Abeilles [The Little Bees]), and children's clothing distribution. In addition, the Milk Droplet (La Goutte de Lait) provided pregnant women with healthy meat dishes, and the Kids Basket (La Layette) supplied young mothers with baby diapers and cradles.

When the National Aid and Nutrition Committee started its extensive food distribution and job placement services, the Patriotic Union of Belgian Women proceeded to their third and final phase: providing seamstresses, knitters, and lace workers with work-from-home opportunities. Poor women could earn between 3.50 and 4 Belgian francs (BEF) per week in this manner. By comparison, a nurse's monthly wage before the war would have been somewhere between 50.70 and 80 BEF.[5] A few thousand lace workers could be employed.

Because lace was not allowed to be sold in occupied Belgium, they found a customer in Boston. The union also had another special division, led by Countess Jean de Mérode, that was responsible for assisting spouses of officers and noncommissioned officers. Ladies from the upper bourgeoisie founded and led most charity organizations. They did not wear uniforms or even a mark of identification such as a bracelet or badge. But they were, nonetheless, swept up in a dramatic transformation of women's fashions.

WOMEN'S FASHION TRANSFORMED

The war and the large-scale entry of women into what was oftentimes a new work environment marked an important turning point in the history of women's fashion in Belgium as in all the Western world.[6] Women's uniforms were at once cause and beneficiary of this transformation. Now, the emphasis would be on simplicity: away with such unnecessary decorations as lace, rushes, and buttons, goodbye to corsets and padding. War-caused shortage of textiles resulted in a number of fashion casualties, including wide skirts, crinolines, and underskirts. Hemlines became shorter (above the ankle), allowing women to move more freely while working. A shorter and more straightforward female silhouette became popular, resulting in the rise of the two-piece tailored suit (*costume-tailleur*). Introduced by fashion designers Jeanne Lanvin and Coco Chanel, the suit remained popular throughout the twentieth century, eventually becoming the most characteristic way to identify independent working women.[7] It was no coincidence that this women's suit had elements of men's clothing and that it can be seen as an expression of the pursuit of equal rights.

The cut of dresses, and even nurses' uniforms, often acquired a degree of tailoring: skirt section with waistband just slightly hugging the torso. Black became fashionable for the first time, not only for widows but for everyone mourning for their country. Black suits (*costume-tailleur*) became popular among the many volunteers working for charity organizations. Such clothing allowed women to exhibit their love for their country in a very visual manner. Khaki also became fashionable, symbolizing solidarity with the soldiers on the front lines.

Women's clothing became a lot more functional. The corset, which had constrained women for decades, gradually faded into oblivion. The corset's demise literally liberated the female body. For a small group of elite women, this liberation had already happened on the eve of the war. In Belgium, it was exemplified by Maria Sèthe, the wife of the famous art nouveau architect Henry van de Velde, who designed functional clothing that would promote freedom of movement and used flexible fabrics. She claimed the right for women to dress in a manner that would fit their personal sense of style and personality, freed from fashion dictatorship.[8] The reformation and health movements (around 1900) had previously protested against corsets as causing health problems. Hardly anyone listened, however. First, there were corsets without reinforcements that did not need to be threaded. They were succeeded by bra-like garments.

Sport also contributed to the disappearance of the corset and the introduction of the bra, as well as more flexible fabrics, such as jersey and tricot. Before the war, these fabrics were used only for sports or underwear. During the war, however, tricot became a kind of replacement material. Fashion magazines indeed encouraged their readers not to wear wool or cotton. Silk or velvet or jersey were still acceptable and could be used to keep producing women's fashion. Wool and cotton, used exclusively for war uniforms, were in short supply. The bra therefore became popular, and by the end of the war, the bra had, in fact, replaced the corset. The main reason why clothing had to become more functional, however, was that women—from upper to lower class—were entering into new working environments on a large scale. When women entered regular occupations, their working clothes tended to become standardized, as exemplified by the black *costume-tailleur*.[9] Although such a standardized costume might be considered a kind of uniform, only nurses in the Belgian context consistently wore uniforms in the normal sense.

EVOLUTION OF THE BELGIAN NURSE'S UNIFORM

The uniform Belgian nurses wore during the Great War was largely based on the uniform that had gradually taken shape at the schools for nurses newly established just before the war. There were four such schools. After failed attempts in Liège and Brussels, the first school for nurses was established in Antwerp in 1902. Article 16 of this school's first rules and regulations, issued 18 March 1910, stipulated that student nurses, nurses, and head nurses were to wear a uniform made available by the governing Council of Houses of Worship in Antwerp—forerunner of the current Public Center for Social Welfare; the council retained ownership of the uniforms.[10] The Stuivenberg hospital, where classes were held, provided the uniforms that all nurses were required to wear.[11] The school continued its activities under German occupation, during the war.

The Brussels Council of Houses of Worship decreed a special uniform for nurses on 5 January 1906: "white blouse, cap, red cross on the sleeve."[12] When school started in 1907, the council provided students with the uniform, as well as lodging, meals, and a monthly stipend.[13] In June 1910, the uniform requirement was extended to graduate nurses.[14] Regulations issued in 1911 added that "the white blouse is mandatory during service and to be worn under a uniform outfit," to be "replaced by the apron outside of service duties."[15] In the same year, the Brussels Council of Houses of Worship also released a lavish presentation brochure on nurse training.

Figure 8.2.
Nurses of the nursing school of the Brussels Council of Houses of Worship during their recreation. In 1906, this school was the first Belgian school to decree a uniform. Archives of the Public Center for Social Welfare (PCSW), Brussels.

It stressed that the student nurse's uniform signified the discipline expected of her. Before putting on this uniform, the student nurse must first ask herself whether she had the necessary qualities and perseverance to effectively perform the tasks that the nursing profession would require of her.[16] Remarkably, the rules and regulations of 1915 said nothing about this uniform.[17]

Brussels surgeon Antoine Depage developed a training program for lay nurses, starting in October 1907. The Belgian School for Qualified Nurses had a difficult time at the beginning. The uniform, a "blue cotton dress, white apron, collar and cuffs," was one of the problems because uniforms for women were something new. Masons in the vicinity of the school, for instance, threw stones and shouted at the uniformed student nurses that it was not carnival time.[18] The elements of this uniform and their costs are shown in Table 8.1. The meeting minutes explained some of the costs:

> This total represents an initial expense for the first year. The two coats will serve for two years. Therefore, there is a deduction of 67 BEF for the second year, which finally remains at 160 BEF. The indicated prices represent a minimum. The hats, gloves, collars, and shoes are listed at a wholesale price, but on the condition that they are purchased in corresponding quantities. The Vaxelaire House [a very well-known Brussels warehouse] provides the other articles and forfeit all profit. Naturally, the orders are supposed to be of importance.[19]

TABLE 8.1. The cost of outfitting a Belgian student nurse in 1907. All costs are in Belgian francs (1 BEF = $1.60, equivalent to about $39 in today's dollars). Source: Ecole Belge d'Infirmières Diplomées, Comité des Dames, 1907 to [9 November 1926], session of 8 June 1907, Archives of the Hospital Cavell-Depage, State Archives of Belgium repository 2, Brussels.

UNIFORM ELEMENT AND TOTAL	COST
Alpine coat (summer), 1	32.00
Woollen coat (winter), 1	35.00
Hats, 2	3.00
Cotton dresses, 4	60.00
Mixed canvas aprons, 12	42.00
Pairs of sleeves, 12	10.20
House bonnets, 4	3.00
Apron blouses, 2	13.50
Cotton bonnets, 2	1.50
Pairs of shoes, 3	14.65
Pairs of gloves, 4	5.00
Collars, 12	7.50
Total	227.35

As school director Edith Cavell further explained in a 1908 letter addressed to candidate students, this uniform was developed in line with that worn by British nurses.[20]

The school's internal rules and regulations, which were adopted two weeks later by the school's administration, stated that both the student nurses (article VII) and the qualified nurses (article XII) were given the uniform free of charge, as was the case with education, lodging, meals, and laundry.[21] Shortly thereafter came a small addition to the rules: student nurses must complete a two-month probationary period before being allowed to wear the uniform. Because these students were also directly involved in caring for the sick, however, they were permitted to wear the uniform immediately. At that time, the new school only had six students, and their uniforms were promptly ordered.[22]

This decision conformed to views that Edith Cavell had expressed before she became the school's principal. In a letter dated 8 August 1907, she had already requested that the uniform be made compulsory for the students on probation. She added that any other uniform would be inappropriate for hospitals and that it could even be dangerous (perhaps

Figure 8.3.
Student nurses in Dr. Depage's school for nurses. Remarkably, the uniform of these lay nurses looks similar to that of the religious nurses. Archives of the Belgian Red Cross, Brussels.

Figure 8.4.
Marie Depage, secretary of her spouse's school for nurses, working at the Royal Palace hospital at the beginning of the war. In May 1915, she was one of the victims of the sinking of the Lusitania. Archives of Belgian Red Cross, Brussels.

she referred to arousing the lust of male patients).[23] Nelly Graux, who chaired the hospital's ladies' committee, believed no such action was needed. Pointedly excluding Cavell, who had not yet been appointed principal, Graux wrote to school secretary Marie Depage. Wearing the uniform, she thought, was a practical matter, to be resolved as the school took shape and nurses tended to the sick.[24]

At a February 1908 board meeting, the directors decided that graduate nurses should be distinguished from students by distinctive uniforms. At the same meeting, they learned that the school uniform would be registered with the Conseil de Prud'hommes (the former Labor Court) in Brussels.[25] The reason was clear: registering with this court, which had jurisdiction over labor disputes, would prevent others from copying their uniform and claiming its prestige. In April 1910, Dr. Depage suggested to the board of directors that all graduate nurses be given a badge to wear on their uniforms. This proposal was accepted.[26] It took another two years before the model was approved: a round pin, with an edelweiss in white enamel on a golden background and the inscription "Ecole Belge d'Infirmières Diplomées" on a blue background.[27] In 1911, the board appointed a five-member committee to review the nurses' service uniform and report their conclusions to the board.[28] This review resulted in adoption of the cloak and hat models, which until then had been only provisionally approved.[29]

The establishment of two training programs for lay nurses in Brussels led, in late November 1907, to the beginning of classes at the Catholic School for Nurses of Saint-Camillus. The uniform of this school was described as simple and elegant in a brochure published to commemorate the twenty-fifth anniversary of the school in 1932. The uniform was an explicit way to underline the catholic identity of the school. According to the brochure, the school's uniform comprised a

> dark colored serge dress with gold buttons with S.C. [Saint Camillus] monogrammed initials, white reps collar and cuffs, white stockings, white gloves, blue silk veil, loose woollen blue fabric marked with a Christian red cross (the same as Saint-Camillus), which is exemplary of the outdoor outfit. In the summer, the wool dress makes way for the white reps dress with gold buttons, which is cut in the same model. During service, it's a white canvas blouse with well-ironed creases, large pockets, white lino veil, white thread stockings, canvas shoes with low white leather heels which make no noise. No jewelry. The more deserving among former nurses carry the medallion from the School. Others clip their veil with the Saint-Camille barrette. Those who are very decorated wear ribbons associated with their duties.[30]

Documentation is lacking. As late as 1910, the school did not yet have its own uniform. This can be deduced from the fact that only the uniforms of various religious orders, members of which were students at the school, were on display on 20 mannequins at the school's booth at the World Exposition in Brussels. Photographs further suggest that the uniform most likely originated just before the Great War, and an excerpt from the school's internal regulations requires every nurse to own three blouses and one linen or cotton nurse cap as per the school's model.[31] Presumably, this uniform was also worn during the war.

During the war, specifically in mid-1916, the board decided that both student and graduate nurses must wear their uniform outside the school, except when on holiday. The board was also examining changes to both the design and color of the nursing hood and the head covering of the service uniform.[32] However, afterward, nothing was heard of the planned changes. At the last meeting before the end of the war, the board considered a proposal for a black or blue veil as head covering when nurses went out and in the hair a small rush in white or in the Belgian tricolor. The board accepted the veil in principle but postponed a final decision to the postwar period. Until then, nurses who wished to wear the veil would be allowed to do so.[33]

THE BELGIAN RED CROSS

Like the Patriotic Union of Belgian Women and the National Aid and Nutrition Committee, the Belgian Red Cross quickly began to open hospitals and to give medical aid when war began. Within a few days, Brussels had 20,000 beds available, and the provinces followed suit.[34] Queen Elisabeth asked the same Dr. Depage who had established the Belgian School for Qualified Nurses in 1907 to set up a hospital near the royal villas in De Panne. Although some military officials opposed the site as being too close to the front lines, the Ministry of War approved. The Red Cross Hospital L'Océan opened in De Panne on 20 December 1914.[35] Ultimately becoming Belgium's largest field hospital, it treated around 24,000 soldiers and civilians during the course of the war. Dr. Depage, the hospital's chief medical officer, established 12 principles to ensure the proper functioning of this hospital. One applied to nurses, who were to exhibit exemplary behavior and keep their uniform in perfect condition.[36] A badge bearing the motto "sometimes curing, most of the time relieving, always comforting" may have been part of the uniform, but it might also have been a distinction awarded by the hospital for exemplary service.[37]

During wartime, the nurse's uniform served as a form of protection in several ways. Like the nun's habit, although to a lesser extent, the nurse's uniform desexualized its wearer, emphasizing her role as caregiver rather than woman. The uniform also called attention to the nurse's association with modern medical practice and became a code against the strict prewar gender restrictions and a sign of unity between the wearers. So it contributed to the professional identity of nurses during the war. Last, but certainly not least, the uniform identified the nurse as an important member of a powerful organization. In her uniform, the

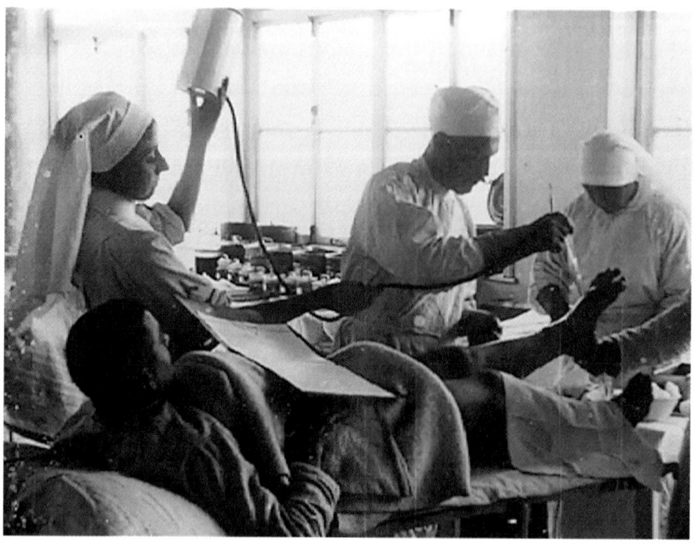

Figure 8.5.
Belgian nurse Jane de Launoy (left) at work at the Hospital L'Océan in De Panne. De Launoy was the only Belgian front nurse who published her diary after the war. CINEMATEK (Royal Belgian Film Archive), Brussels.

Figure 8.6. At the end of the war, nurse Elvire Massaer of L'Océan was photographed in her uniform wearing a badge reading "sometimes curing, most of the time relieving, always comforting." This phrase was already used in the sixteenth century by the famous French surgeon Ambroise Paré. Private Collection Gilberte Arnalsteen, Louvain.

nurse inspired the admiration of civilians and commanded the respect of soldiers, who were expected to salute her, even outside the hospital.[38]

Some nurses belonged to religious orders. The Belgian army felt that the habits worn by nursing sisters were unhygienic. Long and very wide sleeves were a particular matter of concern. At the end of 1915, Inspector General Léopold Mélis of the Belgian army's Medical Service urged Belgian Archbishop Mercier to authorize adjusting the habit by providing more hygienic sleeves.[39] Monseigneur De Wachter, the archbishop's representative in London, requested Rome to exempt nursing sisters from wearing not only the long-sleeved habit during the war but also the nun's hood and chinstrap. Otherwise, he warned, their impractical clothing would bar them from the operating room in favor of lay nurses.[40]

During the war, Red Cross nurses in nonoccupied Belgium received a free uniform. They also received a compensation of 80 BEF (equivalent to about $1,955 in today's dollars). Initially, this was not the case for nurses in military hospitals, who had to buy their dresses and aprons themselves. A note from 1915 provided an overview of uniform costs, which compares the expenses of 1915 with the previous cost (presumably it relates to the cost just before the start of the war). These costs are shown in Table 8.2. Here, it was once again emphasized that Red Cross nurses received this uniform free of charge, with the exception of the blue veil they wore outside the wards.[41] Army nurses received no such largesse.

On the basis of a ministerial decision dated 12 August 1915, nurses who were employed at military hospitals also received a one-time uniform allowance of 80 BEF. Because this compensation was considered insufficient to enable a nurse to afford a regular change of uniform, however, the army Medical Service decided on 11 November 1916 to make the payment annual. The military hospital where the nurse worked would bear the cost.[42] Remarkably, nurses accepted for temporary service during the final offensive in September–October 1918 received no uniform allowance; only those who received permanent appointments

TABLE 8.2. Prewar and wartime uniform costs compared, in Belgian francs (1 BEF = $1.60, equivalent to about $39 in today's dollars). Source: Infirmières, undated [1915] and unsigned note, folder 809, Archives of the Personal Secretary of King Albert and Queen Elisabeth, Royal Palace Archives, Brussels.

UNIFORM ELEMENT AND TOTAL	PREWAR COST	COST IN 1915
Dresses, 3	22.50	60.00
Aprons, 6	9.00	36.00
Pairs of cuffs, 3	2.25	4.50
Belts, 3	2.85	3.75
Collars, 3	3.00	6.00
Veil covering, 1	7.00	15.00
Total	46.60	125.25

were entitled to the allowance.[43] During the same period, it was also decided that nurses could have their shoes repaired in the army workshops, but at their own expense.[44]

FIELD HOSPITAL UNIFORMS

Photographs generally show nurses in field hospitals wearing a white uniform in the wards: dress with sleeves that could be rolled up, apron, and cap. The outside uniform was blue. The Royal Museum of the Armed Forces and Military History in Brussels, one of the military museum sites of the War Heritage Institute, has in its collection a Belgian Red Cross nurse's uniform dating from 1917: light-blue dress, with belt fastener closure and blousing body, with white apron, white socks and shoes, and a white headscarf. The headscarf is missing, as is the bracelet and the Red Cross emblems that were embroidered or sewn onto the breast pocket and cap. For winter, nurses were provided dark-blue woolen coats with a double closure. Because of the shortage of textiles, the skirt had minimal pleating and, as per changing fashion, ended just above the ankles. The Royal Museum of the Armed Forces and Military History collection's nurse's uniform closely resembles the image in Charles Buchel's 1915 poster "Belgian Red Cross": light-blue dress with white cap, collar, sleeves, and apron.[45] This poster was undoubtedly the Anglo-Belgian committee's best-known fund-raising poster.[46]

Countess Maria van den Steen de Jehay, director of the Elisabeth Hospital in Poperinghe (the largest civilian field hospital in nonoccupied Belgium), wrote of her apparel at a royal reception in June 1915: "At that time, we wore a khaki uniform. My silk blouse was light." When, later in the war, Queen Elisabeth's lady-in-waiting painted a portrait of Countess van den Steen, she noted that "the nurses from Poperinghe . . . wore unflattering khaki outfits, cut in British military serge, boots and a felt hat which followed the Australian

Figure 8.7.
Winter uniform of a nurse of the Belgian Red Cross in 1917 to work in the infirmary: white veil, blue dress, separate white starched cuffs, white apron, navy-blue overcoat, white knee socks, and white shoes. The emblems of the Red Cross are missing. © Royal Museum of the Armed Forces and Military History, Brussels (inv. 800963-69).

Figure 8.8.
In 1915, the British painter Charles Buchel (1872–1950) made this poster for the Belgian Red Cross. It became the most well-known poster for the recruitment of funds for the organization. © War Heritage Institute, Brussels (inv. C. 9.3.1.).

style."[47] The obvious British influence on nurses' uniforms in the Elisabeth Hospital, which was situated in the British zone, is not surprising.

The opinion of the lady-in-waiting was not shared by British military officials in Poperinghe, as the countess learned upon investigating reports of "nurses" consorting with soldiers on the streets and in cafes. British headquarters "had created a laundry service and had concocted the elegant idea of copying our uniform and have laundry service workers dress up in them. We could guess that young women had the time to take up another job outside of working hours." Her objections to the practice received a bland reply. "The nurses' outfits are very pretty. We respect and pay homage by copying it through our laundry services." The irate countess countered with a scribbled note to British headquarters: "If General X finds the uniforms of Belgian military nurses flattering on his servants, the Elisabeth Hospital will

Figure 8.9.
Countess Maria van den Steen, cofounder of the Saint Camillus school for nurses, in the uniform of the school. During the war, she became director of the Elisabeth Hospital in Poperinghe, the largest civilian hospital in nonoccupied Belgium. Private collection, Florence de Moreau de Villegas de Saint-Pierre, Louvignies.

take the same measures. Its laundry workers and nurses will from now on dress as officers of the British army." The general ceased and desisted well before the countess' three-day deadline expired.[48]

British officers were not alone in admiring the nurse's uniform. Fashion magazines also acclaimed the Red Cross nurses' uniform as extremely fashionable. They published patterns showing how readers could sew their own nurse costume. The 23 August 1914 edition of *La Mode Illustrée*, a French family newspaper, exclaimed that "the happiest among us are those who are already integrated in our troops: blessed nurses from the Red Cross." Its fashion pages claimed "the only outfit that we, the women of France, think of currently donning is the dress of an ambulance woman." Practical advice followed: "We can wear under the nurse's blouse a short skirt which is all flat and sufficiently large to not hinder movements. Above all, no wool or fabric susceptible to carrying germs, but 'washable cotton fabric.'"[49]

Figure 8.10.
A postwar doll of a front nurse clothed in a uniform to work in the infirmary: white veil, blue dress, separate white starched cuffs, and white apron. It was an illustration of the image of the "white angel," which became popular after the war. The doll would have been molded to the portrait of Queen Elisabeth. © War Heritage Institute (inv. 4501893).

In 1916, the Parisian fashion house Jeanne Lanvin, known for its practical and stylish ladies' apparel, even launched a two-piece cream-colored serge ensemble with light-blue decoration, alluding to the nurse's uniform, including a bracelet inspired by a Red Cross accessory.[50] The reverse also happened. In 1916, the International Red Cross Committee in Geneva commissioned the English fashion house Redfern in Paris to design an official nurse's uniform.[51]

It is understandable that the nurse's uniform was so prized, as it was so much more than just a hygienic working uniform. That is because this omnipresent and emblematic uniform embodied the new social developments, not only in terms of healthier and practical clothing that was easy to wash and did not restrict movement but also in terms of transcending classes in society.[52] Apart from the simple lines of the uniform, which corresponded perfectly to the reform movement, the nurse's uniform was so popular that wearing it was experienced as a patriotic act. Who did not dream of being a white angel for those poor front soldiers?

At the meeting of its board of directors on 6 October 1920, the newly founded Provincial School for Nurses of Ghent requested that a nurse's uniform be adopted for all qualified Belgian nurses. This matter was presented to the Professional Union of Belgian Nurses (Union Professionnelle des Infirmières Belges), founded in 1919 by about 40 Brussels nurses, but that seems to have been the end of it.[53] This proposal for a standard postwar uniform for all Belgian nurses does not seem to have ever materialized.

A standard working uniform for military nurses, however, was accepted the following year. The organic statutes of the nurses in Belgian military hospitals were defined in February 1922. Article 14 stipulated the nurse's working uniform comprise two blue cotton dresses, four white veils, six collars, six pairs of cuffs, three belts, and four white aprons. Article 14 also stipulated that the working uniform would not be worn as a service uniform, except while serving with the army of occupation in Germany. Article 15 required nurses to wear a copper badge on their uniform, with the letters SSAB (Service de Santé de l'Armée Belge).[54]

It would take three more years before a standard uniform for nurses was accepted. In 1925, the three-year-old National Federation of Belgian Nurses (Fédération Nationale des Infirmières Belges), the successor to the Union Professionnelle, conceptualized and designed a service uniform for nurses in "Belgian blue" fabric (dress and coat, felt hat, and dark-blue veil).[55] The National Work for Child Welfare (Œuvre Nationale de l'Enfance, founded in 1919) also agreed to adopt this uniform. In July 1925, the seven Belgian nurses who attended the congress of the International Council of Nurses in Helsinki wore their brand-new uniforms. According to one of them, the uniform made a great impression on congress participants and rivaled the uniforms of their Finnish hostesses.[56]

Throughout the Great War era, the Belgian army did not regulate women's uniforms because women were not officially part of the army. The Belgian Red Cross also lacked a regulation uniform. Variations in cut and color evolved over time—from longer to shorter, from wider to narrower, from light colored to white. In contrast, nursing schools had regulated clothing for student and graduate nurses beginning a decade before the war. A black two-piece suit would be the civilian uniform of women actively involved in the numerous aid and charity organizations in occupied Belgium. Simplicity and functionality were the keywords for women's military attire during the Great War in Belgium. It was somewhat contradictory that the liberating attire—ultimately without a corset—was especially worn in a previously traditional context of caring and nursing women. In this way, their uniform contributed to the professional identity of Belgian nurses during the war. It was a mark of cohesion between them and gave them a sense of belonging to a corps. More generally, the uniform was an element in the recognition of the new and important role played by Belgian women during the Great War. In that sense, it contributed to the emancipation of these Belgian women.

NOTES

We thank Natasja Peeters and Michel Jaupart, War Heritage Institute, Brussels, and Jon Arrizabalaga, Institución Milà I Fontanals-Consejo Superior de Investigaciones Cientificas (IMF-CSIC), Barcelona, for their support. We also thank Joris Vandendriessche, KU Leuven (Catholic University of Leuven), and Luc Vandeweyer, State Archives of Belgium, for their useful comments on the first draft of this article.

1. See Krisztina Robert (ch. 2); see also Samantha Philo-Gill, *The Women's Army Auxiliary Corps in France, 1917–1921: Women Urgently Wanted* (Barnsley, U.K.: Pen & Sword Books, 2017), 10.

2. Diane Atkinson, *Elsie and Mairi Go to War: Two Extraordinary Women on the Western Front* (New York: Pegasus Books, 2010).

3. Denise De Weerdt, *De vrouwen van de Eerste Wereldoorlog* [The women of the First World War] (Ghent: Stichting Mens en Kultuur, 1993), 82–87. For a brief, authoritative English language summary of women in wartime Belgium, see Eliane Gubin, Els Flour, and Marie Kympers, "Women's Mobilization for War (Belgium)," in *1914–1918-Online: International Encyclopedia of the First World War*, ed. Ute Daniel, Peter Gatrell, Oliver Janz, Heather Jones, Jennifer Keene, Alan Kramer, and Bill Nasson (Berlin: Freie Universität Berlin, 21 September 2016), https://doi.org/10.15463/ie1418.10967.

4. Sophie De Schaepdrijver, *De Groote Oorlog: Het koninkrijk België tijdens de Eerste Wereldoorlog* [The Great War: The Kingdom of Belgium during the First World War] (Amsterdam: Uitgeverij Atlas, 1997), 109.

5. Note sur l'Ecole d'Infirmières, [1908], folder 6, Fonds Infirmières, Archives of the Public Center for Social Welfare, Brussels (hereafter PCSW).

6. K.P.C. De Leeuw, *Kleding in Nederland 1813–1920: Van een traditioneel bepaald kleedpatroon naar het begin van een modern kleedgedrag* [Clothing in the Netherlands: From a traditional defined dress pattern to the beginning of a modern dress pattern], Publikaties van de Faculteit der Historische en Kunstwetenschappen, Erasmus Universiteit Rotterdam, No. 8 (Hilversum, Netherlands: Verloren, 1992), 482; François Boucher, *Histoire du costume en Occident, de l'Antiquité à nos jours* (Paris: Flammarion, 1983), 418–419.

7. Adelheld Rasche, *Wardrobes in Wartime: Fashion and Fashion Images during the First World War, 1914–1918* (Berlin: E.A. Seemann, 2014), 24.

8. Denise De Weerdt, *En de vrouwen? Vrouw, vrouwenbeweging en feminisme in België (1830–1960)* [And the women? Woman, women's movement and feminism in Belgium (1830–1960)] (Ghent: Masereelfonds, 1980), 126.

9. François Boucher, *Histoire du costume en Occident, de l'Antiquité à nos jours* (Paris: Flammarion, 1983), 408.

10. Verordening no. 184 School voor Ziekenverplegers en -verpleegsters [Regulation no. 184 School for Nurses], Antwerp, 5 May 1911, 4, folder 4, 2294#2367 Briefwisseling betreffende de instructies voor de organisatie en werking van de School voor Ziekenverpleging in het Stuivenberggasthuis [Correspondence concerning the instructions for the organization and working of the School for Nurses in the Stuivenberghospital], Antwerp City Archives.

11. Inwendig Reglement voor den Verpleegdienst [Internal Rules and Regulations for the Nursing Service], [Antwerp, 1911], 2, folder 4, 2294#2367 Briefwisseling betreffende de instructies voor de organisatie en werking van de School voor Ziekenverpleging in het Stuivenberggasthuis [Correspondence concerning the instructions for the organization and working of the School for Nurses in the Stuivenberghospital], Antwerp City Archives.

12. Les rétroactes de l'Ecole d'Infirmières, 1889–1911, [Brussels, 1911], p. 9, folder 1, Fonds Infirmières, Archives of the PCWS, Brussels.

13. Note sur l'Ecole d'Infirmières, [Brussels, 1908], 1, folder 6, Fonds Infirmières, Archives of the PCWS, Brussels.

14. Les rétroactes de l'Ecole d'Infirmières, 1889–1911, [Brussels, 1911], 10, folder 1, Fonds Infirmières, Archives of the PCWS, Brussels. No information was subsequently found regarding this badge.

15. Règlement pour les Elèves Infirmières et pour les Infirmières de l'Administration des Hospices de Bruxelles, [Brussels, 1911], 11, folder 8, Fonds Infirmières, Archives of the PCWS, Brussels.

16. Administration des hospices et secours de la ville de Bruxelles, Ecole des Infirmières, [Brussels, 1911], 4, folder 13, Fonds Infirmières, Archives of the PCWS, Brussels.

17. Administration des hospices et secours de la ville de Bruxelles, Règlement concernant l'Ecole et le Service des Infirmières, [Brussels, 1915], folder 33, Fonds Infirmières, Archives of the PCWS, Brussels.

18. Marie-Madeleine Bihet, *Histoire du nursing* (Liège: Desoer, 1947), 178.

19. Ecole Belge d'Infirmières Diplomées, Comité des Dames, 1907 to [9 November 1926], session of 8 June 1907, Archives of the Nursing School Cavell-Depage, State Archives of Belgium repository 2, Brussels.

20. Edith Cavell to candidate students, Brussels, 14 January 1908, E.01.03.II.32.10, Archives of the Nursing School Hospital Cavell-Depage, State Archives of Belgium repository 2, Brussels.

21. Ecole Belge d'Infirmières Diplomées, Procès[-]verbaux [Conseil d'administration] May 1907–1916, session of 20 June 1907, Archives of the Nursing School Cavell-Depage, State Archives of Belgium repository 2, Brussels.

22. G. Vandevelde to Monsieur [Antoine Depage], [Brussels], 6 September [1907], E.01.03.II.12.61, Archives of the Nursing School Cavell-Depage, State Archives of Belgium repository 2, Brussels.

23. Edith Cavell to Madame [Nelly Graux], Sussex, 8 August 1907, E.01.03.I.8.41-43, Archives of the Nursing School Cavell-Depage, State Archives of Belgium repository 2, Brussels.

24. Nelly Graux to Marie Depage, Dinant, 12 August 1907, E.01.03.I.8.45, Archives of the Nursing School Cavell-Depage, State Archives of Belgium repository 2, Brussels.

25. Ecole Belge d'Infirmières Diplomées, Procès[-]verbaux [Conseil d'administration] May 1907–1916, session of 28 February 1908, Archives of the Nursing School Cavell-Depage, State Archives of Belgium repository 2, Brussels.

26. Ecole Belge d'Infirmières Diplomées, Procès[-]verbaux [Conseil d'administration] May 1907–1916, session of 26 April 1910, Archives of the Nursing School Cavell-Depage, State Archives of Belgium repository 2, Brussels.

27. Ecole Belge d'Infirmières Diplomées, Procès[-]verbaux [Conseil d'administration] May 1907–1916, session of 23 May 1912, Archives of the Nursing School Cavell-Depage, State Archives of Belgium repository 2, Brussels.

28. Ecole Belge d'Infirmières Diplomées, Procès[-]verbaux [Conseil d'administration] May 1907–1916, session of 4 May 1911, Archives of the Nursing School Cavell-Depage, State Archives of Belgium repository 2, Brussels.

29. Ecole Belge d'Infirmières Diplomées, Procès[-]verbaux [Conseil d'administration] May 1907–1916, session of 29 June 1911, Archives of the Nursing School Cavell-Depage, State Archives of Belgium repository 2, Brussels.

30. L'École d'infirmières Saint-Camille, *L'Institut des Deux-Alice, 1907–1932* (Brussels: L'École d'infirmières Saint-Camille, 1932), 83.

31. Albertine De Villegas de St.-Pierre, "Les origines de l'Ecole St.-Camille," *La Voix de l'Infirmière* 3 (1960): 6; École Saint-Camille, *Infirmières diplomées Religieuses et Laïques* (Brussels: École Saint-Camille, n.d.), 11.

32. Ecole Belge d'Infirmières Diplomées, Procès[-]verbaux [Conseil d'administration] May 1907–1916, session of 26 July 1916 and session of 30 August 1916, Archives of the Nursing School Cavell-Depage, State Archives of Belgium repository 2, Brussels.

33. Ecole Belge d'Infirmières Diplomées, Procès[-]verbaux [Conseil d'administration] May 1907–1916, session of 7 October 1918, Archives of the Nursing School Cavell-Depage, State Archives of Belgium repository 2, Brussels.

34. Luc De Munck, *De Grote Moeder in de Grote Oorlog: De hulpverlening van het Rode Kruis tijdens de Eerste Wereldoorlog* [The Great Mother in the Great War: Medical aid of the Red Cross during the First World War] (Ypres: In Flanders Fields Museum, 2000), 5–7.

35. Luc De Munck and Luc Vandeweyer, *Het hospitaal van de Koningin: Rode Kruis, L'Océan en De Panne, 1914–1918* [The Hospital of the Queen: The Red Cross, L'Océan and De Panne, 1914–1918] (De Panne, Belgium: Gemeentebestuur De Panne, 2012), 63.

36. Antoine Depage, "L'ambulance de l'Océan à La Panne: Sa fondation, son évolution, son organisation," in *Ambulance de "l'Océan,"* ed. Antoine Depage (Paris: Masson, 1917), vol. 1, fasc. 1, 12.

37. Luc De Munck, "'Soms genezen, dikwijls verlichten, altijd troosten': Belgische verpleegsters tijdens de Eerste Wereldoorlog" ["Sometimes healing, most of the time relieving, always comforting": Belgian nurses during the First World War], M.A. thesis, KU Leuven (Catholic University of Leuven), 2017, 191.

38. Luc De Munck, *Altijd troosten: Belgische verpleegsters tijdens de Eerste Wereldoorlog* [Always comforting: Belgian nurses during the First World War] (Amsterdam: Amsterdam University Press, 2018), 28; Eliane Gubin and Valérie Montens, "La symbolique de la souffrance: Les infirmières en 1914–1918," *Sextant: Revue du Groupe Interdisciplinaire d'*Études *sur les Femmes*, no. 3 (Winter 1994–1995): 100.

39. Léopold Melis, *Contribution à l'histoire du Service de Santé de l'Armée au cours de la guerre 1914–1918* (Brussels: Institut Cartographique Militaire, 1932), 39.

40. Inventory no. XII, 312, 14, Subarchive Mgr. De Wachter, Archives of Cardinal Mercier, Archiepiscopal Archives, Mechelen; Pierre Lierneux, ed., *Het Belgische leger in de Grote Oorlog: Uniformen en uitrusting* [The Belgian army during the Great War: Uniforms and outfit] (Vienna: Militaria Stefan Rest, 2015), 330.

41. Infirmières, undated [1915] and unsigned note, folder 809, Archives of the Personal Secretary of King Albert and Queen Elisabeth, Royal Palace Archives, Brussels.

42. Day order 18 November 1916, item 5, folder 958, Archives of the Inspector General of the Army Medical Service, War Heritage Institute/Royal Museum of the Armed Forces and Military History, Brussels.

43. Day order 22 October 1918, item 7, folder 960, Archives of the Inspector General of the Army Medical Service, War Heritage Institute/Royal Museum of the Armed Forces and Military History, Brussels.

44. Day order 22 October 1918, item 9, folder 960, Archives of the Inspector General of the Army Medical Service, War Heritage Institute/Royal Museum of the Armed Forces and Military History, Brussels.

45. Jean-Pierre Gaume, *Profession: Infirmière / Profession: Nurse, Images 1900–1930* (Geneva: Musée international de la Croix-Rouge et du Croissant-Rouge, 1995), 29.

46. De Munck and Vandeweyer, *Het hospitaal van de Koningin*, 72–73.

47. Maria van den Steen, "L'autre guerre (suite de Mon Journal d'Infirmière)," vol. 3, "Les Souverains," 283, 302, personal archives of Florence de Moreau of Villegas de Saint-Pierre, Louvignies Castle, Louvignies.

48. Van den Steen, "L'autre guerre," vol. 2, "Les Britanniques," 253.

49. M. Thévenot, "A travers la mode," *La Mode Illustrée: Journal de la Famille*, no. 34 (23 August 1914): 46.

50. Florence Brachet Champsaur, "French Fashion during the First World War," *Business and Economic History On-Line* 2 (2004): 2–3, http://www.thebhc.org/sites/default/files/Champsaur_0.pdf (access date 24 October 2017); Rassche, *Wardrobes in Wartime*, 19. The original Jeanne Lanvin nurse-inspired ensemble was exhibited in 2017 in the Forney Library (Paris) during the exposition about fashion in France: *Le vestiaire feminine au début du XXe siècle*. The suit belongs to the collection of Palais Galliera.

51. Brachet Champsaur, "French Fashion during the First World War," 208. The Archives of the International Red Cross Committee in Geneva has no information about a Redfern design, according to an email from archivist F. Bensi, "Uniforme infirmière Croix-Rouge," 4 September 2017.

52. Brachet Champsaur, "French Fashion during the First World War," 1–2; De Leeuw, *Kleding in Nederland*, 418.

53. La Famille de l'Infirmière [Procès-verbaux Conseil d'Administration], session of 6 October 1920, Archives La Famille de l'Infirmière, Brussels.

54. National Ministry of Defense, "Statut organique des infirmières en service dans les hôpitaux militaires Belges," Brussels, 1921, 9–10. Appendix 3 of this decision contained a sketch of the uniform, bearing the badge.

55. Cécile Mechelynck, *La genèse et le développement du nursing laïque et quarante ans de la Fédération Nationale des Infirmières Belges* (Brussels: La Gerbe, 1962), 30.

56. Mechelynck, *La genèse et le développement du nursing laïque*, 31.

NINE

IDENTIFYING PATRIOTS

Women in Uniform in Italy

ALLISON SCARDINO BELZER

Staring out at us, smiling through lipstick with a bejeweled hand on her hips, the woman in uniform in Figure 9.1 embodies an elusive vision of modernity. Italians had few precedents for conceiving of what women's participation in the Great War would look like. Although the artist, Bonora, emphasized sex appeal, most other conceptions of women in uniform were more nuanced and conflicted.

Italy entered the Great War late and only after secret negotiations and substantial national debate. Tied to Germany and Austria-Hungary in the Triple Alliance since 1882, Italy opted to remain neutral when war broke out in August 1914. Unprepared militarily, the Liberal government negotiated the Treaty of London with the Allied powers (formerly called the Triple Entente), promising a "return" of the irredenta, land held by Austria but populated by Italian speakers. Many in the upper and middle classes welcomed the chance to expand Italy's borders at Austria's expense, but socialists and others in the working classes resisted the call to join the war. In fact, the Italian Socialist Party, uniquely across Europe, never abandoned its commitment to international pacifism; it remained steadfastly opposed to the war for the duration. Those within the party who demanded intervention, such as Benito Mussolini, simply left the Italian Socialist Party to forge new alliances. When the government formally entered the war on 24 May 1915, nationalists celebrated across Italy. This widespread public support for the war eclipsed the voices of those who continued to feel anxious or downright opposed to intervention. The patriotic, pro-war contingent would dominate Italian culture for the rest of the war.

Figure 9.1.
A postcard created in 1915 by the artist Bonora shows a confident Italian woman wearing a Bersagliere's hat with a modified sailor's uniform tucked into high-heeled boots. She personifies a futuristic, and fictional, view of women in war. Reprinted in Enrico Sturani, La Donna del soldato: L'immagine della donna nella cartolina italiana *(Rovereto: Museo Storico Italiano della Guerra, 2005), 98.*

Like all belligerent nations, Italy needed support from a wide variety of its population in order to participate in its first total war. Men of service age had to show up when drafted and follow orders on the battlefields, processes that never ran smoothly in Italy. Meanwhile, civilians shouldered many other responsibilities. Public speeches and newspaper articles charged women, even those without uniforms, to contribute. For many, women became the keepers of morale. A pamphlet distributed in 1918 by the government-run office of propaganda addressed "Mothers, Wives, and Sisters" about their behavior during the soldiers' winter leave, saying, "Every man who comes home must find you a fount of new force and new generous energy." It concluded with a stirring call: "Women of Italy, incite your men to fight and to win in order to hurry the peace that will return them to you for good."[1] The message was clear; women must resist reducing their men's will to fight by complaining about the hardships of the long war or by discouraging soldiers' return to the front. Influential women writers also called for emotional support for the combatants. Anna Franchi, a leading feminist author who lost her only son in the war, published an article entitled "To the Women!" that reminded her readers, "We Italian women are writing a page in history today. . . . Our sacrifice can speak to our spirit, more than our troubled mind can imagine, women's work will affect the fate of Italy."[2] Her essay came out just after the Italian army had suffered a humiliating retreat in October 1917 at Caporetto that snapped the exigencies of war back into focus. She called on women to watch out for falsified news (one imagines her today offering similar warnings about the proliferation of "fake news") and to maintain their strength in order to drive out the German and Austrian invaders. She, like many others, saw women as the defenders of morale at home and (via letters) at the front, too. Franchi and many others believed women's contributions were essential to victory. The question at hand was how far beyond traditional norms would Italian society, which had long subjected women to second-class status, allow them to go? How would people recognize women who worked for victory?

454 IL SECOLO XX

rinascere i sorrisi, di richiamare le donne alle gaiezze, alle superfluità della vita normale, sopravvennero troppo presto, per nostra sventura, le fatali giornate di Custoza.

L'atterrita cronista di mode grida disperata: «Le mie signore non leggono più il bollettino di mode, ma quello di guerra! Non sono le mode francesi, ma le armate francesi che si desiderano ora! Dio ci mandi un soccorso generoso! Provatevi ora in mezzo a crudeli sospetti, a parlare di mode, di merletti ecc. Chi ci ascolterebbe? Forse Trieste bloccata e gridante pace? Forse Venezia dove stringe il nemico? Forse il Piemonte generoso della sua primogenitura e insofferente di qualsiasi supremazia? Nessuno al certo ci ascolta!».

Rievocando queste angosciose speranze delle donne del 48, cui pur troppo si preparavano invece le tristezze infinite dell'anno terribile e glorioso in cui rifulse il disperato eroismo italico sui campi di Novara e sotto le mura di Roma, ritorniamo con un senso di fervido orgoglio ai giorni nostri in cui la meta vittoriosa ci sta dinnanzi, non prossima forse, ma sicura. Appunto per questa nostra serena certezza dell'esito, la moda di questa guerra non solo non subisce le alternative di sconfitte e di trionfi, ma fa anzi fiorire, come per il passato, giornali e riviste, ispirando nobile gara d'arte e di gusto fra gli artisti delle nazioni alleate. Come agli uomini non verranno mai a mancare, per questa comunione di sforzi, le atroci armi dello sterminio, così non saran mai prive le donne delle loro armi di seduzione! Se anzi vi fu qualche sommessa nota di stupore o di biasimo verso il moderno mondo femminile, che pure si è rivelato dotato d'intelligente attività, è stato appunto a proposito della sua eccessiva eleganza e della improvvisa rivoluzione di tutte le foggie. La *silhouette* femminile che nel tragico agosto del 1914 si disegnava ancora nelle audaci attillature delle gonne strettissime, si è oggi arricchita di tutti i rigonfi e degli svolazzi cari alle nostre nonne del 48. Nè soltanto la linea generale di quell'epoca, sacra ai fasti della libertà, hanno voluto far rivivere i nostri artisti; anche nei particolari tornano volentieri a quei modelli. Così dalla scarpetta *tango* denudante tutto il piede, siamo passati agli altissimi *coturni;* dalla pratica e sgraziata borsa di pelle alla civettuola *ridicule,* dal troppo semplice *en-tous-cas* al pomposo ombrellino a frange e svolazzi. Tutto questo sbocciare di inattese e gaie eleganze, che contrastano colle gloriose gramaglie ineluttabilmente crescenti, potrà bensì rappresentare uno sperpero o peccare talvolta di inopportuna spensieratezza, ma vincendo queste prime impressioni non dimentichiamo che esse rappresentano intanto un'affermazione di serena vigoria delle nostre industrie nazionali e della nostra vita economica.

Non è della moda, ma di tutta la nostra vita l'atroce contrasto fra il mondo della gioia e quello delle lacrime, fra le sublimità dei sanguinosi olocausti e la miseria degli avidi egoismi...

Perchè stupirsi se questa seconda primavera di guerra — che riconduce nella natura la vita gioiosa, senza poter ricondurre tante primavere umane dormenti sui campi di gloria — ha fiori per la tristezza della morte, come per le gioie dell'amore?!

Lina.

Figure 9.2.
The uniform of a war relief worker, bottom right, is portrayed as the pinnacle of style in 1916 in an article discussing wartime fashions since 1848. Lina, "La moda durante la Guerra, 1848-1916" Il secolo XX *14 no. 5 (May 1916), 453.*

Unlike in Britain, America, Canada, and Australasia, no custom developed in Italy of girls and women wearing quasi-military outfits before or during the Great War. But Italian women working in munitions, in a few public sector jobs, and in nursing did put on uniforms. Marked visibly as modern women, these wartime recruits were departing from long-held Italian mores that kept respectable women and girls literally behind closed doors. In part, uniforms helped disguise their sex and their personalities, whether delivering mail or working in military hospitals. This anonymity could be useful, especially for the few women working in public jobs formerly done by men. Professional uniforms, by design, demonstrate one's authority and special standing in society, and women embraced them. As one American visitor noted, women in France, Britain, and Italy, "young and old," were racing "to don the picturesque Red Cross uniform."[3] An article focusing on "fashion during wartime" explained that even though fashion is "frivolous, delicate, feminine," it has always coexisted with war, reflecting the mood of the times (Figure 9.2). The author compared dresses worn in the Risorgimento struggle to those from the Great War. Noticing that flowers can symbolize both the joy of love and the sadness of death, she made the case for fashion as an indicator of national vigor and economic health. She ended the article with a sketch of a relief worker in uniform, showing her as just as stylish as her predecessors.[4]

A leaflet from 1917, *You Are Still Wasting Too Much Money*, makes a similar point by showing women wearing expensive clothes and jewelry (Figure 9.3).[5] On the backside, the text warns, "We are tired of the foolish woman." It reminds women "from every social class" that the men who are fighting are judging them and highlights the sacrifices made by mothers of fallen soldiers. The message is clear: Women need to focus more on saving money and to appear more involved with the war. Everyone could see that women wearing uniforms were not wasting money on frippery. They were virtuous and patriotic citizens, making real contributions to the war effort.

Figure 9.3.
The sketches from the frontside of a leaflet highlight the high cost of trying to dress fashionably, "You are still wasting too much money." Alle donne di ogni classe sociale, *[1917], Biblioteca Universitaria Alessandrina, RML0347523.*

As the chapters in this book demonstrate, the idea of visible patriotism had widespread appeal. Women in Italy were no less interested than their international sisters and their own brothers and cousins in showing their patriotism (and being identified as patriots) by being in uniform.

Wearing uniforms literally opened doors for women. Hoping for even more visibility, some Italian women unsuccessfully called for the government to award decorations and badges for war work.[6] Meanwhile, volunteers with the Italian Red Cross (CRI), called *crocerossine*, were easily identifiable. As in many other countries, they wore long white dresses and wimples. In her diary, one woman noted how her distinctive appearance facilitated her work. She glided among the throngs at the Verona train station, entering and exiting freely, "thanks to my nurse's uniform."[7] The uniform gave her a mobility that other women civilians lacked. The new sight of so many women in uniform attracted public attention and clearly distinguished these women from others. One British aid volunteer in Italy noted that the "general public" was "terrifically interested" in her uniform as she passed through Milan on her way to the front.[8] A vast array of archetypes of uniformed women appeared in the Italian press during the war in photographs, drawings, articles, and short stories; they were courageous, competent, empathetic, and sociable.

Women in uniform projected a new type of participant in Italian civic life. After the war, as Italy reeled from a peace treaty that felt humiliating, people of both sexes felt the allure of Fascism. Mussolini built on the foundations laid during the war, calling for continued personal sacrifice for the greater good and claiming to make a place for all Italians to contribute to a national resurgence. It is no coincidence that Fascism offered uniforms for just about everyone, a compelling proposal for many women eager to continue to be identified as patriots.

A "GREAT FEMALE ARMY" AND THE CALL TO MOBILIZE WOMEN

Although the government did not seriously consider mobilizing women alongside men, some Italians called for mandatory female participation in the war effort and looked closely at what other countries were requiring of women. The goal was to destigmatize women's war work by making it mandatory for all women of a certain age. Most vociferously, Elma Vercelloni, president of the Armed Women's Committee for Home Front Resistance, spearheaded a movement to demand mandatory mobilization and hosted a conference in Rome on 3 March 1918.[9] Others also published articles that discussed the issue of women's mobilization. *Assistenza civile* in particular engaged its audience about the role of women in wartime; it was the mouthpiece of the Federation of National Civilian Assistance Committees, created in a merger between feminist groups in Milan and a male-run war relief committee.[10] Dr. Ernesta Fasciotti, a prominent scientist and relief worker, spoke on the subject of mobilization in April 1917; her speech was reprinted in *Assistenza civile*. Noting the efforts underway that put women to work in Germany, France, and Britain, Fasciotti explained that "we [Italian women], having remained in our comfortable homes, feel the duty to offer ourselves to the Patria in order to form a second army, with no less discipline and valor, to organize the home front defense."[11] Six months later, Stefano Conio published an article on women's mobilization in *Assistenza civile*. He wanted women working "for resistance and for victory" but stopped short of calling for mandatory mobilization.[12] Refuting those who claimed that mobilizing men would be sufficient, Fasciotti claimed that the war needs were too great to limit participation by sex. She called on women from all generations to help, in part to free up men to go to the front. To Fasciotti, it was a waste of soldiers to have men working in administrative offices, in factories, and in the fields—all work that women could do capably. She also wanted to ensure that men and women made equal wartime contributions.

Fasciotti and others saw mobilization as an antidote to discrimination against women. Italians had long-standing prejudices against seeing women as independent agents. Although Italian high politics in this era had more in common with Britain or France (in that they were all parliamentary democracies), Italian cultural mores were more old-fashioned and conservative. Women had few legal rights and, outside of cities, few opportunities for independence. Carla Cadorna, the daughter of the general who led Italian military operations until 1917, addressed "the prejudice that a strong woman is that horrible thing—a woman without a heart."[13] She wanted to convince readers that love and courage could coexist. She herself was no twenty-first century feminist; for example, she wrote that there were things "too serious for our [women's] incompetence" to understand and that woman's natural constitution made her well suited for acts of "spiritual maternity."[14] But her insistence that women must play a role in the war effort shows how frequently social commentators conflated wartime contributions with being socially valuable. Conio quoted one observer: "I confess that I have nourished for a long time the strong opinion that the work of women, in these extraordinary times, would be enough to overcome, with the irresistible force of experience, every inveterate and traditional male prejudice. But experience does not support this opinion."[15] Noticing this same dichotomy, Fasciotti called on Italians to overcome their old biases against women. She believed total mobilization would equalize civilian and soldier contributions, helping each recognize the other's sacrifices. Similarly, Conio hoped that women's abilities would become impossible to ignore once enough of them showed up on the "field of duty."[16] For Vercelloni, the shocking military failures of Caporetto proved that Italian war efforts demanded a new approach. Misunderstanding the nature of that rout, she maintained that if women had been mobilized from the moment of Italy's entrance into the war and taught military discipline, the morale of the soldiers and civilians would have been stronger and the defeat avoided.[17] In her mind, the civilians' low morale at home exacerbated military problems.

Vercelloni, Fasciotti, and others looked outside Italy for models. The Hapsburg Empire's auxiliary program was voluntary; it involved tens of thousands of women working as provisional employees behind the lines doing everything from providing medical care to answering telephones.[18] Vercelloni wanted compulsory participation, explaining voluntary mobilization worked well in Britain because of their organized society and "maybe more virile" temperament.[19] Fasciotti quoted the British minister of business and agriculture as saying, "The woman who helps in agriculture during the war serves her country as faithfully as the men who fight at sea and in the trenches."[20] She wanted Italians to follow suit, and she encouraged women to stay and run their farms and businesses after male relatives had left for military service. Women were needed in all sectors. She concluded her speech with a stirring call to "this great female army that must fight the industrial and economic battle at the home front." It was necessary, Fasciotti believed, not only to win the war but also to provide "a luminous example" to the combatants who would, she predicted, be energized by knowing of women's accomplishments.[21] Making a similar argument in a pamphlet about women and war, Alessandro Schiavi noted the well-functioning administration of women's efforts in England, France, and Germany, emphasizing the creation of courses in professional development and codes regulating work hours and salaries.[22]

Fasciotti offered a plan for Italy that would begin with a period of voluntary enrollment and then move to obligatory mobilization of women from ages 18 through 48, taking into account women's marital status and family needs. They would serve in all sectors of the home front economy: civilian assistance, hospitals, civil administration offices, warehouses, workshops making furniture and textiles, and agriculture. Like the rest of Italy, the local civilian assistance committees were split on this issue. Over 50 branches supported mandatory male and female civilian mobilization; just under 20 rejected both; 9 wanted only male mobilization; and 4 wanted only female.[23]

Vercelloni vigorously argued for her proposal with politicians. She sent her demand to Vittorio Orlando when he served as president of the Council of Ministers and to Minister Leonida Bissolati. Bissolati rebuffed her idea, telling her that women already were working usefully for the war effort.[24] Bissolati spoke for the majority; women in Italy were not mobilized, but they did go to work for the war effort by the thousands, many in uniforms.

WORKING FOR WAGES IN UNIFORM

The home front economy had to produce sufficient munitions to keep the war effort going while also providing enough goods and services for noncombatants to avoid desperation and revolt. Schiavi reported that women needed salaries to sustain their own families now that male breadwinners had been drafted; war work was not only patriotic but, for many, economically essential.[25] Even though a relatively low number of Italian women wore uniforms in the Great War, they were responsible for making the ones worn by men. In an ad hoc system run as a welfare program, 600,000 women sewed military uniforms at home, as a preindustrial cottage industry. Disrupted by rivalries among government branches, the scheme was, according to one expert, "poorly organized" and resulted in underpaid employees and ill-equipped soldiers.[26] Meanwhile, many other women worked outside of the home for the war effort.

Historian Barbara Curli has written the definitive study of Italian women workers during the war. She explains that women did not, by and large, replace men; in fact, most conscripted men were replaced by other men. The total war effort pushed Italy to full employment by absorbing all chronically unemployed and underemployed men. And because of dwindling emigration and increased repatriation, more men reentered the labor pool. When women did take on new jobs, they were supplementary and temporary workers in the eyes of their employers and society.[27] But munitions firms did have to hire women as young men working in unskilled jobs were conscripted or moved to doing "heavier and more difficult" work.[28] The war needs favored heavy industry, work typically designated as masculine.[29] Only in a very few cases did women replace men, but many of these were in public roles such as tram operators.

Women workers in uniforms were a minority in the wartime labor force, but they disproportionately provoked controversy and altered public opinions about women's roles in society. Especially among the older generations, independent women with their own salaries caused anxiety about morality. What luxury goods might they be buying with their wages? Who was chaperoning their behavior both inside and outside the workplace? In September 1916, the Italian undersecretary of arms and munitions explained that women workers would live in settlements to protect their "health and morality," especially when, on occasion, they had to work night shifts.[30] As more women went to work, the government increasingly regulated not only the economic structure but also the social and health-related aspects of their employment.[31] Rules included how long pregnant women could work (not during the last month of pregnancy or the first month after birth) and how they would be supervised (by women, with men working in separate departments).[32] These concerns echoed across Europe.[33]

Italians noted what women from other countries were contributing and felt their own efforts lagging. Three articles appeared in the popular Milan magazine *La lettura* focusing attention on Allied women's war efforts, especially the ways they were replacing men at the home front.[34] Drawings and photographs showed French women working on explosives and packing barrels, American women tilling fields and parading as policewomen, and English women mounting propellers and sweeping streets. The stories reported on the wide range of relief work undertaken, praising the new courses offered at a variety of colleges, from Vassar to Washington State, to train young women in nursing, mechanics, and agriculture. The tone was heroic; these Allied women were doing exceptional and important work that the Italians should imitate. In 1918, an article in *Il secolo XX* (another popular weekly magazine based in Milan) unfavorably compared Italian women with those in Britain, who were officially mobilized and had to "dress in uniforms and live in special housing." Meanwhile, the author continued, Italian efforts to create a unified female army, although "generous," seemed destined for failure because there were too many individual agencies and efforts to coordinate.[35] Even their enemies seemed to be outflanking them; another article in *Il secolo XX* exhibited photos of German women working as coach drivers, chauffeurs, ticket collectors, machine operators, street cleaners and sweepers, mail sorters and carriers, window washers, police agents, paper mill workers, ice cream vendors, and munitions workers.[36] Although it is curious that Italians would look at the successes of their enemy, the point of the story was to call for utilizing women for the war effort. How could Italy win if it pushed aside the assistance of half its population? As Bruna Guarducci, an Italian journalist, noted in *Assistenza civile*, "The war is fought from within, in the city, just as at the front."[37] The Italian public seemed to need some convincing.

The demands of the Great War facilitated a new place for women in the body politic. Working for the war effort in uniform made women visible as participants on the national stage. Women were offered no tangible benefits in exchange for their services to the war effort, but many assumed their faithful contributions would yield the vote and other political gains after victory, and many politicians promised them as much. The minister of finance noted how the war was changing women's position in society. After explaining that before the war, he "had never had much faith nor much hope in the *movimento femminile,*" by 1916, he realized women had made contributions of great "moral" and "economic value." He predicted that after the war "the country will be right to consider female activity as one of the most vital elements" needed to rebuild a successful peacetime society.[38] In June 1916 at the Campidoglio in Rome, a speaker exhorted the crowd, which was meeting to discuss legal reforms and protections for soldiers' families, to "go forward, go forward, messengers armed with faith and valor, continue your work; reverence and national gratitude will accompany you." He cheered "women who work in military plants, in private offices, on the tram lines, in offices, in banks, and wherever they offer proof of strength, of wisdom, and of heart." In return, he promised, Italy would give women "a place worthy of their high valor."[39] Senator Pio Foa opined that "the present war has so much multiplied good examples of feminine potential in Italy as in all of Europe" that it will be necessary to consider what women's roles will be in peacetime.[40]

During the war, some politicians predicted that women's contributions would open new doors, in particular expanding voting rights (even if only in local elections) and repealing inequalities in the marriage laws. For example, in 1916 the mayor of Pavia speculated that after the war women would be the same as they had been before and during the war: "the sweetest founts of life and love, uninterrupted examples of devotion and sacrifice." But he noted how their wartime contributions to "sanitary, moral, and material assistance to the army" and to "civil assistance that contributed to the intellectual and economic development of the Nation" were changing views of what women were like. Men have been holding themselves above women, he noted, and he claimed that now that women's worth was widely apparent, the government should grant them legal equality.[41] Senator Luigi Federzoni expressed similar ideas a few months later, praising Italian women for providing "a marvelous example of patriotism, abnegation, and intellectual energy." He called on legislators to "do our moral duty" after the war ended by granting women better judicial and social conditions.[42]

Senator Luigi Valli came to the same conclusions, but from a different premise. He believed the Great War had imbued women with "a new spirit." Yes, he acknowledged, there were women heroes during the fight for Italian unification in the nineteenth century, but those had been aristocrats. Women from the lower classes were not involved in that struggle, and women did not embrace the cause with any "special fervor," he believed. But "now, it is reversed." Valli listed multiple examples of women who "emerged from the shadow of family [obligations] in order to become hospital nurses, activists in civilian assistance committees," and relief workers in the city and the countryside. The war, he claimed, had created "a new woman" with a conscience who looks beyond herself, making feminism "not only words" but actions.[43] Clearly, women's wartime efforts sparked new ideas about their essential natures and capabilities. Even as one senator favorably cited Rousseau's ideas about women (never a good sign for feminism), he acknowledged that women's current involvement "in the national economy" was elevating them; they worked "without cancelling their character," referring to femininity (as something distinct from masculinity).[44] With these comments, he addressed a widespread anxiety that women taking on new roles and participating in civic engagements would desex them.

In Italy, the women working in public service came under intense scrutiny in large part because of these long-standing prejudices. Other nations, including the neighboring Hapsburg Empire, seemed to have had an easier time accepting the novelty of women in public service. In 1918, Umberto Brunelleschi (1879–1949) celebrated the modern working woman through an Art Deco series of postcards (Figure 9.4). Brunelleschi had studied art in Florence, then moved to Paris in 1901, where he befriended Picasso, Modigliani, Derain, and others. He returned to Italy to serve in the war, during which he cofounded and illustrated a trench newspaper for the Third Army, *La tradotta* (literally, "the troop train").[45] His women are tall and sleek; they wear makeup and uniforms and have tucked their hair under their caps. Even though they work in traditionally male-dominated fields, they maintain their femininity and even keep on their high heels. These postcards seem designed to assuage the fear that work would masculinize women, a worry the soldiers serving at the front shared. These are sexy women, the stuff of dreams. Historian Thomas Row explains that the postcards, published by *La tradotta*, were aimed squarely at men serving in the front lines, functioning as "chaste precursors of the pin-ups of World War II."[46] Brunelleschi's images promote women workers by depicting them as attractive individuals doing dynamic work.

This elegant image stands in stark contrast to the public debate over women working in this role. According to a government survey, people believed women tram operators were inept, accusing them of promiscuity and inattention.[47] Some complaints were valid, and women who were not up to the task were fired. Others quit because of the low pay, long hours, and hard work. Photographs show a more realistic view. Like their fantasy counterparts, but less stylishly, the real *donne tranvieri* wore uniform coats and tied their hair back under their caps. Figure 9.5 comes from *L'Illustrazione italiana*, a weekly magazine with a wide general readership, which sent a positive message about their predicament, presenting them

Figure 9.4.
Umberto Brunelleschi's woman tram operator wears her brown uniform coat over her flowery dress, her ticket pouch slung over her shoulder. She towers over a red streetcar and gazes directly at the viewer, confident she knows how to do her job. Art deco postcard by Umberto Brunelleschi, Donna tranviere, *1917.*

Figure 9.5.
A real-life colleague of Brunelleschi's Donna tranviere *is portrayed as enjoying her work while she counts the day's receipts. This woman, the magazine seems to say, does not deserve public scorn.* L'Illustrazione italiana, *20 May 1917, 425.*

as competent and happy.[48] Austrian magazines, as Claudia Reichl-Ham observes, offered similarly rosy views about how women tram conductors enriched street life.[49]

In his postcard series, Brunelleschi also depicted women in other public sector jobs: the *donna postino* (woman mail carrier), the *donna spazzino* (woman street sweeper), and the *donna facchino* (woman porter), all wearing distinctive uniform smocks. Like the tram operator, these women's own dresses emerge from under the uniform, a message that their femininity (and individuality, too, perhaps) will not disappear just because they are doing men's jobs. And like their *donna tranviere* counterpart, they are fashionable, young women performing their work with élan. It is difficult to track the reaction to these postcards, but it is easy to understand the messages Brunelleschi and *La tradotta* were sending to the servicemen about the allure of a woman in uniform.

As Brunelleschi's postcards reflect, the war effort did have a substantial impact on attitudes about women working. It brought about irreversible changes in society: an unprecedented mobility and a new visibility for women.[50] Women had always worked, but agriculture labor and domestic service were hidden from the pubic gaze. When women in uniform collected tickets or swept the streets, they stepped into the civic sphere, showcasing a new type of modern woman. Curli notes that the war defined the modern woman as one who works and has a sense of participating in the world outside the home. She agrees that the war created a new definition of female citizenship, albeit only a "partial, auxiliary" one.[51]

In addition to those in the public sector, women working in factories making munitions wore uniforms. A contemporary government report remarked that at the end of October 1915 (when Italy had been in the war for five months), some 14,000 women had jobs in skilled war industries. By the end of the war, that number ballooned to almost 200,000.[52] They fabricated projectiles and bombs, operated machinery, lifted materials, and worked in front offices. In the first year of the war, the Office of Industrial Mobilization focused on persuading more firms to hire semiskilled workers (i.e., women) without requiring they hire women per se. One official memo explained that in addition to the reluctance of industries to hire women who had yet to prove that they could work as well as men, there existed the biases of "thousand year old customs of civil and domestic life" that as yet were untouched by the "turbine" of war. Many Italians simply could not imagine women working in these types of jobs.[53] Bice Viallet published several articles in *Assistenza civile* pleading for women's work to be recognized as vital. She called on the minister of munitions to do more to support women laborers and pointed out to readers that wartime jobs were undoing the stigmas attached to women who did paid work.[54] The first wave of women taking on skilled munitions work must have reduced the prejudices against women workers, although Italy developed no public recruitment campaigns along the lines of those produced in Britain and the United States that celebrated the woman worker as "doing her bit" and making fundamental contributions.

As war needs grew exponentially, the government began to require that munitions industries hire women and juveniles, suggesting that firms were slow to employ them. A report from June 1917 set quotas: Half of the total number of skilled workers manufacturing projectiles of medium caliber had to be women and minors, as did those in foundries producing weights under five kilograms. These factories would have to modify their means of transport to accommodate the less strong employees; regional committees were charged with ensuring compliance or dispensing waivers.[55] The Central Committee for Industrial Mobilization set up special training schools for women to learn factory skills.[56] By the end of the war, it was clear that women had mastered their new jobs, and the official government reports credited them with helping Italy successfully produce war materials. Nevertheless, images of these workers wearing uniforms were not widely distributed in mainstream media.

VOLUNTEERS: WOMEN IN UNIFORM

Women employed in munitions and the public sector were not the only ones newly outfitted in distinctive clothes; the thousands of women working in the medical field or doing aid work also wore uniforms. Typical of the period, the uniforms of Italian women aid

Figure 9.6.
A wartime postcard from 1916-1918, signed Ballester, depicts the nurse as charity incarnate. Reprinted in Enrico Sturani, La Donna del soldato: L'immagine della donna nella cartolina italiana *(Rovereto: Museo Storico Italiano della Guerra, 2005), 107.*

workers resembled those of nuns. Long white aprons or long-sleeved dresses hid their arms and legs, and headdresses inching over their foreheads with fabric flowing behind encased their hair. In a poem celebrating the Red Cross nurse, Gemma de Daninos described a "white shadow" and a "holy angel" ministering in the "realm of grief."[57] This ideal nurse was caring, kind, and, like the Madonna, full of unselfish love. She was otherworldly; her outfit erased the body and any traces of femininity, in large part to desexualize women who were attending to men's bodies. To counteract their intimate contact with men, these women were supposed to be charity incarnate, as Figure 9.6, a wartime postcard, makes clear. The uniform signaled to patients that women were unavailable for sex or romantic love. They were pillars of purity; stiff white fabric forbade access to the (possibly corruptible or corrupting) body. Photographs of these women appeared in popular magazines. Whether caring for soldiers' children in group homes or attending a nursing school, they all looked alike.[58] To some degree, the desexualizing project worked; despite Ernest Hemingway's and Mark Helprin's romantic fantasies of patient–nurse relationships, few real-life love affairs seem to have existed between these wealthier and more educated women volunteers and their sickly soldier charges.[59] More often, women spoke of forming a parent–child bond, with nurses standing in for absent mothers, cajoling uncomfortable boys back to health.

When the Great War began, about 4,000 women were already serving as *crocerossine* under the able direction of Duchess Elena d'Aosta, a veteran of the Libyan war (Figure 9.7).[60] She brought an international perspective with her, having been born in England and raised in France.[61] Almost all the women working under the auspices of aid organizations (including the CRI, the Green Cross, and the Samaritans) came from the middle and upper classes because, in Italy, they were volunteers receiving no compensation. They had to pay their own way through nursing school to get accredited. Coming from these social classes, they would have been more conservative and more traditionally patriotic than their working-class sisters. Most of them were also single and childless. They were eager recruits; by the end of the war, there were about 10,000 women volunteers in the CRI.[62] One article noted the

Figure 9.7.
Duchess Elena d'Aosta served as the director of the Italian Red Cross. She is shown in this portrait wearing her uniform. Reprinted in Vittorio Brizzolesi, Gli italiani-americani alla guerra *(Milan: Alfieri & Lacroix, 1919), between 96 and 97.*

Figure 9.8.
The cover of this popular magazine shows a nurse behind two servicemen carrying an injured man. Il secolo XX *14, no. 5 (May 1916).*

pent-up demand among the women of Milan; 10 new nursing schools were created in the first months of the war with 1,500 students already enrolled. It took two months to complete the 30 lessons required on topics such as anatomy, surgery, infectious disease, and bandaging wounds. The author praised the women but undercut their contributions by highlighting their desire to provide "sweet and affectionate assistance to our brave wounded."[63] In reality, nurses and other medical staff did much more than offer affection. Originally conceived as extra hands to help with hygiene and psychological well-being (changing bandages and sheets, writing letters to family, sitting in comfort by a bedside), women found themselves much more involved in providing medical care. They dispensed medicine, helped in amputations, and sorted patients for triage, often working 12- or even 24-hour shifts.[64] Famously, three Italian nurses serving at a field hospital refused to abandon their patients during the Caporetto retreat in October 1917 and ended up in an Austrian concentration camp once the area was retaken.[65] Their story circulated widely, and both the CRI and the Italian government awarded them medals of bravery.[66]

The press showcased nurses and aid workers using several different archetypes, and among the most common was the courageous volunteer. Figure 9.8 shows the only cover of *Il secolo XX* depicting a woman in uniform. Wearing her trademark attire, this Red Cross nurse seems to be stationed close enough to the fighting to be part of the team helping wounded soldiers off the field. Although she is plainly in the thick of the action, her obscured face offers a vivid reminder that women's work remained subordinate to men's.

About 1,320 Italian women served along the Italian front as nurses, up to 720 at a time.[67] These positions were highly competitive; only well-connected women could arrange to serve so close to the action. Most nurses worked on transport trains and in military hospitals at the home front. These women were portrayed as stoic and dutiful. For instance, a short story by Amilda Pons entitled "La Signorina" told the story of a young *crocerossina* who receives news that her father, a general, has died.[68] Heartbroken and physically weakened by the news, she vows to remain on duty all day to emulate his example. Her attention to her patients is her only concern:

> That closed room of her soul remained hermetically sealed: the body continued to be covered in the pure uniform of charity. White wimple, the bandage, white apron and tunic; only the cross, ruby colored, glittering on her whiteness, remained to remind her of the red tears that were oozing in her heart.[69]

Her pain hides under her uniform; her individuality shielded by her patriotic duty. She dies at the end, and the author directly links her determination to serve Italy with her father's military service and praises her commitment to her work.

Many images of women aid workers highlight their capability, perhaps in response to public anxiety about women taking on so many new responsibilities. Nursing could be categorized as "maternal" and was thus deemed appropriate work, but the concern lingered that medical work brought women too close to men's bodies and gave them too much independence. Photographs showing groups of women, either in training or in practice, highlight their efficiency. Although neither society nor the women themselves considered their contributions as equal to men's, a spirit of collaboration existed between servicemen and aid workers. Sita Camperio Meyer, one of the pioneers of the Italian Red Cross movement and a volunteer during the war, noted that "nurses, maybe, were the closest to the spirit of the infantry."[70] She may have meant nurses knew their patients' hearts better than anyone, but it seems she also was eliding their war contributions, saying both are motivated by the same spirit. Yet Italian nurses resembled nuns far more than soldiers. Women from other countries serving in Italy looked much closer to being equals with soldiers. As Figure 9.9 shows, the trench newspaper *La tradotta* called the newly arrived American and British Red Cross workers "the courageous new sisters of the infantryman." Brunelleschi portrayed Allied women as very unlike their Italian "sisters," as all nurses were called in Italy. These foreign women dressed for adventure and mobility, not sainthood, a very different approach that was not common in Italy. For his part, at least, this infantryman seems to approve of women in khaki.[71]

Officially, gender norms restricted the range of Italian women's contributions to the war. As one father told his daughter when she began working with the CRI, "I don't have

Figure 9.9.
Umberto Brunelleschi drew an Italian infantryman at the front flanked by newly arrived American and British Red Cross workers wearing sporty, military-style uniforms. Umberto Brunelleschi, "Crocerossine americane e inglesi in linea durante la battaglia," La tradotta, *29 August 1918, 8.*

any males to send to the front. I send you to the hospitals, because we must give the most possible to the Patria."[72] He felt that giving up his daughter to nurse was the most he could give. A handful of women went farther, forsaking the *crocerossina* uniform for a soldier's. In her book celebrating women's wartime contributions, Donna Paola (the pen name of Paola Baronchelli Grosson) mentioned two women caught cross-dressing to join the army; she imagined, likely in vain, that many more women served undiscovered.[73] A resident of the Austrian territory contested by Italy during the war, Maria von Hauler exchanged her Austrian Red Cross uniform for infantry fatigues after her father died in March 1917. She served in combat as Wolf Hauler and was discovered only when she was hospitalized after a gas attack. It seems some of her fellow soldiers knew she was a woman before officials unmasked her, but they protected her secret, powerful testimony to the bond they must have formed with their comrade in arms.[74] In the Great War, Russia alone allowed women to serve in combat and only after the overthrow of the tsarist regime.[75] For Italy and the other belligerent nations, encouraging women to enter onto the public stage as active and essential participants in the national struggle was as much novelty as they could handle.

POSTWAR LEGACY

Feminist advocates, like Donna Paola, hoped that wartime work was setting a model that would allow women to continue to work outside the home after the war ended. She was careful to note, however, that not even "the most fanatical feminist" would deny that family is fundamental. Donna Paola wanted a postwar world filled with more equal couples who were committed to repopulating Italy and promoting its culture. These mothers of tomorrow must be "conscious citizens," able to educate sons and daughters in an "exclusively Italian spirit."[76] In a later article, she wondered what would happen to all the women who had earned salaries during the war; she worried that pushing them out of the workforce after the war ended would result in not only lost wages but also lost pride, independence, and authority.[77] Similarly, Bice Viallet hoped wartime work was setting an irreversible precedent that would allow women to continue to work outside the home after the war ended.[78]

These predictions would turn out to be too optimistic. After the war, most women left the workforce, and the Italian government (like the French) refused to grant women suffrage. The passage of the Sacchi Law in 1919 opened some new doors for women's work and made wives financially independent from their husbands, but it was not as far reaching as many wished in equalizing women's place in society.[79] It is impossible for historians to measure accurately a change in values, but published and private texts show that public ideas about women and femininity changed because of the war. The women who tasted independence for the first time must have shared their memories with the next generation coming along behind them. The same could be true for the men who had experienced a new model of womanhood: politically active and self-sufficient. Whether they liked it or not, they had witnessed women present in the public sector, visible in their distinctive uniforms. The patriotic wartime woman worker was a long way from the prewar matriarch who might have run the private sphere with force but was secluded from the gaze of the outside world. But these cultural changes did not immediately result in tangible advancements for women. There were few real "flapper girls" (called *maschiette* in Italy) in the postwar years, and the Fascist Party, which came to power in 1922, worked hard to ensure that this image of a short-haired, sassy, corsetless young woman was not held up as a model.[80]

Women who had been proud to be in uniform, serving their country, had choices to make after the war ended. The most profound legacy of the new gender roles developed during the war manifested itself in the Fascist call for women to be good citizens by being prolific mothers and supporters of Mussolini's ideology. Although he ultimately failed, Mussolini wanted to politicize all aspects of life, asking for people to continue to sacrifice their own needs for those of the state even long past the Armistice. The idea was that women would help renew Italy by having lots of babies who would grow up to be good soldiers and good mothers. Fascism cloaked demands for obedience in patriotic terms that echoed the rhetoric of the Great War, and many women responded affirmatively to being included in a national project that celebrated them as (nominal) citizens. In Italy, wearing uniforms could provide a way to step outside traditional norms that denied women civic agency, but it is important to remember that uniforms were also a means of disguising a citizen's individuality and encouraging her to put her nation's needs ahead of her own.

NOTES

1. Edito a cura dell'Ufficio Propaganda presso il Com., in Capo, *Licenze invernali . . .*, Spezia, 1918, collection AST B.N.E./37, sheet 6, Museo Storico del Trentino, Trento.
2. Anna Franchi, "Alle donne!" *Assistenza civile* 1, no. 24 (16 Dec. 1917): 1033.
3. William J. Guard, *The Spirit of Italy: Impressions and Observations of an American Newspaper Man during the Early Months of the War against Austria* (New York: H. Rogowski, 1916), 191.
4. Lina, "La moda durante la guerra," *Il secolo XX* 14, no. 5 (May 1916): 451–454.
5. *Alle donne di ogni classe sociale*, [1917], Biblioteca Universitaria Alessandrina, RML0347523. http://www.14-18.it/foglio/RML0347523_01 (accessed 24 February 2019).
6. Perry Willson, *Women in Twentieth-Century Italy* (New York: Palgrave, 2010), 49.
7. Mario Forano, ed., "Nella tormenta 1915–1919: Diario di Margherita d'Incisa Rossi Passavanti," in *Le crocerossine nella Grande Guerra: Aristocratiche e borghesi nei diari e negli ospedali militari: Una via all'emancipazione femminile*, ed. Paolo Scandaletti and Giuliana Variola (Udine, Italy: Gaspari, 2012), 70.
8. Vera Woodroffe, letter, 13 July 1917, Documents Collection, Imperial War Museum, London.
9. For more about her arguments, see Allison Scardino Belzer, *Women and the Great War: Femininity under Fire* (New York: Palgrave, 2010), 61–65. For the conference proceedings, see Elma Vercelloni, *Perché la coscrizione femminile deve essere obbligatoria: Discorso-programma tenuto al Teatro comunale Argentina in Roma il 3 Marzo del 1918* (Rome: Stabilamento Cromo-Tip. Carlo Colombo, 1918). For an image of a poster advertising the event, see the collection of the Biblioteca Universitaria Alessandrina, http://www.14-18.it/manifesto/RML0217793_01?bt=europeanaapi (accessed 13 June 2017).
10. Willson, *Women in Twentieth-Century Italy*, 48.
11. Ernesta Fasciotti, "Mobilitazione civile," reprinted speech, *Assistenza civile* 1, nos. 7–8 (1–16 Apr. 1917): 351. On Fasciotti, see *Atti della Reale accademia delle scienze di Torino*, 41:12.
12. Stefano Conio, "Bisogna mobilitare le donne per la resistenza e per la vittoria," *Assistenza civile* 1, no. 20 (16 Oct. 1917): 882–884.
13. Carla Cadorna, *La guerra nelle retrovie* (Florence: Bemporad, 1917), 22–23.
14. Cadorna, *La guerra nelle retrovie*, 41, 101.
15. Conio, "Bisogna mobilitare le donne," 882.
16. Conio, "Bisogna mobilitare le donne," 882.
17. Vercelloni, *Perché la coscrizione femminile*, 6–7.
18. For more on Austria-Hungary, see Claudia Reichl-Ham in this volume (ch. 11).
19. Vercelloni, *Perché la coscrizione femminile,* 10.
20. Fasciotti, "Mobilitazione civile," 354.
21. Fasciotti, "Mobilitazione civile," 356.
22. Alessandro Schiavi, *La guerra e la mano d'opera femminile* (Florence: Bemporad, 1915), 3–5.
23. Fasciotti, "Mobilitazione civile," 352.

24. Vercelloni, *Perché la coscrizione femminile*, 8–12.

25. Schiavi, *La guerra e la mano d'opera femminile*, 3.

26. Willson, *Women in Twentieth-Century Italy*, 52.

27. Barbara Curli, *Italiane al lavoro 1914–1920* (Venice: Marsilio, 1998), 13, 32, 33.

28. From a circular dated 19 Mar. 1917, quoted in Ufficio della Mano d'Opera Femminile del Ministero Armi e Munizioni (Direzione Generale Mobilitazione Industriale), *Le donne d'Italia nelle industrie di guerra* (Rome: Tipografia dell'instituto internazionale d'agricoltura, 1918), 4.

29. For more on the gendering of wartime labor, see Margaret R. Higonnet and Patrice L.-R. Higonnet, "The Double Helix," in *Behind the Lines: Gender and the Two World Wars,* eds. Margaret R. Higonnet, Jane Jenson, Soyna Michel, and Margaret Collins Weitz (New Haven, Conn.: Yale University Press, 1987), 31–50.

30. Ufficio della Mano d'Opera Femminile, *Le donne d'Italia nelle industrie di guerra*, 4.

31. For a list of some of the rules, see the "Vigilaza igenienico-sanitaria" published in spring 1917 in the *Gazzetta ufficiale*, reprinted in Ufficio della Mano d'Opera Femminile, *Le donne d'Italia nelle industrie di guerra*, 15–16.

32. Ufficio della Mano d'Opera Femminile, *Le donne d'Italia nelle industrie di guerra*, 22–23.

33. Susan Grayzel, *Women and the First World War* (New York: Pearson, 2002), ch. 3.

34. P. Croci, "Penelope moderna," *La lettura* 16, no. 8 (1 Aug. 1916): 698–704; Romeo Gallenga, "Il lavoro della donna in Inghilterra durante la guerra," *La lettura* 17, no. 11 (1 Nov. 1917), 854–858; Armando Laurini, "Le americane in Guerra," *La lettura* 18, no. 9 (1 Sept. 1918): 623–629. All three articles are reprinted in Enrico Sturani, *La donna del soldato: L'immagine della donna nella cartolina italiana* (Rovereto: Museo Storico Italiano della Guerra, 2005).

35. P.T. [Paolina Tarugi], "Le armate femminili," *Assistenza civile* 2, no. 1 (1 Jan. 1918): 19–22.

36. Davide Guiduci, "Le donne tedesche," *Il secolo XX* 15, no. 7 (Oct. 1916): 641–644.

37. Bruna Guarducci, "Le 'cucine materne,'" *Assistenza civile* 1, no. 15 (1 Aug. 1917): 678.

38. Filippo Meda, 25 Sept. 1916, Rome, quoted in Donna Paola [Paola Baronchelli Grosson], *La donna della nuova Italia: Documenti del contributo femminile alla guerra (Maggio 1915–maggio 1917)* (Milan: R. Quintieri, 1917), 11.

39. As quoted in Donna Paola, *La donna della nuova Italia*, 12.

40. Pio Foa, 22 Oct. 1916, quoted in Donna Paola, *La donna della nuova Italia*, 13.

41. Eteocle Lorini, 20 Sept. 1916, quoted in Donna Paola, *La donna della nuova Italia*, 14.

42. Luigi Federzoni, 19 Nov. 1916, quoted in Donna Paola, *La donna della nuova Italia*, 15.

43. Luigi Valli, 9 July 1916, quoted in Donna Paola, *La donna della nuova Italia*, 17–18.

44. Alfredo Baccelli, quoted in Donna Paola, *La donna della nuova Italia*, 19.

45. After the Armistice, Brunelleschi moved back to Paris and made his name as a costume and set designer. He was involved enough with Fascism to produce in 1935 a poster for a show of contemporary Italian art at the Jeu de Palme; see Thomas Row, "Mobilizing the Nation: Italian Propaganda in the Great War," *Journal of Decorative and Propaganda Arts* 24 (2002): 168–169.

46. On *La tradotta*, see Row, "Mobilizing the Nation," 164; Wolfsonian–Florida International University, "Women and the First World War: Some Artifacts," https://wolfsonianfiulibrary.wordpress.com/2014/10/03/women-and-the-first-world-war-some-artifacts-from-the-wolfsonian-fiu-library-collection (accessed 21 June 2017).

47. Survey sponsored by the Ufficio Storiografico della Mobilitazione; Curli, *Italiane al lavoro*, 155–157.

48. *L'Illustrazione italiana*, 20 May 1917, 425.

49. Claudia Reichl-Ham in this volume (ch. 11).

50. Curli, *Italiane al lavoro*, 13.

51. Curli, *Italiane al lavoro*, 19–20.

52. Figures are valid for August 1918. At that time, almost 300,000 men without military obligations were working in war industries alongside 320,000 men with military ties, 60,000 minors (boys and girls), and 24,000 others (e.g., prisoners, colonials); see Ufficio della Mano d'Opera Femminile, *Le donne d'Italia nelle industrie di guerra*, 3, 51–52.

53. Ufficio della Mano d'Opera Femminile, *Le donne d'Italia nelle industrie di guerra*, 4.

54. Bice Viallet, "L'utilizzazione della mano d'opera femminile," *Assistenza civile* 2, no. 7 (June 1918): 343–344; Bice Viallet, "Quello che il ministero delle arme e munizioni ha fatto per il lavoro femminile e quello che dovrebbe ancora fare," *Assistenza civile* 2, no. 9 (Sept. 1918): 373–375.

55. Ufficio della Mano d'Opera Femminile, *Le donne d'Italia nelle industrie di guerra*, 9–10.

56. For more on these schools, see Ufficio della Mano d'Opera Femminile, *Le donne d'Italia nelle industrie di guerra*, 30.

57. Gemma De Daninos, "Infermiera di Croce Rossa," in *Impressioni di guerra, 1915–1918* (Milan: Coen, 1919), 39–40.

58. See, e.g., Bruna Guarducci, "Tra i figli di nostril soldati alla casa materna," *Il secolo XX* 14, no. 1 (Jan. 1916): 88–89; Ciro Morselli, "La scuola per le infermiere," *Il secolo XX* 14, no. 10 (Oct. 1915): 968–969. Wartime issues are available at http://patrimonio.fondazionefeltrinelli.it (accessed 16 June 2017).

59. See Ernest Hemingway, *A Farewell to Arms*, and Mark Helprin, *A Soldier of the Great War* for examples of fiction featuring a wounded soldier having an affair with his nurse along the Italian front.

60. S.A.R. Duchessa Elena d'Aosta in Vittorio Brizzolesi, *Gli italiani-americani alla guerra* (Milan: Alfieri & Lacroix, 1919), between 96 and 97.

61. Elena Doni, "Il bianco esercito," in *Donne nella Grande Guerra*, eds. Marta Boneschi, Paola Cioni, Elena Doni, Claudia Galimberti, Lia Levi, Maria Serena Palieri, Cristiana Di San Marzano, Francesca Sancin, Mirella Serri, Federica Tagliaventi, Simona Tagliaventiet al. (Bologna: il Mulino, 2014), 37.

62. Doni, "Il bianco esercito," 37.

63. Morselli, "La scuola per le infermiere," 968–969.

64. For more on the responsibilities of the CRI nurses, see Belzer, *Women and the Great War*, ch. 4.

65. Allison Scardino Belzer, "Nurses, Spies, and Sacrifice: Female Citizenship and Patriotism in Italy," in *Italy and the Cultural Politics of World War I*, ed. Graziella Parati (Madison, N.J.: Farleigh Dickinson University Press, 2016), 60–61.

66. Along with Duchess Elena d'Aosta, Clara Barton, Maria Antonietta Clerici, Maria Andina, and Maria Concetta Cludzinska received the inaugural Medaglia Nightingale from the CRI.

67. Gina De Franchesi, "L'attivita delle infermiere volontarie negli ospedali military friuliani," in Scandaletti and Variola, *Le crocerossine nella Grande Guerra*, 46.

68. Amilda A. Pons, "La signorina," in *Piccole storie della storia grande, 1915–1916* (Milan: Società Editrice Dante Alighieri, 1916), 97–103.

69. Pons, "La signorina," 99.

70. The more commonly used spelling of her last name is Meyer; Fornaro uses Mejer. Sita Camperio Mejer, "Il diario di Sita Camperio Mejer," ed. Mario Fornaro, in Scandaletti and Variola, *Le crocerossine nella Grande Guerra*, 158.

71. See, e.g., Grace Cleveland Porter (later Nobili), the great-niece of President Cleveland, clad in either plain clothes or a scouting-style uniform for her YMCA and Red Cross work in photographs held by the University of Minnesota Libraries, Kautz Family YMCA Archives, http://purl.umn.edu/65169 and http://purl.umn.edu/77301(accessed 9 Oct. 2019).

72. Luciana Mion, "I diari delle crocerossine," in Scandaletti and Variola, *Le crocerossine nella Grande Guerra*, 56.

73. For more on these women and other women acting as comrades in arms with men, see Belzer, "Nurses, Spies, and Sacrifice."

74. After the war she married a Japanese diplomat and became May Senta; see Marco Rech, "May Senta Wolf Hauler. Una donna come soldato: La storia di una crocerossina particolare," in Scandaletti and Variola, *Le crocerossine nella Grande Guerra*, 61–66.

75. See Laurie S. Stoff (ch. 10); Melissa K. Stockdale, "'My Death for the Motherland is Happiness': Women, Patriotism, and Soldiering in Russia's Great War, 1914–1917," *American Historical Review* 109, no. 1 (Feb. 2004): 78–116.

76. Donna Paola, *La donna della nuova Italia*, 288–292.

77. Donna Paola, "La donna nel domani di pace," *Assistenza civile* 1, no. 18 (Sept. 1917): 795–796.

78. Viallet, "L'utilizzazione della mano d'opera femminile," 343–344.

79. Belzer, *Women and the Great War*, 171–173.

80. Belzer, *Women and the Great War*, 161–162, 177–188. For more on women in Fascist Italy, see Victoria De Grazia, *How Fascism Ruled Women: Italy, 1922–1945* (Berkeley: University of California Press, 1992).

TEN

THE CLOTHES MAKE THE WOMAN

Russian Women in Uniform

LAURIE S. STOFF

During the Great War, thousands of Russian women wore uniforms as part of their extensive involvement in the war effort.[1] Most did so in more traditional roles as nurses, or Sisters of Mercy as they were called in Russia. But others did so in decidedly nonconventional ways as soldiers. Their uniforms were not only indicative of their specific functions in the conflict but represented significantly transformative experiences in several substantive ways, as civilians and as women. In both cases (nurses and soldiers), the wearing of the uniform, as well as the attire itself, proved to be complex and transmutative, both symbolically and practically. Both uniforms removed women from the traditional domestic context and gave them license to operate in the male zone of the front, allowing women to subvert normative values associated with war, femininity, and masculinity. Nursing uniforms distinguished women from civilians as well as from other military personnel, signaling their national service. It afforded those who wore it a considerable level of prestige and became something of a status symbol. During the war, however, the Sister of Mercy uniform took on additional meaning as a specifically gendered form of dress that, while outwardly conforming to notions of traditional femininity, demonstrated the limitations of such conceptions and even challenged them, raising anxieties over the use of women in such service. Donning military uniforms was the most transgressive act of Russian women during this conflict. Dressing in military uniform was essential in defining function, but also significantly subverted convention. Military uniforms gave women the opportunity to engage in actions previously deemed off limits to them and to prove their abilities in this arena. Moreover, women's wartime uniforms (both nursing and military) served as visible reminders of women's valuable and necessary contribution to the war effort, one that many participants expected to be rewarded with rights of citizenship. As such, they were vitally important to the burgeoning women's movement and efforts to achieve greater gender equality. Indeed, one could argue that women's wartime service was essential in the process of achieving such rights, as Russia granted women the rights to vote and hold public office in July 1917, prior to any other great power. Yet neither women wearing official uniforms nor their actions served to dissipate the anxieties and ambiguities that accompanied women's participation in wartime service.

RUSSIAN NURSING AND THE GREAT WAR

The first Russian women to wear nursing uniforms during wartime were those who served in the Crimean War (1854–1856) as part of the Community of the Exaltation of the Cross (later the Russian Society of the Red Cross),[2] which dispatched approximately a thousand Russian women to care for the wounded in the conflict.[3] Like their British and French counterparts (whom they greatly outnumbered), they wore uniforms to distinguish them from camp followers. In the Russian case, those uniforms distinctly resembled the habits of Orthodox Christian nuns, at least partially in attempt to give them "respectability" and stem concerns about the sexual impropriety of women serving in a perceived male sphere. Unlike Western nurses, however, Russian sisters were not confined to base hospitals but served very

Figure 10.1.
Russian nurses of the Crimean War. "Sister of the Community of the Exaltation of the Cross Attending Wounded at Sevastopol in 1855," Illiustrirovannyi obzor minuvshego stoletiia: XIX vek *(St. Petersburg: Izdanie A.F. Marksa, 1901), 132.*

close to the actual fighting. Despite the valuable contribution they made to the war, their efforts did not lead to the development of a professional nursing corps. Nurses in Russia remained members of quasi-religious communities and continued to be referred to as Sisters of Mercy. The daily lives of these women "in form and spirit" closely resembled that of a convent, although their actions were carried out in the public sphere and they did not take formal religious vows. Not unsurprisingly, the Russian nursing uniform retained its strong resemblance to the nun's habit.[4]

Upon the outbreak of hostilities in August 1914, the Russian government undertook extensive recruitment of women for nursing service. The scale of the hostilities, in which millions of soldiers and civilians would require medical attention, made clear that the existing cadre of approximately 4,000 trained nurses was insufficient. As early as September 1914, the Russian Red Cross shortened training courses, which normally lasted an entire year, to two months in order to get women into medical service as quickly as possible; later that year, courses were reduced to six weeks.[5] Other organizations also engaged in the recruitment and training of nurses for wartime service; they served "under the flag" of the Red Cross. These included the voluntary organs of the Union of Zemstvos (local government agencies) and the Union of Towns (collectively known as Zemgor), which played a vital role in the provision of wartime auxiliary services. By 1917, the number of Sisters of Mercy exceeded 31,000.[6]

Enlistment in nursing service was limited to literate women with at least some secondary education. Most nurses came from the educated middle and upper classes, but there were those of peasantry and working classes among their ranks as well, especially those who had already been members of the existing nursing communities. Placement in service required formal training according to established Red Cross standards. Only women who had completed this training could bear the designation "Sister of Mercy" and wear the official uniform, and only these individuals were given the right to be compensated for their work.[7] Women who did not meet these criteria were accepted as voluntary aids. They wore uniforms as well, but these were distinguished from those of full-fledged Sisters of Mercy.

Wearing the wartime nursing uniform was rife with meaning. For many, it was a transformative act, part of a distinct change from prewar selves, distinguishing them from civilian women. Lidiia Zakharova, who enlisted after her husband was drafted, felt as if she had been "swallowed up" in a new life, "carried away in a powerful stream." She recalled that she

> quickly came to the realization that from this moment I was not that previous woman, who lived, suffered and enjoyed up to this minute, that something else had begun, that I did not even have my previous name, I was "sister," a new person with a name that came before all other interests, sadness and happiness.[8]

For others, the Sister of Mercy uniform proved to be a class leveler, removing identifiable markers of social status and identity visible in civilian clothing. The Grand Duchess Maria Pavlovna (first cousin of the tsar) remarked that in her modest nursing uniform, "almost no one knew me . . . we all lived the same life and had the same interests."[9]

Figure 10.2.
Image of Russian nurse used in pro-war recruitment efforts: Argus, "Kogda muzhchiny na fronte, vot gde vashe mesto, zhenshchiny!" [When men go to the front, this is your place, women!] (Russkoe Obshchestvo Pechatnogo Dela, n.d.), Hoover Institution Poster Collection RU/SU 1107.

The nursing uniform also signified devotion to national service. It not only separated "real" nurses from those with unofficial status but also, as Barton Hacker has indicated for nurses in other countries, "validated their claim to citizenship."[10] The image of the Russian woman in nursing uniform became a patriotic symbol imbued with a level of respect that (nearly) equated the female nurse to the male soldier and was reproduced in numerous wartime publications with the aim of recruiting other women into wartime medical service. Nursing was viewed as the most appropriate way for women to serve the nation in its time of crisis.[11] The nurse was celebrated not only as a figure of support and care but as a strong and active contributor to the war.[12] Members of the women's movement saw the war as an opportunity to demonstrate women's value to the state through war work, which they were convinced would be rewarded with civil, legal, and political rights. Many of the women who enlisted as nurses were themselves avowedly progressive in their views and often expressed ideas about their service in feminist terms.

As a result of its positive connotation in Russian public imagination and association with national service, the Red Cross nursing uniform also became a status symbol. Clothing is highly relevant to identity and status, particularly with regard to gender, as often, Helena Goscilo explains, "fashion privileges image over character."[13] Observers lamented the sight of society women merely "dressing the part" but carrying out no real medical service during the war.[14] Thus, although many women were dedicated to carrying out vital medical services, some were seen as primarily desiring the prestige associated with wearing the nursing uniform and being only superficially committed to the war effort.

The Sister of Mercy uniform was also indicative of attempts to control women's behavior by holding nurses to narrowly conceived expectations. Since the Crimean War, the sexual behavior of Russian nurses had been of primary concern to both military and civilian authorities. According to the Red Cross's rules of conduct, all Sisters of Mercy were to be of the "highest moral caliber."[15] A standard of "propriety" had been set in an attempt to preclude intimate interaction between male military or medical personnel and nurses. Indeed, in some cases, this seemed a higher priority than ensuring quality of medical care.

Red Cross authorities closely scrutinized women who enlisted in its nursing communities and training courses. Women who did not adhere to the moral standards risked punishment and expulsion.

The uniform of the Sister of Mercy was an essential part of this policing. Not only was the nurse to be "morally upright," but her very appearance was to remove any suggestions of sexuality. The uniform consisted of an ankle-length nondescript gray or black cotton or wool dress covered by a long white apron embroidered with a red cross and a white or black head kerchief.[16] These elements intentionally concealed the feminine physical characteristics of her body: The long dress and apron hid any suggestion of curves made by female breasts or hips; the head scarf covered long hair. The uniform also gave the wearer considerable mobility in the public sphere, particularly the war zone. Therefore, it was essential for Sisters of Mercy to be properly dressed. Failure to abide by these regulations was considered a serious disciplinary infraction, often with significant repercussions, including expulsion from the ranks.[17] A shortage of gray wool, however, complicated matters for women enlisted in Red Cross service by making it difficult for sisters to acquire appropriate dress, which was a nurse's own responsibility.[18] Inability, or unwillingness, to conform to military standards on the part of women in the wartime medical service caused tensions and hampered efforts to tend to the nation's ill and wounded.

Not only were nurses required to wear appropriate uniforms, they had to wear the uniforms appropriately, which was understood to reflect behavior. The illustration featured in the highly popular journal *Ogonek* in November 1915 demonstrating the "proper" and "improper" ways for Sisters of Mercy to dress reveals these anxieties. The captions indicate that if Sisters of Mercy appeared only as represented in the second examples rather than the

Figure 10.3.
Hospital Uniforms of Russian Sisters of Mercy. "Her Imperial Highness Empress Aleksandra Fedorovna and Their Imperial Highnesses Grand Duchesses Ol'ga Nikolaevna and Tat'iana Nikolaevna among the personnel of the Tsarkoe Selo Palace Infirmary (Petrograd)," Vechernaiia Gazeta *(n.d.).*

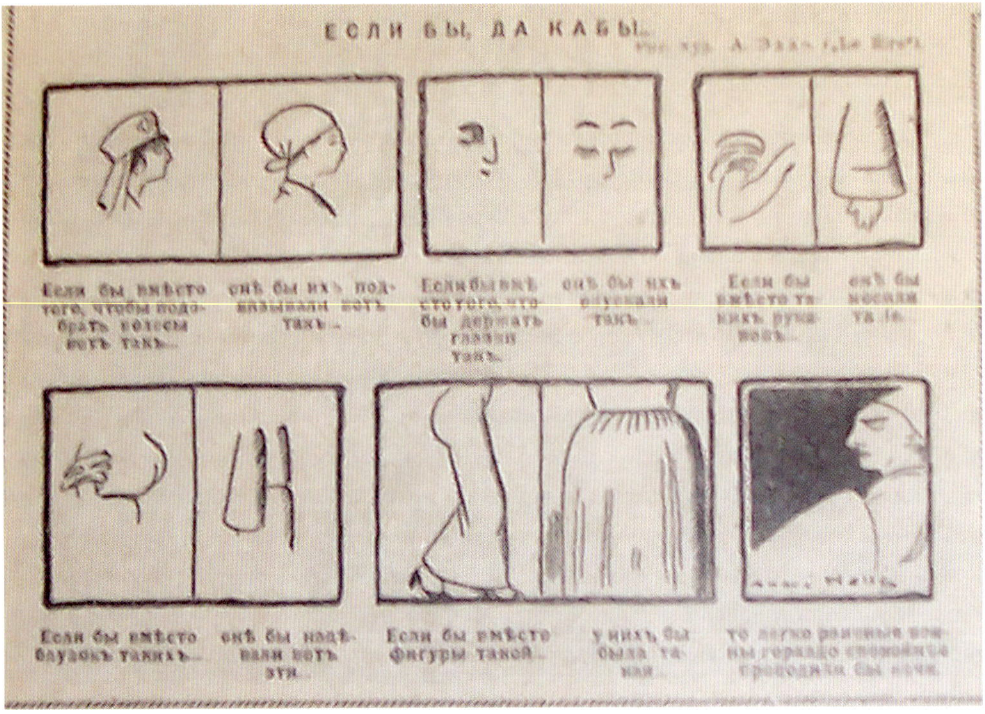

Figure 10.4.
Illustration indicating the "proper" way to wear the Sister of Mercy uniform. "Esli by, da kaby" [If yes, only], Ogonek, *45 (8 November 1915): 5.*

first, soldiers in their care could rest easier. Here again, the emphasis was on desexualizing the female nurse.

Furthermore, issues concerning the Sister of Mercy uniform also concerned those *not* authorized to wear it, precisely because of the freedom of movement it afforded. During the war, prostitution (a perennial concern for the military establishment as a result of its association with the spread of disease and potential for use in espionage) became increasingly troubling. In an attempt to control and limit sex work, regulations were now put in place that allowed local authorities to arrest women for merely walking on the streets. *Any* woman found walking on the streets in some locations near the front was at risk of arrest under suspicion of prostitution. To avoid drawing attention, some adopted nurses' garb, using the mobility afforded to wearers of the Red Cross uniform to engage in sex work.

Ultimately, the nursing disguise proved limited in its effectiveness. As increasing numbers of reports indicated, many unauthorized women were found walking the streets wearing the uniforms of Red Cross sisters. The Red Cross organ, *Vestnik Krasnogo Kresta*, lamented that

> many frivolous creatures have begun to dress themselves in the uniform of the Sister of Mercy, and in this way to profane the sacred work of helping the suffering by looking for adventures in the streets. . . . The public has taken notice of this outrageous occurrence and have come to the [Red Cross] communities with all sorts

> of groundless rumors. . . . The majority of these "ladies," strolling with bandages for suspicious purposes, are just using the emblem of the Red Cross for their own personal, low goals.[19]

Instead of protecting the wearer from unwanted suspicion, the uniform itself began to raise suspicions as associations of nurses with sex work increased over the course of the war.

Attempts to control the wearing of Red Cross uniforms proved insufficient to stop unauthorized occurrences, and the organization decided to take further measures. In a somewhat ironic move considering the previous use of "yellow tickets" to regulate sex work, the Red Cross began issuing special identification "tickets" (these were white) to nursing personnel. Not only was this measure an attempt to hinder sex workers from plying their trade in disguise, it was also a conscious effort to preserve the honor of the Sister of Mercy by identifying and separating imposters. The implication was that "real" nurses would not engage in such immoral behavior. Indeed, the organization was careful to distinguish these women from those officially registered in medical services, who, Red Cross officials insisted, "are seldom seen on the streets, as they are too busy carrying out their highly humane work."[20] In reality, nursing work could not be limited to the hospital or dressing station, and nurses often had to appear in public wearing their uniforms. Their official duties required them to transport patients from one location to another, to obtain supplies and equipment from other facilities, and to engage in other responsibilities that demanded their public presence. When they entered such spaces, suspicions were raised. The lines of respectability were distinctly drawn between the "protected" space of the medical facility, where nurses carried out their "sacred work," and the street or other public places, which for women, were associated with a lack of respectability. When the Sister of Mercy left the medical facility, her purpose became muddled in the public view.[21]

The Red Cross took the threat posed to the image of the Sister of Mercy seriously, so much so that it established a "Commission for the Fight against the Misuse of the Name of the Sister of Mercy." Determined to remove from the ranks those women who had "no right to wear the symbol of the Red Cross," the organization wanted to ensure that only those who had been members of the communities of the Red Cross and had undergone the vetting process through those organs would be designated as Sisters of Mercy and wear the nursing uniform.[22] This proved to be an impractical measure in a total war requiring mass mobilization, including many women who had not passed through the Red Cross nursing communities, but rather were trained and assigned to nursing duties by other organizations.

Nurses who appeared in public spaces in their uniforms, particularly in the company of men and in unofficial capacities, continued to be troubling to some. In a further effort to curtail such incidences, the Red Cross issued an order that restricted the wearing of uniforms to assigned work periods, prohibiting nurses from "walking the streets or visiting entertainment establishments in the uniform of a Sister of Mercy."[23] This measure seems to have been similarly ineffective, and the problem of distinguishing between "respectable" nurses and "unrespectable" poseurs continued throughout the war.

Nor did the attempt to separate "real" nurses from sex workers save Russia's wartime nursing from associations with moral impropriety. Rather than distinguishing the immoral "false" nurses from the pure "true" sisters, to some members of the Russian public, the former became largely indistinguishable from the latter. The lines of demarcations between nursing and prostitution became blurred, and the rumor that Sisters of Mercy were little more than "sisters of comfort" providing sexual services to soldiers circulated through Russian society. Although wartime nursing had come to be seen as an appropriate way for women to serve the nation in times of crisis, fears about their conduct had not dissipated since first expressed in the mid-nineteenth century.[24]

At the heart of this problem was the fact that very few of the women who became wartime nurses were members of religious communities or had any desire to be. A large number of the Sisters of Mercy were young women, who, upon entering wartime medical services, were emancipated from the controlling atmosphere of life at home. This freedom was attractive to many young women who chafed under the constraints of their lives and saw wartime nursing as a means of escape.[25] Nursing often allowed women the opportunity to pursue relationships with men on their own terms while simultaneously exposing them to sexual harassment by male military and medical personnel.[26] For many members of Russian society, this was much too much freedom given to women, whose honor was still derived from their sexual purity. When women failed to conform to the rigid standards of sexual propriety, their behavior became a point of contention. The sight of young women on the arms of men strolling through the streets, attending concerts and theater performances, and eating in restaurants was disconcerting to those who believed that given this kind of unfettered freedom, women would enter into inappropriate sexual relations. Moreover, it is clear from the records of punishments meted out to those accused of "immorality" and "depraved behavior" that Sisters of Mercy did indeed engage in such intimate relationships with men.[27] This behavior opened the door not only to accusations of impropriety but also to those of prostitution as a result of social expectations that rooted female honor in chastity.

Concerns over the sexual respectability of Russian wartime nurses and the intersection of such concerns with clothing were part of the larger issue in a modernizing Russia, where anxieties were expressed not only over women's increasing public presence but also over their involvement in activities understood to be outside traditional behavior. As Christine Ruane has demonstrated, these activities included women's conspicuous consumption of products like clothing. Thus, even the act of shopping for fashionable apparel was seen by some as morally questionable. Ruane argues,

> All these women had abandoned appropriate "female" behavior emphasizing modesty, restraint and self-sacrifice to participate in the world of commerce. Thus, a simple commercial transaction became, in the eyes of many commentators, a defiant and deviant expression of a woman's sexuality. In this sense any woman who participated in commercial activity was a *publichnaya zhenshchina*, a public woman who sold her body for men's pleasure.[28]

Because wearing the nursing uniform often was seen as a "fashionable" activity, it overlapped directly with public concerns about women's respectability. The uniform, which for so many was a symbol of self-sacrifice, modesty, and service, for others was transformed into an indicator of immorality.

Concomitantly, the uniform itself proved to be something of a hindrance to effective service provision for Russian nurses at the front in other ways. Unlike the nurses of other belligerents, Sisters of Mercy in Russia often served very close to the fighting. This proximity was the result of the very different nature of the war on the Eastern Front, which was considerably more mobile and where the front lines shifted so often it was nearly impossible to consistently delineate between "front" and "rear." The result was that Russian nurses were quite frequently required to operate in battle zones and therefore exposed to conditions similar to those of soldiers. The traditional elements of female clothing that comprised the nurse's uniform, a long dress, a smock covering the dress, and a head kerchief, were not really problematic for work in medical facilities away from the forward positions. But for women in medical service at the front, it was often necessary to adopt more practical attire. The long, loose dress and women's shoes hindered the carrying out of service at the front, where nurses faced the extremes of weather and ever-present mud. Frontline nurses needed protection from the elements and the ability to move about freely under difficult conditions. As a result, many adapted their clothing, choosing to wear high leather soldiers' boots and men's leather jackets. Some communities of sisters even recommended that nurses acquire these items before leaving for the front. A few even abandoned their dresses in favor of trousers. Numerous photographs of nurses at the front, such as the one depicted in Figure 10.5, attest to this and give a very different visual impression than that of the saintly white-veiled Sister of Mercy of conventional opinion. In early 1915, the popular journal *Niva* published a picture of a Sister of Mercy who was awarded a St. George's medal for carrying out difficult work under enemy fire on the front lines. She was dressed in pants, a leather jacket, high boots, and a Cossack hat, sitting on horseback. The only indication of her status as a nurse was the white armband emblazoned with the Red Cross.[29] Florence Farmborough, an Englishwoman who enlisted with the Russian Red Cross, appears in a photograph on the cover of her memoir garbed in leather jacket, pants, hat, and high boots—again, with the white armband decorated with a red cross the only indication of her status as a nurse.[30]

Modifying one's clothing often had internal effects on wartime nurses. Lidiia Zakharova wrote that she underwent something of a gender transformation, commenting that over time "there remained in me less and less of the feminine." Her change, like that of other women in war service, took on physical manifestations, and she remarked that she felt more comfortable in her role after purchasing a man's leather coat. She also felt very fortunate to acquire a pair of "excellent men's boots," which came in handy on a number of occasions when she was trudging through the deep, sticky mud that was ubiquitous throughout much of the front.[31] After merely a month with her mobile unit, Aleksandra Tolstaia (youngest daughter of famed writer Leo Tolstoy) commented that she had been "completely weaned from civilization and

Figure 10.5.
Sisters of Mercy in leather jackets. "Sisters of Mercy of the 4th Flying Column of the Field of the South-Western Zemskii Organization," Ogonek, *35 (30 August 1915): 2.*

no longer paid any attention to my appearance. Indeed, this would have been impossible to do during campaigns." In order to travel easily by horseback, she discarded the long dress uniform of a Sister of Mercy in favor of Caucasian dress that included trousers, high boots, and a black sheepskin hat with a white hood to block the sun.[32]

Although nursing culture was largely understood as distinctly feminine because of its consistency with normative associations of women as caring and nurturing, the act of engaging in wartime medical service proved to be a transgressive act. Although women may have entered nursing service without any contemplation of gender transgression, many underwent significant transformative processes that led them away from these conventional gendered notions. Confronted with the realities of the war, the women who became nurses in Russia, both consciously and unconsciously, entered a much more nebulous terrain with regard to both gender and sexuality, as well as public roles. Changing their civilian clothing for nursing uniforms was an important part of this process.

RUSSIA'S FEMALE SOLDIERS OF THE GREAT WAR

The lines of demarcation between masculine and feminine were most strikingly blurred by the Russian women who put on military uniforms and became soldiers in this war. The presence of women in the ranks of armies long predates the Great War and is not exclusive to Russia. In Russia specifically, women served as warriors from its earliest history, hiding their true sex by wearing men's clothing and calling themselves by male names.[33] The Great

War experience in Russia, however, is exceptional. Some scholars have estimated that perhaps close to a thousand women fought in the ranks of Russia's armies between 1914 and 1917.[34] But what makes the Russian experience even more remarkable is that in the summer of 1917, an even larger number of women, approximately 5,000, were actively recruited as soldiers and organized to serve in combat.

Before the organization of the all-female units, because imperial Russian law prohibited female enlistment, women could enter the armed forces through two avenues. The much less common means was direct appeal to authorities for special permission to enlist. A handful of women were able to join in this way, without having to hide their true sexual identities. They often gained entry as the result of the personal prerogative of individual officers. Some even received authorization from the highest levels, including from the tsar himself.[35] Most, however, had to adopt male guise to enter the ranks. This was made possible as a result of a lack of consistent medical examinations in enlistment procedures. The example of women disguising themselves as men in order to fight demonstrates the importance of a uniform in the strongest way. It allowed for a complete transformation—so much so that most of these women remained undetected (unless they were injured and examined by medical personnel). In both instances, however, military uniforms were essential for women joining the Russian armed forces and reveal a significant failure of centralized control.

Women who became soldiers in the Russian army during the Great War came from a variety of backgrounds. They were aristocrats, middle class, urban workers, and peasants. They ranged in age from as young as 14 to mid-40s. Most were motivated by strong patriotic feelings, but other factors provided impetus as well. Dissatisfied with roles of passive support, women soldiers were convinced that they could serve their country better in combat.[36] Like many men at the time, some women soldiers had romanticized conceptions of war, believing it would provide them with escape from mundane lives.[37] The fact that all the women soldiers were volunteers, however, is extremely important for understanding their experiences and the phenomenon as a whole. All of them *chose* to enlist, electing to risk their lives in the war, unlike the majority of men, who were conscripted into service and who often lacked the same zeal.[38]

In the spring and summer of 1917, the Russian Provisional Government made the unprecedented decision to create all-female military units. The formation of these units was the result of a combination of two specific contextual factors: pressure put on the Provisional Government by those seeking to expand female participation in the war and the significantly deteriorating conditions of the army in the face of preparations for a new offensive. The first was spearheaded by progressive women who believed that service in the war was the best way to demonstrate civic value. They created organizations, recruited members, held fundraisers, and petitioned the new minister of war, Alexander Kerensky, to allow women into the ranks of the active army. This included forming separate women's military units.[39] The second factor was the need to prepare the army prior for the upcoming offensive scheduled to begin in June 1917. The Russian army was not in a suitable condition to engage in such

Figure 10.6.
Individual woman soldier dressed in Russian imperial military uniform during the Great War. The Graphic, *15 May 1915.*

an attack; in many places along the front it was suffering from lack of discipline, insubordination, fraternization, desertion, and overall war weariness.[40] There was a desire to restore morale and provide the soldiers with badly needed incentive to continue risking their lives. The women's units were part of a larger effort to create "shock" and "revolutionary" battalions intended to lead by example. All able-bodied men (and even those not so able bodied, including disabled veterans) were called to participate in this effort. By using women specifically, there was also a simultaneous impulse to "shame" the male soldiers, who were seen as shirking their duties as defenders of the nation, into continuing to fight.[41]

Ultimately, Prime Minister Kerensky agreed, authorizing the establishment of the 1st Russian Women's Battalion of Death in Petrograd, under the command of veteran soldier and newly commissioned officer Maria Bochkareva. Bochkareva was one of the few women who served as a woman, having managed to secure personal permission from the tsar to enlist.[42] The unit initially recruited over 2,000 women, who were provided with barracks, weapons, equipment, uniforms, and male officers (as a result of a lack of sufficiently trained female officers) to prepare them for combat. Their uniforms were emblazoned with a special insignia designed for battalions of death: red and black chevrons and skull-and-crossbones emblems. These symbolized the willingness of the members of these units to "fight to the death" for the defense of the nation. As such, the women were simultaneously identifiable as combatants, with the intention of integrating them into military culture, but also set apart from regular infantry units.

Figure 10.7.
Bochkareva and the volunteers of the 1st Russian Women's Battalion of Death. Courtesy Museum of the Revolution, Moscow.

Figure 10.8.
Female noncommissioned officers of Bochkareva's battalion. Courtesy Museum of the Revolution, Moscow.

As commander, Bochkareva was not convinced that all the female volunteers were suitable candidates for military service and that merely outfitting them in military uniform would affect a suitable transformation. Having served at the front for three years, she understood soldiering in specifically gendered terms, that is, as "masculine." She insisted that women could make good soldiers only if they completely transformed themselves, sublimating any "feminine" behaviors or characteristics and adopting appropriate masculine attributes. She told them, "I will make strong those of you from the 'weaker sex'. . . . Forget that you are women, you are now soldiers."[43] Uniforming them in military attire was essential in this process. But for Bochkareva, the uniform was not enough; she also demanded that they forgo any aspect of what she perceived as femininity. Recruits were required to shave their heads and relinquish items of personal hygiene, even toothbrushes. They were encouraged to spit, smoke, and swear so as to act more "manly." The slightest hint of femininity was considered grounds for removal from the unit, as Bochkareva strove to "beat the domestic foolishness out of them."[44]

Although the commander insisted that her methods were vital for purposes of thorough combat preparation, a number of women did not see soldiering as an exclusively masculine endeavor and did not believe that such gendered alteration was essential to becoming effective combatants. Bochkareva had little patience for these women and ultimately drove out those who refused to adhere to her strictures. Many of those who were rejected or left her command entered other women's military units, formed shortly after Bochkareva's was organized. Ultimately, she was left with only around 300 volunteers willing to submit to her demands.[45]

A number of other women's combat units were formed following the example of Bochkareva's efforts. Many of them were privately initiated by individuals or groups that sought to increase female participation in the war effort for politically progressive aims, convinced that women's wartime service would be rewarded with rights and opportunities. Indeed, one of the arguments used against granting women the franchise was that they did not participate in the defense of the nation. Becoming military servitors was thus seen as an effective way to demonstrate that women deserved full citizenship. Their actions constituted a socially significant phenomenon, a "women's military movement," as contemporaries referred to it.[46] The result of these grassroots initiatives was the formation of 10 units in cities around the empire.

Women who desired to become soldiers continued to pressure the Provisional Government throughout the summer of 1917.[47] In the end, the Ministry of War relented, not only as a result of public influence but also because it wanted to bring the privately created units under its control. There was considerable anxiety over these units, which were uniformed, armed, and trained without any control by the military authorities. Most disconcerting to the Provisional Government was its inability to determine whether these military formations would be loyal to the government. The Provisional Government existed in a situation that historians have described as "dual power," competing for authority with the Petrograd Soviet of Workers' and Soldiers' Deputies. The latter often commanded greater loyalty from the working class and peasant population.[48] To stem the growth of unofficial units and satisfy public demand, the Ministry of War ultimately allowed for the organization of 14 additional women's units. These included three more all-female combat battalions: an additional unit in Petrograd (the 1st Petrograd Women's Battalion), one in Moscow (the 2nd Moscow Women's Battalion of Death), and one in Ekaterinodar (the 3rd Kuban Women's Shock Battalion). The Petrograd and Moscow units were to be complemented by two women's communications detachments each. Five additional communications detachments were to be created in Kiev, as well as two more such units in the city of Saratov.[49] A women's naval

Figure 10.9.
Recruits of the 1st Russian Women's Naval Detachment. Courtesy Museum of the Revolution, Moscow.

unit, the 1st Women's Naval Detachment, was also created at the Kolsk Naval Base.[50] Although supposed to be entirely female, these units initially were not, as insufficient numbers of trained women officers meant the first commanders and training officers were men. Once women had received proper officer preparation, the men in the unit were to be replaced. To accomplish this, 25 women were chosen from the Moscow Women's Battalion to attend the Aleskandrovskii Military Academy for officer instruction.[51]

The women's military units were organized under the auspices of the local military command in the cities of their formation, which were responsible for recruiting, equipping, arming, and training them.[52] Essential to this was the provision of regulation military uniforms. In the Russian army, as in all other cotemporary armed forces, uniforms meant clothing that was designed to fit to the male body. Financial and temporal limitations dictated the impossibility of waiting for uniforms fitted to female forms to be made, so women soldiers had to make do with those that were extant, as ill-suited to their physiques as they were. Boots were a particular problem, as male shoe sizes ran considerably larger than women's, as were trousers, which often failed to accommodate women's wider hips.[53] The problems of properly outfitting the members of the women's unit did not go unnoticed. When Bochkareva visited the Moscow battalion in July 1917, she was appalled at the absence of martial appearance among the women volunteers. "When I arrived at the barracks," she recalled "I nearly fainted at the sight of them. They were nearly all rouged, wearing slippers and fancy stockings, loosely dressed and of very nonchalant bearing."[54] Her comments concerning the women's dress are indicative of the problems of securing military uniforms for women. The

Moscow district warehouses had been ordered to provide the unit with all necessary supplies, including uniforms. But it did not deliver all the required items. One newspaper reported that the quartermaster actually refused the unit's request for uniforms, claiming that uniforms designed for men were unsuitable for women. This refusal meant that the battalion was forced to procure uniforms by its own means.[55] Collections were taken up at public gatherings for this purpose.[56] The women soldiers wore civilian footwear because they had not been supplied with sufficient numbers of army boots. A scarcity of leather in the city aggravated this problem and delayed the order for boots made to fit women's feet.[57] In addition, there were shortages of needed equipment and provisions. What Bochkareva perceived as the women's disregard for military regulations was actually the result of the central military authorities' inattentiveness and inability to fulfill the needs of the unit.

By contrast, the Kuban Women's Shock Battalion seemed better attuned to the problems of outfitting women soldiers. Its organizer, Matriona Zalesskaia, appealed to the Ministry of War in an effort to ensure that the equipment, uniforms, and supplies issued to the unit were compatible with female bodies.[58] Uniforms, therefore, were to be specially made to fit the measurements of the members of the battalion. The Women's Naval Detachment also attempted to compensate for female bodies. Realizing that existing standard-issue uniforms and footwear would be inadequate for women, the commander asked that a sufficient number of boots and caps be made in small sizes and that five or six experienced tailors be assigned to the unit, along with appropriate material and sewing machines, to make necessary alterations to uniforms.[59] Additionally, ribbons were ordered for the women's caps that read "Women's Naval Detachment."[60]

News of the creation of all-female military units was greeted by many members of Russian society positively, as a symbol of women's devotion to the cause of the war. As with nurses, progressive women were highly supportive of these endeavors as a means to demonstrate their worth as citizens. Some even likened the actions of the women soldiers to those of Joan of Arc. Indeed, the figure of the woman in military uniform garnered significant attention, especially from the contemporary media, which immediately recognized the sensational character of the phenomenon. Female soldiers were featured in both domestic and foreign publications from the very start of the war as the press fell in love with the image of the girl volunteer in military uniform. Their exploits received extensive coverage in newspapers and journals from Petrograd to New York.[61] Coverage amplified dramatically with the creation of the women's units in 1917. Pictures of women in soldiers' uniforms were featured on the pages of nearly every major publication in Russia, all over Europe, and in the United States. These women were recognized for their propaganda value by both the beleaguered Provisional Government and its Western allies, who were desperately trying to convince Russia to remain in the war. Western journalists published numerous melodramatic tales of Russia's women in uniform, many of which included photographs to prove to any doubting readers that such "Amazons" really did exist. A British newsreel covered the visit of suffragettes Emmeline Pankhurst and Florence Harper to Bochkareva's unit in Petrograd and the

Russian Women Disprove Belief That Their Sex Lacks Martial Spirit by Forming Battalion to Fight for Their Country

Figure 10.10.
Media coverage of the Russian women's military units. "Russian Women Disprove Belief That Their Sex Lacks Martial Spirit by Forming Battalion to Fight for Their Country," New York Times Mid-Week Pictorial, *23 August 1917.*

benediction ceremony of the Moscow battalion on Red Square.[62] As Ann Eliot Griese and Richard Stites comment, this was "the first instance in modern history in which women were used in all-female fighting units as models of military valor and performance."[63]

The act of putting women in military uniforms and training them to fight was not without controversy, however. Considerable ambiguity existed in public opinion concerning the women's units. The creation of sexually segregated combat formations was a radical social experiment that contravened widely held essentialist assumptions concerning women as life-giving, caring, and nurturing. A female soldier ran counter to these notions, and the sight of a woman military uniform caused considerably anxiety for many. Even some who admired the women soldiers for their bravery sometimes expressed reservations about the cultural wisdom of employing women in the violence of war. And underlying the support for the women's units was a sense of failure on the part of Russia's men, who were perceived as being either unwilling or unable to do their part in defending their homeland.

A number of observers believed that the women soldiers had little value aside from pro-war propaganda and wanted evidence that they could be effective in battle.[64] This proof meant not only competent performance of combat duties but also a morale-boosting effect on male soldiers. The latter was much more difficult to achieve than the former. The battle test for the 1st Russian Women's Battalion of Death came on 9 July 1917 (o.s.), in fighting near the Belorussian town of Smorgon. The unit carried out a successful charge and drove the Germans back from the first and second line of trenches, even managing to capture 200 prisoners and inspiring about half of the corps to follow them into the attack.[65] But they were unable to sustain the forward momentum or the positive influence on the male troops, who were reluctant to go on the offensive in the first place and completely halted their advance when they discovered stores of alcohol left behind by retreating Germans in the third line of trenches. Ultimately, the entire offensive proved to be a failure. The women's military movement was deemed ineffective, and the military establishment withdrew its formal support of the all-female units.[66] The commanders of the women's units were authorized to discharge volunteers who desired to leave the ranks, as regular rules of enlistment did not apply to them.[67]

Although the military authorities and many in the general public had become convinced that the women's military movement was a futile effort, the women's military organizations did not share that opinion. The Organizational Committee of the Petrograd Women's Military Union, with the support of district military headquarters, submitted a proposal to form women's reserve units to replenish existing women's battalions. Individual women continued to apply for acceptance into the women's military units. The military administration, however, refused to approve new requests, believing such formations to be superfluous and unwilling to commit state funds to what they considered unjustified expenses.[68] In an attempt to coordinate the disparate efforts of the various individuals and groups engaged in the women's military movement, a Women's Military Congress convened in August 1917. More than 50 individual women soldiers and representatives of both official and grassroots women's military units and quasi-military organizations from all over the country, as well as nursing and medical units, attended. Of primary importance was the consolidation of all activities associated with the movement into the hands of a central authoritative body. To accomplish this, the attendees resolved to create an All-Russian Women's Military Union.[69] Equally significant was the status of women serving in military capacities. The delegates insisted that female military servitors be afforded the same rights as male soldiers, including the same pay, leave, rights, and privileges, as well as assistance to women veterans and their families and the establishment of a home for disabled women soldiers. As such, they were seeking to legitimize the participation of women in the armed forces, to make it a regulated and standardized aspect of military service. They were also concerned with the legacy of female participation in military activities and promoted the construction of memorials for those women soldiers who had given their lives on the battlefields.[70] In so doing, they were consciously attempting to include women's combat participation in the ritualized national mythos of warfare.

The last formal act of the formations created under the Provisional Government was the participation of a company from the 1st Petrograd Women's Battalion in the defense of the Winter Palace during the Bolshevik Revolution on 24–25 October 1917 (7–8 November 1917 [n.s.]). The entire battalion was ordered to the palace square on 23 October, ostensibly for review prior to being sent to the front. When the women arrived, it became clear that

Figure 10.11.
Women of the 1st Petrograd Women's Battalion on the square in front of the Winter Palace, Petrograd, Courtesy of the State Central Museum of Contemporary History of Russia, 24 October 1917 (7 November 1917 [n.s.]).

they were not going to be dispatched for combat service, but rather used as part of the Provisional Government's last-ditch attempts to defend itself against the Bolsheviks and their supporters, after most of the other military units assigned to this task had refused. The women soldiers expressed their opposition to becoming embroiled in the internal political battles of the nation, insisting their purpose was to fight external enemies. As a result, most of the unit departed, but a small company of 137 women soldiers remained at the request of the Petrograd military commander. Their participation in the defense of the Winter Palace was short-lived, for while they fought to prevent the Bolshevik Red Guards, soldiers, and sailors from breeching the building, they were overwhelmed by vastly superior numbers and forced to surrender.[71]

The new Bolshevik government had little use for female soldiers who had, in their view, been "duped" into fighting for the bourgeois Provisional Government and therefore were ideologically unreliable. As a result, they ordered the Petrograd unit, as well as all of the remaining women's military formations, disbanded. Initially, a number of women resisted the order and remained in their encampment outside of Petrograd. In fact, eventually, the Bolsheviks had to send soldiers to forcibly disarm the women. Following the October Revolution, however, the sight of a woman in the uniform of one of the all-female units proved highly problematic. These women were targeted for abuse from members of the both the military and civilian population who perceived them as "enemies of the Revolution." Some were attacked physically, even raped, by Bolshevik supporters. But many had little choice but to continue wearing their uniforms despite the negative attention it garnered them, as a result of a shortage of women's clothing.[72] Bochkareva's small battalion (now numbering only around 200), which was actually still at the front when the October Revolution occurred, faced increasing hostility from male soldiers, who saw them as representatives of efforts to continue a war from which they wanted to be extricated. Therefore, the decision was made to disband the battalion in mid-December. Those members of the unit desiring to continue their military service were offered entrance into the active army as part of male units.[73] Those wishing to return to their homes were granted permission to do so. The volunteers dispersed. Bochkareva, sullen and disappointed, commented that it was "a pitiful finale to a heroic chapter in the history of Russian womanhood."[74]

This did not signal the end of women in military uniform in Russia, however. Thousands of women went on to serve on both sides of the conflict during the Civil War (1918–1921). Although the White (anti-Bolshevik) forces were, for the most part, much more conservative in their attitudes and largely resisted the use of women in combat capacities, some women did fight with them. More served as medical personnel. The newly created Red Army, however, made extensive use of women during this war and subsequently in future armed conflicts. The Bolsheviks, in keeping with Communist ideology concerning gender equality, had no theoretical opposition to the use of women in military capacities and actively encouraged women to participate in national defense. As a result, approximately 80,000 women served in military uniform in a variety of capacities, from infantry to auxiliary. The vast majority, however, did not participate in combat, but rather in medical, clerical, and political positions, and considerable opposition to the use of women in combat remained in the Soviet military establishment. The result was something of a contradiction within the new Soviet government itself. The Main Staff of the Red Army indicated clear opposition to women in combat roles and ultimately forbade their participation as such, whereas its Universal Military Training Administration promoted women's training for combat positions.[75]

Both the theoretical acceptance and the actual use of women in military roles by the Soviets, once again, should not be interpreted as a radical reorientation of gender ideology. Deeply entrenched notions of the exclusive "masculinity" of military culture were not overturned, despite official efforts to encourage women to be involved. The precedent established by the Great War of using women only as a result of the exigencies of war, precipitating national crises that required the active involvement in all members of society, was retained. The use of women in military capacities, specifically in combat, was seen as temporarily acceptable as a result of necessity. But in "normal" peacetime conditions, the prevailing notion was that women should not be integrated into the Soviet armed forces. Moreover, views of women who served as nurses remained problematic in association with notions of female sexuality in the World War II, as many were accused of promiscuity, earning the derogatory label of "mobile field wives," which referred to their engaging in sexual relationships with officers during the war.[76]

LEGACIES OF WOMEN IN UNIFORM

An examination of the uniforms and the women who wore them in Russia during the Great War indicates that strict demarcations of gender were impossible to maintain and ultimately breached the lines of separation of the division of labor. However, this created a paradox in which the ideologies of gender and sexuality, which insisted on rigid dichotomies and double standards, were undermined and counteracted by the realities of war and women's participation. And although insufficient to deter the use of women in wartime nursing and even in combat capacities, it gave rise to significant anxieties that would plague wartime participation of women in Russia during the Great War, where women and war intersected in ways that clearly indicate the inability to maintain gendered boundaries.

Somewhat remarkably, within a span of merely half a century, what was once understood to be a male endeavor, considered strictly off-limits to women (at least respectable women), performed in a space designated exclusively masculine where it had been unthinkable to introduce (again, respectable) women, had been transformed into a space for women's participation in a variety of capacities, including the most sacrosanct of masculine endeavors: combat. Wartime nursing in particular had become a service that not only was deemed appropriate for women but was, for the most part, now seen as honorable, dutiful, and even best undertaken by women as a result of their specific "nature." Despite reservations concerning the ability of women to endure the rigors of war, most early twentieth-century observers had come to view nursing as something specifically feminine, and necessary, even in the male zone of war. Thus, although war itself was still considered "men's work," nursing, even in wartime, was now viewed as "women's work" and respectable women's work at that. Men would fight on the battlefields, and women would bind their wounds and care for them in medical facilities, the two activities perceived as worlds apart, but in proper balance, akin to the separation of public and private spheres in peacetime society. Moreover, when necessary, women would also participate in military activity, engaging in combat that was justified for reasons of extreme necessity, when the nation faced its greatest moments of crisis and required all citizens' involvement in national defense.

Essential for such wartime activity for women was the wearing of official uniforms, which gave sanction to their otherwise transgressive acts. The uniforms legitimated the crossing of gendered lines. Their intention, not always successful, was to indicate that the roles engaged in by women were acceptable, at least temporarily. The Red Cross uniform worn by nurses was intended to clearly delineate wartime servitor from the civilian, the "true" Sister of Mercy from the "false" dissolute woman, by hiding markers of identity and sexuality. Over time, however, the uniform itself became conflated with the disreputable. The gendered design of the dress also proved impractical in the difficult conditions of wartime nursing at the front. The military uniform worn by female soldiers similarly aimed, and often successfully worked, to transform civilian women into genderless, or even masculinized, combatants, marked their ability to engage in warfare, and enabled their integration into masculine military culture. But rather than signaling a reassessment of the gendered nature of that culture and of the specific function of combat, the uniform merely provided a means for women, who were largely seen as exceptional rather than representative of their sex, to temporarily recode their functions. As such, neither nursing nor military uniforms proved sufficient to completely overturn deeply entrenched ideologies of gender in Russia but did provide women with opportunities to demonstrate the increasing lack of validity of such ideologies, convincingly engaging in wartime service that proved invaluable to the nation.

NOTES

1. For a much more expansive and detailed account of the themes and events discussed in this chapter, see Laurie S. Stoff, *Russia's Sisters of Mercy and the Great War: More Than Binding Men's Wounds* (Lawrence: University of Kansas Press, 2015).

2. V.P. Romaniuk, V.A. Lapotnikov, and Ia.A. Nakatis, *Istoriia sestrinskogo dela v Rossii* [The history of nursing in Russia] (St. Petersburg: Sankt-Peterburgskaia gosudarstvennyi meditsinskaia akademiia imeni I.I. Mechnikova, 1998), 35.

3. Yuri Bessonov, "Russian Nurses after the Crimean War: Bureaucracy and Prejudice Against Nurses," *RN: Journal of Nursing*, https://rn-journal.com/journal-of-nursing/russian-nurses-after-the-crimean-war (accessed 23 Oct. 2019).

4. A.V. Posternak, "Istorii obshchin sester miloserdiia" [History of societies of Sisters of Mercy], in *Blagotvoritel'nost' v Rossii: Istoricheskie i sotsial'no-ekonomicheskie issledovaniia* [Charity in Russia: Historical and social-economic papers], ed. O.L. Leikinda (St. Petersburg: Liki Rossii, 2003), 29.

5. Circular from the Main Directorate of the Russian Society of the Red Cross to the district and local committees and the committees and fiduciary councils of the communities of sisters of mercy of the society, 4 Sept. 1914, Fond 12674, opis. 2, delo. 1, list 54, Rossiiskii gosudarstvennyi voenno-istoricheskii arkhiv [Russian State Military-Historical Archive], Moscow (hereafter RGVIA).

6. Directory of the quantity of medical personnel in the establishments of the Red Cross according to data on July 1, 1917, f. 12651, op. 3, d. 456, l. 71, RGVIA.

7. Preliminary report of the Mobilization Council of the ROKK, 16 Oct. 1914, f. 12651, op. 3, d. 346, l. 388, RGVIA.

8. Lidiia Zakharova, *Dnevnik sestry miloserdiia*: *Na peredovykh pozitsiiakh* [The diary of a Sister of Mercy (in forward positions)] (St. Petersburg: Izdatel'stvo Biblioteka "Velikoi Voiny," 1915), 46.

9. Marie, Grand Duchess of Russia, *Education of a Princess* (London: Viking Press, 1930), 172.

10. Barton C. Hacker, "Reformers, Nurses, and Ladies in Uniform," in *A Companion to Women's Military History*, ed. Barton C. Hacker and Margaret Vining (Leiden: Brill, 2012), 137–138.

11. Rochelle Goldberg Ruthchild, *Equality and Revolution: Women's Rights in the Russian Empire, 1905–1917* (Pittsburgh: University of Pittsburgh Press, 2010), 215.

12. For a fuller discussion of the positive connotation of nursing during this war in Russia, see of Stoff, *Russia's Sisters of Mercy and the Great War*, ch. 7.

13. Helen Goscilo, "Keeping A-breast of the Waist-Land: Women's Fashion in Early 19th Century Russia," in *Russia—Women—Culture*, ed. Helen Goscilo and Beth Holmgren (Bloomington: Indiana University Press, 1996), 32.

14. See, e.g., Khristina D. Semina, *Tragediia russkoi armii: Pervoi velikoi voiny 1914–1918: Zapiski setry miloserdia Kavkazkogo fronta* [The tragedy of the Russian army in the First World War 1914–1918: Notes of a Sister of Mercy on the Caucasus Front] (New Mexico: Privately published, 1963), 69–70; Tatiana Alexinsky, *With the Russian Wounded*, trans. Gilbert Cannan (London: Fisher Unwin, 1916), 70–71; Florence Farmborough, *With the Armies of the Tsar: A Nurse at the Russian Front in War and Revolution, 1914–1918* (New York: Cooper Square, 2000), 151.

15. D. Mikhailov, *Krasnii Krest i sestry miliserdiia v Rossii i za-granitsei* [The Red Cross and Sisters of Mercy in Russia and abroad] (Petrograd: Knigoizdatel'stvo "Sotrudnik," 1914), 78.

16. Pravila noshcheniia formy ses. mil. i litsami zhenskago sanitarnogo personala ROKK [Regulations concerning the wearing of uniforms for sisters of mercy and female sanitary personnel of the Russian Society of the Red Cross], f. 12675, op. 2, d. 1, l. 61, RGVIA.

17. Resolution of the trustee of the Committee of the Omsk Community of the Red Cross from 3 Jan. 1915, f. 12651, op. 3, d. 373, l. 5, no. 19, RGVIA.

18. Session #13 of the Mobilization Committee of ROKK, 18 Mar. 1917, f. 12651, op. 3, d. 452, l. 130, RGVIA.

19. "O zloupotreblenii zvaniem sester miloserdiia" [On the abuse of the title of Sisters of Mercy], *Vestnik Krasnogo Kresta* [Herald of the Red Cross] 3 (Mar. 1915): 917–918.

20. "O zloupotreblenii zvaniem sester miloserdiia," 917.

21. For a fuller discussion of the negative connotation of nursing during this war, see Stoff, *Russia's Sisters of Mercy and the Great War*, ch. 8.

22. Commission for the Fight against the Misuse of the Name of Sister of Mercy, 20 Jan. 1915, f. 12651, op. 10, d. 23, l. 33, RGVIA.

23. "O zloupotreblenii zvaniem sester miloserdiia," 918.

24. John C. Curtiss, "Russian Sisters of Mercy in the Crimea, 1854–1855," *Slavic Review* 25, no. 1 (Mar. 1966): 84–100.

25. See the memoirs of nurses who indicate this sentiment, including N. Chelakova, "Iz zapisok sestry miloserdiia" [From the notes of a Sister of Mercy], *Novoe Russkoe Slovo* [New Russian word], 13 June 1969, 6; Zakharova, *Dnevnik sestry miloserdiia*: *Na peredovykh pozitsiiakh*; Vanda Kazimirovna Stepanova, "Zapiski velikoi voiny 1914–1918 gg." [Notes of the Great War 1914–1918], holograph, box 1, Hoover Institution Archives, Stanford University, Stanford, Calif.

26. See, e.g., Stepanova, "Zapiski velikoi voiny 1914–1918 gg."

27. The journals of sessions of the Mobilization Committee of the Russian Society of the Red Cross, f. 12651, op. 3, RGVIA, contain numerous documents pertaining to this problem.

28. Christine Ruane, "Clothes Shopping in Imperial Russia: The Development of a Consumer Culture," *Journal of Society History* 28, no. 4 (Summer 1995): 773–774.

29. Photograph and caption, *Niva*, no. 2 (10 Jan. 1915): 30.

30. Farmborough, *With the Armies of the Tsar*, front cover and frontispiece photograph.

31. Zakharova, *Dnevnik Sestry Miloserdiia*, 73, 95.

32. Aleksandra Tolstaia, *Doch'* [Daughter] (Moscow: Vagrius, 2000), 239, 245.

33. For a brief overview of women's participation in warfare in Russia, see Iulia N. Ivanova, "Zhenshchiny v istorii rossiiskoi armii" [Women in the history of the Russian army], *Voenno-Istoricheskii Zhurnal* [Military-historical journal] 3 (1992): 86.

34. Ann Eliot Griese and Richard Stites, "Russia: Revolution and War," in *Female Soldiers: Combatants or Noncombatants? Historical and Contemporary Perspectives*, ed. Nancy Loring Goldman (Westport, Conn.: Greenwood Press, 1982), 67. Although some of the sources of information must be viewed with caution, emanating as they do largely from the pages of sensationalist contemporary periodicals, there is enough corroborating evidence to indicate that a significant number of women successfully entered the Russian army and performed combat roles. I have located nearly 60 examples in contemporary periodicals and accounts and about 10 more in other published and unpublished sources.

35. See RGVIA, f. 2003, op. 2, d. 28, ll. 23, 45, 71–72, 131, for numerous examples of petitions sent to the Russian high command by women requesting permission to enlist in the active army.

36. Rheta Childe Dorr, *Inside the Russian Revolution* (New York: Macmillan, 1917), 75.

37. For the desire for adventure and romanticized notions of war among male soldiers, see George L. Mosse, "Two World Wars and the Myth of the War Experience," *Journal of Contemporary History* 21, no. 4 (Oct. 1986): 493.

38. For soldiers' attitudes about the war, see Nikolai N. Golovin, *The Russian Army in the World War* (New Haven, Conn.: Yale University Press, 1931); Allan K. Wildman, *The End of the Russian Imperial Army*, vol. 1, *The Old Army and the Soldiers' Revolt (March–April 1917)* (Princeton, N.J.: Princeton University Press, 1980).

39. All-Russian Women's Military Union to Aid the Homeland, telegram to the minister of war, f. 2000, op. 2, d. 1557, ll. 15 and 194, RGVIA; report of the Organizational Committee of the Women's Military Detachments to the Minister of War, Alexander Kerenskii, f. 2000, op. 2, d. 1557, l. 3, RGVIA.

40. Wildman, *The Old Army and the Soldiers' Revolt.*

41. "Zhenshchiny idut na front!" [Women go to the front!] *Petrogradskii listok* [Petrograd leaf], 26 May 1917, 2; "Zhenskii Voenno-Narodnyi Soiuz Dobrovol'stev—Manifest" [Female Military People's Union of Volunteers—Manifesto], *Novoe vremia* 8 (June 1917): 5; Sofia Zarechnaia, "Amazonki velikoi voiny" [Amazons of the Great War], *Zhenskoe delo* [Women's work] 14 (1 July 1917): 10–11.

42. Although Bochkareva claims to be the originator of the idea, it is clear that it was already circulating in Russian society. Maria Botchkareva [*sic*], *Yashka: My Life as Peasant, Officer, and Exile*, as told to Isaac Don Levine (New York: Frederick A. Stokes, 1919), 156–161.

43. Boris Solonevich, *Zhenshchina s vintovkoi: Istoricheskii roman* [Woman with a rifle: A historical novel] (Buenos Aires: Privately published, 1955), 51.

44. Solonevich, *Zhenshchina s vintovkoi*, 58.

45. For the complete story of the expulsion of those who did not conform to Bochkareva's demands, see Laurie S. Stoff, *They Fought for the Motherland: Russia's Women Soldiers in World War I and the Revolution* (Lawrence: University Press of Kansas, 2006), ch. 3.

46. See, e.g., "Zhenskii dobrovol'cheskii komitet" [Women's Voluntary Committee], *Armiia i flot svobodnoi Rossii* [Army and navy of free Russia], 2 July 1917, 3; "Ustav Vserossiskago voennago zhenskago soiza 'Pomoshchi Rodine'" [The Charter of the All-Russian Military Women's Union "Help for the Motherland"], f. 2000, op. 2, d. 1557, l. 194, RGVIA; Dokladnaia zapiska voennomu ministru iz Organizatsionogo Komiteta Zhenskei Armii [Statement by the defense ministers about the organization of the Women's Army Committee], f. 2000, op. 2, d. 1557, l. 48, RGVIA; "Zhenskiia Voennyia Organizatsii: Soiuz aktivnoi pomoshchi rodine" [Women's military organizations: Union for Active Help for the Motherland], *Utro Rossii* [Russia morning], 6 June 1917, 6.

47. RGVIA contains many examples of such petitions, as do such contemporary periodicals as *Novoe vremia* and *Utro Rossii*. See also "Telegramma kvartirmeistra Stavky kommandiru iugo-zapadnom fronte" [Telegram, quartermaster staff to commander, southwest front], in *Razlozhenie armii v 1917 godu* [Distintegration of the army 1917], ed. N.E. Kakurin and Ia.A. Iakovleva (Moscow: Gosudarstvennoe izdatel'stvo, 1925), 72.

48. Report by Glavnoe Upravlenie Generalnogo Shtaba (GUGSh), 17 Oct. 1917, f. 2000, op. 2, d. 1557, l. 211, RGVIA.

49. RGVIA holds documents on the four women's army units.

50. Order to the navy and naval military authorities in Petrograd, 12 July 1917, No. 397, f. 417, op. 4, d. 6571, l. 1, Rossiskii gosudarstvennyi arkhiv voenno-morskogo flota [Russian State Archive of the Navy] (hereafter RGAVMF).

51. List of cadets of the Moscow Women's Battalion of Death, f. 725, op. 54, d. 489, l. 19, RGVIA.

52. List of the staff of the Reserve Company of the 1st Petrograd Women's Battalion, f. 2000, op. 2, d. 1557, l. 188, RGVIA; documents of the Moscow Women's Battalion of Death, f. 3474, op. 2, d. 5, l. 7, RGVIA.

53. Solonevich, *Zhenshchina s vintovkoi*, 48.

54. Botchkareva, *Yashka*, 222.

55. "Zhenskii batal'on" [Women's battalion], *Russkoe slovo* [Russian word] 1 (Aug. 1917): 4.

56. "Miting i sbor dlia zhenskago batal'ona" [Rally and collection for the women's battalion], *Vremia*, 23 June 1917, 2; "Zhenskii batal'on" [Women's battalion], *Vremia*, 27 June 1917, 2.

57. Louise Bryant, *Six Red Months in Russia: An Observer's Account of Russia before and during the Proletarian Dictatorship* (New York: George H. Doran, 1918), 211–212.

58. Memorandum to the Minister of War from the Chairwoman of the Organizational Bureau of the Kuban Women's Shock Battalion, Citizen of the Kuban Oblast, Ekaterinodar, Matriona Leontevna Zalesskaia, 3 Aug. 1917, f. 2000, op. 2, d. 1557, l. 69, RGIVA.

59. Report of the Commander of the Naval Infantry Training Unit to Main Naval Headquarters, 19 July 1917, f. 620, op. 1, d. 406, l. 1, RGAVMF.

60. Note to the Office of the Naval Infantry Training Unit No. 25, 31 July 1917, f. 620, op. 1, d. 406, l. 3, RGAVMF.

61. See, e.g., such Russian wartime newspapers as *Birzhevye vedemosti, Novoe vremia, Petrogradskii listok, Rech', Russkoe slovo,* and *Utro Rossii*; such Russian journals as *Iskry, Ogonek, Niva, Sinii zhurnal,* and *20-yi Vek*; and such international periodicals as the *New York Times, Times* (London), *Jus Suffragi*, *Literary Digest,* and the *London Graphic.*

62. Herman Axelbank Film Collection, reel 19, segment 1 (June–July 1917), Hoover Institution Archives, Stanford University, Stanford, Calif.

63. Griese and Stites, "Russia: Revolution and War," 64.

64. See, e.g., correspondence from the Adjutant General of the Commander in Chief of the Western Front to the Chief of Staff of the 10th Army, 8/9 July 1917, f. 2277, op. 1, d. 368, l. 8, 1, RGVIA.

65. Botchkareva, *Yashka*, 211; telegram from the Chief of Staff of the I Siberian Army Corp on the actions of the Women's Battalion of Death in the battle of 9 July 1917 at Novospasskii forest, f. 2277, op. 1, d. 1, l. 1, RGVIA; Solonevich, *Zhenshchina s vintovkoi,* 125–126.

66. Informational report from the Department of Organization and Service of Troops, 27 Sept. 1917, f. 2000, op. 2, d. 1557, l. 190, RGVIA.

67. Telegram from the Duty General of the Southwestern Front, 4 Oct. 1917, f. 2003, op. 2, d. 349, l. 39, RGVIA.

68. Report by GUGSh, 4 Oct. 1917, f. 2003, op. 2, d. 349, l. 39, RGVIA.

69. "Vserossiskii zhenskii voennyi s'ezd" [All-Russian women's military congress], *Novoe vremia*, 13 July 1917, 4.

70. "Zhenshchiny-voiny (zakrytie zhenskago voennago s'ezda)" [Female warriors, closing of the women's military congress], *Petrogradskii Listok*, 6 Aug. 1917, 3.

71. For a detailed account of women soldiers in the defense of the Winter Palace, see Stoff, *They Fought for the Motherland*, 151–160.

72. Documents 5940, 276, and 2655, in *Petrogradskii Voenni-Revoliutsionyi Komitet: dokumenty i materiali* [Petrograd Military-Revolutionary Committee: Documents and materials] (Moscow: Nauka, 1966), 3:113, 116.

73. Copy of the *Journal of Military Activity*, 14–15 Dec. 1917, operations of the 27th Infantry Division, f. 2357, op. 1, d. 520, l. 8, RGVIA.

74. Botchkareva, *Yashka*, 263.

75. Joshua A. Sanborn, *Drafting the Russian Nation: Military Conscription, Total War, and Mass Politics, 1905–1925* (DeKalb: Northern Illinois University Press), 154–155.

76. Roger D. Markwick and Euridice Charon Cardona, *Soviet Women on the Frontline in the Second World War* (London: Palgrave Macmillan, 2012), 239–241.

ELEVEN

"WAR IS MAN STUFF!"? *"Uniformed" Women in the (Military) Service of the Habsburg Empire*

CLAUDIA REICHL-HAM

Henriette Herzfelder, an Austrian writer and suffragette, in 1915 challenged the chauvinist assumption that war is man stuff! This perception, deeply entrenched since time immemorial, had a corollary: Military service defined the full citizen. Because women failed to bear the burden of war, they were widely seen and treated as second-class citizens. Yet war never left women unscathed, Herzfelder observed. They have always suffered its effects. Now, however, we see active female participation in the present war. Not as warriors—two dozen Polish Legionaries and a few other heroines notwithstanding—but as stalwarts of the home front. What millions of women have achieved and accomplished far from the front lines, day in and day out since the beginning of hostilities, she concluded, is just as important and essential for the progress of the war as the sacrifice of millions of nameless soldiers on the firing line. Both give their best and last for the threatened home—themselves.[1]

Herzfelder's challenge to war as an all-male preserve struck at a cliché cherished by politicians and the military and perpetuated by Austrian historians. Traditional military and diplomatic history centered on male elites, even ignoring for the most part the men who did the actual fighting, to say nothing of ubiquitous women camp followers and the occasional cross-dressing female soldier. Although it is true that the increasing professionalization, standardization, and bureaucratization of the Austrian army in the late nineteenth century ushered in a fleeting period when the "military got male-only,"[2] the historiographical prejudice persisted long afterward. As recently as 2014, Christa Hämmerle, the doyenne of Austrian gender and women's studies, criticized the neglect of women in Great War historiography, noting that topics "centered on women and gender history were only hesitantly integrated into Austrian research. A theoretically and methodologically highly developed field of modern historiography is still neglected or marginalized by many Austrian military and war historians."[3]

PREWAR THINKING ABOUT WOMEN'S SERVICE

History belied the historiography. As early as the 1890s, articles in Austrian periodicals were addressing the concept of a female service obligation (*Dienstpflicht*) comparable to men's military service, a topic also broadly discussed in the German Empire. The takeover of "responsibility for the public good" in the form of social, educational, and nursing duties became a desideratum in the public sector. Franziska Wessely entered police service in 1904, becoming the first "police assistant for youth questions."[4] This idea, however, soon fell into oblivion and was taken up again only in the Great War.[5]

Efforts to mobilize women began even before the formal outbreak of war. At the end of July 1914, upon partial mobilization of the Austro-Hungarian army, Helene Granitsch, head of the Imperial Organization of Austrian Housewives, published an urgent appeal to "Austria's women." It called upon them "to perform service in the time of war," display "the strongest solidarity," and put aside all political and social "differences."[6] War propaganda and the state strengthened traditional role stereotypes—the peaceful (i.e., female) and the martial (i.e., male). Language, however, became more and more militarized: Women became "soldiers of the hinterland" or "soldiers of the home front," comparable to the male soldiers in the front lines. While men were fighting in the trenches, women were fighting at home—"for economic continuity and productivity, for social stability, for the management of shortage and hunger." This was at least the scenario created by the propaganda machines of the warring countries in billboards, postcards, posters, and even patriotic poetry.[7]

Large-scale troop mobilization and growing casualties required more and more men to be conscripted for military service. Women filled the places they left in industry, agriculture, public service, and other areas often deemed only male. Women replaced men as streetcar drivers, conductors, letter carriers, street maintenance workers, firefighters, farm hands, and factory workers, especially in armament industries. And they were also employed as auxiliary labor near the front lines; working in the army's service sector, women entered the "male" domain of the Austro-Hungarian army.

Not every woman reacted to the outbreak of war with excessive joy and patriotic feelings. The alleged unique spirit of unity and enthusiasm at the outbreak of the Great War, the so-called spirit of 1914 (*Augusterlebnis*), was, in fact, a myth, initially propagated by the governments of Austria-Hungary and Germany and their religious communities. Scholars have found little evidence of public enthusiasm in general; it spread mostly in the bigger cities and varied with social class.[8] Many women were, nevertheless, ready and willing to serve their homeland. Many others, of course, had no choice; economic necessity and, as the war progressed, the fight for survival forced many women to work, whatever their feelings about the war.

WOMEN IN UNIFORM ON THE HOME FRONT

Contemporaries, especially in bigger cities, soon noticed the replacement of male labor by female, most prominently in those occupations that enjoyed great visibility. Uniformed female mail carriers, streetcar drivers and conductors, and delivery wagon drivers would have been unimaginable before the war. Especially in the first months, women in uniform were a bewildering sight for the civil population and irritated many; women in uniform—at least due to their outer appearance—diverged from the traditional role model of motherly caring and cherished femininity.[9] But after a few months of war, they had become part of everyday life and a common sight on city streets.

> We see the woman's efficiency not only in mental work but also [in areas] where up to now only the "stronger" sex was considered due to its physique. . . . In many businesses, women perform male duties in a diligent and solid way. This official metamorphose has naturally also become evident in the clothes [they wear] and after a first irritation our adaptability in war has led us to accept the idea of seeing women in male, vigorous garments.[10]

Above all, the conductresses quickly became popular figures in bigger cities. Following the example of Graz, Budapest, and Bratislava, Vienna in the spring of 1915 also decided to employ women as tram conductors. Their numbers grew rapidly, from about 600 at the beginning to 4,000 two years later. By 1918, they numbered 7,500—54% of all conductors.[11] For weeks, the newspapers had been full of reports on the activities of the conductresses. The weekly *Das interessante Blatt* reported on 1 July 1915,

> Viennese street life has recently been enriched by a female character type. The first streetcar conductresses entered service. The equal status of the woman has occupied a new area hitherto belonging exclusively to men. . . . They wear as official clothing an ankle-length skirt of the same color as the streetcar-driver uniform, a jacket in the same color with a back clasp and stand-up collar, onto which red braids and cuffs are sewed. The uniform jacket does not cover the neck and allows a view to the blouse worn below. A cap covers the head.[12]

Female carters also became a common sight in the streets of Vienna. Many of the hard-working female laborers who maneuvered heavy bread, ice, milk, or coal wagons through the city wore trousers because they were practical and comfortable. In peacetimes, this clothing would have caused a scandal. Indeed, the first deliveries by women did not go smoothly; some female clients felt themselves threatened "in their noble femininity" at the sight of the women in male garments. As a result, some female carters had to be accompanied by male supervisors on their first rides.[13] But soon they attracted the complacent attention of pedestrians. Mostly sturdy women in a smart uniform with a short skirt and breeches in gray-green fabric, a cap of the same fabric with a yellow silk ribbon and black company logo, as well as ankle gaiters made of jersey. This smart amazon corps are the first bread deliverers . . . recruited and recently employed by the "Erste Wiener Kronenbrotwerke," who resolutely drive their vehicles through the streets of Vienna.[14]

However much war propaganda and the press hyped them, women workers, whether or not in uniform, were never considered equal to their male counterparts. Not only did they receive lower pay; they were, especially at the beginning, confronted with the open hostility of their male colleagues (and their families), who feared losing their safe jobs and being sent

Figure 11.1.
Conductress in uniform, ca. 1916. By war's end, women outnumbered men on Vienna's tramways. Courtesy Heeresgeschichtliches Museum, Vienna.

to the front. The women in uniform additionally had to face an irritated public, initially unable to cope with women who had left traditional roles behind and entered the male sphere.

THE AUSTRO-HUNGARIAN WOMEN'S AUXILIARY LABOR FORCE IN THE FIELD

Austria-Hungary's tremendous wartime losses up to 1917 "prompted the state to recruit women for positions that would take them beyond the home front and for which they were not naturally suited."[15] At that time, numerous female auxiliaries were already working for the "army in the field." Apart from auxiliary nurses, they were mostly local women, recruited individually by military authorities and working in military offices on a nonofficial basis. In the early stages of war, the Army High Command hesitated to employ women officially in military offices. Only after hope of a quick military decision was finally dashed in 1916 did rising casualties compel army authorities to rethink their position. In a letter dated 12 July 1916 "to the armies, the military general governments, etc.," the Army High Command recommended employing female workers in all kinds of military institutions: "The rising demand for labor . . . , connected with the growing restriction of male labor in the hinterland, makes it advisable to employ [women] for all services, which . . . can be done by female labor."[16]

A memorandum of the XXth Corps command (replacement branch), on the "organization of female labor in the field army and in the hinterland," estimated the numbers of female workers necessary:

> A rough calculation shows that in the field army and in the hinterland about 250,000 female workers and auxiliary labor could be employed . . . , for the army in the field 100,000, for the hinterland (the central authorities, military commands, local authorities and military industrial enterprises) ca. 150,000 female auxiliary workers.[17]

As a consequence, in 1917, the Army High Command established the Women's Auxiliary Labor Force in the Field in the newly created office of Replacement Affairs of the Joint Armed Forces, headed by former Hungarian honvéd minister Col.-Gen. Baron Samuel von Hazai.[18] The Army High Command intended to replenish the depleted ranks of its soldiers, announcing an ambitious program to free up the "greatest possible number of troops" for war service for the trenches by replacing men in army support positions with women.[19]

Until the end of the war, between 36,000 and 50,000 women—most of them citizens of Austria, Hungary, and Bosnia-Herzegovina, aged 16 to 40, unmarried, and with "a strong moral character and political reliability"[20]—were recruited as auxiliary laborers and thus became part of the military establishment.[21] As yet, no overall statistics for the social background of the female auxiliaries of the Austro-Hungarian armed forces in general are available. An analysis of the 11th Army shows, however, that 7% of the auxiliaries belonged to the upper class, 31% were middle class, and 45% were lower class; on the remainder, there is no specified information.[22] They were recruited "through the press, posters, employment

Figure 11.2.
Employees of the Kronenbrotwerke. Das interessante Blatt *14 (6 April 1916): 13.*

offices, and through direct appeal to women's organizations." What is important (especially for the time after the war) is that the authorities always stressed "the provisional nature of the assignments."[23] Harsh criticism came from the Army High Command as the armies in the field and other military institutions began to publish job ads in the local newspapers on their own initiative and sometimes recruited women without previous education and adequate training.[24]

As army employees working in areas behind the lines in support areas, these women referred to themselves as "enlisted" and served, among other things, as laboratory assistants, secretaries, technicians, telephone and telegraph operators, and nonprofessional nurses. According to the Regulations for the Enlistment of Female Auxiliary Workers and Their Employment in the Army in the Field, they were urged to wear uniform-like dresses, uniform shoes, and headgear; sketches of these clothes appear in Appendix 4 of the regulations. Different buttons on the garments distinguished the categories of workers.[25] Furthermore, every auxiliary laborer was to wear a black-and-yellow brassard (red and yellow for Hungarians). The Army High Command was very anxious to stress that the prescribed garments were "in no way aimed to uniform" the women; rather, the regulations "intended to simplify the production of garments and curtail special wishes or demands."[26] Category A workers received a clothing allowance of 90 crowns; category B workers received 45 crowns. The women were to purchase shoes and cloth, the cloth to be made according to a prescribed model into garments like blouses, jackets, and skirts. Photographs of female auxiliary workers show, however, that they, in reality, did not wear uniform garments.[27] This flouting of the rules annoyed

Figure 11.3.
Female post office employees amid their male colleagues in Banjaluka, 1917. Courtesy Heeresgeschichtliches Museum, Vienna.

the responsible authorities, who complained that "the equipment with garments and shoes with which the female auxiliary labor force come to the Army in the Field, does not at all correspond to the actual needs. . . . Silk dresses and high-heeled patent-leather shoes are not only unpractical, they seem indecent and ridiculous in their work environment."[28]

The motives that induced women to apply as female auxiliaries were diverse. On the one hand, the majority were motivated by patriotism, solidarity, enthusiasm, and the desire to actively participate in the "Great War." They were eager to "serve their beloved fatherland," as Agathe Fessler, a nurse from Bregenz who worked close behind the Eastern Front in October 1914, put it.[29] Another nurse, Evelina Hrouda, admits in her memoirs that she applied "with utmost enthusiasm" for medical service "out of an irresistible inner desire and my great inclination towards medical care."[30] Others were driven by the desire to accompany their husbands, brothers, or fathers into the field, and for some, it was an act of necessity to maintain their families.[31]

On the other hand, the auxiliary service attracted many women because it offered them the opportunity to break out of the limited role that the hinterland imposed on women (the traditional three *K*'s—*Kinder, Kirche, Küche*) and to lead an independent and self-determined life. It was also an adventure, as most of these women, for the first time, left their homes to travel, often far away, and to work with men, a challenge that was to put their lives on a completely new basis. They were relatively well paid and were promised free lodging and food, as well as social care, which may have been further motives for their service. They had the chance to attend professional courses for telegraphers, telephone operators, typists, and

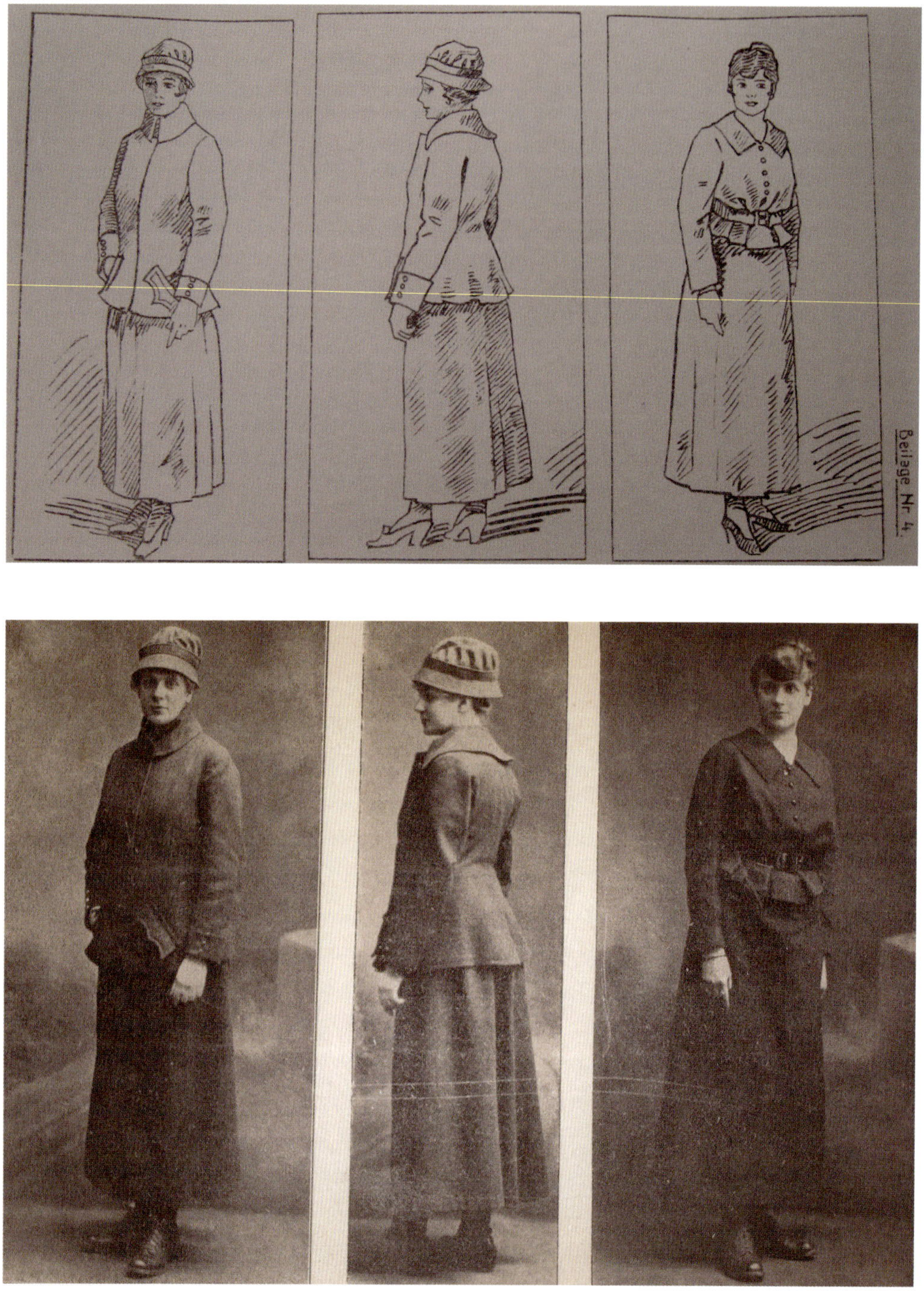

Figure 11.4.
Women's Auxiliary Labor Force in the Field, summer and winter garments (no dates): (top) sketches and (bottom) women modeling. Bestimmungen für die Aufnahme weiblicher Hilfskräfte und deren Verwendung bei der Armee im Felde, *Supplement 4.*

Figure 11.5.
Telegraph operator Eva Baráth. Kriegsbilder, *3 (1915): 2.*

other secretarial staff.[32] For some women, the war also meant the chance to make a career and offered them hitherto undreamed-of possibilities.

Despite the rapidly rising number of female auxiliaries, their image was generally not positive. Unlike Red Cross nurses, who were publicly celebrated for the specifically feminine virtues of their service, the volunteers of the Women's Auxiliary Labor Force met with official resistance as well as public derision and contempt. Despite the repeated declarations of the Army High Command that the Women's Auxiliary Labor Force was essential to the Austrian war effort, social reservations among the civil population toward the military employment of women persisted, although according to the regulations, widows and orphans of former active officers were given preference at first.[33]

Women were criticized for being unreliable and physically incapable of doing their work properly. Suspicions remained that female service for the army in the field was more frivolous or sexual than patriotic or professional. Critical voices charged that the feminine virtues of these women were endangered in the process, or as Maureen Healy put it,

> they were accused of a laundry list of feminine violations. They didn't display selflessness (adventure seeking); they were immoral (prostitutes posing as office workers); they were frivolous (novels and cinema); they did not dress like women (uniforms); and they neglected key feminine duties (poor housekeeping). . . . [They] were not performing their work in a recognizable family capacity as mothers, sisters, or daughters.[34]

Female auxiliaries were not subject to military justice, even when assigned to military commands. In cases of misconduct, they could just be cautioned or reprimanded. Severe offences, such as theft, fraud, or embezzlement, resulted in immediate dismissal, so did immoral lifestyle, unpatriotic sentiments, or defamation.[35]

Public controversy was matched by military resistance. Army commanders complained about the inefficiency and unwillingness of the female staff. But it was also the uncontrolled recruitment by the army commands and other military organizations that had many unqualified and even shady women join the army service. Although such women were finally dismissed—and army commands published their names in official bulletins—they did lasting harm to the good reputation of the Auxiliary Labor Force in the Field, overshadowing the good job that most of the other women did.[36]

Complaints also came from soldiers still working in military offices, who understandably considered the arrival of the female auxiliaries a personal threat: "Stationed comfortably behind the lines in office or support positions with the designation 'indispensable,' these men were suddenly rendered dispensable by a program whose clear aim was an 'increase in troops.' They accused the newcomers of being unqualified, frivolous adventure-seekers."[37] As the situation at the home front steadily deteriorated, the *Illustrirtes Wiener Extrablatt* started stirring up opposition to the auxiliary labor force. It painted a picture of luxurious volunteer life, informing its readers that apart from high pay, these women enjoyed free lodging and board, free travel to and from their assignments, and a yearly clothing allowance.[38] They did receive these benefits, of course, but the same criticism was never leveled at soldiers who received the same benefits for their military service. And the pay was not so "high." In urban areas, high wages paid by the armaments industry made it a serious competitor to the auxiliary service. The number of female applicants for service in the Austro-Hungarian army also varied greatly according to the areas and branches of service. Military organizations in Galicia, the Bukovina, and the Balkans, for instance, offered unusually attractive and popular terms.[39]

The vehement opposition to the Women's Auxiliary Labor Force program suggests that "Austrian society in 1917 and 1918 was not ready for women's service that extended beyond traditional, familial roles."[40] The strong headwind, to which the female labor force was exposed in the Austro-Hungarian army as well as in public, shows that the traditional image of women was put under very heavy strain during the war.[41] For the women themselves, military employment meant further education through the professional courses they were offered. It also helped break them out from the strict limits that their traditional roles imposed, marking a big step toward consciousness, self-reliance, and emancipation.

MEDICAL AND NURSING SERVICES

Even in peacetime, army authorities were well aware that the military medical staff would not be sufficient to provide adequate care of the wounded in the case of a larger conflict. Civil voluntary organizations like the Austrian and Hungarian Red Cross organizations,[42] as well as the Teutonic Order and the Sovereign Military Order of Malta,[43] made provisions to support the army with trained personnel, material, and medical care facilities. In July 1914, the government decreed that "all matters concerning the army's wounded and sick will be managed by the Society of the Red Cross," integrated into the military structures, and placed under the command of the inspector general of the Voluntary Medical Service, a position entrusted to Archduke Franz Salvator.[44] In the course of the war, the "voluntary" medical service proved to be of high importance. By 1916, the Austrian Red Cross alone claimed 1,500 doctors, 2,800 female nurses, and 5,000 male nurses.[45]

At the outbreak of the war, thousands of women in the Habsburg monarchy were fascinated by the idea of working as army nurses, not only in the relatively safe hinterland but also in the mobile field hospitals near the front lines. "Frontline nursing" became very trendy. It is hardly surprising that this kind of work was defined as the ideal profession for women in peacetime and in wartime, perfectly matching the peaceful nature of women. Only a minority of female applicants had a proper education as qualified nurses, however, as the professionalization of female nursing in Austria-Hungary had only begun in the 1880s. It was, in fact, the Balkan Wars of 1912–1913 that accelerated Austria-Hungary's earlier efforts to institutionalize the education of nurses. In a law of 25 June 1914, the state officially regulated "female" nursing for the first time and prescribed two years of training.[46]

The Red Cross Department for Female Nurses assumed the main responsibility for recruiting female nurses.[47] At first, it recruited only professional and auxiliary nurses with a proper education. Soon, it became clear that it would not be able to provide a sufficient number. Therefore, professional nurses from abroad (Switzerland, Sweden, Germany, the United States) as well as voluntary auxiliary nurses were employed. The latter attended a course lasting for only two or three weeks—a short and not very substantial training, which soon impaired the quality of nursing—and were then sent to medical facilities in the hinterland and the rear area of each army.[48]

At first, women of all social classes applied for nursing jobs, as the professional nurses received a guaranteed income of 50 to 90 kronen and the auxiliary nurses received 30 to 40 kronen. But as social and economic conditions deteriorated and food prices rose rapidly because of massive wartime inflation, many dropped out. Only women who had enough money and were not dependent on their salary were able to continue to work, especially as auxiliary nurses.[49] Most voluntary auxiliary nurses, who received no income at all, came from bourgeois and noble classes and were unmarried. For these volunteers, nursing was a relief from the normal everyday routine and corresponded to the image of social motherliness, which put womanhood on a level with empathy and loving care.[50]

The service or work dress for the nurses was a long-sleeved apron that was to be worn "over washable clothing."[51] Voluntary nurses additionally wore a service badge in the form of a round metal brooch with the inscription "Freiw. Hilfskrankenpflegerin vom Roten Kreuze" (voluntary auxiliary nurse of the Red Cross) on their blouse or apron and a Red Cross brassard on their left arms.[52] For professional and auxiliary nurses, most likely pike-gray uniform-like garments[53] and peak caps with the Red Cross badge were handed out. Mary Gasch describes the field garb and equipment as "very nice light-gray [most likely pike-gray] uniforms, a Red-Cross brassard, posh caps, nice nurse caps and an ID card as army nurse."[54] The fact that she writes of a uniform also hints at the military terminology the nurses used and that the term *uniform* was quite common, although not army approved. For Hrouda, they were "extremely practical but too male and too similar to a soldier's uniform"; they did not make a "pleasant and female impression, which should be immanent to a real nurse."[55]

To avoid inconsistencies and provide uniform procedures as to the recruitment, training, and equipment of nurses, the Austro-Hungarian army administration and the Austrian Red Cross signed an agreement on 18 December 1915.[56] It established the Central Office for Austrian Red Cross Nurses, which was responsible for the registration of all female Red

Figure 11.6.
Army nurse of the Red Cross of the Imperial and Royal Army, 1917. Erhard Koppensteiner, Salzburg Museum (FO FOT 00248).

Cross nurses and their assignment to the respective medical institutions. It also had to provide the necessary equipment.

The nurses were now called Red Cross army nurses and were obliged to wear so-called field uniforms (*Feldtrachten*), which were handed out to them after recruitment.[57] The uniform included "a field-gray jacket with covered buttons and set-in pockets. On the turndown collar of the field jacket there were white, square collar patches with a red cross stitched on."[58] The Red Cross nurse's badge was worn centrally below the jacket neckline. Army nurses dressed in an ankle-length field-gray skirt and, for indoor duty, a white cap or headscarf.

For outdoor duty, they had a pike-gray peaked cap (model 1915) of soft fabric with a round or square Red Cross badge, which was soon replaced by a field-gray peaked cap with a leather visor. An overcoat, mostly in the form of a pelerine (cape) complemented the garb. On the left arm, on the sleeve of the outermost garment, they wore a white brassard with the black inscription "Armeeschwester vom Roten Kreuze" (Red Cross army nurse). As this brassard did not guarantee protection according to the Geneva Convention, the nurses working near the front lines rather wore the normal Red Cross brassard. They also carried an Austrian (or Hungarian) Red Cross legitimation booklet that identified them as army nurses.[59] On the left breast side of the jacket or the overcoat, they wore the society badge of the Austrian Red Cross. Introduced in March 1915, it was an oval metal badge with a black double-headed eagle in yellow bearing the shield with the red cross in white.[60]

Despite the strict regulations, the nurses wore field garb of varying nature. Photos also show nurses dressed in dark gray or even black. Dark gray was actually the color of male Red Cross auxiliaries. According to a Ministry of the Interior decree of 4 March 1916 regulating uniforms for male auxiliary staff, "all items of clothing . . . worn by members of the Red Cross had [actually] to be of a uniform dark gray color."[61] The caps differed in color and form as well. There were also caps cut like the 1871 army field cap but made of stiff pike-gray fabric with a leather visor.[62] Field garb was handed out in the form of winter or summer garments according to season. Army nurses who worked at the Italian front or in Syria got their own tropical garb and equipment.[63] The garments and equipment belonged to the army and had to be returned when women left service.

Initially, army nurses were not intended to be assigned to brigade or division medical facilities close to the front lines but to field hospitals in the communications zone and to rear area hospitals. This placement would have perfectly corresponded to the hegemonic gender order and the concept of strictly separated spheres. From 1915 onward, however, female Austro-Hungarian nurses also worked in the actual fighting zones in mobile field hospitals and surgical facilities close to the front or in medical care trains and ships, thus entering the male sphere.[64] Voluntary auxiliary nurses, who had received hardly any training, were also soon assigned to service in field hospitals.

As in other countries, Austro-Hungarian war nurses documented their experiences in letters, diaries, and memoirs.[65] They used a military terminology, writing that they had "enlisted for military service," had received their "march routes," and "went to the front." In fact, they displayed a kind of self-assessment similar to that of men. Army nurse R.M. Konrad, who at first worked in military hospitals in the hinterland, volunteered for frontline duty and was pleased when she received her marching orders and could go to the front, a journey that brought her to Gorizia.[66] Eveline Hrouda, then member of surgeon group IV of the Order of Malta, was also pleased to go to the Isonzo Front but soon after her arrival became disillusioned and bitterly disappointed because of the hostile behavior of nurses and physicians.[67]

The memoirs of these women did not find their way into the collective memory of postwar society; their great importance and discursive impact during the war contrasted with public neglect and oblivion after 1918, which may apply to all other women's war activities as well. It was only in the early 1930s, and thus in the wake of Fascism and National Socialism, that the memoirs of former army nurses—who were then once again heroized as "front fighters," "front sisters," or "comrades"—became known to a broader public. In 1936, Hugo Kerchnawe, a high-ranking Austrian officer, published a short text on female war nurses, in which he called these women "upright, brave sisters, our sisters, our comrades, these female soldiers. . . . We soldiers in war (no less than in peace) have to award no higher title [to them] than the proud word: 'soldier.'"[68]

The widespread desire to serve as war nurses was partly explained by a kind of naïve casualty romanticism (*Verwundetenromantik*). Misleading and naïve conceptions regarding the actual requirements and challenges of military nursing as well as the wish to provide medical treatment to injured soldiers close to the front reveal an entirely erroneous view on the nature of modern warfare, a fact that was also noted and criticized by Karl Kraus in his 1918 satirical play, *Die letzten Tage der Menschheit* (*The Last Days of Mankind*).[69] In reality, enthusiasm and fascination soon gave way to disappointment and disillusion, as many nurses had to experience the cruelty of war at close range and were directly confronted not only with often disastrous working conditions but also with the misery, the terrible, often incurable wounds, and the death of thousands of soldiers. Many nurses showed a tireless commitment in the care of the wounded, worked under the most difficult and dangerous conditions, and often went beyond the limits of their physical and psychological capacity. The view of huge numbers of dead and badly wounded soldiers put them under enormous psychic stress.[70] They often shared the same fate as the soldiers, suffering from lack of food and sleep and coming under enemy fire. Many were traumatized during their service. Eveline Hrouda, for one, had a breakdown but recovered. Many voluntary auxiliary nurses, and quite a few professionals, quit service after a short time or had to be removed.[71]

The appreciation shown for nurses differed substantially. On the one hand, it was soon recognized that they were better suited for patient care than male nurses. In contrast to the rough military tone in hospitals that often hindered patient recovery, their more moderate habits brought female nurses a lot of sympathy. War propaganda strongly idealized the image of the war nurse by stressing her self-sacrificing, caring, and loving femininity and extolling her as angel in white or mother of the sick warrior.[72] It even elevated these women to the status of "comrades" and "soldiers," making them virtually part of the front community (*Frontgemeinschaft*).[73] The integration of the nurses into military hierarchies, to which most of them were unaccustomed, often resulted in friction. Many suffered under the military hierarchical organization of medical care in wartime, especially under the demanded unquestioning obedience.[74] As historian Elisabeth Malleier observed, "Without doubt, demanded and expected characteristics such as passivity, self-sacrifice, devotion, and subordination quickly hint at a patriarchal gender construction. So far, so bad."[75]

Although the military held the professional army nurses of the Red Cross in high esteem, the contrary was true for the voluntary auxiliary nursing staff. Officers and common soldiers alike criticized their work, sometimes quite strongly, sometimes with blistering sarcasm. Military men often stigmatized, sexualized, and judged them derogatively, imputing to them base motives, pure thirst for adventure, and selfishness.[76] Despite the tireless, sometimes dangerous, commitment of female nurses, their work received scant official appreciation. Few nurses received military or even civil decorations.[77]

Another neglected topic of military historiography is that of female doctors in military service during the Great War.[78] It bears special mention that they entered military service very early in the war. On 1 September 1914, Dr. Janina Witoszynska (Filz) participated in the Carpathian campaign with the 2nd Brigade of the Polish Legion.[79] Countess Maria Desfours-Walderode, one of Vienna's most highly qualified female surgeons, went to the southeastern front area as a regimental doctor on 5 December 1914.[80] So did Countess Dr. Friederike Marschall in January 1915.[81] Only then did the military authorities begin to reflect on the employment of female doctors in military medical facilities. In a letter of 27 April 1915, Honvéd Minister Baron Samuel von Hazai forwarded a request by the Faculty of Medicine in Budapest to Imperial War Minister Baron Alexander von Krobatin to employ female doctors in military medical facilities.[82] Responding on 9 May, the Ministry of War acknowledged that some female doctors already worked in military medical facilities and saw no objection to the practice "in limited numbers."[83] The growing shortage of military surgeons induced well-qualified female doctors to enlist voluntarily for army service, which offered them the unique chance to gain experience in treating and operating on patients right behind the front lines.[84] They also enjoyed a state income equal to that of their male colleagues![85]

The growing number of women entering military service also increased the demand for female doctors to carry out the medical examination required before women were allowed to work. One of these doctors was Dr. Gisela Januszewska. Too many of the applicants she judged unfit for service, she complained, had arrived with marching orders already signed.[86] What is more, in the Replacement Department of the Military General Government in Poland, female workers soon preferred female doctors and explicitly asked for them: "It is to be expected that the female auxiliary labor force would confide and confess their physical ailments with more confidence to a female physician."[87]

Apart from surgery, where there was an urgent demand for trained experts, many female doctors worked in the epidemiological service, treating persons with infectious diseases; in this service, they even had the chance to become heads of military medical facilities or principal consultants. Dr. Klara Reiniger was appointed head of the bacteriological facility of the quarantine hospitals at Mährisch-Weißkirchen; Dr. Ada Hirsch became the head of the infection department and the laboratory of the reserve hospital at Klosterneuburg.[88] Dr. Desfours-Walderode and Dr. Witoszynska, mentioned above, even became heads of military hospitals.[89]

The status of female doctors within the military hierarchy remains to be thoroughly investigated. Historian Angelika Stadler writes that we must assume at this time that all female doctors were civilians or volunteers who did not hold officer's rank, although they can be considered as "having the same standing as officers."[90] Their names were listed together with those of male doctors in the quartermasters' lists, and they defined themselves as "military doctors." They worked for the army and got the same salary as male doctors. They were also decorated like male officers. Dr. Friederike Ameisen and Dr. Anna Gruszecka (Birnbaum) received medals for their perseverance in the besieged fortress of Cracow.[91] Dr. Desfours-Walderode was awarded the Dame's Cross of the Imperial Order of Franz Joseph. Her file of application was stored among the officers' applications.[92]

Stadler claims that female doctors did not wear uniforms but civilian clothes under their white doctor's coats.[93] A picture published in several Viennese magazines, however, shows a woman in uniform, which has similarities to the nurse's uniform described above, wearing a Silver Cross of Merit.[94] The interesting fact is that on the standup collar, a collar patch with a star and a golden braid for "Assistenzarzt-Stellvertreter" (substitute to the assistant doctor) sewn on is to been seen, which, in fact, indicates a military rank—this position corresponds to a Kadett-Offiziersstellvertreter, or ensign, the lowest rank for a male doctor; like all military doctors, he was uniformed and armed.[95] The name of the person was given as Dr. Emmy Spindler, who was reported to have served on several fronts from the beginning of the war, to have become Assistenzarzt-Stellvertreter, and to have received a medal.[96] Further investigation showed, however, that the alleged Dr. Spindler was an imposter. She was, in

Figure 11.7.
The alleged Assistenzarzt-Stellvertreter Emmy Spindler. Maria Schrell, "Ein Weihnachtsmärchen," Wiener Bilder, *26 December 1915, 12.*

fact, a nurse who had been dismissed on moral grounds. She was put on trial for fraud, false report, and the unauthorized use of a decoration.[97]

Although female doctors were to have the same standing as officers, there was a permanent conflict potential between male and—often better qualified—female doctors. Male doctors were often not willing to work under a female doctor. Younger female doctors, especially, had to fight for recognition of their professional competence against age discrimination and their alleged lack of experience; often, they were taken for nurses. They also had to assert their rights forcefully, as did Dr. Käte Frankenthal, who finally got access to the officers' mess: "In the officers' mess the [male] colleagues later told me . . . that they had the best intentions to scare me away as quickly as possible. They had not feared about the discipline but the whole war business was man stuff then."[98] Again, "man stuff" appears prominently in the memoirs of a woman.

WOMEN AS COMBATANTS

Officially, none of the branches of the Austrian-Hungarian military intended women to become combatants, nor was it ever desired. The assignment of female combatants met with fierce opposition in the army as well as in society. Nevertheless, some women (other than army nurses) served at the front, exposing themselves to fighting, although they were not active fighters. Spies were one example, sneaking across enemy lines to gather military intelligence and information concerning the strength or movement of the enemy. Others were telephone operators who stayed at their posts despite enemy shelling. Still other women provided the fighting soldiers of local voluntary formations like the Tyrolian and Vorarlberg Landesschützen near or at the front line with food and ammunition. The patriotic press and propaganda readily picked up on such cases and labeled the women as "heroines" or "heroic girls." One such was the 12-year-old Polish-speaking Rosa Zenoch, who became known as the "girl hero from Rawa Ruska," a "model child" of the empire. She had carried water and fruit to the soldiers in the line of fire near her native village, was injured by a grenade splinter, and lost her foot.[99]

Women accompanied their fathers, husbands, or fiancés to the front and, if necessary, engaged in fighting. Female "military protagonists" ranged from the auxiliaries and voluntary car drivers to real female fighters. Stella von Turnau, the wife of the later district commander of Lublin, was awarded the Knight's Cross of the Order of Franz Joseph for fighting side by side with her husband and motivating the soldiers in the trenches during the fighting in the Carpathian Mountains.[100]

Among some women, the enthusiasm to engage in active combat went so far that they concealed their gender and entered military service disguised as male soldiers. One of the best-known female volunteers was Viktoria Savs. Many stories and legends tell about her alleged heroic behavior. With the special permission of the commander of the Southwestern Front, Archduke Eugen, she accompanied her father, who had enlisted for the k.k. Landsturm, and fought in the Landsturm infantry battalion Innsbruck No. II as Viktor or Hansl Savs. In contrast to her superiors, her comrades were not informed about her real identity.[101] Later, she summarized her motives as follows: "I found it boring to play with dolls and I did not understand why I should stand around doing nothing while my playmates lost their lives."[102] Viktor(ia) worked as dispatch runner and pack animal driver and went on patrol. She also escorted Italian prisoners. In May 1917, she was severely injured by a rock avalanche. When her right leg was amputated below the knee, it was discovered that she was a woman. Unfit for future service in the army, she was discharged. But in recognition of her bravery, she received the Medal for Bravery as well as the Karl Troop Cross. Labeled a heroic girl by the propaganda machinery of the Habsburg Empire, Savs also became an icon of National Socialist propaganda in the 1930s.[103]

Stephanie Hollenstein, later to become a famous Austrian painter, was another woman who served in the ranks. After she failed to receive an assignment as a nurse because of her "weak constitution," she changed her identity, procured a militia uniform, and registered with the militia volunteers (Standschützen) of Vorarlberg in May 1915. As medical orderly Stephan, she worked at the Italian front in the Dolomites around Bolzano for more than three months, from May to June. Her comrades-in-arms soon recognized her as a woman but respected her for her bravery and endurance. Her superiors, however, took quite some time to discover her real sex, which finally led to her dismissal.[104] Both patriotism and art moved her to enlist, as she explained in a letter: "Then came the great clash of nations. I felt drawn out as well, partly for reasons of patriotism, partly due to artistic interest. [I] therefore hid in a uniform to have a closer look, as I could not work there." She claimed that on the order of the Army High Command, "all women" were recalled from the front lines on 18 August 1915—"Unfortunately an order came which put a swift end to my interests and my artistic incentives"[105]—but there is no written evidence of such an order to be found in the War Archive.[106]

Later that year, Hollenstein was admitted to the art section of the Military Press Corps. She was not the only one; the press corps also admitted other painters like Fritzi Ulreich and Helene Arnau, as well as the only female war reporter, Alice Schalek. Hollenstein served as a war artist for the remainder of the war. On at least three occasions in 1916, she traveled to the front on official assignment. During the National Socialist era, Hollenstein became

Figure 11.8.
Stephanie Hollenstein. Vorarlberg Chronik.

president of the Artist Association of Viennese Women; like Viktoria Savs, she played a prominent role in Nazi propaganda.[107]

In the northernmost province of the Habsburg Empire, Galicia, female combatants found a larger role in the Polish and Ukrainian Legions of the Habsburg army. National elites in the eastern Habsburg Empire used the patriotic attitude at the outbreak of war to pursue their own political ambitions. They hoped to advance the cause of national liberation, seeking complete independence, or at least emancipation and limited autonomy under the Austro-Hungarian monarchy. Women played an active part in these efforts. With respect to Poland, this development culminated in the proclamation of the emperors of Germany and Austria-Hungary of 5 November 1916 promising the creation of the Kingdom of Poland. Although the kingdom was conceived by its architects as a puppet state controlled by the Central powers, it came to be regarded by Poles as a promise of Polish independence.[108]

Formed in Galicia in August 1914, both the Polish and Ukrainian Legions were voluntary armed formations (as was the Albanian Legion formed later). Although organized as part of the Imperial-Royal Landwehr, they acted almost independently. The Polish and Ukrainian Legions fought against the armies of the Russian Empire, both in Galicia and in the Carpathian Mountains, suffering horrendous casualties.[109] These legions comprised mainly prewar Galician paramilitary organizations, such as the Polskich Drużyn Strzeleckich (Polish Riflemen) and Żwiązek Strzeleckich (Riflemen Association) in Cracow and Lviv. They included women's units, formed between 1910 and 1912. Most of these women were students, office clerks, and craftswomen. Although their training program spanned "signalling, gymnastics, organization, terrain instructions, medical-care training, firing practice, drill, and exercises on tactics and battlefield communication,"[110] they served mainly in the fields of administration, medical service, and intelligence.[111]

At the outbreak of the war, the Army High Command decided that the Polish Legion was to form two brigades with around 3,500 men. In March 1915, a third brigade was formed. In the course of the war, the legion was turned into an auxiliary corps of the Austro-Hungarian army. Reaching a total strength of about 16,500 men, the legion fought exclusively on the Eastern Front in those (former Polish) territories incorporated into the Russian Empire. To distinguish them from the regular army, members of the Polish Legion were to receive their own uniforms with the typical Polish headgear, a square-topped Polish lancer cap with an eagle emblem.[112]

The women's units of the paramilitary organizations Związek Strzeleckich and Polskich Drużyn Strzeleckich began to mobilize at the same time as the Polish Legion. In August 1914, 30 out of more than 100 candidates were recruited for a women's unit in Cracow; they were to work in the Commissariat, which was responsible for supply, equipment, and logistics. Another women's administrative unit was recruited in Lviv. A few women were employed as medical orderlies or supply officers. Others, such as Zofia Zawiszanka, served as messengers or scouts; her task was to spy out military operations of the enemy and to act as a messenger of the 1st Infantry Battalion. The use of women as messengers and spies was quite common, as women in uniform more easily than men passed as civilians. Less meticulously controlled when crossing borders, women also proved adept at smuggling weapons and explosives.[113]

Female members of paramilitary organizations soon became aware that their mobilization and active participation in combat was neither intended nor wanted. With the establishment of the Naczelny Komitet Narodowy (Polish Supreme National Committee), women's service was limited even more. On the order of Władysław Sikorski, the committee's head, all women were to be dismissed from the Polish Legion.[114] Legion commander Józef Piłsudski approved the decision. Women who had wanted to go to the front and fight with their male comrades had to resort to cross-dressing, much like Viktoria Savs and her female comrades-in-arms. Whether they were allowed to stay or had to quit service when they were discovered depended on the good will, acceptance, or ignorance on the part of superiors or comrades.

Cross-dressing began in the earliest months of the war, as exemplified by the widely reported case of Stanisława Ordyńska. As Alfred Woloszynski, she saw action in the battles of Kielce and Jedrezejów, rising to the rank of sergeant. Suffering from shell shock, she was evacuated to Cracow and later to a reserve hospital in Vienna. There she came to the attention of Archduchess Maria Theresa, who was working as a Red Cross army nurse. The duchess drove Ordyńska to the officer's hospital in her own automobile and saw to it that the traumatized woman got the best treatment possible.[115] Cross-dressers such as Ludwika Daszkiewiczowa were especially prominent in the hard-fought 1915–1916 battles in the Carpathian Mountains and Volhynia. Working as a medical orderly with the 2nd Infantry Regiment of the 2nd Brigade, she was captured by the Russians at the battle at Kostiuchnowka in November 1915. After her release, she went back to the front, winning the Medal for Bravery for her participation in the fighting at the Beresina.[116]

In the Ukrainian Legion, the situation of women was very similar. Growing Ukrainian national consciousness led to the establishment, especially in Galicia, of a number of paramilitary youth organizations during the early years of the twentieth century. In August 1914, the Supreme Ukrainian Council united the Ukrainian Sich Riflemen Association and the Plast National Scout Organization of Ukraine into the Ukrainian Legion, its main goal being to liberate Ukrainian lands from the Russian Empire. In September 1914, the Habsburg army accepted 2,500 Ukrainians. Placed under the operational control of the Austrian 55th Infantry Division, they were employed tactically as battalions or companies of the 129th and 130th Austrian Brigades.[117]

One such organization, the Sich Rifleman, recruited women, many of them, like the men, college students. They received much the same training as their male comrades, including the use of firearms. They participated in war exercises, formed their own medical care units, and swore an oath to the organization. Like their Polish counterparts, they were trained in the fields of medical care, administration, supply, and guard duties. In peacetime, the women's unit had its own uniforms, consisting of a dark-green skirt, a cap, a light-green shirt, and a jacket. After the outbreak of the war, photos show female members of the Ukrainian Legion in the same uniforms as their male counterparts.

> The Ukrainian Sich Riflemen wore . . . the standard pike-gray Austrian uniform. After 1915 the uniform became field gray and the tunic received a stand-and-fall collar instead of the previous standing pattern. Puttees appear to have been standard from the start. The kappi bore on its left side a blue cloth rosette with a yellow center. The regulation cockade worn on the front was of the 'German pattern'—a dull brass or iron disc with the cut-out letters FJI . . . in some cases it took the form of a lion of Galicia. The collar patch was plain blue; this became a blue and yellow stripe in 1916.[118]

Figure 11.9.
Sophie Haleczko (no date). Courtesy Heeresgeschichtliches Museum, Vienna.

When war began, Ukrainian women's units mobilized as part of the Sich Riflemen II. Ostensibly, they had the same rights and duties as their male comrades. In reality, the Ukrainian Legion high command had no interest in female combatants; no concrete plans were in place for the employment of the women's units or even single women in combat units. Women who wanted to go to the front met with great difficulties. The few who did manage to deploy with their male comrades rarely saw direct combat; instead, they mainly served as medics, clerks, and messengers. Two of the women, Olena Stepanivna and Sophie Haleczko, won the Medal for Bravery.[119] They promptly became fodder for Austro-Hungarian propaganda and for the press, which published detailed accounts of the two "heroines."[120]

Figure 11.10.
Olena Stepanivna (no date). Courtesy Heeresgeschichtliches Museum, Vienna.

Although few female legionaries served in the ranks of the Ukrainian Legion, others may have fought disguised as men. Some highly motivated women adopted male identities to reach the fighting front. Submerging their female identities under male virtues and values allowed them to become real comrades but led to their alienation from traditional feminine roles. When exposed, often after being wounded, they were usually redeployed rearward or even dismissed. Frontline service for any woman did not last long. During the winter of 1915–1916, all female legionnaires were withdrawn from frontline service, attached to the legion's section for recruit training, and banned from participating in actual fighting.[121]

DEMOBILIZATION

Massive and intensive war propaganda notwithstanding, the Habsburg Empire's home front was, from the beginning, characterized by "social contrast and class conflicts, competition and jealousy, grief and sorrow, rapidly incipient disillusion, protest and the longing for peace." It disintegrated long before the end of the war. Hunger and want became the basis for broader resistance. Mass protests against state mismanagement and supply shortages began even before the "hunger winter" of 1916–1917 but then expanded, aggravated by massive inflation, corruption, and usury. Women, adolescents, and children often launched the protests: inflation demonstrations, hunger riots, or bread strikes. Austria-Hungary's collapse was partly a military failure, but it was also a political failure to cope with the demands of female activists on the home front.[122] The disintegration of the Habsburg Empire resulted from the decay of old institutions, a new political orientation, and economic necessity. This naturally had far-reaching consequences for the female population of the newly formed Republic of German-Austria.

During the course of the war, women, especially women in uniform, had transgressed occupational and/or gender borders, which the state and society had tolerated for the time being; historian Maureen Healy calls this development "the political arrival of a new cadre of incipient citizens eager to serve the state. While the state may have been in a process of decline . . . , women themselves were in a process of becoming citizens."[123] What characterized all these women was a high degree of self-initiative, commitment, and self-sacrifice. Their legal and economic interactions with the state had accelerated markedly during wartime. From war, they emerged as more formal citizens whose relationship to the state was licensed but limited by their familial capacities as mothers, wives, daughters, or sisters.[124]

Their efforts during the war are often deemed a decisive impulse for the women's movement, especially for the fight for women's suffrage. Undoubtedly, the Great War affected the roles of women in society, but according to historian Christa Hämmerle, it may be "seen as a possible catalyst of efforts with respect to women's rights but certainly not as its creator." The women's fight for suffrage, education, and the opening of universities and the job market all had been on the agenda of the women's movement long before 1914 and had been included in the Social Democratic Party program since the 1890s. In 1918, Austrian women acquired the vote. Legally, political public space was now equally opened to women and men. The exclusion of women from political associations was abolished, and article 7 of the federal constitution defined their equality before the law.[125] In practice, however, this breakthrough in women's political rights was largely overshadowed by political and economic turmoil.[126]

Women were the "great losers" in the postwar restructuring of the job market that pushed them back into the badly paid, unskilled jobs they had briefly escaped during the war.[127] This development began during the last months of war, when many female members of the Auxiliary Labor Force in the Field were abruptly discharged from army service as war fronts contracted.[128] Female teachers, streetcar conductresses, state employees, and other working women and students were openly criticized as war profiteers. With the end of the war in November 1918, women everywhere whose efforts had been mobilized for the war now faced immediate demobilization. State and army authorities declared openly that they had always considered women's assignments temporary.[129]

For the gender order, the reintegration of millions of demobilized soldiers became a problem. It gave rise to a public discussion on the development of female and male work. Although some women were relieved that they no longer were solely responsible for their families, many others were not willing to leave their jobs voluntarily to men, although it was expected of them.[130] Government regulations set the stage for a fight for jobs between the sexes. State measures ranged from the explicit dismissal of women to the introduction of unemployment benefits. Women were forced to quit those jobs that had been identified as "traditionally male" before the war. Such relatively low-paid jobs as those in the textile industry failed to make the list.

The respective regulations of 14 February and 24 June 1919 were especially directed against those now unemployed women who were unwilling to accept a "respective employment" in traditionally female fields like childcare, farm work, and household service. Refusing such jobs meant being stripped of their unemployment benefit.[131] Even those middle- and upper-class women who had become wartime nurses or physicians were marginalized and had to take lesser and mostly low-paid jobs. Female doctors were explicitly forced out of their jobs by a decree of the Public Health Department of 15 December 1918, which declared that "with respect to the disproportionately high number of [male] applicants it proves to be necessary to terminate the employment . . . of the German-Austrian female *Sekundarärzte*."[132] A prominent example was Dr. Gisela Januszewska, who had worked in Military Hospital No. 2 in Graz and had to quit military service at the end of 1918.

During the interwar period, especially during the Corporate State (Ständestaat) era, working women became victims of the retrogressive ideologies embodied in the slogans "Heim, Herd und Familie" and the three traditional three *K*'s. The long effort to rethink women's place in society did not merely come to an abrupt end; it went into reverse.[133] The old political-military patriarchal order within society still prevailed and quickly restored the traditional separation of roles according to gender. The First Republic of Austria, especially the newly formed Ständestaat, underlined this development by the establishment of party-controlled women's and girls' organizations, the primary purpose of which was to promote women's traditional social roles.[134]

Female mobilization and women's achievements during the Great War long remained lost to public memory. What was remembered of the war was mainly male war heroes, officers' perspectives, and the battles. Women are largely absent from war monuments; when they do appear, it is in the secondary role of mourner or, in the case of the victorious powers, as a symbol of victory. Prominently placed in the center you will always see men.[135] Recent research studies have begun to lift the veil on that long-forgotten past, revealing how

Figure 11.11.
Female youth group of the Graz Heimatschutz march in a parade in Vienna, 1933. Heimatschutz in Österreich: Sein Werden und die Juli-Ereignisse *(Vienna: Zoller, 1935), 123.*

important the roles were that women of the Austro-Hungarian Empire, especially women in uniform, played on the home front and in the war zones of the Great War. These studies show how fully women were integrated into the everyday routine of war, how extensively they were mobilized for war on the home front, and how much they suffered from the negative impacts of the war. What they also show very clearly is that war was by no means only man stuff!

NOTES

1. Henriette Herzfelder, "Unsere Berufsfrauen und der Krieg," *Der Bund: Zentralblatt des Bundes österr. Frauenvereine* 1 (Jan. 1915): 1.

2. Angelika Stadler, "Ärztinnen im Krieg am Beispiel der Ärztinnen Österreich-Ungarns" (Ph.D. diss., University of Graz, 2003), 86.

3. Christa Hämmerle, "Der Erste Weltkrieg aus frauen- und geschlechtergeschichtlicher Perspektive: Forschungsthemen und -desiderate in Österreich," Österreich in Geschichte und Literatur 3 (2012): 219; Christa Hämmerle, *Heimat/Front: Geschlechtergeschichte/n des Ersten Weltkriegs in Österreich-Ungarn* (Vienna: Böhlau Verlag, 2014), 10.

4. Christoph Hatschek, "Von der 'wehrhaften' Frau zum weiblichen Rekruten: Entwicklungshistorische Perspektiven der österreichischen Soldatinnen" (Ph.D. diss., University of Vienna, 2009), 72.

5. Christa Hämmerle, "Soziale Militarisierung," in *1914–2014: Gedenken 1: Weltkrieg Grundlagenpapier österreichischer Wissenschaftlerinnen und Wissenschaftler aus Anlass des Gedenkens des Ausbruchs des Ersten Weltkriegs vor 100 Jahren* (Vienna: Bundesministerium für europäische und internationale Angelegenheiten, Kulturpolitische Sektion, 2014), 16–17, https://www.bmeia.gv.at/fileadmin/user_upload/Zentrale/Kultur/Schwerpunkte/Grundlagenpapier_1914_-_2014.pdf (accessed 16 October 2019). For the *Arbeitspflicht* during the war, the reaction of the press, and the rejection of the respective law, see Reichsgesetz über allgemeine Arbeitspflicht der Männer und Frauen, Österreichisches Staatsarchiv/Kriegsarchiv, Vienna (Austrian State Archive/War Archive, hereafter KA), Allerhöchster Oberbefehl (hereafter AhOB), Chef des Ersatzwesens (hereafter ChdE), 1918, 18-60, Res. No. 3.22005/Abt. 3.

6."Frauenhilfsaktion im Kriege: An Oesterreichs Frauen!" *Neue Freie Presse* 29 (July 1914): 27. See also Helene Granitsch, *Kriegsdienstleistung der Frauen* (Vienna: Hugo Heller, 1915), 8; Maureen Healy, "Becoming Austrian: Women, the State, and Citizenship in World War I," *Central European History* 35, no. 1 (Winter 2002): 1.

7. Ingrid Bauer, "'Im Dienste des Vaterlandes': Frauenarbeit im und für den Krieg," in *Geschlecht und Arbeitswelten: Beiträge zur 4. Frauen-Ringvorlesung an der Universität Salzburg* (Salzburg: Bundesministerium für Arbeit, Gesundheit und Soziales, Abteilung für Grundsätzliche Angelegenheiten der Frauen, 1998), 50.

8. Erik Ringmar, "'The Spirit of 1914': A Redefinition and a Defense," *War in History* 25, no. 1 (Jan. 2018): 1–22.

9. Bauer, "Im Dienste des Vaterlandes," 54.

10. "Was die Frauen alles können," *Das interessante Blatt*, 6 Apr. 1916, 13.

11. Sigrid Augeneder, *Arbeiterinnen im Ersten Weltkrieg. Leben- und Arbeitsbedingungen proletarischer Frauen in Österreich* (Vienna: Europaverlag, 1987), 122; Ernst Bruckmüller, *Sozialgeschichte Österreichs*, 2nd ed. (Vienna: Verlag für Geschichte und Politik/Oldenbourg, 2001), 451.

12. "Die ersten Strassenbahnschaffnerinnen," *Das interessante Blatt*, 1 July 1915, 14. See also Museen der Stadt Wien, *Die Frau im Korsett: Wiener Frauenalltag zwischen Klischee und Wirklichkeit 1848–1920* (Vienna: Museen der Stadt Wien Eigenverlag, 1984), 210.

13. Museen der Stadt Wien, *Die Frau im Korsett*, 209–210.

14. "Was die Frauen alles können," *Das interessante Blatt*, 6 Apr. 1916, 13.

15. Healy, "Becoming Austrian," 29.

16. Heranziehung von weiblichen Hilfskräften, Bericht über bisheriges Resultat dieser Aktion und Vorschläge bezüglich Ausgabe eines speziellen Befehles, Chef des Ersatzwesens für die gesamte bewaffnete Macht, Res. No. 416036/II, Vienna, 22 Apr. 1917, KA, AhOB, ChdE, 1917, 18-1/4. In this report, the chief of replacement

refers to the Army High Command's recommendation of 12 July 1916 to the armies, the military general governments, etc., to employ female labor.

17. Korpskommando (Expositur für Ersatzwesen), zu Res. No. 12000/7 Ew, Die Organisierung der weiblichen Hilfskräfte bei der Armee im Felde und im Hinterlande (Ausbau), KA, AhOB, ChdE, 1917, 18-1/8-50, K.u.k. XX.

18. Manfried Rauchensteiner, *Der Erste Weltkrieg und das Ende der Habsburgermonarchie 1914–1918* (Vienna: Böhlau Verlag, 2013), 712.

19. KA, Manuskripte 1, Weltkrieg Allgemein/111, fol. 02, k.u.k. Kriegsministerium, Abt. 10, No. 104.000 von 1917, 25 Apr. 1917. See also Healy, "Becoming Austrian," 29.

20. Healy, "Becoming Austrian," 30.

21. The number varies according to the sources. Hämmerle, *Heimat/Front*, 216n46; Stadt Salzburg, ed., *Frauen im Ersten Weltkrieg: Einsatz an der (Heimat-)Front* (Salzburg: Stadtgemeinde Salzburg, Frauenbüro 2015), 7, https://www.stadt-salzburg.at/pdf/frauen_im_1__weltkrieg_-_einsatz_an_der__heimat-_f.pdf (accessed 10 July 2017); Maureen Healy, *Vienna and the Fall of the Habsburg Empire: Total War and Everyday Life in World War I* (Cambridge: Cambridge University Press, 2004), 204; Alexandra Hois, "Weibliche Hilfskräfte in der österreichisch-ungarischen Armee im Ersten Weltkrieg" (Diplomarbeit, University of Vienna, 2012), 12n14, referring to Edmund Glaise-Horstenau, ed., *Österreich-Ungarns letzter Krieg, 1914–1918*, vol. 7, *Das Kriegsjahr 1918* (Vienna: Verlag der militärwissenschaftlichen Mitteilungen, 1938), 39n1 (33,000 women in the field and 107,000 in the hinterland). In a statement on 11 September 1918, the chief of replacement remarked that until 1 August 1918, 36,418 women had worked as a female auxiliary labor force in the field. It is most likely, however, that there were many more. See Herabsetzung der Zahl der weibl. Hilfskräfte bei der A.i.F., Stellungnahme ChdE, Abt. 2, 16 Aug. 1918, KA, AhOB, CHdE, 1918, 18-68/2, Res. No. 9.16.097/7.

22. Hois, "Weibliche Hilfskräfte," 137.

23. Healy, "Becoming Austrian," 30.

24. KA, AhOB, CHdE, 1918, 18-58/2 and 3; Chef des Ersatzwesens für die gesamte bewaffnete Macht to Kommando der k.u.k. Luftfahrtruppen, 26 June 1918, KA, AhOB, CHdE, 1918, 18-58/2, Res. No. 6.27.177/7.

25. For more details on the two categories see KA, Manuskripte 1, Weltkrieg Allgemein/111, Bestimmungen für die Aufnahme weiblicher Hilfskräfte und deren Verwendung im Bereiche der A.i.F., Wien [1918], fol. 06-21, here fol. 08, 3.

26. Ibid., fol. 12, 12.

27. KA, AhOB, ChdE, 1917, 18-1/8-50, Beilage C2; Hois, "Weibliche Hilfskräfte," 49.

28. Ausrüstung weibl. Hilfskräfte, K.u.k. 11. Armeekommando, Abteilung für das Ersatzwesen, to k.u.k. Chef des Ersatzwesens für die gesamte bew. Macht, Feldpost No. 511, 6 June 1918, KA, AhOB, ChdE, 1918, 18-6/15.

29. Agathe Fessler, *Aus der Mappe einer ehemaligen Armeeschwester* (Bregenz: Author, 1919), 4, Fessler Papers, Stadtarchiv Bregenz.

30. Eveline Hrouda, *Barmherzigkeit: Als Freiwillige Malteser-Schwester im Weltkrieg* (Graz: Leykam-Verlag, 1935), 12.

31. Heeresgeschichtliches Museum, *WoMen at War: K.u.k. ♀ Bilder 1914–1918, Ausstellungskatalog* (Vienna: Heeresgeschichtliches Museum, 2013), 120.

32. KA, Manuskripte 1, Weltkrieg Allgemein/111, Bestimmungen, fol. 09–10, 6–7.

33. Ibid., fol. 09 (5, KA); KA, AhOB, CHdE, 1917, 18-1/4); k.u.k. Kriegsministerium, Abt. 14, No. 38388/S von 1916, Weibl. Arbeitskräfte, Heranziehung für Mil. San. Anstalten, 3 Jan. 1917, KA, AhOB, CHdE, 1917, 18-1/4.

34. Healy, "Becoming Austrian," 33–34. Cf. Niklas Weber, "Geschlechtersensibler Geschichtsunterricht mit österreichischen Geschichtsschulbüchern" (Diplomarbeit, University of Vienna, 2014), 33.

35. The Austrian State Archive holds numerous printed lists with the names of dismissed female auxiliaries and the reason of their dismissal. Cf. e.g. KA, AhOB, ChdE, 1917, 18-46/2, Res. Nr. 1031072, weibliche Hilfskräfte - Evidenz der strafweise Entlassenen, 18-46/2-2, Res. Nr. 1208062/1, 18-46/2-4, Res. Nr. 1210087/1 etc. ibid., 187.

36. KA, AhOB, CHdE, 1918, K. 102–105; Manuskripte 1, Weltkrieg Allgemein/111, passim, KA, Manuskripte 1, Weltkrieg Allgemein/111, passim.

37. Healy, "Becoming Austrian," 31–32.

38. "Die Frau im Felde," *Illustrirtes Wiener Extrablatt*, 24 Apr. 1918, 1. Cf. Healy, "Becoming Austrian," 31.

39. M. Christian Ortner, "Women in WW1: An Austro-Hungarian Perspective," in *Le donne nel primo conflitto mondiale—dalle linee avanzate al fronte interno: La Grande Guerra delle Italiane*, ed. Annamaria Isastia, Piero Crociani, Paola Ducci, Ada Fichera, and Paolo Formiconi (Rome: Stato Maggiore della Difesa, 2016), 187.

40. Healy, "Becoming Austrian," 35.

41. Hois, "Weibliche Hilfskräfte," 47; Healy, *Vienna and the Fall of the Habsburg Empire*, 204.

42. Austrian Red Cross, *Instruktion für die Freiwilligen Sanitätsabteilungen der Österreichischen Gesellschaft vom Roten Kreuze bei der Armee im Felde* (Vienna: Reisser, 1913).

43. For more information on the Sovereign Military Order of Malta, see Gerhart Feucht, *Die freiwillige Sanitätspflege des Souveränen Malteser-Ritter Ordens, Großpriorat von Böhmen-Österreich, im Kriege 1914–1918 und das Militärhospital in Kierling bei Wien 1866* (Vienna: Author, 2010).

44. "Kundmachung des Kriegshilfsbureaus des Ministeriums des Innern vom 4. August 1914 betreffend die Zentralisierung der Fürsorgeaktion," *Verordnungsblatt des k.k. Ministeriums des Innern*, no. 14, 15 Aug. 1914, suppl. (quote); Stadler, "Ärztinnen im Krieg," 109; Hermann Hinterstoisser, "Die Uniformierung des Österreichischen Roten Kreuzes im Ersten Weltkrieg," *Pallasch: Zeitschrift für Militärgeschichte* 16 (2003): 87.

45. Ortner, "Women in WW1," 183.

46. Präsidiale, F 36 Krankenpflegewesen, No. 6786/M. I., 1914, Ministerium des Innern, Österreichisches Staatsarchiv/Allgemeines Verwaltungsarchiv (Austrian State Archive, Administrative Archive), Vienna. See also Gabriele Dorffner, *"Ein edler und hoher Beruf": Zur Professionalisierung der österreichischen Krankenpflege* (Freistadt, Austria: Vier-Viertel-Verlag, 2000), passim, especially 129–132, 139–168, 255–261; Gabriele Dorffner and Vlastimil Kozon, "Die 'Verordnung des Ministeriums des Innern vom 25. Juni 1914, betreffend die berufsmässige Krankenpflege,'" in *Wider die Geschichtslosigkeit der Pflege*, ed. Ilsemarie Walter Elisabeth Seidl and Vlastimil Kozon (Vienna: ÖGVP-Verlag, 2004), 45–65; Franziska Salm-Reifferscheidt, "Frauen in der Kriegskrankenpflege im Ersten Weltkrieg am Beispiel der Rotkreuzschwester Marianne Jarka" (Diplomarbeit, University of Vienna, 2010), 20–21; Hämmerle, *Heimat/Front*, 37; Susanne Hauber, "Frauen an der Front: Der Einsatz von Frauen im österreichischen Sanitätswesen während des Ersten Weltkrieges" (Diplomarbeit, University of Innsbruck, 2004), 51.

47. Austrian Red Cross, *Bericht über die Kriegstätigkeit der Österreichischen Gesellschaft vom Roten Kreuze 1914–1915* (Vienna: Austrian Red Cross, 1916), 25.

48. Dorffner, *"Ein edler und hoher Beruf,"* 175–176; Brigitte Biwald, *Von Helden und Krüppeln: Das österreichisch-ungarische Militär-Sanitätswesen im Ersten Weltkrieg*, Militärgeschichtliche Dissertationen österreichischer Universitäten, No. 140 (Vienna: ÖBV & HPT, 2002), 1:153–156.

49. Hauber, *Frauen an der Front*, 41, 96, 57; Hämmerle, *Heimat/Front*, 37.

50. Hämmerle, *Heimat/Front*, 34; Hauber, *Frauen an der Front*, 64.

51. Erlass des Ministers des Innern, Zl.11363/S, *Verordnungsblatt des k.k. Ministeriums des Innern*, no. 17, 15 Sept. 1914. For a detailed description of the apron, see Hinterstoisser, "Die Uniformierung des Österreichischen Roten Kreuzes," 87–88.

52. Hinterstoisser, "Die Uniformierung des Österreichischen Roten Kreuzes," 88.

53. As the photos are all in black-and-white, it is difficult to define the exact colors. From the still-existing peak caps, however, we may conclude that the first uniforms were also pike gray.

54. Mary Gasch, *Im Dienste des Nächsten* (Vienna: Author, 1978), 6.

55. Hrouda, *Barmherzigkeit*, 11.

56. Manuskripte 1, Weltkrieg Allgemein/111, fol. 34–36, "Übereinkommen, zwischen der k.u.k. Heeresverwaltung und der Österreichischen Gesellschaft vom Roten Kreuze, betreffend die Beistellung von Krankenpflegerinnen für die Armee im Felde," KA. Cf. Austrian Red Cross, *Bericht über die Kriegstätigkeit*, 25.

57. Austrian Red Cross, *Bericht über die Kriegstätigkeit*, 25; Manuskripte 1, Weltkrieg Allgemein/111, Übereinkommen, fol. 35–36, 14–15, KA.

58. M. Christian Ortner and Hermann Hinterstoisser, *The Austro-Hungarian Army in the First World War—Uniforms and Equipment—from 1914 to 1918* (Vienna: Militaria, 2013), 2:216.

59. Manuskripte 1, Weltkrieg Allgemein/111, Übereinkommen, fol. 35, 14, KA.

60. Hinterstoisser, "Die Uniformierung des Österreichischen Roten Kreuzes," 89.

61. Erlass des Ministers des Innern, Zl. 5207, *Verordnungsblatt des k.k. Ministeriums des Innern*, 1916, as quoted by Hinterstoisser, "Die Uniformierung des Österreichischen Roten Kreuzes," 82.

62. Ortner and Hinterstoisser, *The Austro-Hungarian Army*, 2:221.

63. Ausrüstungsgegenstände für Pflegerinnen, No. 12739, Ö. Gesellschaft vom Roten Kreuze to Kriegsministerium, Abt. 14, 15 May 1916, KA, Kriegsministerium, Abt. 14, 1916, 12-3/51-20; k.u.k. Sanitätsanstalt für Syrien to Kriegsministerium, Abt. 14, Konstantinopel, 5 May 1916, KA, Kriegsministerium, Abt. 14, 1916, 12-3/51-21.

64. Hauber, *Frauen an der Front*, 90–91; Biwald, *Von Helden und Krüppeln*, 1:91.

65. See, e.g., the memoirs of R.M. Konrad, *Schwestern als Menschen: Aus den Aufzeichnungen einer Armeeschwester*, 2 vols. (Innsbruck: Author, 1922–1929); J. von Michaelsburg, *Im belagerten Przemysl: Tagebuchblätter aus grosser Zeit* (Lipsia: C.S. Amelangs Verlag, 1915); Marianne Jarka, "Erinnerungen 1889–1934," typescript, Dokumentation lebensgeschichtlicher Aufzeichnungen, Institut für Wirtschafts- und Sozialgeschichte, University of Vienna; Hrouda, *Barmherzigkeit*; Agathe Fessler, *Selbsterlebtes schlicht und wahrheitsgetreu* (n.p.: Author, 1928); Fessler, *Aus der Mappe einer ehemaligen Armeeschwester*; Gasch, *Im Dienste des Nächsten*. See also Hämmerle, *Heimat/Front*, 13–14.

66. Konrad, *Schwestern als Menschen*, 8.

67. Hrouda, *Barmherzigkeit*, 136–138. See also Biwald, *Von Helden und Krüppeln*, 2:410; Daniela C. Angetter, *Dem Tod geweiht und doch gerettet: Die Sanitätsversorgung am Isonzo und in den Dolomiten 1915–18*, Beiträge zur neueren Geschichte Österreichs, No. 3 (Frankfurt am Main: Peter Lang Verlag, 1995), 234.

68. Hugo Kerchnawe, "Die Schwester," in *Ärzte und ihre Helfer im Weltkriege 1914–1918*, ed. Burghard Breitner (Vienna: Göth, 1936), 246. See the very source-critical study by Regina Schulte, "Die Schwester des kranken Kriegers: Krankenpflege im Ersten Weltkrieg als Forschungsproblem," *BIOS: Zeitschrift für Biographieforschung und Oral History* 7 (1994): 83–100.

69. Karl Kraus, *Die letzten Tage der Menschheit* (1918), act 3, scene 45, http://gutenberg.spiegel.de/buch/die-letzten-tage-der-menschheit-4688/5 (accessed 17 July 2017).

70. Biwald, *Von Helden und Krüppeln*, 2:411–412; Hauber, *Frauen an der Front*, 91, 99.

71. Hrouda, *Barmherzigkeit*, 205–206; Biwald, *Von Helden und Krüppeln*, 1:91–92, 2:411; Angetter, *Dem Tod geweiht*, 237.

72. See, e.g., Regina Schulte, "Die Schwester des kranken Kriegers: Verwundetenpflege im Ersten Weltkrieg," in *Die verkehrte Welt des Krieges: Studien zu Geschlecht, Religion und Tod* (Frankfurt am Main: Campus-Verlag, 1998), 95–115; Hanna Hacker, *Gewalt ist: Keine Frau: Der Akteurin oder eine Geschichte der Transgressionen* (Königstein, Germany: Helmer, 1998), 155.

73. Kerchnawe, "Die Schwester," 246.

74. Biwald, *Von Helden und Krüppeln*, 1:91.

75. Elisabeth Malleier, "Zur Frage der Geschlechterdifferenz in der Professionalisierungsgeschichte der Krankenpflege," in *Körper—Geschlecht—Geschichte: Historische und aktuelle Debatten in der Medizin*, ed. Elisabeth Mixa (Vienna: Studienverlag, 1996), 286.

76. A very critical view on the role of female nurses at the front is presented by Ernst Hanisch, *Männlichkeiten: Eine andere Geschichte des 20. Jahrhunderts* (Vienna: Böhlau Verlag, 2005), 31–32, quoting diaries and memoirs of Great War soldiers. Cf. Hämmerle, *Heimat/Front*, 28.

77. The handful of exceptions who received Medals of Bravery are documented in KA: Mannschaftsbelohnungsanträge (hereafter MBA) 546.158 (Marianne Heinrich); MBA 572.336 (Ilona Esterhazy); MBA 572.335 (Mariska Heinz). See also Ernst Rutkowski, "Ein leuchtendes Beispiel von Pflichttreue—Frauen im Kriegseinsatz 1914–1918," *Scrinium: Zeitschrift des Verbandes österreichischer Archivare* 28 (1983): 350–351; Hatschek, "Von der 'wehrhaften' Frau zum weiblichen Rekruten," 88. For the military and civil Medals of Bravery the nurses received, see Walter A. Schwarz, "Die militärischen Dekorationen der Monarchie," in *Österreichs Orden: Vom Mittelalter bis zur Gegenwart*, ed. Johann Stolzer and Christian Steeb (Graz: Akademische Druck- und Verlagsanstalt, 1996), 240–244; Helmut-Theobald Müller, "Die zivilen Dekorationen der Monarchie," in Stolzer and Steeb, *Österreichs Orden*, 294–297.

78. In fact, only Stadler, "Ärztinnen im Krieg," deals in detail with this topic, with data derived from KA, K. 2316, Armeeoberkommando, Qu-Abt. San-Chef (1914/1918), and KA, San. Anstalten, K. 2, 3, and 4. She also offers a comprehensive list of biographies of the 586 female doctors who had completed their studies before the end of the Great War (i–lxxv).

79. Stadler, "Ärztinnen im Krieg," 129, xviii.

80. Stadler, "Ärztinnen im Krieg," 116–117.

81. The Bildarchiv of the Austrian National Library has a picture of Dr. Marschall with the inscription "Regimentsärztin."

82. Verwendung von Ärztinen [*sic*] in MilSan Anstalten, Magyar Kiralyi Honvédelmi Minister to Kriegsminister Krobatin, No. 84.722, 27.04.1915, KA, Kriegsministerium, Abt. 14, 1915, 68-4/73, No. 9964; Kriegsministerium to Magyar Kiralyi Honvédelmi Minister, 9 May 1915, KA, Kriegsministerium, Abt. 14, 1915, 68-4/73, No. 9964.

83. Kriegsministerium to Magyar Kiralyi Honvédelmi Minister, 9 May 1915, 68-4/73, Kriegsministerium to Magyar Kiralyi Honvédelmi Minister, 9 May 1915, KA, Kriegsministerium, Abt. 14, 1915, 68-4/73, No. 9964.

84. Ingrid Arias, "Und bei allem war man die Erste! Die ersten Ärztinnen in Wiens Spitäler (1900–1938)" (Diplomarbeit, University of Vienna, 2004), 62–63.

85. Stadler, "Ärztinnen im Krieg," 113–114, 159–160.

86. For Dr. Januszewska's biography, see Stadler, "Ärztinnen im Krieg," 12–16.

87. k.u.k. Militärgouvernement in Polen, KA Präs. No. 10091, to k.u.k. Chef des Ersatzwesens f. d. bewaffn. Macht, 19 July 1918, KA, AhOB, ChdE, 1918, K. 105, 18-66/3.

88. Herzfelder, "Unsere Berufsfrauen und der Krieg," 4; Zivilkommissariat SanChef Mappe 1915, Spitäler: Spital 3/I, KA, Neue Feldakten, 1. Armee, K. 565, 1914/16.

89. Stadler, "Ärztinnen im Krieg," 145.

90. Stadler, "Ärztinnen im Krieg," 146.

91. MBA 779.273 (Dr. Friederike Ameisen), KA; MBA 779.274 (Dr. Anna Birnbaum), KA. Cf. Rutkowski, "Ein leuchtendes Beispiel von Pflichttreue," 348–349; Stadler, "Ärztinnen im Krieg," I, XXIII.

92. Offiziersbelohnungsanträge SW-Front, No. 8530 (Desfours-Walderode), KA. See Brigitte Holl and Liselotte Popelka, eds., *Die Frau im Krieg: Katalog der Ausstellung des Heeresgeschichtlichen Museums* (Vienna: Heeresgeschichtliches Museum, 1986), 93n265; Kriegstagebuch Dr. Maria Gräfin Desfours Walderode, Inv. No. 2036, Institut für Geschichte der Medizin, University of Vienna.

93. Stadler, "Ärztinnen im Krieg," 150.

94. Maria Schrell, "Ein Weihnachtsmärchen," *Wiener Bilder*, 26 Dec. 1915, 12; "Bilder vom Tage," *Wiener Illustrierte Zeitung*, 8 Jan. 1916, 2.

95. Paul Myrdacz, *Handbuch für k.u.k. Militärärzte*, 4th ed. (Vienna: Josef Šafář, 1905), 188.

96. Schrell, "Ein Weihnachtsmärchen," 12.

97. "Die Streiche der falschen Assistenzärztin: Ein abenteuerliches Leben," *Neues Wiener Journal*, 18 June 1916, 17; *Tages-Post* (Linz), 19 June 1916, 6. Almost six months earlier, the same paper had reported suspicion of fraud: "Ein weiblicher 'Militärarzt,'" *Tages-Post* (Linz), 3 Jan. 1916, 6.

98. Stadler, "Ärztinnen im Krieg," 115.

99. "Ein zwölfjähriges Heldenmädchen," *Wiener Bilder*, 27 Sept. 1914, 9; Hatschek, "Von der 'wehrhaften' Frau zum weiblichen Rekruten," 97–98; Ortner, "Women in WW1," 188; Healy, *Vienna and the Fall of the Habsburg Empire*, 229–232; Christa Hämmerle, "Frauen zwischen 'Heimatfront' und Front," in *Der Erste Weltkrieg: Die grosse Erschütterung und der Keim des Neuen*, ed. Claudia Gigler (Graz: Edition Kleine Zeitung, 2013), 78–79, 91.

100. "Frauen als Kämpferinnen," in *Illustrierte Geschichte des Weltkrieges 1914/16* (Berlin: Union Deutsche Verlagegesellschaft, 1917), 5:347; Hatschek, "Von der 'wehrhaften' Frau zum weiblichen Rekruten," 100.

101. Frank Gerbert, *Die Kriege der Viktoria Savs: Von der Frontsoldatin 1917 zu Hitlers Gehilfin* (Vienna: Kremayr & Scheriau, 2015); Peter Kübler and Hugo Reider, *Kampf um die Drei Zinnen: Das Herzstück der Sextener Dolomiten 1915–1917 und heute* (Bolzano, Italy: Athesia, 1981), 6.

102. Viktoria Savs, as quoted in Reinhard Heinisch, "Frauen in der Armee—Viktoria Savs, das 'Heldenmädchen von den Drei Zinnen,'" *Pallasch: Zeitschrift für Militärgeschichte* 1 (1997): 41.

103. MBA, fol. 1 aus 100/3391 von 1917 (Viktoria Savs), KA; Gerbert, *Die Kriege der Viktoria Savs*; Kübler and Reider, *Kampf um die Drei Zinnen*, 6.

104. Ilse Krumpöck, "Suffragetten oder Flintenweiber? Kriegsmalerinnen im Ersten Weltkrieg," in *Viribus Unitis. Jahresbericht 1998 des Heeresgeschichtlichen Museums* (Vienna: Heeresgeschichtliches Museum, 1999): 46–48; Evelyn Kain, "Stephanie Hollenstein: Painter, Patriot, Paradox," *Woman's Art Journal* 22, no. 1 (Spring–Summer 2001): 27–33; Galerie Hollenstein—Kunstraum und Sammlung, "Sammlung Stephanie Hollenstein," https://galerie-hollenstein.lustenau.at/de/hollenstein/ (accessed 16 July 2017); Heeresgeschichtliches Museum, *WoMen at War*, 103.

105. Kriegspressequartier, K. 31, no. 13, letter, 1 Jan. 1915, KA. Cf. Krumpöck, "Suffragetten oder Flintenweiber," 46.

106. Some authors (e.g., Krumpöck, "Suffragetten oder Flintenweiber"; Evelyn Kain, "Stephanie Hollenstein") have taken this claim at face value. For the absence of evidence, see also Hacker, *Gewalt ist*, 309n84. I thank Christoph Tepperberg and his colleagues at the Austrian War Archive for this information.

107. Kain, "Stephanie Hollenstein," 32; Vereinigung bildender Künstlerinnen Österreichs, "Historischer Überblick," 3 Feb. 2013, https://www.vbkoe.org/geschichte-2/historischer-uberblick (accessed 16 October 2019).

108. "Proclamation of the German Emperor and the Emperor of Austria, Respecting the Establishment of a Kingdom of Poland, Warsaw, 6 Nov. 1916," *Times* (London), 6 Nov. 1916, http://www.zum.de/psm/div/polen/mowat15.php3 (accessed 17 July 2017). See also Natali Stegmann, "'Wie die Soldaten im Feld': Der widersprüchliche Kampf polnischer Frauen für 'Vaterland' und Frauenrechte im Ersten Weltkrieg," in *Geschlecht und Nationalismus in Mittel- und Osteuropa: 1848–1918*, ed. Sophia Kemlein, Einzelveröffentlichungen des Deutschen Historischen Instituts Warsaw, No. 4 (Osnabrück, Germany: Fibre, 2000), 205.

109. *Verordnungsblatt für die k.k. Landwehr*, no. 91, 28 Nov. 1914; Zirkularverordnung, 21 Nov. 1914, Präs. No. 10203/II: Polnische und ukrainische (ruthenische) Legion; Bestimmungen über Rangstellung, Befehlsgebungsrecht, Distinktion und Ehrenbezeigungen, 762–764; Hermann Hinterstoisser, "Legionen im Dienste des Kaisers: Freiwilligenformationen im Ersten Weltkrieg," *Pallasch: Zeitschrift für Militärgeschichte* 52 (2015): 102.

110. Angelique Leszczawski-Schwerk, "'Töchter des Volkes' und 'stille Heldinnen': Polnische und ukrainische Legionärinnen im Ersten Weltkrieg," in *Soldatinnen. Gewalt und Geschlecht im Krieg vom Mittelalter bis heute*, ed. Kalus Latzel, Franka Maubach, and Silke Satjukow, Krieg in der Geschichte, No. 60 (Paderborn, Germany: Schöningh, 2011), 189.

111. Angelique Leszczawski-Schwerk, "Kriegsspiel? Polnische Frau/Soldaten im Ersten Weltkrieg," *Pallasch: Zeitschrift für Militärgeschichte* 52 (2015): 152; Leszczawski-Schwerk, "Töchter des Volkes," 188–190.

112. Ortner and Hinterstoisser, *The Austro-Hungarian Army*, 2:232, 234–235.

113. Leszczawski-Schwerk, "Töchter des Volkes," 193.

114. Leszczawski-Schwerk, "Kriegsspiel," 153.

115."Polen-Heldin. Frl. Ordynska ist zum Feldwebel befördert worden; Schützling der Erzherzogin Maria Theresia," *New York Herald*, 1 Jan. 1915, 3; "Erzherzogin und Legionärin," *Neue Freie Presse*, 1 Dec. 1914, 12; "Eine junge Heldin," *Neue Freie Presse*, 5 Dec. 1914, 4–5; "Eine Bitte für die junge Heldin," *Neue Freie Presse*, 8 Dec. 1914, 1–3.

116. Leszczawski-Schwerk, "Kriegsspiel," 153–154.

117. Petro Sodol, "Ukrainian Sich Riflemen," in *Encyclopedia of Ukraine*, vol. 5 (1993), http://www.encyclopediaofukraine.com/display.asp?AddButton=pages\U\K\UkrainianSichRiflemen.htm (accessed 16 July 2017).

118. Peter Abbott and Eugene Pinak, *Ukrainian Armies 1914–55*, Men-at-Arms Series, No. 412 (Oxford: Osprey, 2004), 8. See also Jörg Steiner, "Die 'Helden-Mädchen' der Ruthenischen Legion," *Pallasch: Zeitschrift für Militärgeschichte* 6 (1999): 82–83.

119. On Stepanivna, see also Steiner, "Die 'Helden-Mädchen' der Ruthenischen Legion," 80–82; Viacheslaw Artemenko, "Die 'Helden-Mädchen' der Ruthenischen Legion (II)," *Pallasch: Zeitschrift für Militärgeschichte* 25 (2007): 151–153; Ernst Rutkowski, *Die k.k. Ukrainische Legion 1914–1918*, Österreichische militärhistorische Forschungen, Nos. 9/10 (Vienna: Holzhausen, 2009), 318–324; Leszczawski-Schwerk, "Töchter des Volkes," 199–201. On Haleczko, see Ostap Hrycaj, *Ukrainische Legion* (Vienna: Verlag der Zentralleitung der "Ukrainischen Legion," 1917), 14; Artemenko, "Die 'Helden-Mädchen' der Ruthenischen Legion (II)," 152.

120. MBA 18.673 (Olena Stepaniwna), KA; MBA 18.671 (Sofie Halechko), KA. See, e.g., "Die Auszeichnung der ukrainischen Legionärin Sophie Haleczko," *Neue Freie Presse*, 31 Jan. 1915, 15; Franz Molnar, "Wanderungen an der ostgalizischen Front: Kämpfende Mädchen in der Schwarmlinie," *Neue Freie Presse*, 19 Aug. 1915, 4–5.

121. Leszczawski-Schwerk, "Töchter des Volkes," 201–202; Leszczawski-Schwerk, "Kriegsspiel," 157; Ortner, "Women in WW1," 187.

122. Hämmerle, *Heimat/Front*, 18.

123. Healy, "Becoming Austrian," 34.

124. Healy, "Becoming Austrian," 2.

125. Birgitta Bader-Zaar and Christa Hämmerle, "Times of Trouble: Transformationen von Geschlechterordnungen in Nachkriegszeiten des 20. Jahrhunderts—Erster Weltkrieg: Fallbeispiel Österreich" (paper presented at the Conference"Times of Trouble: Transformationen von Geschlechterordnungen in Nachkriegszeiten des 20. Jahrhunderts," University of Hanover, Germany, Maria-Goeppert-Mayer-Gastprofessur für internationale Frauen- und Geschlechterforschung / Gender Studies, 3), http://www.univie.ac.at/Geschichte/salon21/wp-content/bader-zaar_haemmerle_timestrouble.pdf (accessed 10 July 2017).

126. Bader-Zaar and Hämmerle, "Times of Trouble," 5.

127. Edith Rigler, *Frauenleitbild und Frauenarbeit in Österreich vom ausgehenden 19. Jahrhundert bis zum Zweiten Weltkrieg* (Vienna: Verlag für Geschichte und Politik, 1976), 96–154.

128. For more details, see the correspondence in KA, AhOB, ChdE, 1918, 18–68.

129. Andrea Lösch, "'Die Frau hat ihre Schuldigkeit getan . . .': Staatliche Verdrängungspolitik gegenüber erwerbstätigen Frauen," in *Stille Reserve? Erwerbslose Frauen in Österreich*, ed. Erna Appelt, Andrea Lösch, and Edith Prost, Österreichische Texte zur Gesellschaftskritik, No. 31 (Vienna: Verein kritische Sozialwissenschaft und Politische Bildung, 1987), 107–126; Stadler, "Ärztinnen im Krieg," 208.

130. Bader-Zaar and Hämmerle, "Times of Trouble," 12.

131. Hämmerle, *Heimat/Front*, 189.

132. Ingrid Arias, "Die ersten Ärztinnen in Wien: Ärztliche Karrieren von Frauen zwischen 1900 und 1938," in *Töchter des Hippokrates. 100 Jahre akademische Ärztinnen in Österreich*, ed. Birgit Bolognese-Leuchtenmüller and Sonia Horn (Vienna: ÖÄK-Verlag, 2000), 68.

133. Margit Leimer, "'Kübelweise Tee gekoch': Frauen im Spannungsverhältnis von Anpassung und Widerstand 1934–1938" (Diplomarbeit, University of Vienna, 2000), 31–32.

134. *Heimatschutz in Österreich* (Vienna: Zoller, 1935), 171–172.

135. Françoise Thébaud, "Der Erste Weltkrieg: Triumph der Geschlechtertrennung," in *Geschichte der Frauen*, ed. Françoise Thébaud, vol. 5, *20. Jahrhundert* (Frankfurt am Main: Campus Verlag, 1994), 33; Weber, "Geschlechtersensibler Geschichtsunterricht mit österreichischen Geschichtsschulbüchern," 46.

TWELVE

"WE HAVE TO ADMIT WE REMAINED QUITE INADEQUATE"

Ottoman Muslim Women and the Ottoman Red Crescent Society

NICOLE A.N.M. VAN OS

In November 1914, Sheikh ül Islam Hayri Efendi issued a fatwa calling Ottomans to take up arms against those who attacked Islam, who seized and looted Muslim countries, and who made Muslim populations captive. Newspapers and periodicals summoned all Ottoman citizens to jihad.[1] The daily newspaper *İkdam* (*Perseverance*), for instance, invited Ottoman men and women to follow the example of women belonging to the German imperial family in supporting soldiers and their families.[2] Despite stories in the press about historical Ottoman, Muslim, or Turkish women warriors, the general feeling seems to have been that women did not belong on the battlefield side by side with their husbands, brothers, and fathers; their duties lay elsewhere. "Ottoman women will and can fulfill their duty to the fatherland including taking up the weapons," wrote the publisher of *Kadınlar Dünyası* (Women's World), Ulviye Mevlan. She added, however, "today our brave sons, our hero soldiers, do not want their women, their mothers, their sisters to take up weapons." She did not doubt that women had to play a large role, but this role must be fulfilled somewhere else than the front: through giving birth to children to create a stronger army and, for example, by working for the Red Crescent.[3]

The Ottoman Red Crescent Society was one of the three large semipublic organizations founded in the aftermath of the so-called Young Turk Revolution of July 1908 to arouse patriotism and to extract resources from patriotic Ottoman civilians. The first one had been the Navy League; founded only a few days after the revolution, its main goal was raising funds to purchase ships and, later, aircraft.[4] The Red Crescent was reestablished in April 1911 specifically to support soldiers in need of medical care. Two years later, in 1913, the National Defense League was founded to coordinate support for active soldiers in the field and their dependents at home.[5] All three formed women's committees, but their role in the Navy League and National Defense League remained largely undiscussed. Not so the Red Crescent, which in its publications paid ample attention to the activities of its Women's Central Committee.

Using newspaper articles and documents from the Red Crescent archives to build on the work of Nil Sarı, Zuhal Özaydın, and others, this chapter discusses the roles of Ottoman (Muslim) women in founding the Ottoman Red Crescent Society. It briefly explores the founding and the activities of the Women's Central Committee and other women's branches in the Ottoman Empire.[6] It describes Red Crescent efforts to create an army of professional hospital attendants and nurses' aides starting well before 1914, the year in which Ottoman Muslim women started training as nurses' aides according to the official historiography of the Red Crescent Women's Central Committee. These efforts were, at best, partly successful. Finally, this chapter seeks to answer a fundamental question: How did a community that normatively required women to avoid even being seen by male nonrelatives deal with nursing's transgression of traditional gender borders?

A note on periodization should be made here. For most countries involved, the world war of 1914–1918 was a meaningful historical period. For most Ottomans, it was not. To them World War I formed only part of a decade-long series of military conflicts that began with the Turco–Italian War (September 1911–October 1912), followed by the First and Second Balkan Wars (October 1912–May 1913 and June–July 1913). Only a brief interlude separated these wars from World War I, which for the Ottoman Empire began on 2 August 1914 and ended with an armistice signed at Moudros on 30 October 1918. World War I was followed by yet another war, the War of Independence, which ended with the establishment of the Republic of Turkey in 1923. As a consequence, this chapter includes more than only World War I.

FOUNDING THE OTTOMAN RED CRESCENT SOCIETY

The Young Turk Revolution ended the absolutist regime of Abdülhamid II (reigned 1876–1909) in July 1908, forcing him to call elections for a new parliament. In the aftermath of revolution, a sense of freedom spread through the empire. New periodicals and newspapers appeared, as did new civil societies and organizations, among them the revived Ottoman Red Crescent Society. A predecessor of the Red Crescent, the Organization for the Assistance and Support of Wounded and Sick Soldiers, had been founded in July 1865 as a result of the Ottoman government's ratification of the Geneva Convention for the Amelioration of the Condition of the Wounded in Armies in the Field.[7] But it was stillborn. Urged by the

Red Cross organization in Geneva, a new, more successful effort was undertaken during the Serbian–Ottoman and Russo–Ottoman Wars (1876–1878).[8] In April 1877, the Ottoman Red Crescent Society was officially established for the first time. It immediately set to work raising money from the Ottoman population and Muslims elsewhere in the world to support the fighting troops. Although women in the Ottoman Empire contributed to alleviating the burden of Ottoman soldiers, their activities did not, for the most part, take place under the Red Crescent umbrella.[9] The only reported exception was a group of women supervised by Lady Layard, wife of the British ambassador, who gathered in Kadıköy, on Istanbul's Asian shore, to sew linen for wounded soldiers. A gravure shows British women at work being visited by Ottoman Muslim women.[10] (Figure 12.1) Fearing subversion, however, Sultan Abdülhamid II refused to allow the Red Crescent permanent status. Once the war ended, the society was dismantled and revived only briefly during the short Ottoman–Greek War of 1897.[11]

The Young Turk revolution opened the possibility of once again reviving the Ottoman Red Crescent Society. Although the society had never officially been dissolved, other organizations had adopted the Red Crescent name.[12] Some may have had good intentions; others clearly had not. In a letter published only a month after the revolution in *Metin* (Trustworthy), a woman complained that her "donations [we]re not spent on the goals we want, but [we]re getting in the hand of a bunch of cheaters."[13] Just a day earlier, a letter by the same woman in the same newspaper suggested founding a Red Crescent society. Participating in

Figure 12.1.
Muslim women visiting a group of non-Muslim women working for the Red Crescent in Constantinople in 1877. L'Univers Illustré, *20 October 1877, 669.*

such beneficent activities should not be denied to Ottoman (Muslim) women just because they were veiled, she argued. She urged her female readers to spend their money on charity rather than fashion.[14] Her call did not fall on deaf ears. The Association of Ottoman Ladies for the Elevation of the Fatherland, founded at the end of 1909 in Thessaloniki by women close to the Young Turks, for example, explicitly referred to the Red Crescent as one of the beneficiaries of the donations it would collect.[15]

In 1910, the wife of Minister of Foreign Affairs Mehmed Rıfat Pasha organized a lottery, a popular way of raising funds for charitable and philanthropic organizations, to fund the revival of the Ottoman Red Crescent Society. Her status as the wife of a prominent Ottoman diplomat and statesman allowed her to solicit gifts from both domestic and foreign donors to use as lottery prizes. She received so many gifts, in fact, that she decided to organize a Bazar de la Charité at her mansion to display them. Within a few weeks, however, unexpectedly large crowds of visitors forced a move from mansion to theater. Mrs. Rıfat Pasha was also the patroness of a Viennese concert in one of Istanbul's parks to benefit the Red Crescent. Newspapers referred to the organization behind these activities as the Red Crescent Ottoman Women's (or Ladies') Society.[16] With their activities, Mrs. Rıfat Pasha and the women around her succeeded in collecting approximately 3,500 lira, roughly equivalent in buying power to $350,000 of today's U.S. dollars. In 1911, this money became part of the start-up capital for the newly revived Ottoman Red Crescent Society.[17]

On the basis of its statutes, which conformed to those of the International Red Cross, the Red Crescent was obliged to set up a women's branch as well. Once firmly established, the new society called upon women to organize themselves into committees and subcommittees in Istanbul and the provinces. A few months later, after preliminary meetings, the Ottoman Red Crescent Women's Central Committee (Osmanlı Hilal-i Ahmer Hanımlar Heyet-i Merkeziyesi) was officially established on 20 March 1912. The founding members of the Women's Central Committee and its board initially comprised women from prominent Ottoman and Egyptian families of different creeds.[18] During World War I, particularly after the call for jihad, the organization became increasingly Turkified and Islamicized.

BRANCHING OUT

Although the Women's Central Committee, like the Red Crescent, aspired to branch out from the moment it was established, the number of branches founded remained initially limited. In June 1912, for example, a women's branch was founded in Ayastefanos and Makriköy, two neighboring villages on the European side of Istanbul. Another early branch was established in Kastamonu, a town on the Black Sea coast, during the Balkan wars. Mukbile *hanım,* the governor's wife, succeeded in gathering 150 women around her to provide linen to a field hospital in the nearby town of Inebolu.[19]

Two years after its foundation, in March 1914, the Women's Central Committee decided to work more actively on branches. Dispatches urged women anywhere in the empire to assist in establishing them. It was only during World War I, however, that several branches were firmly founded in Istanbul and the major towns of the Ottoman Empire. So, for example, in Bebek, a village on the Bosporus shore in Istanbul, a group of prominent women founded a branch in August 1915 under the patronage of a daughter of former Sultan Abdülhamid II, (Hamide) Ayşe Sultan. Its president was a member of the Egyptian dynasty, Princess İffet Celal. Another branch was opened in Kadıköy, on the city's Asian shore.[20]

In Anatolia towns, the wives of the local governors or other high bureaucrats generally took the initiative in forming Red Crescent branches and usually became their presidents. One of the first of these branches was founded in Bursa, a town close to Istanbul. Another one was founded in Konya, a town in central Anatolia. The women there had been members of the (men's) Red Crescent but decided to found a branch of their own in October 1914. The branch established earlier in Kastamonu, meanwhile, seems to have become dysfunctional and was reestablished in May 1915 by the wife of Governor Melek Reşid. During the bitterly cold winter months of December 1914 and January 1915, in the aftermath of the Ottoman defeat by Russia at Sarıkamış, she had organized an independent women's group to provide Ottoman soldiers with bedding, bandages, and other hospital materials. In April 1915, however, she decided to join forces with the local branch of the Red Crescent and established its local women's branch with subbranches in the smaller towns around Kastamonu.[21]

In Izmir, a major city on the Aegean shore, a women's branch was established as well. This branch was only briefly active in 1915 to collect money and to provide the hospitals with underwear and clothes. It was reactivated in July 1916 by the wife of a certain Tevfik Pasha. This time, it seems to have been more successful; by 1917, the branch had 180 members.[22] Over the years 1915 and 1916, several other women's branches were established not only in such Anatolian towns as Eskişehir, Bolu, and Nazilli but also farther away in Beirut, Yemen, and Baghdad. Ankara followed suit a few years later.

In November 1916, a Red Crescent women's branch opened in Vienna, the Frauenverein vom Ottomanischen Roten Halbmond in Wien. During the Balkan wars and the first years of World War I, women in Vienna, both Ottoman and non-Ottoman, established several charitable committees to actively support "Turkish" soldiers. In November 1916, Besim Ömer (Akalın), a military doctor and Paris-trained obstetrician and acting General Director of the Red Crescent at that moment, visited Vienna, where he encouraged the "Turkish" women living there to establish a women's branch of the local Red Crescent Society. They did so under the presidency of the wife of the Ottoman ambassador to Vienna, Fatma Zehra Hüseyin Hilmi Pasha, and the vice presidency of the wife of the counsellor of the Ottoman embassy, Madame Josephine Blacque Bey. The Verein collected funds to support Austrian hospitals in treating Ottoman soldiers and to buy goods for the Ottoman Red Crescent.[23] None of these women's groups were formally branches of the Women's Central Committee in Istanbul; rather, they acted under the auspices of the local men's organizations.

ACTIVITIES OF THE WOMEN'S CENTRAL COMMITTEE

One of the main activities of the Red Crescent's women's committee was to secure money, goods, and labor from the (female) public. Through large national campaigns, Ottoman men and women, Muslim and non-Muslim, were asked on a regular basis to donate money. Members of the Women's Central Committee were themselves among the more generous donors. Red Crescent yearbooks and calendars published by the women's committee carefully listed the annual financial contribution of each member. In Istanbul, the committee sponsored an annual "flower fest." Male and female members sold rosettes both to passersby on the streets of Istanbul and door to door. The prospect of Muslim women publicly addressing men in the street caused some anxiety. Accordingly, these women were allowed to address only other women (Figure 12.2).[24]

Donations in kind were just as welcome as money. Women were called upon to use their supposed specifically feminine skills to produce underwear, bandages, and bedding for soldiers in Red Crescent hospitals. When World War I began, Red Crescent depots were well stocked. But there was always more to do. When the governor of Istanbul launched a campaign for "winter presents" with an advertisement on 15 September 1914, the Red Crescent women's committee immediately sprang into action, taking over coordination of the campaign. Two days after the ad appeared, the women's committee issued

Figure 12.2.
Ottoman women selling flower rosettes on behalf of the Ottoman Red Crescent. The picture was taken on the largest of the Princes' Islands in the Sea of Marmara, close to Istanbul, where many affluent Istanbulites, Muslim and non-Muslim, spent their summers. The woman in the center is clearly Muslim, and the other two women probably belong to another ethnoreligious community. Note that the Muslim woman is flanked by the two non-Muslim women, one of whom is conversing with a male bystander. Servet-i Fünun, *no. 1214 (31 Ağustos 1330 [13 September 1914]): 678.*

a declaration asking the public to donate "winter presents," meaning clothing like warm underwear, vests, socks, and gloves. With a new winter looming, the call was repeated in late summer 1915.[25]

Whereas these ads addressed a general audience, members of the women's committee themselves and also other elite women were repeatedly invited to contribute in separate advertisements. They could pick up as much cloth and as many patterns from headquarters as they wanted, so they could work at home. Response to the campaign spread beyond Istanbul to the towns in Anatolia. Every day, newspapers reported donations of goods and money by local communities or listed the names of generous donors and the amount they gave to the Red Crescent or the National Defense League.[26]

More affluent women of Istanbul society actually purchased the winter presents they donated from the Red Crescent Ladies' Craftwork Home. This shop had been founded by the women's committee during the Balkan wars to provide female Muslim refugees, especially soldiers' daughters and widows pouring in from the Balkans, with a job to earn an honest living. Four committee women supervised the home's daily operations and reported to the committee monthly. Although the girls and women originally were supposed to produce artistic needlework based on old Turkish models, after the mobilization of 1914, they turned to the preparation of winter presents. By May 1915, the women's center was producing 2,000 pieces of underwear per day, and by November that year, the home had become one of the suppliers for the First Army Corps as well as for the National Defense League. It successfully developed a way to produce much-needed hydrophilic gauze, which could no longer be imported. Using pictures from European newspapers, it also started to produce gas masks for the soldiers at Gallipoli. By then, the Red Crescent was employing 200 women on a daily basis and 300 others two days a week (Figure 12.3).[27]

A similar charity workshop for women was active in Bursa. It was initially founded by the English Red Cross but in March 1914 was transferred to the local branch of the Ottoman Red Crescent, which asked the newly established women's branch to manage it. This workshop employed 150 girls and women producing hydrophilic gauze and unbleached muslin by the end of 1915. In November 1915, the workshop was integrated into an existing factory and turned into a larger enterprise where poor women and girls were educated and where an income could be generated "for our country and organization."[28]

Combining patriotism with philanthropy, the Ottoman Red Crescent Women's Central Committee became in due time an important provider of army goods. It also coordinated similar activities of the other women's organizations active in the Ottoman Empire.[29] While providing daughters, wives, and mothers of Ottoman soldiers with opportunities to earn an honest living, it also collected and distributed goods for soldiers in the field as well as for those in Red Crescent hospitals. Although it provided goods to hospitals, it was not involved at all in the training of hospital attendants and nurses' aides for these hospitals. In fact, it was explicitly forbidden to take any initiative in that direction, as training was the prerogative of the Red Crescent (Men's) Central Committee.

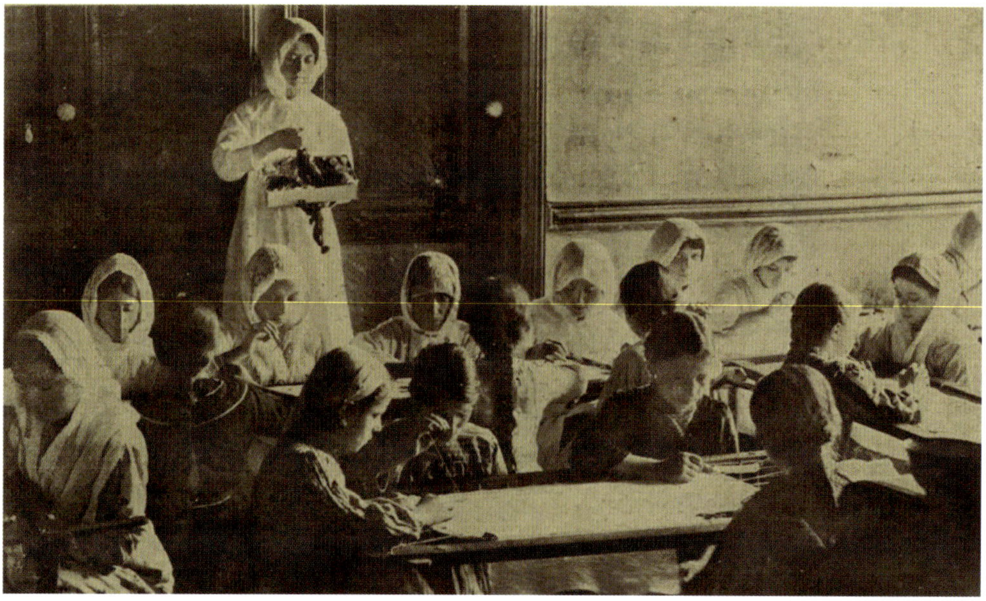

Figure 12.3.
Girls at work at the Red Crescent Ladies' Craftwork Home. The girls seem to be wearing a kind of uniform, but details are unclear. The reason that some of the girls do not wear head covers might be that they are younger and not yet bound by the Muslim dress rules. Or, they might not be Muslims. Servet-i Fünun, *no. 1220 (9 Teşrinievvel 1330 [22 October 1914]): 370.*

BESIM ÖMER AND THE BIRTH OF OTTOMAN MUSLIM NURSING

According to Ottoman Red Crescent Society historiography, the first Ottoman Muslims received training as female hospital attendants in 1914. Actually, Ottoman Muslim women began formal training much earlier. In 1892, Besim Ömer opened a small birth clinic adjacent to the military hospital in Gülhane. The first courses for midwives had started in 1843, but these courses had been quite basic. In 1895, Besim Ömer became clinic director and supervised the first efforts to professionalize midwife training. He introduced entry requirements: Women attending the courses had to speak and understand Turkish, be younger than 30, and, a few years later, also be able to read and write. After 1908, moreover, women would have to have at least a primary school diploma. He also extended the curriculum, introduced elementary training in sick attendance during the first year of studies, and supplemented the theoretical classes with practical demonstrations in the clinic.[30]

Women educated as midwives were, however, not meant to work in hospitals, but rather within the confines of the harems of private homes. It would take a few more years and a political revolution before women would be educated to attend hospital patients. The German director of the military hospital at Gülhane, Julius Wieting, was the first to offer such courses. His predecessor, Robert Rieder, explicitly rejected employing Ottoman females; instead, he brought in three experienced German nurses to train soldiers with at least a year's military experience to become nurses' aides.[31] But Wieting seized the opportunity offered by the Young Turk Revolution's spirit of freedom and loosening of religious restrictions on women's activities to open courses for Ottoman women at the military hospital.

At the end of November 1908, newspapers announced that a "Red Crescent voluntary service" was established at the Gülhane hospital and that courses were to start for women who wanted to become nurses' aides (*hastabakıcı*). Although women without previous education would be accepted, women with at least some education were preferred. The courses, which included both theory and practice, were taught by Asaf Derviş Pasha, a German-trained military doctor and one of the founders of obstetrics in the Ottoman Empire, and Refik Münir Bey, his successor in 1921 as director of the birth clinic. Classes were limited, however, to only two hours per week: one each on Mondays and Wednesdays. A few weeks later, Wieting published a letter in *Tanin* (Echo) in which he referred to the application by a woman who wanted to become a nurses' aide at his hospital. He also noted that an increasing number of *Ottoman* women were attending the "Red Crescent voluntary service" and the courses for "female nurses' aides" at the hospital. It is unclear if these included Muslim women. A remark by Hester Donaldson Jenkins, a professor at the American College for Girls in Istanbul, however, seems to point in this direction. According to her, these early efforts came to a halt in the aftermath of the conservative counterrevolution of April 1909.[32]

In June 1910 *Seda-yı Millet* (People's Voice) announced the start of a new series of courses for women and men at the Gülhane hospital sponsored by a group of Red Crescent "ladies." These unidentified ladies may well have been the group around Mrs. Rıfat Pasha. Just a few months later, in October, the Medical Faculty in Haydarpasha announced the opening of a two-year course for female nurses, either as day students or boarders. During the first year, the students would receive a monthly allowance of 100 kuruş, raised to 200 kuruş per month in the second year. If the aides wished to work in the hospital afterward, their pay would increase to 250 kuruş. The preconditions were that the women must be between 20 and 30, be of good reputation, speak Turkish, and write one other language.[33]

A call upon men and women to become "Red Crescent volunteers" published in April 1912 referred to courses opened for men and women at the Gülhane hospital and to women who "had been taking these classes regularly for two years."[34] While tensions in the Balkan states were rising, *Tanin* published another call upon "Ottoman ladies and gentlemen" to report to the Gülhane Hospital to take courses in "the attendance of and assistance to the wounded" (Figure 12.4).[35] By that time, Besim Ömer was trying to convince the board of the Red Crescent to establish a hospital where professional male and female hospital attendants could be trained. The board rejected building a new facility but did allow him space at the hospital of Kadırga, a birth clinic cum school for midwives, to set up such a "hospital-school" for 10 women. According to Besim Ömer, these women, too, would be trained to assist families in need of medical support at home rather than to be employed at hospitals.[36]

Through announcements in newspapers, both men and women were invited to apply. Men and women would have separate class hours: men 12 hours per week versus 6 hours per week for women.[37] The school never opened, however, because the rooms were needed

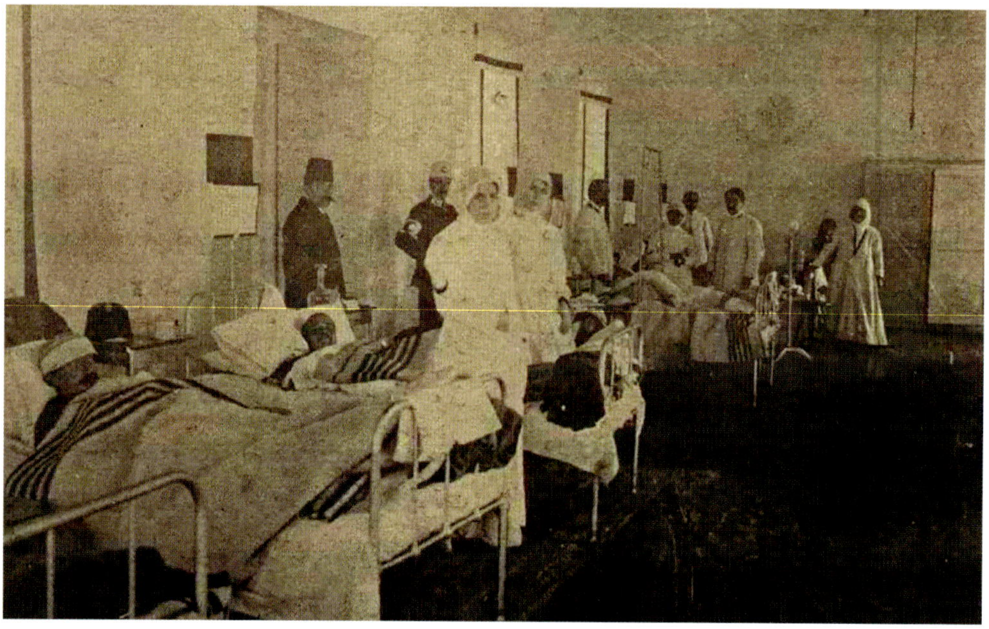

Figure 12.4.
A room at the Gülhane hospital during the Balkan wars with, according to the French caption, Muslim women as nurses for the first time ("on voit pour la première fois les dames turques en infirmières"). Servet-i Fünun, *no. 1118 (25 Teşrinievvel 1328 [7 October 1912]), front page.*

for the wounded from the Balkan wars. Although his idea of a training hospital fell through, Besim Ömer seems to have been inspired by the women, among them nine Muslim women who remained in this hospital to nurse the incoming men. In February 1913, women were invited again to attend a six-month training course to become hospital attendants. Potential candidates had to be healthy, 25–35 years old, able to read and write, and prepared to serve for at least five years with the Red Crescent.[38] It is unclear how many women responded to this call.

Despite Besim Ömer's efforts, the number of Ottoman women, Muslim and non-Muslim, actively working as hospital attendants or nurses' aides, voluntarily or professionally, during the Balkan wars remained limited.[39] This fact was confirmed by Wieting in two articles that appeared in the *Osmanischer Lloyd* in January 1914. He argued that a well-organized army of *professional* hospital attendants was a precondition for the establishment of a well-organized *voluntary* army of hospital attendants (emphasis added). The Ottoman Empire lacked any professional female hospital attendants in its military hospitals, and the education of male and female attendants in civilian hospitals was unregulated. The biggest lack, he believed, was well-educated and well-organized professional female nurses. He blamed the women's movement for talking about women's rights while ignoring women's duties, one of which was taking care of the ill, "their very own profession." He suggested sending a group of Ottoman "ladies" abroad for education. After at least three years of experience, these women would set up professional education for other Ottoman women in the various cities and towns of the empire. Considering the time needed to professionally educate sufficient personnel, Wieting stressed the importance of the training of volunteers by the Red Crescent.[40]

The day after Wieting's articles appeared, Besim Ömer, now president of the Red Crescent, at a women's committee meeting discussed establishing a school for hospital attendants. He announced that while the Red Crescent was looking for an alternative location for the Kadırga hospital, he had permission to teach two theoretical classes per week to women at Red Crescent headquarters and one practical class only in the Kadırga hospital. A month later, in February, the Red Crescent announced the start of a course for nurses' aides, which would consist of 18 lessons of two hours each on Fridays and Sundays for five months. Besim Ömer himself taught the classes together with Akıl Muhtar (Özden). At the end of the course, 27 of the original 45 women successfully took the exam. All 27 women were Muslim, and all were wives and daughters of prominent Ottoman officials. They received their certificates during a ceremony in the presence of the first wife of the sultan, other palace women, and the wives of some prominent statesmen.[41] Writing in retrospect a year later, Besim Ömer declared that the aim had been "the creation and instruction of a corps of *Muslim* male and female nurses' aides."[42] The women's committee calendar explicitly stated that for the first time, *Muslim* women had been certified.[43] This course meant for volunteers was followed by similar courses in Istanbul and Bursa.[44]

Professional hospital attendants cum midwives continued to be educated at the Kadırga hospital (Figure 12.5).[45] But the Red Crescent also set out to develop new schools where women (and men) could be educated to become professional hospital attendants while it was also actively working to create an army of trained female Muslim volunteers. In October 1914, just

Figure 12.5.
Women being trained and working at the Kadırga hospital. According to the French caption, they were all Muslim (infirmières turques). Servet-i Fünun, *no. 1249 (30 Nisan 1331 [13 May 1915]): 4.*

a few months after the widely publicized graduation ceremony of the Ottoman Muslim ladies, the Red Crescent announced the opening in Istanbul of two evening schools, one for male and one for female hospital attendants. Students attending the six-month courses received free meals and a small stipend. They had to be under 35 and to read and write Turkish. The society required them to pay the rather high fee of 30 lira as a kind of security bond and expected a five-year commitment to work for the Red Crescent. Initially, nine Muslim women and one non-Muslim woman were admitted to the course, but others were invited to apply.[46]

The Red Crescent's Izmir branch opened a school for hospital attendants in the fall of 1915. It was expected to educate 30 of them per year. Initially, textbooks were in French and English, but the president of the Izmir branch soon requested books in Turkish. A note scribbled on his letter in the Red Crescent archives confirmed that the books were coming; they "would be printed by the organization within two or three days." A second note indicated that a German *Schwester*, Margot Konrad, would be appointed as instructor. In July 1916, the school graduated its first class; 25 women passed their exams.[47] Similar initiatives were taken in Edirne and Erzurum, whereas organizations of Jewish and Armenian doctors also started classes for hospital attendants, in Beyoğlu and in Istanbul, respectively.[48]

In May 1915, the Women's Central Committee asked the board of the Red Crescent for permission to release a press communiqué announcing the start of new courses with theoretical and practical classes for women. The communiqué clearly stated that women, like men, had duties to the fatherland, but not the same duties as men: While men were defending the fatherland against its enemies, woman should "be prepared, just in case, as an army of mother-and-sister nurses, which is active and sacrificing, educated and trained."[49] The women's committee proposed to conduct the practical side of training hospital attendants in military hospitals. The board, however, coldly pointed out that Red Crescent statutes and bylaws allowed only the board to organize courses, to advertise them, and to make practical arrangements. The board, moreover, did not expect military authorities to welcome using military hospitals for such training, which might discomfort wounded soldiers.[50] The women's committee thus was forced to abandon the plan.

A few months later, Besim Ömer made yet another effort. On 24 November 1915, he sent a pressing letter to the Red Crescent Board of Directors urging action. Stressing the importance of a properly working health care system with well-educated, professional hospital attendants and nurses in times of war, he asked them to actually establish a nursing school with a hospital, meanwhile organizing good teaching facilities at existing Red Crescent military hospitals. Added to his letter was a document suggesting the formation of a Red Crescent Nurses' Committee of both men and women (with, as explicitly stated, more men than women). Although the document listed several conditions that potential committee members had to fulfill, it offered no clues as to what their work was to be. A year later, the general inspector for field hygiene, Süleyman Numan, actually asked the Red Crescent to set up a course to train women as hospital attendants and nurses. He also expressed willingness to allow practical training at a military hospital.[51]

Only in 1917, however, was it decided to allocate 10,000 lira to open a boarding school for female nurses, where 30 to 50 women per year could be trained by professional nurse educators. While education at the Kadırga hospital continued, the opening of a special school for female nurses at the Medical Faculty was announced in April 1918. The students were to be boarders and would receive free medical treatment when necessary. They also had to meet certain requirements, namely, they must be (1) Ottoman nationals; (2) healthy, with professionally appropriate height and posture; (3) able to show a certificate attesting to their good behavior; (4) between 25 and 30 years of age and single; and (5) able to read and write Turkish, preferably having a secondary school education. Furthermore, they had to be willing to respond promptly to any call of the Red Crescent during times of war or when otherwise necessary for a period of at least five years. The response must not have been overwhelming since the ad reappeared several times in the newspapers. Sixteen women, all Muslim, applied, passed the entrance exam, and were invited for a medical examination. When the course started, however, only 10 of the 20 available places were filled. In January 1919, other Ottoman Muslim women passed the entrance exam and started their education at the school.[52] Because of the post–World War I occupation and the subsequent War of Independence, however, this school never had many graduates.

NURSING IN TIMES OF WAR

Although Besim Ömer failed to establish a school for professional nursing, a limited number of Ottoman Muslim women worked voluntarily and professionally as hospital attendants and nurses' aides during World War I, mostly in Istanbul hospitals initially, but later also in Anatolian hospitals and in field hospitals. Only a few days after mobilization began in August 1914, the Red Crescent called upon certified hospital attendants and nurses' aides to report to its headquarters.[53] Both Muslim and non-Muslim women reportedly applied to the Gülhane hospital to offer their services.[54] From the start of Dardanelles Campaign in April 1915, high numbers of wounded soldiers poured into Istanbul. Numerous military and private hospitals opened to meet the demand for beds, and the Red Crescent urgently appealed to women who had trained as hospital attendants or nurses' aides to offer their much-needed services.[55] These requests did not fall on deaf ears. Muslim and non-Muslim women, including some from the Ottoman elite, responded positively and became voluntary or paid hospital attendants and nurses' aides (Figure 12.6).[56]

The rapid influx of volunteers raised Red Crescent concerns about the qualifications of new workers. The organization reminded military hospitals that volunteers were obliged to attend Red Crescent courses and urged the doctors in charge to make sure they did. They replied that most of the women either were attending the courses or had received diplomas. In May 1915, the Red Crescent reported that approximately 150 women were working as hospital attendants and nurses' aides in various Istanbul hospitals. The majority had trained at the Kadırga hospital or had taken courses at either the university or Red Crescent.

Figure 12.6.
Photograph with three doctors; two Ottoman Muslim women, Nuriye and Belkıs (top row left and front row right, although it is not clear who is who); and two non-Muslim sisters, Corinne (front row left) and Edith (top row right) Tercüman, at the hospital at the Military Academy. In the background are two Ottoman officers(?). L.M. Gräfin von Lubieńska, "Türkische Soldaten," Sport und Salon, *7 October 1916, 5–6.*

According to the periodical *Servet-i Fünun* (Treasury of Science), this was no less than a "national social revolution." The Red Crescent Women's Committee agenda for 1916–1917, probably prepared in late 1915 or early 1916, identified 353 women who had applied to work in a military or civilian hospital, of whom 284 were actually employed. Of these 284, only 20 had received a Red Crescent diploma, 35 had certificates of hospital service during the Balkan wars, and 73 were following classes at the university (Darülfünun) or the Kadırga hospital. The remaining 156 did not have any education or experience at all (Figure 12.7).[57]

Who were these women, and what was their background? Lists of names from the Red Crescent archives reveal some information on the women's socioethnic background, but registers of women decorated with Red Crescent Medals tell us more. The women taking care of wounded soldiers could be divided into four categories. First, a limited number of them were professional, well-trained nurses (*hemşire*). In most cases, they were either foreign or non-Muslim Ottomans who had received training abroad, at the hospitals of their own religious or foreign communities, or at one of the colleges set up by missionary organizations (Figure 12.8).[58] Second, a small number of Ottoman women were professional hospital attendants (*hastabakıcı*), who had a degree of theoretical and, sometimes, practical education. The third and largest group comprised Ottoman voluntary nurses' aides (*muavin* or *fahri hastabakıcı*) who had attended one of the special training courses. Finally, at the bottom were

Figure 12.7.
Photograph showing a group of volunteers working at one of the hospitals in Istanbul. The intimate poses of the women in the two front rows suggest that most of these women are non-Muslim; the position and the body language of the woman in the center seems to indicate she is in charge. Is she one of the (foreign) professional nurses? L.M. Gräfin von Lubieńska, "Frauenwirken in der Türkei," Sport und Salon, *11 March 1917, 13.*

Figure 12.8.
Personnel of the Red Crescent hospital in Edirne. All the women in this photograph seem to be non-Muslim. Given the way they are positioned, the three women sitting fourth, fifth, and sixth from the left in the second row might be the heads of the three different groups of women distinguishable in this photograph. The Catholic nun sitting fourth from the left is probably in charge of the five nuns in the third row wearing the same habit. The woman sitting next to her must be in charge of the seven women to the right in the same row. It is difficult to identify what they are wearing: is it a religious habit (Bulgarian Orthodox, Sisters of St. Paul) or a secular uniform of some kind? The third woman looks similar to the two women to the left in the second row. Servet-i Fünun, *no. 1212 (14 Ağustos 1330 [27 August 1914]): 250–251.*

the *hademe*, lower-class men and women in such menial jobs as cleaning floors, changing beds, and making tea.

Registers of recipients of Red Crescent Medals give us more information on these women. This medal was created shortly after the start of the Balkan wars in November 1912 to be awarded to anyone—male or female, Ottoman or foreign—who "rendered beneficent services, materially or morally, to the Ottoman Red Crescent Society."[59] According to the registers, the number of Ottoman Muslim women receiving medals for work as hospital attendants or voluntary nurses' aides in Istanbul or elsewhere in the empire increased rapidly after 1915, whereas the number of non-Muslim and foreign women declined.[60] The decoration registers also provide us with information on the women's socioeconomic background. A woman is often referred to with the name of her closest male relative. She is the wife, daughter, sister, or granddaughter of that male. Not only do we learn his name but, generally, also his profession, his rank, and other information. These lists clearly show that some voluntary nurses' aides belonged to the Ottoman society's higher social strata.

Registers dated toward the end of World War I, however, contain no information on most women's male relatives. The reason is unclear. It might be that the multiplication of decorations left no time for jotting down such details. Another reason may have been that many of these men's whereabouts were unknown. Possibly, the positions of the male relatives were not deemed worth mentioning. Although earlier registers reported most women working as volunteers, later registers do not. It is likely that these women were, in most cases, not volunteering but working to earn a living. The war and the many new hospitals offered impoverished women such opportunities. These women had little choice but to cross gender boundaries seeking to earn a meager income, which was—more importantly—often supplemented with a daily meal and sometimes even housing.[61]

References to male relatives also inform us about the place in the life cycle of the decorated women. The absence of references to any Muslim daughters of a particular man rewarded for work as nurses' aides in one of the hospitals in the older registers, for example, suggests that the Ottoman Muslim women working as hospital volunteers were more mature, married women. Since such references were omitted in later records, we lack the information regarding unmarried women working in hospitals toward the end of the war. Further research in the Red Crescent archives might reveal more on this topic.

MANAGING PUBLIC OPINION

The entrance of, in particular, middle- and upper-class Muslim women into hospitals to take care of men who did not belong to their inner family circle must have caused anxiety in a community for which the ideal was the (almost) complete separation of female and male activities. That Besim Ömer was very much aware of the opposition these Ottoman Muslim hospital attendants and nurses' aides might evoke is clear from his speech at the commencement ceremony of the 27 Muslim women who had taken the course in 1914. He stressed the importance of the event and pointed out that these women, belonging to the Ottoman establishment, would serve as examples. Thus, he hoped to counter any potential, social resistance against the professional nursing school the Red Crescent wanted to establish.[62]

Involvement of several female members of the Ottoman dynasty and its household in the Red Crescent helped legitimize its activities. Their patronage of the Women's Central Committee, widely published donations to the society, presence at the commencement ceremony, and visits to soldiers in hospitals to give them presents—none of this would have been possible without the sultan's approval. As he was also the caliph, head of the Muslim community (the *ummah*), this approval, however implicit and indirect, legitimized the activities of women working for the Red Crescent and constrained opposition from conservative religious forces.

Furthermore, the Red Crescent consciously and consistently pursued what today is called a public relations campaign. It included regularly dispatching announcements, messages, and communiqués to newspapers, public lectures by Besim Ömer and other members of the Red Crescent, the publication of approving articles and photographs in popular magazines, and the "vulgarization of the work of the Red Crescent through illustrated post cards."[63] The publications of the Red Crescent itself—its yearbooks, teaching materials, and the Women's Central Committee agendas—also formed part of its public relations offensive.

Although seclusion remained the Ottoman ideal, by the time Ottoman Muslim women started to take their nursing courses, the first steps toward the education of women by respected men had already been taken; the home-taught daughters of elite families and the pupils of the first middle schools for girls, which was opened during the second half of the nineteenth century, as well as those of the first high schools for girls established in the 1910s, had been receiving education from elderly, respectable men. The women at the teacher's college in Istanbul, which had been opened in 1870, were taught partly by men, and famous men had started to address female audiences in public conferences after the Young Turk Revolution. At almost the same time that the Red Crescent started to teach its courses, the University for Women was opening its doors.[64] In short, women attending nursing courses taught by highly respected men such as Besim Ömer only continued a trend already well under way.

To what extent Ottoman Muslim hospital attendants and nurses' aides interacted with male doctors is not clear. Although information is sparse, it is likely that the professional nurses, who in most cases were non-Muslim or foreign, actually supervised the Ottoman Muslim female volunteers, forming a buffer between them and the male doctors. No such buffer seems possible between Ottoman Muslim volunteers and wounded soldiers. Looking after patients required physical contact, which severely infringed prevailing gender boundaries. One device for coping with this transgression was metaphorical: Contact could be desexualized by establishing a pseudofamily relationship between two persons unknown to each other.

In his speech at the diploma ceremony, Besim Ömer pointed at the supposedly innate qualities of women that so well befit motherhood. Although men could make themselves into nurses, women were nurses by nature. They had "softness and gentleness, mercy and compassion." As mothers, they were "patient, perseverant and tender." Thus, he concluded, a woman looked after a patient as a mother looked after her child.[65] Several months later, the same periodical that had published Besim Ömer's remarks carried a lengthy article by the famous author Fatma Aliye. She also used the mother–child metaphor. Not only were hospitalized soldiers in dire need of motherly comfort and protection, she noted, but nurse and soldier assumed the roles of mother and child. She described a scene in which the soldier-patient addressed his female caretaker as "my dear mother" (*anneciğim*) and she called him "my son" (*oğlum*).[66]

In another article, Fatma Aliye observed how the wounded addressed their caretakers as *doktor nine* (doctor granny), *doktor teyze* (doctor aunty), or *doktor abla* (doctor sister).[67] Physical caring for relatives in the home, normally expected of women, was thus transposed into physical caring for metaphorical grandsons, nephews, and brothers in the hospital.[68] Some well-to-do women took this metaphor even further: They literally took care of wounded soldiers "at home" by turning their mansions into small hospitals.[69]

(NOT) TALKING ABOUT UNIFORMS

Observant readers will have noticed the absence of any discussion of uniforms in this chapter so far. The reason is simple. There seems to be hardly anything in writing—no uniform regulations, no discourse on the pros and cons of uniforms, no published or unpublished letters, diaries, memoirs, or other personal records that discuss uniforms.

One exception is an article that was published in *Servet-i Fünun* in May 1917. Using the rules of hygiene to frame the argument, the author stressed that a hospital attendant's body needed to be fully covered. Her hair should be stacked neatly away not to become "a nest for germs." The "*uniforma*" (quotation marks in the original) should be respected and could be worn outside the hospital only when accompanying a patient, whereas the only "jewel" allowed was the *broş* (insignia) that women received from the Red Crescent upon finishing their course. Fashion, the author wrote, was not relevant for such a uniform; simplicity and a sense of respect were.[70]

Although the unknown author uses a nonreligious context to argue in favor of full coverage of the body, the description, very conveniently, conforms with the Islamic rules of *tesettür,* which requires Muslim women meeting unrelated men to cover themselves to desexualize their interaction. Muslim women are required to dress according to these rules when stepping outside the private quarters of their home into an environment where they might meet nonrelated men.

That not only Muslim women wore this uniform is clear from the visual materials available: a few postcards issued by the Red Crescent, the (propaganda) photographs appearing in the illustrated press, and some private photographs that have recently surfaced on internet. These materials show us that the Red Crescent uniforms were similar for Muslims and non-Muslims but that there were also other uniforms in use.

The women in the photograph of the Red Crescent hospital in Edirne just after the mobilization in August 1914 wear, for example, three different "uniforms." Nuns of two different orders wear their habit, whereas two other nurses wear a dark underdress with a white apron and a white collar. Their hair is uncovered. Like some of the men in the picture (male nurses' aides?), they wear a brassard, which probably carried a Red Crescent.[71]

In a photograph taken at the Armenian hospital of Surp Prgich in Istanbul somewhat earlier, in June 1914, we also see two different kinds of uniform. Some women wear a dark (blue) colored dress with a white collar covered by a white apron. Five other women are dressed in long white uniforms. All of them wear white nurses' caps that leave a large part of their hair visible. The reason for the difference is unclear: Are the women in blue and white fully trained nurses, whereas the others are nurses' aides? Or have they had their training at different places: the women in blue and white at the hospital or, for example, one of the missionary schools and the others at the Red Crescent? Another photograph including one of the five women in white shows that she was trained by the Red Crescent: She carries its insignia on her collar. In this photograph of three women, the white nurse's cap is replaced by a white head scarf knotted at the back of the neck. Although the two women identified as Armenian sisters wear their head scarves pushed back showing their hair, the hair of the other, unidentified woman is hardly visible.[72] She wears her head scarf in the so-called *sıkmabaş* way, that is, a head cover going over the forehead and falling over the back while tied low at the back of the neck. Was this woman, therefore, perhaps a Muslim like the women in Figure 12.5? Making this conclusion on the basis of only the photograph is problematic.

The photographs in this chapter corroborate the description by the unknown author of the article mentioned above: The Red Crescent uniforms, with their long skirts and long sleeves, covered the bodies of the wearers completely to leave only their hands and heads free. The hair could be neatly tucked away under the head scarves, completing the outfit, a unique feature of the Red Crescent uniforms that made them wearable by Muslim and non-Muslim women alike.

From the photographs above it is difficult to distinguish between Muslim and non-Muslim women. Non-Muslim women did not have to adhere to the rules of *tesettür* and were, in theory, allowed to show their hair. Does this mean that the women whose hair was peeping from under their scarves were non-Muslim? Even such a modest interpretation is problematic. The image of a nurse showing some hair might have been that of a non-Muslim, but she might as well have been a "modernized" Ottoman Muslim woman who felt less constrained by tradition. On the other hand, some of the women known to be non-Muslim wore their head scarves in such a way that their hair did not show.

Besides the white, indoor uniforms, the Red Crescent also had an official outfit to wear while traveling outdoors. This outfit was clearly in line with the contemporaneous Muslim rules for outside gear: It consisted of a long, dark-colored overcoat with long sleeves and,

Figure 12.9.
The caption beneath the original photograph reads "Official dress of voluntary nurses of the Red Crescent." This outfit is clearly in line with the contemporaneous Muslim rules for outside gear: a long, dark-colored overcoat with a short pelerine covering the breast and a so-called sıkmabaş, a head cover going over the forehead and falling over the back while tied low at the back of the neck. This woman also carries the symbols of a trained volunteer: the insignia, the Red Crescent signs on the collar, and a Red Crescent medal. L.M. Gräfin von Lubieńska, "Türkische Soldaten," Sport und Salon, *7 October 1916, 5–6.*

on its collar, had the red crescent sign. A short pelerine covered the breast, and the outfit was completed by a matching head scarf also tied in *sıkmabaş* (Figures 12.9 and 12.10).[73]

Both uniforms worn by the Red Crescent hospital attendants and nurses' aides—for indoor and outdoor use—were *tesettür* proof and thus distinct from the garb a woman would wear in the private sphere of her home. Like the metaphors discussed above suggesting a kind of desexualized intimacy between caretaker and patient, these uniforms thus served as an additional shield against true intimacy with the wounded soldiers. The poses of some of the women in the photographs, however, certainly indicate that the uniforms did not prevent a degree of intimacy with male colleagues.

Figure 12.10.
Ottoman Muslim women in the official volunteers' uniform leaving for the front. Servet-i Fünun, *no. 1350 (31 Mayıs 1333 [May 1917]), front page.*

CONCLUSION

After the Young Turk Revolution of 1908, women belonging to the highest Ottoman circles were actively involved in reestablishing the Ottoman Red Crescent Society as one of the three semiofficial organizations. Through its women's center, it successfully mobilized women of the urban upper and middle classes to work to improve the circumstances of wounded soldiers. Much of the work did not transgress existing (spatial) gender boundaries. Sewing to produce winter presents could be done within elite homes, organization workshops, and all-female environments.

Physically taking care of wounded soldiers was, however, different. Although Besim Ömer initiated several courses to engage volunteers in attending the sick, the women who took these courses were trained to look after the wounded and ill at home, rather than at hospitals. The battles at Gallipoli, where Ottomans successfully fought against the Allied forces, proved to be a turning point in this regard. The influx of wounded men from the battlefields and a victory-inspired wave of patriotism seem to have served as a catalyst: Increasing numbers of Muslim women not only started to attend courses, they also started to work in the many hospitals in Istanbul and elsewhere. The efforts of Besim Ömer to firmly establish a nursing school to train professional nurses and nurses' aides, however, remained unsuccessful, partly because of the lack of cooperation from the authorities.

One reason for their hesitance to cooperate might have been that they did not want to upset a public for whom nursing those other than close relatives constituted a severe trespassing of the existing gender norms. In a society where seclusion was the prevalent ideal, the Red Crescent worked hard to point out to the public that nursing was not a break in these gender norms, but rather a confirmation. Through their rhetoric, the Red Crescent turned the wounded soldiers into close relatives of their caretakers and desexualized the male–female contacts in the context of nursing. Moreover, by portraying these women as the mothers and sisters of wounded sons and brothers, they remained the performers of culturally conventional caring tasks that confirmed rather than opposed their feminine roles. The indoor and outdoor uniforms of the Muslim hospital attendants and nurses' aides, which were both in accordance with the Islamic rules of *tesettür*, should have further smoothened the way for the development of an army of professional Muslim nurses, hospital attendants and nurses' aides.

The number of Ottoman Muslims taking up sick attendance as volunteers or professionals remained rather limited, however. There was, therefore, ample reason for the board of the Red Crescent to sigh in its 1919 report, which covered the years from 1914 through 1918: "We have to admit we remained quite inadequate."[74]

NOTES

1. Erik Jan Zürcher, ed., *Jihad and Islam in World War I: Studies on the Ottoman Jihad at the Centenary of Snouck Hurgronje's "Holy War Made in Germany"* (Leiden: Leiden University Press, 2016).

2. "Seferberlikte ahalinin vazifesi," *İkdam*, 23 Sept. 1914, 1. See also "Herkese düşen vazifeler," *İkdam*, 13 Sept. 1914, 1.

3. Ulviye Mevlan, "Hal-ı hazırda kadın," *Kadınlar Dünyası*, no. 154 (29 Teşrinisani 1330 [12 Dec. 1914]): 1.

4. Selahittin Özçelik, *Donanma-yı Osmanî Muavenet-i Milliye Cemiyeti* (Ankara: Türk Tarihi Kurumu, 2000); Mehmet Beşikçi, *The Ottoman Mobilization of Manpower in the First World War: Between Voluntarism and Resistance* (Leiden: Brill, 2012), 44–51.

5. Nâzım H. Polat, *Müdâfaa-i Milliye Cemiyeti* (Ankara: Kültür Bakanlığı, 1991); Ayşe Zamacı, "Müdafaa-i Milliye Cemiyeti ve faaliyetleri" (Ph.D. diss., Trakya Üniversitesi Edirne, 2015).

6. Nil Sarı and Zuhal Özaydın, "Türk hemşireliğine Osmanlı hanımefendileri'nin ve Hilâl-i Ahmer (Kızılay)'in desteği," *Sendrom* 4, no. 3 (1992): 66–78; Nil Sarı and Zuhal Özaydın, "Dr. Besim Ömer Paşa ve kadın hastabakıcı eğitiminin nedenleri (I)," *Sendrom* 4, no. 4 (1992): 10–18; Nil Sarı and Zuhal Özaydın, "Dr. Besim Ömer Paşa ve kadın hastabakıcı eğitiminin nedenleri (II)," *Sendrom* 4, no. 5 (1992): 72–80; Muzaffer Tepekaya and Leyla Kaplan, "Hilâl Ahmer Hanımlar Merkezi'nin kuruluşu ve faaliyetleri (1877–1923)," *Selçuk Üniversitesi Sosyal Bilimler Enstitüsü Dergisi*, no. 10 (2003): 147–202; Mesut Çapa, *Kızılay (Hilal-i Ahmer) Cemiyeti (1914–1925)* (Ankara: Türk Kızılayı, 2009); Seçil Karal Akgün and Murat Uluğtekin, *Hilal-i Ahmer'den Kızılaya* (Ankara: Kızılay, 2002); Hüsnü Ada, "The First Ottoman Civil Society Organization in the Service of the Ottoman State: The Case of the Ottoman Red Crescent (Osmanlı *Hilal-i Ahmer* Cemiyeti)" (M.A. thesis, Sabancı University, 2004); Hüsnü Ada, "Osmanlı Devleti'nin hizmetinde ilk modern Osmanlı sivil toplum örgütü: Osmanlı Hilal-i Ahmer Cemiyeti (1868–1911)" (Ph.D. diss., Marmara Üniversitesi, 2011); Mehmet Polat, "Hilal-i Ahmer Teşkilatının kuruluşu ve teşkilatlanması" (M.A. thesis, Fırat Üniversitesi, 2005).

7. Besim Ömer, "La fondation, la réorganisation du Croissant-Rouge et son action pendant les guerres de Tripolitaine et des Balkans," *Bulletin International des Sociétés de la Croix-Rouge* 46, no. 183 (1915): 419–428. See, for an extensive history of the Ottoman Red Crescent Society to 1914, Osmanlı Hilal-i Ahmer Cemiyeti, *Osmanlı Hilal-i Ahmer Cemiyeti Salnamesi, 1329–1331* (İstanbul: Ahmet İhsan ve Şürekası, [1914]), 20–50.

8. Wikipedia, "Russo-Turkish War (1877–1878)," https://en.wikipedia.org/wiki/Russo-Turkish_War_(1877-1878) (accessed 1 Mar. 2018).

9. Nicole A.N.M. van Os, "Feminism, Philanthropy & Patriotism: Female Associational Life in the Ottoman Empire" (Ph.D. diss., Leiden University, 2013), 56–60.

10. Charles Murato, "La guèrre d'Orient," *L'Univers Illustré*, 20 Oct. 1877, 633, 669.

11. Nadir Özbek, *Osmanlı* İmparatorluğu*'nda sosyal devlet: Siyaset, iktidar ve meşruiyet (1876–1914)* (İstanbul: İletişim Yayınları, 2002), 307–323; Ada, "Osmanlı Devleti'nin hizmetinde ilk modern Osmanlı sivil toplum örgütü."

12. Yavuz Selim Karakısla, "Osmanlı Hilal-i Ahmer ve Terakkiperver Cemiyet-i Nisvaniyesi ve Hilal-i Ahmer ve Fukuraperver Cemiyet-i Hayriye-i Nisvaniyesi: Dolandırıcıların 'sahte' Osmanlı kadın örgütü," *Tarih ve Toplum* 3, no. 220 (2002): 11–16; Nicole A.N.M. van Os, "Osmanlı Hilal-i Ahmer ve Terakkiperver Cemiyet-i Nisvaniyesi ve Hilal-i Ahmer ve Fukuraperver Cemiyet-i Hayriye-i Nisvaniyesi: Dolandırıcıların 'sahte' Osmanlı kadın örgütü - 2," *Tarih ve Toplum* 37, no. 226 (2002): 22–27.

13. Hayriye bint-i Salih, "Hamiyetperver Feride Hanım," *Metin*, 10 Ağustos 1324 [23 Aug. 1908], 3.

14. Feride bint-i Yaver, "Hilal-i Ahmer Cemiyeti teşkili," *Metin*, 9 Ağustos 1324 [22 Aug. 1908], 4.

15. "Association des Dames Ottomanes pour le relèvement de la patrie," *Journal de Salonique*, 8 Mar. 1908, 2. See, for more on this organization, Zafer Toprak, "İttihad ve Terakki ve Teali-i Vatan Osmanlı Hanımlar Cemiyeti," *Toplum ve Bilim* 43–44 (1989): 34–38.

16. "Hilal-i Ahmer Şefkat Pazarı," *Seda-yı Millet*, 17 Mart 1326 [30 Mar. 1910], 3; "Hilal-i Ahmer Şefkat Pazarı," *Yeni Gazete*, 22 Mart 1326 [4 Apr. 1910], 3; "Hilal-i Ahmer Cemiyeti," *Yeni Gazete*, 15 Nisan 1326 [28 Apr. 1910], 2; "Hariciye Nazırı Paşa hazretlerinin . . . ," *Seda-yı Millet*, 8 Mayıs 1326 [21 May 1910], 4; "Hilal-i Ahmer Cemiyeti," *Yeni Gazete*, 14 Mayıs 1326 [27 May 1910], 4; "Croissant Rouge," *Journal de Salonique*, 7 June 1908, 2; "Hilal-i Ahmer Sergisi," *Yeni Gazete*, 8 Haziran 1326 [21 June 1910], 3; "Tepebaşı sergisini ziyaret," *Yeni Gazete*, 20 Haziran 1326 [3 July 1910], 3 "Hilal-i Ahmer Cemiyeti menfaatına," *Yeni Gazete*, 30 Nisan 1326 [13 May 1910], 3; "Konser," *Yeni Gazete*, 1 Mayıs 1326 [14 May 1910], 4; "Hilal-i Ahmer Sergisi," *Yeni Gazete*, 20 Nisan 1326 [3 Apr. 1910], 1; "Hilal-i Ahmer Cemiyeti," *Yeni Gazete*, 6 Mayıs 1326 [19 May 1910], 3.

17. Historical Currency Converter, http://www.historicalstatistics.org/Currencyconverter.html (accessed 30 Mar. 2018); Ada, "Osmanlı Devleti'nin hizmetinde ilk modern Osmanlı sivil toplum örgütü"; Akgün and Uluğtekin, *Hilal-i Ahmer'den Kızılaya*, 36–40; Besim Ömer, "La fondation, la réorganisation du Croissant-Rouge."

18. "Ein Aufruf des 'Roten Halbmonds,'" *Osmanischer Lloyd*, 9. Dec. 1911, 1–2; Osmanlı Hilal-i Ahmer Cemiyeti Hanımlar Heyet-i Merkeziyesi, *Takvim - 1 -* (İstanbul: Osmanlı Hilal-i Ahmer Cemiyeti Hanımlar Heyet-i

Merkeziyesi, 1331 [1915-1916]), 56; Osmanlı Hilal-i Ahmer Cemiyeti, *Osmanlı Hilal-i Ahmer Cemiyeti Salnamesi, 1329–1331*, 53–56; Tepekaya and Kaplan, "Hilâl Ahmer Hanımlar Merkezi'nin kuruluşu ve faaliyetleri," 150–153.

19. "Frauenverein des Roten Halbmondes in Kastamoni," *Osmanischer Lloyd*, 22 Feb. 1913, 2. See also Mustafa Eski, "İlk kadın mitingi," in *Kastamonu'da ilk kadın mitingi'nin 75. yıldönümü uluslararası sempozyumu* (Ankara: Atatürk Araştırma Merkezi, 1996), 33–46.

20. "Hilal-i Ahmer'in yeni hanımlar şubesi," *Tanin*, Temmuz 1331 [9 Aug. 1915], 4; "Bebek'te Hilal-i Ahmer Hanımlar şubesi," İkdam, 27 Temmuz 1331 [9 Aug. 1915], 2; "Mecruh gazilerimizin şefkatlı validesi Hilal-i Ahmer menfaatine" *Sabah*, 19 Mayıs 1331 [1 June 1915], 3; "Osmanlı Hilal-i Ahmer Cemiyeti Hanımlar Merkezi'nden," *Tasvir-i Efkar*, 25 Mayıs 1331 [7 June 1915], 1.

21. Letter from the president of the Konya branch, Türkiye Kızılayı Arşivi (hereafter TKA), box 28, document 16 (herafter, 28/16), 26 Ağustos 1330 [8 Sept. 1914]; Letter from the president of the Kastamonu branch, Governor Mehmed Reşid, TKA, 28/160, 2 Mayıs 1331 [15 May 1915]; Letter from the vice-president of the Kastamonu women's branch, TKA, 28/177; Letter from the governor of the Province of Hüdavendigar, TKA, 156/17, 1 Mart 1330 [14 Mar. 1914]; Letter from the president of the Bursa branch, TKA, 156/121, 5 Mart 1330 [18 Mar. 1914]; Letter from the president of the Konya branch, TKA, 28/24, 13 Teşrinievvel 1330 [26 Oct. 1914]; Letter from the president of the Konya branch, TKA, 28/29, 9 Teşrinisani 1330 [22 Nov. 1914]; Telegraph from the governor of the Kastamonu, Reşid, TKA, 82/19, 25 Kanunuevvel 1330 [7 Jan. 1915]; Letter from the president of the Kastamonu Women's branch, Melek Reşid, TKA, 28/166, 28 Temmuz 1331 [10 Aug. 1915]; Letter from the president of the Kastamonu Women's branch, Melek Reşid, TKA, 28/167, 28 Temmuz 1331 [10 Aug. 1915]; "Kastamonu'da faaliyet-i vatanperverane," *Tasvir-i Efkar*, 10 Nisan 1331 [23 Apr. 1915], 3. See also "Hilal-i Ahmer takvimleri," *Köroğlu*, 18 Haziran 1331 [1 July 1915], 2.

22. "İzmir Hilal-i Ahmer Hanımlar Cemiyeti," *Tasvir-i Efkar*, 30 Haziran 1332 [13 July 1916], 2; Çapa, *Kızılay (Hilal-i Ahmer) Cemiyeti (1914–1925)*, 33.

23. *Frauenverein vom Ottomanischen Roten Halbmond in Wien, Bericht des unter dem Allerhöchsten Protektorate Seiner Majestät des Sultan stehenden Frauenvereines vom Ottomanischen Roten Halbmond in Wien für die Zeit vom 20. November 1916 bis 31. Dezember 1917* (Vienna: Im Selbstverlag, 1918), Austrian literature online, http://www.literature.at (accessed 14 Oct. 2019). See also "Viyena'da Hilal-i Ahmer Hanımlarının faaliyeti," *Tanin*, 2 Mayıs 1334 [2 May 1918], 3; "Der Rote Halbmond in Wien," *Osmanischer Lloyd*, 2 May 1918, 3. A local "men's branch" had been established in December 1914. "Viyena'da Hilal-i Ahmer Cemiyeti," *Tasvir-i Efkar*, 25 Teşrinisani 1330 [8 Dec. 1914], 2; "Hilal-i Ahmer'in Avusturya şubesi," *Tasvir-i Efkar*, 26 Teşrinisani 1330 [9 Dec. 1914], 4.

24. "Hilal-i Ahmer çiçekleri alınız," İkdam, 30 Temmuz 1330 [12 Aug. 1915], 1; Letter from the vice-president of the Red Crescent Society to the president of the Kadıköy Women's branch, TKA, 395/23, 1334 [1918]; Letter from the vice-president of the Red Crescent Society to the president of the Kadıköy Women's branch, TKA, 395/25, 14 Temmuz 1333 [14 July 1917]; Letter from Women's Center of the Red Crescent, TKA, 27/205, 15 Teşrinievvel 1332 [28 Oct. 1916]. See also Çetin Aykurt, "Birinci Dünya Savaşı'nda Osmanlı Hilal-i Ahmer Cemiyeti'nin sanatsal faaliyetleri," *Tarih İncelemeleri Dergisi* 30, no. 2 (2015): 413–428. For lists of (female) donors, see, e.g., Osmanlı Hilal-i Ahmer Cemiyeti, *Osmanlı Hilal-i Ahmer Cemiyeti Salnamesi*, 56–58, 306–401; Tepekaya and Kaplan, "Hilâl Ahmer Hanımlar Merkezi'nin kuruluşu ve faaliyetleri," 152–158.

25. "Askere hedaya-yı şitaiye," *Tasvir-i Efkar*, 2 Eylül 1330 [15 Sept. 1914], 3; Osmanlı Hilal-i Ahmer Cemiyeti Hanımlar Heyet-i Merkeziyesi, *Takvim - 1 -*, 64–65; "Gazilerimize hedaya-yı şitaiye hazırlayalım," *Tasvir-i Efkar*, 11 Ağustos 1331 [24 Aug. 1915], 2; "Askerlerimize hediye-i şitaiye," *Tasvir-i Efkar*, 19 Ağustos 1331 [1 Sept. 1915], 2.

26. "Ein Aufruf an die türkischen Frauen," *Osmanischer Lloyd*, 2. Dec. 1914, 3; Osmanlı Hilal-i Ahmer Cemiyeti Hanımlar Heyet-i Merkeziyesi, *Takvim - 1 -*, 58; "Hilal-i Ahmer'deki dikişler," *Tasvir-i Efkar*, 7 Kanunuevvel 1330 [20 Dec. 1914], 3; "Osmanlı hanımlarına," *Tasvir-i Efkar*, 18 Şubat 1330 [3 Mar. 1915], 4; "Osmanlı hanımlarına," İkdam, 18 Şubat 1330 [3 Mar. 1915], 2; "Vom Roten Halbmond," *Osmanischer Lloyd*, 5 Mar. 1915, 3; "Dikişe davet," *Tasvir-i Efkar*, 19 Nisan 1331 [2 May 1915], 4; "Mecruhin gazata yardım," *Tasvir-i Efkar*, 28 Kanunusani 1330 [10 Feb. 1915], 4; "Hedaya-yı şitaiye," *Tasvir-i Efkar*, 6 Teşrinievvel 1330 [19 Oct. 1914], 3; "Hedaya-yı şitaiye," *Tasvir-i Efkar*, 1 Kanunuevvel 1330 [14 Dec. 1914], 3; "Agence Milli," *Lloyd Ottoman*, 13 Feb. 1915, 5; "Adana'da Yardımcı Hanımlar," *Tasvir-i Efkar*, 28 Nisan 1331 [11 May 1915], 2; "L'oeuvre patriotique dans les provinces . . . ," *Lloyd Ottoman*, 11 May 1915, back page.

27. *Türkiye Hilal-i Ahmer Cemiyeti Hanımlar Merkezi Darüssanaası: Eytam ve Eramil-i Şuhedaya Muavenet* ([İstanbul]: Ahmed İhsan ve Şürekası, 1339 [1923]), 3–4, 21–22; "Osmanlı Hilal-i Ahmer Cemiyeti Hanımlar Merkezi'nin taht-ı idare himayesinde 'Hilal-i Ahmer Darüssanaası'nin asakir-i Osmaniyemize hidematı," *Servet-i Fünun*, no. 1210 (9 Teşrinievvel 1330 [22 Oct. 1914]): 368; "Osmanlı Hilal-i Ahmer Cemiyeti Hanımlar Merkez-i umumisi'nde

humalı bir faali'nin taht-ı idare himayesinde 'Hilal-i Ahmer Darüssanaası'nin asakir-i Osmaniyemize hidematı," *Servet-i Fünun*, no. 1249 (30 Nisan 1331 [13 May 1915]): 5; "Hilal-i Ahmer'in hidematından," *Tasvir-i Efkar,* 22 Teşrinievvel 1331 [4 Nov. 1915], 2; Lebib Selim, "Türk kadınlığın harb-ı umumideki faaliyeti," *Türk Yurdu* 9, no. 4 (22 Teşrinievvel 1331 [4 Nov. 1915]): 2797–2799; "Türkische Frauen des Roten Halbmondes," *Die Islamische Welt* 1, no. 5 (Apr. 1917): 257–262.

28. Correspondence between the president of the Bursa branch and the Central Committee of the Red Crescent Society and, also, the Directorate of Health of the Ministry of Interior on this workshop and its production, TKA, 156/7, 29 Kanunusani 1329 [11 Feb. 1914]; TKA, 156/17, 1 Mart 1330 [14 Mar. 1914]; TKA, 156/121, 5 Mart 1330 [18 Mar. 1914]; TKA, 156/28, 5 Ağustos 1330 [18 Aug. 1915]; TKA, 156/31, 14 Ağustos 1330 [27 Aug. 1915]; TKA, 156/32, 14 Ağustos 1330 [27 Aug. 1915]; TKA, 156/123, 7 Kanunuevvel 1331 [20 Dec. 1915]; Besim Ömer, "La fondation, la réorganisation du Croissant-Rouge et son action pendant les guerres de Tripolitaine et des Balkans," 427. For documents in the Red Crescent Archives pertaining to the sending of various quantities of hydrophilic gauze from Bursa to Istanbul between November 1914 and March 1915, see TKA, 156/44, 30 Teşrinievvel 1330 [12 Nov. 1914] and TKA, 156/92, 17 Mart 1331 [30 Mar. 1915].

29. van Os, "Feminism, Philanthropy & Patriotism," especially chs. 12, 13.

30. Ayten Altıntaş, "Türkiye'de hemşireliğin başlangıcı," in *Sağlık alanında Türk kadını: Cumhuriyet'in ve Tıp Fakültesi'ne kız* öğrenci *kabulünün 75. Yılı*, ed. Nuran Yıldırım (İstanbul: Novartis,, 1998), 373–387; Yeşim Işıl Ülmen, "Besim Ömer Akalın (1862–1940): Ange gardien des femmes et des enfants," in *Médecins et ingénieurs ottomans à l'*âge *des nationalismes*, ed. Méropi Anastassiadou-Dumont (Paris: Maisonneuve & Larose, 2003), 101–123; Mary Mills Patrick, "Among the Educated Women of Turkey," in *Daylight in the Harem: A New Era for Moslem Women,* ed. Annie van Sommer and Samuel M. Zwemer (New York: Fleming H. Revell, 1911), 71–90. See, for more on the history of midwifery in the Ottoman Empire and Turkey, Gülhan Balsoy, "Gender and the Politics of Female Body: Midwifery, Abortion and Pregnancy in Ottoman society, 1838–1890s" (Ph.D. diss., State University of New York at Binghamton, 2009); Fatma Gökçen Dinç, "'Ignorant, Dirty, Superstitious Crones': Degrading of Midwifery and Midwives in Modern Turkey" (M.A. thesis, Istanbul Bilgi University, 2011).

31. Robert Rieder, *Für die Türkei: Selbstgelebtes und Gewohltes* (Jena: Verlag von Gustav Fischer, 1903), 1:21–35, 175–182, 205.

32. "Fevkalade mühim bir teşebbüs," *Yeni Gazete,* 3 Teşrinisani 1324 [17 Nov. 1908], 2; "İstanbul," *İttihad ve Terakki*, 8 Teşrinisani 1324 [21 Nov. 1908], 4; "Şuun-ı nisvan: İstanbul Gülhane Seririyat Hastahanesi'nde . . . ," *Kadın* 6 (17 Teşrinisani 1324 [30 Nov. 1908]): 15; "Hastabakıcı kadınlar," *Tanin*, 6 Kanunuevvel 1324 [19 Dec. 1908], 3; "Gülhane Seririyat Hastahanesi'nden," *Yeni Gazete,* 16 Kanunuevvel 1324 [29 Dec. 1908], 4; Hester Donaldson Jenkins, *Behind Turkish Lattices: The Story of a Turkish Woman's Life* (London: Collins, 1911), 155.

33. "Hilal-i Ahmer Cemiyeti," *Seda-yı Millet*, 27 Mayıs 1326 [9 June 1910], 3; "Eine Schule für Krankenpflegerinnen," *Osmanischer Lloyd,* 21 Oct. 1910, 1.

34. "Hilal-i Ahmer için: Gönüllü aza," *Tanin*, 30 Mart 1328 [12 Apr. 1912], 4.

35. "Vatana hizmet: Vatanın hamiyetli kadınlarına ve erkeklerine," *Tanin*, 22 Eylül 1328 [5 Oct. 1912], 3.

36. Besim Ömer, *Hanımefendilere Hilal-i Ahmer'e dair konferans,* (İstanbul: Ahmed İhsan ve Şürekası, 1330 [1914-1915], 75–77.

37. "Hilal-i Ahmer," *Tanin,* 25 Eylül 1328 [8 Oct. 1912], 5.

38. Text of advertisement, TKA, 193/23, 23 Kanunusani 1328 [5 Feb. 1913].

39. Nicole van Os, "Gendering Jihad: Ottoman Muslim Women and War during the Early Twentieth Century," in Zürcher, *Jihad and Islam in World War I*, 153–178.

40. [Julius] Wieting Pascha, "Die Forderungen des Krankenpflegedienstes I," *Osmanischer Lloyd*, 7 Jan. 1914, 1–2; [Julius] Wieting Pascha, "Die Forderungen des Krankenpflegedienstes II," *Osmanischer Lloyd*, 8 Jan. 1914, 1–2.

41. "Der Frauenverein des 'Roten Halbmonds,'" *Osmanischer Lloyd*, 9 Jan. 1914, 1; "Die Kurse für Krankenpflegerinnen," *Osmanischer Lloyd*, 15 Feb. 1914, 2; "Havadis-i dünya: Kadınlar hastabakıcılığı," *Kadınlar Dünyası,* no. 130 (8 Şubat 1329 [21 Feb. 1914]): 9; "Der Rote Halbmond," *Osmanischer Lloyd*, 14 July 1914, 3; "Hilal-i Ahmer'de bir resm-i bihin," *Servet-i Fünun,* no. 1206 (3 Temmuz 1330 [16 July 1914]): 74. The last article contains a full list of all the women receiving their diploma, including the names and ranks of their fathers and husbands.

42. Besim Ömer, "La fondation, la réorganisation du Croissant-Rouge," 428 (emphasis added).

43. Osmanlı Hilal-i Ahmer Cemiyeti Hanımlar Heyet-i Merkeziyesi, *Takvim - 1 -*, 57; Besim Ömer, *Hanımefendilere Hilal-i Ahmer'e dair konferans*, 77–78 (fn).

44. Letter from the president of the Bursa branch, TKA, 156/27, 5 Ağustos 1330 [18 Aug. 1914]; For examples of texts for advertisements in newspapers to announce these courses, see TKA, 193/112, 10 Teşrinisani 1330 [23 Nov. 1914], TKA, 336/1, 10 Nisan 1330 [23 Apr. 1914], and TKA, 193/183, 17 Temmuz 1330 [30 July 1914]; Osmanlı Hilal-i Ahmer Cemiyeti Hanımlar Heyet-i Merkeziyesi, *Takvim - 5 -* (İstanbul: Osmanlı Hilal-i Ahmer Cemiyeti Hanımlar Heyet-i Merkeziyesi, 1335 [1919]), 155; "Hastabakıcılık dersleri," *Tasvir-i Efkar,* 11 Teşrinisani 1330 [24 Nov. 1914], 4; "Veliahd-ı Sultan Hilal-i Ahmer Hanımlar Merkezi'nde," *Tasvir-i Efkar,* 1 Teşrinisani 1330 [14 Nov. 1914], 3.

45. In September 1914, for example, six Muslim women graduated from the courses at the Kadırga Hospital for female hospital attendants. For a list with their names see TKA, 331/5, 11 Eylül 1330 [24 Sept. 1914].

46. Although men needed to actually deposit the sum of money, women did not; they needed a guarantor. Thirty lira was a substantial amount of money in 1914, but a qualified nurses' aide would earn that in less than a year. For examples of texts for advertisements in newspapers to announce these courses, see TKA, 193/88, 23 Eylül 1330 [6 Oct. 1914] andTKA, 193/95, 12 Teşrinievvel 1330 [25 Oct. 1914]; "Hilal-i Ahmer Cemiyeti'nden," *Tasvir-i Efkar,* 11 Teşrinievvel 1330 [24 Oct. 1914], 4.

47. Letter from the president of the Izmir Central Committee, TKA, 336/2, 6 Teşrinievvel 1331 [19 Oct. 1915]. The books referred to must be the two-volume work *Hastabakıcılık*, of which the first volume was written by Nureddin Ali and the second by Besim Ömer (İstanbul: Hilal Matbaası, 1331 [1915]). On the German nurse instructor, see also N.O., "Eine Krankenpflegerinnenschule in Smyrna," *Welt des Islams (1)* 3, nos. 3/4 (25 Mar. 1916): 225. "İzmir'de hastabakıcı hanımlar," *Tasvir-i Efkar,* 30 Haziran 1332 [13 July 1916], 2.

48. Letter of the secretary of the Edirne Men's Center, TKA, 157/24, 23 Eylül 1330 [6 Oct. 1914]; Letter of the secretary of the Edirne Men's Center, TKA, 157/30, 4 Teşrinisani 1330 [17 Nov. 1914]; Letter of the secretary of the Association des Médecins Israélites de l'Empire Ottoman, TKA, 331/6, 27 Teşrinisani 133 [10 Dec. 1914], "Hastabakıcılık dershanesi," *Tasvir-i Efkar,* 15 Teşrinisani 1330 [28 Nov. 1914], 3; "Hastabakıcılık dershanelerinde," *Tasvir-i Efkar,* 27 Teşrinisani 1330 [10 Dec. 1914], 4.

49. Letter from Hilal-i Ahmer Cemiyeti Hanımlar Merkezi, dated 9 Mayıs 1331 [22 May 1915], as quoted in Sarı and Özaydın, "Dr. Besim Ömer Paşa ve kadın hastabakıcı eğitiminin nedenleri (I)," 13.

50. Sarı and Özaydın, "Dr. Besim Ömer Paşa ve kadın hastabakıcı eğitiminin nedenleri (I)," 13–14.

51. Letter from Besim Ömer, TKA, 336/3, 11 Teşrinisani 1331 [24 Nov. 1915]; Sarı and Özaydın, "Dr. Besim Ömer Paşa ve kadın hastabakıcı eğitiminin nedenleri (I)," 15.

52. "Hastabakıcılık ulvi bir hizmettir: Hilal-i Ahmer Cemiyeti'nin müfid bir teşebbüsü," in Osmanlı Hilal-i Ahmer Cemiyeti Hanımlar Heyet-i Merkeziyesi, *Takvim - 4 -* (İstanbul: Osmanlı Hilal-i Ahmer Cemiyeti Hanımlar Heyet-i Merkeziyesi, 1918), 167–170. See also "Hilal-i Ahmer bir senede ne yaptı," *Vakit,* 17 May 1918, 2; Osmanlı Hilâl-i Ahmer Cemiyeti Merkezi, *Osmanlı Hilâl-i Ahmer Cemiyeti Merkezi Umumi Raporu (1330–1334)*, (Istanbul: Hilal-i Ahmer Cemiyeti, 1335), 35, 61; "Kadın hastabakıcı mektebi," *Tasvir-i Efkar,* 21 Nisan 1334 [21 Apr. 1918], 2; "Hastabakıcılık öğrenmek isteyenlere . . . ," *Vakit,* 19 Nisan 1334 [19 Apr. 1918], 2; "Hilal-i Ahmer'in kadın hastabakıcı mektebi," *Tanin,* 1 Mayıs 1334 [1 May 1918], 4; "Kadın Hastabakıcı Mektebi," *Vakit,* 8 Mayıs 1334 [8 May 1918], 2; "Hastabakıcı olmak isteyenlere," *Tanin,* 11 Haziran 1334 [11 June 1918], 4; "Kadın hastabakıcılık mektebi," *Tasvir-i Efkar,* 12 Haziran 1334 [12 June 1918], 2; "Hastabakıcılık mektebine kabul olunacaklar," *Vakit,* 2 Ağustos 1334 [2 Aug. 1918], 2; "Hastabakıcılık mektebine girecek hanımlar," *Tanin,* 12 Ağustos 1334 [12 Aug. 1918], 4; For letters from the Internal Director of the Faculty of Medicine regarding the courses opened, see TKA, 336/5, 22 Kanunusani 1335 [22 Jan. 1919]; TKA, 336/7, 30 Kanunusani 1335 [30 Jan. 1919]; TKA, 336/8, 22 Kanunusani 1335 [22 Jan. 1919]; and TKA, 336/9, 30 Kanunusani 1335 [30 Jan. 1919].

53. "Hilal-i Ahmer mensubunu," İkdam, 25 Temmuz 1330 [7 Aug. 1914], 3.

54. "Hastabakıcı hanımlar," İkdam, 20 Ağustos 1330 [2 Sept. 1914], 2.

55. Text for advertisement, TKA, 193/314, 18 Nisan 1331 [1 May 1915]; Text for newspaper article and advertisement, TKA, 193/315, 19 Nisan 1331 [2 May 1915]; "Hastabakıcı hanımlara," *Tasvir-i Efkar,* 19 Nisan 1331 [2 May 1915], 2; "Hastabakıcı hanımlarımıza," *İkdam,* 19 Nisan 1331 [2 May 1915], 2; "Hastabakıcı hanımlara," *Tasvir-i Efkar,* 20 Nisan 1331 [3 May 1915], 2.

56. Letter of the chief of staff of the Red Crescent Çağaloğlu hospital, TKA, 331/12, 2 Mayıs 1331 [15 May 1915]; Lists of personnel of various hospitals, TKA, 44/97, Mayıs 1331 [May/June 1915]; Letter of the chief of staff of the Marine hospital, TKA, 331/10, 31 Mayıs 1331 [13 June 1915]; Letter of the chief of staff of the Red Crescent Çağaloğlu hospital, TKA, 520/12, 10 Haziran 1331 [23 June 1915]; Letter of the chief of staff of the Red Crescent Beyoğlu hospital TKA, 223/61, 7 Temmuz 1331 [20 July 1915]; Lists of personnel of the Red Crescent

Çağaloğlu hospital TKA, 520/51, 10 Eylül 1331 [23 Sept. 1915]; Letter of the chief of staff of the Marine hospital, TKA, 223/68, 20 Teşrinievvel 1331 [2 Nov. 1915].

57. Document on obligatory participation in courses, TKA, 331/11, 29 Eylül 1331 [12 Oct. 1915]; Letter from the chief of staff of the Military Academy, TKA, 331/39, 4 Teşrinievvel 1331 [17 Oct. 1915]; List of names of volunteers, TKA, 331/51, 6 Teşrinievvel 1331 [19 Oct. 1915]; Letter of the chief of staff of the Taşkışla hospital, TKA, 331/48, 12 Teşrinievvel 1331 [25 Oct. 1915]; "Bir inkilab-i içtimai-i milli," *Servet-i Fünun,* no. 1249 (30 Nisan 1331 [13 May 1915]): 4–5; Osmanlı Hilal-i Ahmer Cemiyeti Hanımlar Heyet-i Merkeziyesi, *Takvim - 2* (İstanbul: Osmanlı Hilal-i Ahmer Cemiyeti Hanımlar Heyet-i Merkeziyesi, 1332 [1916-1917]).

58. L.M. Gräfin von Lubieńska, "Türkische Soldaten," *Sport und Salon,* 7 Oct. 1916, 5–6; Hilde Mordtmann, *Als ich die Türken pflegte* (Weimar, Germany: Verlag Gustav Kiepenheuer, 1916); Betty S. Anderson, *The American University of Beirut: Arab Nationalism and Liberal Education* (Austin: University of Texas Press, 2011); Isabel Kaprelian-Churchill, *Sisters of Mercy and Survival: Armenian Nurses, 1900–1930* (Antelias, Lebanon: Armenian Catholicosate of Cilicia, 2012).

59. "Osmanlı Hilal-i Ahmer Cemiyeti Madalyaları Nizamnamesi," in Başbakanlık Osmanlı Arşivi (Prime Ministerial Ottoman Archives; hereafter BOA), Nişan Defterleri No. 31: Hilal-i Ahmer Madalyaları.

60 BOA, Nişan Defterleri No. 31: Hilal-i Ahmer Madalyaları; BOA, Nişan Defterleri No. 32: Hilal-i Ahmer Madalyalar; BOA, Nişan Defterleri No. 33: Hilal-i Ahmer Madalyaları.

61. See, e.g., the following newspaper ads: "Hastahane hemşiresi," *Vakit,* 20 Teşrinisani 1333 [20 Nov. 1917], 2; "Kadınları Çalıştırma Cemiyet-i İslamiyesi'nden" *Vakit,* 5 Mayıs 1334 [5 May 1918], 2; "Hastabakıcı aranıyor," *Tanin,* 5 Mayıs 1334 [5 May 1918], 4; "Kolordu için hanım aranıyor," *Tanin,* 6 Haziran 1334 [6 June 1918], 4.

62. "Hilal-i Ahmer Cemiyeti reis-i sanisi muallim doktor Besim Ömer Paşa nutku," *Servet-i Fünun,* no. 1212 (14 Ağustos 1330 [27 Aug. 1914]): 124–125.

63. Besim Ömer, "La fondation, la réorganisation du Croissant-Rouge," 428. For examples of magazine photos, see *Servet-i Fünun,* no. 1249 (30 Nisan 1331 [13 May 1915]): 4–5; "Mecruh gazilerimiz İstanbul'da (Hilal-i Ahmer) hastahanelerinde," *Harb Mecmuası,* no. 3 (Kanunusani 1331 [Jan./Feb. 1916]): 46; "Taşkışla hastahanesinde. . . ," *Harb Mecmuası,* no. 7 (Mart 1332 [Mar./Apr. 1916]): 111; "Yaralı gazilerimiz: beşinci ordu dört numeralı menzil hastahanesinde—İslam hanım kardeşlerimizin şefkatlı mahir ellerinde," *Harb Mecmuası,* no. 14 (Teşrinisani 1332 [Nov./Dec. 1916]): 215; "Merzifon 'Şifa Yurdu' hastanesinde . . . ,"*Harb Mecmuası,* no. 17 (Mar. 1917): 267; "Ladik'te hastabakıcı kızlarımız," *Kadınlar Dünyası,* no. 169 (13 Nisan 1334 [13 Apr. 1918]): 1; "Hilal-i Ahmer'de kadınlığın faaliyeti," *Kadınlar Dünyası,* no. 185 (3 Ağustos 1334 [3 Aug. 1918]): 1.

64. Selçuk Akşin Somel, "Osmanlı modernleşme döneminde kız eğitimi," *Kebikeç,* 10 (2000): 223–238. On the opening of the Women's University, see Bahar Baskın, "II. Meşrutiyet'te kadın eğitimine yönelik bir girişim: İnas Darülfünunu," *Siyasal Bilgiler Fakültesi Dergisi* 38 (Mar. 2008): 89–124.

65. "Hilal-i Ahmer Cemiyeti reis-i sanisi muallim doktor Besim Ömer Paşa nutku," *Servet-i Fünun,* no. 1212 (14 Ağustos 1330 [27 Aug. 1914]): 124–125. See also, e.g., "Hastabakıcılık ulvi bir hizmettir."

66. Fatma Aliye, "Hilal," *Servet-i Fünun,* no. 1251 (14 Mayıs 1331 [27 May 1915]): 34–35.

67. Fatma Aliye, "Kahraman kadınlarımız," *Servet-i Fünun,* no. 1253 (28 Mayıs 1331 [10 June 1915]): 66–67. See also Fatma Aliye, "Kadınlar hakkında," *Servet-i Fünun,* no. 1289 (18 Şubat 1331 [4 Mar. 1916]): 178–179.

68. See also, e.g., Hasim Nahit, "Yaralılar ve hanımlarımız," *Servet-i Fünun,* no. 1263 (13 Ağustos 1331 [26 Aug. 1915]): 226–229.

69. "Hastahane tesisi," *İkdam,* 7 June 1915, 2; "Gazileri ziyaret—takdir," İkdam, 13 July 1915, 2.

70. "'Hilal-i Ahmer'hanımları; 'Hilal-i Ahmer' hastabakıcı hanımları," *Servet-i Fünun,* no. 1350 (31 Mayıs 1917 [31 May 1917]): 401–404.

71. See, for an example, Imperial War Museum, "Brassard, Turkish Red Crescent," https://www.iwm.org.uk/collections/item/object/30076664 (accessed 14 October 2019).

72. Houshamadyan, "Mona Selyan collection (part 1) - Toronto," https://www.houshamadyan.org/en/oda/americas/mona-selyan-collection-ca.html, specifically, https://www.houshamadyan.org/fileadmin/_processed_/d/1/csm_Mona-Selyan-16_e2279a3ae1.jpg and https://www.houshamadyan.org/fileadmin/_processed_/2/2/csm_Mona-Selyan-17_202401bcbe.jpg (accessed 14 October 2019).

73. See, for an elaborate discussion of (the changes in) Ottoman Muslim women's dresses in the Second Constitutional Period, van Os, "Feminism, Philanthropy & Patriotism," in particular ch. 7.

74. Murat Uluğtekin and M. Gül Uluğtekin, eds., *Osmanlı'dan Cumhuriyet'e Hilal-i Ahmer icraat raporları 1914–1928* (Ankara: Türkiye Kızılay, 2013), 32.

THIRTEEN

SWORN VIRGINS AND MOTHERS OF THE WOUNDED

Balkan Women and the Great War

MARIA BUCUR

"Sworn virgins" and "mothers of the wounded": these two familiar images are often conjured up by references to women in uniform during the Great War in the Balkans. This chapter explores the impact of women in uniform on Balkan societies and policy makers, including the military and public health fields. On the basis of available historiography and my own research, this chapter focuses on Romania, Serbia, and Bulgaria. A rich trove of evidence documents the activities women undertook in support of the war. Unfortunately, these aspects of the war effort have remained marginally studied and even less integrated in the historiography of the Great War.[1] My analysis touches comparatively on some commonalities and differences that can be observed among the three countries. In evaluating the impact of their activities, I conclude that despite often spectacular individual achievements or flamboyant self-presentation, women's voluntary war work achieved little in shifting gender norms, enhancing citizenship rights, or even changing nursing in the military. Foremost among the reasons for this failure was the reluctance of the exclusively male political establishment and other powerful patriarchal social institutions—educational, professional, military, and religious—to respond to women's organizations calling for reforms in suffrage, education, professional development, and economic rights.[2]

UNIFORMS AND MODERNITY: THE BALKAN CONTEXT

Uniforms are par excellence intentional markers of homogeneity, shoring up the group's unitary purpose by masking their wearers' heterogeneity. They are also sartorial markers of established hierarchies inside military, religious, state, and educational institutions. Uniforms seek to put people "in their place" at a glance.[3]

In the Balkans, the state's regulation of clothing to mark social status was a longstanding practice.[4] Over 80% of the population lived in rural poverty well into the twentieth century; their clothing marked them clearly as a peasant underclass. From the homemade rough sandals worn by both genders to the coarse homespun cloth used to make shirts, skirts, and pants, peasants put their poverty on everyday display, if only to themselves; interactions with other classes of people were rare. Balkan literature of the nineteenth and twentieth is rife with descriptions of dress as a powerful marker of peasant economic and social standing.[5]

Wearing specific types of head coverings flagged the status, religion, gender, and age of both men and women. For instance, the color of head scarves worn by Orthodox Christian women marked their marital status. Certain kaftans and fur trims communicated elite social standing. Wearing equestrian garb—boots, whip, and a specific type of both pants and jacket—was a sign of elite social status and often religion. Riding horses was reserved for Muslim men in areas ruled directly by the Ottomans and for notables in areas where Christians were a majority, as in Romania and parts of Greece.

Within this larger ensemble of sartorial regulations and practices, military uniforms played a particularly important role by offering easy-to-grasp visual classifications of the male population. Until the eighteenth century, many janissaries, the backbone of the Ottoman army, came to Istanbul from all over the Balkans through the forced-recruitment policy, *devshirme*. Not only the empire's foot soldiers, they were also members of a guild and therefore part of a social group that offered exclusive educational and economic privileges to its members.[6]

In the mid-nineteenth century, military uniforms were redesigned to resemble those worn by the European (read modern) armies that the sultans and their pro-European advisers sought to emulate. This is also the period when Greece (1821), Serbia (1878), and Romania (1878) were recognized as independent states and began to build their military institutions, uniforms and all. Other Balkan states gained independence later, less than a decade before the Great War began: Bulgaria in 1908, Montenegro in 1910, and Albania in 1913. Several Balkan territories, such as Croatia and Bosnia-Herzegovina, remained under imperial rule until after the Great War ended.

For these young states, having their own uniformed military forces was an important symbol of independence, national pride, and the ability to act as sovereign powers. They had all gained independence by bringing together a variety of fighting forces, a motley crew of uneven skill and commitment to the cause. Shifting from that messy structure to a crisp hierarchy was more than a symbolic move. Wearing national military uniforms was a means to create a unified fighting force, mobilize the male population, and justify the rising costs the state imposed on its citizenry for building the military. All but a few leaders of Bulgaria, Romania, and Serbia were raised as military officers, and their identity and authority as prince/king was inextricably bound with the uniform they always wore in public.

WOMEN IN BALKAN SOCIETIES BEFORE 1914

It is no surprise that modernization in these newly founded states rested on profoundly masculinist assumptions about citizenship and public roles; social norms in the European states they emulated were patriarchal to the core.[7] Despite Florence Nightingale's much-touted contribution to rendering nursing a visible, respectable, and even socially important role, Balkan societies were nowhere ready to contemplate the entry of women in professional and political roles. At the start of the Great War, most people in the Balkans lived in the countryside with very little access to education. Women were, by and large, illiterate. Although the state had just begun to consider literacy and public education important responsibilities, boys were mainly the beneficiaries. In Romania, for instance, over 90% of the rural female population was illiterate, and the rate was only slightly better in cities. The situation was similar in Bulgaria and Serbia.[8]

In 1914, men interested in pursuing an education and employment or military service in medical capacities had several options: doctor, under-surgeon, sanitary agent, and nurse. Women's options were far more limited. A handful of women had been trained as doctors, and a very few found educational nursing opportunities. In the second half of the nineteenth century, the first generation of women to receive medical training was those with the economic means and familial support to travel abroad to Switzerland, Austria-Hungary, France, or Germany.[9] The Serbian Draga Ljočić-Milošević traveled to Zurich in 1872 to study medicine and returned to Belgrade in 1879 to become the first female doctor in that country.[10] Similarly, the Romanian Maria Cuțarida-Crăciunescu had to travel abroad to Zurich and, eventually, Montpellier and Paris to complete her medical doctorate in 1884. The two women, both ardent feminists, overlapped in Zurich, one of the few medical schools in Europe that offered women admission at that time.

Their paths differed, however, once they returned home. Cuțarida-Crăciunescu was able to have her Parisian doctorate recognized in Bucharest and became active in medical practice and education, working in the gynecological section of a prominent hospital and offering courses in hygiene to the few other women admitted to the Bucharest Medical School starting in the 1880s. During the Great War, she served as a doctor in a military hospital.[11] Ljočić-Milošević volunteered in her medical capacity during the Balkan wars and the Great War and was decorated multiple times, but her credentials were recognized officially only after the war. Other women with medical training in the Balkans followed similar paths: They faced an uphill battle in terms of admission to medical education in their countries, seldom receiving positions commensurate with their training and skill level. They volunteered in hospitals during the war. The total number of female doctors for the two decades between 1900 and 1920 did not surpass a few hundred for the entire region.

Female nursing did not fare much better before the Great War. No nursing schools existed in Bulgaria or Serbia in 1914. There were efforts in both countries to train women in nursing, but these courses were short (four months in the case of Serbia), had no accreditation, and offered no clear path for professional development or employment afterward. The first accredited state nursing school in the Balkans opened in Bucharest in 1913 and had around 100 graduates by the beginning of Romania's entry into the war in 1916.[12]

Looking back from 2017, it is hard to comprehend why there was so little interest in developing this field. The Crimean War had been fought next door to these countries, and all of them had fought multiple wars with heavy casualties since the 1870s. As Laurie Stoff shows elsewhere in this volume, Russian women tried to use the Crimean experience to promote greater professionalization of women nurses, but to little effect. The larger social context discussed above helps explain this costly blind spot: In a population overwhelmingly rural, illiterate, and patriarchal, few political and educational leaders had the foresight to see women's potential in the field of medicine. It was primarily ambitious women with a feminist bent, like those mentioned above, who pushed for the development of nursing education and women's admission into the medical profession. In the Balkans, as in most of Europe before the Great War, a few exceptional figures succeeded, but only despite the opprobrium of the male establishment.

THE BALKAN WARS

This was the situation during the Balkan wars (1912–1913), when large numbers of wounded began to overcrowd military and civilian hospitals in areas affected by the conflict, from Belgrade to Adrianople.[13] The Second Balkan War in 1913, especially, served as an important test case for the role women in uniform could play in terms of serving the state, engaging with the destruction wrought by the conflict. In 1912, British feminist Mabel St Clair Stobart founded the Women's Sick and Wounded Convoy Corps, an all-women medical unit, the first of its kind, which served in Bulgaria.[14] Initially disregarded by the British Red Cross, which had emphatically rejected the idea of sending women nurses to the Balkan front, Bulgaria's Queen Eleonora and its military authorities warmly received Stobart. Her unit spent the war caring for 729 wounded soldiers, both Bulgarian and Turkish, in an improvised hospital near the front. Stobart proudly claimed in her memoir that only one of these patients died, not from his wounds, but rather a heart condition.[15]

Stobart left behind a rich account of her experiences, together with several valuable photographs she took along the way, all in the service of a specific goal: normalizing women's service in uniform on the battlefield as a means to alter the experience and results of war, as well as a way to prove women's patriotism and therefore justify full legal and civic equality with men. In fact, Stobart left a long paean to the uniform: "Uniforms are representative of Ideas that are unnameable." She ended her extended musings as follows: "Women will never, as a sex, do useful work till they wear clothes which are appropriate to work and—though this may come as a revelation to many—there is no physiological reason against this. 'The essence of all science' says Carlyle 'lies in the philosophy of clothes.'"[16]

Stobart provided a first-hand account of women's participation in the war, as well as the engagement by the Balkan authorities with women as participants. As she visited hospitals in Belgrade, Sofia, Adrianople, and Kirk Kilisse, Stobart noted seeing local women volunteers everywhere. She identified most of these volunteers as drawn from social elites, an observation confirmed by my own research on Romania.[17] Given that most Balkan women were rural, poor, and responsible for families and farms while husbands and sons were at the front, it is not hard to understand why few peasant women could be found in these hospitals. Volunteers were women with spare time who could afford not to worry about their daily survival because of personal financial resources.[18] As in Western Europe, those with some education were also more likely to volunteer for this sort of work.

In describing the experiences of the Women's Sick and Wounded Convoy Corps, Stobart highlighted the ease with which the Bulgarian military and wounded soldiers received them. In fact, she described a conversation with Queen Eleonora that suggested the Bulgarian sovereign was eager to apply some of the principles and training of the convoy corps to the Bulgarian context.[19] Although glad to see many women willing to volunteer, Stobart called for a professional training program that would fully engage these energies in effective ways, rather than as a "game" or "past time" for the aristocracy. This unflattering diagnosis is relevant for understanding how Balkan governments dealt with women wishing to volunteer for the war effort after 1914.

Stobart's experience was exceptional. She was invited to serve at the front because she was an outsider and citizen of a country that many among the Bulgarian elite admired. Arriving with a unit that was already fully staffed by women and needing no Bulgarian logistical support, Stobart imposed few burdens on Bulgarian resources. Nor did Stobart upset existing Balkan gender regimes; she asked no local women to assist her directly, with one exception. While stationed in Kirk Kilisse, Stobart sought peasant women to help with laundry needs. She attributed her success in recruiting them to the promise of better nourishment as volunteers. In addition, the job of washerwoman upset no gender norms in Bulgaria at that time. In short, Stobart's help was easy to accept as exceptional and necessary without disturbing local gender norms. The Women's Sick and Wounded Convoy Corps stood out, clearly separated from other women and male medical personnel they came in contact with. Finally, because this was a small group of 16 (3 doctors, 6 nurses, 3 cooks, and 4 helpers), the Women's Sick and Wounded Convoy Corps was barely visible in the larger picture of the war. This pattern of West European exceptionalism in terms of women's participation in uniform was repeated during the Great War.

A similar picture of women's participation in the Balkan wars in Serbia emerges from journals and memoirs penned by other Red Cross volunteers from Great Britain. Although these women's presence in nursing uniforms was easily accepted by the military and civilians, the Serbian authorities did little to enhance the ranks of their own nurses through any sustained support. Serbian historian Božica Mladenović, however, provides data that suggest some important achievements in this regard: "At the beginning of the First Balkan War, the female humanitarian society '*Kolo srpskih sestara* [Serbian women's circle]' gave to the '*Ministarstvo vojno* [War Ministry]' a list of 1,500 military nurses from all social groups."[20] Mladenović provides no further details about the training of these nurses. But their number and social diversity are impressive in the larger context painted here. It suggests that in 1914, Serbian society was potentially better prepared than Romania or Bulgaria to deal with the casualties of the war and certainly more welcoming of women in uniform than the other two. In Serbia, we already see another element of social acceptance of women in uniform during the Balkan wars, their characterization as soldiers volunteering directly for frontline service.

Romania's involvement in the Balkan wars was far less extensive than other Balkan countries, and women played a minor role in this regard. Yet the cholera epidemic that exploded among Romanian troops in the summer of 1913 brought to the front a number of volunteer nurses and caught the attention of Princess Marie, the future queen. In her memoir, Marie stated that the horrendous ravages made by the cholera epidemic in those days became a turning point for her.[21] She understood what public role she would have to play as a moral leader and caretaker of the Romanian people. But the queen initiated no measures at that time. The nursing school that opened in Bucharest in 1913 was a starting point for the Sanitary Division to enhance the training of women nurses.

THE GREAT WAR: LESSONS NOT LEARNED

Though most of the Balkans had been embroiled in wars for several years before 1914, these states were ill prepared for the total mobilization that started that summer. The effects of military campaigns in the First and Second Balkan Wars had been disastrous for both soldiers and civilians. Adequate care for the wounded remained in short supply, as Stobart had noted and as Queen Elenora of Bulgaria and Queen Marie of Romania recognized. Where trained female personnel like those of the Women's Sick and Wounded Convoy Corps could be brought in, they substantially benefited the wounded soldiers. Casualties were significantly higher when such trained personnel were unavailable. To make matters worse, the unsanitary conditions in many overcrowded areas where civilians had found refuge gave rise to epidemics like cholera and typhoid fever, which spread quickly and killed many. Yet these countries' military and political leaders took no substantial measures to train their large and willing female populations in providing essential medical and logistical support for the war effort.

The Red Cross sent numerous units into the Balkans, and some members left detailed firsthand accounts of these problems:

> The greatest lack [in Romania] seems to be nurses. There seems to be none except a few who have come out with special units and cannot leave them. In these Roumanian hospitals, practically any woman who wears a cap is allowed to do surgical dressings and operating-room work. All other work is considered uninteresting and is left to the servants. One wishes that the nurses could be scattered about where the need is greatest.[22]

Outside observers were left to note these problems with frustration. They could assist and observe but had no authority over the general organization and allocation of medical personnel in the military.

Few reliable institutions offered good-quality medical assistance to the war effort. One was the Red Cross. In hospitals run by the Red Cross, women featured prominently as nurses, volunteers, and various types of assistants, much as they had in the Balkan wars. Yet most of these units, especially in Romania and Serbia, were run by doctors and nurses from England, France, and the United States. In joining the Entente, Serbia and Romania continued to receive support from the American and British Red Cross. Nationals of the Allied powers withdrew, however, when Bulgaria entered the war on the side of the Central powers.

Local women were seldom the leaders of Balkan medical endeavors, in part because so few of them had proper training: Serbia boasted 25 female doctors in an army of around 500,000 mobilized soldiers at the beginning of the war. We have no reliable total accounts for Romania, but the numbers were proportionally around the same—tiny. Neither the Red Cross nor any other organization stipulated a standard nursing uniform. In general, women wore white outfits with a red cross featured somewhere prominently on their headdress, an armband, or on an apron.

Another group of foreign female volunteers provided substantial support in Serbia and Romania, the Scottish Women's Hospitals founded by Dr. Elsie Inglis. Motivated by the same combination of suffragist aspirations and dedication to medical care as Stobart, Inglis spent two tours of duty in Serbia and later in Romania, including time as a prisoner of war. She died in 1917, on her way back to Edinburgh, having served thousands of wounded soldiers on both sides of the conflict and led numerous all-women medical units close to fighting zones.

These women in uniform provided medical care for the wounded, as well as a powerful example of the efficacy of women's caretaking efforts in the war. The Scottish Women's Hospitals, particularly Inglis's example, inspired Serbian women to take up similar professional and political goals:

> To the great joy of our Serbian women, [male surgeons] no longer proclaimed the fact that surgery was not a woman's sphere. This is but one of the services Dr. Inglis has rendered our woman movement in Serbia. Today we have several active societies working for the enfranchisement of women, and there is no doubt that the record of the Scottish Women's Hospital, organized and equipped by a Suffrage society and entirely run by women, is helping us greatly towards the realization of our goal. It was a cause of delight to our women and of no small surprise to our men that the Scottish Units that came out never had male administrators.

Inglis extended her feminist aspirations toward Serbian women themselves, declaring in 1915, "When the war is over, I want to do something lasting for your country. I want to help the women and children; so little has been done for them, and they need so much. I should like to see Serbian qualified nurses and up-to-date women's and children's hospitals."[23] In 1917, as she was dying, Inglis spoke with regret about work left unfinished, and it is possible this is one of the issues she had in mind.

Despite Serbian adulation of the Scottish Women's Hospitals volunteers during the war and the admiration many in Serbia professed towards Inglis, there is no evidence that the Scottish medical units or any other activism by foreign women in uniform had a substantial impact on either military officials or politicians. Serbian women received no political rights at the end of the war. Nursing continued to be provided primarily by the Red Cross, with little support from the newly established Yugoslav state. Women's education lagged men's; higher education was primarily for professions to which women were generally not admitted. Though women were admitted into medical schools at the very end of the nineteenth century, they had a hard time finding employment. Other professions, like architecture, engineering, and law, restricted licensure exams to men until well into the interwar period.

Several historians have written about how uniforms marked the women of the Scottish Women's Hospitals and freed them from the normal gender restrictions. Lesbian volunteers serving near the front, for instance, found an openness and freedom in intimate relations they would not have enjoyed at home. Vera "Jack" Holme and Evelina Haverfield served in the same unit primarily in Serbia; they were able to experience intimacy out in the open: "Eve and I sleep out and I have rigged up our moskito [*sic*] net in quite a swell manner."[24] Holme was part of a "small lesbian circle" that served in Romania as well, where Inglis also spent some time.[25] Several scholars have hinted that Inglis herself may have been a lesbian.[26]

Whether or not same-sex unencumbered intimacy was one of the rewards for these women volunteers, they greatly relished the homosociality offered by camp conditions. Ishobel Ross left a journal of her months in Serbia with the Scottish Women's Hospitals. Her daily jottings revolve around the moments she was able to steal away from the drudgery of intense work to prank her companions, go swimming, or visit nearby areas on horseback. The sense of adventure that animated many young men who went into war in the summer of 1914 seemed to characterize the attitude of these young women as well, enabling them to confront fear and death more easily.[27] It is also possible that the lightheartedness these women projected in their autobiographies had something to do with not being part of the local communities. I have found no autobiographical writings by any Balkan women who volunteered in the war that offer such a whimsical, even campy, portrait of life at the front.

The impact of Western European women donning Red Cross, Scottish Women's Hospitals, or Women's Sick and Wounded Convoy Corps uniforms was felt in Romania, Serbia, and, to some extent, Bulgaria, especially among the soldiers who benefitted from their services. Some civilians, especially other local women volunteers, also interacted with these foreigners. Queen Marie, in particular, wrote effusively about these foreign nurses and doctors.[28] But foreign volunteers, few in number and widely scattered, could not match the visibility and interconnectedness of local volunteers in their own communities. Assessing the impact of Balkan women in uniform on their societies is difficult. The paucity of materials on this topic contrasts greatly with the wealth of diaries, memoirs, and photographs left by the British volunteers who spent time in the Balkans. What follows is perforce impressionistic; it cannot pretend to be a comprehensive account of developments in the Balkans between 1914 and 1919. Instead, reflecting my personal research interests, it will focus predominantly on Romania.

ROMANIA

The medical assistance effort in Romania during the war shifted with the fortunes of the Romanian armies. Initially, Romania sided with the Central powers, but between 1914 and 1916, the country split between supporters of the old alliance, among them King Carol I and the Conservative Party, and supporters of the Triple Entente, especially Prince Ferdinand and Princess Marie. In August 1916, Romania changed sides, and its armies were quickly challenged by the Central powers. By December, the armies retreated northward; they returned to the southern part of the country only after March 1918.

Initially, the military's all-male sanitary corps was assisted by the Red Cross, headed after May 1915 by one of Romania's prominent politicians, Alexandru Marghiloman. Before 1916, the male leaders of the Romanian Red Cross neither sought nor obtained voluntary support from many women. Irina Câmpineanu founded a separate Red Cross of the Ladies of Romania in 1906 to bypass the interdiction against women in the older Red Cross organization. Absent this effort led by women themselves, the male leaders of the Romanian Red Cross would have not seen fit to engage 50% of the population in wartime medical assistance.

In 1915, the two organizations came together, with Câmpineanu now honorary director and Marghiloman as managing director. One complicating factor was that Marghiloman supported the Central powers. In fact, while the Romanian government and army retreated toward Moldova and set up a temporary government in Iași, Marghiloman stayed in Bucharest and continued to manage the Red Cross under the German occupation. Câmpineanu, on the other hand, favored the Entente, as did future Queen Marie, who took a personal interest in the Red Cross.

Marghiloman seems to have made no special effort to attract female volunteers to Red Cross hospitals that operated in the occupied parts of Romania. An interesting oral testimony suggests that, at most, he responded to women's own offers to volunteer.[29] The memoirs of several women who spent the war under occupation and volunteered for the Red Cross confirm the somewhat disorganized and certainly decentralized operation of these hospitals.[30] We have substantial evidence from many sources that women wanted to volunteer and were present in these hospitals, tending to the needs of wounded soldiers, sometimes even facilitating the escape of Romanian prisoners of war to unoccupied Romania.[31]

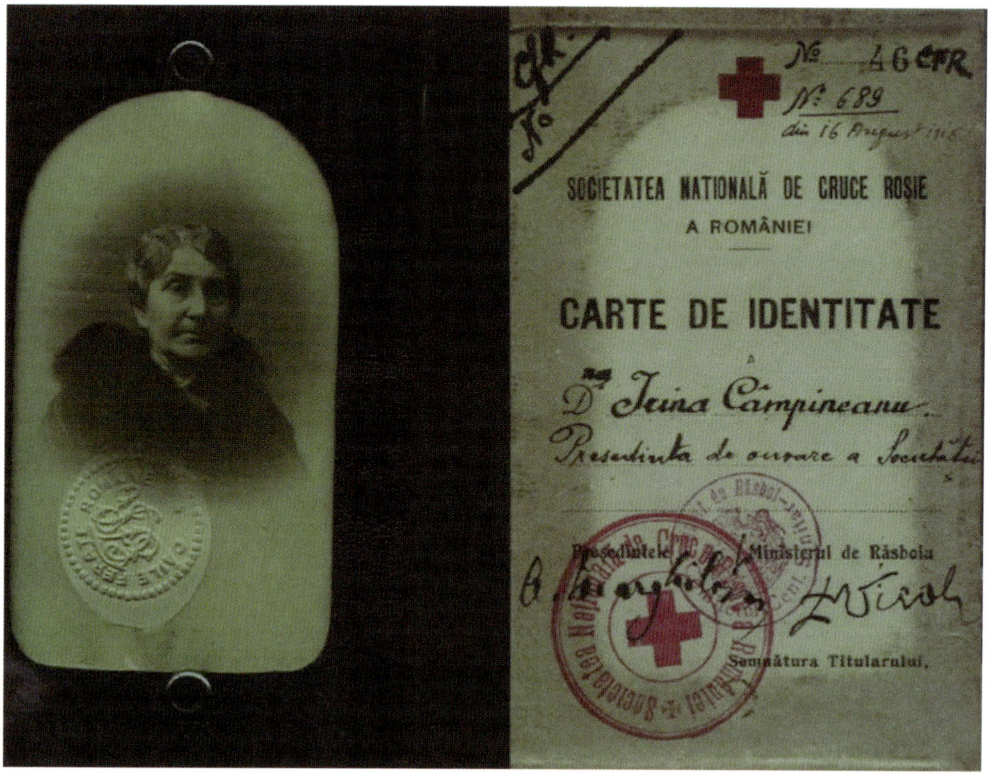

Figure 13.1.
Irina Câmpineanu (1854–1919), founder in 1906 and president of the Red Cross of the Ladies of Romania. Used by permission, collection of Rucsandra Pop.

The most efficient Bucharest hospital operated under the auspices of the National Orthodox Society of Romanian Women and its president, Alexandrina Cantacuzino.

As the country split in two, the Red Cross leadership itself split into several efforts that lessened the effectiveness of medical support. Red Cross hospitals in Moldova operated more autonomously and benefited from the direct help of French, British, Russian, and American allies. Local women sometimes volunteered in these places, but most had not received much, if any, training; professional personnel tended to keep them at arm's length or send them to menial work like laundry and cooking. Autobiographical writings attest to the tension between the trained personnel and volunteers.[32]

Several fictional accounts of the war provide an even more colorful picture of these tensions. One short story published after the war, entitled "The Lady from the Red Cross," describes the work done by some elite women as a fashion fad that largely interfered with the actual work of the male doctors.[33] From ill-fitting uniforms to overpowering perfume, these women were described as vapid and useless, as the cover of the volume illustrates.

A novel written soon after the war focuses intensely on the erotic adventures of the nurses and doctors stationed at a hospital for the wounded, modeled after a real hospital that Queen Marie helped set up during the war with the financial and logistical support of wealthy friends. *Neamul coţofănesc* (The magpie people) is quite unusual in its themes and its

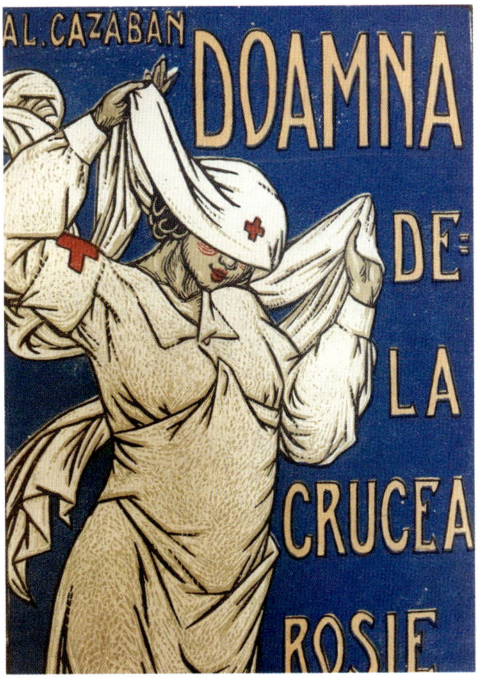

Figure 13.2.
Front cover, Alexandru Cazaban, Doamna de la Crucea Roșie *(Bucharest: Minerva, 1919).*

insistence in painting nurses' effort in the war in terms of their sexual escapades.[34] Depicted by literary critics and historians as a scandalous satire, the book is a great deal more.[35] It offers a modernist analysis of total war, with female characters present front and center in articulating the author's vision. The nurses' complete dedication to the wounded extends into the erotic: They "performed their nursing duties with a crazed energy; even better than before. They found new strength in their erotic excitement, especially in the opportunity they had to tend to the wounded and sneak once in a while in the bed of some with lesser wounds."[36] Dumitru Barnoschi depicted this eroticism as a form of assertiveness derived from the nurses' understanding of the horrors of war and their new roles in the world wrought by war: "a new social psychology and a new morality of relations between men and women. This oeuvre is the avant-garde of a transformation that will encompass humanity."[37] This combination of Eros and Thanatos is reminiscent of the playful eroticism of the British nurses mentioned above. Though rendered in sexually explicit and satirical images, the message seems to come close to the embattled experiences of so many hundreds of thousands of young men who found themselves fighting and rotting in a war without end.

Although this observer found a somewhat sympathetic and nuanced way to depict the extreme experiences of nurses on the front, most women who left autobiographical writings about the wartime were starker in their portrayals. On the one hand, there is little sympathy for women less than completely dedicated to the nursing effort: "If all the nurses had been as dedicated to their duties as Mrs. Demetriade, we wouldn't have had any defections, but they weren't; there were always some who refused one thing or another to my wounded."[38] On the other hand, volunteer female medical personnel hinted at the lack of respect for their efforts by the male doctors with whom they worked. Jeana Fodoreanu, one of the few female doctors, ran a sanitary train during the war; she overheard interactions such as this one:

> "Doctor, we have here a madam [*cocoană*] with relations in Jerusalem, and things will go badly for you when she starts to give orders; you saw how she swept the floor with the other doctor, even though he was the nephew of a general." And then I hear the voice of the doctor: "no worries, buddy, if she messes with me I'll send her flying through the window, I'm not afraid of any hag [*muiere*]."[39]

Figure 13.3.
Postcard of a hospital at the front (1917). Personal collection.

Among the comments made by men and the press, such disrespectful references to women who volunteered their time without any compensation were noticeably more frequent than any praise.

Queen Marie, who wore a variety of uniforms and took on a variety of personas, settled on a white nurse's outfit and the moniker "mother of the wounded" during the war. Marie's autobiographical writings are peppered with references to this term; she took a great deal of pride in her special name. But it may not have been unique. Contemporary writings indicate that the term was used more widely for other nurses and women doctors. Before Marie, Queen Elisabeth had also borne the title.[40]

Between 1916 and 1918, Marie helped raise funds for an ambulance service to the front, as well as several hospitals and soup kitchens. She spent a great deal of time and effort visiting these hospitals, providing direct assistance to the wounded. The fund-raising efforts, in particular, banked on the currency of the nursing uniform as a symbol of purity and patriotism and on Queen Marie's modeling of it. The Romanian Red Cross committee in France sold thousands of postcards featuring the queen in her Red Cross uniform; it was a favorite souvenir for those who wished to contribute money. She spent many hours over the course of the war signing these postcards as thank you gifts to those who attended her fund-raising events.[41]

The queen's fund-raising talents and generous spirit are undeniable. Yet her self-identification with nursing and her leadership in efforts to improve the poor quality

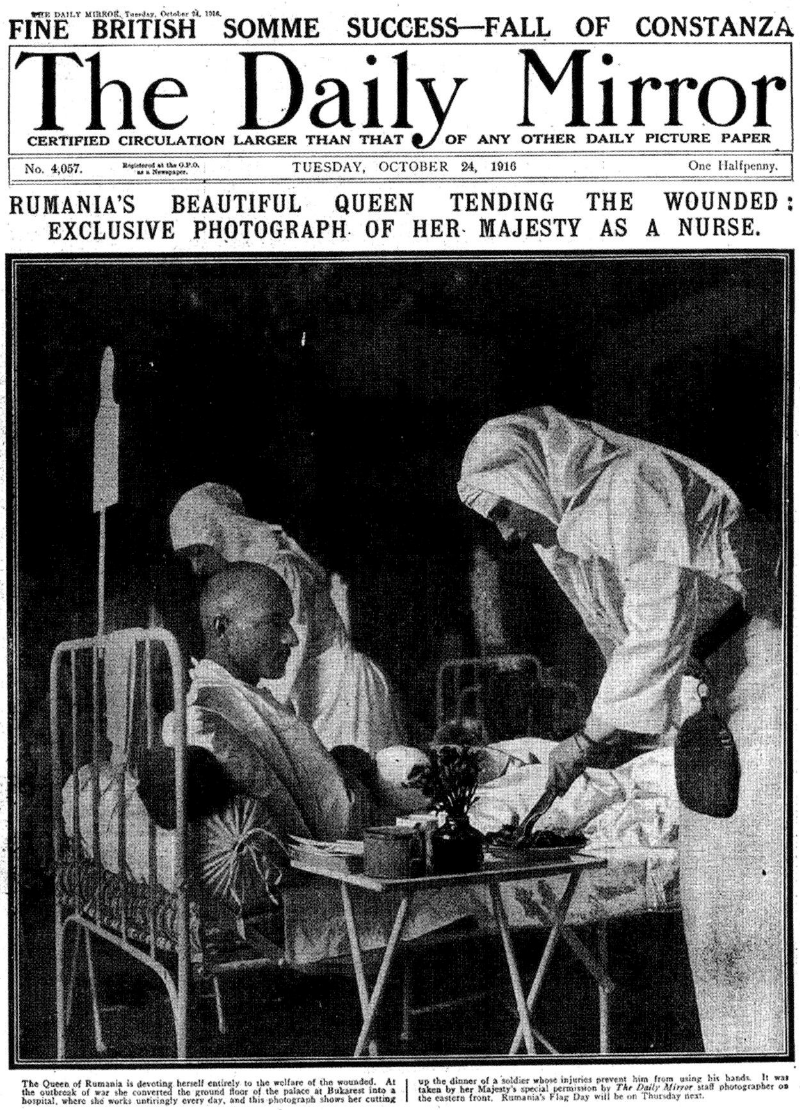

THE DAILY MIRROR, Tuesday, October 24, 1916.

FINE BRITISH SOMME SUCCESS—FALL OF CONSTANZA

The Daily Mirror

CERTIFIED CIRCULATION LARGER THAN THAT OF ANY OTHER DAILY PICTURE PAPER

No. 4,057. Registered at the G.P.O. as a Newspaper. TUESDAY, OCTOBER 24, 1916 One Halfpenny.

RUMANIA'S BEAUTIFUL QUEEN TENDING THE WOUNDED: EXCLUSIVE PHOTOGRAPH OF HER MAJESTY AS A NURSE.

The Queen of Rumania is devoting herself entirely to the welfare of the wounded. At the outbreak of war she converted the ground floor of the palace at Bukarest into a hospital, where she works untiringly every day, and this photograph shows her cutting up the dinner of a soldier whose injuries prevent him from using his hands. It was taken by her Majesty's special permission by *The Daily Mirror* staff photographer on the eastern front. Rumania's Flag Day will be on Thursday next.

Figure 13.4.
Front page, Daily Mirror, *24 October 1916.*

of medical support for the army and civilians had deleterious effects as well. She was ill equipped to make any decisions about the urgent needs of the army, a task she often delegated to others more qualified. Marie seems to have made no concerted effort to push for training more nurses from among the many women volunteers in the hospitals. She modeled a certain image of the caretaker that appealed to many women, offering a kind word, cigarettes, flowers, but little else. This image, beautiful yet inadequate for the needs of the war, provided a false sense of ease for those who wished to volunteer for the effort. To the queen's credit, her intentions were most likely of a propaganda type—aiming to get money and human resources for medical care. But the results were not adequate in terms of the quality of the services offered.

In addition, although professionally trained nurses (the few hundred from among both Romanian and foreign Red Cross ranks) received a modest stipend for their efforts, the overwhelming majority of women donning the nurse's uniform were unremunerated volunteers. In essence, they were considered financially self-sustaining, despite a regime that denied them any legal right to the familial resources administered solely by their husbands or fathers.[42] Any cash not expressly theirs could not be drawn from the bank or, in the case of a husband's death, from the insurance company. Nelli Cornea, an elderly woman who volunteered for the Red Cross during the war, became destitute over months of rising prices and dwindling food supplies. In addition to spending hours every day in a hospital tending to the wounded, she took care of her ailing husband. When he died and she attempted to collect on his life insurance, she was told unceremoniously that only her son, who was off fighting the war, could cash it.[43] Similar financial pressures drove some nurses who received the Queen Marie Sanitary Cross for their sacrifice and heroism to ask for financial rewards instead. Their efforts went unheeded.[44]

What were the larger economic and social implications of wearing a uniform, even being decorated for one's patriotism, during and after the war? Over a thousand Romanian women received the Queen Marie Cross.[45] The decoration was not awarded solely to women (or men) in uniform, but it was overwhelmingly associated with the nursing uniform. Women took pride in receiving this decoration, as several autobiographical accounts show.[46] But did this wartime honor translate into wider social recognition, elevated status, or the gratitude of the state they had served? Anecdotal evidence suggests social rewards were both hard to come by and fleeting. No economic benefits were to be derived from women's decorations, in contrast to decorations offered exclusively to men in uniform, who after the war received entitlements to reduced prices for various public goods, lifelong pensions they could pass down to their heirs, and property rights over public lands. At least three women received the otherwise male Military Virtue medal for their sacrifices in the war. This decoration, according to the postwar veterans' law, entitled recipients and their heirs to receive land and such benefits as pensions and free access to public transportation. There is no evidence these women or their heirs ever received such benefits, which suggests the male exclusivist intention of the policy.[47]

At best, on occasion, decorated women could stand taller and challenge some of the male leaders in the military when they sought support or tried to defend themselves against false accusations. Jeana Fodoreanu narrated one incident in which she came to blows with one of the medical officers she served with. Although she did not report to him, the officer sought to control Fodoreanu's activities and eventually falsely accused her of stealing supplies. When this happened, she took to wearing her Queen Marie Cross, together with another war decoration received from the French government, as a means of representing her unimpeachable honor.[48] Sometimes the strategy worked; other times, it led male officers to further insults, such as stating that they needed no tin adornments to do their jobs properly. It is inconceivable that such a remark would be addressed to any decorated male soldier. A double standard operated even in this case of selfless dedication to the war cause and heroism.

No exact figures are available for how many women in Romania volunteered as nurses. We do know that over a thousand women were decorated, and it is clear that many more served in nurses' uniform. Evidence about them is meager. Memoirs and diaries such as Fodoreanu's are few; autobiography was a novel genre in Romania and especially sparse among women.[49] This lack makes broader generalizations far more difficult for Romanian women in uniform than for British, who were far more prolific in recounting their experience.

The impact of Romanian women's activities as uniformed members of voluntary medical groups remained marginal in relation to the wider society. The press had little to say about them, lavishing instead all its attention on the charismatic queen as the "mother of the wounded." Only faint echoes of how these women understood their participation and wished to be seen more broadly in society appear in the few autobiographical writings published in the postwar decade or in speeches made at war commemorations by leaders of women's organizations years after the conclusion of hostilities.[50] Their frustrations became palpable as the postwar political establishment came to ignore calls by a variety of women's groups to enfranchise women, partly on the basis of the activities they had undertaken during the war in support of Romania's cause.

There is a tangible tension in how various individuals, very much along gender lines, understood these actions as being linked to larger questions of citizenship rights and obligations. In 1931, Radu R. Rosetti, who had served on the front during the war and had observed the activities of the women volunteers for the Red Cross, wrote:

> It must stated that, regarding [the recruitment of voluntary female medical assistants], the Red Cross has been greatly disappointed. Too few ladies and young women answered our appeal. . . . The great majority seem not to understand that today, when woman asks for rights, she also has obligations to satisfy, and the more she will show conscientiousness in upholding her duties—among them taking care of her fellow men is one of the most natural—the easier it will be for her to convince many more about the necessity to grant them new rights.[51]

The article continued by articulating the additional important benefit to be derived from attending voluntary courses: "Notions of hygiene that are necessary for every woman for whom the role of mother, wife, and housekeeper is not just boring and unworthy of the modern woman."[52]

This barely masked derogatory depiction of feminism in Romania says more about the reaction of the political and military male establishment to women's initial demands that the state recognize and reward their contribution to the war effort than it does about the radicalism of the feminist requests or the lack of interest on the part of women to enter the medical profession. Rosetti was not unaware of women's contributions in the war. Both his direct experience and his role after the war as manager of the National Military Museum exposed him to evidence of the actions of women as volunteers with the sanitary service on the front and to requests by those women to have a marker for their contributions supported by the military establishment. The request went unanswered.[53] Rosetti seemed uninterested in responding to those who had already contributed and received no recognition for their efforts, other than the Queen Marie Cross.

In 1919, the Romanian government and army made it perfectly clear how they regarded women's war contributions.[54] The parliament passed a law that defined heroism as exclusively masculine and linked it strictly to serving on the front (though male medical officers and aids were included) and listed what benefits war veterans, war wounded, widows, and orphans would receive. The gender of these various categories is unambiguous in Romanian, where the universalizing masculine often hides institutionalized sexism. In this case, however, things were very clear: Soldiers, veterans, and the war wounded were all men, widows were all women, and orphans were both genders. Thus, any woman who had been deemed a soldier during the war, as, for instance, Fodoreanu had been called by high officers of the Romanian army, were relegated to invisibility and inconsequentiality. Overall, the nursing uniform and the decorations women had received for heroism amounted to nothing after the war. Only if their husbands or sons had died in the war in uniform would women receive any direct benefits from the Romanian state.

The time spent, work undertaken, and sacrifices made on behalf of the war effort, placing country and army above the safety and needs of one's family, had no material value when it came to women, whether they were in uniform or not. Rather, these activities fell under Rosetti's definition of "natural" female duties. And if "natural," the gender logic of the day went, why would women need training and remuneration for such work? As in other Balkan states, this shortsighted view of caretaking gender roles on the part of the Red Cross hampered the development of nursing as a profession.

Though Romanian women had not experienced as many opportunities for employment and empowerment before and during the war as women in Britain, the work many did in hospitals and on the front between 1916 and 1918 were experiences they valued and wished to capitalize on as professionals, not just volunteers. The male leadership of the Red Cross refused to grant them this opportunity. Instead, other initiatives came to fill this void; prominent among them was the eugenicist inspired Institute for Social Assistance, founded in 1929 by Veturia Manuilă.[55] Romanian women's experience in uniform during the Great War remained fruitless and a lesson in the unflinching patriarchal conservatism of the political class and military leadership.

SERBIA AND BULGARIA

In her multiple trips through the Balkans during the Second Balkan War and then the Great War, Stobart remarked on occasion about the numerous women who had stepped out of the home to volunteer for the war effort that she encountered in hospitals throughout

Serbia and Bulgaria.[56] Other foreign witnesses included similar observations in their diaries or memoirs from the war. On the basis of these anecdotal accounts and several studies focusing on women's organizations in the Balkans during and after the Great War, we can surmise that there was little broad coordination between philanthropic work done during the war and the postwar development of women's rights.[57] Though thousands of volunteers served in Red Cross or other improvised nurse uniforms during the war, women did not succeed in making the case for greater citizenship rights after the Great War. The contexts of the two countries were vastly different by 1919, though the results in terms of women's position in society ended up somewhat similar.

After the war, Serbia saw its role increase manifold in relation to the territories acquired from the Habsburg Empire. Political and military leaders came to define contributions in the war and rewards for the service offered in very specific ways that privileged a Serbian, Orthodox Christian, and ethnonationalist version of patriotism and self-sacrifice. In this universe, many categories of individuals who had fought or offered assistance during the war as volunteers came to be excluded or marginalized. The worthiness of Croatian soldiers' service in the war in the Habsburg army came to be questioned as worthy of pensions or commemorations.[58] In Romania, soldiers from Transylvania who had served in the Habsburg army during the war met similar fates.[59] The service of women from areas acquired from the Habsburg Empire became similarly silenced or disregarded in public considerations of the war effort.[60]

As in Romania, thousands of Serbian and Montenegrin women volunteered for the war as doctors or nurses.[61] Given their Orthodox allegiance and open nationalist sentiments, one might have expected these organizations and their members to be recognized by the Serbian-dominated postwar government. There is no evidence, however, that any such recognition took place at the national level. Though a number of women serving as soldiers on the front did receive recognition through medals, monuments, and other symbolic actions, after the war, life continued unchanged for those who volunteered in noncombatant uniforms. As in Romania, only widows and orphans received benefits as family members of soldiers who died in the war.[62]

In Bulgaria, similar informal efforts to work with the Red Cross and under the leadership of Queen Eleonora resulted in some temporary relief for the wounded but did not give rise to longer-term recognition of women's contributions or a change in how nursing connected to sanitary assistance in the military. Already during the Balkan wars, the queen had invited and welcomed Red Cross doctors and other international medical support to help with the wounded as well as to provide models for the Bulgarian women who sought to participate in the war effort. In 1914 and in view of the huge gaps in medical assistance during the Balkan wars, Eleonora asked Helen Scott Hay, the seasoned administrator of a nursing school in the United States and representative of the Red Cross, to come to Bulgaria to establish a nursing school. The queen provided funds with the goal of emulating the curriculum in Hay's school and preparing many more Bulgarian women to become professionally trained and ready for the sorts of medical challenges that soon engulfed the army during the Great War. Hay was able to stay in Bulgaria long enough to establish a small class of six at one of the central hospitals in Sofia but left with Bulgaria's entry into the war on the side of the Central powers.[63] Though the six women used their training successfully during the war, the initiative never grew beyond that initial small effort.

The queen's death in 1917 put an end to the work she had been involved with. When Hay returned to Bulgaria in 1921 to restart the nursing school, Eleonora's son, King Boris, was decidedly less effusive about the initiative than his mother had been. In a meeting with Hay, he stated, "It is my most earnest hope . . . that the best families of Bulgaria will permit their daughters to take up the study of nursing."[64] But he did nothing to further this idea. Several more years passed before a nursing school was reestablished, with the first public health nurse, Boyana Christova, taking a leading role in this profession in 1924.[65]

In essence, the experience women had serving as nurses or in other medical support capacities during the Great War had only a faint impact on how women as citizens and nursing as a profession relevant in the military were treated after 1918 in the Balkans. Even though a high level of support for female nursing existed in all Balkan countries among the queens and princesses of these young states, the efforts made by women in hospitals, in train stations, on the front, and in public spaces affected by the fighting soon faded from public attention and have remained largely invisible in the historiography of the war. The only exception is the feats of women fighting as soldiers.

SWORN VIRGINS AND MANLY GIRLS

The Serbian case stands out in terms of the number of women who served as soldiers in the Great War. This level of participation needs to be contextualized in relation to a longer tradition, the "sworn virgins," prevalent in Albania but with historic examples in Serbia, Montenegro, and Macedonia. In some communities that today are part of these respective countries, young women occasionally took on a cross-dressing gender presentation and committed themselves to representing their family's interests by acting as male warriors rather than according to customary female gender roles.[66] Some of these sworn virgins returned to more traditional female roles later in life. There are cases documented by foreign travelers from the early nineteenth century, and this tradition continues today.

In 1914, therefore, there were relatively more women in the western Balkans trained to handle firearms and who dressed as male than in other parts of the peninsula. The normality of the practice rendered these transgender individuals—who presented themselves as male and whose families acknowledged them as such—an occurrence that did not raise eyebrows among the rank and file when some of these sworn virgins signed up to serve in the war in uniform. But can we even consider these individuals as "women," in a sociocultural rather than biological sense?

This is a complicated question, which pertains primarily to how we understand gender norms in the Balkans at that time. Those who have studied the institution of the sworn virgin have come to little consensus, but the controversy with this issue rests primarily in the binary heteronormative framework through which observers and most scholars have insisted on understanding these transgender individuals.[67] The language for what the sworn virgins represented has done very little in moving us beyond the binary. Being sworn virgins represents only a small fraction of what these individuals took on as gender roles. These cis women renounced their traditional gender roles for a variety of reasons (familial, financial, military, or sexual) and lived in the company of men, self-presenting as men and participating in the social roles usually assigned to cis men. They were transgressors of the biological binary undergirding gender norms, but not of the social gender order overall. This becomes clearest when we view the return of some of these transgender individuals to traditional, heterosexual gender roles by resuming female dress, marrying, and having children. In short, while these individuals dressed and assumed male roles, they were to be considered males, and socially, we cannot define them as women. Therefore, there is a category of Serbian soldiers who fought in the war as men, though biologically they had been born women and might have left behind records as female.

It is possible, though I am simply speculating here, that this tradition rendered the presence of cis women in male uniform as regular soldiers a more acceptable occurrence in Serbia than in other combatant Balkan states. If we compare the number of women who served in the Serbian army as soldiers with those in other Balkan states, there is a remarkable difference. The historiography on this topic is sparse, so again, one must rely on incomplete and often anecdotal information. But according to a recent overview, there was some acceptance in the military that women would, on occasion, volunteer to fight on the front.[68] Some had volunteered in the Balkan wars. Others fought as partisans in occupation zones, as part of a guerrilla war tradition that went back centuries, primarily as wives or lovers or daughters of men in these paramilitary units. Of course, the partisans were not uniformed individuals, but the presence of women among these armed forces most likely rendered more acceptable requests by women to join the official armed forces in the Great War.

One evocative case is that of Milunka Savić, who served as a soldier with unparalleled distinction. Savić volunteered early in the war, by some accounts impersonating her brother.[69] Savić distinguished herself through remarkable feats, such as capturing 23 Bulgarian soldiers single-handedly.[70] Over the course of the war, she became the most decorated woman, with at least eight decorations to her credit, including two Legion d'Honneur medals from France, the Cross of St. George from Russia, the Most Distinguished Order of St. Michael from Great Britain, and the Milos Obilić Medal from Serbia. She was also the only woman to receive the Croix de Guerre in the Great War and "could have received a French pension if she had moved there."[71]

As spectacular as Savić's accomplishments were, so was the disregard of the Yugoslav state, political establishment, and military leadership after the war toward this soldier. Savić received no official recognition for her service in the Serbian army as a veteran. Had she wanted to move to France, she would have become a celebrated war veteran with a handsome pension. Instead, she became a janitor and lived in obscurity and poverty for the rest of her life. According to one account, the few benefits Savić enjoyed on the basis of her service in the war were having her life spared in a concentration camp in World War II because a German officer recognized her contributions in the Great War, being buried with military honors, and having a street named after her.[72] This case shows similarities to the way women who served heroically in Romania during the war were treated.

If the Yugoslav state did not do anything for Savić until she was dead, one can only surmise that it did even less for other less decorated women who served in uniform or as partisans during the war. Starting in World War II, the contribution of women to various partisan groups paved the way to the rise of female figures in the Yugoslav army and Communist Party as leaders and to the beginnings of women's fuller participation in the armed forces. Military institutions in communist regimes established in the Balkans after World War II never attempted to bring about gender equality. One cannot therefore speak of any long-term institutional effects of women's participation in the Great War as soldiers.[73] This is a view confirmed by historian Jelena Batinić, who in a recent study concluded that "these women were, for the most part, exceptional, and all of them together do not constitute a 'female military tradition.'"[74] In her chapter in this volume, Laurie Stoff concludes similarly that the much larger number of female soldiers who served Russia in the Great War did not manage to dislodge the notion that their efforts were "exceptional" in relation to "normal" gender roles.

I am not aware of any Bulgarian examples similar to that of Savić, but Romania offers a handful of cases, most prominently that of Ecaterina Teodoroiu, though we know of at least two other women, Lucreția Cânja and Maria Manciulea, who served on the front and received the Military Virtue decoration. Teodoroiu volunteered after her brother was killed and fought in male garb as a way to blend in. She was not a sworn virgin, though she has often been referred to as a "virgin" in the literature.[75] In real life, Teodoroiu was a teacher engaged to be married when her fiancé left for the front, the state of her sexual activities unknown. After being wounded in battle, Teodoroiu was made an officer in the Romanian army and soon returned to the front. She died in one of the most horrendous battles of the war and was buried with military honors at the site of the battle.[76]

Rather than a virgin or a Romanian Joan of Arc, as historians have insisted in identifying her, Teodoroiu can be better understood as simply a case of uncommon courage and dedication. According to a Romanian law passed in 1919, her sacrifice as a soldier should have entitled Teodoroiu's parents to a pension.[77] I am not aware of any such pension being awarded to the Teodoroiu family. Instead, a number of monuments were erected during the interwar period in parts of Romania connected to her life story, celebrating her heroism and sacrifice, always in the same exceptionalist language used in the press: "the virgin from Jiu" and "the manly girl."[78] To date, the Romanian army, though it now has several generations of female officers in its ranks, refuses to use the female form for soldier, officer, or any other rank in the army. In short, the masculinist universalist assumptions about military service that dominated this institution in 1918 continue unabated, silencing women's participation.

BALKAN WOMEN AND UNIFORMS

Balkan women participated in the wars between 1912 and 1918 in a number of ways. In the Great War, they donned uniforms as nurses and soldiers to assist the military effort directly or to engage with the effects of the war on the civilian population. We do not have a systematic accounting of how many women served in any of these capacities since they mostly volunteered informally. But we know from personal accounts that they were visible to many wounded soldiers and other needy individuals and that they provided essential assistance for the survival and well-being of the people they came in contact with.

Most visible in these roles were urban educated women from the upper classes, who served in hospitals set up by the Red Cross and other international and local organizations. Peasant and lower-class women, most of the female population in the Balkan states, predominantly served by taking on the economic roles needed for the survival of their families. Putting on a uniform was neither a realistic option nor the most necessary role in societies in which the vast majority of men ages 18–45 were mobilized. In the case of Romania and Serbia, in particular, with as much as 25% of the male population off to war, someone had to take care of the crops, the children, and the elderly left behind—women. Continuing to participate in these caretaking roles under foreign occupation (in the case of Serbia and Romania) was no small matter, and many women engaged in remarkable feats of hiding, dissimulation, and resistance that have gone largely unacknowledged in the historiography.[79] When the war ended, none of these states was willing to consider women's contributions to the war and to the safety of their population as worthy of full citizenship rights, precisely at the moment when full benefits were being extended to all men for the very same reason.

The few women who served as soldiers represent exceptional examples of how women in uniform came to be regarded during and after the war. It would take another few decades and radical change in the ideological orientation of these countries before women's presence in military uniform came to be regarded as unexceptional. In 1918, however, despite the appearance of queens and princes in military garb at parades and other military events, the soldier uniform remained largely a costume, rather than the marker of an accepted social role. For women in uniform, modernity would have to wait until after the communist takeover.

NOTES

I thank Valeria Bălescu and the staff at the National Museum of Military History for their help in locating some important sources for this project. My thanks go out also to Rucsandra Pop for sharing stories and materials about Irina Câmpineanu.

1. Božica Mladenović, "Women's Mobilization for War (South East Europe)," in *1914-1918-Online: International Encyclopedia of the First World War*, ed. Ute Daniel, Peter Gatrell, Oliver Janz, Heather Jones, Jennifer Keene, Alan Kramer, and Bill Nasson (Berlin: Freie Universität Berlin, 8 Oct. 2014, https://encyclopedia.1914-1918-online.net/article/womens_mobilization_for_war_south_east_europe. (accessed 19 August 2017).

2. Maria Bucur, "The Economics of Citizenship: Gender Regimes and Property Rights in Romania in the 20th Century," in *Gender and Citizenship in Historical and Transnational Perspective*, ed. Anne Epstein and Rachel Fuchs (Basingstoke, U.K.: Palgrave, 2016), 143–165; Alin Ciupală, *Bătălia lor: Femeile din România* **în** *primul război mondial*

[Their fight: Women in Romani during the First World War] (Iași, Romania: Polirom, 2017); Krassimira Daskalova, *Women, Gender, and Modernization in Bulgaria, 1878–1944* (Sofia: Sofia University Press, 2012); Marina Vujnović, *Forging the Bubikopf Nation: Journalism, Gender, and Modernity in Interwar Yugoslavia* (New York: Peter Lang, 2009).

3. Jennifer Craik, *Uniforms Exposed: From Conformity to Transgression* (Oxford: Berg, 2005).

4. Paul Petrescu and Elena Secoșan, *Romanian Folk Costume* (Bucharest: Meridiane, 1985); Linda Welters, ed., *Folk Dress in Europe and Anatolia: Beliefs about Protection and Fertility* (Oxford: Berg, 1999).

5. See Ivo Andrić, *The Bridge on the Drina* (Chicago: University of Chicago Press, 1977 [1945]); Aleko Konstantinov, *Bai Ganyo: Incredible Tales of a Modern Bulgarian* (1895), ed. Victor A. Friedman, trans. Christina E. Kramer, Grace E. Fielder, and Catherine Rudin. (Madison: University of Wisconsin Press, 2010); Liviu Rebreanu, *Ion* (Chester Springs, Pa.: Dufour, 1965 [1920]).

6. Eunjeong Yi, *Guild Dynamics in Seventeenth-Century Istanbul: Fluidity and Leverage* (Leiden: Brill, 2004).

7. Bucur, "Economics of Citizenship"; Daskalova, *Women, Gender, and Modernization in Bulgaria*; Vujnović, *Forging the Bubikopf Nation*.

8. Dennis Hupchick, *The Balkans: From Constantinople to Communism* (New York: Springer, 2002).

9. Georgeta Nazarska, "Bulgarian Women Medical Doctors in the Social Modernization of the Bulgarian Nation State (1878–1944)," *Historical Social Research* 33, no. 2 (2008): 232–246; Christian Promitzer, Sevasti Trubeta, and Marius Turda, eds., *Health, Hygiene and Eugenics in Southeastern Europe to 1945* (Budapest: Central European University Press, 2011).

10. Ivana Pantelić, "Draga Ljočić-Milošević," in Francisca de Haan, Krassimira Daskalova, and Anna Loutfi, eds., *Biographical Dictionary of Women's Movements and Feminisms in Central, Eastern, and South Eastern Europe: 19th and 20th Centuries* (Budapest: Central European University Press, 2008), 290–292.

11. Raluca Băjenaru, "Maria Cuțarida-Crăciunescu—prima femeie medic din Romania" [Maria Cuțarida-Crăciunescu—The first woman doctor in Romania], *Medica Academica*, 1 Sept. 2011, http://medicaacademica.ro/maria-cutzarida-cra%C8%9Bunescu-prima-femeie-medic-din-romania/ (accessed 19 August 2017).

12. Ministère de la santé publique, du travail, et de l'assistance sociale, *Exposé general de l'état sanitaire de la Roumanie* (Bucharest: Cartea medicală, 1923).

13. Richard C. Hall, *The Balkan Wars 1912–1913: Prelude to the First World War* (London: Routledge, 2000).

14. Angela K. Smith, "'The Woman Who Dared': Major Mabel St Clair Stobart," in *The Women's Movement in Wartime*, ed. Alison S. Fell and Ingrid Sharp (London: Palgrave Macmillan, 2007), 158–174.

15. Mabel St Clair Stobart, *War and Women: From Experience in the Balkans and Elsewhere* (London: G. Bell & Sons, 1913), 167.

16. Stobart, *War and Women*, 65–66.

17. Ciupală, *Bătălia lor.*

18. See Bucur, "Economics of Citizenship."

19. Stobart, *War and Women*, 64.

20. Mladenović, "Women's Mobilization."

21. Marie, Queen of Roumania, *Ordeal: The Story of My Life*, vol. 1 (New York: Charles Scribner's Sons, 1935), ch. 27.

22. Sarah Elizabeth Pickett, "Nursing Service to the Civilian Population of the Allies," in *History of American Red Cross Nursing* (New York: Macmillan, 1922), 881.

23. Eva McLaren, *Elsie Inglis: The Woman with the Torch* (New York: MacMillan, 1920), 54.

24. Olga Dimitrijević and Catherine Baker, "British-Yugoslav Lesbian Networks during and after the Great War," in *Gender in 20th Century Eastern Europe and the USSR*, ed. Catherine Baker (London: Palgrave Macmillan, 2017), 55.

25. Jill Liddington, "Britain in the Balkans: The Response of the Scottish Women's Hospital Units," in *Aftermaths of the War: Women's Movements and Female Activists, 1918–1923*, ed. Ingrid Sharp and Matthew Stribbe (Leiden: Brill, 2011), 409.

26. Dimitrijević and Baker, "British-Yugoslav Lesbian Networks."

27. Ishobel Ross, *Little Grey Partridge: First World War Diary of Ishobel Ross Who Served with the Scottish Women's Hospitals Unit in Serbia* (Aberdeen: Aberdeen University Press, 1988).

28. Marie, *Ordeal.*

29. V. Brădățeanu, "'Să ne înclinăm în fața geniului rasei noastre': Alexandru Marghiloman" ["Let's bow before the genius of our race": Alexandru Marghiloman], RADOR, 26 Jan. 2016, http://www.rador.ro/2016/01/26/sa-ne-inclinam-in-fa%E1%B9%ADa-geniului-rasei-noastre-alexandru-marghiloman/ (accessed 19 August 2017).

30. Nelli Cornea, *Insemnări din vremea războiului* [Notes from wartime] (Bucharest: Ed. Librăriei H. Steinberg şi fiu, 1921); Elena Negrescu, *Jurnal de război, 1916–1918* [Wartime journal, 1916–1918] (Bucharest: Editura detectiv, 2006).

31. Maria Bucur, "Women's Stories as Sites of Memory: Remembering Romania's World Wars," in *Gender and War in Twentieth-Century Eastern Europe*, ed. Nancy M. Wingfield and Maria Bucur (Bloomington: Indiana University Press, 2006), 171–192; Ciupală, *Bătălia lor*.

32. Ciupală, *Bătălia lor*.

33. Alexandru Cazaban, *Doamna de la Crucea Roșie* [The lady from the Red Cross] (Bucharest: Minerva, 1919).

34. Dumitru V. Barnoschi, *Neamul coţofănesc* [The magpie people] (Bucharest: Cultura Românească, 1930).

35. Ciupală, *Bătălia lor*.

36. Barnoschi, *Neamul coţofănesc*, 36–37.

37. Barnoschi, *Neamul coţofănesc*, 62.

38. Cornea, *Insemnări din vremea războiului*, 66.

39. Jeana Fodoreanu, *Femee-soldat* [Woman-soldier] (Oradea: Tipografia Adolf Sonnenfeld, 1928), 87.

40. Ciupală, *Bătălia lor*; Cornea, *Insemnări din vremea războiului*.

41. Ciupală, *Bătălia lor*.

42. Bucur, "Economics of Citizenship."

43. Cornea, *Insemnări din vremea războiului*.

44. Ciupală, *Bătălia lor*.

45. Ciupală, *Bătălia lor*.

46. Fodoreanu, *Femee-soldat*; Marie, *Ordeal*.

47. Ministerul Justiţiei, *Colecţiune de legi, decrete-legi, regulamente, decrete, deciziuni ministeriale* şi *orice alte măsuri luate* în *vederea stării de război (14 aprilie 1919–31 martie 1920)* [Collection of laws, decrees, rules, ministerial decisions, and any other measures taken in regard to the state of war (14 April 1919–31 March 1920)], 3 vols. (Bucharest: Imprimeria Statului, 1920).

48. Fodoreanu, *Femee-Soldat*, 88.

49. Maria Bucur, *Heroes and Victims: Remembering War in Twentieth-Century Romania* (Bloomington: Indiana University Press, 2009).

50. Bucur, *Heroes and Victims*.

51. Radu R. Rosetti, "Crucea Roșie" [The Red Cross], *Boabe de Grâu* [Grains of wheat] 1, no. 9 (1930): 543.

52. Rosetti, "Crucea Roșie."

53. Bucur, *Heroes and Victims*.

54. Ministerul Justiţiei, *Colecţiune de legi*.

55. Maria Bucur, *Eugenics and Modernization in Interwar Romania* (Pittsburgh: Pittsburgh University Press, 2002).

56. Stobart, *War and Women*.

57. Daskalova, *Women, Gender, and Modernization in Bulgaria*; Vujnović, *Forging the Bubikopf Nation*.

58. John Paul Newman, *Yugoslavia in the Shadow of War: Veterans and the Limits of State-Building 1903–1945* (Cambridge: Cambridge University Press, 2015).

59. Bucur, *Heroes and Victims*.

60. Tina Bahoveć, "Love for the Nation in Times of War: Strategies and Discourses of the National and Political Mobilization of Slovene Women in Carinthia from 1917 to 1920," in *Gender and the First World War*, ed. Christa Hämmerle, Osvald Überegger, and Brigitta Bader-Zaar (London: Palgrave, 2014), 231–250.

61. Mladenović, "Women's Mobilization."

62. Newman, *Yugoslavia in the Shadow of War*.

63. Clara D. Noyes, "American Influence in Bulgaria Lives On: Leaves from the Note Book of Miss Noyes, Director, Red Cross Nursing Service," *Red Cross Bulletin* 5, no. 15 (11 April 1921): 5–6.

64. Noyes, "American Influence in Bulgaria," 6.

65. Kristina Popova, "Between Public Health and Social Work: Visiting Nurses in the Struggle against Poverty and Infant Mortality in Bulgaria, 1923–1934," *Social Work and Society* 9, no. 2 (2011), http://www.socwork.net/sws/article/view/271/599, (accessed 19 August 2017).

66. Mildred Dickemann, "The Balkan Sworn Virgin: A Traditional European Transperson," in *Gender Blending*, ed. Bonnie Bullough, Vern Bullough, and Charles Elias (Amherst, Mass.: Prometheus Books, 1997), 248–255; Antonia Young, *Women Who Become Men: Albanian Sworn Virgins* (London: Bloomsbury Academic, 2001).

67. Dickemann, "Balkan Sworn Virgin."

68. Mladenović, "Women's Mobilization."

69. Jelena Batinić, *Women and Yugoslav Partisans: A History of World War II Resistance* (New York: Cambridge University Press, 2015).

70. Holly Godbey, "Milunka Savić: Possibly the Most Decorated Female in the History of Warfare," War History Online, 3 Dec. 2016, https://www.warhistoryonline.com/instant-articles/milunka-savic-possibly-decorated-female-history-warfare.html/2 (accessed 19 August 2017).

71. Godbey, "Milunka Savić."

72. George Daly, "Milunka Savić," *The Female Soldier* (blog), 20 April 2015, http://thefemalesoldier.com/blog/milunka-savi (accessed August 19, 2017).

73. For a discussion of women's participation in the army in communist Romania, see Maria Bucur and Mihaela Miroiu, *The Birth of Citizenship: Women and Power Regimes in Romania (1940–2010)* (Bloomington: Indiana University Press, 2018). For a discussion of the position of women partisans in communist Bulgaria, see Kristen Ghodsee, *The Left Side of History: World War II and the Unfulfilled Promise of Communism in Eastern Europe* (Raleigh, N.C.: Duke University Press, 2015).

74. Batinić, *Women and Yugoslav Partisans*, 64.

75. Maria Bucur, "Between the Mother of the Wounded and the Virgin from Jiu: Romanian Women and the Gender of Heroism during the Great War," *Journal of Women's History* 12. no. 2 (Summer 2000): 30–56.

76. Bucur, "Between the Mother."

77. "'Decretul-Lege nr. 4017 privitor la pensiunile celor care au luat parte la războiul pentru întregirea neamului' din 14 septembrie 1919" ["Law-Decree no. 4017 regarding the pensions of those who took part in the war for the reunification of the nation" from 14 September 1919], in *Codul general al României* [The general code of Romania] (Bucharest, 1919–1922), 9:207–215.

78. Bucur, "Between the Mother."

79. Nancy M. Wingfield and Maria Bucur, eds., *Gender and War in Twentieth-Century Eastern Europe* (Bloomington: Indiana University Press, 2006).

FOURTEEN

CALL TO ACTION

American Women in War Relief and Preparedness, 1914–1917

BARTON C. HACKER

American women's active participation in the Great War was unprecedented. Equally unprecedented was the large number of women who wore uniforms as members of a wide range of medical, preparedness, relief, and welfare organizations, as well as the armed forces. Many acted long before the United States entered the war, and many continued to serve for years after the Armistice. How many, precisely, is hard to say—the number of organizations is beyond counting, and the size of many is also uncertain—but it was clearly substantial, hundreds of thousands in total. Chapter 15 in this volume discusses the American women who volunteered for medical service from the very beginning of the war in Europe, mostly as nurses but also in a variety of other capacities. Chapter 16 focuses on the women who served in or with the armed forces after the United States declared war in April 1917. This chapter follows the many American women who donned uniforms as members of a wide variety of relief, welfare, and preparedness organizations from 1914 onward, but mainly before April 1917. Its inspiration is the unparalleled Smithsonian collection of women's Great War uniforms, a gift of the National Society of the Colonial Dames of America, one of the many hereditary and patriotic societies formed in late nineteenth-century America. For the first time in American history, civilians donned military-style garb for the duration.[1]

THE COLONIAL DAMES COLLECTION OF UNIFORMS WORN BY WOMEN IN THE GREAT WAR

The manifest significance of women's uniformed war participation in the passage of the Nineteenth Amendment struck many contemporaries. That included the Colonial Dames;

Figure 14.1.
From 1919 to 1929, the National Museum (Smithsonian Institution) exhibited uniforms worn by American women during the Great War on behalf of the National Society of the Colonial Dames of America. One of the 17 exhibit cases displayed (left to right) uniforms of the National League for Women's Service, the First National Service School, and the American Friends Service Committee. Courtesy of the National Museum of American History, Smithsonian Institution, Washington, D.C.

they judged "that it would be a good thing if [the society] would undertake to preserve, in suitable place, the uniforms that were worn during this war."[2] The society proposed to "collect at once and offer to the [Smithsonian] Institution as an exhibit in connection with the war museum the uniforms and equipment of the women connected with the various activities during the war."[3] In June 1920, the National Museum formally thanked the Colonial Dames for loaning "the collection of uniforms of the type worn by American women members of war organizations during the World War, 1914–1918."[4] The uniforms remained on display until 1929 (Figure 14.1). With the Colonial Dames' permission, the museum removed the uniforms from display and stored them.[5] Seven decades later, the Colonial Dames formally donated the stored collection to the National Museum of American History.[6]

Despite its unparalleled scope, the Colonial Dames collection is far from comprehensive. The collection is understandingly biased toward the uniforms worn by the kind of middle- and upper-class women who formed the membership of such societies as the Colonial Dames. But even in that restricted area, it is incomplete. Our research has identified many other women's organizations whose members wore uniforms, as well as other organizations that employed uniformed women. Perhaps the most glaring absence from the collection is any representation of uniforms predominantly worn by working-class women, such as munitions workers or other factory operatives, streetcar conductors, mail carriers, and police. Yet for all its gaps, the Colonial Dames collection provides an indispensable and thought-provoking resource for studying women's uniformed participation in the Great War.

Women wore two basic types of uniform. One can best be described as nurse-like; in addition to nurses proper, it was worn by many in organizations that specialized in relief and welfare, especially those involving refugees. Its distinctive characteristics were a full apron over a white or dark ankle-length dress, with flat shoes and a head covering, usually with a badge designating the organization. The second type of uniform was modeled on the male military officer's uniform. It normally featured a Norfolk-style jacket with four front patch pockets, two at the bodice and two at the skirt. It was worn over a shirtwaist, often with a tie. Most women's uniforms substituted an ankle-length skirt for the male trousers, but some included bloomers or another form of pants beneath a shorter skirt. Motor drivers from a wide range of organization typically wore breeches rather than skirts. Fabrics and colors varied, but blue, gray, and khaki were favored. Low-heeled black or tan boots or shoes; some kind of headgear, most often a military-style broad-brimmed campaign hat with badge; and insignia completed the ensemble.

UNIFORMED AMERICAN WOMEN AT WORK IN EUROPE

The 1914 outbreak of war spurred American women living in Europe to action. Much of their activism took the form of organizing efforts to provide aid to wounded soldiers and displaced civilians. They typically identified themselves by wearing uniforms. By far the most important such organization was the American Fund for French Wounded (AFFW), formed in France by American expatriates in December 1915; its 1918 offshoot, the Comité Américain pour les Régions Dévastées de France (American Committee for Devastated France), usually referred to by its French acronym as CARD, remained active well into the 1920s. In the early months of the war, Americans in France had joined the London-based French Wounded Emergency Fund, an unofficial organization distributing supplies to French military hospitals. By December 1915, in the interests of greater efficiency, they reorganized themselves as AFFW and moved operations to Paris. Anne Morgan—the heiress whose brother, John Pierpont Morgan Jr., was by then the exclusive purchasing agent and chief financier in the United States for both Britain and France—became AFFW treasurer and assumed chief responsibility for obtaining supplies and getting them to Paris. Committees in 80 U.S. municipalities raised funds for the organization. AFFW female volunteers chiefly came from wealthy families and could come or go as they pleased.[7]

AFFW deployed a team of female motor car drivers to distribute goods to French military hospitals. Amy Owen Bradley began driving a Ford for AFFW in November 1916. She felt a little conspicuous in her uniform, new both to her and to AFFW:

> The car, whose name is "Lizzie," is painted gray, with red crosses and "Comite Americain pour les Blesses Francais" on one side, and "American Fund for French Wounded" on the other. . . . I also wear a uniform which consists of my leather coat with shoulder straps, marked A. F. F. W., and a blue felt hat with A. F. F. W. on the hatband. Nobody in Paris knows what it means, as the Motor Service of the A. F. F. W. has had uniforms only a week. Hence every one stares, especially as most women in France don't wear uniforms in the street (one does not even see many uniformed nurses).[8]

In 1917, AFFW added a Civil Division to assist refugees and other civilians. Dr. Anne Murray Dike, Morgan's long-time friend, headed the new division, which initially comprised seven volunteers, though the number grew quickly. With the blessing of Marshal Pétain, they set up their base of operations at a ruined chateau in the Aisne village of Blérancourt, formerly occupied by the Germans. Morgan tended to choose volunteers from her own social class, which meant they had relatively limited skills, with the notable exception of driving and repairing autos, then still a mainly upper-class pastime. Morgan's group survived the German 1918 spring offensive but not a schism with AFFW, which led to the reconstitution of the Civil Division as the independent Comité Américain pour les Régions Dévastées de France (CARD). An executive committee in New York vetted most of the 328 CARD volunteers who served abroad at some time from 1918 to 1923. Dike and Morgan also recruited 297 British and French women, bringing the total to 625 who rebuilt the Aisne. With the end of the war, CARD imposed six-month terms on volunteers and began to pay some volunteers a small salary.[9]

CARD retained its headquarters in Blérancourt and expanded its network of field centers and dispensaries throughout the region. To support its far-flung activities, CARD, like AFFW, formed its own transport system, which also relied on young women who not only knew how to drive but were able to maintain and repair their autos. CARD, again like AFFW, dressed its members in military-style uniforms, though the colors differed: AFFW wore aubergine; CARD wore French army blue (Figure 14.2). Uniforms provided the women both recognition and protection in the French countryside.[10]

Two other particularly significant uniformed women's groups active before 1917, both founded by well-known authors, were Duryea War Relief and Le Bien-être du Blessé Women's Motor Unit. Nina Duryea before the war had regularly summered in France, a country for which she developed deep affection. She was in Dinard (Normandy) when war broke out in the summer of 1914. By September, she had organized Secours Duryea, more widely known as Duryea War Relief, to provide food and clothing for the flood of Belgian and French refugees. She established good relations with French officials, who arranged free transport from New York of the supplies she raised in the United States. When the American Expeditionary Force arrived in France, General Pershing designated the Red Cross as sole provider of charity. Most organizations complied, but Duryea remained independent. She

Figure 14.2.
Chauffeurs of the American Fund for French Wounded, 1918. Library of Congress Prints and Photographs Division.

continued her fund-raising efforts and her work well past the Armistice. Duryea and her volunteers, many of them well-to-do American women, wore nurse-like white uniforms with ankle-length skirts and flowing headdresses.[11]

Grace Gallatin Seton in May 1916 founded Le Bien-être du Blessé Women's Motor Unit under the auspices of the War Service Committee of the Woman's Club of New York. Gertrude Atherton, like Duryea and Seton a well-known author, became its American fund-raiser and publicist. Its well-to-do female volunteers delivered by motor car fresh food and delicacies to French soldiers recuperating in hospital; by 1917 they had also deployed mobile diet kitchens. Drivers wore military-style uniforms.[12] Several foreign relief organizations established American branches, chiefly for fund-raising purposes. The Serbian Relief Committee of America, founded in 1915, was the only one that included women who wore military-style uniforms.[13] The activities of American women in uniform abroad persisted throughout the war and well into the 1920s, increasing sharply after America's declaration of war. That development will be further discussed in chapter 16.

UNIFORMED WOMEN IN POLICING, PUBLIC UTILITIES, AND INDUSTRY

Meanwhile, at home, the spectacle of women in uniform became ever more common as well, beginning with the increased flow of women into policing, public utilities, and industry. Before the Great War began, women had begun moving into uniformed public service, most obviously as members of police forces and as tram workers in cities across the country. This trend accelerated after the outbreak of war, becoming even more marked when the United States entered the war in 1917. Women even began to appear in uniform as elevator operators, taxi callers, railroad workers, and mail carriers.[14] Women factory workers in uniform followed much the same pattern, becoming increasingly commonplace during the course of the war.

Women had been moving into police work well before the Great War, but the trend accelerated after 1914 and even more so after 1917. Policewomen, sometime in uniform, sometimes not, often focused on protecting women and children. When the United States entered the war, policewomen played a particularly significant role in what was then called "suppressing vice" around army camps in cooperation with the War Department Commission on Training Camp Activities.[15] But they also took on more mundane police activities, such as directing traffic. A 1918 photograph shows a female officer in Chicago directing traffic in a knee-length jacket over breeches with knee-high boots (Figure 14.3). Women had also been moving into street railway systems. The shift from horse-drawn to electric-powered urban transit from the 1890s onward cleared the way for women to take on jobs like conductor and fare collector formerly held exclusively by men. Although begun well before the United States entered the war, conscription of men for military service after April 1917 greatly accelerated the movement of women into these positions. That they wore uniforms similar to men's roused criticism—many deemed such garb for women immodest—but defenders also rallied around women's uniforms.[16]

Figure 14.3.
Chicago policewoman directing traffic, ca. 1918. Everett Collection, Database: Bridgeman Education.

Issues of modesty also plagued female factory workers, but managers found uniforms useful for controlling the work force and promoting worker safety. For munitions workers, the uniform was a button-down blouse over khaki overalls with an aviator-style cap.[17] Workers loved their overalls, an emotion that those at a Vermont machine tool plant expressed at length in verse:

> My man, you're really out of date.
> And now before it is too late,
> I'll try to set you right;
> We never mixed our bloomers, clown,
> They fit just like a Paris gown.
> . . .
> Now we're the ones who set the pace,
> You'll have to hustle in the race
> Or you'll get left behind.
> We're independent now you see,
> Your bald head don't appeal to me,
> I love my overalls;
> And I would rather polish steel
> Than get you up a tasty meal.
> . . .
> We stand erect now by your side.
> And surmount obstacles with pride,
> We're equal, free, at last
> We're truly glad we got the chance
> To work like men and wear men's pants,
> And proud that we made good
> My suit a badge of honor is. . . .[18]

And for some at least, it was not just a work uniform. The YWCA, which played a major role in providing women workers with housing, welfare, and recreation, promoted thinking of them as a "Women's Industrial Army," the female equivalent of the men's army. It was not merely rhetorical. The YWCA organized military-style activities for munitions workers, who elected captains and drilled in uniform during off hours; some also learned semaphore signaling.[19] This reflected the growing participation of women in the military preparedness movement.

PREPAREDNESS AND WOMEN

The American military preparedness movement that flowered in 1916 produced a number of local and regional paramilitary groups to provide women with some of the same kind of military training that the Plattsburg training camps offered men.[20] The creation of such units continued even after the United States formally declared war. The most important national organization was the Women's Section of the Navy League. On 4 July 1915, a group of women in Washington, D.C., formed the Women's Section of the 14-year-old Navy League. Its motto, "Patriotism, Americanism, and National Defense," found enthusiastic support from women throughout the country who rapidly organized local chapters. In

November 1915, the section sponsored the first woman's national defense conference ever held in the United States, drawing 2,000 women nationwide to meet in the ballroom of the new Willard Hotel in Washington, D.C., to hear lectures on the importance of preparedness by government officials and prominent women.[21] Perhaps the Women's Section's most notable achievement was establishing the First National Service School in spring 1916. The school was widely recognized as a manifestation of the preparedness movement and sometimes referred to as the women's Plattsburg.[22]

Two hundred mostly well-to-do, some socially prominent, young women came to Chevy Chase, Maryland, a Washington suburb, from all over the country for the initial class in May 1916. They lived in tents under army discipline, ate marine corps rations, and experienced two weeks of military training that included mandatory calisthenics, drill, marching, and preparation of surgical dressings; they also enjoyed optional courses in wigwagging, wireless and telegraphy, first aid, dietetics, and knitting, among others.[23] Campers paid their own expenses, including a substantial fee to participate; they also purchased their own khaki uniforms.[24] "Khaki skirts, flannel blouses, and campaign hats may not be the most beautiful of garments," in the words of one camper, "but they are among the most comfortable and the easiest to work in—and with plenty of pockets."[25] Once in uniform, another remarked, the team submerged the individual: "First we must lose that individual feeling, and the beginning of this was when we donned those suits, designed for durability only. Now outwardly we were alike each other as possible. . . . We ceased to think whether we looked well but whether we looked right."[26] To another young woman, "merely wearing [khaki] seems to compel forgetfulness of the petty things and unessentials of life and brings right thinking in a clear honest way."[27] Similar schools were held elsewhere in the country later that summer.[28] The Washington area hosted another service school following year.[29]

Perhaps the best-known local women's military unit was the American Woman's League for Self Defense and Preparedness in New York City. Unexpectedly, it had prewar roots. Jane Hungerford Milbank helped found the International Order of Military Women in 1913. In November, believing that women's suffrage demanded military readiness, she organized as part of the order a women's regiment known as the Army of Columbians. In fact, the "regiment" comprised fewer than 10 members, but they did wear khaki uniforms (designed by Jane Milbank with Norfolk-style jacket, ankle-length skirt, and boots) and drill with wooden rifles at the 47th Regiment Armory in Brooklyn.[30] With the outbreak of war and the growth of the American preparedness movement, the group's mission expanded: Not only would it instill the self-discipline and teamwork that suffrage demanded, it would offer to serve on the Mexican border and defend the home against possible German attack.[31]

General Milbank, as she styled herself, also became a prominent figure in the American Woman's League for Self Defense and Preparedness, into which her Columbians merged. The new organization went public in January 1916 and in March brought together 200 women for its first public drill at the 9th Regiment Armory in Manhattan. Some like General Milbank, who led the drill, were in uniforms of one kind or another; others wore gym suits, and still others wore civilian clothes. None yet wore the regulation uniform, which was to be khaki jacket, short (knee-length) skirt, and knickers, with flat-soled shoes and leggings. The league's cavalry unit, some 20 strong, opted for breeches rather than skirts.[32] The league soon extended its range of activities to include field exercises and summer camp, as well as fund-raising.[33] It also expanded geographically, establishing branch organization beyond New York in New Jersey, Pennsylvania, Ohio, Wisconsin, and California. Membership grew rapidly. Despite a breakaway faction that termed itself the Women's Military Reserve of the United States, the league had almost 1,500 members by early 1917.[34]

New York was not alone. The Emergency Services Corps was a case in point. Organized by a wealthy young woman, Candace Hewitt, the corps brought 30 debutantes in June 1916 to a three-week training camp at Wewappo Farm, the Hewitt summer estate in New Jersey. Run with military precision and discipline, the intensive program included drills, calisthenics, horsemanship, bicycle riding, swimming, flag signaling, rifle practice, long hikes, and first aid training. The trainees lived in canvas tents, which they were responsible for policing; they also did their own cooking, cleaning, and stable duty. Garbed in khaki shirt with red tie, khaki breeches, and leather gaiters, they looked smart and worked hard.[35] Much harder, in fact, than the women at the near-simultaneous National Service School in Chevy Chase, Maryland. Or so at least journalist Marguerite Mooers Marshall believed. These young women displayed, in her view, "all the sincerity, the practicality, the real spirit of self-sacrifice which seemed to me so conspicuously lacking when I visited the nationally exploited 'female Plattsburg' at Chevy Chase" (Figure 14.4).[36]

In Boston, another wealthy young woman, Nora Saltonstall, created her own Action Corps as part of the Massachusetts Branch of the Special Aid Society. Founded in New York City in January 1915, the woman-led National Special Aid Society soon metamorphosed into the Special Aid Society for American Preparedness. By 1917, it had grown to 2,000 members in New York and 30,000 nationwide. The goal of both the national organization and state and local branches was making women active participants in military preparedness. The society's Massachusetts Branch, established in November 1915, became one of its most active.[37] For the most part, there is little evidence of uniform wearing by Special Aid Society members. Saltonstall's Active Corps was a notable exception. Seeking volunteers for the Active Corps in February 1917, she announced that "the aim primarily is to mobilize the women for war preparedness and for peace efficiency and to conduct a combined training school and placement bureau for the Red Cross and other organizations." Compulsory drill was part of the program. Training focused on six areas: (1) Red Cross classes, surgical dressings, first aid care, and dietetics; (2) canteen and emergency cooking; (3) civic instruction and emergency social service relief work; (4) motor section, repairing, and driving; (5) wireless and telegraphy; and (6) clerical, bookkeeping, shorthand, and typewriting. Colonel Saltonstall's first drill at the Boston Armory drew 60 volunteers. She provided the uniforms. The ambitious program, which had soon drawn as many as 300 to her banner, does not seem to have survived Saltonstall's departure for service in France.[38]

Figure 14.4.
Candace Hewitt's Emergency Services Corps, 1917. Library of Congress Prints and Photographs Division.

Other groups can only be glimpsed. The New York City Police Department was particularly active in establishing a wide range of wartime training and reserve corps for women with a strong military cast, going so far as to form a reserve Women's Machine Gun Squad, in 1918, known only from an archival photograph (Figure 14.5).[39] And it was not just government organizations. One example is the American Women's Battalion of Death, founded in Lowell, Massachusetts, apparently inspired by its Russia namesake. It is known only from a 1917 photograph that shows four serious young women wearing Norfolk-style jackets and a fifth who has an overcoat; all five are saluting with their hands on the brims of their campaign hats. Local records and newspapers from the wartime period may have information about these and other groups of women in uniform.

GIRLS IN UNIFORM

Preparedness also extended to young women and girls. Like young men and boys, they also participated in military training in colleges, high schools, and even elementary schools. Military training for male students had been one of the mandates of the American land-grant college system established in 1862. As early as the 1870s, young women demanded that they, too, be allowed to participate in uniformed drill and to learn the manual of arms. They succeeded. The sight of women in uniform drilling on campus had become almost

Figure 14.5.
Women's Machine Gun Squad Police Reserves, New York City, 1918. Library of Congress Prints and Photographs Division.

commonplace by the late nineteenth century. The war opened vast new fields to college women throughout the country, opportunities they seized with alacrity. And women's uniformed service was by no means limited to land-grant schools.[40] Military training was slower to reach high school and grade school girls. The advocates of discipline and hierarchy in American schools who had begun to promote uniforms and military-style drill early in the twentieth century had their eyes on boys. Their efforts received a strong but controversial impetus from the preparedness movement.[41] One direct result of the preparedness movement was the 1916 founding of the Junior Reserve Officer Training Corps in American secondary schools. In the years after its 1916 founding, for instance, it aimed to Americanize the children of southern and eastern European immigrants while easing upper-class fears of social tensions and building support for the military.[42]

Preparedness concerns also brought girls into the fold, as they now sometimes acquired uniforms and received military-style training in school. For girls perhaps more than boys, school uniforms tended to enforce gender norms.[43] Organizations outside school also contributed to the militarization of girls. Camp Fire Girls began informally in 1910 and incorporated in 1912, the same year Juliette Gordon Low organized the first American Girl Guide troop, 18 strong, in Savannah, Georgia; she soon changed the name to the more American-sounding Girl Scouts.[44] Both organizations, of course, like the Boy Scouts that served as their model, wore uniforms. A proposed merger in 1913 went nowhere, partly because the much larger Camp Fire Girls organization was not interested but also because the two organizations differed in their goals. Camp Fire Girls learned only what was needed to become good wives and mothers, whereas the Girl Scouts sought proficiency further afield.[45] Despite their differences, Girl Scouts regularly joined forces during the war with Camp Fire Girls as particularly active agents of Americanization, Liberty Bond sales, and food conservation.[46] The two organizations had something else in common, which they shared with many others; they sponsored summer camps. Everyone wore uniforms, which is what "a new girl . . . likes best about camp," wrote Anna Worthington Coale. "She never knew before what a difference clothes could make." Once you exchange "your troublesome skirts and waists for bloomers and a middy blouse, . . . you never want to go back to your city clothes."[47]

When the United States entered the war, Luther H. Gulick, cofounder and president of Camp Fire Girls, wired President Woodrow Wilson to offer the service of 94,000 girls in uniform to the war effort. "A uniform is needed just as much by the women as it is by the soldier and for the same reasons," he insisted.[48] Gulick proposed the newly adopted Minute Girl uniform, not only for Camp Fire Girls but also for every girl and woman in the country. The red, white, and blue uniform—red tie, white middy blouse, navy hat, and blue serge skirt and bloomers—visibly expressed patriotism, utility, and national unity. It submerged the individual and obliterated class distinctions.[49] Although Gulick's proposal went unheeded, it nonetheless demonstrated the significance many attached to uniforms.

There were many similar organizations. As Salvation Army national commander in America, Evangeline Booth—daughter of Salvation Army founders William and Catherine Booth—established the first Life-Saving Girl Guard troop in the United States in May 1916. The organization had begun in London a year earlier. The girls hiked, camped, marched, exercised, and learned such useful military skills as first aid, Morse code, and flag signaling. They wore forest-green khaki uniforms with campaign hats.[50] Also in 1916, Theodora Booth, William and Catherine's granddaughter and herself a social reformer, established the Girls' National Honor Guard to promote patriotism among American girls and do war relief work. Its members wore military-style uniforms (Figure 14.6). Working closely with the Red Cross, the honor guard engaged in such activities as hosting dances for servicemen, promoting Liberty Loans, and visiting the hospitalized. Although it spread from New York City across the country, the Girls' National Honor Guard never attained very large numbers, and it ended with the war.[51]

Other organizations, although less overtly military, nonetheless found uniforms a useful means of identifying and inspiring their members. A case in point was Emergency Aid of Pennsylvania. Purely homegrown, it was organized by Philadelphia clubwomen in October 1914 to provide aid to those suffering from the war in Europe. It grew rapidly and spread throughout the state, especially after the United States entered the war. Its youth auxiliary, Emergency Aid of Pennsylvania Aides, was a semimilitary organization of 250 girls in

Figure 14.6.
A posed photo from the National Archives captioned "Girls of the National Honor Guard on an Errand of Mercy, May 1918" shows an automobile with several young women; they wear light-colored military-style uniforms. National Archives and Records Administration, American unofficial collection of World War I photographs, 1917–1918, Identifier 6423774, Record Group 165: Records of the War Department General and Special Staffs, 1860–1952.

Philadelphia and 550 in branches elsewhere in the state who engaged in a variety of domestic tasks such as assisting in war bond drives. All wore uniforms.[52]

NATIONAL LEAGUE FOR WOMAN'S SERVICE

By far the largest and most significant women's service organization to grow out of the preparedness movement was the National League for Woman's Service. It was based on a program proposed by Grace Parker, a member of the Women's Section of the Navy League, who spent November and December 1916 in England studying how women had organized to support the war. Shortly after her return, on 25 January 1917, Parker spoke at the National Security League's Congress of Constructive Patriotism in Washington, D.C. She discussed what she had learned in England and proposed a plan for American women. Two days later, 500 women delegates assembled to accept her plan and establish the National League for Woman's Service. They also named Parker national commandant of the newly formed organization.[53]

The National League for Woman's Service organized itself along military lines. Detachments—10 to 30 women under the command of a lieutenant—handled the work on the ground; two or more detachments might be united under a captain. The league also strongly encouraged regular physical drill "for the development of discipline, self-control, team work, endurance and esprit de corps."[54] And the league recognize the "subtle power" of uniforms, as journalist Edward Hungerford observed. "It knows that the trig coat and short skirt, the military boots and puttees, even the small round officers' cap are apt to bring an enthusiasm in the heart of their wearer that can be translated into actual endeavor."[55] Most members wore military-style uniforms.[56] The league also formed a junior branch, the Girl's Patriotic League; its members wore their own distinctive uniform and worked closely with similar groups organized by the YWCA and War Camp Community Service.[57]

Although the work of the National League for Woman's Service was almost entirely domestic, it did have a Division of Home and Overseas Relief that regularly cooperated with such Europe-centered organizations as Belgian Relief and American Committee for Devastated France.[58] A major exception to the league's home service was its Camouflage Division, initiated by the New York City branch early in 1918. Formally known as the Women's Reserve Camouflage Corps, it comprised two platoons of artists and art students. They started training under army and navy experts in April 1918 and finished in mid-July. Three graduates worked for the navy in Washington, and seven assisted the army in France. The Armistice aborted a planned second corps. Even more than the league itself, the Camouflage Division featured military organization, adding target practice and map making to uniforms, officers, drill, and calisthenics.[59]

Another notably militarized division was the Women's Radio Corps of the league's Wireless Division. Its members, like those of the Camouflage Division, always appeared in uniform, which was not true of league members in general. On 7 March 1917, a month before the U.S. declaration of war, the first training program for female wireless operators began at Hunter College in New York. Courses rapidly spread across the country. Graduates of the three-month program worked for the U.S. Army Signal Corps as teachers of male recruits and as inspectors of radio equipment. A few also worked for the Signal Corps' Radio Research and Development Section.[60]

By far, the league's best-known, certainly most widely reported, work involved its Motor Corps. That work included chauffeuring civilian and military officials (mostly in the drivers' own cars), responding to emergencies, and driving ambulances. Most of the driving was domestic, but some members of the Motor Corps also served abroad. Although more women applied to join the Motor Corps than any other league division, its stringent requirements, demanding training, and hard work kept down the membership; it counted some 500 drivers nationwide. Captain Helen Russell Bastedo was the officer in charge.[61] Choosing the Motor Corps' distinctive uniform presented something of a problem, as the league's historian, Bessie R. James, explained: "Something attractive, yet conservative and not provocative of criticism must be chosen. It must be military in appearance, but not like the United States Army uniform. Few women have ever approved the beltless clothes with their inadequate pockets worn by our soldiers." After much discussion, the league authorized "a khaki uniform," comprising "riding breeches, a wide plain skirt buttoned down the front, and a coat patterned after the model of the British officer." Officers wore a Sam Browne belt with shoulder strap; others wore only the belt. "In the beginning, the hat was an American Officer's dress parade cap. Later, however, the overseas cap was adopted because it sticks close to the driver's head on a windy day; also, it can be rolled down for protection against the cold."[62] Reporter Elene Foster observed "trim young figures, dressed alike in khaki uniforms very like those worn by the regular army, save that the trousers are hidden by the short khaki skirt and the army cap bears the insignia of the corps—a tire surrounded by Mercury wings."[63]

During the early years of the Great War, as we have seen, before America's entry, such relief organizations as the American Fund for French Wounded had established uniformed women's motor services, a practice that continued with the American Committee for Devastated France well into the 1920s.[64] But the National League of Woman's Service Motor Corps was the first of three major women's uniformed motor services established during America's Great War. The other two were its offshoots. In November 1917, Captain Helen Bastedo resigned from the league Motor Corps to found the Motor Corps of America, bringing a number of league drivers with her.[65] Until February 1918, the National League for Woman's Service Motor Corps served as the official Red Cross motor service. Only then did the Red Cross form its own Motor Corps, taking over several league Motor Corps units in the process. It had 12,000 members working in 300 cities at the time of the Armistice, and they kept working well into the 1920s.[66] In the eyes of reporter John Walker Harrington, the "smart uniforms" worn by members of all three motor services loomed large:

> What with their jaunty overseas caps on the side of their heads, their trig Sam Browne belts, their short skirts and leather leggins, they have a military appearance which grips attention. The brown gabardines and khakis of the league, with the green stripe on the sleeve denoting active service; the light brown of the Motor Corps of America, with its bit of blue at the collars; the blue gray of the Red Cross drivers, all are quickly distinguished aside from the attractive insignia, of which the motifs are flying wings.[67]

Great as the number of American women in uniform had been before America's entry into the war, their numbers expanded rapidly in 1917 and 1918. An important factor in this expansion was the decision by leaders of the women's suffrage movement to support the war effort.

SUFFRAGISTS MOBILIZE

The mobilization of women in support of suffrage had intensified in the first decade of the twentieth century, propelled by the multiplying membership of the reunified National American Woman Suffrage Association (NAWSA). Drawing on the long-standing American tradition of political parades, marching suffragists in cities throughout the country made the movement's growing strength visible, emphasized by the adoption of uniform sashes and badges. Other forms of public action underscored the impact of parades.[68] American suffragists initially sought to attain their goal through local action, a state-by-state series of campaigns that achieved a degree of success but had come to seem too slow and uncertain.[69] Alice Paul's National Woman's Party focused its militant attention on President Woodrow Wilson and a constitutional amendment through a vigorous campaign of direct nonviolent action.[70]

In 1916 NAWSA, too, shifted its efforts to winning the vote through a constitutional amendment. Although still a federation of state suffrage organizations, it committed itself under the vigorous leadership of Carrie Chapman Catt to what historians Robert Booth Fowler and Spencer Jones characterized as a distinctly more "hierarchical, militarylike organization."[71] Catt's rhetoric reflected the new orientation. In introducing the so-called "winning plan" at NAWSA's annual convention in September 1916, she likened herself to "a general . . . about to make an attack upon the enemy at a fortified point," who "begins to feint elsewhere in order to draw off attention and forces"—that is, focus on a constitutional amendment but keep the pressure on the state legislatures.[72] This strategy meshed well with the headline-grabbing militancy of the National Woman's Party. Despite their strained relations, neither would likely have succeeded without the other.[73]

As the prospect of war loomed early in 1917, NAWSA offered its services in support of the war effort to President Woodrow Wilson; when the United States declared war on Germany, the organized suffrage movement immediately swung into action.[74] The last great suffrage parade took place on 17 October 1917. Though smaller than earlier parades, its impact may have been all the greater for foreshadowing the great postwar victory parades as it did by drawing on women in uniform, marching "divisions of farmerettes, women workers in industry, doctors, and Red Cross nurses for overseas service."[75] Suffrage would remain the central goal, but working to support the war effort now assumed great significance in demonstrating the loyalty and patriotism of the organized women's movement.[76]

Not all women shared militaristic and nationalist sentiments, trusting instead to the century's growing international peace movements. They hoped to forestall armed conflict and, failing that, to stop the bloodshed as soon as possible. Americans as well as Europeans shared this viewpoint as part of the international peace movement that had achieved such prominence in the late nineteenth and early twentieth centuries.[77] The homegrown American peace movement had also attracted many American feminists in the years before the Great War, and some continued to resist.[78] The women's peace movement reached its apogee with the International Congress of Women at The Hague in 1915, but even so illustrious a gathering could do little to halt the juggernaut.[79]

For many suffragists, perhaps most, however, patriotism trumped pacifism. Military preparedness in the United States rapidly eclipsed the peace movement. Women's preparedness organizations like the Woman's Section of the Navy League disputed the peace initiatives of the Woman's Peace Party. Many treated pacifists as traitors in the months before the declaration of war. Although pacifism hardly vanished with the advent of war, many suffragists donned uniforms, and most mobilized themselves, linking their call for suffrage, equal rights, and equal pay to war work and suspending most other reform activism for the duration.[80]

NOTES

1. Margaret Vining and Barton C. Hacker, "Volunteers Inspired by Conscription: Uniformed Women in World War I," in *Total War, Total Defense, 1789–2000*, ed. Per Iko, Lars Ericson, and Gunnar Åselius (Stockholm: Swedish Military History Commission, 2001), 356–362.

2. Minutes of the Fourteenth Biennial Council of the National Society of the Colonial Dames of America, 1919, 69. Unless otherwise specified, all cited documents may be consulted in the Archive of Women's Military History, Division of Armed Forces History, National Museum of American History, Washington, D.C. On the origins and work of the Colonial Dames, see Mrs. Joseph Rucker [Clarinda Pendleton] Lamar, *A History of the National Society of the Colonial Dames of America, from 1891 to 1933* (Atlanta: Walter W. Brown, 1934).

3. W. deC. Ravenel to the Secretary [of the Smithsonian Institution], 4 Jan. 1919.

4. Ravenel to Mrs. Marcus [Caroline Gilbert] Benjamin, 15 June 1920.

5. Ravenel to Mrs. James Carroll [Elizabeth Van Rensselaer] Frazer, 13 March 1929; Frazer, "Report of the Committee on Relics Loaned to the National Museum," Minutes of the Nineteenth Biennial Council of the National Society of the Colonial Dames of America, 1929, 49; Theodore T. Belote to Benjamin, 11 Oct. 1938.

6. For the full history of the Colonial Dames collection, see Margaret Vining and Barton C. Hacker. "Uniforms Make the Woman: Material Culture and Social Technology in the First World War," in *Materializing the Military*, ed. Bernard Finn and Barton C. Hacker (London: Science Museum Press, 2005), 65–76. On the Great War exhibit that included the women's uniforms, see Margaret Vining and Barton C. Hacker, "Displaying the Great War in America: The World War I Exhibition of the United States National Museum in Washington, DC, 1918 and Beyond," in *The Universal Heritage of Arms and Military History: Challenges and Choices in a Changing World*, ed. Claudia Reichl-Ham (Vienna: Heeresgeschichtliches Museum, 2008), 27–38. For images of the 22 cases of women's uniforms displayed in the 1920s, see "Women in World War I: Women's Uniforms," Smithsonian National Museum of American History, http://americanhistory.si.edu/collections/object-groups/women-in-wwi/women-s-uniforms (accessed 19 March 2019). Vivian Lea Young completed a master's thesis based on the Colonial Dames Collection: "'Petticoats Are Part of This Uniform': American Women Volunteers of the First World War and Their Uniforms" (M.A. thesis, Randolph-Macon Woman's College, 10 May 1987). Jill Halcomb Smith also made extensive use of the collection in *Dressed for Duty: America's Women in Uniform, 1898–1973*, 2 vols. (San Jose, Calif.: R. James Bender, 2001–2004).

7. Michael E. McGuire, "'A Highly Successful Experiment in International Partnership?' The Limited Resonance of the American Committee for Devastated France," *First World War Studies* 5, no. 1 (2014): 102–103; Julia Todd and M. Bowling, "Finding Aid for American Fund for French Wounded Records," June 2001, Manuscripts and Archives Division, New York Public Library, http://archives.nypl.org/mss/73; Alan Albright, "Notable American Volunteers of the Great War," in *Les Américains et la Légion d'honneur: 1853–1947*, ed. Véronique Wiesinger and Alan Albright (Paris: Editions de la Réunion des Musées Nationaux, 1993), http://net.lib.byu.edu/estu/wwi/comment/volsnote.html (accessed 5 November 2019); Louise Elliott Dalby, *"An Irrepressible Crew": The Smith College Relief Unit* (Northampton, Mass.: Sophia Smith Collection, Smith College, 1968), 12.

8. Amy Owen Bradley, *Back of the Front in France: Letters from Amy Owen Bradley, Motor Driver of the American Fund for French Wounded* (Boston: W.A. Butterfield, 1918), 4–5. See also Young, "'Petticoats Are Part of This Uniform,'" 85–88.

9. McGuire, "'A Highly Successful Experiment,'" 103–105; Kimberly Chuppa-Cornell, "The U.S. Women's Motor Corps in France, 1914–1921," *Historian* 56, no. 3 (Mar. 1994): 465–479; Anne G. Campbell, "Mary Breckinridge and the American Committee for Devastated France: The Foundations of the Frontier Nursing Service," *Register of the Kentucky Historical Society* 82, no. 3 (Summer 1984): 264.

10. McGuire, "'A Highly Successful Experiment,'" 106; Campbell, "Mary Breckinridge and the American Committee for Devastated France," 264. On AFFW and CARD uniforms, see Young, "'Petticoats Are Part of This Uniform,'" 71–72, 79–84; Smith, *Dressed for Duty*, 1:29–30, 32–35.

11. Ida Clyde Clarke, *American Women and the World War* (New York: D. Appleton, 1918), 483–484; "War Sufferers Needs Vividly Described," *Los Angeles Herald*, 11 Jan. 1919, 3; "The French-American Hall of Fame. Mrs. Nina Larrey Duryea," *La France: An American Magazine* 4, no. 7 (Apr. 1920): 346; Robert Messenger, "Machines à écrire et de secours: Nina Larrey Smith Duryea in France 1914–17," *OzTypewriter: The Wonderful World of Typewriters*

(blog), 28 Jan. 2014, http://oztypewriter.blogspot.com/2014/01/machines-ecrire-et-de-secours-nina.html (accessed 12 Dec. 2016).

12. Gertrude Atherton, "Praise from Petain; New Work Undertaken by Le Bienetre du Blesse," *New York Times*, 31 Mar. 1918, 27; "Activities of Members," *Journal of the National Institute of Social Science* 6 (July 1920): 148; Clarke, *American Women and the World War*, 487–488; Chuppa-Cornell, "The U.S. Women's Motor Corps in France," 468–471; Kathleen Eagen Johnson, "Greenwich Women Face the Great War," *Connecticut Explored* (Winter 2014–2015), http://ctexplored.org/greenwich-women-face-the-great-war/# (accessed 5 November 2019).

13. "Serbian Relief Committee; Morgan Partner Heads List Announced by Madame Groultch," *St. Louis Post-Dispatch*, 31 Jan. 1915, A8; Clarke, *American Women and the World War*, 508. For committee uniforms, see Smith, *Dressed for Duty*, 2:37–38.

14. "She'll Start Taxis; Young Woman to Don Uniform and Direct Machines at Hotel Sherman Station," *Chicago Daily Tribune*, 22 Oct. 1916, A7; "Woman Operates an Elevator at Sage, Allen & Co. Store; Three Others Will Be Put to Work before March 1—Will Have Uniforms," *Hartford Courant*, 15 Feb. 1918, 7; Pauline Goldmark, "Women in the Railroad Service," *Proceedings of the Academy of Political Science in the City of New York* 8, no. 2 (Feb. 1919): 17–22; Janet Frieda Davidson, "Women and the Railroad: The Gendering of Work during the First World War Era, 1917–1920" (Ph.D. diss., University of Delaware, 2000).

15. Chloe Owings, *Women Police: A Study of the Development and Status of the Women Police Movement* (New York: Frederick H. Hitchcock, 1925), 94–117; "Six Policewomen, Just Appointed, Are to Be Armed; They're Going to Wear Uniforms, too, but What Kind Isn't Decided; Will Work at Beaches; New Recruits on the City Force to Attend to Cases Involving girls," *New-York Tribune*, 16 Aug. 1918, 7; "Police Women at Springfield Now; Not in Uniform, but Help in City's Vice Crusade," *Boston Daily Globe*, 10 Nov. 1918, 38; Lois Higgins, "Historical Background of Policewomen's Service," *Journal of Criminal Law and Criminology* 41, no. 6 (Mar.–Apr. 1951): 822–833.

16. "Young Women Conductors for Three Jitney Busses; Wearing Uniforms, They Will Take Charge This Week of 15-Passenger Cars," *St. Louis Post-Dispatch*, 28 Mar. 1915, A10; "Fair Sex Crew of Street Car Success," *Los Angeles Herald*, 31 Aug. 1917, 19; "Woman Given Official Tryout as a Street-Car Conductor; Official Photographs of Our First Woman Conductor," *Los Angeles Times*, 18 Apr. 1918, II1; "What Is Modesty? Shonts, Essayist, Says Bloomers on Conductorettes; President of New York Railways Company, Replying to Unnamed Correspondent, Defends Semi-military Uniform of Women Car Employees—'I Prefer Them to Waistless Theatre Gowns,' He Explains," *New-York Tribune*, 3 Feb. 1918, 6; "500 Women on City Street Cars Prove Their Worth as Conductors," *New-York Tribune*, 23 June 1918, B6; Ronald M. Benson, "Searching for the Antecedents of Affirmative Action: The National War Labor Board and the Cleveland Women Conductors in World War I," *Women's Rights Law Reporter* 5, no. 4 (Summer 1979): 271–282.

17. "They're So Modest in Clintonville," *Los Angeles Herald*, 28 Aug. 1918, 16; C.B. Lord, "How to Deal Successfully with Women in Industry," *Industrial Management* 53 (1917): 838–845; "Safety Uniforms for Women; Workers' Garments on Living Models at Convention Here, Sept. 15–20," *St. Louis Post-Dispatch*, 12 Sept. 1918, 14; "Women Wear Khaki Overalls; Female Workers in Munition Plant Design Their Uniform for Safety," *Washington Post*, 7 Apr. 1918, E4; "Women Gun-Makers Will Wear Overalls," *Los Angeles Herald*, 27 Apr. 1918. See, more generally, Carrie Brown's well-illustrated *Rosie's Mom: Forgotten Women Workers of the First World War* (Boston: Northeastern University Press, 2002).

18. Women Workers in Vermont, "I Love My Overalls," in Caraola M. Cram, "She Hands Him a Lemon," *Springfield Reporter*, 5 Dec. 1918, 2, as reprinted with commentary in Sonya Michel and Robyn Muncy, eds., *Engendering America: A Documentary History, 1865 to the Present* (Boston: McGraw-Hill College, 1999), 145–147.

19. "Girls to Match Our Armies," *War Work Bulletin*, no. 34 (19 July 1918): 1; Elizabeth Porter Wyckoff, "The Girls behind the Men behind the Guns," *Association Monthly* 12, no. 9 (Sept. 1918): 334.

20. On preparedness and Plattsburg, see John Patrick Finnegan, *Against the Specter of a Dragon: The Campaign for American Military Preparedness, 1914–1917* (Westport, Conn.: Greenwood Press, 1974); Michael Pearlman, *To Make Democracy Safe for America: Patricians and Preparedness in the Progressive Era* (Urbana: University of Illinois Press, 1984); John Garry Clifford, *The Citizen Soldiers: The Plattsburg Training Camp Movement, 1913–1920*, 2nd ed. (Lexington: University Press of Kentucky, 2015). None of these works mention women.

21. "2000 Women to Meet, Urge U.S. Defense; Feminine Leaders from All over Country to Endorse Plan of Preparedness," *Los Angeles Herald*, 15 Nov. 1915, 14; Connecticut State Library staff, finding aid for RG 137 United States Navy League, Comforts Committee, Admiral Bunce Section, Inventory of Records, Connecticut State Library, 2009, http://ctstatelibrary.org/RG137.html (accessed 5 November 2019). See also Barbara J. Steinson, *American Women's Activism in World War I* (New York: Garland, 1982), 175–185.

22. "Training Camp for Women; It Will Be Held in Army Tents in Washington Next May," *New York Times*, 19 Mar. 1916, 6; "This Summer It Will Be the Girl Rookies!" *Atlanta Constitution*, 2 Apr. 1916, D8; "Women to Occupy Tented Camp Today; School for Preparedness in Warfare Aid Near Capital Will Open; Each to Wear a Uniform; Institution Has Help from Navy League Section and Other Well-Wishers," *New York Times*, 1 May 1916, 6.

23. Marguerite Marshall, "Daily Routine of Women's Training Camp Is Described by a Post-Dispatch Writer; Volunteers Rise at 6:30, Work for 10 Hours," *St. Louis Post-Dispatch*, 4 May 1916, 3; "Preparedness Wins Fair Sex Recruits," *Los Angeles Herald*, 10 May 1916, 15; "How the Women of Our Country Are Preparing for Emergencies in Case of War, and How They Will Be Equipped to Do Their Part Should Their Services Be Needed," *Sacramento Union*, 9 July 1916, 8; Miriam Warren Hubbard, "The Soldier-Girls at the National Service School," *St. Nicholas: A Monthly Magazine for Boys and Girls* 44, no. 6 (April 1917): 518–520; Steinson, *American Women's Activism*, 192–194.

24. "L.A. Soldier Women Plan for Camp Duty," *Los Angeles Herald*, 26 Apr. 1916, 13; Steinson, *American Women's Activism*, 196; Young, "'Petticoats Are Part of This Uniform,'" 153–158; Smith, *Dressed for Duty*, 1:391–392.

25. Margaret Dadmun, "The Girls in Khaki," *St. Nicholas: A Monthly Magazine for Boys and Girls* 44, no. 6 (Apr. 1917): 520.

26. Emily S. Wickett, "Obedience and Team Work: What the Fourth National Service School Meant to Me," *Sea Power* 2 (Feb. 1917): 42.

27. Dorothy Potter, "And Then the Women: Women No Longer Sit Home and Weep While Their Men Go to War, but Band Themselves Together for National Service," *Sea Power* 2 (May 1917): 17.

28. "L.A. Soldier Women Plan for Camp Duty," *Los Angeles Herald*, 26 Apr. 1916, 13; "Military Training for Young Women." *Sacramento Union*, 9 Aug. 1916, 10; "Women to Have Training Camp. Two Weeks Courses for Nurses to Be Given at Lake Geneva. Life in Tents Planned," *Chicago Daily Tribune*, 9 July 1916, 4; "Women's Training Camp Ends," *St. Louis Post-Dispatch*, 30 Aug. 1916, 3; Steinson, *American Women's Activism*, 194–195.

29. "Call Women to Flag; 'Prepare for Patriotic Service' Is Training School Cry; 1,000 Expected in Camp Here; Two Courses Will Be Given from April 16 to May 26—Army and Navy Officers to Assist Red Cross as Instructors—Uniforms of Khaki to Give Military Touch," *Washington Post*, 11 Mar. 1917, 8; "Preparing Women for Service in War Time," *Outlook*, 28 March 1917, 540–541; Clarke, *American Women and the World War*, 203; "Rookie Commandant; Wife of Head of Great Lakes Station in South Carolina," *Chicago Daily Tribune*, 12 Sept. 1916, 9.

30. "Mrs. J.H. Milbank to Organize Regiment Composed of Women," *Brooklyn Daily Eagle*, 9 Nov. 1913, 20; "Drill to End Divorce; Many Fair New York 'Soldiers' Now in Awkward Squad," *Washington Post*, 14 Feb. 1914, 4; "Members of Female Regiment," 8 Nov. 1914, Getty Images, http://www.gettyimages.ae/license/516578996; "Female Regiment Performing Drill," 8 Nov. 1914, Getty Images, http://www.gettyimages.ae/license/516015654; "'Army' of 7 Women Trains Its Recruit; General Milbank Complains at Fourteenth Regiment Armory of Too Much Ego; Military Drills the Cure; She Admits One Weakness Because Her Cohorts May Refuse to Take Any 'Talk' from Officers," *New York Times*, 19 May 1915.

31. J. Hungerford Milbank, "Now for an Army of Women Soldiers; the First Women's Regiment Organized to Make Its Members Manly and Able to Fight Side by Side with Their Husbands, Fathers, Sons and Brothers," *Washington Post*, 22 Feb. 1914, 37; "Brooklyn Musters an Amazon Army; Mrs. General Milbank Is in Command, Though She Doesn't Look in the Least Warlike; They Have Regular Drills; Sometimes the Corps Turns out Five or Six Strong on Good Nights—Home Defense Its Aim," *New York Times*, 11 May 1915; "'Army' of 7 Women Trains Its Recruits; "Regiment of Fair Home Defenders Will Drill and Shoot Real Guns; Gen. Jane Hungerford Milbank, of the Columbians, Will Be in Charge of Lessons in Sure Enough Armory; Women Will Be Prepared to Protect Themselves and Children While Males Are off at War," *Washington Post*, 26 Mar. 1916, ES13.

32. "To Train Women for War; Self-Defense League Will Put Rifles in Hands of Members," *Washington Post*, 23 Jan. 1916, ES14; "200 Women Soldiers Give a Public Drill; Gen. Mrs. Millbank, in 'Stunning' Khaki, Heads League for Self-Defense; Their Zeal Wins Praise; Men of Ninth Regiment Put Squads through Brisk Evolutions in Armory Hall—Dozens More Enlist," *New York Times*, 25 Mar. 1916, 8; "Girl Soldiers Drill in Khaki," *San Bernardino Sun*, 11 Apr. 1916, 8; "May Wear Either Skirts or Breeches; Uniforms for Women's Self-Defense League are Finally Decided Upon; Bifurcated in Cavalry; Wearers of Skirts Go in Infantry; Some League Members Balk on Oath of Allegiance," *New York Times*, 2 May 1916, 5.

33. "Women Scout in the Rain; Mrs. Gen. Millbank and Her Self-Defenders Map the Palisades," *New York Times*, 15 May 1916, 9; "Co-education Plan for Military Camp; Both Men and Women to Learn How to Be Soldiers at Birchwood Lake; Nobody Will Be Lonely; Capt. Griffin, at Mrs. Milbank's Mass Meeting, Explains Attractions of New Martial Idea," *New York Times*, 13 June 1916, 11; "Khaki Clad Girls Aid 69th Bazaar; Self-Defence Leaguers, in Natty Uniforms, Sell Fancy Work," *New-York Tribune*, 30 Oct. 1916, 7.

34. “Women’s Reserve Formed; Former Members of League for Self-Defense in New Organization,” *New York Times*, 11 Feb. 1917, 18; “Feminine Rookies Win Approval of General [Leonard] Wood; Review of 102 Women Shows Progress in Drilling, Wireless and First Aid Prepare for Real War Hardening Muscles and Learning Military Manoeuvres to Defend Homes,” *New-York Tribune*, 25 Mar. 1917, 5; “Women Fighters; Valiant Americans Who Would Go to War with Men; Complete Regiment Ready; Colonel N. J. Boardman, One of the Leaders of the Woman Warriors Thinks If They Can’t Go with the Men to France, They Should Help Their Sisters in Russia,” *Red Bluff* (Calif.) *Daily News*, 12 Sept. 1917, 3.

35. “Fifty Society Girls to Study War’s Art; to Be Trained by Army Officers in Camp on Hewitt Estate, at Erskine, N.J.; Plattsburg Their Model; ‘Rookies’ to Do Their Own Cooking and Laundry, Practice Rifle-Shooting, and Take 30-Mile ‘Hikes,’” *New York Times*, 1 June 1916, 14; Marguerite Mooers Marshall, “Thirty New York Debutantes Uniformed in Khaki Breeches Begin Camp as ‘Soldierettes’; Coats ‘That Come to Knees’ When Visitors Are Around Only at the Headquarters of the Emergency Service Corps at Erskine, N. J., Where Captain Candace Hewitt and Her Force are Learning War Lessons—More Work Than at Chevy Chase,” *Washington Post*, 4 June 1916, ES5; Katie Wu, “From Satin to Khaki: Women Join the Military Preparedness Movement of 1916,” *O Say Can You See?* (blog), 6 Jan. 2016, http://americanhistory.si.edu/blog/satin-khaki-women-join-military-preparedness-movement-1916 (accessed 5 November 2019).

36. Marshall, “Thirty New York Debutantes Uniformed in Khaki Breeches,” ES5. Cf. Marshall, “Daily Routine of Women’s Training Camp,” 3.

37. National Special Aid Society, *National Special Aid Society* (New York: National Special Aid Society, ca. 1917), https://iiif.lib.harvard.edu/manifests/view/drs:2574379$1i (accessed 5 November 2019); Clarke, *American Women and the World War*, 433–434; “Women Active in Preparedness Plan; Arranging for New Duties in Case of War; Branch of Special Aid Society Organizing throughout State,” *Boston Daily Globe*, 20 Jan. 1916, 12; “Special Aid Society for American ‘Preparedness,’” *Cambridge* (Mass.) *Tribune*, 29 Jan. 1916, 4; Mrs. Barrett [Edith C.] Wendell, “Special Aid Society for American Preparedness,” *Worcester* (Mass.) *Magazine* 19, no. 3 (March 1916): 63.

38. “Mobilizing Women for War Readiness; Active Corps Planned of Trained Workers; Four Groups to Be Classified with Six Fields of Effort,” *Boston Daily Globe*, 9 Feb. 1917, 2 (quote); “Aid in Every County; Conferences throughout State Are Planned—Preparedness Society Will Show What It Has Accomplished,” *Boston Daily Globe*, 8 July 1917, 54; Nora Saltonstall, *“Out Here at the Front”: The World War I Letters of Nora Saltonstall*, ed. Judith S. Graham (Boston: Northeastern University Press, 2004), 25–26.

39. Chris Eger, “Things Change: There Was a Women’s Machine Gun Squad in 1918 New York (Photos),” Guns.com, 7 Oct. 2016, http://www.guns.com/2016/10/07/things-change-there-was-a-womens-machine-gun-squad-in-1918-new-york-photos/ (accessed 5 November 2019).

40. Andrea G. Radke-Moss, “‘The American Eagle in Bloomers’: ‘Student-Soldieresses’ and Women’s Military Activity,” in *Bright Epoch: Women and Coeducation in the American West* (Lincoln: University of Nebraska Press, 2008), 223–252; Committee on Public Information, *War Work of Women in Colleges* (Washington, D.C.: Government Printing Office, 1918).

41. “Military Training in Public Schools,” in *Issues of the Day: Being a Text-book on the Political Situation, Past and Present* (Chicago: Oliver, 1903), 432–435; L.R. Gignilliat, *Arms and the Boy: Military Training in Schools and Colleges* (Indianapolis: Bobbs-Merrill, 1916); Susan Zeiger, “The Schoolhouse vs. the Armory,” *Journal of Women’s History* 15, no. 2 (Summer 2003): 150–179.

42. L. Bartlett and C. Lutz, “Disciplining Social Difference: Some Cultural Politics of Military Training in Public High Schools,” *Urban Review* 30 (1998): 119–136. Cf. Gene M. Lyons and John W. Masland, *Education and Military Leadership: A Study of the R.O.T.C.* (Princeton, N.J.: Princeton University Press, 1959), especially part 2, “A Brief History of the ROTC,” 27–97. For a British view, see C.B. Otley, “Militarism and Militarization in the Public Schools, 1900–1972,” *British Journal of Sociology* 29 (1978): 321–39.

43. “School Drill Plan Will Pass, Canvass Shows; Real Guns, Uniforms, and Army Requirements Approved by Commission,” *Chicago Daily Tribune*, 10 Jan. 1917, 15; “Women Control School Board; Pasadena Men Not Anxious to Fill Vacancy; Specify High School Uniforms for Boys and Girls,” *Los Angeles Times*, 4 Aug. 1918, I11; Alison Happel, “Ritualized Girling: School Uniforms and the Compulsory Performance of Gender,” *Journal of Gender Studies* 22, no. 1 (Jan. 2013): 92–96.

44. Anastatia Hodgens Sims, “Juliette Gordon Low (1860–1927): Late-Blooming Daisy,” in *Georgia Women: Their Lives and Times*, ed. Ann Short Chirhart and Betty Wood (Athens: University of Georgia Press, 2009), 377–379, 380–385.

45. Sims, “Juliette Gordon Low,” 380–381.

46. Clarke, *American Women and the World War*, 206–207; Anna Steese Richardson, "Soldiers All: This Month—Mostly about Patriotic Work for Young People," *Women's Home Companion* 45, no. 4 (Apr. 1918): 64; "Opportunities for Women," *Woman Citizen* 3, no. 6 (6 July 1918): 115; "Girl Scouts Serve in World War I," Vintage Girl Scout Online Museum, 2016, http://www.vintagegirlscout.com/serww1.html (accessed 5 November 2019); Leslie Hahner, "Practical Patriotism: Camp Fire Girls, Girl Scouts, and Americanization," *Communication and Critical/Cultural Studies* 5, no. 2 (June 2008): 113–134.

47. Anna Worthington Coale, "When Girls Go to Camp," *St. Nicholas: A Monthly Magazine for Boys and Girls* 44, no. 6 (April 1917): 500.

48. Luther H. Gulick to President Wilson, 17 April 1917, as quoted in Gulick, "Girls Enlist," *Journal of Education* 85, no. 18 (3 May 1917): 485.

49. Gulick, "Girls Enlist," 486.

50. Steven C. Hohn, "The Origins of the Girl Guards," *Priority!* 7, no. 1 (Spring 2005); Gary Van Hoesen, "Brief History of Girl Guards," Get Connected, April 2015, http://salarmycentral.org/feature/april-2015/2562/brief-history-of-girl-guards/ (accessed 5 November 2019).

51. "Girls' National Honor Guard," *San Bernardino Sun*, 26 Aug. 1917, 2; "Girls' National Honor Guard," Vintage Kids Club Online Museum, 2016, http://www.vintagekidstuff.com/honor/honor.html (accessed 5 November 2019).

52. "The Philadelphia Plan of Emergency Aid," *Survey* 37, no. 24 (17 Mar. 1917): 697; Philadelphia War History Committee, "Emergency Aid of Pennsylvania," *Philadelphia in the World War, 1914–1919* (New York: Wynkoop Hallenbeck Crawford, 1922), 554–587; Joan C. McCulloh, "Accomplishments of the Mercersburg Branch of the Emergency Aid during World War I," Mercersburg Historical Society, http://mhs.mercersburg.org/blog/5/ (accessed 5 November 2019). For Emergency Aid uniforms, see Young, "'Petticoats Are Part of This Uniform,'" 143–147; Smith, *Dressed for Duty*, 1:312–316.

53. National Security League, *Proceedings of the Congress of Constructive Patriotism Held under the Auspices of the National Security League* (New York: National Service League, 1917), 126–135, 384–385; Bessie R. James, *For God, for Country, for Home: The National League for Woman's Service. A Story of the First National Organization of American Women Mobilized for War Service* (New York: G. P. Putnam's Sons, 1920), 12–18.

54. National League for Woman's Service, *Annual Report for the Year 1918, Including a Summary for the Year 1917* (New York: National League for Woman's Service, 1919), 9, 13 (quote).

55. Edward Hungerford, "She Tackles the Job," *Everybody's Magazine* 37, no. 4 (Oct. 1917): 430.

56. This uniform was depicted in a widely reproduced poster by Charles Dana Gibson. Gibson presented his original drawing to the U.S. Food Administration, which judged it too little related to food and offered it to the National League for Woman's Service (NLWS). Gibson then revised it to depict the NLWS uniform; NLWS, *Annual Report for the Year 1918*, 47, 49. Numerous photos of NLWS members in uniform appear in James, *For God, for Country, for Home*. See also Young, "'Petticoats Are Part of This Uniform,'" 188–196; Smith, *Dressed for Duty*, 1:381–388.

57. "To Counteract Lure of Uniform; Work Planned by Girls' Patriotic League Has Wide Scope," *Hartford Courant*, 17 May 1917, 18; Donna R. Causey, "Girls' Patriotic League Alabama," Alabama Pioneers, http://alabamapioneers.com/girls-patriotic-league-alabama-11959/ (accessed 5 November 2019); R. Louise Fitch, "For Country and for Liberty: The Patriotic League of the Y. W. C. A.," *St. Nicholas: A Monthly Magazine for Boys and Girls* 45, no. 6 (April 1918): 500–502.

58. NLWS, *Annual Report for the Year 1918*, 49, 21–22; "Need for Women's Service Realized; Many Opportunities in National League for Women's Service," *Columbia* (University) *Daily Spectator*, 16 July 1917, 1.

59. NLWS, *Annual Report for the Year 1918*, 46, 48, 118–119, 164–166. For photos of the women at work, see Richard Green, "Hidden Women: The Art of WWI Camouflage," *Unwritten Record* (blog), 19 July 2016, https://unwritten-record.blogs.archives.gov/2016/07/19/hidden-women-the-art-of-wwi-camouflage-photos/ (accessed 5 November 2019).

60. James, *For God, for Country, for Home*, 48–53; Alexander B. Magoun, "Wireless Women of World War I," *Today's Engineer*, Dec. 2012, 1–9.

61. Elene Foster, "The Versatile Errand Girls of Uncle Sam; Women's Motor Corps of the National League for Woman's Service Is Everlastingly 'on the Job'; the Trim, Uniformed Girls Drive Their Own Motor Cars and Ambulances Wherever They Are Needed on Government Service; Most of the Corps Is Kept Busy Just Now at Home, but One Detachment Already Has Been Detailed for Foreign Service," *New-York Tribune*, 21 Oct. 1917, D1; John Walker Harrington, "Women Show Skill as Auto Drivers; Thousands Have Done Splendid War Work

in Motor Corps Divisions at Home and Overseas," *New York Times*, 2 Feb. 1919, 92; James, *For God, for Country, for Home*, 55–57.

62. James, *For God, for Country, for Home*, 58–59. See dskjl, "N.L.W.S Motor Corps Group," U.S. Militaria Forum, 5 Mar. 2013, http://www.usmilitariaforum.com/forums/index.php?/topic/169821-nlws-motor-corps-group-published/ (accessed 5 November 2019); cwnorma, "National League for Women's Service Motor Corps Jacket," U.S. Militaria Forum, 9 Mar. 2007, http://www.usmilitariaforum.com/forums/index.php?/topic/3390-national-league-for-womens-service-motor-corps-jacket/ (accessed 5 November 2019).

63. Foster, "The Versatile Errand Girls of Uncle Sam," D1. See also Young, "'Petticoats Are Part of This Uniform,'" 197–202; Smith, *Dressed for Duty*, 1:383–387.

64. Chuppa-Cornell, "The U.S. Women's Motor Corps in France," 465–479; Virginia Scharff, *Taking the Wheel: Women and the Coming of the Motor Age* (New York: Free Press, 1991), 93–97; Miriam Blagden, "In Humanity's Service," *Motor* 37, no. 4 (Mar. 1922): 30, 84.

65. "Women's Motor Corps on Call Day and Night," *New York Times*, 7 April 1918, 79; "Women's Motor Corps of America," *Recruiter's Bulletin* 4, no. 3 (Jan. 1918): 15. For the Motor Corps of America uniform, see Big G. Cloak and Suit Co. advertisement, "Women's Motor Corps of America Uniform Made of Regulation Army Khaki Serge," *American Cloak and Suit Review* 16, no. 4 (Oct. 1918): 134. See also Young, "'Petticoats Are Part of This Uniform,'" 197–202; Smith, *Dressed for Duty*, 1: 372–377.

66. James, *For God, for Country, for Home*, 65; Amanda Brown, "From the Archives: Women of the Motor Service," America Red Cross, Red Cross chat, 13 Mar. 2014, https://redcrosschat.org/2014/03/13/from-the-archives-women-of-the-motor-service/ (accessed 5 November 2019). For the Red Cross Motor Corps uniform, see Young, "'Petticoats Are Part of This Uniform,'" 103–106; Smith, *Dressed for Duty*, 1:59–63.

67. Harrington, "Women Show Skill as Auto Drivers," 92.

68. Holly J. McCammon, "'Out of the Parlors and into the Streets': The Changing Tactic Repertoire of the U.S. Women's Suffrage Movements," *Social Forces* 81, no. 3 (Mar. 2003): 787–818; Jennifer L. Borda, "The Woman Suffrage Parades of 1910–1913: Possibilities and Limitations of an Early Feminist Rhetorical Strategy," *Western Journal of Communication* 66, no. 1 (Jan. 2002): 25–52; Sarah J. Moore, "Making a Spectacle of Suffrage: The National Woman Suffrage Pageant, 1913," *Journal of American Culture* 20, no.1 (Spring 1997): 89–103; Wendy Parkins, "'The Epidemic of Purple, White, and Green': Fashion and the Suffragette Movement in Britain 1908–14," in *Fashioning the Body Politic: Dress, Gender, Citizenship*, ed. Wendy Parkins (Oxford: Berg, 2002), 97–124; Linda J. Lumsden, *Rampant Women: Suffragists and the Right of Assembly* (Knoxville: University of Tennessee Press, 1997).

69. Holly J. McCammon, Karen E. Campbell, Ellen M. Granberg, and Christine Mowery, "How Movements Win: Gendered Opportunity Structures and U.S. Women's Suffrage Movements, 1866 to 1919," *American Sociological Review* 66, no. 1 (Feb. 2001): 49–70; Holly J. McCammon, "Stirring Up Suffrage Sentiment: The Formation of the State Woman Suffrage Organizations, 1866–1914," *Social Forces* 80, no. 2 (Dec. 2001): 449–480.

70. Sally Hunter Graham, "Woodrow Wilson, Alice Paul, and the Woman Suffrage Movement," *Political Science Quarterly* 98, no. 4 (Winter 1983–1984): 665–679; Christine A. Lunardini, *From Equal Suffrage to Equal Rights: Alice Paul and the National Woman's Party, 1910–1928* (New York: New York University Press, 1986).

71. Robert Booth Fowler and Spencer Jones, "Carrie Chapman Catt and the Last Years of the Struggle for Woman Suffrage," in *Votes for Women: The Struggle for Suffrage Revisited*, ed. Jean H. Baker (New York: Oxford University Press, 2002), 136.

72. As quoted in Eleanor Flexner, *Century of Struggle: The Woman's Rights Movement in the United States* (1959; repr., New York: Atheneum, 1968), 277. See also Sara Hunter Graham, "The Suffrage Machine," in *Woman Suffrage and the New Democracy* (New Haven, Conn.: Yale University Press, 1996), 99–127.

73. David Morgan, *Suffragists and Democrats: The Politics of Woman Suffrage in America* (East Lansing: Michigan State University Press, 1972); Linda Lumsden, "'Excellent Ammunition': Suffrage Newspaper Strategies during World War I," *Journalism History* 25, no. 2 (Summer 1999): 53–63; Alana S. Jeydel, "The Impact of the Activist President on the Lobbying Efforts of the Woman Suffrage Movement," *White House Studies* 2, no. 3 (2002): 271–287.

74. Ida Husted Harper, ed., *History of Woman Suffrage*, vol. 5, *1900–1920* (New York: National American Woman Suffrage Association, 1922), 720–726.

75. Flexner, *Century of Struggle*, 289.

76. Kimberly Jensen, "Women, Citizenship, and Civic Sacrifice: Engendering Patriotism in the First World War," in *Bonds of Affection: Americans Define Their Patriotism*, ed. John Bodnar (Princeton, N.J.: Princeton University Press, 1996), 139–159.

77. Richard J. Evans, "Women's Peace, Men's War?" in *Comrades and Sisters: Feminism, Socialism and Pacifism in Europe, 1870–1945* (Brighton, U.K.: Wheatsheaf Books, 1987), 121–156; Joyce Berkman, "Feminism, War, and Peace Politics: The Case of World War I," in *Women, Militarism, and War: Essays in History, Politics, and Social Theory*, ed. Jean Bethke Elshtain and Shiela Tobias (Savage, Md.: Rowman & Littlefield, 1990), 141–160; Ruth Roach Pierson, "'Did Your Mother Wear Army Boots?': Feminist Theory and Women's Relation to War, Peace and Revolution," in *Images of Women in Peace and War: Cross-Cultural and Historical Perspectives*, ed. Sharon Macdonald, Pat Holden and Shirley Ardener (Madison: University of Wisconsin Press, 1987), 213–217.

78. Erika A. Kuhlman, *Petticoats and White Feathers: Gender, Conformity, Race, the Progressive Peace Movement, and the Debate over War, 1895–1919* (Westport, Conn.: Greenwood Press, 1997); Frances H. Early, *A World without War: How U.S. Feminists and Pacifists Resisted World War I* (Syracuse, N.Y.: Syracuse University Press, 1997); Jean Bethke Elshtain, "Solidarity Which Will Not Waver: Jane Addams in War and Peace," in *Jane Addams and the Dream of American Democracy: A Life* (New York: Basic Books, 2002), 211–250.

79. Jane Addams, Emily G. Balch, and Alice Hamilton, *Women at The Hague: The International Congress of Women and Its Results* (New York: Macmillan, 1915); Gertrude Bussey and Margaret Tims, "Wartime Prelude," in *Pioneers for Peace: Women's International League for Peace and Freedom 1915–1965* (London: WILPF British Section, 1965), 17–24; Jonathan M. Hansen, "Fighting Words," in *The Lost Promise of Patriotism: Debating American Identity, 1890–1920* (Chicago: University of Chicago Press, 2003), 157–184.

80. Harper, *History of Woman Suffrage*, 5:533–537; Kathleen Kennedy, *Disloyal Mothers and Scurrilous Citizens: Women and Subversion during World War I* (Bloomington: Indiana University Press, 1999); Barbara J. Steinson, "'The Mother Half of Humanity": American Women in the Peace and Preparedness Movements in World War I," in *Women, War and Revolution*, ed. Carol R. Berkin and Clara M. Lovett (New York: Holmes & Meier, 1980), 265–268.

FIFTEEN

CAPE, CAP, AND CADUCEUS

American Medical Women and the Politics of Uniforms

MARIAN MOSER JONES

The American Red Cross nurse's cape definitively symbolized U.S. women's participation in World War I. Many full-color fund-raising posters for American Red Cross war relief in 1917 and 1918 featured a fresh-faced nurse wearing this navy wool, scarlet-lined cape flipped over the shoulders of her crisp white uniform, whereas black-and-white images of the nurse in her waist-length cape graced the style pages of newspapers around the country. Captions to these images called attention to "the cape of poems and posters and stories," which nevertheless served the prosaic function of offering "practical protection against cold in the hundred daily errands through corridors and courtyards." The cape's influence even crossed the Atlantic, as Parisian designers of women's outerwear began imitating this distinctive outerwear of "nurses américaines" in designing their coats for the 1917–1918 winter season.[1]

After the war, the scarlet-lined navy cape remained deeply associated with American women's medical service. The caped nurse reappeared in American Red Cross posters for 1920s flood relief, and a navy-and-scarlet cape drapes the shoulders of a towering white-gowned goddess at the center of a painting by a Greek refugee. This painting paid tribute to the volunteer women physicians of the American Women's Hospital who served Greeks fleeing Turkish-occupied territory in the early 1920s. Never mind that these women physicians favored khaki Norfolk jackets and ties worn over long, dark skirts and sometimes even breeches, rather than a white dress with a cape. During this era, this navy-and-scarlet Red Cross nurse's cape served as an internationally legible symbol of American women's medical humanitarianism.[2]

Figure 15.1.
American Red Cross recruitment poster, 1917–1918. Library of Congress, Prints and Photographs Division.

The large penumbra cast by the cape, however, tends to obscure the variation and complexity in uniforms that nurses and other American medical women wore during the World War I era. The nearly 24,000 U.S. Army, Navy, and Red Cross nurses comprised, by far, the largest group of U.S. medical women who served in the war. The Army, however, also recruited some 1,800 women as reconstruction aides (physical and occupational therapists), 356 as dietitians, at least 398 as laboratory assistants, and 55 as civilian contract surgeons. Another 130 women physicians and allied professionals also served in uniform treating civilians in the American Women's Hospitals established in France.[3]

During this era, American medical women's uniforms became instrumental in their efforts to establish professional and military identities. This hardly made American women's uniforms unique; uniforms during this era proved critical in *enabling* women within the Allied nations and the Central powers to serve in unprecedented public, professional, and sometimes military roles, albeit with varying levels of success and social acceptance. Moreover, American medical women's uniforms were similar to those worn by women of other belligerents in enabling their public participation in the war by offering symbolic and practical protection against mud, rain, cold, and infectious disease, as well as unwelcome sexual attention from men.[4]

What, then, is different about U.S. medical women's uniforms? At first glance, not much. Within the broader continuum of "martial femininities" established by women in uniform during the war, as formulated by Krisztina Robert (ch. 2), American medical women stood somewhere in the political and cultural middle. With the exception of uniforms worn by a few female U.S. Army contract surgeons during the last months of the war, American medical women's uniforms did not openly challenge gender norms by directly imitating men's uniforms in the brash manner of the breast-pocketed khaki suit jackets worn by Britain's Women's Army Auxiliary Corps described by Robert (ch. 2) or the Australian Women's Service Corps described by Scates and colleagues (ch. 6). Yet their designers and wearers also eschewed hair-covering nunlike veils worn by most nurses and nursing aides of other Allied nations, as described by Christine Hallett et al. (ch. 3) and Laurie Stoff (ch. 10), as well as high-fashion flourishes, like the gold buttons and belt clasps of the much-envied Canadian nurses discussed by Cynthia Toman (ch. 5) or the impractically high-heeled, white

Figure 15.2.
To the American Women's Hospitals, *painting, ca. 1920, by a Greek refugee, Constantinople. Although American Women's Hospital physicians wore jackets, the Red Cross nurse's cape reappears here. Esther Pohl Lovejoy,* Certain Samaritans *(New York: MacMillan, 1927), inside front cover illustration.*

boots worn by American expatriate millionaire Mary Borden while directing her self-funded hospital for the French army, as discussed by Hallett et al. (ch. 3). Overall, American medical women's uniforms were both distinctly feminine and definitively utilitarian.

However, this precise mix of middle-of-the-road femininity and modern practicality is what made these uniforms unmistakably American. They reflected a uniquely American sensibility, rooted in its Puritanism but dominated by a Progressive Era obsession with efficiency, standardization, and professionalism. The particular cut and color of these uniforms distinguished their wearers as professionals, as members of a modern military, and as modern *American* women. The political importance of clothing in establishing a distinct national identity for U.S. nurses and other medical personnel in the multinational, polyglot world of the war zone cannot be underestimated, given the country's late entry into the war and its insecure status during this era as an emergent world power. When the United States declared war on Germany in 1917, few combat troops were ready to mobilize, but Army medical units had already been organized and (mostly) supplied through the Red Cross. As a result, these units became the first troops to plant the American flag on French soil and signal to the Allies that the Americans had arrived to help.[5] If only a few thousand American doughboys, their khaki and olive drab breast-pocketed coats blending in with the larger armies of the British Empire, would make it to the front before the final pushes in 1918, at least the highly trained professional American Red Cross nurse, in her navy-and-scarlet cape and starched white uniform, would make a splash and let the world know that America, too, had something important to contribute.

THE AMERICAN RED CROSS AND MEDICAL WOMEN'S UNIFORMS

An analysis of World War I women's uniforms must begin with a discussion of the American Red Cross and its involvement in the war effort, as this organization played a leading role in dictating uniform design, supply, and use. Although dozens of organizations doing war work designed uniforms for their women volunteers and paid workers, the Red Cross quickly became the largest organization in the field; it recruited 8 million women volunteers on the home front and employed over 12,700 paid workers, several thousand of them women. The Red Cross issued distinct uniform regulations and patterns for different types of volunteers and paid workers. It also expended about $3 million to supply uniforms to nurses, nurses' aides, dietitians, reconstruction aides, and other workers, even though most of these women were inducted into the Army or Navy.[6]

To understand why a voluntary body like the Red Cross served as quartermaster for military nurses and allied workers requires a look into its history. In the United States, because the federalized nineteenth-century state provided inconsistent benefits to citizens and early American democratic culture emphasized charity as a social and religious obligation, voluntary organizations such as fire brigades and benevolent associations formed to meet Americans' health, safety, and social welfare needs. The American Red Cross, founded in 1881 by Clara Barton of Civil War fame, played a unique role in this system. It not only provided disaster relief on a nationwide basis, it also took charge of volunteer medical assistance to the armed forces in time of war.[7] The American Red Cross belonged to the Geneva-based international Red Cross movement, founded in 1863 to mitigate the human consequences of war. The Geneva Convention, its founding document, bound signatories to form volunteer wartime medical auxiliaries whose members provided neutral aid to all war wounded without regard to nationality. The convention specified that members of these volunteer bodies were to wear a white armband with a red cross while in the battlefield, giving rise to the name "Red Cross" society.[8]

During the Spanish-American war, the Red Cross failed miserably to meet American obligations under the Geneva Convention; such a failure enabled government leaders and elite philanthropists in 1905 to reorganize it along Progressive lines, as a quasi-governmental auxiliary of the War Department. In 1909, the new American Red Cross formed a committee on nursing to enroll professional nurses for service in disaster relief and war. Jane Arminda Delano, former nursing superintendent of New York's Bellevue Hospital, who had just taken charge of a young Army Nurse Corps, agreed to serve as volunteer head of the Red Cross nursing committee. Delano had been involved in the transformation of American nursing from a disreputable, unregulated occupation into a tight sisterhood of hospital-trained professionals based on an educational model established in Great Britain by Florence Nightingale. This model emphasized rigorous application of sanitary science and conformity to strict Victorian moral standards—a reaction to the earlier stereotype that women who nursed the sick for pay had loose morals and lacked refinement, as no respectable, middle-class woman would undertake work that involved intimate contact with the bodies of male strangers.[9] Delano now applied these newer standards of training and morality in shaping the Red Cross and the Army Nurse Corps into efficient, professionalized organizations.

Established in 1901, the Army Nurse Corps had received scant appropriations to enroll and equip nurses and "was in trouble" when Delano took charge. She strengthened the corps in part by negotiating a contract between the Red Cross and the Army Nurse Corps that designated the Red Cross as the official wartime recruiter of Army nurses. The Army Nurse Corps benefited greatly from its association with the amply funded and extensively networked Red Cross. Delano made similar arrangements with the fledgling Navy Nurse Corps, founded in 1908. As official recruiter of military nurses, the Red Cross maintained strict standards for enrollment that placed equal emphasis on training at a respected hospital-based school and character references from a leading nursing superintendent, along with registration or other credentials.[10] These standards and the intertwined relationship between the Red Cross and the military nurse corps would make the American Army, Navy, and Red Cross nurses one of the most tightly regulated and professionalized groups of nurses to serve in the war (matched only by the Canadian nursing sisters that Toman (ch. 5) discusses), effectively preventing all but a few American women without substantial professional training from volunteering for "nursing" in war hospitals in the manner of women who volunteered for British Voluntary Aid Detachments described in chapters 3 (Hallett et al.), 5 (Toman), and 6 (Scates et al.) or the Russian Sisters of Mercy that Stoff discusses (ch. 10). This nearly unrivaled level of professionalization in American war nursing was reflected in regulations on nurses' uniforms and insignia in the years leading up to the war.

Soon after the Red Cross began enrolling nurses, it also began issuing them a distinctive round pin with a red cross on a white enamel background, encircled by a navy-blue ring bearing the words "American National Red Cross Nurse" in gold and bordered by a gold laurel. To control against fraudulent manufacture and wearing, each nurse was assigned a specific number, which was engraved on the back of her pin. From 1906 to 1914, the pin was the Red Cross nurses' only distinctive item. The Army and Navy followed suit with quarter-sized round metal badges. The Army badge featured a caduceus of gold or gilt, superimposed at its center by the letters "A.N.C." in white enamel. The Navy badge was "made of heavy gold plate with dull rough surface," emblazoned with the letters "U.S.N." under "an anchor combined with the caduceus."[11] These Red Cross, Army, and Navy badges served as Progressive Era marks of uniformity and quality, like brand names and safety inspection labels. During this period of increasing regulation and standardization in the United States, such a guarantee assured a wary public that the product met uniform standards of quality; this principle operated no differently when the "product" was a Red Cross nurse than when it was Ivory soap or a Ford automobile.[12]

Figure 15.3.
American Red Cross nurses' original uniform with cape, 1914. American Red Cross Magazine, *July 1914, 171.*

Although the Red Cross initially included no standard uniform specifications, both the Army and Navy services issued such standards in the prewar years. Army Nurse Corps regulations stipulated that the uniform be white and consist of a shirtwaist (a tailored blouse) as well as a belt, a skirt, a bishop collar (a round collar worn close around the neck), and white cap; the regulation allowed the surgeon general of the Army to dictate further specifications. The official Navy nurse's uniform differed from the Army's only in two respects: The material for the white cap must be "Persian lawn" (a very fine cotton used in wedding dresses) and contain a 1-inch black velvet band, and a "Geneva Red Cross" must be embroidered on "the left sleeve of the uniform half-way between the shoulder and elbow."[13] Notably, however, neither the Army nor Navy nurses' uniform during this period included outdoor wear.

In April 1914, the Red Cross issued its own uniform specifications. This uniform, unveiled with great fanfare during the joint national convention of the American Nurses Association, the National Organization for Public Health Nursing, and the National League of Nursing Education, comprised a light-blue crepe dress, a soft white open collar with pointed edges, a single-strap white apron, a white cap with a small red cross on its front, and a white arm brassard bearing a large red cross. As cool-weather outerwear, the uniform included a scarlet-lined, waist-length navy wool cape with a wool red cross stitched onto the outside near the front. According to Delano's official report of the meeting, the new uniform "received enthusiastic approval." Nurses from Red Cross headquarters distributed samples of material to attendees, and the participants made plans to distribute patterns to local Red Cross nursing committees so they could outfit the nurses in their local areas.[14]

The choice of wool cape as outerwear rather than tailored jacket identified nurses as distinctly feminine actors within the masculine military medical setting. As was the case with British nurses, the sartorial contrast between American Red Cross nurses haloed in loose navy-and-scarlet capes and the drably clad men of the battlefield in their form-fitting khaki or blue-gray single-breasted service coats could hardly have been sharper. With its winglike shape and bright avian colors, the cape referenced the Florence Nightingale–inspired ideal of the war nurse as a self-sacrificing feminine angel alighting at the bedside of the sick soldier to firmly but gently guide him back toward health.[15]

On a more profound level, the rich navy blue and flaming scarlet paid homage to one of Christendom's most revered figures, the Virgin Mary. Classic fourteenth century Italian images of Madonna and child, such as Duccio's *Maestà* altarpiece in Siena and Giotto's *Ognissanti Madonna* in Florence's Uffizi Gallery, depict the Virgin draped in a rich navy-blue cloak lined with bright-red hues or with a red dress underneath. Such images were undoubtedly familiar to Delano, who had spent a long sojourn in Italy immediately prior to taking charge of the Army Nurse Corps and the Red Cross nursing committee. Delano and her assistants, while also seeking to gain recognition of the profession as grounded in hard science, gained much from enveloping their nurses in such archetypal symbols of feminine purity. This bold idealization overwrote the prior stereotypes of nurses as boozy, unkempt, and incompetent, like the drunken midwife Sairey Gamp in Dickens' *Martin Chuzzlewit*, or as fallen, promiscuous women, and thus addressed male military leaders' perennial concerns—present in nearly every nation's military, as other chapters attest—that such women working in war hospitals would only distract, weaken, or demoralize their troops.[16] This almost magic cloak of feminine virtue gave Red Cross nurses the power and permission to operate within the masculine war zone.

On a more mundane level, the American Red Cross cape referenced the uniforms of Queen Alexandra's Imperial Military Nursing Service (QA), which had already seen 12 years of service in British imperial wars when World War I began. QA nurses wore long gray dresses with short wool scarlet shoulder capes (tippets), whereas the larger corps of territorial force nurses (the reserve) wore scarlet-bordered tippets. As Hallett et al. (ch. 3) note, the gray dress and tippet clearly distinguished QA nurses from civilian nurses. Moreover, in contrast to the four-pocket uniform jacket, jodhpurs, and puttees worn by male doctors and hospital workers, the QA nurses' shoulder capes and wool or crepe dresses served as a bright-line marker of gender in British field hospitals. Although the exigencies of conflict pushed these medical men and women into close working relationships, the visually distinct uniforms served as reminders that they still occupied separate social spheres.

For the American military nurses, who often were assigned to already-established British or Allied field hospitals, the waist-length navy-and-scarlet cape further distinguished them from their British and Anzac counterparts in their gray dresses and short tippets. Canadian nurses' uniforms also included longer navy capes lined with deep cherry-red material, with gold clasps as outerwear. This cape, introduced in 1904, may, in fact, have inspired the more utilitarian American nurses' cape. But the Canadians were most noted for their blue dress uniforms with two rows of overtly military brass buttons on the chest—their own unique markers of an emergent military femininity and national identity, as Cynthia Toman discusses (ch. 5). Amid these differences, the wearing of a cape united an Anglophone sorority of professional war nurses trained in the Nightingale model.[17]

One notable difference between the U.S. nurses' uniforms and those of other nations' nurses was the fact that the Americans wore nurses' caps and not veils, as Hallett et al. (ch. 3) point out. There are two likely reasons for this unique feature. First, the cap functioned as part of the uniform's overall purpose as envisioned by the pioneer leaders in American professional nursing who designed these uniforms to establish the wearer's professional identity and to distinguish her from an untrained or lesser-trained volunteer. Nurses' caps, adopted in modern American professional nursing schools and hospitals, more clearly communicated this message than veils with their age-old religious connotations. Second, although in other countries the veil served to "identify its wearer as a woman of purity and chastity," as Hallett et al. (ch. 3) note, American nurses had no need for such sartorial moral protection when they were already wearing a long, body-cloaking cape in the Virgin Mary's own colors over a high-necked white uniform. At the same time, from the beginning of the war, elite U.S. women volunteered in France and other countries with the Red Cross or other organizations (Hacker, ch. 14) or nursed with British Voluntary Aid Detachment corps, and many adopted the veil as part of these volunteer uniforms. When the United States entered the war, some American Red Cross volunteer uniforms also incorporated the veil.[18] The nurse's cap made trained American professional nurses stand out from the pack of untrained American volunteers and other nations' nurses.

GRAY WAR UNIFORMS, SHADES OF DISCONTENT

In 1914, Red Cross nurses debuted their new uniforms not in France but on the Mexican border. When notified in May 1914 that the Army needed nurses to support its engagement with Mexican revolutionary forces, Red Cross leaders immediately drew up a circular with "definite instructions concerning uniforms and equipment." It specified "a special field uniform of blue-gray" designed to be "suitable for service in a warm country" that could "launder easily and pack in small space." The uniform's white cap, white collar, and strapless white apron, unlike most white nurses' uniforms, required no starch to launder. But it was also "so unbecoming and washed so poorly" that the nurses obtained special permission to return to their white uniforms.[19]

Despite its shortcomings, this blue-gray crepe uniform outlasted the brief U.S.-Mexican conflict. The outbreak of World War I in August 1914 led the Red Cross to recruit 126 enrolled nurses, along with 30 male surgeons, for service in Europe. When the nurses showed up in New York to board what the press named the "Mercy Ship," they were each issued a set of six "grey chambray uniforms," not the light-blue uniforms introduced the prior April. All other features of the standard uniform remained the same. Each nurse was also issued a brown canvas duffel bag marked with a circular emblem of the American Red Cross, packed with "twelve white aprons, six collars, four caps," along with a white cotton Red Cross brassard, a navy-blue wool cape lined with red, a navy-blue felt hat, a gray wool sweater, an olive-green "steamer robe" (to keep warm on deck chairs), a laundry bag, a shoe bag, and a bag "containing scissors, needles, cotton, buttons and a piece of the uniform material."[20] As was the case in Great Britain (Hallett et al., ch. 3), the American military supply chain did not offer nurses' clothing repair services; nurses were expected to care for and repair their own uniforms.

By issuing these visually distinct uniforms, the Red Cross intended to make the women going to Europe instantly identifiable in the war zone as *American* Red Cross nurses. Writing in 1922, Sarah Elizabeth Pickett, Delano's assistant, recognized the important role the uniform had played at this pivotal moment. She recalled watching the nurses standing in a line against the lower rail of the Mercy Ship as it set sail. "The white caps, the gray uniforms, the line of scarlet as the fresh sea wind blew back the active service capes, *proclaimed their identity*," she wrote. A national identity, of course, but also the identity of a neutral medical worker in the war zone. American Red Cross nurses and doctors were being sent to hospitals in nations on both sides of the conflict, in keeping with the organization's obligations under the Geneva Convention and America's neutral status. Fearing that Red Cross brassards alone did not sufficiently identify the American nurses as neutrals, Delano ordered them to wear full uniforms throughout their transatlantic passage and thereafter for their "protection." Delano and Helen Scott Hay, the chief nurse on the mission, also ordered the nurses to wear their Red Cross badges (pins) at all times and to carry with them their certificates of immunization and official documents.[21]

Some nurses viewed their capes and uniforms as broadly protective against the hazards of nature and war. On the way to Russia in October 1914, Mary Frederika Farley and the other "Kiev nurses" and doctors endured a stormy voyage across a rough Baltic Sea on a "very small boat." The boat's pitching drove Farley from her berth and "on deck at 10 a.m. in my night gown, wrapper [cape] and uniform." Fresh air did not avert seasickness, but the clothing offered some protection from the rain and also may have helped her feel less vulnerable on this strange, turbulent sea. Mary Gladwin, chief nurse for the Red Cross unit in Belgrade, reported using her cape as a form of armor. On 1 December 1914, she awoke to find the Serbians evacuating the city before an invading Austrian army. But all she could think about was breakfast. "This morning, I wanted eggs very much, so threw my cape over my white uniform and ran, literally ran, down to the market, not in fear of the Austrians but in considerable dread of the disapproval of the Chief," she wrote. Luckily, the chief surgeon evidently forgave her, and the invading Austrians decided not to take her prisoner. Gladwin's mention of her white uniform in this passage also indicates that not all Red Cross nurses always wore the official gray. Serving in Antoine Depage's Belgian field hospital close to the front in 1916 (Ilse Bogaerts and Luc De Munck, ch. 8), Florence May Cooper also recalled in her diary wearing her cape during a particularly harrowing incident. Awakened one night by sounds of gunfire and bombs dropping nearby, followed shortly by a maid yelling at her to go downstairs, "I slipped into my red cross coat, for protection."[22]

In August 1915, the Red Cross informed the nurses that it was recalling all units except those in Belgium. Many nurses sought to volunteer with other organizations, such as the American Ambulance, a war hospital in Paris, and scrambled to have white uniforms made or sent to them. Until their new uniforms arrived, some nurses sought to be exempted from Red Cross orders to wear gray uniforms only on Red Cross duty; they also wondered whether or not they could continue to wear their Red Cross pins while working for other organizations.[23] Such correspondence indicates the seriousness with which the Red Cross nurses regarded uniform rules.

A few nurses also celebrated the distinct identity that the Red Cross uniform had given them. In an unsigned 1915 Christmas card, a nurse assigned to duty in Belgium wrote,

> Here's to the American Red Cross uniform which has turned the heads of all Europe—the outdoor costume which rivals the latest from Paris—the uniform which is equally becoming to all, the bewitching cap and collar, the cuffs (where are they?) the apron with its captivating bib and dainty strings which renders all figures alike graceful. May its popularity continue.[24]

The sarcasm may only disguise an underlying affection. But by the time that the last Mercy Ship nurses completed their service in mid-1916, their displeasure at the gray crepe indoor uniform had reached Director Delano. She also received reports that the material was now in short supply. Delano agreed, reluctantly, to allow Red Cross nurses who joined base hospitals to wear the white uniforms of the nursing schools they had attended. But she wrote Bessie Baker, the lead nurse of the unit being organized at Johns Hopkins Hospital, "low neck and short sleeves will not be allowed."[25]

1917: UNIFORMED, BUT HARDLY UNIFORM

When the United States entered the war on the side of the Allies in April 1917, the Red Cross abandoned its neutral stance to become an extension of the American armed forces. For a year prior to the declaration of war, nursing superintendents at each major teaching hospital had worked closely with Red Cross nursing leaders to assemble a roster of respected graduate nurses who met stringent Red Cross requirements for enrolled nurses. Leading physicians at the teaching hospitals also assembled rosters for medical officer positions. All this effective spadework allowed the quick mobilization of base hospital units to serve in both the Army and Navy Medical Corps. Despite nearly 6,000 practicing women physicians in the United States by 1915, neither the Army nor Navy accepted women physicians as medical officers—although the Army later hired women as civilian contract surgeons and women physicians served with volunteer bodies.[26]

Figure 15.4.
Standard gray chambray American Red Cross nurse's uniform. American Journal of Nursing, *November 1917.*

The Lakeside Hospital Unit in Cleveland would be the first American military unit of any kind to sail for France, as Base Hospital No. 4. On 3 May 1917, Maj. H.L. Gilchrist, the unit's commanding officer, ordered nurses and doctors "to uniform themselves."[27] Dr. George Washington Crile, the unit's chief medical officer, went to a quartermaster's depot on New York's Governor's Island to procure Army uniforms for the physicians and male enlisted personnel. On 7 May, the day before the unit sailed, Clara Noyes, director of the Red Cross Bureau of Nursing, personally distributed to each nurse a cape, a hat, two blankets, and $50 spending money.[28] But the rest of the nurses' kit was long delayed. When the nurses arrived at the ship, they "huddled together on the deck of the ferry boat, obviously reflecting upon the unjust lot which gave them no uniforms, no equipment," Crile observed, angry at Noyes and the Red Cross for failing to properly outfit the nurses.[29] These nurses, in fact, did not receive their full kits from the Red Cross until 4 July.[30] So when the British royal family on 23 May officially received the Clevelanders at Buckingham Palace—they were honored as members of the first American military unit to arrive in the war zone—the nurses wore their Red Cross capes over white uniforms.[31]

Although subsequent base hospital units headed for France had less trouble receiving their uniforms, different groups of Red Cross volunteers were responsible for having uniforms made for each unit, meaning that considerable variation persisted. Nurses of the Pennsylvania Hospital in Philadelphia, who would become part of Base Hospital No. 10, were measured for their uniforms a week before they sailed for France. Measurements went to a local Red Cross committee in New York, which then provided them with the uniforms when they boarded ship in New York Harbor on 17 May, the day before sailing. Although the "well made" uniforms "fitted very well under the circumstances," Chief Nurse Margaret A. Dunlop noted in an official history, the indoor uniforms were dark blue rather than regulation gray. Combined with dark-navy wool Ulster coats and hats provided as outwear, the uniforms appeared "very somber and the nurses became known as the Pennsylvania Hospital 'orphans.'" Nonetheless, Dunlop added, "after many months of service, the uniform became very dear to us and the comfort and protection that it secured to us in France were very much appreciated."[32] Photos in the hospital's official history indicate that the nurses did not always wear these dark uniforms on duty: Some wore gray; others varied their collar shape. Similarly, nurses from Base Hospital No. 9, a unit organized at New York Hospital that operated in Savenay, France, are pictured in their unit's official history wearing indoor uniforms of different shades and styles, with variously shaped collars, and white aprons with one or two straps—not just the one-strap, triangular, peaked apron of the official Red Cross nurses' uniform.[33]

Base hospitals mobilized later in 1917 provided their nurses with a standard outdoor uniform in addition to the indoor uniform. This Army Nurse Corps uniform comprised

Figure 15.5.
Nurses and medical officers from Base Hospital No. 12, the Northwestern University Hospital Unit, pictured with Sir Thomas Lipton, at his estate in Southgate, London, on 10 June 1917. Nurses are wearing their Army Nurse Corps–issued dresses as uniforms, without capes. Library of Congress, Prints and Photographs Division.

long, belted double-breasted navy-blue serge dresses, with band collars and rows of dark-blue buttons running down each side of the chest. Official photographs show nurses wearing the dresses as they drilled in training camps, assembled on deck while en route to Europe, or met with Sir Thomas Lipton in Great Britain. Some wore capes, some did not; some wore Red Cross brassards on the left sleeve, some did not. Even within units, the shape and shade of their dark fedora hats varied somewhat.[34]

Part of the variation in nurses' uniforms came from the considerable creativity that nurses exhibited in wearing them. On 4 October 1917, such creativity was on display in the Red Cross parade in New York, where a number of base hospital units were stationed awaiting sailing orders. Maude Essig, a nurse from Base Hospital No. 32 of Indianapolis, marched with other nurses 16 abreast for 69 blocks down Fifth Avenue:

> The nurses for overseas duty followed the Chief dignitaries and Sousa's Band—each unit in different parade dress, i.e.; some in slickers, some in white uniform and cap [,] some in blue dress uniform, some with capes all blue, some with corner of cape thrown back to show red lining, many variations—our unit wore blue dress uniform (no wrap) and dress hat. It was a gorgeous sight. Every type of Red Cross uniform represented.

Or as Ruth Wright, another Base Hospital No. 32 nurse, expressed it more tersely, "Youngstown in Ulsters. Detroit in capes. Indianapolis in Blue Dress."[35]

1918: LOOKING "QUITE MILITARY"

By the end of 1917, the Red Cross had ironed out the problems and inconsistencies of outfitting nurses. Emma Elizabeth Weaver, a nurse who sailed for France in March 1918 with the second group from Philadelphia's Pennsylvania Hospital (Base Hospital No. 20), wrote of how she received her full uniform and underclothing while training at Ellis Island: "Uncle Sam & the Red Cross give us a very adequate & appropriate outfit. Good looking dark-blue serge suits, dark-blue cloth over-coats. We wear the U.S. insignia on the collars, also the A.N.C. medical caduceus—dark-blue hat to match, chin strap for windy weather. When new the outfit looks quite military." The full nurse's kit cataloged by Weaver included rain coat, rubber boots, sweater, two pairs of black tights, three pairs of pajamas, four sets of underwear, ten pairs of socks, four pairs of shoes, three caps, cuff links, aprons, blanket, sleeping bag, "carry all," poncho, and tan gloves. She deemed this a "very adequate and appropriate outfit." Although intended only for Red Cross nurses working with civilians, the white Red Cross brassard also comprised part of the unit's uniform.[36]

Each nurse also received four gray cotton uniforms. Despite nurses' oft-stated preference for white, gray remained the standard for overseas units. Nurses arriving in France often had to do their own laundry in their scant spare time with little equipment: A washboard was a "prized possession," and the nurses at first "often went on duty in unironed uniforms," according to nurse Irene Brewster of Base Hospital No. 65. Brewster expressed sentiments similar to Weaver's but indicated that they were likely influenced by the patriotism of the moment. "Our uniform was probably ill-fitting and unbecoming, but we wore it with all the pride we could muster," she stated, adding, "how we ever managed to walk so lightly in those heavy shoes has always been a mystery to me."[37]

The dark-blue serge suit, which the Army introduced in November 1917 to replace the navy double-breasted long dress, featured a Norfolk jacket—a loose, single-breasted, belted wool suit jacket of a style worn by English country gentlemen in shooting sports but adapted for women's outdoor wear in the early 1900s. Nurses most commonly wore this jacket over a white band-collared shirtwaist (sometimes with tie) and a long navy wool skirt.[38] Because the Army mobilized far more nurses than any other organization, the Army-style jacketed outdoor uniform became the norm for most nurses, overseas and at home. In the war zone, it was never the only option, as illustrated in the 1918 Red Cross pamphlet *All Honor to the War Nurse*, each page of which featured and described a different uniform. In addition to the outdoor Army uniform with its Norfolk jacket and the gray cotton crepe Red Cross indoor uniform, the pamphlet featured a white-capped nurse in white uniform wearing the "famous red-lined cape," its "brilliant lining thrown smartly over the shoulder, following tradition."[39] (A tradition, we may add, no earlier than 1914!) The pamphlet also addressed the "distinctive outdoor uniform of the U.S. Navy nurses"—a double-breasted coat cape with "U.S." and anchor pins on each lapel, worn over a dark band-collared blouse, and the same dark round-brimmed wool fedora hat, long navy wool skirt, dark gloves, and square-heeled, laced leather shoes that comprised the Army nurses' uniform. The pamphlet omitted a variant of the Navy uniform: a single-breasted serge suit, like the newer Army uniform but with a coat that buttoned up the left side all the way to the standing collar.[40]

Figure 15.6.
Army Nurse Corps nurse Mary Welty Christie, Base Hospital No. 12, in uniform (1919) with three service chevrons on the left sleeve to indicate 18 months of overseas service. Christie Collection, Midwest Nursing History Research Center, College of Nursing, University of Illinois at Chicago.

The pamphlet also displayed less common uniforms. One was the summer outdoor uniform of Red Cross nurses stationed in the Mediterranean region—a gray four-pocket Norfolk jacket and skirt, with gloves, boots, and gray straw hat with navy band bearing a Red Cross on the front. Red Cross public health nurses working in France and in rural America wore blue gingham uniforms that differed only in color from the gray crepe Red Cross indoor uniform.[41] Finally came the "rough weather" gear—bell-shaped rain hat, long slicker with tab collar, and rubber boots in one photo and single-breasted heavy Ulster coat with large Puritan collar, buttons down the left side, and "American Red Cross" embroidered midway on the left sleeve in another. France's constant rain and mud made the "rough weather outfit," as Mary Collins of Base Hospital No. 8 noted on a copy of the pamphlet she saved in her scrapbook, "worn most of all in [the] A.E.F."[42]

American Army nurses created a sensation in France. Not only did they serve as welcome, comforting symbols of a friendly country coming to the aid of war-weary France, their uniforms inspired the curiosity and admiration of French women and men alike. In December 1917, a Paris fashion magazine reporter commented that many of the women's coats of the season "seem to be inspired by the nurses' pleated cape, with an enveloping shape. More fantastic than the real cape worn by French nurses, these coats, often lined with strong colors, strongly resemble certain coats of the American nurses."[43]

When on the Fourth of July in 1918 a group of Army nurses marched in a Paris military parade to inaugurate the new Avenue President Wilson, French newspapers devoted special attention to the nurses' uniforms and appearance. The Parisian daily *Le Figaro* described "a section of American Red Cross nurses, commanded by a chief nurse [who were] dressed in dark-blue wool, enhanced with a white collar, and wearing on the lapel of their jackets the initials US next to a Red Cross," which made "a profound impression" on the crowd of spectators.[44] Another report termed the nurses' uniforms "somber" (sober) and noted that "the American female nurses received strong applause." The Paris correspondent of an Algerian colonial weekly commented that the nurse's impression on the crowd partly stemmed from the novelty of viewing women marching in military uniform: "There were young ones and old ones, ugly ones and pretty ones, and it was a bit strange to see them marching in little bird steps."[45] In a country where the military successfully resisted attempts of volunteer women to wear military uniforms, as Margaret Darrow (ch. 7) notes, it is not surprising that the sight of American nurses in military parade produced such an amazed reaction.

FIGHTING FOR INSIGNIA: CHEVRONS, MEDALS, BUT NO RANK

Wearing the uniform and drilling did not immediately make nurses feel like full-fledged military members, but service in the war zone seemed to change their views. The attitude that nurses displayed toward service and wound chevrons reflected this shift. On 11 February 1918, War Department General Orders No. 26, authorized "each officer and enlisted man who has served six months in the Zone of the Advance in the war," including aviators, to wear a gold chevron on the lower left sleeve of his uniform coat. Although the regulation did not expressly include nurses, some in war zone base hospitals were notified that they could wear

Figure 15.7.
Reconstruction Aides of Base Hospital No. 9, the New York Hospital Unit. Official History of Base Hospital No. 9, Raymond Shiland Brown, 1919, 76.

them and embraced this rare accolade. "I have my new suit now and my two gold service stripes on my left sleeve," wrote Mary Welty Christy, a nurse from Base Hospital No. 12 (the Northwestern University Unit). "We four [nurses] feel very proud that we are the first to wear them here."

Winning the right for a woman to wear the wound chevron was another matter, as a scrapbook kept by Beatrice MacDonald, a nurse from Base Hospital No. 2, New York's Presbyterian Hospital unit, clearly demonstrates. In August 1917, MacDonald had been wounded in a night bombing raid while aiding patients in a British casualty clearing station. Despite losing an eye in the attack, she insisted on returning to her unit. Although MacDonald now sported a glass eye and a written commendation from General Pershing for remaining at her post during the attack until wounded, her commanding officer doubted a woman could wear a wound chevron. He informed the adjutant general in a November 1918 memo that MacDonald claimed to be wounded and "now desires authority to wear a 'Wound Chevron.'" He requested an investigation to determine if she was really entitled to such a decoration. Although the adjutant general's response was vague, MacDonald had clearly earned the right to wear the wound chevron.[46]

MacDonald included in her scrapbook official notices and news articles about the medals she earned for her service from the British, French, and American governments. These documents include a newspaper photograph of U.S. Secretary of War Newton Baker pinning the Distinguished Service Cross on the upper left side of her Norfolk jacket. MacDonald stands facing Baker in full uniform, with her dark-blue velour hat, jacket, long serge

Figure 15.8.
Physicians, nurses, and other staff of the American Women's Hospital No. 1 in Luzancy, France, 23 April 1919. This hospital remained in service from July 1918 through 1919, although it was moved twice. Note the variations in hats and uniform shade. Library of Congress, Prints and Photograph Division.

wool skirt, dark-brown gloves, and dark, laced shoes. Importantly, her *right* sleeve displays a single inverted chevron, the gold wound chevron authorized by General Orders No. 26 to be worn on the right sleeve of uniform coats "by each officer, field clerk, and enlisted man who has received or who may hereafter receive a wound in action with the enemy, or as the result of an act of the enemy, which necessitates treatment by a medical officer."[47] Wearing of this chevron on her coat demonstrates MacDonald's pride in being recognized as a wounded combat veteran and her willingness to fight for the right to wear it.

MacDonald's individual campaign for the right to wear a wound chevron (a forerunner of the Purple Heart medal) foreshadowed a larger campaign among Army nurses to be awarded rank. During the war, Army and Navy nurses were neither enlisted personnel nor officers, although they were required to take the officers' oath. Unlike other military personnel, they could wear a nonmilitary symbol, a Red Cross pin, on their uniform; this suggested that they were enrolled by the Red Cross, not inducted into the military. That led some members of the public to think of them as "Red Cross nurses," not military nurses. Yet they were subject to military discipline, were eligible for $10,000 in war risk insurance, and later would be eligible for veterans' benefits. In late 1918, Army nurses began working with members of Congress to develop legislation that would commission them as officers.[48] They achieved a partial victory in 1920, with the award of relative rank at the level of lieutenant, captain, and major but had to wait until 1947 to become commissioned officers.[49]

RECONSTRUCTION AIDES, HOSPITAL DIETITIANS, AND LABORATORY TECHNICIANS

Nurses were not the only medical women to serve in and with the American military forces during World War I. In January 1918, the U.S. Army began recruiting 25- to 40-year-old women with high school diplomas as reconstruction aides to work in Army hospitals in France and at home helping to rehabilitate wounded soldiers. Of the 1,800 women accepted, roughly 700 either had or received training in massage and electro- or hydrotherapy and became physiotherapists (later physical therapists). Other reconstruction aides became occupational therapists, teaching such commercial skills as mechanical drawing and such handicrafts as weaving.[50]

Ora Ruggles, a Southern California teacher raised in western Nebraska, was recruited as an occupational therapist. As the Army recruiter explained to her, "thousands of wounded soldiers are coming home from the war in bad condition. We think it would help them if they could be taught new or interesting occupations. You know, something to take their minds off themselves, sort of reconstruct them." Ruggles began working with wounded and disabled soldiers at Camp McPherson, Georgia, during the sweltering summer of 1918, as the camp's first reconstruction aide. She arrived before the Army had time to issue the aides their uniforms. Like many of the aides, she encountered resistance to her presence from both military doctors and nurses, who believed that these women were, at best, useless and, at worst, distracted the hospital from its more important work. Soon after her arrival, "one particularly officious major threatened to arrest her for being 'out of uniform'" and informed her of a new regulation stipulating that all reconstruction aides were required to wear white-and-blue uniforms. The next day, when the major returned to her basket weaving workshop, he was surprised to find Ruggles in full uniform—light-blue dress with white apron and "perky cap." After the major's reproach, she had obtained the details of the uniform regulations from a friendly captain, asked an acquaintance to drive her to Atlanta to buy the cloth, then had the uniform sewn by "a fast working dressmaker who lived behind the Dixie Cafe"—the camp's local greasy spoon. The uniform matched the regulations closely enough that Ruggles escaped notice once she "made the switch" to the official one.[51]

The reconstruction aide's uniform regulations had already gone through multiple changes by the time Ruggles learned about them. Marguerite Sanderson, a physical education pioneer, served as the only woman in the Division of Special Hospitals and Physical Reconstruction established by the surgeon general in 1917. Sanderson originally pushed for the reconstruction aides to wear "bloomers"—women's loose trousers gathered at the ankle—because she believed that these would be more practical than skirts in the mud and rain of France. But she lost this battle: Bloomers, introduced in the 1890s, were still associated in many men's minds with radical women who wanted to usurp male roles in American society. So the first reconstruction aides, who were sent to Walter Reed Army Hospital in Washington, D.C., were issued dark-blue dresses. Lena Hitchcock, one of the aides, recalled that the aides considered these dresses "hideous" and "several of us, on the grounds that the dark blue hospital uniforms were depressing, succeeded in getting them changed to the present light blue chambray." The standard uniform then became a pale-blue, loose, ankle-length dress, with short sleeves for physical therapists and long sleeves for occupational therapists. Over this, they wore white, V-necked, pointed Chelsea collars, white cuffs, and a white ankle-length skirt apron, with two white wide apron straps that formed a V shape over the blouse. They also wore hats with white, upturned brims and light-blue crowns, whereas the chief reconstruction aide wore the same cap in all white. Because of the color of their uniform, the "re-aides" earned the nickname "bluebirds."[52]

Reconstruction aides often complained about how heavy and ill fitting were the uniforms they had to drill in. Hitchcock suggested the uniform "was designed by a man who believed that women working in the hospitals were a menace to patients."[53] A uniform that flattened out feminine curves and rendered the reconstruction aides as unbecoming as possible nicely complemented a dominant strain in Army thought about rehabilitating injured soldiers. Proponents of this approach discouraged the "sentimental pampering" thought to be practiced by nurses on male patients, seeking to recruit as reconstruction aides less nurturing women trained in physical education or practical arts who could practice "kindly discipline" with soldiers to push them toward masculine self-sufficiency.[54] The aides' uniforms—in color, apron design, and cap design—also clearly distinguished these workers from Army nurses.[55]

By September 1918, when the Army sent its first group of reconstruction aides to France, the Red Cross was ready to outfit each aide with a raincoat and rubber boots similar to those worn by nurses, a gray sweater, three pairs of flannel pajamas, two pairs of wool tights, four suits of wool underwear, and merino wool stockings. Aides received their pale-blue uniforms, along with 12 sets of white collars and cuffs. But unlike nurses, reconstruction aides were required to buy their own outdoor uniform: a dark-blue or dark-gray serge Norfolk jacket, with maroon and white braid on the sleeve, white shirtwaist, black four-in-hand tie, and long skirt, Ulster overcoat, and long cape lined with maroon silk. They were also required to wear a round wool hat with a maroon-and-white cockade. Just as Army nurses wore "U.S." and caduceus pins on their jacket lapels, some reconstruction aides received a bronze caduceus with "R.A." superimposed or a pin with the simple bronze letters "R.A." Others alternatively wore the "U.S." pin on the collars of their capes.[56]

Encouraged to volunteer by Army recruiters, swearing the same oath of office as nurses (and officers), and subject to military discipline while in service, reconstruction aides understandably viewed themselves as members of the Army. That the U.S. Army and Veterans Bureau hospitals continued to employ them throughout the postwar decade at wartime levels could only have reinforced their sense of belonging to the Army. But when they were discharged from service, they learned otherwise. The Army deemed them civilian employees, thus not entitled to veterans' benefits. Not until the 1977 passage of the GI Bill Improvement Act were these women, along with World War I female Army Signal Corps telephone operators, officially recognized as veterans.[57]

The same fight lay before the 356 hospital dietitians who served in Army hospitals, 84 of them overseas. These women, all of whom had advanced technical training in the emerging field of dietetics, were recruited by the Red Cross Bureau of Nursing (even though most were not nurses) and then were attached to the dietitian service of the U.S. Army Medical Department. Like reconstruction aides, dietitians occupied a liminal zone between military and civilian personnel. Officially employed and paid by the U.S. Civil Service Commission, they nonetheless drilled, trained, and bunked with the nurses at Army base hospitals. They also faced similar dangers and displayed no less heroism. During the influenza pandemic of 1918–1919, reported the surgeon general of the Army, "dietitians proved themselves of inestimable value in organizing . . . the feeding of the sick and well. Three dietitians lost their lives . . . and several other were seriously ill."[58]

Dietitians' uniforms reflected this ambiguity. The first dietitians arrived at base hospitals in May 1917 wearing whatever they had brought with them. Not until three months later did the surgeon general issue uniform regulations, and the issue remained unsettled through the following spring.[59] The first regulations specified a white one-piece dress with a "rolled white collar, a white cap, and a caduceus with the letter 'D' on it" as the dietitian's indoor uniform but allowed a blue cotton crepe dress in foreign service if white was impractical. Dietitians already in service when the surgeon general issued regulations had to purchase the uniform themselves. In October 1917, the Red Cross began providing dietitians with outdoor gray uniforms similar in form to those worn by nurses. The dietitian's outdoor uniform comprised a dress, cape, and Ulster all in gray wool, topped by a black velour hat. Like nurses, dietitians in 1918 switched to the Norfolk jacket (with "D" caduceus and "U.S." pins on the lapels) and long wool skirt; they retained the black velour hat for winter but added a black or white straw hat for summer. Gray gloves (rather than tan), black or white shoes (rather than brown), and white or gray shirtwaist with black ribbon tie and plain bar pin completed the ensemble.[60]

Fitting in could be problematic. When Mary Taylor Hungate, a graduate of the University of Nebraska with postgraduate training in dietetics who had served as head of the domestic science department in the Twin Falls, Idaho, public schools, signed up, she was assigned to Base Hospital No. 51—a unit composed of personnel from various parts of the country.[61] Before sailing for France in August 1918, she remembered drilling in uniform with the nurses in New York:

> The hundred nurses all wore street uniforms of blue serge, blue velour hats and tan shoes; while I, the dietitian, the one hundred and oneth, was duly fitted out in a similar suit of gray, a black hat and black shoes. There was no question about it, I was the odd member of the family; my clothes served only to indicate that I was with, but not of the unit.

But after sweating through a "gray silk blouse" during weeks of drill, where the women were organized according to height, "my gray uniform was permitted to blend inconspicuously with the blue ones," she remembered.[62]

At least one photograph shows that dietitians, like nurses, wore the war service chevron. Mary Pascoe, a hospital dietitian who served at three different base hospitals, is pictured in her official portrait wearing two war service chevrons on her lower left sleeve. This chevron and the Service of Supply patch on her left shoulder suggest that she was considered, at least de facto, a member of the Army.[63] Dietitians, however, were no more eligible for military benefits than reconstruction aides. So obvious was the unfair treatment of the dietitians that the normally matter-of-fact annual report of the surgeon general called it out: "It seems unfortunate that these professional women who worked side by side with nurses, doctors, and enlisted men should not have had the privileges of the war risk insurance."[64] Like reconstruction aides, dietitians received recognition as veterans only in 1977.[65]

The third, and perhaps least discussed, group of medical women who served in the war without benefits were laboratory and X-ray technicians. According to the Army surgeon general's annual report, 398 female laboratory technicians were on duty by November 1918. Technicians were trained in special wartime programs in the United States, then sent to hospitals in France and at home. Their work included clinical radiology, pathology, autopsy, bacteriology, serology, and examination of "surgical specimens removed at operation." The central laboratory of the Vichy Hospital Center in France—a complex of 18 converted hotels that France transferred to the Americans and that eventually housed five base hospital units—included an art department where technicians photographed and drew surgical specimens and modeled facial reconstructions in wax.[66]

Unlike dietitians or reconstruction aides, technicians had no designated uniforms, though some apparently wore uniforms nonetheless. A photograph of the Vichy Hospital Center X-ray staff shows four uniformed men along with a woman, Minerva Blaisdell, wearing a civilian blouse and skirt. But in a photograph of the center's laboratory personnel, which includes 33 men in uniform and 4 women, two of the four wear dark dresses and brimless hats, while one wears a white blouse with open collar and dark sweater along with a dark, brimmed hat. The fourth wears a typical nurse's outdoor uniform—light-colored Norfolk jacket with white shirtwaist and dark tie under a wide-brimmed beribboned hat.[67] In sharp contrast to that of dietitians and reconstruction aides, the civilian status of these women was unambiguous. They received no recognition as veterans in the 1977 act, although they had endured the same difficult wartime conditions as those who did.[68]

WOMEN PHYSICIANS IN UNIFORM

Of all medical women to apply for service in World War I, the physicians encountered the stiffest resistance. Although nursing became emblematic of women's role in the war, no belligerent power, with the exception of the shorthanded Russians (Stoff, ch. 10), initially accepted women physicians. Only a few British women served as physicians in the army, after British women doctors had established the Scottish Women's Hospital and other voluntary outfits with charitable support (Marie Bucur, ch. 13).[69] Although some countries lacked significant numbers of women physicians, American women physicians in active practice numbered over 5,000—roughly 3% to 4% of all practicing physicians. Organized in 1915, the Medical Women's National Association (later American Medical Women's Association) initially met resistance from many prominent women physicians, who preferred to be integrated into the profession, not segregated from male physicians; after all, had not the American Medical Association just seated its first female physician? But when both the Army and Navy rejected women's applications for medical corps service in 1917 on grounds that their gender disqualified them for military service, the association campaigned to change this policy, and women physicians closed ranks to support the campaign.[70] They succeeded only in part. Although the Navy never accepted women physicians, the Army in 1918 hired 55 women as civilian contract surgeons without rank, pay, or benefits comparable to those of male doctors. Eleven served in the war zone as physician anesthetists.[71]

In July 1918, the Army issued male contract surgeons official uniforms with an insignia, a 1-inch caduceus bearing the superimposed monogram "C.S."[72] Three months later, it was the women's turn. They received not uniforms, but authorization "to wear a khaki uniform made according to specifications approved by the Acting Surgeon General."[73] The press noted the confusion. "Just what is to be done about uniforming the women contract surgeons does not seem to be thoroughly decided by headquarters in the Surgeon General's department," reported the *Detroit Free Press*. "The arrival of the lady doctors is rather too recent for all the details of her employment to be arranged, apparently." Although Army officials claimed a uniform had been designed, "nobody seems to have seen it yet."[74]

One of these few women contract surgeons, Dr. Loy McAfee, had graduated in 1904 from Indiana Medical College, Indianapolis, then pursued a career in medical publishing in New York. Contracted as an Army surgeon in May 1918, she began working on the multivolume history of the Army Medical Department in World War I; she continued as the civilian associate editor in chief after her discharge in 1921, the year the first volume was published, until the project's completion with volume 15 in 1927.[75] McAfee's uniform is now part of the collections of the Smithsonian Institutions's National Museum of American History (Hacker, ch. 14). The uniform comprises a khaki Norfolk jacket with four pleated flap pockets and four bronze buttons, a matching calf-length skirt buttoning down the front, lace-up brown boots, a red tie, and a high-collared off-white blouse, with pins "US" and "M.C." on either side of the collar at the neck.[76] The Norfolk jacket is substantially shorter than that worn in 1918 by Army nurses but includes shoulder straps and narrower lapels; the belt piece is also sewn into the jacket and includes no buttons. The overall effect is a more tailored-looking jacket like the four-pocket khaki service coats worn by male U.S. and British army personnel in World War I. The hat that accompanies the uniform is identical to the round-brimmed, brown service hat issued to doughboys and officers—with a signature pointed crown with soft creases in the side.[77] At first glance, this uniform's resemblance to men's uniforms does appear to flout gender norms. However, given that women contract surgeons had to custom order their uniforms, it is cut to fit and reveals the feminine curves of the wearer to a greater degree than the often-blousy Army and Navy nurses' uniforms.

Many American Medical Women's Association members, rather than accept second-class status within the Army Medical Corps, decided to raise funds to start their own hospitals to care for civilians in the war zone.[78] By the Armistice, the association had raised $200,000 for the American Women's Hospital Service, had enlisted the deep-pocketed Red Cross to help it organize and equip these hospitals, and had sent over 130 women physicians, nurses, and allied workers to the war zone. Many of these workers arrived after the Armistice but found that the unmet medical needs of refugees and other civilians remained acute. The American Women's Hospitals expanded after the war, with 9 hospitals and 20 dispensaries operating in France, Serbia, and Greece by 1920.[79]

Since each volunteer physician procured and payed for her own uniform, variation in style and color seems inevitable. By June 1918, when the first unit arrived in France, American Women's Hospitals had adopted a signature uniform, which, like the Army contract surgeon's uniform, somewhat imitated men's uniforms. On 15 June 1918, the *Morning Register* of Eugene, Oregon, noted the results:

> The women physicians wear wool or cotton khaki military suits with trimmings of French blue, with their insignia embroidered on the collar and Sam Browne belts. Their skirts are much longer than most military costumes worn by women. Underneath they wear knickerbockers to match the skirts. They have discarded puttees and wear stout, medium height boots. Their hats are army shape of khaki, faced and trimmed with blue.[80]

An accompanying photo illustrated how women physicians adopted these guidelines. In it, six women physicians stand in front of their Model T ambulance, wearing long, loosely fitting Norfolk jackets with wide lapels, white shirtwaist blouses and ties, ankle-length skirts, dark boots, and gloves. These uniforms look similar to Army Nurse Corps uniforms in shape. All but one of the physicians are wearing hats identical to the pointed, wide-brimmed U.S. Army service hats. The last is wearing a cloche-like hat—her own feminine flourish.

The Sam Browne belt comprised a wide leather waistband and a single, diagonal leather strap running across the chest and over the shoulder. Originally designed for (and named after) a British cavalry officer serving in India who lost his arm in combat, these belts became prestigious markers of officer status in the British army during World War I. The U.S. Army barred stateside officers from wearing the belt but required it of all officers serving abroad.[81] That women physicians adopted the belt, a signature symbol of membership in the brotherhood of Anglo-American officers in the war zone, can be read as a form of protest. It displayed the wearers' belief that they were as fit as any man for military medical commissions and war service. (As noted by Vining and Hacker [ch. 16], U.S. Navy yeomen [f] and Marinettes also sometimes wore decidedly nonregulation Sam Browne belts as a way of expressing military identities). Moreover, the belt, service hats, and pants underneath their skirts emphasize that physicians—unlike nurses, dietitians, and reconstruction aides—were not trying to carve a uniquely feminine niche within the masculine war zone; instead, they sought to diminish gender differences and demand respect for their equal skills and knowledge.

UNIFORMS AND WOMEN'S MILITARY IDENTITIES

Uniforms clearly mattered in the creation and expression of female military identities during World War I. Many must have shared Maude Essig's regrets at laying her uniform aside:

> It broke my heart to turn in my precious cape. Some simply said they were "lost in action" but I could not say that, much as I wanted to keep it. History was all wrapped up in that cape, with all the holes burnt into the lower edge where it flipped against our little stoves. Nary a day that it had not been on duty with me, my faithful friend.[82]

Uniforms served as markers of military status but also helped these women to define new identities for themselves, as professional, military, or quasi-military women serving in war. Since women had previously been excluded from official military service, these new identities did not emerge completely formed. As the many inconsistencies and changes show, the process of developing women's uniforms was dynamic and interactive. Women's uniforms not only changed during the war, they multiplied as women were recruited for new or newly important jobs. The professions of occupational and physical therapist, anesthetist, dietitian, and laboratory technician all originated or developed substantially during the war, providing women in the postwar world with new career options. Although the war did not have the same positive effect on women in medicine, the Women's National Medical Association grew during the war into an effective voice for women within the profession and developed a philanthropic program that outlasted the war by decades.

For nurses, the largest group of women to serve in the war, the distinctive uniforms solidified their identities as professional military women. Such professional solidarity undergirded the Army nurses' somewhat successful postwar campaign for officer rank. Although they secured relative rank only in 1920, this first step blazed the path for the much larger, more respected Army and Navy Nurse Corps of World War II and for commissioning of military nurses in 1947.[83] By World War II, the sight of women in uniform was no longer a novelty or a curiosity in American culture, and the United States did not hesitate to put hundreds of thousands of women in uniform to serve in noncombatant positions.[84] The celebrated American women who served in this conflict owed this opportunity to the nearly forgotten American women who served in uniform a generation earlier.

NOTES

1. Harrison Fisher, "Join the Red Cross—All You Need Is a Heart and a Dollar. Red Cross Christmas Roll Call, Dec. 16-23" (Buffalo, N.Y.: Niagara Litho. Co., 1917); Harrison Fisher, "Have You Answered the Red Cross

Christmas Roll Call?" (1918), Prints and Photographs Collection, Library of Congress, Washington, D.C.; "Do you know these American uniforms which every French officer salutes?" *Sun* (Baltimore), 16 June 1918, 10A (quote); "La femme et le foyer, les mantes et la mode," *Les annales politiques et littéraires* (Paris), 19 Dec. 1917, 568.

2. Marian Moser Jones, *The American Red Cross from Clara Barton to the New Deal* (Baltimore: Johns Hopkins University Press, 2012), 260; Esther Pohl Lovejoy, *Certain Samaritans*, rev. ed. (New York: MacMillan, 1933), inside front cover illustration; "First Unit of American Women's Hospitals on Way Abroad," *Morning Register* (Eugene, Ore.), 15 June 1918, 6.

3. American National Red Cross, *The Work of the American Red Cross during the War: A Statement of Finances and Accomplishments for the Period July 1, 1917 to February 28, 1919* (Washington, D.C.: American National Red Cross, 1919), xi; Myra L. McDaniel, "Occupational Therapists before World War II," in *Army Medical Specialist Corps*, eds. Robert S. Anderson, Harriet S. Lee, and Myra L. McDaniel, (Washington, D.C.: Office of the Surgeon General, Department of the Army, 1968), 91; Surgeon General, U.S. Army, *Annual Report of the Surgeon General, U.S. Army, to the Secretary of War, 1919* (Washington, D.C.: Government Printing Office, 1919), 2:1127; Judith Bellafaire and Mercedes Herrera Graf, *Women Doctors in War* (College Station: Texas A&M University Press, 2009), 35–37; Ellen S. More, "The American Medical Women's Association and the Role of the Woman Physician, 1915–1990," *Journal of the American Medical Women's Association* 45, no. 5 (Sept.–Oct. 1990): 167.

4. Barton C. Hacker, "Reformers, Nurses, and Ladies in Uniform," in *A Companion to Women's Military History*, eds. Barton C. Hacker and Margaret Vining (Leiden: Brill, 2012), 137–138; Barton C. Hacker, "Control, Utility, Status, Symbol: Reflections on the Multiple Historical Meanings of Uniforms," in *Uniforms: Yesterday, Today, and Tomorrow*, ed. Phillippe Thilly (Brussels: Musée Royal de l'Armée et d'Histoire Militaire, 2007), 72–81.

5. Mary E. Sarnecky, *A History of the U.S. Army Nurse Corps* (Philadelphia: University of Pennsylvania Press, 1999), 81.

6. National Society of Colonial Dames of America, "List of Uniforms of Women Worn during the War," in *Minutes of the Fourteenth Biennial Council of the National Society of Colonial Dames of America, Washington, D.C., May 21, 22, and 23, 1919* (Washington, D.C.: National Society of Colonial Dames of America, 1919), 87–97; American National Red Cross, *The Work of the American Red Cross During the War*, xiii, 32–33, 47; "Uniform to Be Worn during Roll Call," *American Red Cross Pacific Division Activities* 3, no. 8 (15 Oct. 1920): 4; Lavinia L. Dock and Sarah Elizabeth Pickett, "Mobilization," in *History of American Red Cross Nursing*, ed. Lavinia L. Dock, Sarah Elizabeth Pickett, Clara D. Noyes, Fannie F. Clement, Elizabeth G. Fox, and Anna R. Van Meter (New York: MacMillan, 1922), 277; Sarah Elizabeth Pickett, "The Relation of the Nursing Services to the Army," in Dock et al., *History of American Red Cross Nursing*, 368–370, 381–383.

7. Robert H. Bremner, *American Philanthropy*, 2nd ed. (Chicago: University of Chicago Press, 1987), 40–54; Theda Skocpol, *Protecting Soldiers and Mothers: The Political Origins of Social Policy in the United States* (Cambridge, Mass.: Belknap Press of Harvard University Press, 1992), 87–88; Jones, *American Red Cross*, 25–36.

8. Caroline Moorehead, *Dunant's Dream: War, Switzerland, and the History of the Red Cross* (New York: Carrol & Graf, 1999), 15–17, 36–37; John F. Hutchinson, *Champions of Charity: War and the Rise of the Red Cross* (Boulder, Colo.: Westview Press, 1996), 46–50; Convention for the Amelioration of the Condition of the Wounded in Armies in the Field, Geneva, 22 August 1864, Article 7, International Committee of the Red Cross, https://ihl-databases.icrc.org/applic/ihl/ihl.nsf/Article.xsp?action=openDocument&documentId=7694EEE50D349138C12563CD00515357 (accessed 11 October, 2019).

9. Jones, *American Red Cross*, 102–115, 167; Ruth E. Malone, "Jane A. Delano: Saint or Sellout?" *Nursing History Review* 2, no.2 (1994): 67–69; Patricia D'Antonio, *American Nursing: A History of Knowledge, Authority, and the Meaning of Work* (Baltimore: Johns Hopkins University Press, 2010), 8–9, 28–41.

10. Sarnecky, *History of the U.S. Army Nurse Corps*, 69 (quote), 71–72; Clara Noyes, "The Red Cross," *American Journal of Nursing* 17, no. 7 (April 1917): 620–627; Ester V. Hasson, "The Navy Nurse Corps," *American Journal of Nursing* 9, no. 4 (Jan. 1909): 267–268; Lavinia R. Dock, "Affiliation of the American Red Cross with the Nurses' Association," in Dock et al., *History of American Red Cross Nursing*, 104–105, 120.

11. Portia B. Kernodle, The Red Cross Nurse in Action, 1882-1948 (New York: Harper, 1949), 59; "Tenth Annual Convention of the Nurses' Associated Alumnæ of the United States: Minutes of the Proceedings," *American Journal of Nursing* 7, no. 11 (Aug. 1907): 910; Isabel McIsaac, "The Army Nurse Corps," *American Journal of Nursing* 13, no. 3 (Dec. 1912): 172–176; Hasson, "Navy Nurse Corps," 267.

12. J. D. Norris, *Advertising and the Transformation of American Society, 1865–1920* (New York: Greenwood Press, 1990), 39.

13. McIsaac, "Army Nurse Corps," 175; Hasson, "Navy Nurse Corps," 267.

14. Jane A. Delano, "Activities of the Nursing Service," *Red Cross Magazine* 9, no. 3 (July 1914): 169–172 (quote at 172); "American Nurses Hold Board Meeting Here," *St. Louis Star and Times*, 22 Apr. 1914, 2; Pickett, "The Relation of the Nursing Service to the Army," 359.

15. David Cole, *Survey of U.S. Army Uniforms, Weapons and Accoutrements* (Ft. Sam Houston, Tex.: U.S. Army Medical Museum, 2007), 61; Ronald I. Davis, *Men's Garments, 1830–1900: A Guide to Pattern Cutting and Tailoring* (Studio City, Calif.: Players Press, 1994), 122; Jane Tynan, "Military Dress and Men's Outdoor Leisurewear: Burberry's Trench Coat in First World War," *Journal of Design History* 24, no. 2 (May 2011), 148; Elisabeth Robinson Scovil, "Florence Nightingale," *American Journal of Nursing* 14, no. 1 (Oct. 1913): 28–33; Sandra Holton, "Feminine Authority and Social Order: Florence Nightingale's Conception of Nursing and Health Care," *Social Analysis: The International Journal of Social and Cultural Practice* 15 (Aug. 1984): 59–72.

16. David West, *A Brief Illustrated History of Art* (North Mankato, Minn.: Capstone Press, 2017), 9; Mary Hollingsworth, *Art in World History* (Florence: Giunti Editore, 2008), 207; "The Odd Measure: America's Premier Nurse: Miss Jane Delano and Her Wonderful Work of Organization for the Red Cross," *Munsey's Magazine* 64, no. 3 (Aug. 1918): 639; Annette Summers, "Sairey Gamp: Generating Fact from Fiction," *Nursing Inquiry* 4, no. 1 (Mar. 1997): 14–18; "Nurse Girls and Stablemen: A Lady Complains of Improper Conduct," *San Francisco Chronicle*, 2 Aug. 1871, 3; Sarnecky, *History of the U.S. Army Nurse Corps*, 30.

17. Janet S.K. Watson, *Fighting Different Wars: Experience, Memory and the First World War in Britain* (Cambridge: Cambridge University Press, 2004), 76–77; "Skirt Worn by Sister A. Stewart Wyatt, Queen Alexandra's Imperial Military Nursing Service, 1902," National Army Museum [London] Online Collection, https://collection.nam.ac.uk/detail.php?acc=1981-06-33-1 (accessed 11 October 2019); Juliet Piggott, *Queen Alexandra's Royal Army Nursing Corps* (London: Leo Cooper, 1975), 11.

18. *Sun* (Baltimore), 16 June 1918, 10A.

19. Delano, "Activities of the Nursing Service," 169 (quote); Pickett, "The Relation of the Nursing Services to the Army," 360.

20. Sarah Elizabeth Pickett, "The Mercy Ship," in Dock et al., *History of American Red Cross Nursing*, 143–144.

21. Pickett, "The Mercy Ship," 139 (quote, my emphasis); Delano, "The Nurses and the Requirements," *Red Cross Magazine* 9, no. 4 (Oct. 1914): 226 (quote); Jane A. Delano, "The Red Cross," *American Journal of Nursing* 15, no. 1 (Oct. 1914): 37.

22. Mary Frederika Farley, diary, 3 Oct. 1914, Mary Fredericka Farley Papers, Radcliffe Schlesinger Library, Harvard University, Cambridge, Mass.; Mary Gladwin, diary, 1 Dec. 1914, Mary Gladwin Papers, University of Akron, Ohio; Florence May Cooper, diary, 12 Feb. 1916, Florence May Cooper Papers, Maryland Historical Society, Baltimore.

23. Vashti Bartlett to Alice, 18 August 1915; Bartlett to Jane Delano, 27 Dec. 1915, box 6, Vashti Bartlett Papers, Alan Mason Chesney Medical Archives, Johns Hopkins University, Baltimore.

24. Unsigned postcard, Xmas 1915, box 7, folder 4, Bartlett Papers.

25. Pickett, "The Relation of the Nursing Service to the Army," 360; Jane Delano to Bessie Baker, 29 June and 7 July 1916, folder 1, Bessie Baker Papers, Alan Mason Chesney Medical Archives, Johns Hopkins University, Baltimore (hereafter Baker Papers).

26. Jones, *American Red Cross*, 157; American National Red Cross, *Work of the American Red Cross*, 41; Baker correspondence with Delano, 1916–1917, Baker Papers; Pickett, "The Relation of the Nursing Services to the Army," 315–316; "Thirty Thousand Enrolled," *Red Cross Bulletin* 2, no. 45 (4 Nov. 1918): 3; *History of the Pennsylvania Unit (Base Hospital No. 10, U.S.A.) in the Great War* (New York: Paul B. Hoeber, 1921), 18–25; More, "The American Medical Women's Association," 165.

27. Maj. H.L. Gilchrist, Orders #3, Headquarters Base Hospital #4, Cleveland, Ohio, 3 May 1917, folder 24, Archives of Lakeside Unit, I, Dittrick Medical History Center, Case Western Reserve University, Cleveland, Ohio (hereafter Archives of Lakeside Unit).

28. Diary "A.F.R.," 8 May 1917, folder 1, 1915–1916, May 1917, Archives of Lakeside Unit.

29. G.W. Crile, diary, 8 May 1917, folder 1, Archives of Lakeside Unit (hereafter Crile diary); "U.S. Medical Corps Unit Sails for War Zone Today; Organization Recruited in Cleveland by Red Cross Is in Charge of Army Surgeon," *St. Louis Post- Dispatch*, 8 May 1917, 1.

30. Minnie Victoria Strobel (Base Hospital No. 4 nurse), diary, 4 July 1917, private collection of Dr. Paul Turkeltaub, Bethesda, Md.

31. U.S. Army Base Hospital No. 4, *Album de guerre: Five Hundred Photographs, Seventy Drawings and Thirteen Articles* (Cleveland: Scientific Illustrating Studios, 1919), 8.

32. *History of the Pennsylvania Unit*, 78–79.

33. *History of the Pennsylvania Unit*, 66, 80; Raymond Shiland Brown, *Base Hospital No. 9, A.E.F., a History of the Work of the New York Hospital* (New York: New York Hospital, 1920), 24–26.

34. Sarnecky, *History of the U.S. Army Nurse Corps*, 84; "Nurses of Base Hospital 32 Drilling at Columbia War Hospital, N.Y.," in *A History of Base Hospital 32 [Including Unit R]*, ed. Benjamin D. Hitz (Indianapolis: American Legion, 1922), 10; "Base Hospital 12 Nurses Meeting with Sir Thomas Lipton," 1917, in "Northwestern Remembers the First World War," Northwestern University Archives, http://sites.northwestern.edu/ww1/hospital/ (accessed 7 Feb. 2018); Base Hospital No. 21 photo album, photo 025022, Base Hospital 21 Collection, Special Collections, Becker Medical Library, Washington University in St. Louis.

35. Maude Essig, "My Trip Abroad with Uncle Sam, 1917:1919," unpublished diary, 5 Oct. 1917, Special Collections, Illinois Wesleyan University Library, Bloomington; Ruth Wright (Coppedge), diary, 5 Oct. 1917, Indiana Historical Society, Indianapolis.

36. Emma Elizabeth Weaver, unpublished World War diary, undated entry, 8 (quote), Army Heritage and Education Center Library, Army War College, Carlisle Barracks, Pa. (hereafter Weaver diary); American Red Cross, *All Honor to the War Nurse* (Washington, D.C.: American Red Cross, 1918), 4, pamphlet in Mary Collins (Harvey) scrapbook, Collection of Lucy Harvey, Washington, D.C.

37. Irene Brewster, "The Nurses' Side of It; Being a Story of Their Contributions to the Achievements of Base Hospital #65 Stationed at Kerhoun in France during the World War," 3–4, unpublished memoir, Women in Military Service for America Archives, Arlington, Va.

38. Sven Raphael Schneider, "The Norfolk Jacket Guide: History, Style & How to Buy," *Gentleman's Gazette*, 5 Apr. 2013, https://www.gentlemansgazette.com/norfolk-jacket-guide/ (accessed 11 October 2019); "The Red Cross," *American Journal of Nursing* 18, no. 2 (Nov. 1917): 131; Aurel Baker Pardee (Army Nurse Corps) photo, Pardee Papers, Wisconsin Historical Society, Madison; Mary Welty Christy (Army Nurse Corps) photo, Christie Collection, Midwest Nursing History Research Center, College of Nursing, University of Illinois at Chicago; Edna Dunlap work permit, 1918, in Dunlap Papers, Army Heritage and Education Center, Army War College, Carlisle Barracks, Pa.

39. American Red Cross, *All Honor to the War Nurse*, 7, 8, 11; Collins scrapbook.

40. American Red Cross, *All Honor to the War Nurse*, 10; Elizabeth Wells Neil, "The Experiences of an Ex-Navy Nurse on Recruiting Duty," *American Journal of Nursing* 18, no. 8 (May 1918): 624.

41. American Red Cross, *All Honor to the War Nurse*, 9, 14.

42. American Red Cross, *All Honor to the War Nurse*, 12, 13.

43. "La femme et le foyer," 568.

44. "L'Avenue du Président-Wilson," *Le Figaro*, 5 July 1918, 2. Author's translation of "Elles precedent une section d'infirmières de La Croix-Rouge américaine, commandée par une infirmière-major. Habillées de drap bleu foncé rehaussé d'un col blanc et portant au reverse de leurs jaquettes les initiales US a cote d'une Croix-Rouge, les dames infirmières américaines ont fait sur la foule une impression profonde."

45. "L'inauguration de l'Avenue du President-Wilson," *L'Ouest-Eclair* (Rennes), 5 July 1918, 2; "A Paris," *Annales Africaines: Revue Hebdomadaire de l'Afrique du Nord* (Alger), 1 Aug. 1918, 144–145. Author's translation of "Il y en avait des jeunes et des vieilles, des laides et des belles et c'était assez curieux de les voir marcher au pas comme des petits pioupious."

46. Gen. John Pershing to Nursing Sister Miss Beatrice MacDonald, 15 Apr. 1918, MacDonald scrapbook, 17, Radcliffe Schlesinger Library, Harvard University, Cambridge, Mass.; Amanda Hegarty, "'I've Only Started Doing My Bit,'" blog, 7 Dec. 2012, Schlesinger Library, Radcliffe Institute for Advanced Study, Harvard University, https://www.radcliffe.harvard.edu/schlesinger-library/inside-the-collections/ive-only-started-doing-my-bit (accessed 11 October 2019); Albert Morrow, CO Evacuation Hospital No. 2 to AG H.G. Smith, 27 Nov. 1918, MacDonald scrapbook, 39–40.

47. U.S. War Department General Orders No. 26, Headquarters, A.E.F., Feb. 11, 1918, reprinted in United States Army, *United States Army in the World War, General Orders, GHQ, AEF*, Vol. 16, (Washington, D.C.: United States Army Center of Military History, 1992), 203.

48. Sarnecky, *History of the Army Nurse Corps*, 143–147.

49. Tammy M. Proctor, *Civilians in a World at War, 1914–1918* (New York: New York University Press, 2010), 53; Lettie M. Gavin, *American Women in World War I: They Also Served* (Niwot: University Press of Colorado, 2006),102.

50. Beth Linker, *War's Waste: Rehabilitation in World War I America* (Chicago: University of Chicago Press, 2011), 61–62; Surgeon General, *Annual Report, 1919*, 1172, 1176.

51. John Carlova and Ora Ruggles, *The Healing Heart* (New York: Julian Messner, 1961), 1–5, 39–40 (quote), 65–66 (quotes).

52. Gavin, *American Women in World War I*, 102, 110–111 (quote); Patricia Marks, *Bicycles, Bangs, and Bloomers: The New Woman in the Popular Press* (Lexington: University Press of Kentucky, 1990), 147–149; Brown, *Base Hospital No. 9*, 76–77; A.W. Koester, *Fashion Terms and Styles for Women's Garments*, Extension Circular No. 1382 (Corvallis: Oregon State University Extension Service, 1991), 9.

53. As quoted in Gavin, *American Women in World War I*, 109–110.

54. Linker, *War's Waste*, 61–62, 67–68.

55. Gavin, *American Women in World War I*, 105–106.

56. Gavin, *American Women in World War I*, 104–105; William K. Emerson, *Encyclopedia of United States Army Insignia and Uniforms* (Norman: University of Oklahoma Press, 1996), 196.

57. Gavin, *American Women in World War I*, 118. See also Margaret Vining and Barton C. Hacker, ch. 16, in this volume.

58. Katharine E. Manchester and Helen B. Gearin, "Dietitians before World War II," in *Army Medical Specialist Corps*, ed. Robert S. Anderson (Washington, D.C.: Office of the Surgeon General, Department of the Army, 1968), 16, 20; Mary I. Barber, ed., *History of the American Dietetic Association, 1917–1959* (Philadelphia: J.B. Lippincott, 1959), 198–199; Anna R. Van Meter, "The Dietitian Service," in Dock et al., *History of American Red Cross Nursing*, 1403; Surgeon General, *Annual Report, 1919*, 1127 (quote).

59. Van Meter, "The Dietitian Service," 1400–1401.

60. Manchester and Gearin, "Dietitians before World War II," 24–26.

61. Van Meter, "The Dietitian Service," 1406; Surgeon General, *Annual Report, 1919*, 3673–3674.

62. Van Meter, "The Dietitian Service," 1406.

63. Manchester and Gearin, "Dietitians before World War II," 26; Barber, *History of the American Dietetic Association*, 200. On these chevrons and patches, see David L. Zabecki, "Medals and Decorations," in *World War I Encyclopedia*, ed. Spencer Tucker and Priscilla Mary Roberts, (Santa Barbara, Calif.: ABC-CLIO, 2005), 3:767; Robert E. Wyllie, *Orders, Decorations, and Insignia, Military and Civil; with the History and Romance of Their Origin and a Full Description of Each* (New York: G.P. Putnam's Sons, 1921), 238.

64. Surgeon General, *Annual Report, 1919*, 1127–1128.

65. Gavin, *American Women in World War I*, 118.

66. Surgeon General, *Annual Report, 1919*, 1042, 1163, 1869 (quote); Anne Tjosmland, *Bellevue in France: Anecdotal History of Base Hospital No. 1* (New York: Froben Press, 1941), 106, 109, 113–114.

67. Tjosmland, *Bellevue in France*, 106, 110, 246.

For similar examples of nonuniformed female laboratory personnel, see U.S. Army Base Hospital No. 26, *History of Base Hospital 26, December 15th, 1917–May 3rd, 1919* (Minneapolis: D.D. Getchell, 1920), 66, 113, 180; Brown, *Base Hospital No. 9*, 11.

68. Gavin, *American Women in World War I*, 121n42.

69. Proctor, *Civilians in a World at War*, 164–165; Laurie S. Stoff, *Russia's Sisters of Mercy in the Great War: More Than Binding Men's Wounds* (Lawrence: University of Kansas Press, 2015), 198–199. See, more specifically, Jill Liddington, "Britain in the Balkans: The Response of the Scottish Women's Hospital Units," in *Aftermaths of War: Women's Movements and Female Activists, 1918–1923*, ed. Ingrid Sharp and Matthew Stibbe (Leiden: Brill, 2011), 395–418.

70. Ellen S. More, *Restoring the Balance: Women Physicians and the Profession of Medicine, 1950–1995* (Cambridge, Mass.: Harvard University Press, 1999), 288; More, "American Medical Women's Association," 165–167, 172.

71. Bellafaire and Graf, *Women Doctors in War*, 35–37; Joseph H. Ford, *Administration, American Expeditionary Force*, vol. 2 of *The Medical Department of the United States Army in the World War*, ed. Charles Lynch, Frank W. Weed, and Loy McAfee (Washington, D.C.: Government Printing Office, 1927), 102.

72. Emerson, *Encyclopedia of United States Army Insignia and Uniforms*, 184.

73. Charles Lynch, Frank W. Weed, and Loy McAffee, *The Medical Department of the United States Army in the World War*, vol. 1, *The Surgeon General's Office* (Washington: Government Printing Office, 1923), 152.

74. "Washington Racks Brains to Devise Army Uniforms for Women Camp Doctors," *Detroit Free Press*, 27 Oct. 1918, 6.

75. "Biography of Dr. Loy McAfee," American Medical Women's Association, https://cfmedicine.nlm.nih.gov/physicians/biography_356.html (accessed 11 October 2019); Charles Lynch, Frank W. Weed, and Loy McAfee, eds., *The Medical Department of the United States Army in the World War*, 15 vols. (Washington, D.C.: Government Printing Office, 1921–1927).

76. Barton C. Hacker, "Women in Uniform, World War 1 Edition," *O Say Can You See? Stories from the Museum* (blog), 8 Sept. 2011, photo, https://americanhistory.si.edu/blog/2011/09/women-in-uniform-world-war-i-edition.html (accessed 11 October 2019).

77. Cole, *Survey of U.S. Army Uniforms*, 59.

78. Bellafaire and Graf, *Women Doctors in War*, 33, 35; More, "American Medical Women's Association," 167.

79. More, "American Medical Women's Association," 167; Bellafaire and Graf, *Women Doctors in War*, 46–47.

80. "First Unit of American Women's Hospitals on Way Abroad," *Morning Register* (Eugene, Ore.), 15 June 1918, 6.

81. "That 'Sam Browne Belt,'" *Sun* (Baltimore), 10 Nov. 1917, 6; "'Sam Browne' Belts Are Barred Here," *New York Times*, 18 Oct. 1917, 18; "Army Officers in U.S. Must Give up Sam Browne Belts," *New-York Tribune*, 18 Oct. 1917, 4; "'Sam Browne' Belt Adopted by U.S. Army and Named 'Liberty,'" *Washington Post*, 4 Jan. 1918, 3.

82. Essig, "My Trip Abroad with Uncle Sam."

83. Sarnecky, *History of the U.S. Army Nurse Corps*, 144–147.

84. Catherine Lewis Harker, *Beyond Rosie: A Documentary History of Women and World War II* (Fayetteville: University of Arkansas Press, 2015), 89.

SIXTEEN

CALL TO COLORS

American Women Join the Armed Forces, 1917–1919

MARGARET VINING AND BARTON C. HACKER

When the United States declared war on Germany in April 1917, American women had already been serving in uniform for more than two and a half years as members of a wide variety of relief and welfare organizations. But now their opportunities greatly expanded: The American branches of the Young Men's Christian Association (YMCA), the Salvation Army, the Young Women's Christian Association (YWCA), and the Society of Friends (Quakers) immediately established their own programs distinct from the international organization of which they were part. They were joined by such national organizations as the Jewish Welfare Board, the Knights of Columbus, and the National Catholic War Council. Local organizations, secular as well as faith based, also proliferated. Government agencies at all levels grew ever more reliant on women workers and increasingly expected them to work in uniform. They also collaborated with such civilian organizations as the Humane Society and the American Library Association to further the war effort. And for the first time in American history, women other than nurses were allowed to join the armed forces. At every level, uniform-wearing women played conspicuous and indispensable parts.

UNIFORMED WOMEN IN WAR RELIEF AND WELFARE

With a record of military support dating back to the Civil War, the YMCA promptly received War Department and Navy Department endorsement when the United States entered the war.[1] It became the lead agency in the Commission on Training Camp Activities in the United States. Created in April 1917 by the War Department and led by Raymond B. Fosdick, the commission relied on a coalition of seven welfare organization, the so-called Seven Sisters: YMCA, YWCA, Knights of Columbus, Jewish Welfare Board, Salvation Army, American Library Association, and War Camp Community Service. The commission mainly sought to help keep stateside troops in training out of bars and brothels, aided by a substantial number of women.[2] The War Camp Community Service, organized by the commission with the help of the Playground and Recreation Association of America, operated solely outside the camps. Like the other Seven Sisters, its female members wore uniforms.[3] Its activities were also seconded by a nationwide cadre of policewomen trained to work with delinquent women and to protect young girls. By the end of the war, they numbered 286, with 58 of them paid by the War Department and the others by municipalities or private organizations.[4]

Acting under the auspices of the American Expeditionary Force (AEF), the YMCA also took charge of as much as 90% of the AEF's nonmedical welfare work, ministering to the spiritual needs, morale, entertainment, and comfort of the troops.[5] And for the first time in its history, the Y added women to its field workers; like their male counterparts, the women were called secretaries. For women, the work was mostly in canteens, and it was mostly abroad; twice as many female secretaries served in Europe as in the homeland.[6] Canteen service in a wide range of local and national organizations ranked second only to nursing among women's uniformed wartime activities. One estimate put the number of women who volunteered for canteen service in cities and railway stations throughout the United States during the war at 70,000.[7] How many women worked in overseas canteens for the YMCA, the YWCA, the Red Cross, the Salvation Army, and other organizations is probably unknowable, but it was substantial. The YMCA alone recruited through a purpose-created Women's Bureau some 3,500 women for canteen work in France—though the women did engage in other activities as well. About a thousand women were working in France when the war ended, but that number more than doubled after the Armistice as women increasingly took charge of activities to ease the plight of soldiers anxious to return home.[8]

Like the men of the YMCA, the women served in uniform. The YMCA paid its secretaries and provided their very expensive uniforms. The average total cost of a female secretary's overseas outfit, including the uniform supplied when she arrived in Paris, was $215 (equivalent to $4,475 of today's dollars).[9] Volunteers paid their own expenses and purchased their own uniforms (Figure 16.1).[10] Most women saw the uniform positively, "very good looking," even "stunning."[11] Nora Saltonstall judged "the Y.M.C.A. uniform . . . very smart & attractive," adding that "the whole effect is dignified, stylish & yet military."[12] Good looks aside, the uniform conferred status, protection, and recognition on its wearer.[13] Even someone who disliked the idea of wearing a uniform admitted its value.[14]

The Salvation Army had come to America in 1880. Its female members, like their male counterparts, had been wearing uniforms from the beginning.[15] Wearing a uniform, in other words, was nothing new for Salvation Army women serving in the Great War. According to the Salvation Army's American commander, Evangeline Booth, General Pershing authorized salvationists to bear the rank of Army private and to wear "the regulation khaki uniforms

Figure 16.1.
Eleanor Butler Alexander Roosevelt, 1918. Wikimedia Commons.

Figure 16.2.
A cheerful American Salvation Army "lassie" rolling pie crusts for men of the 26th Division in France, 1918. National Archives.

with the addition of the red Salvation Army shield on the hats, red epaulets, and with skirts for the women."[16] Despite their small numbers—of the 250 American salvationists sent to France, 109 were women—they were perhaps the most highly regarded of all welfare workers. Widely known as lassies, Salvation Army doughnut girls became iconic figures, featured on posters and much photographed at work in their uniform, their smiling faces topped by halo-like helmets (Figure 16.2).[17]

Woman-led and woman-oriented, the YWCA occupied a unique position in the landscape of American relief and welfare. It became very active early in the war, extending its longtime commitment to providing residential, welfare, and leisure activities for women in the cities to the growing numbers of women industrial workers. When the United States entered the war, the YWCA expanded its domestic role to assist female visitors to men in the training camps. Its unique woman-designed hostess houses provided both temporary housing for female visitors and pleasant meeting places for soldiers and their families.[18] The YWCA followed much the same pattern when it sent over 400 of its workers to France, where they were especially active in ministering to French women workers, especially in the munitions industry, and to American women serving overseas.[19] The YWCA assumed a special role in providing quarters and other assistance to the young women recruited by the Army for overseas duty as stenographers and telephone operators.[20]

Although YWCA workers had always identified themselves with pins, badges, or armbands, in 1918, the organization's members donned uniforms. In a talk to the staff at YWCA headquarters in New York, *Woman's Home Companion* staff writer Anna Steese Richardson, just back from a trip to Paris, "spoke fervently of the smartness and trimness of the Y.W.C.A. overseas uniform."[21] Designed and made by a Paris couturier, the uniform comprised "a box plaited skirt and Norfolk jacket with Kitchener pockets, both of horizon blue, and a black hat of the tri-corner design." Right sleeve and hat bore "the blue triangle of the Y.W.C.A."[22] For those who wore the uniform, its meaning ranged from exalted to mundane. Feeling "at first . . . uncomfortably conspicuous [wearing] . . . her uniform," one worker soon became convinced that she was "doing something in these great days that merits a uniform." Another worker enjoyed a "mind . . . free from the cluttery competitive feeling of 'what to put on' each day."[23]

Both the YMCA and the YWCA provided cover for smaller independent organizations. One was America's Over There Theatre League, founded in New York City in April 1918 to entertain the troops of the AEF. League members traveled as YMCA volunteers and wore the YMCA uniform, women and men alike.[24] The YMCA also hosted troupers of Stage Women's War Relief, which sponsored shows in camps and hospitals both at home and abroad. Trouping for the troops was a relatively late addition to the Stage Women's War Relief repertoire. Stage women organized in New York shortly after the declaration of war with the aim of making clothing and surgical dressings and distributing them to military and civilian facilities in Europe. They worked in nurse-like uniforms at their workshop on Fifth Avenue (Figure 16.3).[25]

Another organization to serve under the YMCA umbrella was the Overseas Service Unit of the General Federation of Women's Clubs. The federation had intended the unit's 100 young women for independent canteen work in France but altered plans when General Pershing placed all relief and welfare work under either the Red Cross or the YMCA. As the young women sailed for France in January 1919, their mission was still canteening, but now as part of the YMCA Women's Division.[26] Observing them depart, Delphine Dodge Ashbaugh, chairman of the federation's War Victory Commission, thought "they were so good to look at in the uniform . . . , olive grey with blue trimmings and hat to match. On the right coat sleeve is stitched an arm band bearing these words, 'General Federation Women's Clubs Overseas Unit.'"[27] The YWCA played a central role in assisting the Polish Reconstruction Association in the war's immediate aftermath. Commonly referred to as the Grey Samaritans after the YWCA-style uniform they wore, specially trained young American women of Polish descent spent four years assisting Poland's postwar recovery.[28]

Joining these well-established organizations were several new ones that all employed uniformed women. The American Friends Service Committee (AFSC) began in April 1917 as a temporary organization to provide service alternatives during the Great War for Quaker conscientious objectors. Working in close cooperation with the Red Cross, AFSC expanded to include a wide variety of relief and welfare activities not only in the United States but throughout Europe that lasted will into the 1920s. Of the 600 AFSC members who served abroad, 50 were women. AFSC women's work was gendered along conventional early

Figure 16.3.
Stage Women's War Relief poster, 1918. Library of Congress, Prints and Photographs Division.

twentieth-century lines: nursing, childcare, embroidery oversight, housekeeping supervision, and stenography.[29] But like their male counterparts, they did wear uniforms. British Friends, who had already been hard at work in France for three years, urged "our American Friends to adopt the gray uniform which is now so well known to the authorities and to the people amongst whom we work, and which is so definitely associated with the non-military character of our work."[30] As historian J. William Frost observed, "The gray uniforms . . . made Quakers less visible."[31]

On 9 April 1917, just three days after the declaration of war, several Jewish groups organized a Jewish Welfare Board to help Jewish soldiers and sailors cope with the spiritual, moral, and social challenges of military service. Five months after its formation, the board was named to the War Department's Commission on Training Camp Activities, where it joined the Protestant YMCA, YWCA, and Salvation Army and the Catholic Knights of Columbus. The board began recruiting women as the draft siphoned off Jewish men, with 75 women serving as welfare workers. The women served in uniform chiefly as canteen workers, both at home and abroad.[32]

Two major organizations represented American Catholics in relief and welfare during the Great War. The church hierarchy created the National Catholic War Council, whereas the laity was represented by the Knights of Columbus, a fraternal order founded in 1882. The Knights were actually the first in action, responding immediately after the declaration of war. The American bishops formed their National Catholic War Council in August. The Knights became the Catholic presence in the Commission on Training Camp Activities, along with the YMCA, YWCA, and Jewish Welfare Board. The Knights rigorously avoided employing women in their field operations either at home or abroad but welcomed the service of 75 uniformed young women as clerks and stenographers in their Paris headquarters. The National Catholic War Council, in contrast, arranged for the special training of women in social work to serve both at home and abroad. Those assigned to overseas duty wore uniforms.[33]

Local as well as national organizations emerged as women mobilized for the war. New York, for instance, was home to the League of Catholic Women, whose members donned uniforms to cooperate with other Catholic organizations in relief work and to provide canteen services for military personnel.[34] New York City's Mayor's Committee of Women on National Defense also established a uniformed canteen service.[35]

GOVERNMENT UNIFORMS FOR WOMEN

The number of government agencies that established or endorsed official and quasi-official dress for their female employees testifies to the significance the government attached to uniforms. Although the American Humane Society and the War Department agreed on a plan to establish American Red Star Animal Relief in spring 1916, the organization did not go into action until June 1917, after the United States entered the war. Modeled on an international Swiss organization with the same name, its primary mission was providing medical care and rehabilitation for sick and wounded military equines, though Red Star did extend its care to dogs and other animals. The approved uniform for women members was tan cotton or wool with a military-style coat 27 inches long, standing collar, shoulder straps, four patch pockets; a skirt 34 to 36 inches in length, to be worn over breeches or knickerbockers; a cap of the same material as the uniform; and tan leather riding boots.[36]

Under the auspices of the Library of Congress, the American Library Association (ALA) established its Library War Service in April 1917. Its purpose was to collect books and operate military camp and hospital libraries at home and abroad.[37] The eagerness of women to serve was not always matched by the willingness either of the officers in charge of the camps or of the men in charge of the ALA to accept their service.[38] Yet serve they did. Of the 329 women engaged as librarians in the United States and overseas, 170 worked in hospital libraries, and the others worked in camp libraries, in dispatch offices, and as field supervisors.[39] Caroline Webster, who oversaw hospital libraries in Library War Service headquarters at the Library of Congress, spelled out the need for uniforms: "Our representatives are equipped with a uniform so that they may have standing with the military authorities and be given the respect and attention which an official connection with the military gives." An incomplete uniform was no uniform at all, she warned. "Unless you are willing to conform to the uniform in every detail, do not equip yourself with an outfit either at your own or the Association's expense."[40]

The ALA specified the uniforms and reimbursed a portion of their cost. Hospital librarians wore natural-colored pongee shirtwaist dresses cut much like nurse's uniforms, with a white collar and dark-brown tie. A dark-brown brassard on the sleeve bore the ALA logo; a panama hat with dark-brown band and ALA pin completed the uniform.[41] Those not working in hospitals wore a different uniform. Librarians were responsible for obtaining their own uniforms, for which the association reimbursed them. The procedure required the librarian to send her measurements (taken by a tailor) with payment to Weltman, Pollack & Company in New York, which guaranteed to ship the uniform within 10 days. She then forwarded the signed bill to headquarters for reimbursement. Similar arrangements applied for hats from the Ferry Hat Company and overcoats from Best & Company, both of New York. The ALA directly supplied two ties and three pins, a large one for the hat and two smaller ones for the collars. An official ALA circular specified the required white high-necked madras blouse and tan or black low-heeled shoes. These items workers provided for themselves, but material was available upon request without cost for spats.[42]

America's food supply was widely perceived to be in jeopardy when the United States entered the war for reasons ranging from the growing demand for supplying the Allies to the looming loss of agricultural labor to the draft. The National League for Woman's Service Division of Agriculture acted from the outset to promote women's training and participation in food production. Many other organizations followed suit. Especially significant was the Committee on Agriculture of New York City's Mayor's Committee of Women on National Defense, which played a key role in developing the unit idea—organizing female farm labor in semimilitary self-supporting units responsible for their own maintenance. Barnard College professor Ida H. Ogilvie headed the committee's training camp.[43] She deemed uniforms vital. Trainees wore men's blue overalls and work shirts, cotton gloves, broad-brimmed hats, and stout shoes. "The long trousers and stout material are essential where work in rough places is to be done, and where there is kneeling, as in weeding, any form of skirt or tunic is too much in the way," Ogilvie explained, adding that "although somewhat startling to a conservative neighborhood at first, this costume was accepted remarkably soon as a matter of course."[44] Helen Kennedy Stevens, who became something of a poster girl for the Woman's Land Army, recalled how excited she and her fellow training camp recruits were to receive their uniforms.[45] At another New York training camp, *New-York Tribune* reporter Elene Foster noted the "obligatory" uniform. Everyone was "dressed alike in short khaki skirts, long linen leggings, khaki colored flannel shirts and broad brimmed felt hats of the same khaki color." To her surprise, "the costume was remarkably becoming."[46]

Trainees from these and many other programs around the country proved their value to often reluctant farmers during the 1917 growing season. Denigrated as "farmerettes" by early critics, the women came to embrace the slur as a badge of honor. With 1917 drawing to a close, the National Women's Farm and Garden Association invited delegates from a broad range of interested organizations to a meeting in New York. On the basis of the 1917 experience, they agreed to establish the Woman's Land of Army of America (WLAA). When neither the Department of Agriculture nor the Department of Labor would agree to sponsor the WLAA, it operated as a private labor organization dependent on donations and fund-raising. Piggybacking on already established state-level organizations like those of the National League for Women's Service and the National Women's Farm and Garden League, the Woman's Land Army fielded farm workers all over the country in 1918, some 15,000 in all. Thousands of others served in unofficial units or in units on college and university farms (Figure 16.4).[47]

Figure 16.4.
A farmerette behind a plow in a peach orchard. 1917. Library of Congress, Prints and Photographs Division.

And, as always, the uniform was indispensable. Explaining that "women should not attempt to do farm work hampered by skirts or by clothing that constricts the muscles," the Woman's Land Army eventually adopted "a uniform carefully designed to meet the needs of the woman land-worker," adding that "three-quarter or full height shoes of stout leather with low heels are essential."[48] This standardization came late, however, not until April 1919. During the 1918 growing season, uniforms varied from state to state and even within states. New York City newspapers took note of fund-raising farmerettes proudly wearing blue denim smocks and bloomers on the city's streets.[49] In Hamilton County, Ohio, they wore blue denim bib overalls and white cotton shirtwaists, topped by wide-brimmed straw hats.[50] The uniform was a little different in California, but not the sentiment. Against criticism of their uniform, farmerettes explained "that a practical, serviceable uniform makes not alone for comfort, but for a sense of responsibility." The uniform, they insisted, "affects their whole attitude towards the work—they must live up to it; they must do it credit."[51]

Another response to the perceived food crisis was the U.S. Food Administration (USFA), which led to perhaps the most unexpected of all women's uniforms in the Great War. The notion of putting housewives in uniform underscored a widespread recognition of the symbolic potency of the uniform. Shortly after the U.S. Congress declared war on Germany, President Wilson had recalled Herbert Hoover from his headquarters in Belgium, where he oversaw a massive relief effort, to take charge of the new USFA. Hoover's leadership of Belgian relief had already made him a household name, and he seemed the likeliest choice to organize and manage American food production and voluntary conservation, widely deemed a critical element in the U.S. war effort. By the summer of 1917, the new food administration had begun a massive propaganda campaign aimed at enlisting women to support food conservation.[52]

Recognizing the symbolism of uniforms, the USFA made a uniform for housewives an important part of the campaign. The wives of official Washington led the way, promptly pledging to conserve food and donning the red, white, and blue uniform: blue chambray with white piqué cuffs, collar, and cap, bearing the red USFA insignia on the sleeve and cap. Ordinary folk could make their own with a government-provided pattern for about a dollar or buy one ready-made for about $3. Breathless newspaper and magazine stories reported the progress of Hoover's conservation army, many illustrated with photographs of uniformed matrons.[53] How many women actually worked in the Hoover apron, as it has come to be called, is unknowable. Some, certainly, but likely not that many. Establishing the purported equivalence between uniformed men in the trenches and uniformed women in the kitchen proved a hard sell. The one major exception were the home economists. An emerging profession in the early twentieth century, home economics furnished much of the expertise behind food conservation. And home economists adopted the Hoover apron as a kind of professional uniform (Figure 16.5).[54]

Uniforms also spread through government service. During the war, efforts multiplied to put all female clerical workers into uniform, a move that met some resistance, though it

Figure 16.5.
Mina Van Winkle, head of the Lecture Bureau of the USFA, wears the Hoover apron as she explains Victory gardening and food processing to support the war effort. Library of Congress Prints and Photographs Division.

was strongly supported by most workers themselves.[55] Even such unlikely agencies as the Emergency Fleet Corporation of the U.S. Shipping Board, created in April 1917 explicitly to provide the ships needed to carry American forces to France, required its female clerical workers to wear uniforms.[56] The Emergency Fleet Corporation uniform appeared on the government list of 20 approved uniforms for women issued in mid-1918.[57] In October, the War Department announced plans for all female clerical workers to wear uniforms of "battleship gray," but the Armistice a month later foreclosed the plan.[58]

WOMEN JOIN THE ARMED FORCES

Perhaps the most unexpected aspect of female mobilization for America's Great War was the acceptance of women as regular members of the armed forces. With the approach of war in early 1917, the U.S. Navy faced an immediate need for large numbers of new clerical workers, which normal civil service procedures could not meet. When the Progressive secretary of the Navy, Josephus Daniels, confirmed that existing law did not explicitly bar them, he promptly authorized the recruitment of women as members of the Naval Coast Defense Reserve. Designated yeomen (f), though widely referred to colloquially as yeomanettes, they received the same pay and allowances as their male counterparts. The Navy accepted its first female enlistees in mid-March 1917. Eventually, well over 11,000 served.[59]

The new female members of the U.S. Navy had every reason to expect uniforms, but none were yet available. In fact, the Navy took a year to finalize uniform regulations for women: a single-breasted coat with patch pockets and matching skirt 4 inches above the ankle of navy-blue serge for winter wear and white drill for summer. This uniform became mandatory only in September 1918. Well before then, of course, the Navy had begun distributing uniforms to its new female members, though there was often a long wait; some enlistees made their own or had them made by seamstresses, on occasion straying from the approved design. Others simply served in civilian clothes with an identifying pin or brassard until they were issued uniforms. Even after regulations were issued, however, the women could be quite casual about adhering to them, especially with respect to carrying swagger sticks or wearing unauthorized hats and Sam Browne belts.[60] For the new yeoman (f), receiving the uniform issue was memorable. Lou McPherson Guthrie recalled "the smart ensign-type jackets [with] naval insignia on the sleeves," adding that "when we got our uniforms, we all went downtown and had our pictures made to send home" (Figure 16.6).[61]

Quite different was the way officials handled uniforms for the women who joined the Marine Reserve (f), unofficially dubbed marinettes. As part of the Navy, the U.S. Marine Corps

Figure 16.6.
Yeoman (f) inspection. Library of Congress, Prints and Photographs Division.

was also authorized to recruit women but decided to do so only in August 1918, enlisting only 305. Having learned from the Navy's experience, the marines promptly promulgated uniform regulations, which were strictly enforced (though even the lady marines sometimes found the Sam Browne belt irresistible). The uniform was widely admired, its wearers looking "stylish indeed in their tailormade two-piece suits of green wool in the winter and tan khaki in the summer."[62] Admiration for the yeoman (f) uniform was less universal. Some, like Estelle Kemper and her Vassar friends, really disliked theirs. But Eunice Dessez probably more accurately reflected the view of most her fellows. "No professional couturier could have produced a more suitable model," she insisted. "A belated expression of thanks is long overdue to the original designers of the smart Yeoman F uniform." According to Navy Secretary Daniels, "The uniforms of the Yeomen (F) and the Marines (F) were natty and beautiful, were worn with pride. . . . They were both becoming and suited to the duty assigned."[63]

Secretary of War Newton Baker adamantly opposed allowing women to join the U.S. Army, as did most War Department officials. Even had they favored allowing women to serve, they would have faced an obstacle that the Navy did not. All statutes governing Army recruitment specified men. Various War Department agencies nonetheless seemed perfectly willing to hire women, sometimes as contractors, more often as civilian employees. Like the Navy women, they mainly performed clerical duties. Although civilians, they were required to wear uniforms, which for the most part they did eagerly. Women served in the War Department as Signal Corps telephone operators and inspectors, Ordnance Department clerks and inspectors, and Quartermaster Corps clerks and stenographers. As historian Susan Zeiger points out, no modern bureaucracy could function without stenographers, typists, and telephone operators, all occupations that had become highly feminized by 1910.[64]

Their work kept them only within the continental United States with two notable exceptions. The Quartermaster Corps sent 35 stenographers to serve with the AEF in France. Small numbers of other office workers also joined the Army in France.[65] By far the largest group of nonmedical Army women in France belonged to the Signal Corps telephone operators unit. Cooperating closely with the American Telegraph and Telephone Company, the Army hired 377 women, 223 of whom served in France. They were widely, though unofficially, known as "hello girls," just as female U.S. telephone operators had been since the turn of the century.[66] Because the Army assigned them the status of cadet officers, they were responsible for buying their own Army-specified kit, which cost $250–$350, roughly equivalent to six months' salary. The kit included everything, as historian Elizabeth Cobbs explained, "from tan parade gloves, woolen stockings, sateen bloomers, and union suits to bicarbonate of soda, Lysol, iodine, and sewing kits. Uniform coats, skirts blouses, high-top shoes, and bronze insignia were the most expensive items." Despite the financial burden, Cobbs added, "the women loved their uniforms, which meant full membership in the AEF."[67] Or so they thought.

Because they signed enlistment papers, wore military uniforms, accepted military discipline, and served with the AEF in France, the telephone operators quite naturally believed they were in the Army. Recruiters may have deliberately misled them as well. Only after the Armistice did they learn that the Army regarded them as civilian employees or contractors. A long struggle for official recognition ensued, finally resolved 60 years later when the government acknowledged the survivors as military veterans in the GI Bill Improvement Act of 1977, which granted veteran status to the hello girls and several other groups. Two years later, 18 survivors received their discharge papers and Victory Medals.[68] In a sense, Elizabeth Cobbs' recent study, *The Hello Girls: America's First Women Soldiers*, is a testament of their true military service and the long struggle to undo the injustice perpetuated in 1919.[69]

WOMEN'S UNIFORMS IN CONTEMPORARY EYES

One of the most striking demonstrations of the power of the uniform was the Congress of Allied Women in War Service. On 22 August 1918, 2,000 uniformed women primarily from the France, Britain, and the United States, but drawing women from around the world, assembled in Paris. The purpose was to increase mutual understanding and promote cooperation in war work. But the program also suggested a larger goal: "to improve the unparalleled opportunity of interpreting to one another the women of the nations *in whose hands will rest in increasing measure the formative influences in the building of the new world.* It is believed that such forces, rightly stimulated and directed will shorten the war."[70] "There was no feminist propaganda," according to YWCA secretary Janet Wallace Enrich, but there was no need. "When the women of the great nations can come together on a common ground of a great task they need no longer talk about the principles underlying what they want to do."[71] The British, American, and French Red Cross, YMCA, and YWCA accounted for about three-quarters of the attendees, but a hundred other organizations were represented in all. They included, among many others, Queen Mary's Army Auxiliary Corps, the Women's Army Auxiliary Corps, women motor drivers from all organizations, the Scottish Women's Hospitals, nurses of every description, the Salvation Army, and the American Fund for French Wounded. The French government even supported the attendance of munitionettes from Lyon, St. Etienne, Roanne, Bourgcs, and Paris. Every account of the congress stressed the fact that every one of the 2,000 women who attended was in uniform.[72]

The significance of women's uniforms was not lost on contemporaries. One indication of the fascination of women's uniforms was the publication of numerous newspaper articles on foreign women in uniform early in the war and continuing until well after American entry. The large-scale British mobilization of women both within and outside the armed forces held the limelight,[73] but Italian policewomen and French letter carriers received a nod as well.[74] Newspapers and magazines regularly attended to women's paramilitary units, women's move into uniformed public service, and women workers (both factory and pink collar), to say nothing of articles on female members of the armed forces, the Red Cross, and all the other welfare and relief organizations. Journalists regularly commented on the spectacle of American women in uniform, both at home and abroad.[75] That women themselves so often commented on the meaning uniform wearing had for them across the gamut of organizations may offer the most significant testimony of all.

NOTES

1. General Orders, No. 57, War Department, Washington, D.C., 9 May 1917; General Orders, No. 313, Navy Department, Washington, D.C., 26 July 1917; as reprinted in John R. Mott, "Religious Organizations in War Relief Work: The War Work of the Young Men's Christian Associations of the United States," in "War Relief Work," special issue, *Annals of the American Academy of Political and Social Science* 79 (Sept. 1918): 204–206.

2. Raymond B. Fosdick, "The Commission on Training Camp Activities: The War and Navy Departments Commissions on Training Camp Activities," in "War Relief Work," special issue, *Annals of the American Academy of Political and Social Science* 79 (Sept. 1918): 130–142; Commission on Training Camp Activities, *A Report on the Work of Women in Military Camps in the United State* (Washington, D.C.: Government Printing Office, 1918); Weldon B. Durham, "'Big Brother' and the 'Seven Sisters': Camp Life Reforms in World War I," *Military Affairs* 42, no. 2 (April 1978): 57–60; Susan Zeiger, *In Uncle Sam's Service: Women Workers with the American Expeditionary Force, 1917–1919* (Ithaca, N.Y.: Cornell University Press, 1999), 53–55; Nancy Kathleen Bristow, *Making Men Moral: Social Engineering during the Great War* (New York: New York University Press, 1996).

3. War Camp Community Service, *Handbook of the War Camp Community Service* (New York: WCCS, 1918); Joseph Lee, "The Commission on Training Camp Activities: War Camp Community Service," in "War Relief Work," special issue, *Annals of the American Academy of Political and Social Science* 79 (Sept. 1918): 189–194. On the War Camp Community Service uniform, see Vivian Lea Young, "'Petticoats Are Part of this Uniform': American Women Volunteers of the First World War and Their Uniforms" (M.A. thesis, Randolph-Macon Woman's College, 1987), 278–283; Jill Halcomb Smith, *Dressed for Duty: America's Women in Uniform, 1898–1973* (San Jose, Calif.: R. James Bender, 2001–2004), 2:95–97.

4. Martha P. Falconer, "The Commission on Training Camp Activities: The Segregation of Delinquent Women and Girls as a War Problem," in "War Relief Work," special issue, *Annals of the American Academy of Political and Social Science* 79 (Sept. 1918): 160–166; Margaret Weddemer, "The War Camp Community Service That Is Introducing the Public to the Soldiers," *Touchstone* 4, no. 1 (Oct. 1918): 34–40; "Police Women," *Woman Citizen* 3, no. 49 (3 May 1919): 1055.

5. Young Men's Christian Association, International Committee, *Summary of World War Work of the American Y.M.C.A.: With the Soldiers and Sailors of America at Home, on the Sea, and Overseas, with the Men of the Allied Armies and with the Prisoners of War in All Parts of the World* (New York: YMCA, 1920), 199–203.

6. YMCA, *Summary of World War Work of the American Y.M.C.A.*, 39–41, 112.

7. Frederick Harris, Frederic Houston Kent, and William J. Newlin, eds., *Service with Fighting Men: An Account of the Work of the American Young Men's Christian Associations in the World War* (New York: Association Press, 1922), 1:248.

8. Harris et al., *Service with Fighting Men*, 1:100–101, 258; Barbara Schroeder, "Women YMCA Secretaries in World War I," *Carry On: Women's Overseas Service Magazine* 68, no. 3 (Mar. 1988): 17–19; E.T. Brainerd, "Women's Division, Overseas Service, Y.M.C.A.," *General Federation Magazine* 18, no. 3 (Mar. 1919): 8.

9. Harris et al., *Service with Fighting Men*, 1:528.

10. "War Relief Work," *Hartford Courant*, 23 Mar. 1918, 13.

11. Marian Baldwin, *Canteening Overseas, 1917–1919* (New York: Macmillan, 1920), 38; Frances Gulick, "Y Girl," *American Legion Monthly* 8, no. 2 (Feb. 1930): 1.

12. Eleanor "Nora" Saltonstall, letter to her family, 30 Nov. 1917, 4, Eleanor Saltonstall Papers, Massachusetts Historical Society Collections Online, http://www.masshist.org/database/viewer.php?item_id=2001&img_step=1&mode=dual (accessed 5 November 2019).

13. Baldwin, *Canteening Overseas*, 42; Katherine Mayo, *That Damn Y: A Record of Overseas Service* (Boston: Houghton Mifflin, 1920), 150; Helen Perry, "The Journal Intime of a 'Y' Worker," *Woman Citizen* 3, no. 10 (3 Aug. 1918): 196.

14. Katherine Duncan Morse, *The Uncensored Letters of a Canteen Girl* (New York: Henry Holt, 1920), 7–8, 262–263.

15. Sallie Chesham, *Born to Battle: The Salvation Army in America* (Chicago: Rand McNally, 1965); Edward M. McKinley, *Marching to Glory: The History of the Salvation Army in the USA, 1880–1980* (San Francisco: Harper & Row,

1980); Lillian Talz, *Hallelujah Lads and Lasses: Remaking the Salvation Army in America, 1880–1930* (Chapel Hill: University of North Carolina Press, 2001); Lillian Talz, "Hallelujah Lasses in the Battle for Souls: Working- and Middle-Class Women in the Salvation Army in the United States, 1872–1896," *Journal of Women's History* 9, no. 2 (1997): 84–106. On early Salvation Army women's uniforms, see especially Jennifer Le Zotte, "'Be Odd': The Contradictory Use of Dress in the Gilded Age Salvation Army," *Winterthur Portfolio* 47, no. 4 (Winter 2013): 248–258.

16. Evangeline Booth and Grace Livingston Hill, *The War Romance of the Salvation Army* (Philadelphia: J.B. Lippincott, 1919), 55. Cf. Young, "'Petticoats Are Part of This Uniform,'" 213–222; Smith, *Dressed for Duty*, 2:23–34.

17. William E. Moore and James Crussell, *U. S. Official Pictures of the World War, Showing America's Participation, Selected from the Official Files of the War Department* (Washington, D.C.: Pictorial Bureau, 1920), 541; Dorothy Schneider and Carl J. Schneider, *Into the Breach: American Women Overseas in World War I* (New York: Viking, 1991), 221; Zeiger, *In Uncle Sam's Service*, 143–144. Overall, American salvationists accounted for about a third of the international Salvation Army effort on all fronts in the Great War; see Herbert A. Wisbey Jr., *Soldiers without Swords: A History of the Salvation Army in the United States* (New York: Macmillan, 1955), 160.

18. A. Estelle Paddock, "Religious Organizations in War Relief Work: War Work of Young Women's Christian Association," in "War Relief Work," special issue, *Annals of the American Academy of Political and Social Science* 79 (Sept. 1918): 208–212; Mary S. Sims, *The Natural History of a Social Institution—The Young Women's Christian Association* (New York: Woman's Press, 1936), 183–187; Zeiger, *In Uncle Sam's Service*, 92; Robert H. Moulton, "Women Design Hostess Houses for Army Camps," *Cambridge Sentinel*, 10 Aug. 1918, 6; Cynthia Brandimarte, "Women on the Home Front: Hostess Houses during World War I," *Winterthur Portfolio* 42, no. 4 (Winter 2008): 201–222.

19. Henrietta Roelofs, "The Value of the Association in France," *Association Monthly* 12, no. 9 (Sept. 1918): 314–317; "Work of Y.W.C.A. in Allied Nations," *Madera* (Calif.) *Weekly Tribune*, 26 Sept. 1918, 3; Young Women's Christian Association of the U.S.A., *Young Women's Christian Association Overseas* (New York: YWCA War Work Council, 1919); Sims, *The Natural History of a Social Institution*, 188–190; Nancy Boyd, *Emissaries: The Overseas Work of the American YWCA, 1895–1970* (New York: Woman's Press, 1986), 73.

20. "U. S. Signal Corps Unit at [YWCA] Headquarters," *War Work Bulletin*, no. 29 (26 Apr. 1918): 4; Zeiger, *In Uncle Sam's service*, 92.

21. "The Y. W. C. A. Makes a New Friend," *War Work Bulletin*, no. 37 (16 Aug. 1918): 1. See also Anna Steese Richardson, "The Y.W.C.A. in France," *Association Monthly* 12, no. 10 (Oct. 1918): 386.

22. "Y. W. C. A. Workers to Have Uniforms," *Madera* (Calif.) *Weekly Tribune*, 19 Sept. 1918, 4. See also Young, "'Petticoats Are Part of this Uniform,'" 316–321; Smith, *Dressed for Duty*, 2:446–449.

23. "Variations in Uniform-ity," *Association Monthly* 13, no. 2 (Feb. 1919): 79.

24. Winthrop Ames, "America's Over-There Theatre League," *Bulletin of the Authors' League of America* 6, no. 3 (June 1918): 3–4; E.H. Sothern, "America's 'Over There' Theatre League: A Player on the Fighting Front," *Scribner's Magazine* 64, no. 1 (July 1918): 22–34, 64; no. 2 (Aug. 1918): 129–141; James W. Evans and Gardner L. Harding, *Entertaining the American Army: The American Stage and Lyceum in the World War* (New York: Association Press, 1921); Felicia Hardison Londré, "The Range of Laughter: First Person Reports from Entertainers of the Over There Theatre League," in *Humor, Entertainment, and Popular Culture during World War I*, ed. Clémentine Tholas-Disset and Karen A. Ritzenhoff (New York: Palgrave Macmillan US, 2015), 169–179.

25. "Actresses in Tears over War Appeal; Leaders Join in Forming an Organization for Active Relief Work; Telegram from President; Julia Marlowe, Elsie De Wolfe, and Others Take Part in Meeting at Hudson Theatre," *New York Times*, 14 Apr. 1917, 8; Elene Foster, "Famous Women of the Stage Working for War; Generous and Kindly Players All over the Country Are Giving Every Spare Hour to Sewing, Knitting and Making Bandages for the Men in the Trenches; Work Directed from the Fifth Avenue Headquarters Is Nation-wide," *New-York Tribune*, 10 June 1917, C8; Elene Foster, "'Trouping' for Uncle Sam and His Boys," *New-York Tribune*, 5 May 1918: E4; "Women War Workers of the World: The Third of This Series Presents the Work of the American Stage Women," *Touchstone* 4, no. 1 (Oct. 1918): 19–27, 84; Evans and Harding, *Entertaining the American Army*, 150–153, 197.

26. "News of Our Overseas Unit," *General Federation Magazine* 18, no. 5 (May 1919): 7–9; "Our Girls," *General Federation Magazine* 18, no. 10 (Dec. 1919): 13–15; Mildred White Wells, *Unity in Diversity: The History of the General Federation of Women's Clubs* (Washington, D.C.: General Federation of Women's Clubs, 1953), 231–232.

27. Delphine Dodge Asbaugh, "War Victory Commission," *General Federation Magazine* 18, no. 3 (March 1919): 9.

28. Frank W. Thackeray, "To Serve the Cause of Poland: The Polish Grey Samaritans, 1919–1922," *Polish Review* 35, no. 1 (1990): 37–50; Robert Szymczak, "An Act of Devotion: The Polish Grey Samaritans and the American Relief Effort in Poland, 1919–1921," *Polish American Studies* 43, no. 1 (Spring 1986): 13–36; Matthew Lloyd

Adams, "Herbert Hoover and the Organization of the American Relief Effort in Poland (1919–1923)," *European Journal of American Studies* 14-2 (Autumn 2009), paragraphs 48–52, https://doi.org/10.4000/ejas.7627.

29. Rufus M. Jones, *A Service of Love in War Time: American Friends Relief Work in Europe, 1917–1919* (New York: Macmillan, 1920), 140; J. William Frost, "'Our Deeds Carry Our Message': The Early History of the American Friends Service Committee," *Quaker History* 81, no. 1 (Spring 1992): 15, 23; John Forbes, *The Quaker Star under Seven Flags, 1917–1927* (Philadelphia: University of Pennsylvania Press, 1962), 48–68.

30. Jones, *A Service of Love in War Time*, 43.

31. Frost, "'Our Deeds Carry Our Message,'" 14; Jack Sutters, "The Red and Black Star," AFSC, 30 Mar. 2010, http://www.afsc.org/story/red-and-black-star (accessed 5 November 2019); Young, "'Petticoats Are Part of This Uniform,'" 73–78; Smith, *Dressed for Duty*, 1:31.

32. Chester Jacob Teller, "The Jewish Welfare Board," *American Jewish Year Book 5679* (7 Sept. 1918 to 24 Sept. 1919): 88–102; Cyrus Adler, "The Jewish Welfare Board—Twenty Years Old," *American Jewish Year Book 5698* (6 Sept. 1937 to 25 Sept. 1938): 153; Zeiger, *In Uncle Sam's Service*, 53, 55. For the uniforms, see Young, "'Petticoats Are Part of This Uniform,'" 162–168; Smith, *Dressed for Duty*, 1: 319–325.

33. Maurice Francis Egan and John B. Kennedy, *The Knights of Columbus in Peace and War* (New Haven, Conn.: Knights of Columbus, 1920), 1:374–375; Michael Williams, *American Catholics in the War: National Catholic War Council, 1917–1921* (New York: Macmillan, 1921), 386–441. On the uniforms worn by women who worked for the Knights of Columbus, see Young, "'Petticoats Are Part of This Uniform,'" 169–172; Smith, *Dressed for Duty*, 1:377–380. For the National Catholic War Council women, see Young, "'Petticoats Are Part of This Uniform,'" 183; Smith, *Dressed for Duty*, 1:377–380.

34. Egan and Kennedy, *The Knights of Columbus in Peace and War*, 1:374; Young, "'Petticoats Are Part of This Uniform,'" 173–175; "Catholic Women to Continue Canteen Work; Free Meals on Sunday and Food at Cost on Week Days for Men in Uniform," *New-York Tribune*, 14 Sept. 1919, F1.

35. "Women Volunteers to Wear Uniforms," *Hartford Courant*, 22 Mar. 1917, 8; "Uniform for Canteen Aids; Women on Mayor's Committee to Wear Distinctive Dress," *New York Times*, 17 Sept. 1918, 17; "Gray for Canteen Women; Mayor's Committee Adopts Uniform for Workers," *New York Times*, 27 Sept. 1918, 12; "Uniform for Women's Committee," *New York Times*, 13 Oct. 1918, 20. On the work of the Canteen Division, see Mayor's Committee of Women on National Defense, *The Activities of the Mayor's Committee of Women on National Defense, New York, 1918–1919* (New York: Mayor's Committee, 1919), 43–55.

36. "War Dept. Approves Mrs. Baldwin's Uniform," *Los Angeles Herald*, 9 Oct. 1918, 11; Charles Lynch, Frank W. Weed, and Loy McAfee, "American Red Star Animal Relief," in *The Medical Department of the United States Army in the World War*, ed. Charles Lynch, Frank W. Weed, and Loy McAfee, vol. 1, *The Surgeon General's Office* (Washington, D.C.: Government Printing Office, 1923), 557–558; Janet M. Davis, "'Where Gasoline Can't Go': Equine Patriotism and the American Red Star Animal Relief Campaign during World War I" (paper presented at "War Horses of the World," School of Oriental and African Studies, University of London, May 2014), https://www.soas.ac.uk/history/conferences/war-horses-conference-2014/file94551.pdf (accessed 5 November 2019).

37. Herbert Putnam et al., "American Library Association War Service Committee," *Bulletin of the American Library Association* 12, no. 3 (Sept. 1918): 107–162.

38. Theodore Wesley Koch, *War Service of the American Library Association* (Washington, D.C.: ALA War Service, Library of Congress, 1918), 9–10; Arthur P. Young, *Books for Sammies: The American Library Association and World War I* (Pittsburgh: Beta Phi Mu, 1981), 34; Schneider and Schneider, *Into the Breach*, 149–154; Caroline Daniels, "'The Feminine Touch Has Not Been Wanting': Women Librarians at Camp Zachary Taylor, 1917–1919," *Libraries and the Cultural Record* 43, no. 3 (2008): 286–307.

39. Caroline Webster, assistant to the director, ALA Library War Service Headquarters, Library of Congress, to Mrs. Benjamin, 2 Feb. 1920. Unless otherwise specified, all cited documents may be consulted in the Archive of Women's Military History, Division of Armed Forces History, National Museum of American History, Washington, D.C. See also Ola M. Wyeth, "Library Service in a Base Hospital," *American Journal of Nursing* 18, no. 12 (Sept. 1918): 1153–1154.

40. Caroline Webster to Miss Natalie DeM. Hopper, ALA Library, U.S. General Hospital No. 9, Lakewood, N.J., 22 April 1919.

41. ALA Hospital Informational Circular, "Uniforms," 10 June 1918; "What Are You Doing to Win the War? Camp Library Service," *Chicago Daily Tribune*, 23 June 1918, E7. See also Denise Rayman, "Librarians in Uniform," American Library Association Archives at University of Illinois Archives, 14 Apr. 2014, http://archives.library.illinois.edu/ala/wwi-librarian-uniforms/?utm_source=rss&utm_medium=rss&utm_campaign=wwi-librarian-uniforms.

42. Caroline Webster, for the director, "Uniforms for Women," 7 Oct. 1918; Webster for the director, "Overseas Uniforms for Women," 4 Feb. 1919. See also Rayman, "Librarians in Uniform"; Young, "'Petticoats are Part of this Uniform,'" 89–92; Smith, *Dressed for Duty*, 1:35–37.

43. Woman's Land Army of America, *Women on the Land* (New York: Advisory Council of the Woman's Land Army of America, 1918); Elaine F. Weiss, *Fruits of Victory: The Woman's Land Army of America in the Great War* (Dulles, Va.: Potomac Books, 2008), 40–55; Cecilia Gowdy-Wygant, *Cultivating Victory: The Women's Land Army and the Victory Garden Movement* (Pittsburgh: University of Pittsburgh Press, 2013), 43–44.

44. Women's Land Army of America, *First Annual Report of the Women's Agricultural Camp* (Bedford, N.Y.: Women's Land Army of America, 1917), 7, as quoted in Weiss, *Fruits of Victory*, 52n45.

45. Helen Kennedy Stevens, "City Girl as Farm Worker—Her Own Story: How Nursing the Crops in Westchester County Provided a Healthful Vacation, a Little Fun Now and Then, Much Valuable Experience, and Cash Wages," *New York Times Sunday Magazine*, 24 Feb. 1918, 71.

46. Elene Foster, "Farming with the Farmerettes of Farmingdale; What the Invasion of Enthusiastic Girls Meant to the Little College; They May Look Like the Chorus of a Musical Comedy in Their Smart Khaki Uniforms, But They Are to Learn Everything about Farming," *New-York Tribune*, 15 July 1917, C7.

47. Weiss, *Fruits of Victory*, 107.

48. Woman's Land Army of America, *Handbook of Standards for the Woman's Land Army of America* (Washington, D.C.: Government Printing Office, April 1919), 12. See also Margaret Laughlin, "The Woman's Land Army, 1918–1920," in "Homefront to Front Lines: Women in Wartime," special issue, *Social Education* 58, no. 2 (Feb. 1994): 85–88.

49. "1,000 New Farmerettes; Woman's Land Army Gains Many Members in the City," *New York Times*, 22 Sept. 1918, 8; "Women Farmers Begin Harvest of Money Crop Here; 'Blue Denim Girls' Launch $600,000 Drive as Skies Clear; All Wear Bloomers; Novel Uniform Pleases Soldiers and Helps in Campaign Work," *New-York Tribune*, 22 Sept. 1918, 11.

50. Young, "'Petticoats Are Part of This Uniform,'" 287–289.

51. "The Woman's Land Army," *Los Angeles Times*, 31 May 1918, II4. See also Gowdy-Wygant, *Cultivating Victory*, 52–53.

52. William Clinton Mullendore, *History of the United States Food Administration, 1917–1919* (Stanford, Calif.: Stanford University Press, 1941); John Allen, "The Food Administration of Herbert Hoover and American Voluntarism in the First World War," *Germina Veris* 1, no. 1 (2014), http://www.easternct.edu/germinaveris/the-food-administration-of-herbert-hoover-and-american-voluntarism-in-the-first-world-war/; James H. Smith, "Cultivating Intelligent Consumption: The United States Food Administration and Food Control during World War I" (Ph.D. diss., West Virginia University, 2015).

53. See, e.g., "The House Card, the Uniform and Campaign News," *New-York Tribune*, 29 July 1917, C7; "Nifty. Official Uniform for Women in Food Conservation Army," *Chicago Daily Tribune*, 30 June 1917, 10; Dudley Harmon, "How You May Know Her," inset in "Questions That Women Ask Mr. Hoover: Answered Here So That Every Woman in America May Know What She Can Do to Help the Food Administration," *Ladies' Home Journal* 34, no. 9 (Sept. 1917): 27; Mildred Maddocks, "Good Housekeeping Institute," *Good Housekeeping* 65, no. 3 (Sept. 1917): 74; Clara Savage, "Official Washington Enlists with Mr. Hoover," *Good Housekeeping* 65, no. 4 (Oct. 1917): 54–55.

54. Helen Zoe Veit, *Modern Food, Moral Food: Self-Control, Science, and the Rise of Modern American Eating in the Early Twentieth Century* (Chapel Hill: University of North Carolina Press, 2013), 86; Marsha Gordon, "Onward Kitchen Soldiers: Mobilizing the Domestic during World War I," *Canadian Review of American Studies* 29, no. 2 (Summer 1999): 61–88; Joan L. Sullivan, "In Pursuit of Legitimacy: Home Economists and the Hoover Apron in World War I," *Dress* 26, no. 1 (1999): 31–46.

55. "Styles in Uniforms for Women War Workers," *New York Times*, 27 Jan. 1918, 38; "War Workers Here for Uniform Dress: Appoint Committee to Study Designs—Plan Economy," *Washington Post*, 11 May 1918, 2; "Women Oppose Being Uniformed; Protest That Department Plan Is Useless and Adds to Expenses," *Washington Post*, 14 May 1918: 8; "At Odds over Dress Reform; Women War Workers Say Uniform Would Be Cheaper and Better," *Washington Post*, 15 May 1918, 11.

56. On the Emergency Fleet Corporation and its wartime accomplishments, see Bernard S. Hurley, *The Bridge to France* (Philadelphia: J.B. Lippincott, 1927); Gail Radford, "William Gibbs McAdoo, the Emergency Fleet Corporation, and the Origins of the Public-Authority Model of Government Action," *Journal of Policy History* 11, no. 1 (Jan. 1999): 59–88. On the clerical uniforms, see "Fashion Notes," *Woman Citizen* 3, no. 3 (15 June 1918): 58; Young, "'Petticoats Are Part of This Uniform,'" 270–274; Smith, *Dressed for Duty*, 2:87–88.

57. "20 Uniforms for Women," *Atlanta Constitution*, 1 June 1918, 8; "Twenty Different Uniforms for Women in War Work," *Clothing Designer and Manufacturer* 13, no. 3 (June 1918): 129; "Twenty Uniforms for Women; This Number Is Officially Recognized in the United States," *Los Angeles Times*, 7 July 1918, III-5.

58. "Uniforms for War Workers," *Washington Post*, 19 Sept. 1918, 7; "Uniforms for Women War Clerks Planned," *Los Angeles Times*, 2 Oct. 1918, 16; "Women War Toilers to Wear Gowns of 'Battleship Gray'; Army Department Decides upon Standard Uniform for Workers," *New-York Tribune*, 8 Oct. 1918, 13.

59. Josephus Daniels, *Our Navy at War* (New York: George H. Doran, 1922), 328–329; Jean Ebbert and Marie-Beth Hall, *The First, the Few, the Forgotten: Navy and Marine Corps Women in World War I* (Annapolis, Md.: Naval Institute Press, 2002), 3–4; Nathaniel Patch, "The Story of the Female Yeomen during the First World War," *Prologue* 38, no. 3 (Fall 2006): 55; Naval History and Heritage Command, "100 Years Ago: First Women to Join the Naval Reserve," *CHIPS: The Department of the Navy's Information Technology Magazine*, 14 Mar. 2017, http://www.doncio.navy.mil/chips/ArticleDetails.aspx?ID=6140 (accessed 5 November 2019).

60. Navy Department, "Changes in Uniform Regulations, No. 15. Garments and Articles of Equipment of Enrolled Women of the Naval Reserve Force," 1918, adding articles 264–271 to *Uniform Regulations, United States Navy, Together with Uniforms Common to Both Navy and Marine Corps* (Washington, D.C.: Government Printing Office, 1913), 73ff.; Eunice C. Dessez, *The First Enlisted Women, 1917–1918* (Philadelphia: Dorrance, 1955), 44–51; John A. Stacey, "What Happened to This Man's Navy? A Brief History of the Yeomanettes," *Military Images* 11, no. 1 (July/Aug. 1989): 4–5, 7; Ebbert and Hall, *The First, the Few, the Forgotten*, 28–36; Patch, "The Story of the Female Yeomen during the First World War," 57; Regina T. Akers, "An Historical Overview of the Yeoman F," Naval History and Heritage Command, 18 May 2017. For details on the yeoman (f) uniform, see Young, "'Petticoats Are Part of This Uniform,'" 251–256; Smith, *Dressed for Duty*, 2:216–223.

61. Lou MacPherson Guthrie, "I Was a Yeomanette," *Naval Institute Proceedings* 110, no. 12 (Dec. 1984): 61–62.

62. Linda L. Hewitt, *Women Marines in World War I* (Washington, D.C.: History & Museums Division, Headquarters, U.S. Marine Corps, 1974), 4, 16, 19–24 (quote at 19). See also Young, "'Petticoats Are Part of This Uniform,'" 257–269; Smith, *Dressed for Duty*, 1:332–341.

63. Mrs. Henry F. [Estelle Kemper] Butler, *I was a Yeoman (F)* (Washington, D.C.: Naval Historical Foundation, 1967), 6–7; Dessez, *The First Enlisted Women, 1917–1918*, 44–45; Daniels, *Our Navy at War*, 329. See also Ebbert and Hall, *The First, the Few, the Forgotten*, 35–39.

64. Zeiger, *In Uncle Sam's Service*, 177–178. See also Lynn Dumenil, *The Second Line of Defense: American Women and World War I* (Chapel Hill: University of North Carolina Press, 2017), 194–203.

65. "Stenographers in Uniform," *Woman Citizen* 3, no. 13 (24 Aug. 1918): 255; American Women in the First World War, 2013–2014, https://www.gale.com/binaries/content/assets/au-resources-in-product/wwsessay_grayzel_introduction.pdf (accessed 30 Dec. 2019).

66. Jill Frahm, "Advance to the 'Fighting Lines': The Changing Role of Women Telephone Operators in France during the First World War," *Federal History*, no. 8 (2016): 101; "Topics in Chronicling America—Hello Girls," Library of Congress, Newspaper & Current Periodical Reading Room, 29 Jan. 2015.

67. Elizabeth Cobbs, *The Hello Girls: America's First Women Soldiers* (Cambridge, Mass.: Harvard University Press, 2017), 104. For details on the operators' uniform, see Young, "'Petticoats Are Part of This Uniform,'" 240–244; Smith, *Dressed for Duty*, 2: 56–63, 523–528.

68. Lettie Gavin, *American Women in World War I: They Also Served* (Niwot: University of Colorado Press, 1997), 93.

69. Cobbs, *The Hello Girls.*

70. "The Blue Triangle at the Congress of Allied Women," *War Work Bulletin*, no. 39 (13 Sept. 1918): 2.

71. "Congress of Women," *New-York Tribune*, 29 Sept. 1918, B12.

72. "Congress of Women," B12; "Allies in Paris," *Woman Citizen* 3, no. 23 (2 Nov. 1918): 462–463, 477.

73. "Women in Uniform [from *Manchester Guardian*]," *New-York Tribune*, 1 Aug. 1915, 10; "Women Don War Uniforms in England; Khakis Aid to Discipline; Is Declaration of Volunteer Yeomanry Members," *Los Angeles Herald*, 24 Aug. 1915, 2; "No More Evening Gowns; Uniforms for Court Beauties," *Atlanta Constitution*, 3 Oct. 1915, c14a; "Women of England to Till the Fields; Government Undertakes to Recruit 400,000—to Wear Special Uniform and Armlet," *New York Times*, 15 Feb. 1916, 2; "Uniforms of England's Women Workers," *Boston Daily Globe*, 24 Dec. 1916, 29; A.P. Furmon, "'Waacs': Women in France Lead Military Life; Auxiliary Army Corps under Strict Discipline; Wear Khaki Uniforms, Occupy Regulation Barracks and Have Their Own Organization on Lines of

Men Fighting at the Front," *Los Angeles Times*, 7 Oct. 1917, I4; Mary Brush Williams, "Khaki-Clad British Kitchen Queen Now Reigns in Camp of Mars," *New-York Tribune*, 30 Dec. 1917, C7.

74. "11,000 Women Police Enroll. Italian Force Will Wear Uniform and Undergo Physical Training," *New York Times*, 27 May 1915, 2; "French Women Carry Letters; in Natty Uniforms They Make First Appearance on Paris Streets," *Los Angeles Times*, 1 June 1917, I1.

75. "'Minute Girl' Uniform Urged for U. S. Women by President Wilson," *Atlanta Constitution*, 24 Apr. 1917, 7; "Women's War-Work Uniforms Adding Color to Capital Gatherings—Capital Society Becomes Metropolitan; Cabinet Girls 'in Office,'" *Washington Post*, 24 Feb. 1918, ES6; "Uniforms for Women," *Chicago Daily Tribune*, 14 July 1918, B2; "Women Answer the Call. The Time, the Place and the Costume," *Atlanta Constitution*, 21 July 1918, b8; "Uniforms for War Workers," *Washington Post*, 19 Sept. 1918, 7; "The Uniforms Which the American Women Have Adopted for Their War Work," *Touchstone* 4, no. 1 (Oct. 1918): 63–69; Truman B. Handy, "Milady's Uniform," *Los Angeles Times*, 29 Oct. 1918, II4; "Would Women Wage War without Uniforms?" *Madera* (Calif.) *Weekly Tribune*, 26 Dec. 1918, 2; John S. Steele, "City of Noise and Uniforms," *Chicago Daily Tribune*, 3 Aug. 1919, F9.

ABOUT THE CONTRIBUTORS

Allison Scardino Belzer (Ph.D., History, 2002, Emory University, Atlanta, Ga.) is Associate Professor of History at Georgia Southern University, Savannah.

Ilse Bogaerts (M.A., Textile Studies, 1988, University of Antwerp; M.A., Art History, 1993, Free University of Brussels) heads the textile and uniform collection in the Royal Museum of the Armed Forces and of Military History in Brussels.

Maria Bucur (Ph.D., History, 1996, University of Illinois, Champagne-Urbana) is John W. Hill Professor of East European History, Indiana University, Bloomington.

Margaret H. Darrow (Ph.D., History, 1981, Rutgers, The State University of New Jersey, New Brunswick) is Professor of History at Dartmouth College, Hanover, N.H.

Luc De Munck (M.A., History, University of Louvain) is a doctoral fellow at the University of Louvain, Belgium.

Raelene Frances (Ph.D., History, 1989, Monash University, Melbourne) is Professor of History, Australian National University, Canberra.

Barton C. Hacker (Ph.D., History, 1968, University of Chicago) is Senior Curator Emeritus of Armed Forces History in the National Museum of American History, Smithsonian Institution, Washington, D.C.

Christine E. Hallett (Ph.D., Nursing; 1995; Ph.D., History, 2002, University of Manchester) is Professor of Nursing History at the University of Manchester.

Margaret Harris (B.A., Massey University, Wellington, New Zealand) is a graduate student at Monash University, Melbourne, Australia.

Marian Moser Jones (Ph.D., 2008, Columbia University, New York) is Associate Professor of Family Science at the School of Public Health and is affiliated with the Department of History, University of Maryland, College Park.

Tammy M. Proctor (PhD, History, 1995, Rutgers, The State University of New Jersey, New Brunswick) is Distinguished Professor of History at Utah State University, Logan.

Claudia Reichl-Ham (Ph.D., History, University of Vienna) is Deputy Director of Research in the Military History Museum, Vienna.

Krisztina Robert (Ph.D., History, 1998, University of Houston, Texas) is Senior Lecturer in History, University of Roehampton, London.

Bruce Scates (Ph.D., History, Monash University, Melbourne) is Professor of History at Australian National University, Canberra.

Alison Spires (M.A., Medical Anthropology) is an independent military nursing historian. She retired after twenty-eight years of service as a military nurse.

Keiron Spires is Associate Professor of eLearning and Learning Technologies in the School of Health and Social Care, London South Bank University. A retired army nurse, he chairs the Queen Alexandra's Royal Army Nurse Corps Heritage & Chattels Committee.

Laurie S. Stoff (Ph.D., History, 2002, University of Kansas, Lawrence) is Senior Lecturer in History in the Barrett Honors College, Arizona State University, Tempe.

Cynthia Toman (M.Sc.N., Nursing, 1998; Ph.D., History, 2003, University of Ottawa) is retired Associate Professor of Nursing and History, University of Ottawa.

Nicole A.N.M. van Os (Ph.D., History, 2003, University of Leiden) is Coordinator of Asian Studies and Middle Eastern Studies, University of Leiden.

Margaret Vining (M.A., George Washington University, Washington, D.C.) was Curator Emerita of Armed Forces History in the National Museum of American History, Smithsonian Institution, Washington, D.C.

INDEX